Insolvent Debtors in 19th Century Harford County, Maryland

A Legal and Genealogical Digest

Henry C. Peden, Jr.

HERITAGE BOOKS
2019

HERITAGE BOOKS

AN IMPRINT OF HERITAGE BOOKS, INC.

Books, CDs, and more—Worldwide

For our listing of thousands of titles see our website
at
www.HeritageBooks.com

Published 2019 by
HERITAGE BOOKS, INC.
Publishing Division
5810 Ruatan Street
Berwyn Heights, Md. 20740

International Standard Book Number
Paperbound: 978-0-7884-5750-0

INTRODUCTION

Insolvency has been defined as the condition of having more debts (liabilities) than total assets which might be available to pay them, even if the assets were mortgaged or sold.[1] The Maryland State Archives is in possession of insolvency records from the late 17th century up to the early 20th century. For Harford County they have one book, Insolvent Docket A, which was made available through the efforts of Christopher C. DiJulio and Christopher T. Smithson[2] and I thank them very much for their assistance which in turn made this book more comprehensive. I also consulted three other insolvent books and many court papers in possession of the Historical Society of Harford County.

There were countless individuals in Harford County in the 19th century who were in and out of debt, but this book only addresses those who were insolvent and unable to pay their debts. Some of them, men and women alike, were imprisoned, many sold their property, both real and personal, and many applied for the benefit under the insolvency acts of Maryland. Those acts changed over time and today we know insolvency as bankruptcy. By the mid-1800s imprisonment was discontinued and in Harford County the last person I could find imprisoned for debt was Alexander McDonald in 1851.

This book is a digest of legal information that was gleaned from extant newspapers, court records, insolvent books and judgment books and supplemented thereafter with genealogical notes that identify the insolvent debtors. In many instances a legal description of the case is presented verbatim although some may be abbreviated as was common in docket books. Newspaper notices to creditors also reported the insolvents' situations and trustee's sales listed the property that was sold to pay the debts. Most of the insolvents herein were individuals, but several of them were companies.

Unlike today, insolvency was a matter of shame and embarrassment back in the day, but it did not only affect poor people *per se*. All walks of life, from farmers to canners, and merchants to doctors and lawyers, found themselves in dire straits at one time or another. Some dealt with it and paid as best they could and moved on with their lives while others absconded. All are presented in this book.

It should also be noted that I had researched and published two volumes entitled *Maryland Prisoners Languishing in Gaol, Volume 1, 1635-1765* and *Maryland Prisoners Languishing in Gaol, Volume 2, 1766-1800*. Most of the persons in those books were imprisoned for debt. They were my motivation for continuing on and writing this book about Harford County insolvent debtors in the 19th century.

"An insolvent debtor offered his creditors a compromise of twenty-five cents on the dollar, which they declined. He went into bankruptcy, the lawyers got a nibble at the estate, and now it pays only two and a-half per cent, to the creditors!" This commentary may sound like a recent occurrence, but it was made in 1874.[3] Some things never change.

Henry C. Peden, Jr.
Bel Air, Maryland
November 11, 2019

---

[1] Maryland State Archives Guide to Government Records online at www.mdsa.net.
[2] Smithson also conducted additional genealogical research on some of the insolvent debtors.
[3] *Havre de Grace Republican*, January 30, 1874.

Insolvent Debtors in 19th Century Harford County, Maryland: A Legal and Genealogical Digest

Aberdeen Can Company, 1895/1897. "The machine-making department of the Aberdeen can factory has closed, on account of the scarcity of orders for cans." (*Havre de Grace Republican*, September 14, 1895, p. 3). State Tax Commissioner reported in 1896, "Aberdeen Can Company of Aberdeen – value of stock, $30,000; real property, $11,710; [and] tax due, $32.42." (*Havre de Grace Republican*, February 15, 1896, p. 2). In March 1896 "The Aberdeen can factory has commenced operations for the season and employs thirty-five hands." (*Havre de Grace Republican*, March 21, 1896, p. 2). In October 1896 it was reported, "The Aberdeen can factory has shut down for the season, throwing about thirty persons out of employment." (*Havre de Grace Republican*, October 17, 1896, p. 3). In January 1897 it was reported, "Mr. Septimus Davis, as attorney for J. H. Thiemeyer & Co., of Baltimore, has filed a bill in the Circuit Court asking that a receiver be appointed for the Aberdeen Can Company, alleging that the said company is insolvent." (*The Aegis & Intelligencer*, January 8, 1897, p. 3). In another newspaper it was reported, "The plaintiffs allege that the defendant owes them $385 on a protested note and is insolvent." (*Havre de Grace Republican*, January 9, 1897, p. 3). "Receiver Appointed. Judge Watters, in Court, at Bel Air, last Saturday [January 9, 1897], heard the petition filed in court by J. H. Thiemeyer & Co., of Baltimore, asking that a receiver be appointed for the Aberdeen Can Company. The Court, after hearing the proceedings, declared that the company was insolvent, and appointed Septimus Davis receiver, and Mr. Davis gave bond in the sum of $20,000. The company admitted the allegations of the bill, and consented to the appointment of a receiver." (*Havre de Grace Republican*, January 16, 1897, p. 3). "Receivers' Sale of All the Valuable Property of the Aberdeen Can Company, of Aberdeen, Md., Consisting of Large Can Factory, Large Warehouse, Boiler Room and Press Room. Also Complete Equipment of Tin Can Making Machinery. By Virtue of an Order of the Circuit Court for Harford County, in Chancery, passed in the case of J. H. Thiemeyer & Co. and H. Clay Tunis, Trustee, vs. the Aberdeen Can Company of Harford County, the undersigned, Receivers, will offer at Public Auction, on the premises at Aberdeen, on Saturday, May 8th, 1897, at 11 o'clock A. M., All Those 4 Lots of Ground situate in the town of Aberdeen, in Harford County, Md., fronting in all two hundred and fifteen feet on Edmund street and running back an even depth two hundred feet to Pine Alley, and which are particularly described in a deed from The Aberdeen Land and Improvement Company of Harford County to the Aberdeen Can Company of Harford County, dated the 23rd day of June, in the year 1893, and is recorded amongst the land Record Records of said Harford county, in Liber W.S.F. No. 79, folio 207. Together with the improvements thereon, consisting of a large Tin Can Factory, 40x100 feet, with Boiler Room and Solder Room attached, 20x40 feet, and also attached a Press Room, 20x50 feet, also large Warehouse, 40x160 feet, which will hold two or three million cans. These buildings are in fine condition and were built in the year 1893. Also the complete equipment of the Can Factory, consisting of 40 H. P. Coleman Boiler and 12 H. P. Corliss Engine, Monroe Circular Can Making Machine, Ramsay & Phelps' Circular Can Testing Machine, Westinghouse Pumps, two Stevens Pumps, Cutting Machines, Presses, Dies, etc. Also Office Furniture, consisting of a large Safe, Walnut Roll top Desk, Double Standing Desk, etc. The Factory and Warehouse, with the appurtenances, including the Boiler, Engine Shafting and all Can-making Machinery, will be first offered together, and then the Real Estate without the machinery, and will be sold in such way as to secure the best price. This property is near the line of the B. & O. R. R., and has a siding running to the warehouse. Septimus Davis, Geo. L. Van Bibber, Receivers." (*Havre de Grace Republican*, May 1, 1897, p. 2). "Withdrawn. The receivers, Messrs. Geo. L. Van Bibber and Septimus Davis, of the Aberdeen Can Company, only received a bid of $1,500 for the buildings and machinery at the public sale last Saturday, and it was withdrawn. When it is recollected that the buildings and machinery represent an outlay of nearly $20,000, it will be seen that the price offered was entirely inadequate." (*Havre de Grace Republican*, May 15, 1897, p. 3). "Notice to Creditors. George L. Van Bibber and Septimus Davis, Solicitors. J. H. Thiemeyer and Company and others, vs. The Aberdeen Can Company of Harford County. In the Circuit Court for Harford County in Equity. By Authority of an order of [the] Court passed in the above entitled case, all creditors of The Aberdeen Can Company, of Harford County, are hereby notified to file their claims properly proven with the Clerk of the Circuit Court for Harford County, on or before the first day of November, 1897, or they may be excluded from all participation in the estate. George L. Van Bibber, Septimus Davis, Receivers." (*Havre de Grace Republican*, August 21, 1897, p. 2). "Mr. Chas. W. Baker, of Aberdeen, has purchased from the receivers, Messrs. George L. Van Bibber and Septimus Davis, the real estate of the Aberdeen Can Company, for $3,000." (*Havre de Grace Republican*, August 28, 1897, p. 2). **Genealogical Notes:** The aforementioned Chas. W. Baker was Charles Winfield Baker (1848-1918), son of George Washington Baker (1815-1888) and Elizabeth Greenland (1818-1893). His father is credited with being the founder of the corn canning industry in Harford County. In the 1860s he began canning fruit and later corn. Charles W. Baker started his career in the meat business in Aberdeen and was perhaps the most financially successful of the Bakers with canning and a canned goods brokerage. ("The Baker Family of Aberdeen," by Jon Harlan Livezey, *Harford Historical Bulletin No. 16*, Spring, 1983, pp. 2-6)

Adams, Samuel B., 1835. "Petition, Affidavits, Schedule, personal discharge and order of publication, Bond for Appearance, Trustee's Bond, Trustee's Certificate and Deed to Trustee filed the 26th May 1835. 19th March 1836 Petitioner appears and ..." [nothing further recorded] (Insolvent Docket A, 1807-1843, p. 140, at Maryland State Archives)

Addison, Thomas L., 1835. "Petition, Affidavits, Schedule, personal discharge and order of publication, Bond for Appearance, Trustee's Bond, Trustee's Certificate and Deed to Trustee filed 9th Nov. 1835. 19th March 1836 Petitioner appears, certificate of publication filed and finally discharged." (Insolvent Docket A, 1807-1843, p. 145, at Maryland State Archives)

Aikens, John, 1844. "Notice Is Hereby Given, To the creditors of John Aikens, late an imprisoned debtor of Harford county, that on the application of said debtor by petition in writing to the Hon. Robert W. Holland, chief justice of the Orphan's court of said county, for the benefit of the insolvent laws of Maryland, the said judge on the 24th day of June, 1844, granted to the said debtor a discharge from imprisonment and appointed the first Saturday after the 3rd Monday in November next, for his appearance before the Judges of Harford county court at the court house of said county, for a final hearing before said court, on said petition and to answer such interrogatories as his creditors may propose to him." (*Harford Madisonian and Bel-Air & Havre de Grace Messenger*, October 18, 1844, p. 3)

Alexander, John J. M., 1883. "July 25th 1883. Petition of James A. Fulton, E. Hall Richardson, Josiah M. Herrman, Benjamin Wann filed. Same day Subpoena & copy of petition & order of Court delivered to sheriff of Harford County. This Petition dismissed per order filed August 2nd 1883." [A second petition on August 2nd 1883 signed by these and additional people was filed and "all agreed that this case be tried before the Court, without intervention of a Jury" and it too was dismissed on August 11th 1883 with the petitioners paying the costs.] (Insolvent Docket A. L. J. No. 1, p. 80, in the Court Records Department of the Historical Society of Harford County). **Genealogical Notes:** John J. M. Alexander (1855-1917) was a blacksmith in Bel Air by 1875 and his smithy was located at "the

Flatiron" where Bond and Main Streets split near Gordon Street. He married Mollie E. Denbow on January 10, 1878 and moved to Baltimore after 1883. John died at home on May 27, 1917 and was returned to Harford County for burial at Mt. Tabor M. P. Church. (*The Aegis & Intelligencer*, June 1, 1917; *Bel Air: The Town Through Its Buildings*, by Marilynn M. Larew, 1981, p. 33; marriage record)

Allen, Ebenezer N., Jr., 1827. "Petition, Schedule, Bond, Sheriff's certificate and personal discharge and order for publication filed and Bond of provisional trustee filed and certificate for trustee filed 6th March 1827 … 18th August 1827 petitioner personally discharged." (Insolvent Docket A, 1807-1843, p. 84, at the Maryland State Archives). **Genealogical Notes:** Ebenezer Nunn Allen, Jr. (1777-1840), a native of Latimerstown, County Wexford, Ireland, son of Ebenezer Nunn Allen and ----, married 1st to Elizabeth Chauncey (1792-1816) circa February 13, 1816 (date of license), 2nd to Elecia or Alicia Melvina Monks (1795-1823) on November 20, 1821, 3rd to Mary Ann Billingslea (1801-1826) on December 4, 1823, and 4th to Martha Bond Dickinson (b. 1781) circa May 28, 1827 (date of license). (Harford County Marriage Records; *Baltimore Patriot*, November 23, 1821 and December 8, 1823; Dielman-Hayward File at the Maryland Historical Society; Court Records Document 59.26.8 in 1817 at the Historical Society of Harford County; Research by Kevin Johnston, of Abingdon, MD, 2005)

Allen, Isaac, 1822. Insolvent debtor to be discharged from imprisonment. (*Bond of Union and Harford County Weekly Advertiser*, July 25, 1822). "Petition, Schedule, Bond, Sheriff's Certificate, personal Discharge and order for Publication filed 30th March 1822 … 31st Augt. 1822 petitioner appears … Jason Moore appointed trustee and petitioner discharged." [nothing further recorded] (Insolvent Docket A, 1807-1843, p. 49, at the Maryland State Archives; Insolvent Docket Prior to 1827, Court Records Accession #632 at the Historical Society of Harford County). **Genealogical Note:** Isaac Allen and Mary Herring were married on December 24, 1800. (St. George's P. E. Parish Register)

Allen, Israel, 1860. "Petition, Schedule of property, A list of debts due to & from, Affidavit, Order of Notice to Creditors. Appointment of Henry D. Farnandis, Esqr., Trustee, Trustee's Bond approved & filed & Deed to Trustee filed 7th May 1860. 13th Novr./1860 Certificate of notice to creditors filed and Applicant finally discharged." (Insolvent Docket A. L. J. No. 1, p. 34, in the Court Records Department of the Historical Society of Harford County). "Notice is hereby given, that Israel Allen has made application to the circuit court of Harford county, for the benefit of the Insolvent Laws of Maryland; and that the 1st Monday of August next, has been assigned for him to appear in said court to answer such interrogatories as his creditors may propose or allege against him. Wm. Galloway, Clerk, circuit court for Harford co." (*National American*, June 8, 1860, p. 3) **Genealogical Note:** Israel Allen, for many years the well-known proprietor of the United States Hotel in Havre de Grace, died at his residence on Churchville road on July 20, 1872, age 60, and buried in Angel Hill Cemetery. (*The Havre Republican*, July 26, 1872)

Amos(s), Benjamin, of Wm., 1810. "Whereas we the subscribers Justices of the Peace for Harford County upon the petition of Benjamin Amos, of Wm., who set forth that he had been confined in the gaol [jail] of said county twenty days for debts which he was unable to pay & finding the facts stated to be true we did meet at the gaol of said county on the 5th day of February last and did then and there appoint the 8th day of March instant to meet at the Court House of said county which said appointment we did then and there … at the request of said Sheriff administer to the said Benjamin Amos the following Oath which was taken by the said Benjamin Amos being first duly sworn on the Holy Evangely of Almighty God in the words following – I Benjamin Amos do solemnly swear that the Schedule which I have delivered to the Sheriff of Harford County doth contain a full account to the best of my knowledge & remembrance of my whole estate both real and personal or that I have any title to or interest in and of all debts, credits and effects whatsoever which I or any in trust for me have or at the time of my petition had, or am or was in any respect entitled to in possession,

4

remainder or reversion and that I have not directly or indirectly at any time since my imprisonment or before, sold, leased or otherwise conveyed or disposed of or intrusted all or any part of my estate, Goods, Stock, money or Debts thereby to defraud my Creditors or to secure the same to receive or expect any profit or advantage thereof so help me God, which said duplicate of the Schedule aforesaid we have transmitted to the Clerk of the County Court to be by him preserved in his Office for the information of the Creditors of the said Benjamin Amos. Given under our hands & seals this 8th Day of March 1810. Thomas A. Hays. John C. Bond." (Court Records Document 67.12(5) at the Historical Society of Harford County; copy of the schedule to which he signed his name "Benjamin Amos" was included). **Genealogical Notes**: Benjamin Amoss, son of William Amoss (1718-1814) and 2nd wife Martha Wiley Bull, was born a Quaker on the 29th day of the 6th month 1773, was reported to Friends as being guilty of fighting, swearing and neglecting the attendance of religious meetings, and was disowned at a Gunpowder Monthly Meeting in 1796. He married Margaret Conn on November 5, 1800, after acquiring a license that same day, and removed to Madison Co., OH by 1811. Their children were: Robert Conn Amoss (1801-1859), Ann (Amoss) Rea (1802-1857), Elizabeth (Amoss) Rea, ---- Amoss (daughter died in 1811 in Ohio), and possibly a son John Amoss (*Children of Mt. Soma*, by Gertrude J. Stephens, 1992, pp. 374, 1006-1007). Benjamin's disownment in 1796 explains why he obtained a license in order to get married outside the Society of Friends and it also explains why he swore to an oath rather than an affirming to his statement of indebtedness in 1810.

Amos, Benjamin S., 1891. "Mr. Farnandis, as trustee, advertised for sale the real and personal property of Benj. S. Amos, an insolvent debtor." (*Havre de Grace Republican*, Oct 9, 1891, p. 3). **Genealogical Notes**: Benjamin Scott Amos, son of Zachariah Amos (1818-1890) and Caroline F. Moore (1831-1916), was born in 1856, married Elizabeth H. "Eliza" Streett, daughter of John Streett and Drucilla Johns, on January 31, 1877 and their children were Mary Drucilla Amos (1880-1964), Mary Roberta Amos married a Hudson, and Caroline Amos married a Miller. (*Children of Mt. Soma*, by Gertrude J. Stephens, 1992, p. 416, mistakenly stated they married on January 29, 1877)

Amos, Corbin, 1888. "In the matter of the Insolvency of Corbin Amos. Notice is hereby given to the creditors of Corbin Amos, of Harford county, that he has applied for the benefit of the Insolvent Laws of the State of Maryland, and that a meeting of the creditors of the said Amos will be held in my office, in the town of Bel Air, on Thursday, March 15th, 1888, at 10 o'clock, A. M., for the purpose of electing a permanent trustee for the estate of the said insolvent. John S. Young, Preliminary Trustee." (*The Aegis & Intelligencer*, March 9, 1888, p. 2). "In pursuance of an order passed in the above entitled cause, the undersigned hereby gives notice to the creditors of Corbin Amos, an insolvent debtor, that 14th day of May, 1888, has been fixed upon by the Court for said insolvent to appear and answer such interrogatories or allegations, as his creditors, endorsers or sureties may propose or allege against him. Thomas H. Robinson, Permanent Trustee." (*The Aegis & Intelligencer*, March 23, 1888, p. 2). "Notice To Creditors. In pursuance of an order passed in the above entitled cause, the Creditors of Corbin Amos, who were such upon the date of application of said insolvent for the benefit of the Insolvent laws, to file their claims against said insolvent, duly authenticated, with the Clerk of Circuit Court for Harford County, on or before the 1st day of July, 1888. Thomas H. Robinson, Permanent Trustee." (*The Aegis & Intelligencer*, March 23, 1888, p. 2). **Genealogical Notes**: Corbin Amos, the only son and fourth and last child of Capt. Joshua M. Amos (1780-1860) and Catherine Hanway, was born on January 24, 1837 and married Amanda Jane Holland (1841-1902) daughter of James Holland, on September 11, 1861. They had six children: Joshua Amos (1863-1875), Corbin Amos, Jr. (1864-1935) married Elizabeth Morse, Charles Archer Amos (1866-1930) married Annie Anderson (Dance) Watters, Ella Amos (1869-1885), Clarence Elmer Amos (1871-1899), and Birdette "Etta" Amos (1873-1925) married Dr. W. W. Abbott, of Chicago. Corbin Amos was a farmer and also served as a Harford County Commissioner. A fire destroyed his house, barn and most of the outbuildings [date not known] and this speculatively could be the reason for his insolvency. Corbin advertised in *The Aegis & Intelligencer* in March 18, 1887 that "The undersigned, having sold his farm, known as the 'Merritt Farm' situated on the road from Fallston to the Upper Cross Roads, and having no further use for the stock and farming implements thereon, will sell [them] at Public Sale, on the premises, on Wednesday, March 23rd, 1887." He died on July 27, 1890 and was buried in Friendship Cemetery, now Fallston United Methodist Church Cemetery, in Fallston, MD. (*Children of Mt. Soma*, by Gertrude J. Stephens, 1992, pp. 410-414)

Amos(s), Daniel, 1809. "Petition, Schedule, Bond, &c. filed 23rd of Dec. 1809 … Augt. 18th 1810 the necessary oath was administered to the petitioner and the Court appointed Robert Amoss, Sr., trustee … Certificate of discharge granted 2nd March 1812." (Insolvent Docket A, 1807-1843, p. 6, at the Maryland State Archives; Insolvent Docket Prior to 1827, Court Records Accession #632 at the Historical Society of Harford County). **Genealogical Notes**: Daniel Amos, son of Robert Amos (1741-1818) and Martha McComas (c1745/1749-1832), was born on October 13, 1768, married Sarah Johnson (1771-1858), daughter of John and Ann Johnson, in 1792 and died on March 5, 1854. Daniel and Sarah were members of Old Brick Baptist Church for a time and he farmed between Upper Cross Roads and Jarrettsville on Route 165. They were buried in the Amos Family Cemetery on what is now the Uphill Farm. Their children were John Johnson Amos who possibly married Susan Wiseman, Robert Clarke Amos, Ann Amos married John Chatterton (Baltimore *Sun*, February 4, 1871), Martha Ann Amos, Daniel Amos, Sarah Amos married John Varns, Margaret S. Amos married Rev. William Wilson, and Elizabeth Amos married David Davis. (*Children of Mt. Soma*, by Gertrude J. Stephens, 1992, pp. 382-383)

Amos(s), Mordecai, 1811. "Petition, bond and Schedule filed 16th March 1811 … Ordered by the Court ordered that Mordecai Amoss be discharged from confinement and ordered that he give notice in some of the newspapers printed in the City of Baltimore to his creditors to appear at next August term … [case continued] … 11th March 1813. Objections to the discharge of Mordecai Amoss filed by John Archer's Executors." [nothing further recorded]. (Insolvent Docket A, 1807-1843, p. 9, at the Maryland State Archives; Insolvent Docket Prior to 1827, Court Records Accession #632 at the Historical Society of Harford County). **Genealogical Note**: Mordecai Amos(s) and Mordecai Amos(s), Jr. were both signers of the Association of Freemen in 1775 in Bush River Upper Hundred, both took the Oath of Allegiance to the State of Maryland in 1778. One "Worshipfull" Mordecai Amos administered the oaths as well and one or both served in the militia. (*Revolutionary Patriots of Harford County, Maryland, 1775-1783*, by Henry C. Peden, Jr., 1985, p. 5)

Amos, Robert, 1878. "Petition, 3 Schedules, Affidavit, Order, Trustee's Bond & Deed filed Sept. 4th 1878. Same day recommendation of Elizabeth A. Amos filed. Same day recommendation of J. T. C. Hopkins, S. A. Williams and Archer & Van Bibber to appoint H. D. Farnandis filed … Feby. 10th 1879 Petitioner appears, files Certificate & is finally discharged … Sept. 9th 1879 Petition of Robert Amos & wife … April 26th 1880 Final ratification of Trustee's Report of Sale filed." (Insolvent Docket A. L. J. No. 1, p. 59, in the Court Records Department of the Historical Society of Harford County). "Notice is hereby given that Robert Amos has made application to the Circuit Court of Harford county, for the benefit of the Insolvent Laws of Maryland, and that the second Monday in February, 1879, has been assigned for him to appear in said Court to answer such interrogatories as his creditors may propose or allege against him. A. L. Jarrett, Clerk." (*The Aegis & Intelligencer*, September 13, 1878, p. 2). 1879. "Trustee's Sale. In virtue of an order of the Circuit Court for Harford county, the subscriber, as insolvent's trustee, will sell at public sale, at the residence of Robert Amos, in the 1st election district, about one mile below Emmorton, on Friday, March 7th, 1879, sale commencing at 10 o'clock

A. M., for the personal property at 12 o'clock M., for the realty, all that Tract or Parcel of Land, situate in Harford county, composed of parts of two tracts called *Ann's Dower* and *Littleton*, containing together 117 acres, more or less, on which Robert Amos now resides, being the same and all the land described in a deed from David Harlan and wife to Robert Amos, dated December 1, 1874, and recorded in Liber A.L.J.. No. 31, folio 122, one of the Land Records of the Circuit Court for Harford county. This property lies on the road leading from Demoss' corner to Hall's Mills, adjoins the lands of John H. Bradford, Edward Hall, and others, and is improved by a good Dwelling House, and the usual outbuildings. A large portion of the land is under cultivation, highly improved and well watered and fenced. The woodland on it has valuable building and fencing timber. Also a Parcel of Land, being part of a tract called *Bloom's Bloom*, containing 29 acres, more or less, being the same and all the land described in a deed from W. W. Castner and wife to said Robert Amos, dated June 5, 1871, and recorded in Liber A.L.J. No. 26, folio 167, one of the Land Records aforesaid, except a parcel thereof conveyed by the said Amos and wife to William S. George, by deed dated the 24th day of June, 1871, and recorded in Liber A.L.J. No. 26, folio 167, one of the Land Records of the Circuit Court for Harford county. This land adjoins the farms of W. W. Castner, Jeremiah Black and others. Also 1 Horse, 1 yoke of Oxen, 2 Farm Wagons, 1 Ox Cart, 1 Carriage, 1 Reaper and Mower, 1 Threshing Machine and Power, a lot of Plows, harrows and other Farming Implements. A lot of Cattle, 1 Desk, Corn by the barrel, Hay and Straw, and other articles. Herman Stump, Jr., Trustee. J. S. Richardson, Auctioneer." (*The Aegis & Intelligencer*, February 7, 1879, p. 2; *Harford Democrat*, February 14, 1879, p. 3). **Genealogical Notes**: Robert Amos, son of Benjamin Scott Amos (1786-1865) and Sarah Ann Amos (1792-1869), was born on October 2, 1820, married Elizabeth Ann Hitchcock circa 1847-1850 and died in 1886. Their children were Mary Virginia Amos who married Joseph Waterman in 1877, Sarah O. Amos, Martha Rebecca Amos married John T. McAbee in 1881, Walter Scott Amos married Florence R. Few in 1891, Anna Amos, William Phillip Amos married Sarah Martha ----, Robert Lee Amos married Violet Gertrude Gorrell in 1892, and Benjamin Howear Amos married Sophia Alice Haywood Miller in 1899. (*Children of Mt. Soma*, by Gertrude J. Stephens, 1993, pp. 501-502; Harford County marriage records)

Anderson, Francis D., 1857. "Petition, Schedules, Affidavits, Appointment of Trustee & order of notice, Trustee's Bond & Deed filed 11th Nov 1857. 15th May 1858 Petitioner appears, files certificate of publication & discharged. 1st October/58 Petition of John D. Addicks & others and admr. of Insolvent Trustee filed. 21st April 1859 Allegations of Saml. L. Bird filed … 5th June 1865 Petition of A. H. Jarrett filed. 8th August 1865 Trustee's report of sales filed. Recorded in Judgment Record ALJ No. 1, folio 399." (Insolvent Docket ALJ No. 1, p. 21, in the Court Records Department of the Historical Society of Harford County). "Notice is hereby given that Frank D. Anderson [later as Francis D. Anderson], of Harford County, has made application to the Circuit Court of said County, for the benefit of the Insolvent Laws of Maryland, and that the first Saturday after the second Monday in May, 1858, has been assigned for him to appear in said Court to answer such interrogatories as his creditors may propose or allege against him. William Galloway, Clerk of Circuit Court for Harford County." (*The Southern Aegis*, January 9, 1858, p. 3, and January 16, 1858, p. 3). **Genealogical Notes**: Francis Durbin Anderson (1809-1873), son of John Anderson, married Mary Davis Silver (September 10, 1810 – January 26, 1869), daughter of William Silver (1778-1838) and Elizabeth Davis (1782-1848), on June 13, 1833 and later moved to Howard Co., MD. Their children were John William Anderson, Maria Louisa Anderson (married a Hopkins), Francis Durbin Anderson, Jr., Mary Elizabeth Anderson (married a Webb), Henry Anderson, James Edward Anderson, Edgar S. Anderson, and Frederick Thomas Anderson (married Cassandra Whiteford Brown). (*Independent Citizen*, July 11, 1833; Churchville Presbyterian Church Register of Communicants; *The Whiteford Genealogy*, by Hazel

Whiteford Baldwin, 1992, pp. 322-323; *Our Silver Heritage*, by Benjamin Stump Silver and Frances Aylette (Bowen) Silver, 1976, Volume I, pp. 3151, 3157)

Anderson, George L., 1866. "Petition, Schedule of property, List of debts to & from Affidavit, Order, Bond & Deed filed 14th Oct 1867 & 17th day of February 1868 appointed for his appearance. A. W. Bateman, Trustee." [nothing further recorded] (Insolvent Docket A. L. J. No. 1, p. 49, in the Court Records Department of the Historical Society of Harford County) **Genealogical Notes**: George L. Anderson, son of Mitchell Anderson and Mary Thompson, of NJ, was born on December 10, 1827, worked as a harness maker in Dublin, Harford Co., and married Ann Mariah Singleton. (*Ancestral Charts, Volume 4*, Special Publication No. 1, Harford County Genealogical Society, 1988, pp. 164-168)

Anderson, George W., 1824. "Petition, Schedule, Bond, Sheriffs Certificate and personal Discharge and order for Publication filed 16th January 1824. Aug 14th 1824 Printers certificate of publication filed. Petitioner appears and is discharged." (Insolvent Docket A, 1807-1843, p. 60, at the Maryland State Archives; Insolvent Docket Prior to 1827, Court Records Accession #632 at the Historical Society of Harford County). **Genealogical Notes**: George W. Anderson was born circa 1785 (age 31 in 1817 and age 45 in 1829) and married Hannah Norris circa July 22, 1812. (Harford County Marriage license date; Court Records Documents 82.19.2.E and 89.06.1.1 at the Historical Society of Harford County)

Anderson. Moses (African American}. 1836. "Negro Moses Anderson. Petition, Affidavits, Schedule, personal discharge and order of publication, Bond for Appearance, Trustee's Bond, Trustee's Certificate and Deed to Trustee filed 2nd August 1836. 18th March 1837 Petitioner appears, certificate of publication filed, interrogatories filed and finally discharged." (Insolvent Docket A, 1807-1843, p. 150, at Maryland State Archives). **Genealogical Notes**: Moses Anderson, son of Nelly Anderson, a free woman of colour, was aged about 50 in 1842, dark complexion, 5' 11" tall, born free (Certificates of Freedom, 1818-1842, n.p.n.) He was involved in various legal matters in 1828, 1829, 1836 and 1842 (Court Records Document 91.08.2, 96.26.10, 113.10.5 and 113.20.3 at the Historical Society of Harford County). His age in 1832 was listed as 45 (A List of Free People of Colour Taken in 1832 by Joshua Guyton, Sheriff) and he was enumerated as head of household in 1840 (Harford County Census).

Andrews, Abraham, 1810. "Whereas we the subscribers Justices of the Peace for Harford County upon the petition of Abraham Andrews who set forth therein that he had been confined in the Gaol [jail] of said county twenty days for debts which he was unable to pay & finding the facts stated to be true we did meet at the county Gaol of said county on the 25th Day of June last and we did then and there appoint the 25th Day of July Instant to meet at the court House of said county which said appointment we did then … at the request of the said Sheriff administer to the said Abraham Andrews the following Oath which was taken by the said Abraham Andrews being first duly sworn on the Holy Evangely of Almighty God in the words following, vizt., I Abraham Andrews do Solemnly swear that the Schedule which I have delivered to the Sheriff of Harford County doth contain a full account to the best of my knowledge and remembrance of my whole estate both real and personal or that I have any title to or interest in and of all debts, credits and effects whatsoever which I or any in trust for me have or at the time of my petition had, or am or was in any respect entitled to in possession, remainder or reversion and that I have not directly or indirectly at any time since my imprisonment or before, sold, leased or otherwise conveyed or disposed of or intrusted all or any part of my estate, goods, Stock, money or Debts thereby to defraud my creditors or to secure the same to receive or expect any profit or advantage thereof so help me God, which said duplicate of the Schedule aforesaid we have transmitted to the clerk of the county court to be by him preserved in his Office for the information of the Creditors of the said Abraham Andrews. Given under our hands and seals this 25th Day of July 1810. Thomas A. Hays. Jno. C. Bond. Saml. Bradford." (Court Records Document 67.09.1(A) at the Historical Society of Harford County; a copy of the schedule to which he signed his name "Abraham Andrews" was included and listed this personal property: "2 tables & 4 chairs, 1 Chest & Cutting Box, 2 pair Geers, 3 Axes, 2 Hoes, A Set of Coopers Tools, Some Old Casks, Some Earthen Ware, 1 Bed Stead, 1 looking Glass, 1 Cupboard, 1 Saddle & Bridle, 1 Ox Chain, 2 Straw Beds &c, 1 Mawl, 2 Wedges, 1 Plow, 1 forked chain, Part of a Waggon, 1 Grind Stone"). **Genealogical Notes**: Abraham Andrews served as a private in Capt. William Bradford's Militia Co. No. 15 in 1775 during the Revolutionary War, drove a wagon to deliver blankets to Col. Hall at Head of Elk in 1776, signed the Association of Freemen in 1776 in Harford Upper Hundred, and signed the Oath of Allegiance to the State of Maryland in 1778. He married Mary Hanson circa March 17, 1779 (date of license). (*Revolutionary Patriots of Harford County, Maryland, 1775-1783*, by Henry C. Peden, Jr., 1985, p. 6)

Andrews, George W., 1885. "August 19th 1885. Petition, Schedule, Affidavits, Deed, Order appointing Preliminary Trustee [name not given] filed … Dec 19/85 Certificate of Publication of Notice to Creditors filed … Feby 8/86 Final discharge of George W. Andrews filed." (Insolvent Docket A. L. J. No. 1, p. 99, in the Court Records Department of the Historical Society of Harford County). "In the matter of the Insolvency of George W. Andrews. Notice is hereby given to the creditors of George W. Andrews, of Harford county, Md., that he has made application for the benefit of the insolvent laws of the State of Maryland, and that a meeting of the creditors will be held at the office of the Clerk of the Circuit Court, in Bel Air, on Saturday, the 29th day of August, 1885, at 10½ o'clock, A. M., to chose [sic] a permanent trustee for the estate of the said George W. Andrews. J. Martin McNabb, Preliminary Trustee." (*The Aegis & Intelligencer*, August 21, 1885, p. 2). "In pursuance of an order passed by the Circuit Court for Harford county, on the 14th day of September, 1885, notice is hereby given to George W. Andrews, insolvent debtor, to appear in said Court on the second Monday in February, 1886, to answer such interrogatories or allegations, as his creditors, endorsers or sureties may propose or allege against him. And notice is also hereby given to the creditors of the said insolvent of the day so fixed upon. J. Martin McNabb, Permanent Trustee." (*The Aegis & Intelligencer*, September 25, 1885, p. 3) **Genealogical Notes**: Dr. George Washington Andrews, son of Isaac Andrews (1817-1890) and Ann W. Scarborough, was born on December 24, 1845, married Mary Jane Heaps (September 30, 1858 – January 18, 1936) and died on August 13, 1902 in Fawn Grove, York Co., PA. They had one known child, Mary Ethel Andrews (1883-1932) who married William Thomas Richardson (1881-1940). (Death certificates of Mary J. Andrews and Mary E. Richardson; *The Aegis & Intelligencer*, August 15, 1902 p. 3)

Archer, James H., 1893. "Insolvent Sale. Alexander Norris, Auctioneer. The undersigned, as permanent trustee of James H. Archer, will offer at public sale, on the premises now occupied by the said Archer, about one and a half miles from Emmorton, on the public road from Demoss' blacksmith shop to Patterson's mill, on Tuesday, December 19, 1893, at 10 o'clock A. M., the following Personal Property: Two Horses, 2 Mares, 3 Cows, 1 Heifer, one Wagon, 1 Combined Mower and Reaper, one Horse cart, 1 Corn Worker, 3 Plows, 2 Harrows, 2 Iron Cultivators, 3 Shovel Plows, 1 Corn Sheller, 1 Fan, 3 sets Plow Harness, 3 sets Wagon Harness, 1 Carriage, 1 set Carriage Harness, 1 Grindstone, Mattocks, Hoes, &c. W. Beatty Harlan, Permanent Trustee." (*Harford Democrat*, December 8, 1893, p. 2). "Insolvent Notice. In the matter of the Insolvency of James H. Archer … Ordered, this 1st day of January, 1894, that James H. Archer appear before the Circuit Court of Harford County, in insolvency, on the second Monday in February, 1894, and answer such interrogatories and allegations as his creditors, endorsers or sureties may propose or allege against him; and that the trustee give notice by publication of this order in some newspaper published in Harford county, once a week for three consecutive weeks before the 1st day of February, 1894, to the creditors of said insolvent of the day so fixed upon. Jas. D. Watters. True copy—test: Wm. S. Forwood, Jr., Clerk."

(*Harford Democrat*, January 19, 1894, p. 2). **Genealogical Notes**: James Hendrickson Archer, son of John Archer, of Pennsylvania, and Hannah Trainor, was born on March 21, 1851, married Margaret Ann "Maggie" Magness (October 1, 1856 – October 3, 1931), daughter of Elijah Magness (1813-1876) and Fannie M. Robinson (1817-1880), circa September 28, 1876 (date of license), worked as a farmer near Bel Air and died on October 16, 1925. He was survived by his wife Maggie Archer, daughters Mrs. Walter Boone, Maude M. Archer married Jacob O. Livezey, and Frances Adelaide Archer married Thomas Earl White, and sons James E. Archer and F. Trainor Archer (1888-1948). James and Maggie are buried in Mount Carmel Cemetery in Emmorton. They were preceded in death by two daughters, Lillian A. Archer (1877-1882) and Margaret Edith Archer (1881-1910), and a son Joseph Wilson Archer (1883-1914). (*The Aegis*, October 23, 1925; Mount Carmel United Methodist Church Cemetery tombstone inscriptions; Death certificates of James Hendrickson Archer and Margaret Ann Archer; *Maryland Bible Records, Volume 1*, by Henry C. Peden, Jr., 2003, p. 155)

Armstrong, G. Sidney, 1885. A "deed of trust for the benefit of creditors" [under the Insolvent Laws of the State of Maryland] has "lately been filed in the clerk's office [for] G. Sidney Armstrong, canner, to Herman Stump." (*The Aegis & Intelligencer*, November 20, 1885, p. 2). **Genealogical Notes**: George Sidney Armstrong (1825 – September 21, 1892), farmer and canner near Carsins Run, married Sarah Catharine Gilbert (1829 – June 23, 1905), daughter of Taylor Gilbert and Sophia Baker, circa 9 Jan 1850 (date of license) and died at home near Carsins Run. (*The Aegis & Intelligencer*, September 23, 1892; "Canning Industry in Harford County," by Margaret S. Bishop, *Harford Historical Bulletin No. 42*, Fall 1989, p. 28; Smith's Chapel tombstone inscriptions; Death Certificate of Sarah Catherine Armstrong stated she was the widow of "Sydney Armstrong")

Armstrong, Nehemiah, 1810. "Whereas we the subscribers Justices of the Peace for Harford County together with John C. Bond, Esq., also one of the Justices of the Peace for said County, upon the petition of Nehemiah Armstrong who set forth therein that he had been confined in the Gaol [jail] of said county twenty Days for Debts which he was unable to pay and finding the facts stated to be true we together with John C. Bond, Esq., did meet at the county Gaol of said county on the 19th Day of February last and we did then and there appoint the 22nd Day of March Inst. to meet at the Court House of said county which said appointment we did then and there … at the request of said Sheriff administer to the said Nehemiah Armstrong the following Oath which was taken by the said Nehemiah Armstrong being first duly sworn on the holy Evangely of Almighty God in the words following – I Nehemiah Armstrong do Solemnly swear that the Schedule which I have delivered to the Sheriff of Harford County doth contain a full account to the best of my Knowledge & Remembrance of my whole estate both real and personal or that I have any title to or interest in and of all debts, credits and effects whatsoever which I or any in trust for me have or at the time of my petition had, or am or was in any respect entitled to in possession, remainder or reversion and that I have not directly or indirectly at any time since my imprisonment or before, sold, leased or otherwise conveyed or disposed of or intrusted all or any part of my estate, goods, Stock, money or Debts thereby to defraud my creditors or to secure the same to receive or expect any profit or advantage thereof so help me God, which said duplicate of the Schedule aforesaid we have transmitted to the Clerk of the County Court to be by him preserved in his Office for the information of the Creditors of the said Nehemiah Armstrong. Given under our hands and seals this 22nd Day of March Eighteen hundred and Ten. Thomas A. Hays. Saml. Bradford." (Court Records Document 67.09.4(B) at the Historical Society of Harford County; a copy of the schedule was included to which "Nehemiah Armstrong" had signed his name, but no property was listed). **Genealogical Note**: Nehemiah Armstrong married Hannah Perine, widow of John Perine, some time prior to 1808. (Harford County Estate Distribution, 1808)

Arthur, Henry (Harry) L., 1884. "January 29, 1884. Petition in Insolvency, affidavit and order of Court thereon filed. Same day Subpoena & copy of petition & order of Court delivered to Sheriff, Harford County. 6th February 1884 Petition dismissed without prejudice per order filed." [A second petition was filed on February 13, 1884 but it was dismissed on December 12, 1884 without explanation.] (Insolvent Docket A. L. J. No. 1, p. 84, in Court Records Department of Historical Society of Harford County) **Genealogical Notes**: Henry Lee Arthur, son of Joseph Owen Arthur (1817-1900) and Mary Jane Grier (1824-1874), was born on February 5, 1862, married Etta Virginia Wells (1883-1937), daughter of James Wells (1810-1888) and Semelia Ann Hollis (1820-1896), circa October 4, 1882 (date of license) and died on July 1, 1922 in Church Home Hospital in Baltimore. Their children were Lillie Olivia Arthur (1883-1937) who married Richard Arthur Neu (1880-1971), Mabel S. Arthur (1886-1941), Maud R. Arthur (1890-1961) who married Oscar R. Tarring, Beulah Meta Arthur (1892-1893), Capt. Herbert Hollis Arthur, U.S.N. (1904-1991) who married Elizabeth Baker (1905-1997), and Virginia L. Arthur (b. 1908) (*The Aegis*, July 7, 1922; Baker Cemetery and William Watters Memorial Church tombstones; Historical Society of Harford County cemetery files)

Austin, Edward, 1841. "Petition, 2 Affidavits, Schedules, Appointment of Trustee, Certificate, Order, Personal Discharge, Appearance Bond, Deed and Trustee's Bond filed 29th June 1841. 20th Novr. 1841 Petitioner appears, Certificate of Publication filed & finally discharged." (Insolvent Docket A, 1807-1843, p. 178, at the Maryland State Archives)

Axer, John, 1892. "Circuit Court Proceedings. Messrs. John Axer and ---- Zimmerman, insolvents, appeared at the bar and asked to be discharged." (*Havre de Grace Republican*, November 18, 1892, p. 3). **Genealogical Notes**: John Philip Axer (harness maker) was born in 1843 (age 22 years and 11 months as of January 1866), married Susanna Elizabeth "Lizzie" Heck (born on January 27, 1844 at Sandy Hook, Harford County, daughter of Charles Lewis Heck (1818-1897), of Germany, and 1st wife Cassandra E. Morgan (1824-1852), of Harford Co.), on January 27, 1866 by Rev. William F. Brand, of St. Mary's Episcopal Church, at the pastor's home. Susanna Elizabeth Axer died at home in Madonna on September 1, 1944, aged 100 years, 7 months and 4 days. The children of John and Lizzie Axer were Charles Henry Axer, Mary H. Axer, John Philip Axer, Jr., Mary Elizabeth Axer Glenn Gunn, Mattie M. Axer and Edgar Hamilton Axer. (Harford Co. marriage certificate; *The Aegis & Intelligencer*, February 2, 1866; 1870 Harford County Census, 4th District; *Descendants of the Signers of the Bush Declaration of March 22, 1775, Harford County, Maryland*, by Christopher T. Smithson and Henry C. Peden, Jr., 2010, pp. 234, 239; Death Certificate No. 10848 of Susanna Elizabeth Axer)

Ayres, John T., 1881. "Petition for benefit of the Insolvent Laws, Schedules, Affidavit, Order of Court appointing J. Edwin Webster preliminary trustee [later appointed permanent trustee], trustee's Bond & deed filed Novr 29th 1881 ... May 13th 1882 … Petitioner appeared in open Court & was finally discharged." (Insolvent Docket A. L. J. No. 1, p. 73, in Court Records Department of the Historical Society of Harford County). **Genealogical Notes**: There were two men with this name at this time: One John T. Ayres married Miss Sarah J. Colder, both of Harford Co., on February 12, 1863 by Rev. R. C. Haslup at Mt. Zion Methodist Church. (Harford Co. license; *Southern Aegis*, February 20, 1863) Another John T. Ayres (1839 – March 8, 1895), of Rocks, Harford Co., married Anna E. "Annie" Hazlett (September 19, 1840 – December 27, 1926), daughter of James Hazlett and Ellen Bell Tate, probably circa 1861 (Death certificate of Anna E. Ayres – informant was their son John C. Ayres; William Watters United Methodist Church tombstones – her marker is inscribed 1841-1926; *The Aegis and Intelligencer*, 15 Mar 1894, stated he died while dancing and playing the violin at a dance near Highland, leaving a widow (name not given) and two grown sons, John and James Ayres). Which one of these John T. Ayres was the insolvent debtor has not been determined.

Ayres, Thomas, 1831/1866. "Petition, Schedule, Sheriff's Certificate, personal discharge and Order for Publication, Bond for Appearance, Trustee's Bond, Trustee's Certificate and Deed to Trustee filed the 6th Febry. 1832. March 24th 1832 petition and order for sale and order for publication and reference to Auditor filed … [several claims filed by various people during 1832] … 18th Augt. 1832 Petitioner appears, certificate of publication filed and finally discharged … [additional accounts and reports recorded from 1832 to 1853] … Novr. 18th 1853 Withdrawal of objections to ratification of sale of real estate filed. 23rd Nov/66 Petition of Nicholas Hutchins & order of Court appointing H. D. Farnandis Trustee filed. Recorded in Judgment Liber H.D.G. No. 2, folio 391." (Insolvent Docket A, 1807-1843, p. 115, at Maryland State Archives)

Bailey, John Barnes, 1887. "Notice To Creditors. In the matter of the Insolvency of J. Barnes Bailey ... This is to give notice to the creditors of J. Barnes Bailey, that he has applied for the benefit of the Insolvent Laws of the State of Maryland, and that I have been appointed Preliminary Trustee, and have fixed Friday, the 16th day of September, at 11 o'clock, A. M., at my office in the town of Bel Air, Harford county, as the time and place for the meeting of his creditors, for the election of a permanent trustee, and other business. Herman Stump, Preliminary Trustee." (*The Aegis & Intelligencer*, September 9, 1887, p. 2; *Havre de Grace Republican*, September 16, 1887, p. 3, stated that Bailey resided in the second district). **Genealogical Notes**: John Barnes Bailey, the sixth of thirteen children of William Bailey (1823-1905) and Priscilla Bowman (1831-1886), was born on March 28, 1860 in Churchville, married 1st to Mary Tollinger on October 11, 1881 and they had two sons, Robert Asael Bailey (1882-1893) and William Scott Bailey (1883-1940). Barnes filed for a divorce in 1885, citing desertion and other reasons, as they had been living apart for fifteen months. A divorce *vinculo matrimonii* was later granted and he married 2nd to Catherine O. Beale on January 2, 1896; they had no children. For many years he engaged in canning and was a farmer in Forest Hill for 50 years. Upon his death on July 13, 1933 he was survived by his wife Catherine, son William, a brother Walter Bailey, of Forest Hill, and a sister Mrs. Rachel Elizabeth Runan, wife of John Runan, of Churchville. Barnes was buried in the Mt. Zion Methodist Church Cemetery near Bel Air. (*Barnes-Bailey Genealogy*, by Walter D. Barnes, 1939, pp. G-19, H-43, I-66; Death Certificates of J. Barnes Bailey and Willilam Bailey; *Havre de Grace Republican*, July 3, 1885; *The Aegis*, July 21, 1933, p. 8)

Baker, James, 1810. "Whereas we the subscribers Justices of the Peace for Harford County together with Bennet Bussey, Esq., also a Justice of the Peace for said county, upon the petition of James Baker, who set forth that he had been confined [in jail] twenty days and upwards for debts which he was unable to pay and finding the facts stated to be true together with the said Bennet Bussey, Esq. we did meet at the Gaol of said county on the 25th Day of October last and did then and there appoint the 26th day of November Inst. to meet at the Court House of said county which said appointment we did then and there … at the request of the said Sheriff administer to the said James Baker the following oath which was taken by the said James Baker being first duly sworn on the holy Evangels of Almighty God in the words following, to wit, I James Baker do solemnly swear that the schedule which I have delivered to the Sheriff of Harford County doth contain a full account to the best of my knowledge and remembrance of my whole estate both real and personal or that I have any title to or interest in and of all debts, credits and effects whatsoever which I or any in trust for me have or at the time of my petition had, or am or was in any respect entitled to in possession, remainder or reversion and that I have not directly or indirectly at any time since my imprisonment or before, sold, leased or otherwise conveyed or disposed of or intrusted all or any part of my estate, goods, stock, money or debts thereby to defraud my creditors or to secure the same to receive or expect any profit or advantage thereof so help me God, which said duplicate of the schedule aforesaid we have transmitted to the clerk of the county court to be by him preserved in his office for the information of the creditors of the said James Baker. Given under our hands and seals this 26th Day of November 1810. Thomas A. Hays. Jno. C. Bond." (Court Records Document 67.09.4(B) at the Historical Society of Harford County; a copy of the schedule to which "James Baker" signed his name, but no property was listed)

Baker, John C., 1890. "Creditors of Mr. John C. Baker, a Churchville canner, have filed petitions in the Circuit Court, asking that he be adjudged insolvent." (*Havre de Grace Republican*, February 14, 1890, p. 3) "On Thursday [June 26, 1890] Judge Watters heard the petition in insolvency of Eisenberg & New against John C. Baker, a canner formerly of Churchville. The proceeding was ex parte, no resistance being made by the defence. The court adjudged Baker insolvent and appointed George L. Van Bibber and Wm. H. Harlan preliminary trustees." (*The Aegis & Intelligencer*, June 27, 1890, p. 2). **Genealogical Notes**: John Carsins Baker (June 18, 1841 – October 24, 1927), eldest son of Nicholas Baker (1810-1896) and Elizabeth Carsins (1819-1853), was a carpenter and canner in Aberdeen, later of Baltimore, and married Miss Martha Louise Chapman Wells (1849-1918) on December 10, 1867 by Rev. J. Marshall West at Bush Chapel. The children of John and Martha Baker were Harry R. Baker (1868-1870), Edgar Nicholas Baker (1871-1964), Howard Wells Baker, Walter C. Baker (born c1873), Clarence B. Baker (1874-1876), and Florence Olivia Baker (married Daniel Hope) (Harford County license and marriage certificate; 1850 Harford County Census; "The Baker Family of Aberdeen," by John Harlan Livezey *Harford Historical Bulletin No. 16*, Spring 1983, pp. 3-4; *The Aegis & Intelligencer*, 28 Oct 1927; *Maryland Bible Records, Volume 1*, by Henry C. Peden, Jr., 2003, p. 155)

Baldwin, George, 1844. "Notice is hereby given, to the creditors of George Baldwin, late an imprisoned debtor of Harford county, that on the application of said debtor by petition in writing to the Hon. Robert W. Holland, chief justice of the Orphan's court of said county, for the benefit of the insolvent laws of Maryland, the said judge on the 24th day of November 1844, granted to the said debtor a discharge from imprisonment and appointed the first Saturday after the 3rd Monday in May next, for his appearance before the Judges of Harford county court at the court house of said county, for a final hearing before said court, on said petition and to answer such interrogatories as his creditors may propose to him." (*Harford Madisonian and Bel-Air & Havre de Grace Messenger*, January 3, 1845, p. 3). **Genealogical Note**: George Baldwin (born September 1, 1821) was a son of Tyler and Sarah Baldwin. (Tyler Baldwin Bible, *Maryland Bible Records, Volume. 5*, by Henry C. Peden, Jr., 2004, p. 14)

Baldwin, George H., 1868. "Petition, 3 Schedules, Affidavit, Order, Trustee's Bond & Deed filed 5th Nov/68." [nothing further recorded] (Insolvent Docket A. L. J. No. 1, p. 52, in the Court Records Department of the Historical Society of Harford County). "Notice is hereby given that George H. Baldwin has made application to the Circuit Court of Harford county, for the benefit of the Insolvent Laws of Maryland, and that the second Monday in May, 1869, has been assigned for him to appear in said Court to answer such interrogatories as his creditors may propose or allege against him. A. Lingan Jarrett, Clerk, Circuit Court for Harford county." (*The Aegis & Intelligencer*, November 13, 1868, p. 2)

Baldwin, Timothy, 1842. "Petition, Affidavits, Schedules, Appointment, Order, Personal Discharge, Appearance Bond & Trustee's Bonds filed 13th Septr. 1842. 20 May 1843 Petitioner appears, files certificate of publication & finally discharged." (Insolvent Docket A, 1807-1843, p. 185, at Maryland State Archives). **Genealogical Note**: Timothy Baldwin (born April 7, 1816) was a son of Tyler and Sarah Baldwin and he married Mary Ann R. Bowen circa August 14, 1839 (date of license). ("Tyler Baldwin Bible," *Maryland Bible Records, Volume 5*, by Henry C. Peden, Jr., 2004, p. 14)

Baldwin, William A., 1885. "January 30th 1885. Petition, Order, Affidavit, Schedules, List of Creditors, Debts and Insolvent's Deed filed. Same day Bond of Preliminary Trustee [name was not given] approved & filed … May 11/85 Order of Court discharging Insolvent filed." (Insolvent Docket A. L.

J. No. 1, p. 97, in Court Records Department of the Historical Society of Harford County). "Notice Is Hereby Given, to the creditors of William A. Baldwin, an insolvent debtor, who were such on the 30th day of January, 1885, the date of his application for the benefit of the insolvent laws, to file their claims against the said insolvent, duly proven, with the Clerk of the Circuit Court for Harford county on or before the 1st day of May, 1885. Otho S. Lee, Permanent Trustee." (*The Aegis & Intelligencer*, February 27, 1885, p. 2). "In the matter of the Insolvency of William A. Baldwin ... In pursuance of an order passed by the Circuit Court for Harford county, on the 18th day of April, 1885, notice is hereby given to William A. Baldwin, insolvent debtor, to appear in said Court on Monday, the 11th day of May, 1885, to answer such interrogatories or allegations, as his creditors, endorsers or sureties may propose or allege against him; and notice is also hereby given to the creditors of the said insolvent of the day so fixed upon. Otho S. Lee, Permanent Trustee." (*The Aegis & Intelligencer*, April 24, 1885, p. 3). **Genealogical Notes**: William Alfred Baldwin, son of Jarrett T. Baldwin (1823-1903) and Aliceanna E. "Allie" Keen (1823-1888), was born in 1858 or 1859, married Susan K. "Susie" Murphy circa March 3, 1880 (date of license) and committed suicide (by shooting) at his home in Aberdeen on April 2, 1905. He was survived by his wife Susan and six children, names not given. (*The Aegis & Intelligencer*, April 7, 1905; Death certificate of William Alfred Baldwin; *Harford County, Maryland Marriage References and Family Relationships, 1825-1850*, by Henry C. Peden, Jr., 2014, p. 15)

Baltimore and Lehigh Railroad, 1893. "The Baltimore and Lehigh Railroad is now operated under the direction of the Circuit Court for Harford county by Receiver William H. Bosley and W. R. Crumpton, General Manager. The work of broad-gauging has stopped for want of money to pay for labor and material. This condition of affairs was known and a bill had been prepared by the contractors alleging the insolvency of the corporation managing the road when the application for the appointment of a receiver was made to the Harford court. As soon as Receiver Bosley was appointed the fact was wired to Miller & Co., then operating the road, and who delayed an hour the train to give the insolvent corporation time to file a deed of trust to Winfield S. Taylor, a member of the insolvent firm, before the injunction could be served on them. The deed of trust, which virtually admits the insolvency of the railroad company and the forwarding company, having been given after the appointment of Receiver Bosley and after the Baltimore corporation had actual notice, is believed to be irregular and illegal, a bill in equity has been filed in Baltimore to set aside the deed of trust to Taylor. The action taken in the Harford court has been in contemplation for some time and was delayed in the hope that the money promises of improvement would be realized. When it was definitely ascertained that the Forwarding Company had not the means to pay for broad-gauging the road, and that the contractors had prepared a bill to put the Railroad and Forwarding Company into insolvency, action could no longer be delayed, as it was certain, as has been since proved, that these corporations would make a deed of trust and endeavor to continue the control of the road under the trustee of their selection. Attention was called to the proceedings of John H. Miller and company, who controlled the road some time ago when they changed the name of the corporation and leased several thousand additional shares of stock and appointed as directors employees in their office. They procured from the Deer Creek and Susquehanna Railroad Co. a large block of bonds endorsed by the Maryland Central Railroad Co. under promise of building the former road. They then authorized an issue of seven million general mortgage bonds in the Baltimore and Lehigh Railroad, two and a half millions of which have been actually issued. These various issues of stock and bonds have created an indebtedness of over five million dollars on a road that cost but little more than one million. With this vast indebtedness the property of the company is in little or no better condition than it was when it passed into the control of the Miller management with a stock issue of four hundred thousand dollars and a bonded debt of eight hundred and fifty thousand dollars. The gross earnings of the road are about $200,000 annually. The operating expenses should not exceed sixty per cent. This would leave a surplus of $80,000. Of this sum $34,000 would pay interest on the first mortgage bonds and leave a margin of $46,000, which should go to the stockholders either in the form of dividends or in the improvement of their property. Thursday [May 25, 1893] the court heard the motion for dissolving the injunction issued by the court restraining Winfield Taylor from interfering with Receiver Bosley's operation of the road, and directing Taylor to deliver to the Receiver all the books and other property of the Company was overruled. The court adjudged Taylor to be in contempt, but assuming that it was not intentional he passed an order directing Taylor to purge himself of contempt by complying with the order of the court before Saturday morning at ten o'clock, and said that an attachment would not be issued before that time. It is to ascertain what has become of the proceeds of the new stock and two and half million bonds and of the earnings of the road, to secure an economical and efficient management, including the prompt payment for labor and supplies, and to invite development of the country, that this suit was instituted. There is publicly expressed wish and belief that these results will follow this investigation. (*Harford Democrat*, May 26, 1893, p. 2). "The Railroad Case of Streett vs. B. & L. R. R. and others, in which Wm. Bosley was appointed Receiver, has been removed to the United States Court, on petition of Houseman and Walworth, residents respectively of Pennsylvania and Ohio, who make affidavit that they can not get justice in the State Courts, on account of prejudice against them. A few years ago some of the Directors operating the Maryland Central Railroad were indicted for manslaughter in permitting, by their negligence, accidents on the road. Since then some of these officials and their confreres have a decided conviction that Harford justice is not of the kind that suits their convenience and is not what they what [want]. The evidence taken under the various commissions since the appointment of the Receiver, and the books examined, disclose the fact that the various corporations named in the suit are insolvent, and that it is for the best interest of the railroad to have the management placed in independent and responsible hands." (*Harford Democrat*, June 23, 1893, p. 2). 1894. "The B. & L. Railroad to be Sold. On the petition of Warren F. Walworth, of Ohio, a judgment creditor to the amount of $261,871.66, Judge Bittinger of York, Pa., last Wednesday made an order for the sale of that part of the Baltimore and Lehigh Railroad lying in Pennsylvania, the sale to take place between now and the first Monday in March. The road has been in receivers' hands about a year, and it is stated that as soon as it is delivered from the receivers' hands it will be broadgauged." (*Havre de Grace Republican*, February 2, 1894). "This poor little road seems to be environed by troubles innumerable. Lawsuits affecting it are pending in the United States and in the State Courts in Baltimore city, in Baltimore and Harford County Courts and in Pennsylvania Courts, so that it will be a wonder if it is not litigated to bankruptcy and dissolution. Judge Morris, in the U.S. Circuit Court, yesterday week, dismissed the petition in the case of Joseph M. Streett and others against the Company in an application to remand the case back from the United States Circuit Court to the Circuit Court for Harford county, where it was originally brought, and from which it was removed to the Court in which it now is. Following this, in the same Court, a bill was filed by Gans & Haman, and Marshall, Marbury & Bowdoin, as counsel for Charles E. Lewis, of New York, the trustee appointed by the Circuit Court of Baltimore city, in place of Edwin G. Baetjer, resigned, asking for the foreclosure of the general mortgage bonds, on the ground that the defendant had defaulted in the payment of interest. It is alleged that the road is insolvent, and the Court is again asked for the appointment of a receiver, &c. The bill is very voluminous, but contains little that is new regarding the vexed question of what shall be done with the Baltimore and Lehigh, and what will be the best manner of making it pay. A creditor's bill was filed last week in the Circuit Court for Harford County by F. R. Williams, attorney for Caleb J.

Moore, Christian Westerman and Richard Roberts & Son, against the Railroad. The bill alleges the insolvency of the railroad company, and claims that the removal of the receivership case to the United States Court was illegal, and prays that this Court take jurisdiction." (*Havre de Grace Republican*, March 30, 1894, p. 3). "Charles R. Spence, commissioner under a decree of the United States Court for the District of Maryland, has given notice of a sale of the entire line of the Baltimore and Lehigh Railroad, from Baltimore to York, about forty-four miles, with all its property, franchises, personal property, &c. The sale will take place June 15th. This sale is a result of the suit brought against the Company by Charles E. Lewis, trustee." (*Havre de Grace Republican*, May 11, 1894, p. 3). **Note**: The Baltimore & Lehigh Railroad survived and later became known as the Ma & Pa Railroad. For a comprehensive history of this famous railroad see *The Ma & Pa Remembered: A History of the Maryland & Pennsylvania Railroad*, by Henry C. Peden, Jr. and Jack L. Shagena, Jr., 2011)

Baptist (Babtist), Jesse (African American), 1837. "Negro Jesse Babtist. Petition, Affidavits, Schedule, personal discharge and order of publication, Bond for Appearance, Trustee's Bond, Trustee's Certificate and Deed to Trustee filed 25th September 1837. 17th March 1838 Certificate of Publication filed. Petitioner appears and finally discharged." (Insolvent Docket A, 1807-1843, p. 159, at the Maryland State Archives). **Genealogical Notes**: Jesse Baptist was age 36 in 1832, with Fanny Baptist, age 44, John Baptist, age 8, Thomas Baptist, age 6, Jesse Baptist', age 4, and James Baptist, age 1. (A List of Free People of Colour Taken in 1832 by Joshua Guyton, Sheriff). He was also listed as a free colored person and head of household in 1840. (Harford County Census)

Barclay, John, 1813. "Whereas we the subscribers Justices of the Peace for Harford County upon the petition of John Barclay setting forth therein that he had actually remained in the goal [jail] of said County since the fifth day of August last for debts which he was unable to pay and finding the facts therein stated to be true we did meet at the goal of said County on the third day of September Instant and did then and there appoint the 24th day of September Inst. to meet at the Courthouse of said County, which said appointment we did then and there ... at the request of the said Sheriff administer to the said John Barclay the following oath which was taken by the said John Barclay being first duly sworn on the Holy Evangels of Almighty God in the words following to wit, I do solemnly promise and swear that the schedule which I have delivered to the Sheriff of Harford County doth contain a full account to the best of my knowledge and remembrance of my whole estate both real and personal or that I have any title to or interest in, and of all debts, credits and effects whatsoever which I or any in trust for me have or at the time of my petition had, or am or was in any respect entitled to in possession, remainder or reversion and that I have not directly or indirectly at any time since my imprisonment or before, sold, leased or otherwise conveyed or disposed of or intrusted all or any part of my estate, goods, stock, money or debts thereby to defraud my creditors or to secure the same to receive or expect any profit or advantage thereof so help me God, which said duplicate of the Schedule aforesaid we have transmitted to the Clerk of the County Court to be by him preserved in his office for the information of the creditors of the said John Barclay. Given under our hands and seals this twenty-fourth day of September 1813. Samuel Bradford. Thomas A. Hays. John Guyton." (Court Records Document 67.12(6) at the Historical Society of Harford County; copy of the schedule to which he signed his name "Jno. Barclay" was included, but no property was listed). **Genealogical Note**: John Barclay was deposed on December 6, 1809 and stated he was age 31 and his father showed him the bounded tree of *Betsy's Inheritance* about 15 years ago. (Court Records Document 57.09.1 at the Historical Society of Harford County)

Barclay, William, 1805. "In Harford County Court. March 26th 1805. On application to the Justices of the said County Court by petition in writing of William Barclay, of the said County, praying the benefit of the 'Act for the relief of sundry Insolvent Debtors' and passed at November Session

Eighteen hundred and four, on the terms mentioned in the said Act, a Schedule of his property and a list of his Creditors on oath, as far as he can ascertain them, as directed by the said Act being annexed to his petition, and the said County Court being satisfied by competent testimony that the said William Barclay has resided the two preceding years within the State of Maryland prior to the passage of the said Act – It is thereupon adjudged and ordered by the said Court that the said William Barclay (by causing a Copy of this order to be inserted in the *Baltimore Telegraphe* once a week for four successive weeks and at the Court house door in Harford County before the second Monday in July next) give notice to his creditors to appear before the said County Court at the Court house in the same County for the purpose of recommending a Trustee for their Benefit, on the said William Barclay, then and there taking the oath by the said Act prescribed for delivering up his property. Signed by order- Henry Dorsey, Clk. July 8th 1805. The Creditors of the said William Barclay not attending according to notice it is ruled and ordered here by the Court that the further consideration of the petition of the said William Barclay be continued over and postponed to next Term." (Court Actions in Insolvencies, 1805-1807, p. 1, Court Records Book Accession No. 605 at the Historical Society of Harford County)

Barnes, Amos D., 1857. "Petition, Schedules, Affidavits, Appointment of Trustee & order of notice, Bond & deed filed 8th May 1857." [nothing further recorded] (Insolvent Docket A. L. J. No. 1, p. 15, in the Court Records Department of the Historical Society of Harford County)

Barnes, Ford, 1833. "Petition, Schedule, Affidavit, Personal discharge, Order for Publication, Bond for Appearance, Trustee's Bond, Trustee's Certificate and Deed to Trustee filed 27th Nov. 1833. 15th March 1834. Allegations filed. A. W. Bradford appears for petitioner and moved to continue the case. 22nd August 1834 Certificate and affidavit filed and petitioner appears by A. W. Bradford his attorney & cont'd. by order of Court." (Insolvent Docket A, 1807-1843, p. 129, at the Maryland State Archives). **Genealogical Notes**: Ford Barnes, son of Gregory Barnes (1765-1846) and his 2nd wife Elizabeth Mitchell (1775-1859), was born on August 4, 1801 and married Mary A. Osborn (1802-1880) on January 1, 1822. Their daughter and only child Elizabeth Barnes (1823-1902) married Jarrett E Ward (1802-1898) circa February 3, 1841 (date of license). (*Barnes-Bailey Genealogy*, by Walter D. Barnes, 1939, pp. E-4, F-7, G-10; *Baltimore Patriot*, January 8, 1822; Wesleyan Chapel tombstones)

Barnes, Hosier, 1828. "Petition, Schedule, Affidavit, Certificate, Bond, Deed, Trustee Bond, Discharge and Order for Publication filed 7 Mar 1828." [nothing further recorded] (Insolvent Docket A, 1807-1843, p. 88, at the Maryland State Archives). **Genealogical Notes**: Hosier or Hosea Barnes was born in 1764, worked as a farmer in the 2nd district and appears to have married thrice: 1st to Mary Wood in 1788; 2nd to Elizabeth Lester in 1809; and, 3rd to Mary Garretson in 1812, His parents and date of death are undetermined, but he died in the 1830s. His known children are Amos Barnes, John Lisby Barnes, Joshua Wood Barnes and Rebecca Barnes. (*Barnes-Bailey Genealogy*, by Walter D. Barnes, 1939, pp. E-0, F-2; St. George's Parish Register; Court Records Document 90.29.67 at the Historical Society of Harford County states Hosea was deposed on June 13, 1828, aged 64 years and upwards)

Barnes, Richard, 1823. "Petition, Schedule, Bond, Sheriff's certificate, personal discharge and order for publication filed 8th March 1823. Certificate of publication filed, petitioner appears and personally discharged 30th Aug. 1823." (Insolvent Docket A, 1807-1843, p. 54, at the Maryland State Archives; Insolvent Docket Prior to 1827, Court Records Accession #632 at the Historical Society of Harford County). **Genealogical Notes**: Richard Barnes, son of Bennett and Esther Barnes, was born in 1763 and married Mary K. Myers (1787-1868), daughter of John Kentle Myers and Margaret ----, circa September 27, 1808 (date of license). Their children were George Washington Barnes, Emily M. Barnes Reasin, Arabella Barnes Faulkner, Lydia Barnes Henry and Elizabeth Barnes Barr. (*Barnes-*

Bailey Genealogy, by Walter D. Barnes, 1939, pp. F-1, G-4; Court Records Document 90.20.66 at the Historical Society of Harford County states he was deposed on June 12, 1828, aged 65 and upwards)

Barnes, William, 1830. Insolvent debtor to be discharged from imprisonment (*Independent Citizen*, June 24, 1830). "Petition, Schedule, personal discharge, order of publication, Bond for Appearance & Trustees Bond filed 1st day of June 1830. 19th March 1831 Petitioner appears, certificate of publication filed & finally discharged." (Insolvent Docket A, 1807-1843, p. 105, at Maryland State Archives)

Barnet, George, 1845. "Notice is hereby given, to the creditors of *George Barnet*, late an imprisoned debtor of *Harford County*, that on the application of said debtor by petition in writing to the Hon. Robert W. Holland, chief justice of the Orphan's court of said county, for the benefit of the insolvent laws of Maryland, the said judge on the 13th day of January, 1845, granted to the said debtor a discharge from imprisonment and appointed the first Saturday after the 3rd Monday in May next, for his appearance before the Judges of *Harford* county court at the court house of said county, for a final hearing before said court, on said petition and to answer such interrogatories as his creditors may propose to him." (*Harford Madisonian and Bel-Air & Havre de Grace Messenger*, April 18, 1845, p. 3)

Barton, Benjamin, 1820. "Petition, Schedule, Bond, Sheriff's certificate, personal discharge and order for publication filed 28th November 1820 – March 17th 1821 petitioner appeared … Andrew McAdow appointed Trustee and a personal discharge granted the petitioner." [nothing further recorded] (Insolvent Docket A, 1807-1843, p. 39, at Maryland State Archives; Insolvent Docket Prior to 1827, Court Records Accession #632 at the Historical Society of Harford County)

Barton, George A., 1889. "George A. Barton and Wm. H. Hopkins, insolvents, appeared, and [both] were finally discharged." (*Havre de Grace Republican*, February 15, 1889, p. 4)

Barton, Philip A., 1859. "Petition, Schedule, Affidavit, Appointment of Trustee, Order of Notice, Trustee's Bond and Deed to Trustee filed 9th Aug/59. A. W. Bateman, Esqr., appointed Trustee. 27th February 1860 Petitioner appears, files certificate of notice & finally discharged." (Insolvent Docket A. L. J. No. 1, p. 30, in the Court Records Department of the Historical Society of Harford County). "Notice is hereby given that Philip A. Barton, of Harford County, has made application to the Circuit Court of said County, for the benefit of the Insolvent Laws of Maryland, and that the 4th Monday in February, 1860, has been assigned for him to appear in said Court to answer such interrogatories as his creditors may propose or allege against him. Wm. Galloway, Clerk, Circuit Court for Harford County." (*The Southern Aegis*, August 13, 1859, p. 3)

Bateman, William B., 1823. "Petition, Schedule, Bond, Sheriff's certificate, and personal discharge and order for publication filed 8th March 1823. 30th Augt. 1823 Petitioner appears and finally discharged." (Insolvent Docket A, 1807-1843, p. 54, at the Maryland State Archives; Insolvent Docket Prior to 1827, Court Records Accession #632 at Historical Society of Harford County). **Genealogical Notes**: William B. Bateman (1791-1835), son of William Bateman of England and later of Harford Co., MD, married 1st to Susan J. Worthington circa December 7, 1813 (date of license), served in the War of 1812 (participated in the Battle of North Point on September 12-14, 1814), married 2nd to Sarah L. Birckhead, daughter of Dr. Thomas Howell Birckhead and Elizabeth Waters, circa February 8, 1822 (date of license) and died on January 8, 1835. (*Ancestral Charts, Volume 6*, Special Publication No. 34, Harford County Genealogical Society, 2005, p. 35; marriage records; military records)

Baxter, Benjamin, 1830. "Petition, Schedule, Shffs. certificate, personal discharge and order of publication, Bond for Appearance, Trustee's Bond, Trustee's Certificate and Deed to Trustee filed 8th day of June 1830." [nothing further recorded] (Insolvent Docket A, 1807-1843, p. 105, at Maryland State Archives). Insolvent debtor to be discharged from imprisonment. (*Independent Citizen*, December 9, 1830). **Genealogical Note**: Benjamin Baxter and Miss Ann Reed, of Harford Co., were married on April 3, 1821 in Baltimore City by Rev. Glendy. (*Baltimore Federal Gazette*, April 7, 1821)

Baxter, John T., 1833. "Petition, Schedule, Affidavit, Personal discharge, Order for Publication, Bond for Appearance, Trustee's Bond, Trustee's Certificate and Deed to Trustee filed 5th Nov. 1833. 15th March 1834 Petitioner appears, Certificate of Publication filed and finally discharged." (Insolvent Docket A, 1807-1843, p. 128, at the Maryland State Archives)

Baxter, William, 1830. "William Baxter, insolvent debtor, to be discharged from imprisonment." (*Independent Citizen*, December 9, 1830). "William Baxter, Jnr. Petition, Schedule, Shff's. Certificate, Personal Discharge and Order of Publication, Bond for Appearance, Trustee's Bond, Trustee's Certificate and Deed to Trustee filed 1st day of June 1830. 23rd March 1831 Affidavit & Certificate of Publication filed & finally discharged." (Insolvent Docket A, 1807-1843, p. 104, at the Maryland State Archives). 1833. "Petition, Schedule, Affidavit, Personal discharge, Order for Publication, Bond for Appearance, Trustee's Bond, Trustee's Certificate and Deed to Trustee filed 21st Octr. 1833. 14th March 1834. Allegations of Wm. Robinson filed … 15th March 1834 Petitioner appears, motion to withdraw petition and cont'd." (Insolvent Docket A, 1807-1843, p. 130, at the Maryland State Archives). 1834. "William Baxter, Jnr. Petition, Affidavits, Schedule, personal discharge and order of publication, Bond for Appearance, Trustee's Bond, Trustee's Certificate and Deed to Trustee filed 12th May 1834. 16th Augt. 1834 Petitioner appears, Certificate of Publication filed and finally discharged." (Insolvent Docket A, 1807-1843, p. 134, at the Maryland State Archives). "William Baxter, Senr. 1835. "Petition, Affidavits, Schedule, personal discharge, order of publication, Bond for Appearance, Trustee's Bond, Trustee's Certificate and Deed to Trustee filed 14th March 1835. 15th Augt. 1835. Petitioner appears, Certificate of Publication filed and finally discharged." (Insolvent Docket A, 1807-1843, p. 139, at the Maryland State Archives) **Genealogical Notes**: William Baxter married Sarah Ecoff (born circa 1791), only daughter and third and youngest child of Samuel Ecoff (Eacoff, Eckhoff) and Abigail Pyle (born 1752), of Deer Creek, circa December 8, 1813 (date of license). (*Pyles of Bishops Canning, England*, by Howard Thornton and Jane Weaver, 1980, p. 151)

Beaty, James, 1817. "Petition, Schedule, Bond & Notice to Creditors filed 10th March 1817." [nothing further recorded] (Insolvent Docket A, 1807-1843, p. 20, at the Maryland State Archives; Insolvent Docket Prior to 1827, Court Records Accession #632 at the Historical Society of Harford County). **Genealogical Notes**: James Beaty, son of William Beaty, was born July 22, 1776, married Catharine Demoss (March 5, 1779 - November 13, 1862), daughter of William and Mary Demoss, on April 24, 1806 and died on September 28, 1852. Their children were Mary Harrison Beaty (born 1809), John Demoss Beaty (born 1813) and Catharine Beaty. (Bethel Presbyterian Church cemetery records; *St. James Parish Register, 1787-1815*, by Bill and Martha Reamy, 1987, pp. 7, 45, 47)

Beaumont, Hiram, 1856. "Petition, Schedules, Affidavits, Appointment of Trustee," etc. 6 May/56. 15th Novr. 1856 Petitioner appears, files certificate of publication & is finally discharged." (Insolvent Docket A. L. J. No. 1, p. 14, in the Court Records Department of the Historical Society of Harford County). "Notice Is Hereby Given, that Hiram Beaumont, of Harford county, has made application to the Circuit Court of said county, for the benefit of the Insolvent Laws of Maryland; and that the first Saturday after the second Monday in November next, has been assigned for him to appear in said court to answer such interrogatories as his creditors may propose or allege against him. A. L. Jarrett, Cl'k. Cir. Court for Harford Co." (*National American*, September 5, 1856, p. 3). **Genealogical Notes**: Hiram Beaumont, son of Mifflin Beaumont (1800-1884) and Mary Lake (1798-1877), was born on February 18, 1827, married Cecelia Ann Norris (April 19, 1837 - March 17, 1922 or 1923), daughter of David Norris and Rachel Lockhard, circa May 2, 1854 (date of license), moved to Illinois circa 1857-1858 and then to Piedmont, KS in 1869. He worked as a farmer and died on May 11, 1898. (Mifflin Beaumont Family Bible and research by Sue Beaumont Hughes of Hamilton, KS in 2005; *The Norris Family of Maryland and Virginia*, by Harry Alexander Davis, 1941, pp. 247, 248, 565)

Bel Air Social, Literary, Musical and Dramatic Club, 1890. "The Bel Air Social Club Charter. Judge Watters last Monday [June 23, 1890] heard the motion against the Bel Air Social, Literary, Musical and Dramatic Club by J. Edwin Webster, State's attorney, asking that the charter of the club be revoked. The club was represented by Geo. L. Van Bibber, George Y. Maynadier and William S. Cooley. The club was convicted of violating the local option and sentenced to pay a fine of $6.000 and cost. A *fi fa* [abbreviation for *fieri facias* meaning "a writ of execution against the goods of a debtor"] was issued and returned *nulla bona* [meaning "no goods"]. On this point the State asked for the revoking of the charter under that section of the code which provided that insolvency is a sufficient ground for revoking the charter of a corporation. The defense was that the proper proceeding was to file to have the corporation declared insolvent, and when this was done follow the proceedings by a similar bill as now filed. The case was held *sub curia*." [meaning "under law"] (*Havre de Grace Republican*, June 27, 1890, p. 3)

Bell, Joseph, 1824. "Petition, Schedule, Bond, Sheriffs Certificate and personal Discharge and order for Publication filed 21st January 1824. Aug 14th Petitioner appears." [nothing further recorded] (Insolvent Docket A, 1807-1843, p. 60, at the Maryland State Archives; Insolvent Docket Prior to 1827, Court Records Accession #632 at the Historical Society of Harford County)

Berg, Daniel, 1841. "Feby 2nd 1841. Petition, Affidavits, Schedules, Order of appointment of Trustee, Trustee Certificate, Order of Discharge & Order of Publication, Appearance Bond, Trustee Bond & deed filed. Petitioner appears & files Certificate of Publication and finally discharged 22nd May 1841." (Insolvent Docket A, 1807-1843, p. 176, at the Maryland State Archives)

Bevard, Charles, 1826. "Petition, schedule, bond, Sheriff's certificate and personal discharge and order for publication filed 24th January 1826. Petitioner appears, Printers certificate filed and Personal discharged filed 19th Augt. 1826." (Insolvent Docket A, 1807-1843, p. 77, at the Maryland State Archives; Insolvent Docket Prior to 1827, Court Records Accession #632 at Historical Society of Harford County). **Genealogical Note**: Charles Bevard married Amelia Chance on February 4, 1798 (marriage license stated his name was Charles; St. James Parish Register mistakenly stated James)

Bevard, James, 1802. Petitioned for relief under the act for relief of sundry Insolvent Debtors (*Laws of Maryland*, Vol. III, 1802, Chapter 97, Liber JG No. 4, folio 308-314) [see the Genealogical Note above]

Billingslea, Bennett M., 1830. "Petition, Schedule, Shff's. Certificate, personal discharge and Order for Publication, Bond for Appearance, Trustee's Bond, Trustee's Certificate and Deed to Trustee filed 11th May 1830. 15th August 1830 Petitioner appears and Certificate of Publication filed and finally discharged by order of Court." (Insolvent Docket A, 1807-1843, p. 102, at the Maryland State Archives) **Genealogical Notes**: Bennett M. Billingslea was born circa 1790-1794 and was buried at Cokesbury Memorial Methodist Church, but most of his tombstone is beneath the ground. Beside him rest his wife Elizabeth Freeborn Billingslea (August 27, 1794 – December 18, 1858) and youngest daughter Ethlin H. Baker who died on April 2, 1888, wife of Henry F. Baker. (Cokesbury Memorial Methodist Church tombstones)

Blakey, Thomas, 1860. "Petition, Schedule of property, List of debts due & owing, Affidavit, Order appointing Trustee, Trustee's Bond and Deed to Trustee filed & Henry D. Farnandis, Esqr., appointed Trustee filed 1st October 1860 … 25th February 1861 Petitioner appears & files Certificate of Publication of Notice to Creditors & finally discharged by the Court." (Insolvent Docket A. L. J. No. 1, p. 36, in the Court Records Department of the Historical Society of Harford County)

Bodt, Edward A., 1867. "Petition, 3 Schedules, Affidavit, Order to give Bond & appear. Trustee's Bond & Deed filed 28th Feby. 1868." [nothing further recorded] (Insolvent Docket A. L. J. No. 1, p. 51, in the Court Records Department of the Historical Society of Harford County). **Genealogical Notes**: Edward August Bodt (May 9, 1833, Hanover, Germany – May 2, 1914), a farmer, canner and cabinet maker near Carsins Run, married Fredericka Burkley (November 27, 1835, Württemberg, Germany – April 29, 1904) circa 1855 and their children were William A. Bodt (1856-1937) married Anna A. Preston, Eva Katherine "Kate" Bodt (1860-1924) married Henry Koendries, Elizabeth F. "Lizzie" Bodt (born c1862) married Frederick Wirsing, Andrew P. Bodt (March 17, 1864 – February 7, 1952), Anna M. "Annie" Bodt (1868-1895), Matilda Bodt (1870-1949) married John Henry Smith, and Emma Bodt (born c1874). (1860 Harford Co. Census mistakenly listed them as Alwood and Fredericka Bode and the 1880 census enumerated them as Edward A. and Fredericka Bodt; St. Paul's Lutheran Church tombstone inscriptions; Smith's Chapel tombstone inscriptions; Death certificate of Edward August Bodt; *The Aegis & Intelligencer*, 6 May 1904 and 8 May 1914; Harford Co. marriage licenses)

Boice, James, 1888. "Proceedings of the County Commissioners. The Commissioners met on Monday [June 25, 1888]. An order was passed instructing the collector of the second district to return, as insolvent, $5,000 assessed on the property of James Boice, Spesutia Island." (*The Aegis & Intelligencer*, June 29, 1888, p. 2)

Bolster, William, 1820. "Petition, Schedule, Sheriff's certificate, Bond, order for publication and personal discharge filed 7th March 1820. Sepr. 2nd 1820 petitioner appeared." [nothing further was recorded] (Insolvent Docket A, 1807-1843, p. 28, at the Maryland State Archives; Insolvent Docket Prior to 1827, Court Records Accession #632 at Historical Society of Harford County). **Genealogical Note**: William Bolster married 1st to Frances Hollis on June 8, 1809 and married 2nd to Susan Wilson circa January 27, 1818 (Harford County marriage license; St. James Parish Register)

Bond, James T., 1848. "Petition &c. 9 May/48. Nov/48 Cert. & Discharge – appointment of O. Scott Trustee … Auditor's Report & Order filed 23rd Nov/53. 25 Sept/54 Petition of L. M. Jarrett Admrs. & Jno. A. McKee … Recorded in Judgment Record A.L.J. No. 1, folio 258 &c. See Doc. B, fol. 67." (Insolvent Docket A. L. J. No. 1, p. 3, in the Court Records Department of the Historical Society of Harford County)

Bond, John C., 1810. "On application to the Subscriber in the recess of the Court as Associate Judge of the Sixth Judicial district of the State of Maryland by petition in writing of John C. Bond of Harford County stating that he is in actual confinement and praying the benefit of the Act of the General Assembly of the State of Maryland entitled an Act for the relief of sundry Insolvent debtors, passed at November session 1805 and the several Supplements thereto, on the terms therein mentioned, a schedule of his property and a list of his creditors on oath as far as he can ascertain them being annexed to his petition and the said John C. Bond having satisfied me by competent testimony that he has resided two years within the State of Maryland immediately preceding [sic] the time of his application and having taken the oath by the said act prescribed for Delivering up his Property and given Sufficient Security for his Personal appearance at the County Court of Harford County to answer such allegations as may be made against him I do therefore order and adjudge that the said John C. Bond be discharged from the Imprisonment and that by causing a copy of this order to be inserted in some one of the Public Newspapers for the City of Baltimore once in every week for three months successively before the First Saturday in March Term next he give notice to his creditors to appear before the said Court at the Court House of said county at ten o'clock in the forenoon of said day to show cause if any they have why the said John C. Bond should not have the benefit of the said act and supplements as prayed. Given under my hand this 26th day of October 1810, Thos. Jones." (Court Records Document 67.12(7) at Historical Society of Harford County; a schedule of his creditors was included in the file, property listed as "one house & Lott in Charles Town, Cecil County," signed his name "Jno. C. Bond" and another document gave his full name as John Churchman Bond. "Petition, Schedule and Bond filed for his appearance filed 28th November 1810. March 10th 1811 the petitioner appeared according to the tenor of his bond and not having given the necessary notice the Court refuse to grant him further relief" [nothing further recorded]. (Insolvent Docket A, 1807-1843, p. 8, at the Maryland State Archives; Insolvent Docket Prior to 1827, Court Records Accession #632 at the Historical Society of Harford County). **Genealogical Note**: John C. Bond, aged about 39, was deposed on August 15, 1807, thus he was born in 1768. (Court Records Document 75.00.1(X) in the Court Records Department at the Historical Society of Harford County)

Bond, John H., 1899. "Notice to Creditors. To the Creditors of John H. Bond. Take notice that John H. Bond, of Harford county, State of Maryland, having filed his petition to be discharged from all his debts and liabilities under the insolvent laws of said State, and such petition being now pending, a meeting of the creditors of such insolvent will be held on Monday, 10th day of April, 1899, at 12 o'clock, M., at the office of Robert Archer, Bel Air, Md., for the purpose of proof of claims, propounding interrogatories and the selection of a permanent trustee or trustees. Robert Archer, Preliminary Trustee." (*The Aegis & Intelligencer*, March 21, 1899, p. 2). "Notice to Creditors. In the matter of the Insolvency of John H. Bond. In the Circuit Court for Harford County, In Insolvency. Ordered, this 31st day of May, 1899, that Robert Archer, permanent trustee of John H. Bond, give notice, by the publication of this order, once a week for one month, before the 1st day of July, 1899, in some newspaper published in Harford county, to the creditors of said insolvent to file their claims, duly proven, with the Clerk of the Court on or before the 11th day of September, 1899, and also to said insolvent to appear in this court on Monday, 11th day of September, 1899, to answer such interrogatories or allegations as his creditors, endorsers or sureties may propose or allege against him. James D. Watters. True Copy. Test: Wm. S. Forwood, Jr., Clerk." (*The Aegis & Intelligencer*, June 9, 1899, p. 3). **Genealogical Note**: John H. Bond married Anne E. Bradford circa November 14, 1883 (date of license).

Bond, Mordecai, 1810. "Whereas we the subscribers Justices of the Peace for Harford County together with John C. Bond, Esq., also one of the Justices of the Peace for said County, upon the petition of Mordecai Bond who set forth therein that he had been confined in the Gaol [jail] of said county twenty Days for Debts which he was unable to pay and finding the facts stated to be true we together with John C. Bond, Esq., did meet at the county Gaol of said county on the 25th Day of April Inst. and we did then and there appoint the 26th Day of May Inst. to meet at the Court House of said county which said appointment we did then and there ... at the request of the said Sheriff administer to the said Mordecai Bond the following Oath which was taken by the said Mordecai Bond being first duly sworn on the holy Evangels of Almighty God in the words following, to wit, I Mordecai Bond do solemnly swear that the Schedule which I have delivered to the Sheriff of Harford County doth contain a full account to the best of my knowledge and remembrance of my whole estate both real and personal or that I have any title to or interest in and of all debts, credits and effects whatsoever which I or any in trust for me have or at the time of my petition had, or am or was in any respect entitled to in possession, remainder or reversion and that I have not directly or indirectly at any time since my imprisonment or before, sold, leased or otherwise conveyed or disposed of or intrusted all or any part of my estate, goods, Stock, money or Debts thereby to defraud my creditors or to secure the same to receive or expect any profit or advantage thereof so help me God, which said duplicate of the Schedule aforesaid we have transmitted to the Clerk of the County Court to be by him preserved in his Office for the information of the Creditors of the said Mordecai Bond. Given under our hands & seals this 26th Day of May 1810. Saml. Bradford. Thomas A. Hays." (Court Records Document 67.09.5(B) at the Historical Society of Harford County; a copy of the schedule was included to which "Mord Bond" signed his name, but no property was listed)

Bond, Prush A. (African American), 1826. "Negro Prush A. Bond. Petition, Schedule, Bond, Sheriff's certificate and personal discharge and order for publication and Bond of provisional trustee and

Certificate for Trustee filed 25th July 1826." [nothing further recorded] (Insolvent Docket A, 1807-1843, p. 81, at the Maryland State Archives; Insolvent Docket Prior to 1827, Court Records Accession #632 at the Historical Society of Harford County). 1841. "Feby 2nd 1841. Petition, Affidavits, Schedules, Order of appointment of Trustee, Certificate, Order, personal Discharge, Deed, Appearance Bond & trustee's Bond filed 15th March 1841. 20th Novr. 1841 Allegations filed & Petitioner appears & finally discharged." (Insolvent Docket A, 1807-1843, p. 177, at Maryland State Archives). **Genealogical Notes**: Prush A. Bond, a free black, was born circa 1783-1786 and probably married Rose --- before 1805 (probable daughter Hester born circa 1805 and enumerated in his household in the 1850 census). Rose was still living in 1827 and Prush possibly married 2nd to Hester --- (born circa 1795) before 1834 (probable daughter Elizabeth born circa 1834) and they were still living in 1860. (*African Americans in Harford County, Maryland, 1774-1864*, by Henry C. Peden, Jr., MA, FMGS, published on a computer disk by and for The Historical Society of Harford County, Inc.)

Bond, Thomas T., 1850. David L. Maulsby and Thomas J. Nelson vs. Thomas T. Bond. "20 May/50 Judgt. confessed (subject to his discharge under the Insolvent laws) for $800 ..." (Judgment Docket 1846-1850, p. 65, Court Records Accession #187 at Historical Society of Harford County). "For former entries see Inst. Doc. B, page 79. 23rd May/53 Auditor's Reports Nos. 1 & 2 & orders nisi filed." [nothing further] (Insolvent Docket A. L. J. No. 1, p. 2, at Historical Society of Harford County) **Genealogical Notes**: Thomas Talbott Bond, most likely the son of Thomas Bond and Ann Talbott, was born on August 14, 1792, served in the War of 1812 and defended Baltimore at Fort McHenry on September 12-14, 1814, married Mary Ann Bond (February 15, 1803 – July 30, 1876) on November 24, 1821, died on March 21, 1875 at the White House [an area in Fallston] and was buried in Fallston United Methodist Church cemetery. (*Baltimore Patriot*, December 1, 1821; War of 1812 Pension File SC-12637; Fallston United Methodist Church tombstones; *The Aegis & Intelligencer*, March 26, 1875)

Botts, Isaac, 1842. "Petition, Affidavits, Schedules, Appointment of trustee, certificate, order, personal discharge, trustee's bond & deed to trustee & appearance bond filed 7th June 1842. 26th Novr. 1842 Petitioner appears, files certificate of publication & finally discharged." (Insolvent Docket A, 1807-1843, p. 181, at Maryland State Archives)

Botts, Isaac W., 1897. "The insolvency case of Isaac W. Botts was taken up in the County Court Monday [January 18, 1897], and all that day and next day were consumed by counsel in framing issues to go before a jury. Mr. Botts is a canner, residing at Carsins' Run. Being embarrassed, financially, some time ago, he made a deed of trust to Mr. T. L. Hanway, for the benefit of his creditors. Certain of his creditors claims that before doing so he delivered large quantities of canned goods to certain other of his creditors, thereby creating unlawful preferences, and it is sought to have these goods, or the price thereof, brought into the general trust fund." (*Havre de Grace Republican*, January 23, 1897, p. 3). "The insolvency case of Isaac W. Bootts [sic] is still on trial before Judge Watters and a jury. It will probably occupy the rest of the week." (*The Aegis & Intelligencer*, January 29, 1897, p. 3). "The insolvency case of Mr. Isaac W. Botts, of Carsins' Run, which had been going on in the Circuit Court for over two weeks, was concluded Thursday [February 4, 1897], by a verdict in favor of Mr. Botts. For a case to occupy sixteen days in its trail is unprecedented in the annals of our Court." (*Havre de Grace Republican*, February 6, 1897, p. 3). "The Botts Insolvency Case ... Mr. Botts was a canner, and some months ago executed a deed of trust to Mr. T. L. Hanway, of Aberdeen. It was charged that within four months previous to the execution of this deed, Mr. Botts had transferred large blocks of canned goods, amounting to over $9,000 in value, to certain of his creditors—the First National Bank of Aberdeen, the Aberdeen Can Company, Otho N. Johnson, Charles W. Michael, Michael & Malcolm, and others – and the object of the suit was to compel these preferred creditors to transfer the proceeds of these canned good to the general insolvent fund, for the benefit of all creditors. Mr.

Wm. J. Becker, the principal complainant, is a box manufacturer in Baltimore city. The ground of his defence was that at the time Mr. Botts transferred the goods to the above parties he did not know he was insolvent, nor was he in contemplation of insolvency, and did not intend to prefer these creditors over others." (*Havre de Grace Republican*, February 13, 1897, p. 2; *Harford Democrat*, February 12, 1897, p. 2, reported a similar story and gave some additional indebtedness details and amounts). "Messrs. S. A. Williams, George L. Van Bibber and Willard G. Rouse, left Bel Air for Annapolis on Tuesday afternoon [November 16, 1897]. It is expected that several of the appealed cases from the Harford county Court will be called for trial during the week, prominent among them being then insolvency case of Isaac W. Botts." (*The Aegis & Intelligencer*, November 19, 1897, p. 3). "The appeal in the insolvency case of Isaac W. Botts has been dismissed by the Court of Appeals." (*The Aegis & Intelligencer*, December 10, 1897, p. 3). **Genealogical Notes**: Isaac Wesley Botts married Elizabeth J. Carsins (November 8, 1861 – September 14, 1912), daughter of William S. Carsins and Martha J. Maxwell, circa January 19, 1881 (date of license) and they lived in Michaelsville. (Death certificate of Elizabeth J. Botts states she was born in 1861, but her tombstone states 1853; no tombstone for husband Isaac. William R. Botts, an infant son, died in 1889 and is buried beside her. (St. George's P. E. Church Cemetery). Elizabeth Botts was survived by her husband Isaac, brothers John W. and Edward Carsins, and sister Mrs. Corrine Jewens. (*The Aegis & Intelligencer*, September 20, 1912)

Bouldin, Richard E., 1892. "Notice to Creditors. In the matter of the Insolvency of Richard E. Bouldin. In the Circuit Court for Harford County In Insolvency. To the Creditors of Richard E. Bouldin: Take notice that Richard E. Bouldin has made application in the Circuit Court for Harford County for the benefit of the Insolvent Laws of the State of Maryland, the proceedings under which said application was made being now pending, a meeting of the creditors of said Insolvent debtor, will be held at the office of Frank E. Gorrell, in the Town of Bel Air, Harford county, Maryland, on Monday, the 10th day of October, 1892, at 11 o'clock, A. M., for the purpose proof of claims, propounding interrogatories and the election of a permanent trustee or trustees. Frank E. Gorrell, Preliminary Trustee." (*The Aegis & Intelligencer*, September 30, 1892, p. 2). "Notice to Creditors ... Notice is hereby given to the creditors of Richard E. Bouldin, who were such upon his application for the benefit of the Insolvent Laws of the State of Maryland, to file their claims, duly proven, with the Clerk of the Circuit Court for Harford County, on or before the first day of March, 1893. Frank E. Gorrell, Permanent Trustee." (*The Aegis & Intelligencer*, November 4, 1892, p. 2). "Notice to Creditors ... In pursuance of an order of Court, passed in the above matter on the 1st day of November, 1892, the undersigned hereby gives notice to the creditors of Richard E. Bouldin, an insolvent debtor, that the Second Monday of February, of 1893, has been fixed by the Court for the appearance of said Insolvent, to answer such interrogatories or allegations as his creditors, endorsers or sureties may propose or allege against him. Frank E. Gorrell, Permanent Trustee." (*The Aegis & Intelligencer*, November 2, 1892, p. 2). **Genealogical Notes**: Richard Edwin Bouldin (November 26, 1837 – March 12, 1920), son of Charles Douglas Bouldin (1797-1882) and Mary Gover Wilson (1799-1877), of Cecil Co., later of Jerusalem Mills, Harford Co., was a farmer and captain, 7th MD Volunteers, in the Civil War. He married Martha Christobella Gough (July 15, 1839 – May 29, 1894), daughter of Harry Dorsey Gough (1791-1867, War of 1812 veteran) and Mary Honora O'Brien (1807-1844), of Baltimore, later of Bel Air, on February 4, 1864 by Rev. L. F. Morgan at Charles Street M. E. Church in Baltimore (*The Aegis and Intelligencer*, February 12, 1864, December 6, 1867 and January 3, 1868; Baltimore *Sun*, February 6, 1864; Christ Episcopal Church (Rock Spring Parish) Cemetery tombstones; 1850 Harford County Census; Death certificate of Richard E. Bouldin; 1870 Harford County Census, 3rd District, included their daughters Nora Bouldin, age 5, and Corine Bouldin, age 1; Bouldin family research by Bonnie P. Hedstrom, of Amityville, NY, 2009)

24

Bowyer, Theodore, 1831. "Petition, Schedule, Sheriffs certificate, personal discharge and order for publication, Bond for Appearance, Trustee's Bond, Trustee's Certificate and Deed to Trustee filed the 25th April 1831. 13th August 1831 Petitioner appears, certificate of publication filed, and cont'd. 17th March 1832 answers filed, petitioner appears and finally discharged." (Insolvent Docket A, 1807-1843, p. 109, at Maryland State Archives). **Genealogical Notes**: Theodore Bowyer, son of Thomas Bowyer and Ann Calwell, was born in 1803, married Mary Ann --- circa 1832, died on December 13, 1886 in Baltimore and was buried in Green Mount Cemetery. The children of Theodore and Mary Ann Bowyer were Ann Bowyer, Catherine Bowyer, Frances Bowyer, William Bowyer, Theodore Bowyer, Jr., Johanna Bowyer, Thomas Boyer, Laura Bowyer and Virginia Bowyer. *Descendants of the Signers of the Bush Declaration of March 22, 1775, Harford County, Maryland*, by Christopher T. Smithson and Henry C. Peden, Jr., 2010, pp. 89, 90, 93, and research by J. Andrew Calwell in 2010)

Boyd, Weston, 1844. "Notice Is Hereby Given, to the creditors of *Weston Boyd*, late an imprisoned debtor of Harford county, that on the application of said debtor by petition in writing to the Hon. Robert W. Holland, chief justice of the Orphan's court of said county, for the benefit of the insolvent laws of Maryland, the said judge on the 22nd day of July, 1844, granted to the said debtor a discharge from imprisonment and appointed the first Saturday after the 3rd Monday in November next, for his appearance before the Judges of Harford county court at the court house of said county, for a final hearing before said court, on said petition and to answer such interrogatories as his creditors may propose to him." (*Harford Madisonian and Bel-Air & Havre de Grace Messenger*, October 18, 1844, p. 3) **Genealogical Notes**: Weston Boyd was born in 1812, married Miss Hannah Cook Parsons (July 23, 1817 – June 6, 1905), of Baltimore City, on December 28, 1837 by Rev. Joseph Merriken in Baltimore City, died on June 12, 1857 and was buried in Angel Hill Cemetery. (Baltimore *Sun*, January 1, 1838; Angel Hill Cemetery tombstone inscriptions)

Bradberry, John T., 1865. Cornelia Cooley vs. William Alexander and others. In the Circuit Court for Harford county, as a Court of Chancery. "The object of this suit is to procure a decree to enforce the specific performance of an agreement mentioned in the proceedings therein, and to enforce the complainant's lien for purchase money upon certain lands therein mentioned. The Bill states that the Complainant and her husband, Charles Cooley, who is since deceased, on or about the 5th of February, 1859, sold to one John T. Bradberry, a tract or parcel of land, situated in Harford county, called *Dolph Island* or *Taylor's Island*. That said Bradberry agreed to pay therefore $2,000, with interest, in installments of four hundred dollars each; and it was also agreed that Complainant and her husband, or the survivor, should execute a deed conveying said lands to the purchaser, upon which said Bradberry was to execute and deliver to them a mortgage upon said lands, to secure the payment of said purchase money; and in default of the execution of said deed, the Complainant and her husband would pay to the said Bradberry, his heirs or assigns, all expenses resulting from such default; and also, that said Charles Cooley, during his natural life, should have the privilege of pasturing his cattle upon the marsh on said farm, free of charge. That said Bradberry entered into possession of said lands, but before payment of any part of the purchase money, assigned all his rights to a certain William Alexander, of Baltimore city, who, as assignee, took possession thereof, and agreed to comply with the terms of sale. That Complainant and her husband were willing, and since the decease of her husband Complainant was and is ready and willing to comply with her part of said agreement, but that said Bradberry and Alexander, and each of them, have failed and neglected to comply with their part of said agreement, or to pay any part of said purchase money; and that the two first installments thereof, with the interest, are now over due. That said Bradberry has removed from the State of Maryland and died insolvent, and no administration has been

25

granted upon [his] estate, and whether he left heirs-at-law, and if so, who they are and where they reside, is to the Complainant unknown." (*The Aegis & Intelligencer*, February 10, 1865, p. 2)

Bradford, George W., 1821. "Petition, Schedule, Bond, Sheriff's certificate, personal discharge and order for publication filed 29ᵗʰ June 1821." [nothing further recorded] (Insolvent Docket A, 1807-1843, p. 46, at the Maryland State Archives; Insolvent Docket Prior to 1827, Court Records Accession #632 at the Historical Society of Harford County). **Genealogical Notes:** George W. Bradford was born in 1780, married Jane Mather (1782-1860) circa December 11, 1804 (date of license), died in 1845 and was buried in the Cokesbury Memorial Methodist Church cemetery in Abingdon, MD. (Harford County marriage license; tombstone; Records of the West Harford Circuit of the Methodist Church)

Bradford, Samuel D., 1888. "Public Sale. By virtue of an order of the Circuit Court for Harford county, in the matter of insolvency of Samuel D. Bradford, the undersigned, Permanent Trustee, will offer at Public Sale, on Tuesday, April 10ᵗʰ, 1888, at 11 o'clock, A. M., at the residence of the said Samuel D. Bradford, on the road from Perrymans to Bush River Neck, the following Personal Property, to wit: One Buckeye Binder, 35 barrels of Corn, 1 Colt, 1 Cow, 1 Buggy, 1 Horse Rake. Geo. L. Van Bibber, S. W. Bradford, Permanent Trustees." (*The Aegis & Intelligencer*, March 30, 1888, p. 2). "Insolvent's Notice ... Notice is hereby given to the creditors of Samuel D. Bradford that the 16ᵗʰ day of May, 1888, has been fixed as the day that said Insolvent shall appear before the Circuit Court for Harford county and answer such interrogatories or allegations as his creditors, endorsers and sureties propose or allege against him. Geo. L. Van Bibber, Samuel W. Bradford, Permanent Trustees." (*The Aegis & Intelligencer*, April 6, 1888, p. 3). "Trustee's Sale of Valuable Real Estate. By virtue of a decree of the Circuit Court for Harford County, in Chancery, the undersigned, as trustee, will offer at Public Sale, at the Court House door, in Bel Air, on Monday, April 14ᵗʰ, 1890, at 12 o'clock, M., all that Valuable Farm or Tract of Land, in which Samuel D. Bradford now resides, known as *Shepherd's Choice*, particularly described in a deed dated the 24ᵗʰ of February, 1887, and recorded among the Land Records of Harford County, in Liber A.L.J. No. 58, folio 76, situated in Romney Neck, about 8 miles below Perryman, on both sides of the public road leading into Bush River Neck, adjoining the lands of James Walker and Stockham's Estate, containing 225 Acres, More or Less. The property is well fenced and well wooded, and conveniently situated in a desirable neighborhood, near stores, schools and churches. The land is of excellent quality and in a good state of cultivation. The improvements consist of a two-story Frame Dwelling House, with porch and back building, a large Frame Barn and Stable, Corn House, Meat House and other necessary outbuildings, all in good condition. Walter W. Preston, James J. Archers, Trustees, Bel Air, Md." (*The Aegis & Intelligencer*, April 11, 1890, p. 1). **Genealogical Note:** Samuel D. Bradford (1851-1924) married Mary Belle or Bella Nelson (1854-1926) circa February 19, 1878 (date of license; St. George's Church tombstones).

Bradford, William, 1832. "Petition, Schedule, Affidavit, Personal discharge, Order for Publication, Bond for Appearance, Trustee's Bond, Trustee's Certificate and Deed to Trustee filed 14ᵗʰ December 1832. 16ᵗʰ March 1833 Petitioner appears, Certificate of Publication filed and petitioner finally discharged ... 1ˢᵗ Decr. 1834 Auditor's Report and Order of Confirmation filed." (Insolvent Docket A, 1807-1843, p. 123, at the Maryland State Archives). **Genealogical Notes:** There were two men with this name at this same time. One William Bradford (1783-1835), son of William Bradford and Margaret Hill, married Eliza Fullerton (c1800-1851), daughter of James Fullerton and Sarah Bradford, on May 15, 1817 and some time later moved to Lebanon, St. Clair Co., IL. Eliza Bradford died in St. Louis, MO. Their son James F. Bradford was born on September 10, 1834 in Illinois and died on January 9, 1909 in St. Cloud, MN. Another William Bradford married Susan Drew on June 27, 1811 in Harford County. Which of these William Bradford's was the insolvent debtor is yet to be determined. (Harford County marriages; St. George's P. E. Parish Register; *Descendants of the Signers* *of the Bush Declaration of March 22, 1775, Harford County, Maryland,* by Christopher T. Smithson and Henry C. Peden, Jr., 2010, pp. 79-80)

Bramble, Thomas, 1857. "Petition, Schedules, Affidavits, Appointment of Trustee & order of notice, Trustee's Bond & Deed to Trustee filed 1st June 1857. 14th Novr. 1857 Petitioner appears, files certificate of publication & discharged." (Insolvent Docket A. L. J. No. 1, p. 18, in the Court Records Department of the Historical Society of Harford County). **Genealogical Note**: Thomas Bramble apparently never married, died on September 24, 1879 in his 70th year and was buried in Union Chapel Cemetery (tombstone inscription).

Brannan (Brannon), William, 1830. "Petition, Schedule, Shffs. certificate, personal Discharge and order for Publication, Bond for App., Trustee's Bond, Trustee's Certificate and Deed to Trustee filed 12th October 1830. 17th March 1831 Petitioner appears. Certificate of Publication filed and finally discharged." (Insolvent Docket A, 1807-1843, p. 107, at the Maryland State Archives). 1841. "Petition, 3 Schedules, 2 Affidavits, personal Discharge, Certificate, Appearance Bond, Appointment of Trustee, Trustee's Deed, Trustee's Bond & order filed 20th July 1841. Novr. 20th 1841 Certificate filed, Petitioner appears & finally discharged." (Insolvent Docket A, 1807-1843, p. 178, at the Maryland State Archives). **Genealogical Notes**: There was a William Brannan who married Ann Coale circa January 16, 1822 (date of license) and there was a William Brannon who died in July 1877, age 90, and was buried in Broad Creek Friends Cemetery (tombstone inscription).

Brooke, James W., 1852. "For former entries see Inst. Doc. B, page 92. Same entries as in case of J. W. Hall [which would be as follows]: 19th Decr/52 Order of Sale & Trustee's Report filed … 22nd Nov/53 Creditor's Report & order nisi passed." [nothing further recorded] (Insolvent Docket A. L. J. No. 1, p. 1, in the Court Records Department of the Historical Society of Harford County). **Genealogical Note**: James W. Brooke (1807-1870) married Sarah Ann Lewis (1807-1890), daughter of John Day Lewis and Sophia White Hall, on January 4, 1834. (*Account of the Meeting of the Descendants of Colonel Thomas White of Maryland Held at Sophia's Dairy on the Bush River, Maryland, June 7, 1877*, no author, privately published in Philadelphia, 1879, p. 134; Angel Hill Cemetery tombstones; *Havre de Grace Republican*, October 21, 1870, reports he had died and was removed from the voter registration list)

Brown, Jesse, 1819. "Petition, Schedule, Sheriff's certificate, Bond and personal discharge filed 16th Augt. 1819 – Augt. 28th 1819 petr. appeared – March 18th 1820 petr. appeared." [nothing further recorded] (Insolvent Docket A, 1807-1843, p. 25, at the Maryland State Archives; Insolvent Docket Prior to 1827, Court Records Accession #632 at the Historical Society of Harford County)

Brown, Thomas, 1824. "Petition, Schedule, Bond, Sheriffs Certificate, personal Discharge and order for Publication filed 11th March 1824." [nothing further recorded] (Insolvent Docket Prior to 1827, Court Records Accession #632 at the Historical Society of Harford County). 1825. "Petition, bond, Schedule, affidavit of residence, Shffs. Certificate and personal discharge filed 2nd Aug. 1825. Petitioner appears 18th March 1826 and allegations filed and order filed … 20th March 1827 William B. Bond appointed Trustee … petitioner discharged." (Insolvent Docket A, 1807-1843, p. 73, at the Maryland State Archives; Insolvent Docket Prior to 1827, Court Records Accession #632 at the Historical Society of Harford County). **Genealogical Notes**: Thomas Brown married Clemency G. Mitchell circa July 1, 1820 (date of license). He was deposed on July 31, 1826 and stated he was 38 years old, thus born in 1787 or 1788 (Court Records Document 90.29.68 at the Historical Society of Harford County). Thomas served in the War of 1812 and died on August 27, 1833. (military records)

Buchanan, William, 1887. "Order Nisi. In the matter of the Insolvency of William Buchanan ... In pursuance of an order passed by the Circuit Court for Harford county, on the 2nd day of March, 1887, notice is hereby given to William Buchanan, Insolvent debtor, to appear in said Court on the Monday, the 9th day of May, 1887, to answer such interrogatories or allegations, as his creditors, endorsers or sureties may propose or allege against him; and notice is also hereby given to the creditors of the said insolvent of the day so fixed upon. Otho S. Lee, Permanent Trustee." (*The Aegis & Intelligencer*, March 4, 1887, p. 2)

Buck, Ananias D., 1838. "Petition, Schedule, Affidavits, personal discharge and order of publication, Bond for Appearance, Trustee's Bond, Trustee's Certificate and Deed to Trustee filed 1st Feby 1838. 24th Novr. 1838 Certificate of publication filed and petitioner discharged." (Insolvent Docket A, 1807-1843, p. 163, at the Maryland State Archives)

Buck, John D., 1838. "Petition, Schedule, Affidavits, personal discharge and order of publication, Bond for Appearance, Trustee's Bond, Trustee's Certificate and Deed to Trustee filed 1st February 1838. 24th Novr. 1838 Petitioner appears, certificate of publication filed & discharged. 23rd Jany/49 Petitions & order appointing new Trustee filed. Trustee's Bond filed." [nothing further recorded] (Insolvent Docket A, 1807-1843, p. 162, at the Maryland State Archives)

Buckingham, Hannah, 1810. "Whereas we the subscribers Justices of the Peace for Harford County together with Bennet Bussey, Esq., a Justice of the Peace for said county, upon the petition of Hannah Buckingham, who set forth that she had been confined [in jail] twenty days and upwards for debts which she was unable to pay and finding the facts stated to be true together with the said Bennet Bussey, Esq. we did meet at the gaol of said county on the 25th Day of October last and did then and there appoint the 26th day of November Instant to meet at the Court house of said county which said appointment we did then and there … at the request of the said Sheriff administer to the said Hannah Buckingham the following oath which was taken by the said Hannah Buckingham being first duly sworn on the holy Evangely of Almighty God in the words following, to wit, I Hannah Buckingham do solemnly swear that the schedule which I have delivered to the Sheriff of Harford County doth contain a full account to the best of my knowledge and remembrance of my whole estate both real and personal or that I have any title to or interest in and of all debts, credits and effects whatsoever which I or any in trust for me have or at the time of my petition had, or am or was in any respect entitled to in possession, remainder or reversion and that I have not directly or indirectly at any time since my imprisonment or before, sold, leased or otherwise conveyed or disposed of or intrusted all or any part of my estate, goods, stock, money or debts thereby to defraud my creditors or to secure the same to receive or expect any profit or advantage thereof so help me God, which said duplicate of the schedule aforesaid we have transmitted to the clerk of the county court to be by him preserved in his office for the information of the creditors of the said Hannah Buckingham. Given under our hands and seals this 26th Day of November 1810. Thomas A. Hays. Jno. C. Bond." (Court Records Document 67.14.1(B) at the Historical Society of Harford County; a copy of the schedule to which "Hannah Buckingham" made her "I" mark was included, but no property was listed)

Buckingham, James, 1824. "Petition, Schedule, Bond, Sheriffs certificate and personal discharge and order for publication filed 13th day of January 1824. Aug 14th 1824 Printers certificate of publication filed. Petitioner appears and is discharged. Paid for recording proceedings and certificate of final discharge $2.31¼ by Thomas Scott to JGL." (Insolvent Docket A, 1807-1843, p. 59, at the Maryland State Archives; Insolvent Docket Prior to 1827, Court Records Accession #632 at the Historical Society of Harford County)

Budd, John, 1826. "Petition, Schedule, Bond, Sheriff's certificate and personal discharge and order for publication and Bond of provisional trustee and certificate for Trustee filed 24th July 1826. 17th March 1827. Certificate of Publication filed, Petitioner appears. William B. Bond appointed Trustee and petitioner personally discharged – Jonathan Sutton appointed Trustee … 15th March 1828 appeared by I. D. Maulsby, Esqr., his atty & cont'd. 16th Augt. 1828 Petitioner appears & his case continued …

Augt. 22nd 1833 Petitioner examined on Interrogatories and finally discharged." (Insolvent Docket A, 1807-1843, p. 81, at the Maryland State Archives; Insolvent Docket Prior to 1827, Court Records Accession #632 at the Historical Society of Harford County). **Genealogical Notes**: John Budd was born circa 1785, married Elizabeth ---- some time before 1808, served in the War of 1812 in Capt. Paca Smith's Militia Co., and died on June 26, 1843. (Baltimore *Sun*, July 7, 1843; military records; Court Records Document 56.19.3 at the Historical Society of Harford County)

Bull, Bennett L., 1826. "Petition, Schedule, bond, Sheriff's certificate and personal discharge and order for publication filed 17th March 1826. 22nd August 1826 Printers certificate filed. Petitioner appears and finally discharged. Novr. 20th 1841 Petition and order thereon, bond & order to appoint trustee filed. May 25th 1842 Audr. Report filed." [nothing further recorded] (Insolvent Docket A, 1807-1843, p. 77, at the Maryland State Archives; Insolvent Docket Prior to 1827, Court Records Accession #632 at the Historical Society of Harford County)

Bunce, David, 1900. "David Bunce, of Aldino, has filed a petition in the U.S. District Court, Baltimore, asking that he be declared a bankrupt. His liabilities are $405.68, with no assets. Mr. John L. G. Lee is the attorney." (*Havre de Grace Republican*, March 10, 1900). **Genealogical Note**: There was a David M. Bunce who married Libbie J. Cullum circa October 23, 1892 (date of license).

Burke, David Y., 1884. "September 24th 1884. Petition, Schedule of Property, List of Creditors & Debts, Affidavits, Order appointing Preliminary Trustee [no name given], Insolvent Deed & Preliminary Trustee's Bond filed ... May 11th 1885 Certificate of Publication of Notice to Creditors filed. Same day Petitioner appeared in open Court and was finally discharged per order of Court filed [nothing further recorded] (Insolvent Docket A. L. J. No. 1, p. 91, in the Court Records Department of the Historical Society of Harford County). **Genealogical Notes**: David Y. Burke, a tobacconist in Havre de Grace, was born in 1842, served as Register of Voters in 1882, was issued wild waterfowl gunning licenses in 1895 and 1897, served as a Judge of Elections in 1914, later moved to Baltimore and died in 1926. (*Duck Hunters on the Susquehanna Flats, 1850-1930*, by Henry C. Peden, Jr. & Jack L. Shagena, Jr., 2014, p. 24; *The Harford Democrat*, October 6, 1882, p. 2)

Burkins, Joseph T., 1888. "Insolvent Notice. In the Matter of the Insolvency of Joseph T. Burkins ... Notice is hereby given to the creditors of Joseph T. Burkins, that he has applied for the benefit of the Insolvent Laws of the State of Maryland, and that a meeting of his creditors will be held at my office, in Bel Air, on Friday, September 16th, 1887, at 10 o'clock A. M., for the purpose of the selection of a permanent trustee and other business. Geo. L. Van Bibber, Preliminary Trustee." (*Harford Democrat*, September 9, 1887, p. 2). "On Tuesday [February 14, 1888] Joseph T. Burkins, insolvent, appeared in open court, and no objections being made was finally discharged." (*The Aegis & Intelligencer*, February 17, 1888, p. 3). **Genealogical Notes**: Joseph T. Burkins (1831 – September 22, 1908) married Arabella Preston (August 8, 1832 – September 13, 1905), both of Harford County, on September 7, 1865 by Rev. E. Kinsey, but he neglected to list their marriage in the West Harford Methodist Circuit, Record of Marriages, 1851-1868. (license and marriage certificate; Mount Vernon United Methodist Church tombstones, but no death certificate or obituary for either of them in Harford County)

Bussey, Bennett, 1822. Insolvent debtor to be discharged from imprisonment. (*Bond of Union and Harford County Weekly Advertiser*, July 25, 1822). "Petition, Schedule, Bond, Sheriff's certificate, personal discharge and order for publication filed 13th March 1822 – 31st Augt. 1822 objections filed by Wm. McMath ... 15th March 1823 Petitioner appears. William McMath's death suggested, and [case] cont'd. August 29, 1823. Mary Jourdan, Exx. [sic] of Wm. McMath appears ... 10th Mar 1824 ... Mary Jordan [sic] appointed trustee and ordered to bond in a penalty of $2000 ... 13th Mar 1824 objections withdrawn and Petitioner released." [nothing further recorded] (Insolvent Docket A, 1807-1843, p. 48, at the Maryland State Archives; Insolvent Docket Prior to 1827, Court Records

Accession #632 at Historical Society of Harford County). **Genealogical Notes**: Bennett Bussey was born in 1745, married 1st to Anne Green, daughter of Henry Green and Elizabeth Wheeler, in 1744, served as a captain during the Revolutionary War, married 2nd to Elizabeth Stansbury Slade on July 7, 1806 at St. Peter's Catholic Church in Baltimore and died in 1827. His children were Martha, Elizabeth, Edward and Henry Bussey. (*John Wheeler (1630-1693) of Charles County, Maryland and Some of His Descendants*, by Walter V, Ball, 1066, p. 85; *Maryland Marriages, 1801-1820*, by Robert Barnes, 1993, p. 26; *Revolutionary Patriots of Harford County, Maryland, 1775-1783*, by Henry C. Peden, Jr., M.A., 1985, pp. 29-30; Harford County Will Book AJ No. C, p. 261)

Byrnes, William, 1815. "Whereas we the Subscribers Justices of the Peace for Harford County together with Thomas Jeffery, also a Justice of the peace for said County, upon the petition of William Byrnes stating therein that he had actually remained in the gaol [jail] of said county since the fourteenth day of March last for debts which he was unable to pay and finding the facts stated to be true we did meet at the gaol of said county on the fourteenth of April last and we did then and there appoint the seventeenth day of May instant to meet at the Court house of said county which said appointment we did then and there ... at the request of the said Sheriff administer to the said William Byrnes the following oath which was taken by the said William Byrnes being first duly sworn on the holy Evangely of Almighty God in the words following, to wit, I William Byrnes do solemnly swear that the schedule which I have delivered to the Sheriff of Harford County doth contain a full account to the best of my knowledge and remembrance of my whole estate both real and personal or that I have any title to or interest in and of all debts, credits and effects whatsoever which I or any in trust for me have or at the time of my petition had, or am or was in any respect entitled to in possession, remainder or reversion and that I have not directly or indirectly at any time since my imprisonment or before, sold, leased or otherwise conveyed or disposed of or intrusted all or any part of my estate, goods, stock, money or debts thereby to defraud my creditors or to secure the same to receive or expect any profit or advantage thereof so help me God, which said duplicate of the Schedule aforesaid we have transmitted to the clerk of the county court to be by him preserved in his office for the information of the creditors of the said William Byrnes. Given under our hands and seals this seventeenth of May 1815. James Wallace. Joseph Robinson." (Court Records Document 67.07.8(b) at the Historical Society of Harford County; a copy of the schedule to which "Wm. Byrnes" signed his name was included, but he had no property to list). **Genealogical Note**: William Byrnes, aged 32, appeared in Court on August 31, 1818 and openly stated that he is "a native of Ireland and at present residing in Harford County within the State of Maryland and declares on oath that it is bona fide his intention to become a citizen of the United States and to renounce forever all allegiance and fidelity to the United Kingdoms of Great Britain and Ireland whereof he is at this time a citizen." [He signed his name to the statement.] (County Court Minutes 1816-1822, p. 44, at the Historical Society of Harford County)

Cain, Cumberland (African American), 1822. "To the Honorable John Moores, one of the Justices of the Orphans Court of Harford County. The petition of Negro Cumberland Cain of Harford County respectfully sheweth that your petitioner is now in actual confinement in Harford County Jail for debts which he is unable to pay, that he is willing and offers to deliver up to the use of his creditors all his property real, personal and mixed, the necessary wearing apparel and bedding of himself & family excepted, a schedule whereof together with a list of his creditors and debtors, as far as he can at present ascertain them is hereto on oath annexed. Your petitioner also hereto annexes proof on oath that he has resided two years next preceding this his application within the State of Maryland. Your petitioner therefore prays your Honour to grant him the benefit of the insolvent laws of this State and to relieve him from his present confinement, and your Petitioner will ever pray, &c.

Cumberland Cain." [July 23, 1822] (Court Records Document 68.05.5(b) at the Historical Society of Harford County). "I hereby certify that Negro Cumberland Cain the petitioner above named is now in actual confinement in Harford County Jail for debt at the suit of William McJilton and that is not upon a breach of peace or any of the penal Laws of the State of Maryland or of the United States. Given under my hand this 23rd day of July 1822. Saml. Bradford, Sheriff." (Court Records Document 68.05.5(b), loc. cit.) "State of Maryland Harford County, to wit. On this 23rd day of July 1822 personally appeared Aquila Massey before me the subscriber one of the State of Maryland's Justices of the Peace in and for the County aforesaid and solemnly and sincearly [sic] declared and affirmed that Cumberland Cain the petitioner within named has resided within the State of Maryland the two years next preceding the date hereof and that he still resides therein. Affirmed before Joshua Guyton." (Court Records Document 68.05. 5 (b), loc cit., included a copy of the schedule to which "Cumberland Cain" signed his name, but no property was listed). "Harford County, sct. On application to the subscriber as a Justice of the Orphans Court of Harford County by petition in writing of Cumberland Cain stating that he is an imprisoned debtor in actual confinement in the jail of said County and praying for a discharge from said confinement and for the benefit of the Act of the General Assembly of Maryland Entitled an 'Act for the relief of sundry insolvent debtors' passed at November session in the year eighteen hundred and five and the several supplements thereto on the terms therein mentioned, a schedule of his property and a list of his creditors on oath being annexed to his said petition with competent and satisfactory testimony that he has resided two years within the State of Maryland next before the making of his application as aforesaid and the said Cumberland Cain having taken the oath prescribed by the said act prescribed for delivering up his property and given bond with security and in a penalty by me approved and prescribed for his appearance before the Judges of Harford County Court on the first Saturday after the second Monday in March next at the Court House of said County, being the time by me appointed for hearing before said court in said petition to answer interrogatories which his creditors may propose to him according to the provisions of the said original act. I do hereby order and adjudge that the said Cumberland Cain be discharged from imprisonment and direct that he give notice to his creditors of his said application and discharge, and of the day so by me appointed for a hearing before said Court, by advertisement to be inserted in the Bond of Union once a week for three months before the day so appointed. Given under my hand this 23rd day of July 1822. John Moores." (Court Records Document 68.05.6(a), loc. cit.) "I hereby certify that the annexed advertisement was published three months in the *Bond of Union* agreeably to the order therein specified. Wm. Coale, Jr., March 15th, 1823." (Court Records Document 68.05.5(d), loc. cit.; a copy of the notice was clipped from the newspaper and included in file). "Petition, Schedule, Bond, Sheriff's certificate, personal discharge and order for publication filed 23rd July 1822. March 15th 1823 printers certificate of publication filed. Petitioner appears and discharged." [nothing further recorded] (Insolvent Docket A, 1807-1843, p. 50, at the Maryland State Archives; Insolvent Docket Prior to 1827, Court Records Accession #632 at the Historical Society of Harford County). **Genealogical Notes:** Cumberland Cain (free black), son of Samuel Cain (1752-1830s) and Hannah Tally (born 1758, died after 1832), daughter of Edward K. Tally (all free blacks), was born circa 1784 and married Eliza or Elizabeth ---- (born circa 1795) some time before 1819 at which time their daughter Eliza Cain was born. (Research by descendant Michael Cain, of Aberdeen, MD, in 2006). Cumberland Cain was head of household in 1820 Census. He was age 48 in 1832, with Eliza Cain, age 37, Eliza Cain, age 13, Ellen Cain, age 9, Ann Cain, age 5, Edward Kean, age 12, David Kean, age 8, Samuel Kean, age 7, and Solomon Kean, age 2 (A List of Free People of Colour taken in 1832 by Joshua Guyton, Sheriff). Cumberlin Cain, age 50 [sic] in 1850, b. MD, head of household, laborer, with Elizabeth Cain, age 52, Samuel Cain, age 24, laborer, Solomon Cain, age 18, laborer, Frances Cain, age 15, and William J. Cumberlin [sic], age 12 (Census). Cumberland Cain was age 60 in 1860, head of household, laborer, with Elizabeth Cain, age 50, and Laura Gage, age 7 (Census). He was a builder of stone fences. (*A Journey Through Berkley, Maryland*, by Constance R. Beims and Christine P. Tolbert, 2003, p. 26). Cumberland Cain, son of Samuel Cain (b. 1752, d. by 1840) and Hannah Tally (b. 1748), married Elizabeth ----; his siblings were Henry Cain (b. 1802) and Prina Cain (b. 1805); his children were Eliza Cain (b. 1819), Edward Cain (b. 1822), Ellen Cain (b. 1823), David Cain (b. 1825), Samuel Cain (b. 1826), Ann Cain (b. 1827), Sophia Cain (b. 1830), Solomon R. Cain (1832-1903), Frances Cain (b. 1835), William Cain (b. 1838), John Cain (b. 1839), Henry Cain (b. 1838), and Lewis Cain (b. 1848); Hannah (Tally) Cain was the daughter of Edward K. Tally who was born about 1730 and died in the winter of 1824-1825. (*African-American Families, Harford County, Maryland: Cain, Christie, Boddy, Parker, Presberry, Webster*, by Michael Cain, 2006); Cumberland Cain, Edward Cain and Ned Cain were involved in a legal matter in 1841-1842. (Court Records Document 111.05.8 at the Historical Society of Harford County)

Cain, John, 1819. William Williams and Jane Guyton vs. Jane Cain, exec. and devisee of John Cain, deceased, and Mary Cain. Bill of Complaint stated John Cain died in debt to Jane Guyton who was at that time Jane Cain and she married Benjamin Guyton who also has since died. The sum of money was $1,350.96½ and a bond signed on November 5, 1814. Jane Guyton transferred the bond to William Williams on October 19, 1821 and remains unpaid. John Cain died testate seized of two land tracts and his daughter Ann Cain died thereafter and her sister Mary Cain became entitled to her share of the land. Jane Cain was the widow and executrix of John Cain. Cain's personal estate is insufficient, so the complainants requested his land be sold to pay his debts. A copy of John Cain's will was enclosed and mentioned his wife Jane, daughters Ann and Mary, and John's brother Matthew Cain. The will written on May 2, 1819 was proved on February 25, 1822. Case was finally resolved and the debt paid on May 25, 1829. (Harford County Equity Court Book HD No. 1, pp. 128-136). **Genealogical Notes**: John Cain married Jane Holmes circa May 28, 1816 (date of license). His brother Matthew Cain was born in November, 1781, married Sarah Nagle on October 7, 1820 in Philadelphia and died at home in Harford County on March 11, 1859, aged 77 years and 4 months. (War of 1812 Pension File WC-27416; *The Southern Aegis*, March 26, 1859 and August 20, 1859)

Calary, William F., 1894. "Insolvent's Sale. The undersigned, trustee in insolvency of the estate of Wm. F. Calary, an insolvent debtor, will offer at Public Sale, at the Court House door, in Bel Air, on Saturday, June 30th, 1894, at 11 o'clock, A. M., 1 C. Aultman & Co. New Model Vibrator Threshing Machine, with Clover Huller Attachment. The Machine is now on the farm of Mr. Corbin Amos, near Jarrettsville, where it can be seen and examined at any time. Walter W. Preston, Trustee." (*The Aegis & Intelligencer*, June 15, 1894, p. 2). **Genealogical Note**: William F. Calary married Ida J. Eck circa April 27, 1897 (date of license).

Calwell, Robert, 1832. "Petition, Schedule, personal discharge, Order for Publication, Bond for Appearance, Trustee's Bond, Trustee's Certificate and Deed to Trustee filed 23rd March 1832. 18th Augt. 1832 Petitioner appears, certificate of publication filed, and finally discharged." (Insolvent Docket A, 1807-1843, p. 116, at the Maryland State Archives). **Genealogical Notes**: Robert Calwell, son of Thomas Calwell (1765-1832) and Sarah Gallion (1762-1808), was born on January 31, 1801 and married M. Gasely who was born in Texas on September 22, 1802. Their daughter and only child Caroline S. Calwell married John Calvin Norris on November 26, 1827 in Harford County and died in September 1873 in Baltimore. (*Descendants of the Signers of the Bush Declaration of March 22, 1775, Harford County, Maryland*, by Christopher T. Smithson and Henry C. Peden, Jr., 2010, pp. 90, 94)

Calwell, Thomas, 1826. "Petition, Schedule, Bond, Sheriff's certificate and personal discharge and order for publication filed 15th March 1826. 19th Augt. 1826 Printers certificate filed. Petitioner appears and finally discharged. March 21ˢᵗ 1827 James Reardon appointed Trustee for the benefit of the creditors." (Insolvent Docket A, 1807-1843, p. 78, at the Maryland State Archives; Insolvent Docket Prior to 1827, Court Records Accession #632 at the Historical Society of Harford County). **Genealogical Notes**: Thomas Calwell (1765-1828), son of Samuel Calwell and Ann Richardson, married 1ˢᵗ to Sarah "Sally" Gallion (1762-1808), daughter of James Gallion and Rachel Mariarty, on February 14. 1793 by Rev. Davis at the home of Jacob Norris in Bel Air, and married 2ⁿᵈ to Nancy "Ann" Kelso, daughter of John Russell Kelso and Mary Smith, on March 18, 1813 by Rev. Glendy in Baltimore. Thomas Calwell begat 18 children. The 8 children of Thomas and Sarah Calwell were Ann Calwell Webster, Elizabeth Calwell, Samuel Calwell, Thomas Jefferson Calwell, Robert Calwell, Sophia Calwell, Mary Budden Calwell and Sarah Clarissa Calwell. The 10 children of Thomas and Nancy Calwell were Mary Cordelia Calwell, William Henry Calwell, Sidney Augusta Calwell, Frances Elizabeth Calwell, James S. Calwell, John Kelso Calwell, Sidney Amanda Calwell, Owen Calwell, Samuel Thomas Calwell and Lucien Bonaparte Calwell. (*Descendants of the Signers of the Bush Declaration of March 22, 1775, Harford County, Maryland*, by Christopher T. Smithson and Henry C. Peden, Jr., 2010, pp. 90, 91, citing research by J. Andrew Calwell, of Lutherville, MD, in 2010)

Careins, John, 1810. "Whereas we the subscribers Justices of the Peace for Harford County upon the petition of John Careins who set forth therein that he had actually remained in the Gaol [jail] of said county since the twenty-second day of January last for debts which he was unable to pay and finding the facts stated to be true we did meet at the county Gaol of said County on the fifteenth day of February last and we did then and there appoint the fourteenth day of March instant to meet at the Court house of said county which said appointment we did then and there … at the request of the said Sheriff administer to the said John Careins the following Oath which was taken by the said John Careins being first duly sworn on the Holy Evangely of Almighty God in the words following, to wit, I do solemnly swear that the schedule which I have delivered to the Sheriff of Harford County doth contain a full account to the best of my knowledge and remembrance of my whole estate both real and personal or that I have any title to or interest in and of all debts, credits and effects whatsoever which I or any in trust for me have or at the time of my petition had, or am or was in any respect entitled to in possession, remainder or reversion and that I have not directly or indirectly at any time since my imprisonment or before, sold, leased or otherwise conveyed or disposed of or intrusted all or any part of my estate, goods, Stock, money or Debts thereby to defraud my creditors or to secure the same to receive or expect any profit or advantage thereof so help me God, which said duplicate of the Schedule aforesaid we have transmitted to the clerk of the county court to be by him preserved in his Office for the information of the Creditors of the said John Careins. Given under our hands and seals this fourteenth day of March 1814. Thomas Ayres. Benj. Richardson. James Wallace." (Court Records Document 67.14.2(A) at the Historical Society of Harford County; a copy of the schedule to which he signed his name "John Carins" was included and listed this property: "one yearling heifer, one sow and three pigs")

Carpenter, William T., 1851. "Petition &c. 8ᵗʰ Jany/51 … 12ᵗʰ May/53 Allegations withdrawn & Petitioner discharged." (Insolvent Docket A. L. J. No. 1, p. 1, in the Court Records Department of the Historical Society of Harford County)

Carr, John D., 1832. "Petition, Schedule, Affidavit, Personal discharge, and Order for Publication, Bond for Appearance, Trustee's Bond, Trustee's Certificate and Deed to Trustee filed 6ᵗʰ September 1832. 16ᵗʰ March 1833 Petitioner appears, certificate of publication filed and finally discharged." (Insolvent Docket A, 1807-1843, p. 121, at the Maryland State Archives)

Carroll, Aquilla, 1846. "Notice is hereby given, to creditors of Aquila (sic) Carroll, late an imprisoned debtor of Harford County, that on the application of said debtor by petition in writing to the Hon.

Samuel Bradford, associate justice of the Orphan's Court of said county, for the benefit of the insolvent laws of Maryland, the said judge on the 22nd day of May last, 1846, granted to the said debtor a discharge from imprisonment and appointed the first Saturday after the 3rd Monday in November next, for his appearance before the Judges of Harford county court at the court house of said county, for a final hearing before said court, on said petition and to answer such interrogatories as his creditors may propose to him." (*Harford Madisonian and Havre de Grace Messenger*, August 20, 1846, p. 3) **Genealogical Notes**: Aquilla Carroll, son of William and Margaret Carroll, was born on January 21, 1792, served in the War of 1812, married Rachel Ann Whitaker (January 6, 1792 – March 19, 1871), daughter of Isaac and Ann Whitaker, on January 12, 1815 and died on September 2, 1864. Their children were John Whitaker Carroll (1816-1901), Benjamin F. Carroll (1818-1881), Pamelia A. Carroll (1821-1903) married a Touchton, Isaac N. Carroll (1824-1892), Margaret J. Carroll (1826-1909) married a Treadway, Peter E. Carroll (twin, 1828-1897), William H. Carroll (twin, 1828-1891), Aquilla M. Carroll (1832-1910), Adriannias D. Carroll (1833-1903), and Frederick P. Carroll (1836-1909). (*Maryland Bible Records, Volume 2*, by Henry C. Peden, Jr. 2003, p. 17; Wesleyan Chapel tombstones)

Carroll, Benjamin F., 1855. "Petition, Schedules, Affidavits, Appointment of D. Scott as Trustee. Order of Appearance, Trustee's Bond, deed filed 3rd Decr. 1855. 13th May/56 Petitioner appears & files certificate of publication & finally discharged." (Insolvent Docket A. L. J. No. 1, p. 9, in the Court Records Department of the Historical Society of Harford County). "Notice is hereby given that Benjamin Carroll, of Harford County, has made application to the Circuit Court of said County, for the benefit of the Insolvent Laws of Maryland, and that the first Tuesday of May term, 1856, has been assigned for him to appear in said Court to answer such interrogatories as his creditors may propose or allege against him. A. Lingan Jarrett, Clerk." (*Harford Democrat*, January 18, 1856, p. 2) **Genealogical Notes**: Benjamin F. Carroll, son of Aquilla Carroll (1792-1864) and Rachel Ann Whitaker (1792-1871), was born on July 2, 1818, married 1st to Leuiza Griffith, daughter of Scott Griffith, circa February 15, 1837 (date of license), married 2nd to Clarissa R. "Clara" Martin (1822-1864), daughter of Abraham Martin (1788-1872) and Mary Magness (1793-1842), circa November 6, 1840 (date of license), died on November 20, 1881 and was buried in Cokesbury Memorial Methodist Church cemetery. (*Independent Citizen*, February, 1837; *The Aegis & Intelligencer*, August 9, 1864; *Maryland Bible Records, Volume 2*, by Henry C. Peden, Jr. 2003, p. 17; William Magness Estate, 1854)

Carroll, Isaac N., 1857. "Petition, Schedules, Affidavits, Appointment of Trustee & order of notice, Trustee's Bond & Deed filed 4th Decr. 1857. 2nd August/58 Petition and order filed. 13th Nov/58 Petitioner appears, files certificate of publication & discharged." (Insolvent Docket A. L. J. No. 1, p. 21, in the Court Records Department of the Historical Society of Harford County). "In the matter of the petition of Isaac N. Carroll for the benefit of the Insolvent Laws. In the Circuit Court for Harford County, May term, 1858. Ordered by this Court, this 2nd day of August, 1858, that Isaac N. Carroll be and appear before this Court on the first Saturday after the second Monday in November next, to answer such interrogatories or allegations as his creditors may propose or allege against him, and that he give notice of the day so fixed for his appearance, by publishing a copy of this order in some newspaper printed in Harford County, once a week for one month, the first assertion to be three months before the said first Saturday after the said second Monday in November next. John H. Price. Test: Wm. Galloway, Clk." (*The Southern Aegis*, August 14, 1858, p. 3). **Genealogical Notes**: Isaac N. Carroll, son of Aquilla Carroll and Rachel Ann Whitaker, was born on January 20, 1824, married Margaret ---- (June 19, 1835 – September 22, 1874), died on May 28, 1892 and was buried beside his wife Margaret and daughter Sarah R. Carroll (1860-1880). (Wesleyan Chapel tombstones)

Carroll, James D., 1834. "Petition, Affidavit, Schedule, personal discharge and order of publication, Bond for Appearance, Trustee's Bond, Trustee's Certificate and Deed to Trustee filed 12th May 1834.

16th Augt. 1834 Interrogatories filed. Petitioner appears, Certificate of Publication filed and finally discharged." (Insolvent Docket A, 1807-1843, p. 134, at Maryland State Archives)

Carroll, Patrick, 1836. "Petition, Affidavits, Schedule, personal discharge and order of publication, Bond for Appearance, Trustee's Bond, Trustee's Certificate and Deed to Trustee filed the 5th July 1836. 18th March 1837 Petitioner appears, certificate of publication filed and finally discharged." (Insolvent Docket A, 1807-1843, p. 148, at Maryland State Archives)

Carroll, William, Jr., 1820. "Petition, Schedule, Bond, Sheriff's certificate, personal discharge and order for publication filed 21st Augt. 1820. March 17th 1821 … Reuben Stump appointed Trustee." [nothing further recorded] (Insolvent Docket A, 1807-1843, p. 36, at the Maryland State Archives; Insolvent Docket Prior to 1827, Court Records Accession #632 at the Historical Society of Harford County)

Chamberlain, John H., 1807. "Petition filed and ordered by the Court [August 15, 1807] that he be discharged from the custody of the Sheriff by giving bond with Security in the penalty of $800 for his appearance on the first Saturday of the next term to answer allegations of his creditors" and that he is ordered to give notice in one of newspapers of Baltimore City. (Insolvent Docket A, 1807-1843, p. 1, at the Maryland State Archives; Insolvent Docket Prior to 1827, Court Records Accession #632 at the Historical Society of Harford County)

Chandley, James L., 1837. "Petition, Affidavits, Schedule, personal discharge and order of publication, Bond for Appearance, Trustee's Bond, Trustee's Certificate and Deed to Trustee filed 23rd August 1837. 17th March 1838 Certificate of Publication filed. Petitioner appears and finally discharged." (Insolvent Docket A, 1807-1843, p. 158, at the Maryland State Archives)

Chaney, William, 1836. "Petition, Affidavits, Schedule, personal discharge and order of publication, Bond for Appearance, Trustee's Bond, Trustee's Certificate and Deed to Trustee filed 4th August 1836." [nothing further recorded] (Insolvent Docket A, 1807-1843, p. 151, at the Maryland State Archives)

Chipman, Daniel, 1824. "Petition, Schedule, Bond, Sheriffs Certificate filed 13th March 1824 and personal Discharge and order for Publication filed 13th March 1824. Aug 14th 1824 Petitioner appears and continued." [nothing further recorded] (Insolvent Docket A, 1807-1843, p. 62, at the Maryland State Archives; Insolvent Docket Prior to 1827, Court Records Accession #632 at the Historical Society of Harford County)

Christy, Benjamin W., 1887. "Notice to Creditors. In the matter of the Insolvency of Benj. W. Christy … In pursuance of an order passed in the above entitled cause, the undersigned hereby gives notice to the creditors of Benjamin W. Christy, an insolvent debtor, who were such on the date of his application for the benefit of the insolvent laws of Maryland, to file their claims, duly proven, with the Clerk of the Circuit Court for Harford county on or before the 1st day of June, 1887. Joseph M. Streett, Permanent Trustee." (*Harford Democrat*, March 4, 1887, p. 3). "Insolvent Notice … In pursuance of an order passed in the above entitled cause, the undersigned hereby gives notice to the creditors of Benj. W. Christy, an insolvent debtor, that the 9th day of May, 1887, has been fixed upon by the court for said insolvent to appear and answer such interrogatories or allegations, as his creditors, endorsers or sureties may propose or allege against him. Joseph M. Streett, Permanent Trustee." (*Harford Democrat*, March 4, 1887, p. 3)

Christy, Joseph S., 1887. "Notice to Creditors. In the matter of the Insolvency of Jos. S. Christy … In pursuance of an order passed in the above entitled cause, the undersigned hereby gives notice to the creditors of Joseph S. Christy, an insolvent debtor, who were such on the date of his application for the benefit of the insolvent laws of Maryland, to file their claims, duly proven, with the Clerk of the Circuit Court for Harford county on or before the 1st day of June, 1887. Joseph M. Streett, Permanent Trustee." (*Harford Democrat*, March 4, 1887, p. 3). "Insolvent Notice … In pursuance of an order passed in the above entitled cause, the undersigned hereby gives notice to the creditors of Joseph S. Christy, an insolvent debtor, that the 9th day of May, 1887, has been fixed upon by the court for said insolvent to appear and answer such interrogatories or allegations, as his creditors, endorsers or sureties may propose or allege against him. Joseph M. Streett, Permanent Trustee." (*Harford Democrat*, March 4, 1887, p. 3)

Clap, Enoch, 1841. "Petition, 2 Affidavits, Schedule, Appointment of Trustee, Certificate, Order to appear & personal Discharge, deed, Trustee's Bond & appearance bond filed 19 Octr. 1841. 21 May 1842 [Petitioner] files Certificate of Publication & finally discharged." (Insolvent Docket A, 1807-1843, p. 179, at the Maryland State Archives)

Clark (Clarke), James, 1810. "Petition, Schedule, Bond, &c. filed 22nd Augt. 1810 ... Ordered by the Court that he be discharged from confinement [and] bond filed for his appearance." [nothing further recorded] (Insolvent Docket A, 1807-1843, p. 8, at the Maryland State Archives; Insolvent Docket Prior to 1827, Court Records Accession #632 at the Historical Society of Harford County)

Clark, Thomas, 1821. "Petition, Schedule, Bond, Sheriff's certificate, personal discharge and order for publication filed 23rd January 1821 – 1st September 1821 petitioner appeared in court, Henry McAtee appointed Trustee and ordered that he give bond in the penalty of $500. Bond filed 13th Sept. 1821." [nothing further recorded] (Insolvent Docket A, 1807-1843, p. 41, at the Maryland State Archives; Insolvent Docket Prior to 1827, Court Records Accession #632 at the Historical Society of Harford County). 1836. "Petition, Affidavits, Schedule, personal discharge and order of publication, Bond for Appearance, Trustee's Bond, Trustee's Certificate and Deed to Trustee filed 6th [4th?] November 1836. 18th Mar 1837 Petitioner appears, Certificate of Publication filed & finally discharged." (Insolvent Docket A, 1807-1843, p. 154, at the Maryland State Archives). **Genealogical Note**: Thomas Clark was born circa 1770 and made his "X" mark on a deposition taken on June 3, 1816, age about 46. (Court Records Document 58.21.7 at the Historical Society of Harford County)

Clement, William and David G., 1890. "William and David G. Clement, merchants doing business in Dublin, have made application for the benefit of the insolvent laws. Messrs. S. A. Williams and Thomas H. Robinson have been appointed preliminary trustees." (*The Aegis & Intelligencer*, May 16, 1890, p. 2; Havre de Grace Republican, May 23, 1890, p. 3, added they were "of South Delta" and mistakenly gave their name as William and Charles G. Clements). "Insolvents' Notice. In the matter of the Insolvency of William Clement and David G. Clement, co-partners trading as W. & D. G. Clement ... The creditors of William Clement and David G. Clement, co-partners trading as W. & D. G. Clement, are hereby notified that they have applied for the benefit of the Insolvent Laws of the State of Maryland, and that Saturday, the 24th day of May, 1890, at the office of Thomas H. Robinson, in Bel Air, Md., at 12 o'clock, M., is fixed as the time and place of their creditors to meet and choose a permanent trustee for their estate. Stevenson A. Williams, Thomas H. Robinson, Preliminary Trustees." (*The Aegis & Intelligencer*, May 23, 1890, p. 3). "Notice to Creditors ... Notice is hereby given to the creditors of William Clement and David G. Clement, co-partners trading as W. & D. G. Clement, who were such at the date of their application for the benefit of the Insolvent Laws of the State of Maryland, to file their claims, properly authenticated, with the clerk of the Circuit Court for Harford county, on or before the 8th day of September, 1890, as directed by an order of said Court, passed in the above case; provided, a copy of this order be inserted in some newspaper printed in Harford county, once a week for four successive weeks, before the 1st day of August, 1890. Stevenson A. Williams, Thomas H. Robinson, Preliminary Trustees." (*The Aegis & Intelligencer*, July 4, 1890, p. 2). "Notice to Creditors ... Notice is hereby given to the creditors of William Clement and David G. Clement, that by an order of the Circuit Court for Harford County, the second Monday in September, 1890, is fixed as the day for said Insolvents to appear in said court to answer such interrogatories and allegations as their creditors, endorsers or sureties may propose or allege against them. Stevenson A. Williams, Thomas H. Robinson, Permanent Trustees." (*The Aegis & Intelligencer*, July 18, 1890, p. 3). **Genealogical Notes**: William Clement (born c1858) and David G. Clement (born c1861) were Quakers and sons of Thomas Clement (1821-1890), a farmer near Dublin, and Cassandra McCoy (1830-1900) who are buried in Broad Creek Friends Cemetery. They had an older brother Samuel Clement (born c1854) whose wife Eliza Gulielma Clement (1858-1898) is buried next to his mother, but there is no marker for Samuel) and three younger sisters, Beulah Clement, Sarah Clement and Annie E. Clement. (*The Aegis & Intelligencer*, October 31, 1890, p. 3; Broad Creek Friends Cemetery tombstone inscriptions; Deer Creek Friends Monthly Meeting Register; 1860 Harford County Census). David G. Clement married Ella May Riley circa March 31, 1885 and William Clement married Roberta A. Riley circa May 8, 1894 (dates of licenses). William and David G. Clement kept a general store in Dublin by 1888 and their day book for 1888-1889 is maintained by the Maryland Historical Society. In June 1891 David G. Clement built a new store in Dublin and some time prior to 1908 he relocated to Parkersburg, NC. (Maryland Historical Society Manuscript MS.1516; *The Aegis & Intelligencer*, January 11, 1889, p. 3, and January 31, 1908, p. 3; *Harford Democrat*, June 12, 1891, p. 3)

Clendenon, Isaac, 1840. "Petition, Schedule, Affidavits, personal discharge & order of publication, Trustee's Bond, Appearance Bond, Trustee's Certificate & Deed filed 15th Decr. 1840. May 22 1841 Petitioner appears & files Certificate of Publication. 25 May [1841] Petitioner appears & finally discharged." (Insolvent Docket A, 1807-1843, p. 175, at the Maryland State Archives)

Clendenon, Joshua, 1840. "Petition, Schedule, Affidavits, personal discharge and order of publication, Bond for Appearance, Trustee's Bond, Trustee's Certificate and Deed to Trustee filed 15th Decr. 1840. May 22 [1841] Petitioner appears & files Certificate of Publication & Allegations filed. 25 May 1841 Petitioner appears, allegations withdrawn & Petitioner finally discharged." (Insolvent Docket A, 1807-1843, p. 174, at the Maryland State Archives)

Cloman (Clowman), Edward, 1832. "Petition, Schedule, Affidavit, personal discharge, Order for Publication, Bond for Appearance, Trustee's Bond, Trustee's Certificate and Deed to Trustee filed 25th April 1832. 13th Aug. 1832 Petitioner appears, certificate of publication filed, and petitioner finally discharged." (Insolvent Docket A, 1807-1843, p. 117, at the Maryland State Archives)

Cloman, George, 1856. "Petition, Schedules, Affidavits, Appointment of Trustee (A. W. B.)," etc., 22 April 1856. "11th Novr. 1856 Petitioner appears [name misspelled Cloeman], files certificate of publication of notice to creditors & finally discharged." (Insolvent Docket A. L. J. No. 1, p. 12, in the Court Records Dept. of the Historical Society of Harford County). "Notice is hereby given that George Cloman, of Harford County, has made application to the Circuit Court of said County, for the benefit of the Insolvent Laws of Maryland, and that the first Tuesday of November term, 1856, has been assigned for him to appear in said Court to answer such interrogatories as his creditors may propose or allege against him. A. Lingan Jarrett, Clerk." (*Harford Democrat*, June 13, 1856, p. 3)

Coale, Harry D. and Charles, 1897. "Insolvents' Notice. In the matter of the Insolvency of Harry D. Coale and Charles Coale, co-partners trading as Harry D. Coale & Bro. ... The creditors of Harry D. Coale and Charles Coale, co-partners, trading as Harry D. Coale & Brother, are hereby notified that they have applied for the benefit of the Insolvent Laws of the State of Maryland, and that Monday, September 27th, 1897, at 12 o'clock, M., at W. Beatty Harlan's Office, Main street, Bel Air, is fixed as the time and place of their creditors to meet and choose a permanent trustee for their estate. W. Beatty Harlan, Preliminary Trustee." (*The Aegis & Intelligencer*, September 24, 1897, p. 3). "Messrs. Harry D. Coale & Bro., formerly well-known canners, residing near Churchville, on Tuesday [September 22, 1897] filed in the Circuit Court a petition for the benefit of the insolvent laws, through their attorney, W. Beatty Harlan. Their liabilities amount to over $3,500, the largest creditor being Eliza M. Jackson, of Level, who holds a claim for $2,533.04, balance on a mortgage. Mr. Harlan was appointed trustee." (*Havre de Grace Republican*, September 25, 1897, p. 4). "Insolvent Notice ... Notice is hereby given to the creditors of Harry D. Coale and Charles Coale, partners, trading as Harry D. Coale & Bro., that the first day of November, 1897, has been fixed by the Circuit Court for Harford county when said insolvent will appear and answer such interrogatories or allegations as their creditors, endorsers or sureties may propose or allege against them. Gilbert S. Hawkins, Permanent Trustees." (*The Aegis & Intelligencer*, October 8, 1897, p. 2). "Insolvent Notice ... In pursuance of an order passed by the Circuit Court for Harford county, in insolvency, the under-signed, permanent trustee, hereby gives notice to the creditors of Harry D. Coale and Charles Coale, partners, trading as Harry D. Coale & Bro., who were such on the 21st day of September, 1897, to file their claims, duly proven, with the Clerk of Circuit Court for Harford county, on or before the 1st day of January, 1898. Gilbert S. Hawkins, Permanent Trustee." (*The Aegis & Intelligencer*, October 29, 1897, p. 2). **Genealogical Notes**: Harry Davis Coale, son of Isaac Webster Coale (1823-1904) and Martha Davis (1823-1905), was born on September 22, 1858, married Anne Spalding (1860-1941) circa January 4, 1883 (date of license), and died on December 7, 1934. Charles Coale, brother of Harry, was born on January 4, 1862, married Elizabeth S. James (1876-1940) and died on March 9, 1941. They are all buried in Holy Trinity Episcopal Church cemetery (marrage records; tombstone inscriptions).

Coale, Isaac, 1830. "Petition, Schedule, Shff's. Certificate, copy of Act of Assembly, personal discharge and Order of Publication, Trustee's Bond and Deed to Trustee filed 1st June 1830. 19th March 1831 Petitioner appears, Certificate of Publication filed and finally discharged." (Insolvent Docket A, 1807-1843, p. 104, at Maryland State Archives)

Coale, Joseph A., 1884. "Joseph A. Coale made an assignment, Friday last [February 22], to Stevenson Archer, trustee, of all of his property for the benefit of his creditors. His liabilities are about eight thousand dollars and his assets about five thousand, chiefly covered by liens. Mr. Coale's insolvency is due largely to a sale of canned goods two years ago to a Western buyer who never paid him for the good." (*Harford Democrat*, February 29, 1884, p. 2). **Genealogical Notes**: Joseph A. Coale (born c1842), son of Joseph Reed Coale (1807-1864) and Sarah Ann Watson (c1807-1901), married Mary ---- (born c1842) circa 1868, worked as a butcher in Bel Air, and their children in 1870 were Lylly Coale, age 1, and Harry Coale, born in January 1870. (1850 and 1870 Harford County Censuses, 3rd District)

Cochran, James, 1853/1865. "For former entries see Inst. Doc. B, page 79. 18th March 1853 Petition of Wm. F. Pierce – 2 recommendations & service filed ... 8th April 1853 ... appointment of Wm. B. Bond as Trustee ... 19th May/54 Auditor's Report Nos. 1 & 2 filed ... 3rd December Order referring case to Auditor ... 5th June/65 Withdrawal of objections & plea of limitations ... Same day final order of notification of Creditors Report filed." [nothing further] (Insolvent Docket A. L. J. No. 1, p. 2, in the Court Records Department at the Historical Society of Harford County) **Genealogical Note**: James Cochran (1819-1891), a farmer near Abingdon, never married and was once a tax collector. He was survived by siblings William, T. L., and Miss Eliza Cochran (*The Aegis & Intelligencer*, July 10, 1891)

Conley, Francis E., 1827. "November 27, 1827. Petition, Schedule, Bond, Personal Trustee's Bond, Trustee's Report, and order for Publication filed. 15th March 1828 personally appeared. Notice of publication filed." [nothing further] (Insolvent Docket A, 1807-1843, p. 86, Maryland State Archives)

Connelly (Connoly), Ignatius, 1832. "Petition, Schedule, Affidavit, personal discharge, Order for Publication, Bond for Appearance, Trustee's Bond, Trustee's Certificate and Deed to Trustee filed the 29th March 1832. 18th Augt. 1832 Petitioner appears, certificate of publication filed, and finally discharged." (Insolvent Docket A, 1807-1843, p. 116, at the Maryland State Archives). 1838. "Petition, Schedule, Affidavits, personal discharge and order of publication, Bond for Appearance, Trustee's

Bond, Trustee's Certificate and Deed to Trustee filed 15th January 1838. 28th Novr. 1838 Petitioner appears, Certificate of Publication filed & discharged." (Insolvent Docket A, 1807-1843, p. 161, at the Maryland State Archives)

Connolly, Alexander, 1856. "Petition, Schedules, Affidavits, Appointment of Trustee," etc. 25th Nov/56. 16th May/57 Petitioner appears, files certificate of publication & finally discharged." (Insolvent Docket A. L. J. No. 1, p. 14, in the Court Records Department of the Historical Society of Harford County)

Cooley, Charles, 1830. "Petition, Schedule, Shffs. certificate, personal discharge and order of publication, Bond for App. [Appearance], Trustee's Bond, Trustee's Certificate and Deed to Trustee filed 18th August 1830. March 19th 1831 Certificate of Publication & Interrogatories filed. Petitioner appears and discharged." (Insolvent Docket A, 1807-1843, p. 107, at Maryland State Archives).
Genealogical Notes: Charles Cooley, son of John Cooley (c1755-1807), a Revolutionary War soldier, and Sarah Ann Gilbert (c1760-1836), was born circa 1781 (age 35 and upwards when deposed in 1826 and age about 37 when deposed in 1828) and reportedly served in the War of 1812. He married Cornelia E. Barron (c1801 – February 27, 1875) on January 4, 1837 and died in May 1864, age 77, at *Mr. Friendship*, the home of his brother Daniel M. Cooley. Charles and Cornelia Cooley had no children. (*The Family History and Genealogy of John Cooley (1755-1807) of Harford & Cecil Counties, Maryland*, by Walter Lawson Cooley, 2007, pp. 1, 26-27, which source cites several cases where "Carvel and Charles [brothers] ran into financial difficulties" which led to indebtedness; Equity Court Case No. 33; Court Records Document 90.29.74 at the Historical Society of Harford County)

Cox, Larkin, 1822. Insolvent debtor to be discharged from imprisonment. (*Bond of Union and Harford County Weekly Advertiser*, July 25, 1822). "Petition, Schedule, Bond, Certificate, personal discharge and order for publication filed 15th January 1822. 21st Augt. 1822. Certificate of publication filed. Petitioner appears and Petitioner discharged." (Insolvent Docket A, 1807-1843, p. 48, at Maryland State Archives; Insolvent Docket Prior to 1827, Court Records Accession #632 at the Historical Society of Harford County)

Cox, Nicholas, 1834. "Petition, Affidavits, Schedule, personal discharge and order of publication, Bond for Appearance, Trustee's Bond, Trustee's Certificate and Deed to Trustee filed 5th May 1834. 16th Augt. 1834 Petitioner appears, Certificate of Publication filed and finally discharged." (Insolvent Docket A, 1807-1843, p. 133, at Maryland State Archives)

Creamer, Adam, 1860. "Petition, Schedule of property, List of debts due to & from, Affidavit, Order appointing Trustee & notice to creditors, Trustee's Bond and Deed filed 4th February 1861 & Henry D. Farnandis, Esqr., appointed Trustee. 5th Aug 1861 Cont'd." [nothing further recorded] (Insolvent Docket A.L.J. No. 1, p. 37, in Court Records Department of the Historical Society of Harford County)

Cresmer, John H. and R. Sophia, 1882. "Last Wednesday [December 13, 1882] the court passed an order appointing Wm. H. Harlan permanent trustee of the insolvent estate of John H. and R. Sophia Cresmer." (*Harford Democrat*, December 15, 1882). "Trustee's Sale of Personal Property. In virtue of orders of the Circuit Court for Harford county, passed in the matters of the insolvency of John H. Cresmer and R. Sophia Cresmer, the subscriber as permanent trustee, will offer at public sale, on the farm lately occupied by said insolvents, near Creswell P. O., on Thursday, January 11th, 1883, at 11 o'clock, A. M., the following Personal Property: Two Horses, 2 Mares, 3 Cows, 1 yoke of Oxen, I Sow, 1 four-horse Wagon, 1 two-horse Wagon, with Springs, 1 one-horse Wagon, 1 top Buggy, Roller, Ox Cart, Plows, Harrows, Grain Drill, Mower, Cultivators, &c., 1 Boiler, 10-horse power, Crates, Oil Tank and Pipes, and many other articles. Also a lot of fine 2-pound Tomatoes in the rough, stored in the railroad depot at Perryman, and a large lot of damaged can Goods stored in Baltimore city. Full information in regard to the Canned Goods given on day of sale. Wm. H.

Harlan, Permanent Trustee. J. S. Richardson, Auctioneer." (*Harford Democrat*, December 29, 1882, p. 3). [Summary of many court papers filed in this case and a long list of creditors of the Cresmers through 1883 can be found in Insolvent Docket A. L. J. No. 1, pp. 75-76, 78-79, in the Court Records Department of the Historical Society of Harford County, finally noting that the Court had dismissed the petition of the insolvents as "Recorded in Judgment Record Liber H. D. G. No. 2, ff. 289, 313."]

Cullum, Albert E., 1880. "Petition, Schedules, Affidavits, Order appointing George L. Van Bibber Trustee, Bond & Deed filed January 27th 1880, July 23rd 1880 Objections of Josiah Cope & Co. to discharge filed … 14th Sept 1880 Issues filed & Jury trial prayed. Novr 8th 1880 Objections of Josiah Cope & Co. by O. S. [Otho S.] Lee their atty., withdrawn & the Petitioner finally discharged." (Insolvent Docket A. L. J. No. 1, p. 67, in Court Records Department of the Historical Society of Harford County). "Insolvent Notice. Notice is hereby given, that Albert E. Cullum, of Harford county, has made application to the Circuit Court for said county for the benefit of the insolvent laws of Maryland, and that the second Monday of September, 1880, has been assigned for him to appear and answer such interrogatories as his creditors may propose or allege against him." (*Harford Democrat*, April 30, 1880, p. 2)

Cummins, Mark, 1810. "Whereas we the subscribers Justices of the Peace for Harford County upon the petition of Abraham Parsons, who set forth that he had been confined in the Gaol [jail] of said county twenty days for debts which he was unable to pay & finding the facts stated to be true we did meet at the gaol of said county on the 22nd day of February last and did then and there appoint the 26th day of March Instant to meet at the Court House of said county which said appointment we did then and there … at the request of the said Sheriff administer to the said Mark Cummins the following Oath which was taken by the said Mark Cummins being first duly sworn on the Holy Evangely of Almighty God in the words following – I Mark Cummins do solemnly swear that the Schedule which I have delivered to the Sheriff of Harford County doth contain a full account to the best of my knowledge & remembrance of my whole estate both real and personal or that I have any title to or interest in and of all debts, credits and effects whatsoever which I or any in trust for me have or at the time of my petition had, or am or was in any respect entitled to in possession, remainder or reversion and that I have not directly or indirectly at any time since my imprisonment or before, sold, leased or otherwise conveyed or disposed of or intrusted all or any part of my estate, Goods, Stock, money or Debts thereby to defraud my Creditors or to secure the same to receive or expect any profit or advantage thereof so help me God, which said duplicate of the Schedule aforesaid we have transmitted to the Clerk of the County Court to be by him preserved in his Office for the information of the Creditors of the said Mark Cummins. Given under our hands & seals this 20th Day of March 1810. Saml. Bradford. Benjn. Richardson. Jno C. Bond." (Court Records Document 67.10.4(A) at the Historical Society of Harford County; a copy of the schedule to which "Mark Cummins" made his "X" mark was included, but no property was listed)

Cunningham, Crispin (Chrispin), 1826. "Petition, Schedule, bond, Sheriff's certificate and personal discharge and order for publication filed 9th June 1826. 17th March 1827 Petitioner appears." [nothing further recorded] (Insolvent Docket A, 1807-1843, p. 79, at the Maryland State Archives; Insolvent Docket Prior to 1827, Court Records Accession #632 at the Historical Society of Harford County). **Genealogical Note:** Crispin Cunningham was deposed on February 15, 1820, age 56. (Archives File No. 484, "Josias W. Dallam – Bush River Properties," at the Historical Society of Harford County)

Cunningham, John, 1828. "Petition, Schedule, Affidavit, Certificate, Sheriff's Certificate, Bond, Trustee's Bond and Discharge filed 7th July 1828 … 14th March 1829 Petitioner appears in Court and finally discharged." (Insolvent Docket A, 1807-1843, p. 90, at the Maryland State Archives)

Curren (Curen), John R. and W. W., 1871. "Petition, Schedules, Affidavit, Order, Trustee's Bond & Deed filed 22 July/71. Paid $3." [nothing further recorded] (Insolvent Docket A. L. J. No. 1, p. 56, in the Court Records Department of the Historical Society of Harford County). "Notice is hereby given that John R. Curen has made application to the Circuit Court of Harford county, for the benefit of the Insolvent Laws of Maryland, and that second Monday in November, 1871, has been assigned for him to appear in said Court to answer such interrogatories as his creditors may propose or allege against him. A. Lingan Jarrett, Clerk, Circuit Court for Harford county." (*The Aegis & Intelligencer*, October 13, 1871, p. 3). W. W. Curen & Bro., 1885. "Trustee's Sale. The Undersigned, having been duly appointed Permanent Trustee in the matter of the insolvency of W. W. Curen & Bro., will offer for sale, on Saturday, January 2nd, 1886, commencing at 10 o'clock, A. M., the following property: Real Estate. The equity of redemption in Lots Nos. 89 and 90, situated at the corner of Otsego and Stokes Sts., fronting fifty feet on Otsego street, and running back ninety feet; being the property conveyed to William W. and John R. Curen by Peter Scully, by deed dated November 27th, 1884, and recorded in the Land Records of Harford county, in Liber A.L.J. No. 53, folio 74. Also, The equity of redemption in Lot No. 84 in square No. 214, fronting twenty-five feet on Franklin St. and running back one hundred and twenty feet; being the property conveyed to John R. Curen by Patrick Boyd, by deed dated September 22, 1883; and the following Personal Property: New Farrel Safe, No. 5; set of Office Furniture; 2 Stoves; a large and varied assortment of Carriage Builder's Hardware, consisting of Bolts, Screws, Rivets. Clips, springs, Washers, Gum Cloth, &c.; a lot of Bar Iron and Bar Steel, Sheet Iron, Horse Shoes, &c.; a complete assortment of valuable Blacksmith Tools, of new and improved patterns, consisting of a set of Lightning Screw Plates, Stock and Dies' a set of old style Screw Plates. 2 Leg Vises, 1 Tire Shrinker, 1 Tire Bender, 2 Anvils, 1 Upright Drill and Bits; a complete set of Swedges, Punches, Chisels and Tongs; 2 Hand Hammers, 1 Sledge, 2 sets of Bellows, 3 Tuyere Irons, 1 Bolt Cutter, set of Shoeing Tools, 2 Monkey Wrenches, 1 Grindstone, a Bend Saw, with Hand Power, a lot of Fork and Shovel Handles, Spokes, Plow Handles, Wheel Rims, Single Trees, Shafts, Poles, Yokes and an Unfinished Express Wagon Body, a lot of Paints, Varnish and Brushes; A New Cart, A New Buggy, A New Dayton Wagon, A New Cutter, A Second-Hand Express Wagon, Valuable Lumber, Oak, Ash and Hickory; a lot of Scrap Iron and Second-Hand Wheels; Two New Wheelbarrows, and many other articles. The Sale Will Be Peremptory And Without Reserve. P. L. Hopper, Permanent Trustee. Wm. S. Bowman, Auctioneer." (*Havre de Grace Republican*, December 11, 1885, p. 4). In the Matter of the Insolvency of W. W. Curen & Bro. ... In the above matter it is this 15th day of December, 1885, Ordered that John R. Curen, surviving member of the said insolvent co-partnership, be and appear in this court on the *Second Monday of February, 1886*, to answer such interrogatories or allegations as the creditors, endorsers, or sureties of said insolvent may propose or allege against him, and that P. L. Hopper, the permanent trustees give notice, by the publication of this order in some newspaper published in Harford county, once a week for four successive weeks before the 15th day of January, 1886, to the creditors of the said insolvents of the day so fixed upon. James D. Watters. True Copy—Test: A Lingan Jarrett, Clerk." (*Havre de Grace Republican*, December 18, 1885, p. 4). "Notice is Hereby Given to the Creditors of W. W. Curen & Bro., who were such at the time of the filing of his application for the benefit of the insolvent laws of the State of Maryland, to file their claims, duly proven, with the Clerk of the Circuit Court for Harford County, *on or before the 1st day of April, 1886*. P. L. Hopper, Permanent Trustee." (*Havre de Grace Republican*, December 18, 1885, p. 4). "Order Nisi ... Ordered, this 3rd day of August, in the year 1886, that the sales made and reported by Peter Lesley Hopper, trustee in the above entitled cause, be ratified and confirmed, unless cause to the contrary thereof be shown on or before the 24th day of August, 1886, provided, a copy of this order be inserted in some newspaper printed and published in Harford county, once in each of three successive weeks before the 24th day of August, 1886. The report states the amount of sales to be $1,413.08. A. L. Jarrett, Clerk." (*Bel Air Times*, August 6, 1886, p. 3). **Genealogical Notes**: John R. Curren (August 24. 1846 – February 23, 1897) (wheelwright and blacksmith and later in life an ice business manager), of Harford Co., formerly of Baltimore, son of John P. Curren (1821-1898) and Margaret A. ---- (1821-1883), married Mary A. Harward (March 21, 1851 – October 8, 1917), daughter of Charles Harward and Mary A. Curtis, all of Harford Co., on February 13, 1873 "at parsonage" by Rev. Jesse Shreeve [Hopewell Methodist Protestant Church]. The children of John and Mary Curren were William Curren (b. c1874), Elsie M. Curen (*sic*) (c1880-1954), Thomas Curen (*sic*) (1886-1967), and Adah Curren (b. c1893) (marriage records spelled his name Curren; death certificate of Mary spelled her name Curen and stated she was the daughter of John Harwood; Angel Hill Cemetery tombstones inscribed John's name as Curren, but his son Thomas' and daughter Elsie's names were inscribed Curen; *Havre de Grace Republican*, 27 Feb 1897, spelled John's name Curen). John's brother William Wells Curren (May 25, 1852 – November 24, 1886) married Emma Reasin Schritz (1845 – April 27, 1881) circa July 26, 1875 (date of license that misspelled his name Curens; Harford County marriage book recorded the license date, but the certificate was not returned to the county clerk by the minister; Angel Hill Cemetery tombstones)

Curry, Arthur, 1832. "Petition, Schedule, Affidavit, Personal discharge, Order for Publication, Bond for Appearance, Trustee's Bond, Trustee's Certificate and Deed to Trustee filed 4th Febry. 1833." [nothing further recorded] (Insolvent Docket A, 1807-1843, p. 123, at the Maryland State Archives)

Curry, John Jr., 1830. Insolvent debtor to be discharged from imprisonment. (*Independent Citizen*, April 22, 1830). "Petition, Schedule, Shff's. Certificate, personal discharge, Order for Publication, Bond for Appearance, Trustee's Bond filed 10th April 1830. 13th August 1831 Petitioner appears, Certificate of Publication filed and petitioner finally discharged." (Insolvent Docket A, 1807-1843, p. 101, at the Maryland State Archives)

Dallam, Joseph W., 1837. "Petition, Affidavits, Schedule, personal discharge and order of publication, Bond for Appearance, Trustee's Bond, Trustee's Certificate and Deed to Trustee filed 18th May 1837. 19th Augt. 1837 Petitioner appears, Certificate of Publication filed and finally discharged." (Insolvent Docket A, 1807-1843, p. 156, at the Maryland State Archives)

Dallam, Josias M., 1819. "Petition & Schedule filed 23rd August 1819. Ordered by the Court that the petitioner appear before the Court – appeared and took the necessary oath and ordered to be discharged from the Custody of the Sheriff ... March 18th 1820 petitioner appeared." [nothing further recorded] (Insolvent Docket A, 1807-1843, p. 26, at the Maryland State Archives; Insolvent Docket Prior to 1827, Court Records Accession #632 at the Historical Society of Harford County). **Genealogical Notes**: Josias Middlemore Dallam, son of Josias William Dallam and Sarah Smith, was born on December 14, 1782 in Harford County, married Frances Paca (c1787-1841, daughter of Aquila Paca (1738-1788) and 2nd wife Helen Tootell), moved to Kentucky and later to St. Louis, MO where he died on October 19, 1846. The children of Josias and Frances Dallam were Josiah William Dallam, Richard B. Dallam, Francis Asbury Dallam and Sarah E. Dallam Armes. (*Descendants of the Signers of the Bush Declaration of March 22, 1775, Harford County, Maryland*, by Christopher T. Smithson and Henry C. Peden, Jr., 2010, pp. 296-297)

Daugherty, Henry, 1819. "Petition, Schedule, Sheriff's certificate, Bond and personal discharge filed 16th Augt. 1819 – Augt. 28th 1819 petr. appeared." [nothing further recorded] (Insolvent Docket A, 1807-1843, p. 26, at the Maryland State Archives; Insolvent Docket Prior to 1827, Court Records Accession #632 at the Historical Society of Harford County)

Davis, Isaac, 1808. "£500. Petition, Schedule, Bond, &c. filed 23rd Dec. 1809 ... Augt. 18th 1810 the necessary oath was administered to the petitioner and the Court appointed Danl. Thompson

42

trustee." [nothing further recorded]. (Insolvent Docket A, 1807-1843, p. 4, at the Maryland State Archives; Insolvent Docket Prior to 1827, Court Records Accession #632 at the Historical Society of Harford County)

Davis, Larkin, 1835. "Petition, Affidavits, Schedule, personal discharge and order of publication, Bond for Appearance, Trustee's Bond, Trustee's Certificate and Deed to Trustee filed 8th Decr. 1835. 19th March 1836 Petitioner appears, certificate of publication filed and finally discharged." (Insolvent Docket A, 1807-1843, p. 145, at Maryland State Archives). **Genealogical Note**: Larkin Davis was born on August 25, 1798, died on February 5, 1876 at Dr. E. Hall Richardson's house in Bel Air and was buried at Old Brick Baptist Church. (*The Aegis & Intelligencer*, February 11, 1876; *Harford (Old Brick Baptist) Church, Harford County, Maryland, Records and Members (1742-1974), Tombstones, Burial (1775-2009) and Family Relationships*, by Henry C. Peden, Jr., 2017, p. 47)

Davis, Samuel, 1886. "Notice to Creditors. In the matter of the Insolvency of Samuel Davis ... Notice is hereby given to the creditors of the said Samuel Davis, who were such on the 9th day of March, 1886, upon the date of his application for the benefit of the insolvent laws, to file their claims against the estate of said insolvent, duly proven, with the Clerk of the Circuit Court for Harford county, on or before the 10th day of May, 1886. James W. McNabb, Permanent Trustee." (*Harford Democrat*, April 23, 1886, p. 3). "In pursuance of an order passed by the Circuit Court for Harford county, on the 8th day of April 1886, notice is hereby given to Samuel Davis, insolvent debtor, to appear in said court on the 10th day of May, 1886, to answer such interrogatories or allegations, as his creditors, endorsers or sureties may propose or allege against him; and notice is also hereby given to the creditors of the insolvent of the day so fixed upon. James McNabb, Permanent Trustee." (*Harford Democrat*, April 23, 1886, p. 3). **Genealogical Notes**: Samuel Davis (September 16, 1838 – January 10, 1921), son of Elisha Davis (1807-1891) and Mary James (1801-1881), was a farmer at Cardiff and married Cordelia E. Evans (March 18, 1838 – April 15, 1912), daughter of Amos Evans and Anna Saunders, all of Harford Co., on December 23, 1869 by Rev. Thomas M. Crawford, of York Co., PA, at George Jones' house in Harford Co. (Harford County license and marriage certificate; *Maryland Bible Records, Volume 5*, by Henry C. Peden, Jr., 2003, pp. 60-61, states Samuel died on January 12, 1921; Slateville Presbyterian Cemetery, York Co., PA, tombstones; Harford Co. death certificate of Cordelia E. Davis; Harford Do. death certificate of Samuel Davis states he died on January 10, 1921)

Dawes, Francis, 1808. "Petition, Schedule and Bond filed 12th May 1808. – August 13th 1808 papers delivered to Israel D. Maulsby, Esq., by order of the Court." [nothing further recorded]. (Insolvent Docket A, 1807-1843, p. 2, at the Maryland State Archives; Insolvent Docket Prior to 1827, Court Records Accession #632 at the Historical Society of Harford County)

Day, George W., 1887. "In the Matter of the Insolvency of George W. Day. In the Circuit Court for Harford County. In the above entitled matter, it is this 23rd day of March, 1887, by the Circuit Court for Harford County, ordered that the said George W. Day, the insolvent, be and appear in this Court on the 9th day of <ay, 1887, to answer such interrogatories or allegations as their creditors, endorsers or sureties may propound or allege against them, and that the permanent trustee of said insolvent give notice to the creditors of said insolvent of the day so fixed upon by the publication of this order in some newspaper published in Harford county once a week for one month before the said 9th day of May 1887. Jas. D. Watters. True Copy-Test: A. L. Jarrett, Clerk." (*Bel Air Times*, April 8, 1887, p. 3). "Notice to Creditors ... Notice is hereby given to the creditors of said George W. Day, who were such on the date of his application for the benefit of the insolvent laws of the State of Maryland, to file their claims, duly proven, with the Clerk of said court, on or before the 1st day of July 1887. George L. Van Bibber." (*Bel Air Times*, April 8, 1887, p. 3). **Genealogical Notes**: George Washington Day (August 27, 1847 – February 10, 1925) married Mary Louise Stokes (August 6, 1849 – September 16,

1891), daughter of Nathan Rigby Stokes (1808-1882) and Hannah Jane McFadden (1822-1906), of Harford Co., circa 14 Dec 1870. (Harford Co. license; Chart of the Descendants of John McFadden (1730-1811) posted online in 2006, compiler unknown; no Harford County death certificate in 1925)

Day, William N., 1866. "Petition, Schedule of property, List of debts to & from Affidavit, Order, Bond & Deed filed 14th Aug 1866 … R. B. Duvall, Trustee. 16th Feb/67 … Petitioner appeared & was finally discharged." (Insolvent Docket A.L.J. No. 1, p. 48, in the Court Records Department of the Historical Society of Harford County) **Genealogical Notes:** William N. Day, son of William Day, was born on November 30, 1830, married Fannie R. ----, worked as a stone mason, died on December 17, 1900 at Prospect, MD and was buried in Mount Vernon Methodist Church Cemetery. (Death certificate of William N. Day; tombstone inscription for William Day, but no marker for his wife Fannie R. Day)

Deaver, Aquila, 1828. "Petition, Schedule, Affidavit, Certificate, Bond, Trustee's Bond, Trustee's Certificate, Order of Publication filed 26th November 1828. 14th March 1829 Notice to Creditors filed. Petitioner appeared in Court and finally discharged. 20th August 1832 Jacob Michael appointed trustee & trustee bond filed." (Insolvent Docket A, 1807-1843, p. 92, at the Maryland State Archives) **Genealogical Notes**: Aquila Deaver, aged 66, swore in open Court on September 1, 1820 that he "served in the Revolutionary War and enlisted under Capt. J. Price attached to the 3rd Maryland Regiment of Militia on 14 May 1777 and served until 1783." He referred to Certificate 4358 and stated "I do solemnly swear that I was a resident citizen of the United States on the 18th March 1818, and that I have since that time by gift, sale or in any manner disposed of my property or any part thereof with intent thereby so to diminish it as to bring myself within provisions of an act of Congress entitled an act to provide for certain persons engaged in the land and naval service of the United States in the Revolutionary War, passed on the 18th day of March 1818, and that I have not nor has any person in trust for me, any property or securities, contracts or debts due to me nor have I any income other than what is contained in the schedule hereto annexed and by me subscribed. Schedule of Real and personal property: 1 house and lott, $150; 1 mare and colt, $30; 1 cow and calf, $12; 1 sow and pigs, $10; 1 chest drawers, $5; 1 cupboard and contents, $10; 1 desk, $3; 2 tables, $2; ½ dozen chairs, $1; plow and harness, $2; saddle and bridle, $2; kitchen furniture, $3; 1 stove, $5. [total] $235. I have no trade nor family except a wife." (Court Records Document 25.14.4 at the Historical Society of Harford County). Aquila Deaver is buried in Angel Hill Cemetery in Havre de Grace.

Deaver, James, 1838. "Petition, Schedule, Affidavits, personal discharge and order of publication, Bond for Appearance, Trustee's Bond, Trustee's Certificate and Deed to Trustee filed 19th March 1838. 24th Novr. 1838 Petitioner appears, certificate of publication filed & discharged." (Insolvent Docket A, 1807-1843, p. 164, at the Maryland State Archives)

Deckman, Isaac, 1879. "Notice is hereby given that Isaac Deckman has made application to the Circuit Court of Harford county, for the benefit of the Insolvent Laws of Maryland, and that the second Monday in May, 1879, has been assigned for him to appear in said Court to answer such interrogatories as his creditors may propose or allege against him. A. Lingan Jarrett, Clerk, Circuit Court for Harford County." (*The Aegis & Intelligencer*, January 24, 1879, p. 2). "Petition, Affidavit, Schedules, Order, Appointment of Trustee, Bond & Deed filed 23rd Jany 1879 … [also mentioned several claims filed by various individuals one of whom was E. M. Allen whose claim was heard before a jury and the verdict was in his favor] … See Trial Docket 1880, folio 58, No. 45." (Insolvent Docket A. L. J. No. 1, p. 61, in Court Records Department of the Historical Society of Harford County). "Court Proceedings. E. M. Allen, objectant, vs. Isaac Deckman; application for a discharge under insolvent laws; tried before jury; verdict for Allen. Judge Price, Williams and Young for objectant, H. W. Archer for defendant." (*Harford Democrat*, February 20, 1880, p. 2). **Genealogical**

Note: Isaac Deckman (July 9, 1851 – December 25, 1892) married Mary Martha Irwin circa April 2, 1874 (date of license; Dublin Southern Cemetery tombstone)

Deer Creek & Susquehanna Railroad, 1895. "A bill for foreclosure was filed in our Circuit Court, at Bel Air, Tuesday [September 10, 1895] by Hugh J. Jewett, Jr., solicitor for the Mercantile Trust and Deposit Company of Baltimore, trustee, against the Deer Creek & Susquehanna Railroad Company. The bill states that the railroad was begun under the terms of its charter, but was never completed; that a mortgage was given to the complainant, as trustee, to secure bonds to the amount of $300,000; that default has been made in the payment of all the interest due on the payment of all the interest due on the bonds, and that the railroad company is insolvent, and cannot pay its debts; that a large amount of subscription is due and has not been collected; that a large quantity of trestle timber is lying out unprotected and going to ruin. The bill further states that George M. Jewett and Stevenson A. Williams hold a lien upon the railroad by way of judgment, for $1,200 and interest and costs. It asks the Court to appoint a receiver or receivers, and that a decree for the sale of the railroad property and roadbed may be issued. On Wednesday [September 11, 1895] Judge Watters appointed Hugh J. Jewett, Jr., receiver for the road, and he gave bond in the sum of $25,000. The road was surveyed from Bel Air to Conowingo, and part of it has been graded. It is stated that the road will be sold." (*Havre de Grace Republican*, September 14, 1895, p. 3). **Note**: The railroad was never completed.

Devoe, Thomas B., 1862. "Petition, List of debts due to & from, Affidavit, Order, Schedule of property, Trustee's Bond & approval & Deed to Trustee filed 30th December 1862. A. W. Bateman, Esqr., appointed Trustee. 3rd August 1863 Petitioner appears, files Certificate & finally discharged." (Insolvent Docket A. L. J. No. 1, p. 41, in the Court Records Department of the Historical Society of Harford County). "Notice is hereby given that Thomas Devoe has made application to the Circuit Court of Harford county, for the benefit of the Insolvent Laws of Maryland, and that the first Monday in August, 1863, has been assigned for him to appear in said Court to answer such interrogatories as his creditors may propose or allege against him. Wm. Galloway, Clerk, Circuit Court for Harford County." (*The Southern Aegis*, February 13, 1863, p. 2, listed him as Thomas Devoe, but on February 27, 1863 and subsequent editions listed him as Thomas B. Devoe). **Genealogical Notes**: Thomas B. Devoe was born on February 1, 1817, married Mary O. Lytle (September 24, 1820 – January 28, 1895) on February 22, 1840 by Rev. John R. Keech, died on May 3, 1894 and was buried in Christ Church (Rock Spring Parish) Cemetery. (Keech's pastoral records; tombstone inscriptions)

Dinsmore, Samuel, 1842. "Petition, Affidavits, Schedules, Appointment, Certificate, Order, Personal Discharge, Appearance bond & Trustee's bond filed 8th Novr. 1842 – 20 May 1843 Interrogatories filed – 24th May 1843 Certificate of Publication filed and ordered that the petitioner republish the notice to his creditors & cont'd. 25th Novr. 1843 Petitioner appears & files certificate of publication & finally discharged." (Insolvent Docket A, 1807-1843, p. 186, at the Maryland State Archives). **Genealogical Note**: On March 12, 1817 Samuel Dinsmore, age not given, stated he was "a native of Ireland and at present residing in Harford County in the State of Maryland, appeared in open Court here and prays to become a citizen of the United States, and it appearing to the satisfaction of the Court here by John Sample and Morgan Richardson, citizens of the United States duly sworn in open Court here, that the said Samuel Dinsmore was a resident within the limits and under the jurisdiction of the United States between the twenty ninth day of January seventeen hundred and ninety five and the eighteenth day of June seventeen hundred and ninety eight, that he was a resident five years and upwards within and under the jurisdiction of the United States and one year and upwards immediately preceding this application within the State of Maryland and that during the said time of five years he has behaved as a man of good moral character attached to the principles of the Constitution of the United States, and well disposed to the good order and happiness of the same, and the said Samuel Dinsmore having declared on oath taken within open Court here that he would support the Constitution of the United States, and that he doth absolutely and entirely renounce and adjure all allegiance and fidelity to every Prince, Potentate, State and Sovereignty whatever and particularly all allegiance and fidelity to the United Kingdoms of Great Britain and Ireland. The Court thereupon admits the said Samuel Dinsmore to become a citizen of the United States." (County Court Minutes 1816-1822, p. 19, at Historical Society of Harford County)

Donahoo, Joseph F., 1856. "Petition, Schedules, Affidavits, Appoint. of Trustee (A. W. Bateman)," etc., 4 April 1856. "11th Novr. 1856 Petitioner appears, files certificate of publication & finally discharged." (Insolvent Docket A. L. J. No. 1, p. 11, in the Court Records Department of the Historical Society of Harford County). "Notice is hereby given that Joseph F. Donahoo, of Harford County, has made application to the Circuit Court of said County, for the benefit of the Insolvent Laws of Maryland, and that the first Tuesday after the second Monday in November next has been assigned for him to appear in said Court to answer such interrogatories as his creditors may propose or allege against him. A. Lingan Jarrett, Clerk." (*Harford Democrat*, June 20, 1856, p. 3). 1865. "Administratrix' Notice. This is to give notice, that the subscriber has obtained from the Register of Wills of Harford county, Md., Letters of Administration on the personal estate of Joseph F. Donahoo, late of said County, deceased. All persons having claims against said deceased, are hereby notified to exhibit the same, with the legal vouchers thereof, on or before the 6th Day of December 1866, or they may otherwise, by law, be excluded from all benefit of said estate. All persons indebted to said estate are requested to make immediate payment. Given under my hand and seal this 6th day of December, 1865. Mary E. Donahoo, Administratrix." (*National American*, December 29, 1865)

Donn, John, 1829. "Insolvent debtor to be discharged from imprisonment." (*Independent Citizen*, December 10, 1829). "Petition, Schedule, Shff's Certificate, personal discharge, Order for Publication, Bond for Appearance, Trustee's Certificate, Trustee's Bond and Deed to Trustee filed 30th Oct 1829. 13th March 1830 Petitioner appears and Notice of Publication filed. 15th March 1830 Oath prescribed by law administered and Petitioner discharged." (Insolvent Docket A, 1807-1843, p. 99, at Maryland State Archives). **Genealogical Notes**: John Donn was a wheelwright in Havre de Grace by 1798 and a coach maker by 1803. He was likely the father of John M. Donn and Thomas C. Donn who began making saddles and harnesses in Havre de Grace in July 1825. The sons had moved to Washington, D. C. by 1830 and John M. Donn married Caroline Boteler in May 1831. John Donn probably removed there as well as no further record about him is found in Harford Co. By 1850 John M. Donn was a merchant in Bladensburg, Maryland. (*Carriages Back in the Day*, by Jack L. Shagena, Jr. and Henry C. Peden, Jr., 2016, p. 47; *Bond of Union and Harford County Weekly Advertiser*, July 28, 1825)

Dorney, Henry, 1818. "Petition, schedule and bond filed 2nd Sepr. 1818 … and ordered by the Court that he be discharged from the custody of the Sheriff and that he give the usual notice to his creditors." (Insolvent Docket A, 1807-1843, p. 22, at the Maryland State Archives; Insolvent Docket Prior to 1827, Court Records Accession #632 at Historical Society of Harford County) **Genealogical Notes** Henry Dorney, son of John Dorney (1744-1785) and Martha Woodland, was born in 1779, married Martha Hill, daughter of Thomas Hill and Martha Dorney, on September 12, 1799 and they had a son Henry Dorney, Jr. (St. John's P. E. Church and George's P. E. Church Registers)

Doyle, Hugh, 1860. "Petition, Schedules, Affidavit, Order appointing Trustee, List of debts due to & from, Trustee's Bond and Deed to Trustee filed 15th September 1860 … 22nd April/61 Cont'd." [nothing further recorded] (Insolvent Docket A. L. J. No. 1, p. 35, in the Court Records Department of the Historical Society of Harford County)

Duff, Francis, 1821. "Petition, Schedule, Bond, Sheriff's certificate, personal discharge & order for publication filed 14th March 1821 – 1st September 1821 petitioner appeared & Thomas Baxter [was] appointed Trustee and ordered that he give bond in the penalty of $500." [nothing further recorded] (Insolvent Docket A, 1807-1843, p. 44, at the Maryland State Archives; Insolvent Docket Prior to 1827, Court Records Accession #632 at the Historical Society of Harford County). 1836. "This Indenture made this second day of May in the year of our Lord One Thousand Eight Hundred and Thirty Six between Francis Duff of Harford County in the State of Maryland of the one part, and John D. Connelly, of the other part: Whereas, on the application of the said Francis Duff for the Benefit of the Acts of Assembly for the relief of Insolvent Debtors on the second day of May instant the above named John D. Connelly was appointed Trustee for the benefit of the Creditors of the said Francis Duff agreeable to the provisions of the Act of Assembly in such cases made and provided. Now this Indenture Witnesseth, that the said Francis Duff in pursuance of the premises, and in consideration of one dollar current money, to be paid by the said John D. Connelly – hath granted, bargained and sold, released, conveyed, assigned, transferred and set over, and by these presents doth freely and obsolutely [sic] grant, bargain and sell, release, convey, assign, transfer and set over, unto the said John D. Connelly, his heirs, executors and administrators, all and every the household goods and furniture, effects and chattels, debts and sum and sums of money belonging to, and due or owing to the said Francis Duff as are in the schedule of the said Francis Duff particularly mentioned: and also, all other property and estate, real, personal and mixed, of what kind, nature or quality soever (excepting the wearing apparel, bed and bedding of the said Francis Duff) which the said Francis Duff has or claims any title to, or in any respect entitled to, in possession, remainder or reversion; To Have and To Hold the same, and every part and parcel thereof, unto him the said John D. Connelly, heirs, executors, administrators and assigns, forever, in trust, for the Creditors of the said Francis Duff and for their use and benefit, agreeably to the Act of Assembly, entitled 'An Act for the relief of sundry Insolvent Debtors, and the several Supplements thereto.' In witness whereof the said Francis Duff hath hereunto set his hand and affixed his seal, the day and year first above mentioned. Signed, sealed and delivered in the presence of Thomas A. Hays." ("Deed. Francis Duff, An Insolvent Debtor, To John D. Connelly, Trustee" in the Archives of the Historical Society of Harford County; also recorded in Harford County land records HD-19-99). 1836. "Petition, Affidavits, Schedule, personal discharge and order of publication, Bond for Appearance, Trustee's Bond, Trustee's Certificate and Deed to Trustee filed 2nd May 1836. August 13th 1836 Petitioner appears, certificate of publication filed and finally discharged." (Insolvent Docket A, 1807-1843, p. 147, at the Maryland State Archives)

Duff, John, 1816. "Whereas we the Subscribers, Justices of the Peace for Harford County upon the petition of John Duff stating therein that he had actually been confined in the gaol [jail] of said county since the nineth day of July last for debts which he was unable to pay and finding the facts therein stated to be true we did on the twenty-ninth day of July 1816 appoint the 31st day of Augt. instant to meet at the Court house of said county which said appointment we did there certify to the Sheriff of said County in whose custody the said John Duff was … [and] … at the Request of the said Sheriff administer to the said John Duff the following oath which was taken by the said John Duff being first duly sworn on the holy Evangely of Almighty God in the words following, to wit: I, John Duff do solemnly promise and swear that the Schedule which I have delivered to the Sheriff of Harford County doth contain a full account to the best of my knowledge and rembrance of my whole estate both real and personal or that I have any title to, or interest in, and of all debts, credits and effects whatsoever which I or any in trust for me, have or at the time of my petition had, or now or was in any respect entitled to in possession, remainder or reversion and that I have not directly or indirectly at any time since my imprisonment or before, sold, leased or otherwise conveyed or disposed of or intrusted all or any part of my estate, goods, stock, money or debts thereby to defraud his creditors or to secure the same to receive or expect any profit or advantage thereof, so help me God. Which said duplicate of the schedule aforesaid we have transmitted to the Clerk of the County Court to be by him preserved in his office for the information of the creditors of the said John Duff. Given under our hands ands seals this 31st day of August 1816. James Wallace, Benjn. Richardson and Joseph Robinson. (Court Records Document 67.10.5(A) at the Historical Society of Harford County; a copy of the schedule to which "John Duff" made his "X" mark was included, but did not list any property). 1820. "Petition, Schedule, Bond, Sheriff's certificate, order for personal discharge and publication filed 18th July 1820. March 17th 1821 petr. appeared and filed a certificate of publication." [nothing further recorded] (Insolvent Docket A, 1807-1843, p. 34, at the Maryland State Archives; Insolvent Docket Prior to 1827, Court Records Accession #632 at the Historical Society of Harford County). 1832. "Petition, Schedule, personal discharge, Order for Publication, Bond for Appearance, Trustee's Bond, Trustee's Certificate and Deed to Trustee filed the 29th February 1832. 18th Augt. 1832 Petitioner appears, certificate of publication filed, and finally discharged." (Insolvent Docket A, 1807-1843, p. 115, at the Maryland State Archives)

Durham, David, 1862. "Petition, List of debts due to & from, Affidavit, Order appointing Trustee, Schedule of property, Trustee's Bond & approval & Deed to Trustee filed 17th day of May 1862 ... 10th Nov 1862 Petitioner appears, files Certificate of Notice & is finally discharged." (Insolvent Docket A. L. J. No. 1, p. 41, in the Court Records Department of the Historical Society of Harford County). "Notice is hereby given that David Durham has made application to the Circuit Court of Harford county, for the benefit of the Insolvent Laws of Maryland, and that the second Monday in November, 1862, has been assigned for him to appear in said Court to answer such interrogatories as his creditors may propose or allege against him. Wm. Galloway, Clk." (*The Southern Aegis*, August 2, 1862, p. 3; his name was misspelled Darham in the July 26, 1862 issue). **Genealogical Notes**: This was probably David Devoe Durham (July 3, 1820 – January 6, 1877), son of Abel Anderson Durham (1791-1875) and Sarah Devoe (1797-1866), who married 1st to Ann Dorcas Woods (1806-1842) and 2nd to Mrs. Mary A. Harker, of Baltimore City, on 5 Apr 1864 by Rev. Dr. Hawkes at Christ Church and divorced February 10, 1868. The children of David D. and Ann Durham were Sarah Elizabeth Texas Durham (married Silas Lowe), Marie Antoinette Pocahontas Durham (married Howard Poteet), Dorcas Florida Monterey Durham (married Israel Scarff), Alphonso Beuna Vista Durham (never married), Morgianna Wilena Matermora Durham (married Philip West), Abel James Durham (married Clara Kennedy, moved to Texas), and Josephine Pamelia Burlington Durham. (marriage licenses; Baltimore *Sun*, April 13, 1864; Divorce Case No. 1736 filed by David Durham on August 4, 1866 in Harford County; *Clark, Rigdon, Wilson and Durham Families of Harford County, Maryland*, by Ella Harrison Rowe, 1987, p. 67, states Mary Durham had "a violent and turbulent temper" and it was a very stormy marriage with destruction of personal property; "she left home without cause on August 19, 1865, her whereabouts unknown;" he filed for and was granted a divorce one year later)

Duval, William J., 1825. "Petition, Schedule, Bond, Sheriff Certificate and personal discharge and order for publication filed 20th July 1825. 18th March 1826 Printers certificate filed." [nothing further recorded] (Insolvent Docket A, 1807-1843, p. 72, at the Maryland State Archives; Insolvent Docket Prior to 1827, Court Records Accession #632 at the Historical Society of Harford County)

Edelin, William M., 1896. "A petition was filed in the Circuit Court on Tuesday by William M. Edelin asking for the benefit of the insolvent law. Mr. S. A. Williams was appointed trustee." (*The Aegis & Intelligencer*, September 18, 1896, p. 3)

Edie, Arthur E., 1894. Judgment against Edie for $603.66. (*The Aegis & Intelligencer*, November 16, 1894). "Arthur E. Edie, of Dublin district, has applied for the benefit of the insolvent laws, and Wm. W. (sic) Whiteford of Cambria, is his insolvent trustee." (*Havre de Grace Republican*, December 21, 1894,

p. 3). "Insolvency Notice. Roberts and Son and others vs. Arthur E. Edie and Henry C. Brenneman, Trustee. In the Circuit Court for Harford County, In Insolvency. By virtue of an order of said Court, passed on the 4th day of January, 1895, notice is hereby given that the 11th day of February, 1895, is fixed as the day for said Arthur E. Edie, insolvent, to appear in said Court, to answer such interrogatories or allegations as his creditors, endorsers or sureties may propose or allege against him. William M. (sic) Whiteford, Permanent Trustee." (*The Aegis & Intelligencer*, January 11, 1895, p. 2). "Notice to Creditors. Roberts and Sons and others vs. Arthur E. Edie and Henry C. Brenneman, Trustee. In the Circuit Court for Harford County, In Insolvency. Notice is hereby given to all creditors of Arthur E. Edie, who were such on the 14th day of November, 1892 (sic), to file their claims, duly proven with the Clerk of the Circuit Court for Harford County, on or before the 4th day of March, 1895. William M. (sic) Whiteford, Permanent Trustee." (*The Aegis & Intelligencer*, Ibid.)

Edie, David A., 1891. "Notice to Creditors. In the matter of the Insolvency of David A. Edie ... This is to give notice to the creditors of David A. Edie, an insolvent debtor, of the pendency of proceedings in insolvency in regard to the estate of said Edie, and that Tuesday, the 9th day of June, 1891, at 10 o'clock, A. M., at my office in Bel Air, in said county, is the time and place fixed for a meeting of the creditors of said insolvent to choose a permanent trustee for said estate. William Young, Preliminary Trustee." (*The Aegis & Intelligencer*, June 5, 1891, p. 3). "Insolvent's Notice ... In pursuance of an order of the Circuit Court for Harford county, passed in the above matter, notice is hereby given that the 14th day of September, 1891, is fixed as the day for the said David A. Edie to appear in said Court, to answer such interrogatories or allegations as his creditors, endorsers or sureties may propose or allege against him. Wm. Young, Permanent Trustee." (*The Aegis & Intelligencer*, August 14, 1891, p. 3). "Notice to Creditors ... In pursuance of an order of the Circuit Court for Harford county, passed in the above matter, notice is hereby given to the creditors of said David A. Edie, who were such on the 1st day of June, 1891, to file their claims, duly authenticated, with the Clerk of said Court, on or before the 1st day of November 1891. Wm. Young, Permanent Trustee." (*The Aegis & Intelligencer*, August 14, 1891, p. 3). **Genealogical Notes**: David A. Edie (born c1832, PA) married Mary E. Payne (born c1839, PA) circa February 25, 1856 (date of license), worked as a farmer and their children in 1860 were Laura Edie (age 3) and John Edie (age 1). (1860 Harford County Census)

Emmord, John H., 1885. "September 10th 1885. Petition, Schedules, Affidavit, Order appointing Preliminary Trustee [name not given], Bond & Deed filed ... Nov 19/85 Permanent Trustee's Bond [name not given] approved & filed, certificate of notice of creditors & insolvent notice is filed, same day order of Final discharge filed." (Insolvent Docket A. L. J. No. 1, p. 100, in the Court Records Department of the Historical Society of Harford County). "In the matter of the Insolvency of John H. Emmord ... In pursuance of an order passed by the Circuit Court for Harford County, notice is hereby given to the Creditors of John H. Emmord, an insolvent debtor, to file their claims, duly authenticated and proven, with the Clerk of said court, on or before the second Monday of February, 1886. Herman Stump, Permanent Trustee." (*The Aegis & Intelligencer*, November 27, 1885, p. 3). "To the Creditors of John H. Emmord. Take notice that John H. Emmord, of Harford county, an Insolvent Debtor, having filed his petition to be discharged from all his debts and inabilities under the provisions of the Insolvent Laws of the State of Maryland, and such petition being now pending, a meeting of the creditors of said insolvent debtor will be held at my office, in the town of Bel Air, Harford county, Md., on the 22nd day of October, 1885, at 12 o'clock, M., for the purpose of proof of claims, propounding interrogatories, selection of a permanent Trustee and for such other business as may properly come before said meeting. Herman Stump, Preliminary Trustee." (*The Aegis & Intelligencer*, October 16, 1885, p. 2). **Genealogical Notes**: John Henry Emmord (1850-1927), son of Frederick H. Emmord and Mary Louisa Bauersfeld, married Laura E. Lantz, of Baltimore, daughter of John George Lantz and Mary Margaret Elizabeth Rieger, on March 12, 1878 at 144 Barre Street by Rev. Henry Scheib. Their children were Harry Oscar Emmord (1879-1966) married Eva Grace Forwood, and Laura Winifred Emmord (born 1882) married Maurice Julius Boeschel. John Henry Emmord was the B&O Railroad agent at Perryman and afterwards kept a store at "The Square" before 1880. He was in partnership with J. W. Taylor, trading as Emmord & Taylor, in 1885. Emmord transformed his farming implement warehouse into a general merchandise store and had a grand opening on May 1, 1890. James McDonald, who had been acting as "confidential clerk" for J. H. Emmord, moved to Baltimore. It was reported in April 1891, "The public watering trough at the Emmord store has been replaced for the season." The following month Emmord's store displayed a "Mother Goose Egg" that weighed 8½ ounces. In February 1892 the store was robbed of about $125 worth of goods, as were several other stores in this part of the county, and the robbers were eventually apprehended. Undeterred by the burglary, Emmord built a 16x38 feet addition to his store the following month. In 1893 J. Frank Cole was hired as a clerk and in 1894 arrangements were made to have a night school and public library in the hall over the store. In 1900 John Emmord was enumerated in the Second District, Third Precinct, as a merchant and his son Harry Oscar Emmord worked in his store. In 1914 a newspaper advertisement stated anyone interested in young pigs of any kind could obtain them from C. S. Clark's wagon at the Emmord & Co. Store in Emmorton. In 1920 Emmord sold his Perryman store to Samuel Sutton and his son Harry O. Emmord became the manager of the A & P Store in Havre de Grace in 1921. John Emmord stated in 1921 that he had resided in Perryman for 44 years and owned three acres in the "center of town" where he kept a 30x60 store. After Aberdeen Proving Ground was established he rented the store for $50 a month and disposed of it after 1919. He then rented another store, but "business is probably dead" as people were forced to sell their land and move away because of the proving ground. Emmord's Store was torn down sometime between 1942 and 1953. (Sources: General License Book; *The Aegis & Intelligencer*, June 26, 1885, November 11, 1887 (Business Index), May 9, 1890, April 10, 1891, March 4, 1892, April 8, 1892, April 21, 1893, January 12, 1894, May 1, 1914, April 16, 1920 and December 2, 1921; Harford County Censuses; Maryland Directory, 1880; *Harford Democrat*, April 18, 1890, April 25, 1890 and May 15, 1891; Maryland and District of Columbia Gazetteer and Business Directory, 1894-1895; Maryland State Gazetteer, 1902-1903; Polk's Maryland State Gazetteer and Business Directory, 1915-16-17, misspelled the name as Emmard; *Portrait and Biographical Record of Harford and Cecil Counties, Maryland*, 1897, repr. 1989, p. 567; *The Aegis*, July 29, 1927; Aberdeen Proving Ground Claims File #8 - Donald A. Norris Collection, Historical Society of Harford County Archives; *Harford County in Vintage Postcards*, by Bill Bates, 2005, p. 64; *Harford County Directory 1953*, p. 82; *Our Harford Heritage*, by C. Milton Wright, 1967, p. 352; *Harford County Place Names, Past and Present*, by Henry C. Peden, Jr. and Jack L. Shagena, Jr., 2014, p. 76; Historical Society of Harford County, Archives, Photograph Collection Drawers A-231, A-237, A-681, B-2315 and C-3079; John Henry Emmord Bible, *Maryland Bible Records, Volume 1*, by Henry C. Peden, Jr., 2003, pp. 79-80)

Enlows, Abraham, 1832. "Petition, Schedule, Affidavit, Personal Discharge, Order for Publication, Bond for Appearance, Trustee's Bond, Trustee's Certificate and Deed to Trustee filed 28th April 1832. 18th August 1832 Petitioner appears, certificate of publication filed, and cont'd. 16th March 1833 Allegations filed, petitioner appears and finally discharged." (Insolvent Docket A, 1807-1843, p. 118, at the Maryland State Archives)

Erwin, John, 1816. "Petition, Schedule, Bond and Notice to Creditors filed 10th August 1816 – March 13th 1817 the petitioner appeared agreeably to the tenor of his bond and Philip Doran appointed Trustee and ordered to give bond in $500 and ordered by the Court that the petitioner be personally discharged – bond of trustee recorded." [nothing further recorded] (Insolvent Docket A, 1807-1843,

p. 18, at the Maryland State Archives; Insolvent Docket Prior to 1827, Court Records Accession #632 at the Historical Society of Harford County)

Evans, George W., 1885. "October 14/85. Petition, Schedules, Affidavit, Order appointing Preliminary Trustee [name not given], Bond & Deed filed … Dec 11ᵗʰ 1885 Bond of Permanent Trustee [name not given] approved and filed. April 13ᵗʰ 1886 Order of Court discharging Insolvent filed." (Insolvent Docket A. L. J. No. 1, p. 101, in the Court Records Department of the Historical Society of Harford County). "Insolvent Notice. In the matter of the Insolvency of George W. Evans … In the above matter it is ordered, this 8ᵗʰ day of December, 1885, that the said George W. Evans, the insolvent, be and appear in this Court, on the second Monday of February, 1886, to answer such interrogatories or allegations, as his creditors, endorsers or sureties may propose or allege against him; and that the permanent trustee give notice, by the publication of this order in some newspaper published at Bel Air, in Harford county, once a week for three successive weeks, before the 15ᵗʰ day of January, 1886, to the creditors of said insolvent of the day so fixed upon. Jas. D. Watters. A. L. Jarrett, Clerk." (*Harford Democrat*, December 18, 1885, p. 3). **Genealogical Note**: He may have been the George W. Evans who married Fannie W. Pritchard circa June 9, 1891 (date of license).

Evans, Isaac, Jr., 1811. "Petition, Schedule, Bond and Notice to Creditors filed 13ᵗʰ December 1811 … August Term 1812 petitioner appeared and the Court appointed John Marche Trustee, bond to be taken in the penalty of $4000. Trustee refuses to serve … Court appoints John B. Onion Trustee. Bond and deed filed 1ˢᵗ Sept. 1812. Petitioner ordered to be discharged from his debts." (Insolvent Docket A, 1807-1843, p. 11, at the Maryland State Archives; Insolvent Docket Prior to 1827, Court Records Accession #632 at the Historical Society of Harford County)

Evans, Jeremiah, 1833. "Petition, Schedule, Affidavit, Personal discharge, Order for Publication, Bond for Appearance, Trustee's Bond, Trustee's Certificate and Deed to Trustee filed 5ᵗʰ March 1833. 17ᵗʰ August 1833 Petitioner appears, Certificate of Publication filed and finally discharged." (Insolvent Docket A, 1807-1843, p. 124, at the Maryland State Archives)

Evans, John, 1821. "Petition, Schedule, Bond, Sheriff's certificate, personal discharge and order for publication filed 15ᵗʰ January 1821." [nothing further recorded] (Insolvent Docket A, 1807-1843, at the Maryland State Archives; Insolvent Docket Prior to 1827, Court Records Accession #632 at the Historical Society of Harford County)

Everett, Nathaniel, 1824. "Petition, Bond, Schedule, Certificate of residence, Shffs Certificate, personal discharge and order for publication filed 14ᵗʰ Augt. 1824. March 19ᵗʰ 1825 Printers Certificate filed. Petitioner appears and is discharged." (Insolvent Docket A, 1807-1843, p. 67, at the Maryland State Archives; Insolvent Docket Prior to 1827, Court Records Accession #632 at the Historical Society of Harford County)

Everett, William, 1824. "Petition, Bond, Schedule, Sheriff certificate, Personal Discharge and order for Publication filed 2ⁿᵈ October 1824. March 19ᵗʰ 1825 Printers Certificate filed. Petitioner appears and is discharged." (Insolvent Docket A, 1807-1843, p. 69, at the Maryland State Archives; Insolvent Docket Prior to 1827, Court Records Accession #632 at the Historical Society of Harford County)

Famous, Andrew J., 1887. "Notice to Creditors. In the matter of the Insolvency of Andrew J. Famous … Notice is hereby given, that the 14th day of November, 1887, has been fixed as the day when said insolvent shall appear to answer such interrogatories or allegations as his creditors, endorsers or sureties may propose or allege against him. Geo. L. Van Bibber, Permanent Trustee." (*Harford Democrat*, September 9, 1887, p. 2). "Notice is hereby given to the creditors of Andrew J. Famous, who were such upon the date of his application for the benefit of the insolvent laws of the State of Maryland, to file their claims, duly proven, with the Clerk of the Circuit Court for Harford county on or before the 14ᵗʰ day of November, 1887. Geo. L. Van Bibber, Permanent Trustee." (*Harford*

Democrat, September 9, 1887, p. 2). **Genealogical Notes**: Andrew J. Famous (December 25, 1837 – March 1, 1920), son of Samuel R. Famous and Sarah A. Jarrett, both of Chester Co., PA, was a farmer and Civil War Veteran, and married Mary A. Carr (February 9, 1840 – January 9, 1911), daughter of James Carr, of Maryland, and Julia Hickey, of Germany, circa May 19, 1860 (Harford County license; Emory United Methodist Church tombstones; Death certificates of Andrew J. and Mary A. Famous)

Field, William O., 1883. "July 26th 1883. Petition, affidavit, Schedules, Order of Court appointing S. A. Williams preliminary trustee [later appointed permanent trustee] filed … Nov 12/83 … Petitioner appears in open Court & was finally discharged … Dec 15/85 Auditor's Report filed & Order Nisi filed … Recorded in Liber H. D. G. No. 2, folio 250, one of the Judgment Records of Harford County circuit Court." (Insolvent Docket A. L. J. No. 1, p. 81, in Court Records Department of the Historical Society of Harford County). "Trustee's Sale! In pursuance of an order of the Circuit Court for Harford county the undersigned, permanent trustee of the estate of William O. Field, an insolvent debtor, will sell at Public Sale at the Harford House, in the city of Havre de Grace, on Saturday, the 1st day of September, in the year 1883, at 12 o'clock M., all that lot of ground, with improvements thereon, situate on Washington street in said city, known as lot No. 325, in square No. 233, fronting 60 feet on said street, and particularly described in a deed from John Pratt and wife to the said W. O. Field, dated October 13th, in the year 1868, and recorded amongst the Land Records of Harford county in Liber A.L.J., No. 21, folio 117. This lot is improved by a comfortable Two-Story Frame Dwelling, with Porch, and Two-Story Back Building. Stevenson A. Williams, Permanent Trustee." (*Havre de Grace Republican*, August 17, 1883, p. 3). **Genealogical Notes**: William Oliver Field (July 8, 1843 – November 25, 1927), of Williamsport, PA, later of Havre de Grace, son of Cornelius P. Field, of New Jersey, and Mary S. Collar, of Pennsylvania, married Laura Emma Sadler (March 26, 1845 – June 14, 1916), of Havre de Grace, daughter of Thomas S. Sadler (1796-1889), of Dorchester Co., MD, later of Havre de Grace, and Mary A. Findlay (1809-1882), of Baltimore, on December 31, 1868 in Havre de Grace, and their son John Field was born in November 1869. William O. Field was a carpenter, millwright and employee of John E. Dubois Lumber Co. (Harford Co. license; Havre de Grace United Methodist Church, Record of Marriages, 1862-1874, p. 66; 1870 Harford Co. Census listed him as Oliver Field, age 23, with Laura Field, age 21, and John Field, age 6 months; Angel Hill Cemetery tombstones; Death certificates of William Oliver Field and Laura Emma Field; *Havre de Grace Republican*, 26 Nov 1927, obituary spelled his name Fields, stated he moved to Havre de Grace in 1860 and reported their only child, Mrs. John E. Green, died about three years ago, but there was no mention of their son John Field)

Finley, William B., 1867. "Petition, 3 Schedules, Affidavit, Order to give Bond & appear on 1st Saturday after 2nd Monday of February, Trustee's Bond & Deed filed 2nd Decr. 1867. 15th Feby. 1867 Petitioner appears, files Cert. of Publication & finally discharged." (Insolvent Docket A. L. J. No. 1, p. 50, in the Court Records Department of the Historical Society of Harford County). "Notice is hereby given that William B. Finley has made application to the Circuit Court of Harford county, for the benefit of the Insolvent Laws of Maryland, and that the first Saturday after the second Monday in February, 1868, has been assigned for him to appear in said Court to answer such interrogatories as his creditors may propose or allege against him. A. Lingan Jarrett, Clerk, Circuit Court for Harford county." (*The Aegis & Intelligencer*, December 13, 1867, p. 2)

Finney, George J., 1897. "Insolvent Notice. Notice is hereby given to all the creditors of George J. Finney, of Harford county, that he has applied for the benefit of the insolvent laws of the State of Maryland, and that a meeting of his creditors will be held at the office of Harlan & Webster, in Bel Air, on Wednesday, December 29th, 1897, for proof of claims, choice of permanent trustee, etc. William W. Finney, Preliminary Trustee." (*The Aegis & Intelligencer*, December 24, 1897, p. 3). "Notice to Creditors. In the matter of the Insolvency of George J. Finney ... In pursuance of an order of Court, passed in the above case on the 30th day of December, 1897, the undersigned trustee hereby gives notice to the creditors of George J. Finney, an insolvent debtor, to file their claims, duly authenticated, with the Clerk of the Circuit Court for Harford county, on or before the 1st day of March, 1898. William W. Finney, Permanent trustee." (*The Aegis & Intelligencer*, January 7, 1898, p. 2). "W. H. Harlan, Attorney. Trustee's Sale ... The undersigned, permanent trustee, will offer at Public auction, at the Court House door in Bel Air, on Monday, January 31st, 1898, at 11 o'clock A.M., all the said George J. Finney's equity of redemption, in and to all that Farm or Tract of Land, situate and lying in Harford county, Maryland, on the public road leading from Churchville to Davis' Mill, and containing 190 Acres, More or Less, upon which he now resides, being the same and all the land described in a mortgage from said George J. Finney to Edwin H. Webster, trustee, dated May 5th, 1879, and recorded amongst the Land Records of Harford county, in Liber A.L.J., No. 39, folio 133. This property is offered and will be sold subject to the legal operation and effect of the aforesaid mortgage to Webster, trustee, to secure the sum of $6,394, with interest from the day of sale. The improvements consist of a large Frame Dwelling in good condition, frame Barn, Granary, Hog House, Ice House, Smoke House and other buildings The land is of fine quality and well improved. About 150 acres are cleared, balance in wood. William W. Finney, Permanent Trustee. W. S. Bowman, Auctioneer." (*The Aegis & Intelligencer*, January 7, 1898, p. 2). "Trustee's Sale of Valuable Personal Property, By virtue of an order of the Circuit Court ... the undersigned will sell at Public Sale, at his residence, near Churchville, on Friday, February 25th, 1898, at 2 o'clock P. M., the following Personal Property: Three Mules, 2 Cows, 2 Heifers, 2 Calves, 7 Pigs, four-horse Broad-Tread Wagon (Brown) and Harness, 1 Cart, 1 Hay Carriage, 1 Dearborn, 1 Syracuse Plows, 2 Cultivators, 1 Corn Marker, 1 Sulky Corn Worker, Wheat Drill, Horse Rake, small Platform scales, Corn Barrel, Corn Sheller, Wheat Fan, Tomato Boxes, Grindstone, Shovels, Rakes, Forks, &c. About 75 barrels of Corn, about 30 bushels of Oats, 1 roller and other things. Wm. W. Finney, Permanent Trustee. Wm. S. Bowman, Auctioneer." (*The Aegis & Intelligencer*, February 25, 1898, p. 2). "Notice to Creditors ... In pursuance of an order of Court, passed in the above case on the 30th day of December, 1897, the undersigned trustee hereby gives notice to the creditors of George J. Finney, an insolvent debtor, that he had been ordered to appear before the Court on the first day of the February term, 1898, the same being the 14th day of said month, to answer such interrogatories and allegations as his creditors, endorsers and sureties may propose or allege against him. William W. Finney, Permanent trustee." (*The Aegis & Intelligencer*, January 14, 1898, p. 2). "Notice to Creditors ... Ordered, this 1st day of February, 1898, that the sale made and reported in the above entitled cause by William W. Finney, Permanent Trustee, be ratified and confirmed, unless cause to the contrary thereof be shown on or before the 28th day of February, 1898; provided, a copy of this order be inserted in some newspaper published in Harford county once in each of three (3) successive weeks before the 28th day of February, 1898. The report states the amount of sales to be $50. William S. Forwood, Jr., Clerk." (*The Aegis & Intelligencer*, February 18, 1898, p. 2). **Genealogical Notes**: George Jenkins Finney was born on September 28, 1830, married Louisa Lyons Webster (January 29, 1838 – March 28, 1927) on April 26, 1865 in Baltimore and died on December 17, 1906. Their children were John Clark Finney, Margaret Finney, Walter Finney, William Webster Finney, George Jenkins Finney, Jr. and Edwin Webster Finney. (*Descendants of the Signers of the Bush Declaration of March 22, 1775, Harford County, Maryland*, by Christopher T. Smithson and Henry C. Peden, Jr., 2010, p. 99)

Fisher, George W., 1829. "Petition, Schedule, Sheriff's certificate, personal discharge, order for publication, bond for appearance, Trustee's bond and Trustee's certificate and Deed to trustee filed the 11th July 1829 ... 13th March 1830 Petitioner appears. 15th March 1830 interrogatories withdrawn, oath prescribed by law administered and petitioner discharged." (Insolvent Docket A, 1807-1843, p. 98, at Maryland State Archives)

Fletcher, A. Ringold, 1893. "Notice to Creditors. This is to give notice to the creditors of A. Ringold Fletcher, of Harford County, an insolvent debtor, of the pendency of proceedings in Insolvency, in relation to his estate, and that Monday, April 17th, 1893, at 11 o'clock, A. M., at the office of George Y. Maynadier, in Bel Air, Md., is the time and place fixed for a meeting of the creditors of said insolvent to choose a permanent trustee or trustees for said estate and other business. George Y. Maynadier, Preliminary Trustee." (*The Aegis & Intelligencer*, April 7, 1893, p. 3)

Flowers, David, 1828. "Petition, Schedule, Affidavit, Certificate, Bond, Certificate [sic] and Order of Publication filed 26th Novr. 1828. March 14th 1829 Petitioner bond approved and filed, Trustee appointed [name not given] and prisoner discharged." (Insolvent Docket A, 1807-1843, p. 93, at the Maryland State Archives, spelled his name Flower). **Genealogical Note**: David Flowers married Phoebe Watters, daughter of Robert Watters, but their marriage date was not given. (Harford County Equity Court Paper #77, Watters vs. Onion, at the Maryland State Archives)

Flowers, John, 1820. "Petition, Schedule, Bond, Sheriff's Certificate, order for publication & personal discharge filed 26th July 1820 ... George McCausland appointed Trustee and personal discharge granted the petitioner." [nothing further recorded] (Insolvent Docket A, 1807-1843, p. 35, at the Maryland State Archives; Insolvent Docket Prior to 1827, Court Records Accession #632 at the Historical Society of Harford County)

Flowers, William, 1835. "Petition, Affidavits, Schedule, personal discharge and order of publication, Bond for Appearance, Trustee's Bond, Trustee's Certificate and Deed to Trustee filed the 29th June 1835. 19th Mar 1836 Petitioner appears, certificate of publication filed and finally discharged." (Insolvent Docket A, 1807-1843, p. 141, at Maryland State Archives)

Foard, George O., 1895. "Walter W. Preston, Attorney, Notice to Insolvent and Creditors. In the matter of the Insolvency of George O. Foard ... In the above matter it is ordered, this 1st day of April, 1895, that the said George O. Foard, the insolvent, appear in this Court, on Monday, May 13th, 1895, to answer such interrogatories or allegations, as his creditors, endorsers or sureties may propose or allege against him, and that the permanent trustee give notice, by the publication of this order in some newspaper published in Harford county, once a week for three successive weeks, before the 1st day of May, 1895, to the creditors of said insolvent of the day so fixed upon. Jas. D. Watters. True copy—test: Wm. S. Forwood, Jr., Clerk." (*Harford Democrat*, April 5, 1895, p. 2). **Genealogical Notes**: George Oliver Foard, son of William Foard and Mary Ford (sic), both of Baltimore Co., was born on April 20, 1852, married Annie Mary Stansbury (July 23, 1858 – September 3, 1947), daughter of Tobias Emerson Stansbury III and Amanda Rutledge, worked as a farmer and canner and died on his birthday on April 20, 1925 at Federal Hill. They are buried in William Watters Memorial United Methodist Church Cemetery in Cooptown (tombstones; death certificates). The children of George and Annie Foard in 1947 were Samuel B. Foard, William M. Foard, Robert S. Foard, J. Edward Foard, Mary F. (Mrs. Walter) Burton, Miss Margaret Foard and Grace (Mrs. Cecil) Denton. (*The Aegis*, April 24, 1925 and September 12, 1947)

Foard, John Calvin, 1859. "Petition, Schedule of property, List of debts due & owing to & from, Affidavit, Order & appointment of A. W. Bateman, Trustee. Trustee's Bond and Deed to Trustee filed 9th August 1859." [nothing further recorded] (Insolvent Docket A. L. J. No. 1, p. 29, in the Court Records Department of the Historical Society of Harford County). "Notice is hereby given that John Calvin Foard, of Harford County, has made application to the Circuit Court of said County, for the benefit of the Insolvent Laws of Maryland, and that the 4th Monday in February, 1860, has been assigned for him to appear in said Court to answer such interrogatories as his creditors may propose or allege against him. Wm. Galloway, Clerk, Circuit Court for Harford County." (*The Southern Aegis*, August 13, 1859, p. 3)

Foard, Lloyd J., 1836. "Petition, Affidavits, Schedule, personal discharge and order of publication, Bond for Appearance, Trustee's Bond, Trustee's Certificate and Deed to Trustee filed the 13th July 1836. 18th March 1837 Petitioner appears, certificate of publication filed and finally discharged." (Insolvent Docket A, 1807-1843, p. 148, at Maryland State Archives)

Foard, Lorenzo W., 1896. "Mr. Lorenzo W. Foard, of Aldino, has made application for the benefit of the insolvent laws of the State. Mr. Geo. L. Van Bibber is preliminary trustee." (*Havre de Grace Republican*, October 17, 1896, p. 3). "Lorenzo W. Foard, of Aberdeen, has made an assignment for the benefit of his creditors to George L. Van Bibber." (*The Aegis & Intelligencer*, October 23, 1896, p. 3). "In the matter of the Insolvency of Lorenzo W. Foard ... The creditors of Lorenzo W. Foard, of Harford County, are hereby notified that he has made application to the Circuit Court of Harford County for the benefit of the Insolvent Laws of the State of Maryland, and that a meeting of his creditors will be held at the office of George L. Van Bibber, in Bel Air, on Saturday, October 24, 1896, at 10 o'clock A. M. for the purpose of choosing a permanent trustee for the estate of said insolvent. George L. Van Bibber, Preliminary Trustee." (*The Aegis & Intelligencer*, October 16, 1896, p. 2). "Mr. Foard is a member of the firm of Foard Bros., who formerly ran a large canning house at Aberdeen. He states that he is liable for a large amount of the firm's indebtedness, which he is unable to pay. The liabilities amount to $4,550. Wallace & Neitze, of Baltimore, are the largest creditors, having a claim of $2,000." (*Havre de Grace Republican*, October 24, 1896, p. 3). **Genealogical Notes**: Lorenzo Wesley Foard (1863 – September 1, 1941) married Sarah Ellen Barrow (1869, Havre de Grace – April 12, 1951, Baltimore), daughter of Lewis H. Barrow and Sarah Parker, circa November 15, 1893 (date of license) and died at home in Aldino, but there is no death certificate for him in Harford County. Their children were James H. Foard, Mrs. John Wellington Thompson and Mrs. John H. Janssen. (*The Aegis*, September 5, 1941 and April 20, 1951; Baker Cemetery tombstones)

Foley, Maurice, 1832. "Petition, Schedule, Affidavit, Personal discharge, and Order for Publication, Bond for Appearance, Trustee's Bond, Trustee's Certificate and Deed to Trustee filed 31st July 1832." [nothing further recorded] (Insolvent Docket A, 1807-1843, p. 120, at the Maryland State Archives)

Ford, Joseph, 1824. "Petition, Bond, Schedule, Sheriffs Certificate and Personal Discharge and order for Publication filed 6th August 1824. 14th March 1825 Printers certificate, petitioner appears and is discharged." (Insolvent Docket A, 1807-1843, p. 65, at the Maryland State Archives; Insolvent Docket Prior to 1827, Court Records Accession #632 at the Historical Society of Harford County)

Forsythe, Alexander, 1858. "Jacob Hoke vs. Cornelia Forsythe, administratrix of Alexander Forsythe, et al. Bill of Complaint states that a certain Alexander Forsythe, late of Harford County, deceased, being indebted to Jacob Hoke for $100, on March 10, 1856 gave his promissory note for that amount payable on demand. Forsythe died about August 1, 1857, intestate, seized of a lot in Havre de Grace fronting 60 feet on Washington Street and 140 feet on Congress Avenue, which was conveyed to him by Hannah M. Boyce, and said lot he and his wife mortgaged to Robert R. Vandiver on July 9, 1855 to secure payment of $500. No part of the above sums were ever paid and are still due. Forsythe's estate is wholly insufficient to pay his debts. He left a widow Cornelia, who is the administratrix of his estate, and children Melvina, William and Marcellus Forsythe, heirs at law, all of whom are non-residents of Maryland. The bill requested that the real estate be sold to pay the debts. On February 15, 1858 it was ordered by the Court that the heirs of Alexander Forsythe appear to answer this complaint on or before January 20, 1859 or a decree *pro confesso* would be passed in default thereof. An order was decreed on June 22, 1859 that the sale made and reported by A. Lingan Jarrett, Trustee, was to be ratified and confirmed unless the heirs appeared in Court on or before August 1,

1859 to show cause to the contrary." (*The Southern Aegis*, September 25, 1858 and July 16, 1859).

Genealogical Notes: Alexander Forsythe, son of Samuel Forsythe and Amelia Gorrell, was born on June 3, 1813 in Pennsylvania, married Cornelia ---- (born c1824, PA) circa 1842, moved to Maryland circa 1845 and was listed as a cooper in Havre de Grace in 1850 census. The children of Alexander and Cornelia Forsythe were Melvina Forsythe, William Forsythe, Laura Forsythe, and Marcellus Forsythe. "Alexander Forsyth (adult)" was baptized on June 21, 1857 at Havre de Grace United Methodist Church and died circa August 1, 1857. His widow moved to Pennsylvania with their children in 1858. (Forsythe Typescript in The Henry C. Peden, Jr. Research Library at the Historical Society of Harford County; *Harford Historical Bulletin No. 4*, 1973, p. 14; Havre de Grace United Methodist Church Records, p. 206; Harford County 1850 Census)

Forsythe, Samuel, 1827. "Petition, Schedule, Bond, Sheriffs Certificate and personal discharge and order for publication filed. Bond of provisional trustee filed & Certificate of trustee filed September 21st 1827. 15th March 1828 Petitioner appears. Crawford Gorrell appointed Trustee ... bond with security ... in the penalty of $500 ... personal discharge granted." (Insolvent Docket A, 1807-1843, p. 86, at the Maryland State Archives). **Genealogical Notes**: Samuel Forsythe, son of Samuel Forsythe (c1759-1804) and Martha Crosan, was born August 15, 1787, was indentured to learn to be a cooper in 1804 and married Amelia Gorrell (born January 11, 1792), probable daughter of Thomas Gorrell and Sarah Silver, circa January 5, 1811 (date of license). They lived in Aberdeen and they both died between 1860 and 1870. The children of Samuel and Amelia Forsythe were John Forsythe, Alexander Forsythe (married Cornelia ----), James Forsythe (married Juliann Landis), Sarah Forsythe (married James Harmon Baldwin), Martha Forsythe (married Elijah Thompson), Margaret Forsythe (married Alexander W. Barr), Phoebe Forsythe, Samuel Forsythe (married Catherine Bailey), Elizabeth Forsythe (married William A. Bair), Hannah Forsythe, Ruth Silver Forsythe (married James Thomas Pritchard), Mary R. Forsythe (married David H. German), and Cornelia Forysthe (married William Finney Bayless). (Forsythe Typescript in The Henry C. Peden, Jr. Research Library at the Historical Society of Harford County; *Harford Historical Bulletin No. 4*, 1973, p. 14; Harford County Marriage Licenses; Havre de Grace United Methodist Church Records, p. 108; Harford County Censuses; Court Records Documents 37.06.6 and 81.15.10 at the Historical Society of Harford County; Land Records WHD No. 17, p. 343; Research by Jean H. Scrogin, of Miami, FL, Robert F. Phillips, of Chillicothe, OH, Jon H. Livezey, of Aberdeen, MD, Henry C. Peden, Jr., of Bel Air, MD, Dale E. Martz, of Lillian, AL, Karen P. Myers, of Columbia, MO, and Joyce Gorrell, of Salt Lake City, UT)

Forwood, Ebenezer, 1815. "Whereas we the Subscribers Justices of the Peace for Harford County, upon the petition of Ebenezer Forwood stating therein that he had actually remained in the gaol [jail] of said county since the twenty seventh day of February last for debts which he was unable to pay and finding the facts stated to be true we did meet at the gaol of said county on eighteenth of April last and we did then and there appoint the eighteenth day of May instant to meet at the Court house of said county which said appointment we did then and there ... at the request of the said Sheriff administer to the said Ebenezer Forwood the following oath which was taken by the said Ebenezer Forwood being first duly sworn on the holy Evangely of Almighty God in the words following, to wit, I Ebenezer Forwood do solemnly swear that the schedule which I have delivered to the Sheriff of Harford County doth contain a full account to the best of my knowledge and remembrance of my whole estate both real and personal or that I have any title to or interest in and of all debts, credits and effects whatsoever which I or any in trust for me have or at the time of my petition had, or am or was in any respect entitled to in possession, remainder or reversion and that I have not directly or indirectly at any time since my imprisonment or before, sold, leased or otherwise conveyed or disposed of or intrusted all or any part of my Estate, Goods, Stock, money or Debts thereby to defraud my creditors or to secure the same to Receive or expect any Profit or advantage thereof so help me God, which said duplicate of the Schedule aforesaid we have transmitted to the clerk of the county court to be by him Preserved in his Office for the information of the Creditors of the said Ebenezer Forwood. Given under our hands & seals this eighteenth day of May 1815. James Wallace. Joseph Robinson." (Court Records Document 67.01.5(C) at the Historical Society of Harford County; a copy of the schedule to which "Ebenezer Forwood" signed his name was included, but listed no property)

Forwood, Jacob, 1810. "Whereas we the Subscribers Justices of the Peace for Harford County, upon the petition of Jacob Forwood who set forth that he had been confined in the gaol [jail] twenty Days & upwards for debts which he was unable to pay and finding the facts stated to be true we did meet at the gaol of said county on the 20th Day of July last and we did then and there appoint the 20th Day of August Inst. to meet at the Court house of said county which said appointment we did then and there ... at the request of the said Sheriff administer to the said Jacob Forwood the following oath which was taken by the said Jacob Forwood being first duly sworn on the holy Evangely of Almighty God in the words following, to wit, I Jacob Forwood do solemnly swear that the schedule which I have delivered to the Sheriff of Harford County doth contain a full account to the best of my knowledge and remembrance of my whole estate both real and personal or that I have any title to or interest in and of all debts, credits and effects whatsoever which I or any in trust for me have or at the time of my petition had, or am or was in any respect entitled to in possession, remainder or reversion and that I have not directly or indirectly at any time since my imprisonment or before, sold, leased or otherwise conveyed or disposed of or intrusted all or any part of my Estate, Goods, Stock, money or Debts thereby to defraud my creditors or to secure the same to Receive or expect any Profit or advantage thereof so help me God, which said duplicate of the Schedule aforesaid we have transmitted to the clerk of the county court to be by him Preserved in his Office for the information of the Creditors of the said Jacob Forwood. Given under our hands and seals this 20th Day of August 1810. Saml. Bradford. Thomas A. Hays. Jno. C. Bond." (Court Records Document 67.01.6(B) at the Historical Society of Harford County; a copy of the schedule to which "Jacob Forwood" signed his name and listed this personal property: "2 Smoothing Irons, 2 Phials, 1 Kettle, 1 Barrel, 1 Sifter"). 1828. "Petition, Schedule, Affidavit, Certificate, Bond, Deed, Provisional Trustee's Bond, Trustee's Certificate, Discharge and Order for Publication filed 17th June 1828." [nothing further recorded] (Insolvent Docket A, 1807-1843, p. 89, at Maryland State Archives) **Genealogical Note**: Jacob Forwood was born on September 30, 1761 and died on November 24, 1840 (inscription on tombstone once at Sharon Quaker Cemetery and since removed to Forest Hill Friends Cemetery)

Forwood, Loami R., 1884. "December 29th 1884. Petition, Schedule, List of Debts & Credits, Deed & Order of Court appointing Preliminary Trustee [name was not given] filed ... April 17/86 ... Order appointing Permanent Trustee [name was not given] & Insolvent to appear & answer Interrogatories filed ... 24th May/86 ... Certificate of Pubn. [Publication] of Notice to Creditors & Final discharge of Insolvent filed." [nothing further recorded] (Insolvent Docket A. L. J. No. 1, p. 95, in the Court Records Department of the Historical Society of Harford County). "Notice to Creditors. In the matter of the Insolvency of Loami Forwood ... Notice is hereby given to the creditors of the said Loami Forwood, who were such on the 29th day of December, 1884, upon the date of the application for the benefit of the insolvent laws, to file their claims against the estate of said insolvent, duly proven, with the Clerk of the Circuit Court for Harford county, on or before the 24th day of May, 1886. Wm. H. Doxen, Permanent Trustee." (*Harford Democrat*, April 23, 1886, p. 2). "In pursuance of an order passed by the Circuit Court for Harford county, on the 17th day of April 1886, notice is hereby given to Loami Forwood, insolvent debtor, to appear in said court on the 24th day of May,

1886, to answer such interrogatories or allegations, as his creditors, endorsers or sureties may propose or allege against him; and notice is also hereby given to the creditors of the insolvent of the day so fixed upon. Wm. H. Doxen, Permanent Trustee." (*Harford Democrat*, April 23, 1886, p. 2). **Genealogical Note**: Loammie Forwood, son of William Forwood (1787-1860), a War of 1812 soldier, and Sarah Forwood (1796-1888, married February 12, 1818 in Delaware), was born on November 27, 1843. (*Maryland Bible Records, Volume 1*, by Henry C. Peden, Jr., 2003, p. 86; 1812 Pension WC-26094)

Forwood, Reuben, 1832. "Petition, Schedule, Affidavit, Personal discharge, and Order for Publication, Bond for Appearance, Trustee's Bond, Trustee's Certificate and Deed to Trustee filed 21st July 1832. 16th March 1833 Petitioner appears, certificate of publication filed and finally discharged." (Insolvent Docket A, 1807-1843, p. 119, at the Maryland State Archives)

Forwood, William, 1838. "Petition, Schedule, Affidavits, personal discharge and order of publication, Bond for Appearance, Trustee's Bond, Trustee's Certificate and Deed to Trustee filed 19th May 1838. 24th Novr. 1838 Petitioner appears, certificate of publication filed & discharged." (Insolvent Docket A, 1807-1843, p. 166, at the Maryland State Archives) **Genealogical Note**: William Forwood (1787-1860), a War of 1812 soldier, son of John and Hannah Forwood, was born on August 30, 1787, married Sarah Forwood (October 19, 1796 – May 17, 1888) on February 12, 1818 in Delaware and died on September 11, 1860. (*Maryland Bible Records, Volume 1*, by Henry C. Peden, Jr., 2003, pp. 85-86; 1812 Pension WC-26094)

Forwood, William & Son, 1895. "Messrs. Percival LeRoy & Co., of Baltimore, have petitioned our Circuit Court to declare Wm. Forwood & Son, of this county, involuntary insolvents." (*Havre de Grace Republican*, January 19, 1895, p. 3)

Forwood, William Smithson, 1878. "Petition, Affidavit, 2 Schedules, Appointment of Trustee & Order, Trustee's Bond & Deed filed 19th December 1878. 12th May 1879 Petitioner appears, files Certificate of Publication and finally discharged by the Court." (Insolvent Docket A. L. J. No. 1, p. 60, in the Court Records Department of the Historical Society of Harford County) "Notice is hereby given that W. Smithson Forwood has made application to the Circuit Court of Harford county, for the benefit of the Insolvent Laws of Maryland, and that the second Monday in May, 1879, has been assigned for him to appear in said Court to answer such interrogatories as his creditors may propose or allege against him. A. Lingan Jarrett, Clerk, Circuit Court for Harford County." (*The Aegis & Intelligencer*, January 10, 1879, p. 2). **Genealogical Notes**: William Smithson Forwood (March 17, 1834 – February 28, 1905), son of Dr. Parker Forwood (1797-1866) and his second wife Mary Hall Smithson, worked as a farmer and married Rebecca Glenn (March 16, 1832 – July 20, 1906), daughter of Nathan Glenn and Elizabeth Butler, after December 29, 1860 (date of license) and probably on January 2, 1861. (*Colonial Families of the United States of America*, by George Norbury Mackenzie, 1907, Volume I, p. 168, mistakenly stated they married January 2, 1860) The children of William and Rebecca Forwood were Thomas Glenn Forwood (1861-1903), William Smithson Forwood (1863-1926), Charles Clarence Forwood (1866-1927), married Bertha Martin, Dr. Francis Frederick Forwood (1869-1902), Lillian Rebecca Forwood (c1871-1951), Priscilla Frances Webster Forwood, and Mary Elizabeth Forwood married George Norbury Mackenzie in 1902. (Death certificates of William Smithson Forwood and Rebecca Glenn Forwood; John Forwood Bible, *Maryland Bible Records, Volume 1*, by Henry C. Peden, Jr., 2003, pp. 82-84; "Family Group Sheets of the Forwood Family of Harford County, MD" on file in The Henry C. Peden, Jr. Research Library at the Historical Society of Harford County, Bel Air, MD)

Forwood, William W., 1835. "Petition, Affidavits, Schedule, personal discharge and order of publication, Bond for Appearance, Trustee's Bond, Trustee's Certificate and Deed to Trustee filed 15th Augt. 1835. 19th Mar 1836 Petitioner appears, certificate of publication filed and finally discharged." (Insolvent Docket A, 1807-1843, p. 143, at Maryland State Archives) **Genealogical Notes**: William

Warner Forwood served in the War of 1812, married Sarah F. Gilbert on February 25, 1816 and died on or about July 9, 1852 in Placer Co., CA. (*Maryland Militia War of 1812, Volume 3, Cecil & Harford Counties*, by F. Edward Wright, 1980, p. 49; War of 1812 Bounty Land Warrant 55-120-28261)

Fowler, David P., 1839. "Petition, Schedule, Affidavits, personal discharge and order of publication, Bond for Appearance, Trustee's Bond, Trustee's Certificate and Deed to Trustee filed 5th Novr. 1839. 23rd May 1840 Certificate of publication filed, petitioner appears and finally discharged." (Insolvent Docket A, 1807-1843, p. 171, at the Maryland State Archives)

Foy, Samuel, 1832. "Petition, Schedule, Affidavit, Personal discharge, and Order for Publication, Bond for Appearance, Trustee's Bond, Trustee's Certificate and Deed to Trustee filed 25th June 1832. 16th March 1833 Petitioner appears, certificate of publication filed and finally discharged." (Insolvent Docket A, 1807-1843, p. 119, at the Maryland State Archives)

Frank, Aaron, 1860. "Petition, Schedules, Affidavit, Order appointing Trustee, List of debts due to & from, Trustee's Bond and Deed to George Y. Maynadier his Trustee filed July 23rd 1860 ... 13th Nov 1860 Petitioner appeared, filed Certificate of Notice to creditors and was finally discharged." (Insolvent Docket A. L. J. No. 1, p. 35, in the Court Records Department of the Historical Society of Harford County)

Frederick, John N., 1897. "Creditors' Meeting. In the Matter of the Insolvency of John N. Frederick. In the Circuit Court for Harford County in Equity. Notice Is Hereby Given to the creditors of John N. Frederick, that he has made application for the benefit of the insolvent laws of the State of Maryland and such application being now pending a meeting of the creditors of said insolvent debtor will be held on *Saturday, the 15th day of May, 1897*, at 12 o'clock M., at the office of the Clerk of the Circuit Court for Harford County, at Bel Air, Md., for the purpose of proof of claims, propounding interrogatories and the selection of a permanent trustee or trustees. Oliver T. Rogers, Preliminary Trustee." (*Havre de Grace Republican*, May 8, 1897, p. 2). **Genealogical Note**: John N. Frederick was born in 1854 in Havre de Grace, married Maud M. Walker (August 1, 1872 – February 14, 1920), daughter of John C. Walker and Mary Francis, and died on January 2, 1935 in Princeton, WV. The children of John and Maud Frederick were Alonzo B. Frederick (1897-1967), of Havre de Grace, George Frederick, of East Hampton, MA, Jacob Frederick, of East Hampton, MA, John N. Frederick, Jr., of Havre de Grace, and Mrs. William H. Whittaker, of Princeton, WV. (Angel Hill Cemetery tombstones; *The Aegis*, January 25, 1935)

Fulford, Henry, 1889. "Notice To Creditors. In the matter of the Insolvency of Henry Fulford ... To the Creditors of Henry Fulford. Take notice that Henry Fulford, of Harford County, an insolvent debtor, having filed his petition to be discharged from all his debts and liabilities, under the Insolvent laws of the State of Maryland, and such petition being now pending, a meeting of the creditors of such insolvent debtor will be held on Thursday, the 11th day of July, 1889, at 10 o'clock, A. M., at the office of the undersigned, in the town of Bel Air, for the purpose of proof of claims, propounding of interrogatories and the selection of permanent trustee or trustees. James J. Archer, Preliminary Trustee." (*The Aegis & Intelligencer*, July 12, 1889, p. 2). "Meeting of Creditors ... Notice is hereby given, that the 9th day of September, 1889, has been fixed as the day when said insolvent shall appear to answer such interrogatories or allegations as his creditors, endorsers or sureties may propose or allege against him. James J. Archer, Permanent Trustee." (*The Aegis & Intelligencer*, July 26, 1889, p. 3)

Galbreath, Alexander Finney, 1886. "Notice to Creditors. In the Matter of the Insolvency of Alex. Finney Galbreath ... In pursuance of an order of Court, passed in the above matter on the 2nd day of June, 1886, the undersigned hereby gives notice to the creditors of Alexander Finney Galbreath, an insolvent debtor, that Monday, the 13th day of September 1886, has been fixed by the Court for the appearance of said Insolvent, to answer such interrogatories or allegations as his creditors, endorsers or sureties may propose or allege against him. Wm. H. Harlan, Permanent Trustee." (*Bel Air Times*, June 4, 1886, p. 3). **Genealogical Notes**: Alexander Finney Galbreath was born in 1852, became principal of Darlington Academy in 1878, married Sara W. Wilson (1856, Darlington - March 13, 1932, Warren, OH), daughter of William Worthington Wilson and Anna Elizabeth Ferguson, circa January 19, 1882 (date of license) and died on January 12, 1922. They had a son William Wilson Galbreath (1882-1952) who married Natalie Cole (1884-1959) and lived in Warren, OH. (*The Aegis & Intelligencer*, January 13, 1922 and March 18, 1932; Darlington Cemetery tombstone inscriptions)

Galbreath, William H., 1886. "Notice to Creditors. In the Matter of the Insolvency of William H. Galbreath ... In pursuance of an order of Court, passed in the above matter on the 2ⁿᵈ day of June, 1886, the undersigned hereby gives notice to the creditors of William H. Galbreath, an insolvent debtor, that Monday, the 13ᵗʰ day of September 1886, has been fixed by the Court for the appearance of said Insolvent, to answer such interrogatories or allegations as his creditors, endorsers or sureties may propose or allege against him. Wm. H. Harlan, Permanent Trustee." (*Bel Air Times*, June 4, 1886)

Gale, Henry G., 1835. "Petition, Affidavits, Schedule, personal discharge and order of publication, Bond for Appearance, Trustee's Bond, Trustee's Certificate and Deed to Trustee filed the 26ᵗʰ May 1835." (Insolvent Docket A, 1807-1843, p. 140, at Maryland State Archives)

Gallagher, John, 1846. "Petition, 2 Affidavits, 3 Schedules, Appointment of Trustee [name not given], bond, deed, certificate, order [of] appearance, & certificate & personal discharge filed 1ˢᵗ Sept./46 ... 23 Jany/56 Hon. John H. Price being Trustee & counsel in this case ... 3ʳᵈ Nov/56 Order of Notice to Creditors filed." [nothing further recorded] (Insolvent Docket A. L. J. No. 1, p. 9, in the Court Records Department of the Historical Society of Harford County)

Gallion, Aquila S., 1842. "Petition, Affidavits, Schedules, Appointment, Certificate, Order, Personal Discharge, Deed, Appearance & Trustee's Bonds filed 20ᵗʰ Augst. 1842. 20ᵗʰ May 1843 Petitioner appears, files Certificate of Publication. Petition dismissed 20ᵗʰ Novr. 1843." (Insolvent Docket A, 1807-1843, p. 183, at Maryland State Archives)

Gallion, John W., 1858. "Petition, Schedules, Affidavits, Appointment of Trustee, Order of Notice, Trustee's Bond and Deed filed February 11ᵗʰ 1858. 13ᵗʰ Nov/58 Petition & ordered filed. 13ᵗʰ Novr. 1858 Petitioner appears and files certificate of publication & finally discharged." (Insolvent Docket A. L. J. No. 1, p. 23, in the Court Records Department of the Historical Society of Harford County). "Notice is hereby given that John W. Gallion, of Harford County, has made application to the Circuit Court of said County, for the benefit of the Insolvent Laws of Maryland, and that the 1ˢᵗ Saturday after the second Monday in May, 1858, has been assigned for him to appear in said Court to answer such interrogatories as his creditors may propose or allege against him. Wm. Galloway, Clerk of Circuit Court for Harford County." (*The Southern Aegis*, March 20, 1858, p. 3). 1872. "Petition, 3 Schedules, Affidavit, Order, Trustee's Bond & Deed filed 19 February 1872. 21 May/72 Order extending time for applicant's appearance filed. 18ᵗʰ Nov/72 Order extending time for applicant's appearance filed to 2ⁿᵈ Monday of May/73 & to give notice to creditors filed." [nothing further recorded] (Insolvent Docket A. L. J. No. 1, p. 57, in Court Records Department of the Historical Society of Harford County). **Genealogical Notes**: John W. Gallion (born circa 1813) married Martha ---- (born circa 1823), of Perryman, and their son John W. Gallion, Jr. (born circa 1845) married Mary E. Aaronson (born circa 1853) on March 11, 1873 at home by Rev. J. C. Sedwick (Harford County marriage record; *The Aegis and Intelligencer*, March 28, 1873, noting "*Balto. Sun* and the *Epis. Methodist* please copy")

Galloway, John, 1837. "Petition, Affidavits, Schedule, personal discharge and order of publication, Bond for Appearance, Trustee's Bond, Trustee's Certificate and Deed to Trustee filed 19ᵗʰ Augt. 1837.

17th March 1838 Certificate of Publication filed. Petitioner appears and finally discharged." (Insolvent Docket A, 1807-1843, p. 158, at the Maryland State Archives)

Galloway, Moses, 1824. "Petition, Bond, Schedule, Sheriffs Certificate and personal Discharge and order for Publication filed 27th April 1824." [nothing further was recorded] (Insolvent Docket A, 1807-1843, p. 63, at the Maryland State Archives; Insolvent Docket Prior to 1827, Court Records Accession #632 at the Historical Society of Harford County). **Genealogical Note**: Moses Galloway was a son of Aquila and Berthia Galloway. (Court Records Document 72.26.2.E at the Historical Society of Harford County)

Galloway, William K., 1820. "Petition, Schedule, Bond, Sheriff's Certificate, order for personal discharge and publication filed 27th June 1820. Allegations of fraud filed 17th March 1821. Certificate of publication filed. 1st Sepr. 1821 petitioner appeared & cont'd." [nothing further recorded] (Insolvent Docket A, 1807-1843, p. 33, at the Maryland State Archives; Insolvent Docket Prior to 1827, Court Records Accession #632 at the Historical Society of Harford County). 1824. "Petition, Bond, Schedule, Certificate and personal Discharge and order for Publication filed 20th April 1824." [nothing further recorded] (Insolvent Docket A, 1807-1843, p. 63, at the Maryland State Archives; Insolvent Docket Prior to 1827, Court Records Accession #632 at the Historical Society of Harford County). **Genealogical Note**: William K. Galloway was a son of Aquila and Berthia Galloway. (Court Records Document 72.26.2.E at the Historical Society of Harford County)

Gallup, Edward Beach, 1856. "Petition, Schedules, Affidavits, Appointment of Trustee," etc., 4th June 1856. "15th Novr. 1856 Petitioner appears, files certificate of publication & finally discharged." (Insolvent Docket A. L. J. No. 1, p. 13, in the Court Records Department of the Historical Society of Harford County). "Notice is hereby given that Edward Beach Gallup, of Harford County, has made application to the Circuit Court of said County, for the benefit of the Insolvent Laws of Maryland, and that the first Tuesday after the second Saturday in November next has been assigned for him to appear in said Court to answer such interrogatories as his creditors may propose or allege against him. A. Lingan Jarrett, Clerk." (*Harford Democrat*, June 20, 1856, p. 3). **Genealogical Notes**: Edward Beach "Ned" Gallup (1818 – November 25, 1903), son of Edward Gallup and Katherine James, was a sailor, boat captain on Spesutia Island, later of Havre de Grace, and manager of a freighting vessel. He was issued wild waterfowl gunning licenses in 1876 and 1877 and in November and December 1891 Capt. E. B. Gallup was at Nathan Barron's property on Bush River Neck acting as a policeman since Barron had requested him to look after the interests of the Taylor's Island Ducking Club. His death certificate stated he was age 85, thus born in 1818, but his obituary stated he was born in 1819. He was survived by his widow (name not given) sons Capt. Eldridge B. Gallup, of Boston, and Charles T. Gallup, of Havre de Grace, and a daughter Clara Osmond, wife of H. C. Osmond, of Havre de Grace He was buried in Angel Hill Cemetery. (*Duck Hunters on the Susquehanna Flats, 1850-1930*, by Henry C. Peden, Jr. and Jack L. Shagena, Jr., 2014, p. 46; Death certificate of Edward B. Gallup; *The Aegis & Intelligencer*, December 4, 1903, p. 3)

Garbers, John, 1835. "Petition, Affidavits, Schedule, personal discharge and order of publication, Bond for Appearance, Trustee's Bond, Trustee's Certificate and Deed to Trustee filed 9th November 1835. 19th Mar 1836 Petitioner appears, certificate of publication filed and finally discharged." (Insol-vent Docket A, 1807-1843, p. 144, at Maryland State Archives)

Garrett, Charles, 1880. "Petition, Schedules, Affidavits, Order appointing Henry Harlan Trustee, Bond & Deed filed March 12th 1880. Sept 13th 1880 Certificate of pub. of notice filed & Petitioner finally discharged." (Insolvent Docket A. L. J. No. 1, p. 67, in Court Records Department of the Historical Society of Harford County). "Insolvent's Notice. Notice is hereby given, that Charles Garrett, of Harford county, has made application to the Circuit Court for said county for the benefit of the insolvent laws of Maryland, and that the second Monday of September, 1880, has been assigned for him to appear and answer such interrogatories as his creditors may propose or allege against him. A. L. Jarrett, Clerk." (*Harford Democrat*, March 12, 1880, p. 2). **Genealogical Notes**: Charles Garrett (African American) (born circa 1820, MD), worked as a farmer, married Emily ---- (born circa 1830, MD) circa 1852 and their children in 1860 were Alice Garrett (age 7), Henry Garrett (age 5) and Mary and Martha Garrett (twins, age 2). (Harford County 1860 Census)

Gatchell, Increase, 1824. "Petition, Schedule, Bond, Sheriffs Certificate and personal Discharge and order for Publication filed 16th March 1824. August 14th 1824 Printers certificate of notice of publication filed. Petitioner appears and is discharged. John Donahoo appointed Trustee by the Court." (Insolvent Docket A, 1807-1843, p. 62, at Maryland State Archives; Insolvent Docket Prior to 1827, Court Records Accession #632 at the Historical Society of Harford County)

Gaunt, Elwood B., 1875. "Petition, 3 Schedules, Affidavit, Order, Trustee's Bond & Deed filed 13th Decr. 1875. Certificate of Publication of Insolvent Notice & is finally discharged." (Insolvent Docket A. L. J. No. 1, p. 58, in the Court Records Department of the Historical Society of Harford County). "Notice is hereby given that Elwood B. Gaunt has made application to the Circuit Court of Harford county, for the benefit of the Insolvent Laws of Maryland, and that the 10th day of May, 1876 has been assigned for him to appear in said Court to answer such interrogatories as his creditors may propose or allege against him. A. L. Jarrett, Clerk." (*Harford Democrat*, December 17, 1875, p. 2)

Gibson, Benjamin, 1820. "Petition, Schedule, Bond, Sheriff's certificate, personal discharge and order for publication filed 2nd December 1820 – objections filed 17th March 1821 [and] petr. appd. on the 17th March 1821 and filed certificate of publication." [nothing further recorded] (Insolvent Docket A, 1807-1843, p. 40, at the Maryland State Archives; Insolvent Docket Prior to 1827, Court Records Accession #632 at the Historical Society of Harford County)

Gibson, John L., 1828. "Petition, Schedule, Affidavit, Certificate, Bond, Deed, Trustee's Bond, Trustee's Certificate and Order of Publication filed 26th Novr. 1828. March 14th 1829 Petitioner appeared and discharged." (Insolvent Docket A, 1807-1843, p. 92, at the Maryland State Archives)

Gibson, William, 1819. "Petition, Schedule, Bond, Order for publication, Sheriff's certificate and personal discharge filed 16th April 1819 – Augt. 28th 1819 petr. appeared." [nothing further recorded] (Insolvent Docket A, 1807-1843, p. 24, at Maryland State Archives; Insolvent Docket Prior to 1827, Court Records Accession #632 at Historical Society of Harford County). 1820. "Petition, Schedule, Bond, Sheriff's Certificate, order for publication and personal discharge filed 22nd June 1820. [nothing further]. (Insolvent Docket A, 1807-1843, p. 32, at Maryland State Archives; Insolvent Docket Prior to 1827, Court Records Accession #632 at Historical Society of Harford County).

Gilbert, Bennett A., 1895. "Insolvent Notice. In the matter of the Insolvency of Bennett A. Gilbert ... *To the Creditors of Bennett A. Gilbert*: Take notice that Bennett A. Gilbert, of Harford County, an insolvent debtor, having filed his petition to be discharged from all his debts and liabilities, under the insolvent laws of the State of Maryland, and such petition being now pending, a meeting of the creditors of said insolvent debtor will be held on Monday, the 14th day of January, 1895, at 12 o'clock, M., at the office of the undersigned, in the town of Bel Air, for the purpose of proof of claims, propounding of interrogatories and the selection of permanent trustee or trustees. Robert Archer, Preliminary Trustee." (*Harford Democrat*, January 4, 1895, p. 2). "At a meeting of the creditors of Bennett A. Gilbert, insolvent, last Monday [January 16, 1895], Judge Watters selected Willard G. Rouse as permanent trustee." (*Havre de Grace Republican*, January 19, 1895, p. 3). "Notice To Creditors ... In Pursuance of an order of Court, passed in the above matter on the 17th day of January, 1895, the undersigned hereby gives notice to the creditors of Bennett A. Gilbert, who were such upon the date of application of his insolvent for the benefit of the insolvent laws, to file their claims, duly proven, with the Clerk of Circuit Court for Harford county, on or before the 1st day of May, 1895. Willard G. Rouse, Permanent Trustee." (*The Aegis & Intelligencer*, January 18, 1895, p. 2). "Notice To Creditors ... In Pursuance of an order of Court, passed in the above matter on the 17th day of January, 1895, the undersigned, permanent trustee of Bennett A. Gilbert, an insolvent debtor, hereby gives notice that the 11th day of February, 1895, has been fixed by the Court for appearance of said insolvent to answer such interrogatories or allegations as his creditors, endorsers or sureties may propose or allege against him. Willard G. Rouse, Permanent Trustee." (*The Aegis & Intelligencer*, January 18, 1895, p. 2). "Dallam & Rouse, Solicitors. Order Nisi ... Ordered this 28th day of February, 1896, that the sales made and reported in the above entitled cause by Willard G. Rouse, permanent trustee, be finally confirmed, unless cause to the contrary thereof be shown on or before the 23rd day of March, 1895; provided, a copy of this order be inserted in some newspaper published in Harford county, once in each of three successive weeks, before the 23rd day of March, 1895. The report states the amount of sale to be $300. Wm. S. Forwood, Jr., Clerk." (*Harford Democrat*, March 1, 1895, p. 2). **Genealogical Note**: Bennett A. Gilbert married Katie A. Saverd circa Dec. 18, 1877 (date of license).

Gilbert, James, 1821. "Petition, Schedule, Bond, Sheriff's certificate, and personal discharge & order for publication filed 5th June 1821 – 1822 Mar 16th petitioner appeared in Court." [nothing further recorded] (Insolvent Docket A, 1807-1843, p. 46, at the Maryland State Archives; Insolvent Docket Prior to 1827, Court Records Accession #632 at the Historical Society of Harford County)

Gilbert, Nicholas R., 1886. "Insolvent Notice. In the Matter of the Insolvency of Nicholas R. Gilbert ... Notice is hereby given to the creditors of Nicholas R. Gilbert, of Harford county, that he has applied for the benefit of the Insolvent Laws of the State of Maryland, and that a meeting of the creditors of the said Gilbert will be held at my office, in the town of Bel Air, on Friday, February 5th, 1886, at 10 o'clock A. M., for the purpose of electing a permanent trustee for the estate of the said insolvent. William H. Harlan, Preliminary Trustee." (*Bel Air Times*, January 29, 1886, p. 3). "Insolvent Creditors' Notice ... In pursuance of an order of Court passed in the above case on the 10th day of February, 1886, the subscriber hereby gives notice to Nicholas R. Gilbert, an insolvent debtor, to be and appear in the Circuit Court for Harford county on Monday, May 10, 1886 to answer such interrogatories and allegations as his creditors, endorsers or sureties may propose or allege against him, and also to the creditors of the said Nicholas R. Gilbert that the said 10th day of May, 1886, has been affixed by said court for the appearance of said insolvent. William H. Harlan, Permanent Trustee." (*Bel Air Times*, February 19, 1886, p. 3)

Gilbert, Taylor, 1831. "Petition, Schedule, personal discharge and order for publication, bond for appearance, Trustee's bond, Trustee's certificate and deed to Trustee filed 4th July 1831. 18th Augt. 1832 Petitioner appears, certificate of publication filed and finally discharged." [nothing further recorded] (Insolvent Docket A, 1807-1843, p. 111, at the Maryland State Archives)

Gillespie, William B., 1854. "Petition, 2 Affidavits, 3 Schedules, appointment of Jno. H. Price, Esq., Trustee & Deed filed 17 Oct/54 ... Aug/54 Qualification of Edwin H. Webster as Special Judge filed & final order of ratification filed. Augt 7th 1856 Order of Notice to Creditors filed ... Recorded in Judgment Record A.L.J. No. 1, folio 160 &c. See Doc. B, fol. 67." (Insolvent Docket A. L. J. No. 1, p. 4, in the Court Records Department of the Historical Society of Harford County)

Godwin, James, 1856. "Petition, Schedules, Affidavits, Appointment of Trustee," etc., 20 Feb 1856. "14th Nov. 1857 Petitioner appears, files Certificate of Publication and discharged." [nothing further recorded} (Insolvent Docket A. L. J. No. 1, p. 10, in the Court Records Department of the Historical Society of Harford County). "Notice is hereby given that James Godwin, of Harford County, has made application to the Circuit Court of said County, for the benefit of the Insolvent Laws of Maryland, and that the first Tuesday of November term, 1856, has been assigned for him to appear in said Court to answer such interrogatories as his creditors may propose or allege against him. A. Lingan Jarrett, Clerk." (*Harford Democrat*, March 14, 1856, p. 3). "In the matter of the petition of James Godwin for the benefit of the Insolvent Laws. In the Circuit Court for Harford County, May Term, 1857. Ordered By The Court, That James Godwin be and appear before this Court on the first Saturday after the second Monday in November next, to answer such interrogatories or allegations as his creditors may propose or allege against him, and that he give notice of the day so fixed for his appearance, by publishing a copy of this order in some newspaper printed in Harford County for one month, three months before the first Saturday after the said second Monday in November next. 23rd May, 1857. John H. Price. True copy. Test: A. L. Jarrett, Clk. Circuit Court for Harford County." (*Harford Democrat*, June 12, 1857, p. 3)

Gordon, Abraham, 1837. "Petition, Affidavits, Schedule, personal discharge and order of publication, Bond for Appearance, Trustee's Bond, Trustee's Certificate and Deed to Trustee filed 11th July 1837. 17h March 1838 Petitioner appears, certificate of publication filed and finally discharged." (Insolvent Docket A, 1807-1843, p. 155, at Maryland State Archives)

Gorrell, Andrew J., 1841. "Petition, Affidavits, Schedules, Appointment of Trustee, Certificate, order, personal discharge, Trustee's Bond & deed to Trustee, Appearance Bond filed 19th Octr. 1841. 21 May 1842 Petitioner appears & files Certificate of Publication & finally discharged." (Insolvent Docket A, 1807-1843, p. 180, at the Maryland State Archives). 1863. "Petition, Schedule, List of Debts to him, Affidavit, Order, Trustee's Bond and Deed filed 3rd November 1863 & John H. Mitchell appointed Trustee. 22nd Feb 1864 Petitioner appeared, filed Certificate of Notice to Creditors & was finally discharged." [additional information recorded regarding various reports filed through February 1868] (Insolvent Docket A. L. J. No. 1, p. 44, in the Court Records Department of the Historical Society of Harford County). "Notice is hereby given that Andrew J. Gorrell has made application to the Circuit Court of Harford county, for the benefit of the Insolvent Laws of Maryland, and that the fourth Monday in February, 1864, has been assigned for him to appear in said Court to answer such interrogatories as his creditors may propose or allege against him. Wm. Galloway, Clerk, Circuit Court for Harford County." (*The Southern Aegis*, November 6, 1863, p. 2). "Trustee's Sale. In Virtue of an order of the Circuit Court for Harford county, the subscriber, an Insolvent Trustee of A. J. Gorrell, will offer at Public Sale, at Hopewell Cross Roads, on Monday, the 11th Day of April, 1864, at 11 o'clock, A. M., all that Tract or Parcel of Land on which Andrew J. Gorrell lately resided, called *Westwood*, Situated in Harford county, on the road leading from Churchville to Hopewell X Roads, and about one mile from the latter place, containing 2 Acres & 70 Perches, more or less, Being the same land particularly described in a Mortgage Deed from A. J. Gorrell and wife to John H. Mitchell, bearing date the 18th day of July, 1860, and recorded in Liber W. G. No. 12, folio 6, one of the Land Records of the Circuit Court for Harford county. The improvements thereon consist of a two-story Brick Dwelling House, Frame Stable, Corn House, Smoke House, Wagon House, Carpenter Shop, A good Apple Orchard, a well of water, a good pailed Garden, &c. Also at the same time and place, and described in the above named Mortgage Deed, a Tract of Land containing 40 Acres, 2 Roods and 35 Perches, more or less, Occupied by James Dick, situated on the road leading from Mudtown to Bush, and about one mile from the former place. The improvements are a comfortable Dwelling House and Garden. The land is of good quality, red soil, and susceptible of improvement. The Terms of Sale as prescribed by the Order are—that one-third of the purchase money shall be paid in Cash on the day of sale, or the ratification thereof, one-third in six months, and the balance in twelve months thereafter, the credit payments to be secured by notes or bonds of the purchaser, bearing interest from the day of sale, with security to be approved by the Trustee. John H. Mitchell, Trustee." (*The Aegis & Intelligencer*, March 18, 1864, p. 3). "In the matter of the insolvency of Andrew J Gorrell

... Ordered, this 14th day of April, A.D. 1864, that the sales made and reported by John H. Mitchell, Trustee for the benefit of the creditors of Andrew J. Gorrell, be ratified and confirmed, unless cause to the contrary be shown on or before the 14th day of May next; provided a copy of this order be published in some newspaper printed in Harford county, once in each of three successive weeks, before the said 14th day of May next. The report states the amount of sale to be $1,600. Wm. H. Dallam, Clerk." (*The Southern Aegis*, May 13, 1864, p. 3). **Genealogical Notes**: Andrew Jackson Gorrell, son of Abraham Gorrell and Elizabeth Carroll, was born on April 11, 1815, worked as a carpenter, married 1st to Ellen Ewing (1817-1861) circa April 3, 1837 (date of license), married 2nd to Margaret Everist (1831-1893) circa October 22, 1862 (date of license), lived near Aberdeen and died on November 11, 1898 at his daughter's home in Havre de Grace. His surviving children were Mrs. Frederick McClintock, of Havre de Grace, Mrs. William Harkins, of Aberdeen, Mrs. Ava McCord, of Paradise, and N. Gorrell, of Joppa. (Rock Run United Methodist Church tombstone inscriptions; Death certificate of Andrew J. Gorrell; *The Aegis & Intelligencer*, November 18, 1898)

Gorrell, Charles Lee, 1885. "December 29th 1884. Petition, Schedules, List of Debts, Affidavits, Deed, Appointment of Preliminary Trustee [name was not given] & Trustee's Bond filed ... May 11/85 Petitioner discharged per Order of Court filed." (Insolvent Docket A. L. J. No. 1, p. 95, in the Court Records Department of the Historical Society of Harford County). **Genealogical Note**: Charles Lee Gorrell, son of James L. Gorrell (1822-1900) and his third wife Sarah A. Donnelly (1825 - October 4, 1901), was born in 1857, married Mary Alice Gorrell (d. June 5, 1923), daughter of Theodore and Margaret Gorrell, worked as a contractor and builder in Baltimore and died on March 12, 1909 at Walbrook in Baltimore. They had no children. (1860 Harford County Census; tombstones at Holy Trinity Episcopal Church, Cokesbury Memorial Methodist Church and Grove Presbyterian Church; *The Aegis & Intelligencer*, March 19, 1909 and June 8, 1923)

Gorrell, Elizabeth M., 1879. "Petition, Schedules, Affidavit, Order of Court appointing Geo. L. Van Bibber, Trustee, Trustee's Bond & Deed filed March 26th 1879 ... Sept 8th 1879 Petitioner appears in open Court, files certificate of publication and is finally discharged ... Recorded in Judgment Record Liber H. D. G. No. 2, folio 352." (Insolvent Docket A. L. J. No. 1, p. 63, in Court Records Department of the Historical Society of Harford County). "Insolvent's Notice. Notice is hereby given, that Elizabeth M. Gorrell, by her husband and next friend, J. Thomas Gorrell, both of Harford county, has made application to the Circuit Court for said county for the benefit of the Insolvent Laws of Maryland, and that the second Monday of September, 1879, has been assigned for her to appear and answer such interrogatories as her creditors may propose or allege against her. A. Lingan Jarrett, Clerk, Circuit Court for Harford Co." (*Harford Democrat*, March 28, 1879, p. 2). "Trustee's Sale. In virtue of an order of the Circuit Court for Harford county, in the matter of the insolvency of Elizabeth M. Gorrell, wife of J. Thomas Gorrell, the subscriber, as trustee, will sell at public auction, to the highest bidder, on the farm now occupied by J. Thomas Gorrell and wife, situated on the road from Bel Air to Mitchell's Mill, on Saturday, April 19, 1879, at 10 o'clock, A. M., the following Personal Property: 1 Bay Mare and Colt, 1 Express Wagon, 1 Horse Cart, 1 Cow, 1 Heifer, 3 Steers, Plow, Cultivator, Harrow, and other Farming Utensils. Geo. L. Van Bibber, Trustee. J. S. Richardson, Auctioneer." (*Harford Democrat*, April 4, 1879, p. 3). "Trustee's Sale. In virtue of an order of the Circuit Court ... the subscriber, as trustee, will offer for sale at public auction, at the Court House door, in Bel Air, on Monday, April 21st, 1879, at 11 o'clock, A. M. all that certain Piece or Parcel of Land situated in said county, whereon J. Thomas Gorrell and Elizabeth M. Gorrell, his wife, now reside, containing 35 acres, more or less. This land is situated on the north side of the public road leading from Bel Air to Mitchell's Mill, about two miles from the former place, adjoining the lands of Wm. H. Waters and others, being the same and all the land described and comprehended in a deed from George Y. Maynadier, bearing date the 7th day of January, 1876, and recorded among the land records of Harford county in Liber A. L. J., No. 22, folio 464. The land is nearly all under cultivation, and is of good quality. The improvements consist of a comfortable two-story frame Dwelling House, Barn, Stabling and other buildings. There is also a good Peach and Apple Orchard on the place, and A Lot or Parcel of Woodland, containing Four Acres, More or Less. Geo. L. Van Bibber, Trustee. J. S. Richardson, Auctioneer." (*Harford Democrat*, April 18, 1879, p. 3). "Order Nisi ... Ordered this 30th day of April, 1879, that the sales made and reported by George L. Van Bibber, insolvent trustee of Elizabeth M. Gorrell, wife of J. Thomas Gorrell, be ratified and confirmed, unless cause to the contrary thereof be shown on or before the 26th day of May, 1879; provided a copy of this order be inserted in some newspaper printed and published at Bel Air, in Harford county, once a week for three successive weeks before the said 26th day of May, 1879. The report states the amount of sale of real estate to be $1,315.00 and amount of sales of per. Property $144.95 [totaling] $1,458.95. A. L. Jarrett, Clerk." (*Harford Democrat*, May 9, 1879, p. 3) **Genealogical Note**: see J. Thomas Gorrell below.

Gorrell, J. Thomas, 1879. "Petition, Affidavit, Schedules, Appointment of Trustee, Order of Appearance, Trustee's Bond & Deed filed 24 March 1879 ... Sept 8th 1879 Petitioner appears in open Court, files certificate of publication and finally discharged ... 7th October 1884 Final order, Auditor's Report filed ... Recorded in Judgment Record Liber H. D. G. No. 2, folio 342." (Insolvent Docket A. L. J. No. 1, p. 64, in the Court Records Department of the Historical Society of Harford County). "Insolvent Notice. Notice is hereby given, that J. Thomas Gorrell, of Harford county, has made application to the Circuit Court for said county for the benefit of the Insolvent Laws of Maryland, and that the second Monday of February, 1880, has been assigned for him to appear and answer such interrogatories as his creditors may propose or allege against him. A. Lingan Jarrett, Clerk, Circuit Court for Harford Co." (*Harford Democrat*, March 28, 1879, p. 2). "Trustee's Sale. In virtue of an order of the Circuit Court for Harford county, in the matter of the insolvency of J. Thomas Gorrell, the subscriber, as trustee, will sell at public sale, at the Court House door, in Bel Air, on Monday, April 21st, 1879, at 11 o'clock, A. M. all that certain Piece or Parcel of Land situated in Harford county, on the road leading from Churchville to Hopewell X Roads, about one mile from the later place, containing 2 Acres and 70 Perches, more or less, being the same land particularly described in a deed from John H. Mitchell to J. Thomas Gorrell, dated February 6th 1869, and recorded amongst the land records of Circuit Court for Harford county in Liber A. L. J., No, 21, folio 395. The improvements consist of a good and comfortable two-story Brick Dwelling House, frame Carpenter's Shop, Stabling, and other outbuildings. The land is in a very high state of cultivation, having on it good fruit of various kinds. Geo. L. Van Bibber, Trustee. J. S. Richardson, Auctioneer." (*Harford Democrat*, April 18, 1879, p. 3). "Order Nisi ... Ordered this 30th day of April, 1879, that the sales made and reported by George L. Van Bibber, trustee of J. Thomas Gorrell, insolvent, be ratified and confirmed, unless cause to the contrary thereof be shown on or before the 26th day of May, 1879; provided a copy of this order be inserted in some newspaper printed and published at Bel Air, in Harford county, once a week for three successive weeks before the said 26th day of May, 1879. The report states the amount of sale to be $515. A. L. Jarrett, Clerk." (*Harford Democrat*, May 9, 1879, p. 3). **Genealogical Notes**: James Thomas Gorrell (September 3, 1836 – December 27, 1903), son of John Gorrell and Elizabeth Bell, of Hopewell, Harford Co., married Mary Elizabeth Hendon (born May 8, 1850), daughter of Benjamin Hendon and Elizabeth Ann Treadwell, circa 1870 and worked as a carpenter. (Death certificate of James Thomas Gorrell states he died in Bel Air and the informant was his son Harry B. Gorrell; Treadwell-Hendon Family research by Carol Lynn Vanderherchen, of Richmond, VA, in 2004)

Gorrell, James O., 1885. "January 21st 1885. Petition, Order, Affidavits, Schedules, List of Creditors, Debts and Insolvent's Deed filed. Same day Bond of Preliminary Trustee [name was not given] approved & filed ... Sept. 14/85 Order of Court discharging Insolvent filed." (Insolvent Docket A. L. J. No. 1, p. 96, in the Court Records Department of the Historical Society of Harford County) "Insolvent Notice. In the matter of the Insolvency of James O. Gorrell ... In the above matter it is ordered, this 25th day of May, 1885, that the said James O. Gorrell, the insolvent, be and appear in this Court, on the second Monday of September, 1885, to answer such interrogatories or allegations, as his creditors, endorsers or sureties may propose or allege against him; and that the permanent trustee give notice, by the publication of this order in some newspaper published at Bel Air, in Harford county, once a week for three successive weeks, before the first day of July, 1885, to the creditors of said insolvent of the day so fixed upon. Jas. D. Watters. A. L. Jarrett, Clerk." (*Harford Democrat*, May 29, 1885, p. 2). **Genealogical Notes**: James Oliver Gorrell, son of James L. Gorrell, of Maryland, and Sarah A. Donnelly, of Pennsylvania, was born on December 21, 1860, married Angie V. Hopkins on February 4, 1888, worked as a nurseryman and died on June 4, 1933 at home in Aberdeen. They had no children, but his siblings were Zadoc Gorrell, William R. Gorrell and Mrs. Sarah Holloway. (Death certificate; marriage record; *Havre de Grace Republican*, June 10, 1933)

Gorrell, Rezin, 1835. "Petition, Affidavits, Schedule, personal discharge and order of publication, Bond for Appearance, Trustee's Bond, Trustee's Certificate and Deed to Trustee filed 17th Aug. 1835. 19th Mar 1836 Petitioner appears and continued. Augt. 13th 1836 Petition to appoint Trustee filed, Certificate of Publication filed and finally discharged." (Insolvent Docket A, 1807-1843, p. 143, at the Maryland State Archives). **Genealogical Notes**: Reasin Gorrell married Martha West and their son Joshua S. Gorrell was born November 9, 1829, married Sallie E. Knight on January 2, 1855, worked as a blacksmith in Darlington and died on January 13, 1916. (*Maryland Bible Records, Volume 5*, by Henry C. Peden, Jr., 2004, p. 83; Death certificate of Joshua S. Gorrell)

Gorrell, Vincent, 1839. "Petition, Schedule, Affidavits, personal discharge and order of publication, Bond for Appearance, Trustee's Bond, Trustee's Certificate and Deed to Trustee filed March 28th 1839. Novr. 23rd 1839 Petitioner appears and finally discharged." (Insolvent Docket A, 1807-1843, p. 169, at the Maryland State Archives)

Gorrell, William R., 1885. "January 21st 1885. Petition, Order, Affidavits, Schedules, List of Creditors, Debts & Insolvent's Deed filed. Same day Bond of Preliminary Trustee [name not given] approved & filed ... Sept. 14/85 Order of Court discharging Insolvent filed." (Insolvent Docket A. L. J. No. 1, p. 96, in the Court Records Department of the Historical Society of Harford County). "Insolvent Notice. In the matter of the Insolvency of William R. Gorrell ... In the above matter it is ordered, this 25th day of May, 1885, that the said William R. Gorrell, the insolvent, be and appear in this Court, on the second Monday of September, 1885, to answer such interrogatories or allegations, as his creditors, endorsers or sureties may propose or allege against him; and that the permanent trustee give notice, by the publication of this order in some newspaper published at Bel Air, in Harford county, once a week for three successive weeks, before the first day of July, 1885, to the creditors of said insolvent of the day so fixed upon. Jas. D. Watters. A. L. Jarrett, Clerk." (*Harford Democrat*, May 29, 1885, p. 2). **Genealogical Note**: William R. Gorrell, a brother of James Oliver Gorrell, q.v., was living in Los Angeles, CA at the time of James' death in 1933. (*Havre de Grace Republican*, June 10, 1933)

Gorrell, Winston, 1817. "Petition, Schedule and Bond filed 27th Augt. 1817, the necessary oath was administered to the Petitioner and ordered by the Court that he give the necessary notice to his creditors and that he be discharged from the custody of the Sheriff of Harford County ... March 12th 1818 the petitioner appeared and filed a certificate of his publication." [nothing further recorded] (Insolvent Docket A, 1807-1843, p. 21, at the Maryland State Archives, misspelled his name Winson

Gorrell and indexed it as Winston Gorrel; Insolvent Docket Prior to 1827, Court Records Accession #632 at the Historical Society of Harford County, listed is as Vinson Gorrell)

Gover, George P., 1862. "Petition, List of debts due to & from, Affidavit, Order appointing Trustee, Trustee's Bond, Deed &c. filed 3rd March 1862 S. Archer appointed Trustee … 4th Aug 1862 Petitioner appears, files Certificate and is finally discharged." (Insolvent Docket A. L. J. No. 1, p. 40, in the Court Records Department of the Historical Society of Harford County). "Notice is hereby given, that George P. Gover has made application to the Circuit Court of Harford county, for the benefit of the Insolvent Laws of Maryland; and that the 1st Monday of August next, has been assigned for him to appear in said court to answer such interrogatories as his creditors may propose or allege against him. Wm. Galloway, Clerk, Circuit Court for Harford County." (*National American*, April 4, 1862, p. 3). **Genealogical Notes**: George Presbury Gover married Juliet Onion Evans and their daughter Bettie Belle Gover married Stevenson Archer (1850-1933) in 1876. (*Descendants of the Signers of the Bush Declaration of March 22, 1775, Harford County, Maryland*, by Christopher T. Smithson and Henry C. Peden, Jr., 2010, p. 52, citing *The Archer Family Record* compiled by Henry Wilson Archer in 1888)

Gover, Robert, 1810. "Petition, Schedule, Bond, &c. filed 22nd Augt. 1810 … Court appoints Jno. Streett, trustee." [nothing further recorded]. (Insolvent Docket A, 1807-1843, p. 7, at the Maryland State Archives; Insolvent Docket Prior to 1827, Court Records Accession #632 at the Historical Society of Harford County). 1827. "Petition, Schedule, Bond, Sheriff's certificate and personal discharge and order for publication filed and Bond of provisional trustee filed and Certificate for Trustee filed 15th January 1827. 18th Augt. 1827 petitioner appeared. Petition & order filed. 15th March 1828 petitioner appears, ordered that he give notice to his creditors against the first Saturday of next Augt. term. 22nd August 1832 leave given to the Petitioner to withdraw his application." (Insolvent Docket A, 1807-1843, p. 83, at the Maryland State Archives). 1832. "Petition, Schedule, Affidavit, Personal discharge, and Order for Publication, Bond for Appearance, Trustee's Bond, Trustee's Certificate and Deed to Trustee filed 29th August 1832. 16th March 1833 Petitioner appears, certificate of publication filed and finally discharged." (Insolvent Docket A, 1807-1843, p. 120, at the Maryland State Archives). **Genealogical Note**: Robert Gover died in November 1850, age 81, and was buried in Deer Creek Quaker Cemetery in Darlington beside his wife Casandra Gover who died in October 1841, age 66, and their son Samuel Gover who died in March 1839, age 39 (tombstones).

Grafton, Curtis, 1835. "Petition, Affidavits, Schedule, personal discharge and order of publication, Bond for Appearance, Trustee's Bond, Trustee's Certificate and Deed to Trustee filed the 22nd June 1835. 19th Mar 1836 Petitioner appears, certificate of publication filed and finally discharged." (Insolvent Docket A, 1807-1843, p. 141, at the Maryland State Archives). **Genealogical Note**: Curtis Grafton was a son of William and Martha Grafton. (Harford Co. Equity Book HD No. 2, pp. 162-169)

Grafton, W. Charles and T. Burlington, 1884. "October 27/84. Petition, Schedule of Property, List of Debts & Credits, Affidavits, Order appointing Preliminary Trustee & Insolvent's Deed filed … Nov 10/84 Wm. H. Doxen trustee … [several claims and notices filed from 1884 to 1886] … March 2/86 Certificate of Publication of Notice to Creditors & Final Discharge filed … Mar 17/86 Auditor's Report & Order Nisi filed." (Insolvent Docket A. L. J. No. 1, pp. 92, 105, in the Court Records Department of the Historical Society of Harford County). "In the matter of the insolvency of W. Charles and T. Burlington Grafton … Ordered, this 8th day of July 1885, that the sales of property made and reported by Wm. H. Doxen, permanent trustee in the above cause, be ratified and confirmed, unless cause to the contrary thereof be shown on or before the 7th day of august, 1885; provided a copy of this order be inserted in some newspaper printed and published in Bel Air, in Harford county, once a week for three successive weeks before the said 7th day of Augst, 1885. The report states the amount of sales to be $581.50. A. L. Jarrett, Clerk." (*Harford Democrat*, July 24, 1885,

68

p. 3). "Insolvent Notice. In the matter of the Insolvency of the Grafton Brothers ... In the above matter it is ordered, this 3rd day of October, 1885, that the said insolvents be and appear in this Court, on the 1st day of February, 1886, to answer such interrogatories or allegations, as his creditors, endorsers or sureties may propose or allege against him; and that the permanent trustee give notice, by the publication of this order in some newspaper published at Bel Air, in Harford county, once a week for three successive weeks, before the 1st day of December, 1885, to the creditors of said insolvent of the day so fixed upon. Jas. D. Watters. A. L. Jarrett, Clerk." (*Harford Democrat*, October 9, 1885, p. 2)

Gray, Joseph, 1835. "Petition, Affidavits, Schedule, personal discharge and order of publication, Bond for Appearance, Trustee's Bond, Trustee's Certificate and Deed to Trustee filed 24th day of February 1835. 15th Augt. 1835. Petitioner appears and cont'd. 19th March 1836 Petitioner appears, Certificate of Publication filed and finally discharged." (Insolvent Docket A, 1807-1843, p. 138, at Maryland State Archives)

Green, Clement, 1825. "Petition, Schedule, Bond, Sheriff's Certificate and personal Discharge and order for publication filed [on] 15th day of August 1825. March 18th 1826 printers certificate filed. Petitioner appeared and John Fowood appointed Trustee." [nothing further recorded] (Insolvent Docket A, 1807-1843, p. 74, at the Maryland State Archives; Insolvent Docket Prior to 1827, Court Records Accession #632 at the Historical Society of Harford County)

Green, Henry, 1810. "Whereas we the subscribers Justices of the Peace for Harford County together with Thomas A. Hays, Esq., also one of the Justices of the Peace for said county, upon the petition of Henry Green, who set forth that he had been confined in the Gaol jail] of said county twenty Days for Debts which he was unable to pay and finding the facts stated to be true together with Thomas A. Hays, Esq. we did meet at the county Gaol on the 18th day of April last and did then and there appoint the 17th day of May Instant to meet at the Court house of said county which said appointment we did then and there ... at the request of the said Sheriff administer to said Henry Green the following oath which was taken by the said Henry Green being first duly sworn on the holy Evangely of Almighty God in the words following, to wit, I Henry Green do solemnly swear that the schedule which I have delivered to the Sheriff of Harford County doth contain a full account to the best of my knowledge and remembrance of my whole estate both real & personal or that I have any title to or interest in and of all debts, credits and effects whatsoever which I or any in trust for me have or at the time of my petition had, or am or was in any respect entitled to in possession, remainder or reversion and that I have not directly or indirectly at any time since my imprisonment or before, sold, leased or otherwise conveyed or disposed of or intrusted all or any part of my estate, goods, stock, money or debts thereby to defraud my creditors or to secure the same to receive or expect any profit or advantage thereof so help me God, which said duplicate of the schedule aforesaid we have transmitted to the clerk of the county court to be by him preserved in his office for the information of the creditors of the said Henry Green. Given under our hands and seals this 17th Day of May 1810. Saml. Bradford. Jno. C. Bond." (Court Records Document 67.10.7(A) at the Historical Society of Harford County; copy of schedule which "Henry Green" signed was included and this property was listed: "2 Old Scythes, 2 Old Sugar Hogsheads, 2 Old Hoes, 1 Old Shovel Plow, 2 Old Axes, 1 Old Dung fork, 1 Old fire shovel, 1 Old Bottle Case, 1 Old Augur, 1 Old Chizle")

Green, James, 1838. "Petition, Schedule, Affidavits, personal discharge and order of publication, Bond for Appearance, Trustee's Bond, Trustee's Certificate and Deed to Trustee filed 15th January 1838. 24th Novr. 1838 Petitioner appears, certificate of publication filed & discharged." (Insolvent Docket A, 1807-1843, p. 162, at the Maryland State Archives)

Green, John W., 1830. "Petition, Schedule, Shff's. Certificate, Personal Discharge, Order of Publication, Bond for Appearance, Trustee's Bond, Trustee's Certificate and Deed to Trustee filed 25th May 1830. 14th August 1830 Petitioner appears and Certificate of Publication filed and petitioner finally discharged … 20th August 1834 petition and ordered filed and Trustee's Bond filed." (Insolvent Docket A, 1807-1843, p. 103, at Maryland State Archives)

Green, William, 1832. "Petition, Schedule, Affidavit, Personal discharge, and Order for Publication, and Bond for Appearance, Trustee's Bond, Trustee's Certificate and Deed to Trustee filed 22nd Oct 1832. 16th March 1833 Petitioner appears and cont'd." [nothing further recorded] (Insolvent Docket A, 1807-1843, p. 121, at the Maryland State Archives)

Greenfield, James, 1810. "Whereas we the Subscribers, Justices of the Peace for Harford County upon the petition of James Greenfield, who set forth that he had been confined in the Goal [jail] of said county twenty Days and upwards for Debts which he was unable to pay and finding the facts stated to be true we did meet at the county Gaol of said county on the 23rd Day of July last and did then and there appoint the 23rd day of August Inst. to meet at the Court House of said county which said appointment we did then and there … at the request of the said Sheriff administer to the said James Greenfield the following oath which was taken by the said James Greenfield being first duly sworn on the holy Evangely of Almighty God in the words following, viz., I James Greenfield do solemnly swear that the schedule which I have delivered to the Sheriff of Harford County doth contain a full account to the best of my knowledge and remembrance of my whole estate both real and personal or that I have any title to or interest in and of all debts, credits and effects whatsoever which I or any in trust for me have or at the time of my petition had, or am or was in any respect entitled to in possession, remainder or reversion and that I have not directly or indirectly at any time since my imprisonment or before, sold, leased or otherwise conveyed or disposed of or intrusted all or any part of my estate, goods, stock, money or debts thereby to defraud my creditors or to secure the same to receive or expect any profit or advantage thereof, which said duplicate of the schedule aforesaid we have transmitted to the clerk of the county court to be by him preserved in his office for the information of the creditors of the said James Greenfield Given under our hands and seals this 23rd day of August 1810. Thomas A. Hays. Saml. Bradford. Jno. C. Bond" (Court Records Document 67.11.1(A) at the Historical Society of Harford County; a copy of the schedule to which "James Greenfield" signed his name was included and this property was listed: "An Interest in Six Lots of Land in Allegany County 50 acres each")

Gregory, John, 1820. "Petition, Schedule, Bond, Sheriff's certificate, personal discharge and order for publication filed 10th October 1820. March 17th 1821 petitioner appeared." [nothing further recorded] (Insolvent Docket A, 1807-1843, p. 38, at the Maryland State Archives; Insolvent Docket Prior to 1827, Court Records Accession #632 at the Historical Society of Harford County)

Griffin, Henry, 1864. "Petition, Schedule, List of debts to & from, Affidavit, Order, Bond and Deed & filed 24th January 1864 … Henry D. Farnandis, Esqr., Trustee … 14th Nov 1864 Petitioner appeared, filed Certificate of Notice to Creditors and was finally discharged. 5th Dec 1864 Final Order of Confirmation of Sales filed." (Insolvent Docket A. L. J. No. 1, p. 45, in the Court Records Department of the Historical Society of Harford County). "Notice is hereby given that Henry Griffin has made application to the Circuit Court of Harford county, for the benefit of the Insolvent Laws of Maryland, and that the 1st Monday in August, 1864, has been assigned for him to appear in said Court to answer such interrogatories as his creditors may propose or allege against him. Wm. H. Dallam, Clerk, Circuit Court for Harford county." (*The Southern Aegis*, February 5, 1864, p. 2). "In the matter of the insolvency of Henry Griffin. In the Circuit Court for Harford County. Ordered, this 11th day of August, 1864, that the sale made and reported by Henry D. Farnandis, Trustee of Henry

Griffin, an insolvent debtor, be and the same is confirmed, unless cause to the contrary be shown on or before the 11th day of September next, provided a copy of this order be published in some newspaper printed in Harford county, once in each of three successive weeks, before the said 11th day of September next. The report states the amount of sales to be $600. Wm. H. Dallam, Clerk." (*The Aegis & Intelligencer*, September 2, 1864, p. 3)

Griffith, George, 1831. "Petition, Schedule, Sheriff's Certificate, personal discharge and Order for Publication, Bond for Appearance, Trustee's Bond, Trustee's Certificate and Deed to Trustee filed 12th Dec 1831. March 17th 1832 Interrogatories filed and certificate of publication filed, petitioner appears. 17 March 1832 [sic] Petitioner sworn. Interroged [sic] at bar and final discharge granted." (Insolvent Docket A, 1807-1843, p. 113, at the Maryland State Archives)

Grill, Franklin, 1890. "Franklin Grill, of the second district, has made application for the benefit of the insolvent laws. Charles M. Hinkle was appointed preliminary trustee." (*The Aegis & Intelligencer*, November 14, 1890, p. 2)

Gwynn (Gwinn), Charles (African American), 1823. "Negro Charles Gwynn. Petition, Schedule, Bond, Sheriff's certificate and personal discharge and order for publication filed 26th March 1823. Augt. 30th 1823 petitioner appears & cont'd." [nothing further recorded] (Insolvent Docket A, 1807-1843, p. 55, at the Maryland State Archives, spelled his name Gwinn; Insolvent Docket Prior to 1827, Court Records Accession #632 at the Historical Society of Harford County, spelled his name Gwinn). **Genealogical Notes**: Charles Gwynn (Gwinn, Guinn), born circa 1774, was head of household in 1810 (Census) and master of John Gibbs, an indentured negro, in 1812. (General Entries Book, 1801-1830). He was involved in legal matters in 1815, 1818, 1821 and 1822. (Court Record Documents 57.06.7, 61.02.2, 74.18.9, 78.19.22, 79.07.10, 79.11.2, 88.09.1 and 93.12.1 at the Historical Society of Harford). Charles Gwinn was listed in Sheriff Benjamin Guyton's Account Book in 1815. (Benjamin Guyton folder in the Archives of the Historical Society of Harford County). Charles Guinn was age 58 in 1832. (A List of Free People of Colour Taken in 1832 by Joshua Guyton, Sheriff)

Haines, Jeremiah, 1891. "Proceedings of the County Commissioners. Jacob A. Grafton, collector of taxes for the 5th district, for 1886 and 1887, was authorized to return as insolvent $724 of the assessment of Jeremiah Haines." (*The Aegis & Intelligencer*, March 20, 1891, p. 2)

Haines, John H., 1884. "February 11th 1884. Petition in Insolvency, affidavit and order of Court thereon filed. Same day Subpoena & copy of petition & order of Court delivered to Sheriff, Harford County. ... 18th Feby 1884 Answer of John H. Haines filed ... February 23rd 1884 Petition dismissed by the Court." [no explanation given] (Insolvent Docket A. L. J. No. 1, p. 85, in Court Records Department of Historical Society of Harford County). **Genealogical Notes:** John Hastings Haines (October 1, 1842 – August 27, 1904), son of Thomas Haines and Mary ----, of Lancaster Co., PA, married Margaret Jane "Maggie" Knight (June 17, 1855 – March 14, 1945), daughter of William Knight (1825-1898), of Harford Co., and Jane Scott (c1837-1898), of County Tyrone, Ireland, on November 26, 1874 at the parsonage in Havre de Grace by Rev. J. H. M. Lemon. John worked as a canner in Havre de Grace and was later superintendent on the farm of Harry Hopper near Dublin. The children of John and Margaret Haines were John Hopper Haines (b. c1876), William T. Haines (b. c1877), Charles Haines (b. c1879), Edwin Haines, Helen Haines (married Will Main), and Fulton P. Haines (1891-1944). (Havre de Grace United Methodist Church Register, 1862-1875, p. 72; Death certificates of John H. Haines and Margarett K. Haines; Dublin Southern Cemetery tombstones; *The Aegis and Intelligencer*, September 3, 1904, stated he died suddenly while running the engine in the canning house of Wilbur McCann, survived by his wife and several children, but no names were given; 1880 Harford County Census; Haines-Knight Family research by Julia M. Haynes, of Naples, FL, in 2008)

Hair, Jehu, 1839. "Petition, Schedule, Affidavits, personal discharge and order of publication, Bond for Appearance, Trustee's Bond, Trustee's Certificate and Deed to Trustee filed 4th June 1839. Novr. 23rd 1839 Petitioner appears, certificate of publication filed and finally discharged." (Insolvent Docket A, 1807-1843, p. 169, at the Maryland State Archives)

Hall, Andrew, 1838. "Petition, Schedule, Affidavits, personal discharge and order of publication, Bond for Appearance, Trustee's Bond, Trustee's Certificate and Deed to Trustee filed 8th May 1838. 24th Novr. 1838 Petitioner appears, certificate of publication filed & discharged. 1840 26th May Petition of Trustee fee and Order of Court." [nothing further recorded] (Insolvent Docket A, 1807-1843, p. 165, at the Maryland State Archives). **Genealogical Note**: Andrew Hall died on June 9, 1857 and was buried in St. George's P. E. Church cemetery (tombstone inscription).

Hall, James W., 1852. "For former entries see Inst. Doc. B, page 92. 19th Decr/52 Order of Sale & Trustee's Report filed … 22nd Nov/53 Creditor's Report & order nisi passed." [nothing further recorded] (Insolvent Docket A. L. J. No. 1, p. 1, in the Court Records Department of the Historical Society of Harford County). **Genealogical Notes**: James White Hall, son of George Washington Hall (1788-1853) and Sophia White Hall (1787-1859), was born on July 20, 1823, died on August 21, 1897 and was buried in Angel Hill Cemetery in Havre de Grace. (*Descendants of the Signers of the Bush Declaration of March 22, 1775, Harford County, Maryland*, by Christopher T. Smithson and Henry C. Peden, Jr., 2010, pp. 137-139, citing the 1897 meeting of the descendants of Colonel Thomas White)

Hall, John H., 1894. "Insolvent Notice … *To the Creditors of John H. Hall*: Take notice that John H. Hall, of Harford county, Maryland, an insolvent debtor, having filed his petition to be discharged from all his debts and liabilities, under the insolvent laws of the State of Maryland, and such petition being now pending, a meeting of the creditors of said insolvent debtor will be held on Saturday, the 9th day of June, 1894, at 10 o'clock A. M., at the office of the undersigned, in the town of Bel Air, for the purpose of proof of claims, propounding of interrogatories and the selection of permanent trustee or trustees. James J. Archer, Preliminary Trustee." (*Harford Democrat*, June 8, 1894, p. 2). **Genealogical Notes**: This might have been John H. Hall (African American), probable son of James and Phoebe Hall, who was born circa 1838 and married Mary P. Lee (African American) born circa 1851, all of Harford County, on February 8, 1872 at Dublin by Rev. Jonathan H. Lemmon (Harford County marriage records; 1860 Harford County Census). He appears to have been the John Hall, a resident of Glenville, who was drafted into the U. S. Army in 1864. (*The Aegis and Intelligencer*, 27 May 1864)

Hall, Walter T., 1807. "Petition filed 11th Augt. 1807. Schedule filed same day and the petitioner [was] discharged from confinement and ordered that he give bond for his appearance before the court on the first Saturday of March term next to answer the allegations of his creditors … [case continued] … Petitioner appeared and discharged from his bond on the 18th March 1809." (Insolvent Docket A, 1807-1843, p. 1, at the Maryland State Archives; Insolvent Docket Prior to 1827, Court Records Accession #632 at the Historical Society of Harford County). **Genealogical Notes**: Walter Tolley Hall, oldest child and son of Aquila Hall, Jr. (1750-1815) and Ann Tolley (1756-1830), was born on October 2, 1776, married Charlotte White Hall on January 5, 1801 and died on April 17, 1846. Their children were Mary Ann Hall, John Sidney Hall and Delia More Hall Penniman. (*Descendants of the Signers of the Bush Declaration of March 22, 1775, Harford County, Maryland*, by Christopher T. Smithson and Henry C. Peden, Jr., 2010, p. 161)

Hamby, William, 1838. "Notice Is Hereby Given to the creditors of William Hamby, late an imprisoned debtor of Harford county, that on the application of said debtor by petition in writing to the Honorable Thomas A. Hays, one of the Justices of the Orphan's court for said county, for the benefit of the insolvent laws of Maryland, the said Judge on the 28th day of July, 1838, granted to the said debtor a discharge from imprisonment and appointed the first Saturday after the third Monday in

November next, for his appearance before the Judges of Harford county court at the court house of said county, for a final hearing before said court, on said petition and to answer such interrogatories as his creditors may propose to him." (*Harford Madisonian and Bel-Air & Havre de Grace Messenger*, October 18, 1838, p. 3). 1838. "Petition, Schedule, Affidavits, personal discharge and order of publication, Bond for Appearance, Trustee's Bond, Trustee's Certificate and Deed to Trustee filed 30th July 1838. 24th Novr. 1838 Petitioner appears, certificate of publication filed & discharged." (Insolvent Docket A, 1807-1843, p. 165, at the Maryland State Archives)

Hamby, William I., 1858. "Petition, Schedules, Affidavits, Order, Trustee's Bond & Deed filed 7th September 1858." [nothing further recorded] (Insolvent Docket A. L. J. No. 1, p. 24, in the Court Records Department of the Historical Society of Harford County)

Hamilton, Edward, 1833. "Petition, Schedule, Affidavit, Personal discharge, Order for Publication, Bond for Appearance, Trustee's Bond, Trustee's Certificate and Deed to Trustee filed 30th April 1833. 17th Augt. 1833 Petitioner appears, Certificate of Publication filed and petitioner finally discharged." (Insolvent Docket A, 1807-1843, p. 125, at the Maryland State Archives)

Haney, Daniel, 1828. "Petition, Schedule, Affidavit, Certificate, Bond, Deed, Trustee Bond, Discharge and Order for Publication filed 15 Jany 1828. 16th August 1828 Notice of publication filed, petitioner appears and finally discharged." (Insolvent Docket A, 1807-1843, p. 88, at the Maryland State Archives)

Haney, Thomas, 1810. "Whereas we the subscribers Justices of the Peace for Harford County together with Bennet Bussey, Esq., also one of the Justices of the Peace for said county, upon the petition of Thomas Haney, who set forth that he had been confined [in jail] twenty days and upwards for debts which he was unable to pay and finding the facts stated to be true together with the said Bennet Bussey, Esq. we did meet at the gaol of said county on the 18th day of September last and did then and there appoint the 19th day of October Instant to meet at the Court house of said county which said appointment we did then and there ... at the request of the said Sheriff administer to the said Thomas Haney the following oath which was taken by the said Thomas Haney being first duly sworn on the holy Evangely of Almighty God in the words following, to wit, I Thomas Haney do solemnly swear that the schedule which I have delivered to the Sheriff of Harford County doth contain a full account to the best of my knowledge and remembrance of my whole estate both real & personal or that I have any title to or interest in and of all debts, credits and effects whatsoever which I or any in trust for me have or at the time of my petition had, or am or was in any respect entitled to in possession, remainder or reversion and that I have not directly or indirectly at any time since my imprisonment or before, sold, leased or otherwise conveyed or disposed of or intrusted all or any part of my estate, goods, stock, money or debts thereby to defraud my creditors or to secure the same to receive or expect any profit or advantage thereof so help me God, which said duplicate of the schedule aforesaid we have transmitted to the clerk of the county court to be by him preserved in his office for the information of the creditors of the said Thomas Haney. Given under our hands and seals this 19th Day of October 1810. Saml. Bradford. Thomas A. Hays." (Court Records Document 67.14.4(A) at the Historical Society of Harford County; copy of the schedule to which "Thomas Haney" signed his name was included, but no property was listed)

Hanson, Aquila B., 1880. "May 7th 1880. Petition, Schedule, Affidavit, Order & Trustee Bond filed & George L. Van Bibber appointed Trustee. Feby. 16th 1881 claim of Marston & Co. filed ... 22nd February 1883 ... Order of Court appointing George L. Van Bibber permanent Trustee filed. Same day Bond approved & filed." [nothing further recorded] (Insolvent Docket A. L. J. No. 1, p. 70, in Court Records Department of the Historical Society of Harford County). "Notice to Creditors. "In the matter of the Insolvency of Aquila B. Hanson ... Notice is hereby given to the creditors of Aquila

B, Hanson, that he has applied to the Circuit Court of Harford county for the benefit of the insolvent laws; and that a meeting of his creditors will be held at my office, in the town of Bel Air, on Saturday, February 17th, 1883, at 10 o'clock, A. M., for the purpose of choosing a permanent trustee for the estate of said insolvent. Geo. L. Van Bibber, Preliminary Trustee." (*Harford Democrat*, February 9, 1883, p. 3). "Insolvent Notice. Notice is hereby given, that Aquila B. Hanson, of Harford county, has made application to the Circuit Court of Harford county for the benefit of the insolvent laws of Maryland, and that the second Monday in May, 1883, being the 14th day of the month, has been assigned for him to appear in said court and answer such interrogatories or allegations as his creditors, endorsers or sureties may propose or allege against him. Geo. L. Van Bibber, Permanent Trustee." (*Harford Democrat*, March 23, 1883, p. 3). **Genealogical Notes**: Aquila Brown Hanson, second son of Benedict Henry Hanson (1809-1882) and Lydia S. Barnes (1809-1881), was born on August 26, 1833, married Ann Elizabeth "Annie" Middleton (January 30, 1846 – March 25, 1925) on December 1, 1864 by Rev. Hays and was a merchant in Churchville by 1878. Their sons were John Middleton Hanson (born 1865) who was a clerk in his father's store in 1880 and Aquila Brown Hanson, Jr. (1880-1955) who married Eleanor Gittings Williams. Aquila B. Hanson advertised his stock of store goods for sale in 1880 and his dwelling and store for sale in 1881, describing the store as "a large new two-story frame storehouse with warehouse attached." In 1885 he sold the store to John G. Rouse and Robert C. Richardson and was employed by them for about two years. In 1887 he opened another store at the Churchville Post Office in partnership with John H. Michael, but by June of that year he was in partnership with John H. Nagle. Hanson retired by 1903. (Harford County 1878 Directory; Harford County 1870 and 1880 Censuses; General License Book; Maryland 1880 Directory; *The Aegis and Intelligencer*, April 2, 1880, March 18, 1874, January 7, 1887, June 3, 1887 and April 17, 1903; *Harford Democrat*, January 21, 1881 and March 27, 1885; Historical Society of Harford County Photograph Collection Box R3-7565; *Descendants of the Signers of the Bush Declaration of March 22, 1775, Harford County, Maryland*, by Christopher T. Smithson and Henry C. Peden, Jr., 2010, p. 117; Hanson Family records; Baltimore *Sun*, December 2, 1864; *Country Stores: Harford County's Rural Heritage*, by Henry C. Peden, Jr. and Jack L. Shagena, Jr., 2015, p. 122)

Hardgrove (Hargrove), Ephraim, 1815. "Whereas we the Subscribers, Justices of the Peace for Harford County together with Thomas Jeffery, also a Justice of the peace for said County, upon the petition of Ephraim Hardgrove stating therein that he had actually remained in the goal [jail] of said county since the twenty-seventh day of January last for debts which he was unable to pay and finding the facts stated to be true we did meet at the goal of said county on the twenty-eighth day of February last and we did then and there appoint the 18th day of March instant to meet at the Court house of said county which said appointment we did then and there … at the request of the said Sheriff administer to the said Ephraim Hardgrove the following oath which was taken by the said Ephraim Hargrove being first duly sworn on the Holy Evangels of Almighty God in the words following, to wit, I Ephraim Hardgrove do solemnly swear that the schedule which I have delivered to the Sheriff of Harford County doth contain a full account to the best of my knowledge and remembrance of my whole estate both real and personal or that I have any title to or interest in and of all debts, credits and effects whatsoever which I or any in trust for me have or at the time of my petition had, or am or was in any respect entitled to in possession, remainder or reversion and that I have not directly or indirectly at any time since my imprisonment or before, sold, leased or otherwise conveyed or disposed of or intrusted all or any part of my estate, goods, stock, money or debts thereby to defraud my creditors or to secure the same to receive or expect any profit or advantage thereof so help me God, which said duplicate of the Schedule aforesaid we have transmitted to the clerk of the county court to be by him preserved in his office for the information of the creditors of the said

Ephraim Hardgrove. Given under our hands and seals this eighteenth day of March 1815. James Wallace. Joseph Robinson." (Court Records Document 67.11.2(B) at the Historical Society of Harford County; a copy of the schedule to which "Ephraim Hardgrove" signed his name was included, but no property was listed)

Harford County Farm Dairy Co., 1899. "Receiver Appointed. James H. Quinby was Tuesday [October 10] appointed by Judge Wickes, of Baltimore City, receiver for the Harford County Farm Dairy Company of Baltimore under a bond for $10,000. The bill of complaint, filed in the Circuit Court by Stephen H. Harkins, stated that the company owes him $72.90 for milk furnished by him and alleged that the company is largely insolvent. The liabilities of the company, it was stated, are over $11,000 and it assets about $5,000. Mr. Quinby is treasurer and manager of the company. The company, in its answer, admitted the allegations in the bill of complaint." (*Aegis & Intelligencer*, October 13, 1899, p. 3)

Harry, David, 1823. "Petition, Schedule, certificate of residence, Shff's certificate, bond, personal discharge and order for publication filed 11th July 1823. 13th March 1824 Petitioner remanded to the custody of the Sheriff and petition dismissed." [nothing further recorded]. In a later entry: "Petition, Schedule, Bond, Sheriffs Certificate and personal Discharge and order for Publication filed 13th March 1824. March 18th 1826 [sic] Petitioner appears [nothing further recorded]. And in a third entry: "Petition, schedule, bond, Shffs Certificate, affidavit of residence, personal discharge and order for publication filed 1st Sept. 1825. 18th March 1826 Printers Certificate filed and petitioner appears." [nothing further]. (Insolvent Docket A, 1807-1843, pp. 57, 74, at Maryland State Archives; Insolvent Docket Prior to 1827, Court Records Accession #632 at the Historical Society of Harford County)

Haughey, Richard T., 1837. "Petition, Affidavits, Schedule, personal discharge and order of publication, Bond for Appearance, Trustee's Bond, Trustee's Certificate and Deed to Trustee filed 15th April 1837. 19th Augt. 1837 Petitioner appears, Certificate of Publication filed and finally discharged." (Insolvent Docket A, 1807-1843, p. 155, at the Maryland State Archives)

Haviland, Edward, 1891. "May Term of Court … Edward Haviland, insolvent, appeared, and was discharged." (*Havre de Grace Republican*, May 15, 1891, p. 3)

Havlin, Patrick, 1836. "Petition, Affidavits, Schedule, personal discharge and order of publication, Bond for Appearance, Trustee's Bond, Trustee's Certificate and Deed to Trustee filed 4th August 1836. 18th March 1837 Petitioner appears, certificate of publication filed and petitioner finally discharged." (Insolvent Docket A, 1807-1843, p. 151, at the Maryland State Archives). **Genealogical Note**: Patrick Havlin, aged 30, appeared in Court on March 15, 1824 and openly stated he is "a native of Londonderry, Ireland, intending to settle in Harford County in State of Maryland, reports himself and declares on oath that it is bona fide his intention to become a citizen of the United States and to renounce forever all allegiance and fidelity to the United Kingdoms of Great Britain and Ireland, whereof he is, at this time, a citizen." [He signed his name to the statement.] (County Court Minutes 1822-1830, p. 26, at the Historical Society of Harford County)

Havre de Grace Water Company, 1893. "Proceedings of the County Commissioners. Christopher De Swan, Collector of the second district, was directed to return $5,000 of the assessment of the Havre de Grace Water Co. insolvent." (*The Aegis & Intelligencer*, February 17, 1893, p. 3)

Hawkins, Charles, 1823. "Petition, Schedule, certificate of residence, Shff's certificate, bond, personal discharge and order for publication filed 23 July 1823. 13th March 1824 Petitioner appears & cont'd." [nothing further recorded] (Insolvent Docket A, 1807-1843, p. 58, at the Maryland State Archives; Insolvent Docket Prior to 1827, Court Records Accession #632 at the Historical Society of Harford County)

Hawkins, Isaiah, 1834. "Petition, Affidavits, Schedule, personal discharge and order of publication, Bond for Appearance, Trustee's Bond, Trustee's Certificate and Deed to Trustee filed 14th Augt.1834. 15th Augt. 1835. Petitioner appears, Certificate of Publication filed and finally discharged." (Insolvent Docket A, 1807-1843, p. 136, at Maryland State Archives)

Hays, Nathaniel W. S., 1885. "July 2nd 1885. Petition, Schedules, Affidavits, Order of Court & Deed filed. Same day Preliminary Trustee [name not given], Bond of Preliminary Trustee & Deed filed ... Sept 1/85 Claim of Hartman, Bach & Co. filed ... April 13/86 Order of Court discharging Insolvent filed." (Insolvent Docket A. L. J. No. 1, p. 99, in the Court Records Department of the Historical Society of Harford County). "Insolvent Notice. In the matter of the Insolvency of Nathaniel W. S. Hays ... In the above matter it is ordered, this 8th day of December, 1885, that the said Nathaniel W. S. Hays, the insolvent, be and appear in this Court, on the second Monday of February, 1886, to answer such interrogatories or allegations, as his creditors, endorsers or sureties may propose or allege against him; and that the permanent trustee give notice, by the publication of this order in some newspaper published at Bel Air, in Harford county, once a week for three successive weeks, before the 15th day of January, 1886, to the creditors of said insolvent of the day so fixed upon. Jas. D. Watters. A. L. Jarrett, Clerk." (*Harford Democrat*, December 18, 1885, p. 3). **Genealogical Notes**: Nathaniel William Smith Hays, son of Thomas Archer Hays, Jr. (1810-1868) and Sarah A. Fulford, was born on August 16, 1855 near Churchville, worked as a farmer near Bel Air and married 1st to Hattie Hanson (1867 – February 5, 1896, at the home of her brother-in-law J. E. Dean, of Fountain Green, aged about 30 years) on November 27, 1883. Nathaniel married 2nd to Dorothea Y. Pyle (March 4, 1880 – July 31, 1942), daughter of Harman T. Pyle and Florence B. Monks, on March 30, 1903, died on March 5, 1934 at his home on Thomas Street in Bel Air, and was buried in Christ Church (Rock Spring Parish) Cemetery. Lloyd Colburn Hayes, son of Nathaniel and Hattie Hays, died on July 28, 1897, age 18 months. Nathaniel W. S. Hays, son of Nathaniel and Dorothea Hays, died on November 1, 1904, and Rosamond Lavinia Hays, their daughter, was born on March 14, 1916 and died on September 23, 1923 at Fountain Green. The obituary of Nathaniel W. S. Hays in 1934 stated he was survived by his widow Dorothea Pyle Hays, sons George E. Hays, of 5301 Grindon Ave., Baltimore, and Nathaniel W. S. Hays, Jr., of Bel Air, a daughter, Miss Margaret Hays at home in Bel Air, and a brother George Hays, of near Bel Air. (Harford County Marriage Records; Death Certificates of Nathaniel Wm. S. Hays, Dorothea P. Hays and Rosamond L. Hays; *Colonial Families of the United States of America*, by George Norbury Mackenzie, 1907, Volume III, p. 222; Christ Episcopal Church and Holy Trinity Episcopal Church tombstones for Nathaniel and his two wives and three of his children; *The Aegis and Intelligencer*, February 7, 1897 and March 9, 1934)

Healey, Patrick, 1859. "Petition, Schedule of property, List of debts due & owing to & from, Affidavit, Order & Appointment of Daniel Scott, Esqr., Trustee, Trustee's Bond approved and filed 21st April 1859 and Deed to Trustee filed. 6th August/59 Petitioner appears, files certificate of publication & finally discharged ... 28th Sept/60 Trustee's Report of Sales filed ... 4th Mach 1861 Petition of Peter Hughes & Order of Court filed ... 23rd May/61 Order of Court for Writ of Habere filed ... 25th May/61 Shff's return filed. 27th February 1862 Final order of Auditor's Report filed ... 7th May/62 Petition of A. G. Lyon & others & order of Court filed." [nothing further after this entry] (Insolvent Docket A. L. J. No. 1, p. 27, in the Court Records Department of the Historical Society of Harford County). "Notice is hereby given that Patrick Healey, of Harford County, has made application to the Circuit Court of said County, for the benefit of the Insolvent Laws of Maryland, and that the 1st Saturday after the 1st Monday in August, 1859, has been assigned for him to appear in said Court to answer such interrogatories as his creditors may propose or allege against him. Wm. Galloway, Clerk, Circuit Court for Harford County." (*The Southern Aegis*, May 7, 1859, p. 3) "Trustee's Sale. By Virtue of a Decree of the Circuit Court for Harford County, sitting as a Court of Equity, the undersigned, as Insolvent Trustee of Patrick Haley [sic], will offer at public sale to the highest bidder, at the United States Hotel in the town of Havre de Grace, on Wednesday, the 18th Day of July, 1860, at 12 o'clock M., The Following Property, 1 Gilling Boat, Seine and Tackle, in complete order, and the appurtenances thereto belonging, and 1 First Rate Milch Cow, and other personal property. Terms of sale, all sums under ten dollars, cash; all sums over ten dollars, will be one third cash, one-third in six months, and the balance in twelve months from the day of sale, the credit payments to be secured by notes of the purchers [sic], bearing interest from the day of sale, with surety approved by the trustee. Dan. Scott, Trustee." (*The Southern Aegis*, July 14, 1860, p. 3). **Genealogical Notes**: Patrick Healey (1813-1888) married Ellen ---- (1818 – September 19, 1887) in 1836. Her obituary stated, in part: "She was an educated Irish lady who many years ago left the land of her birth to find a home in free America, and for nearly fifty years has been a resident of Havre de Grace. She was a sincere and devout Catholic … About a year ago Mr. and Mrs. Healey quietly celebrated the fiftieth anniversary of their marriage. Several children, all grown, survive to share the sorrow of the aged husband." One of their children was Patrick L. Healy (1851 - March 7, 1933) who married Mary Koendress (1865-1937) and died at home in Baltimore City. (*Havre de Grace Republican*, September 23, 1887 and March 11, 1933; Mt. Erin Cemetery tombstone inscriptions spelled the name Healy)

Heaps, Hugh Henry, William C. and John T., 1885. "May 21st 1885. Petition, Affidavits, Schedules, Order of Court & Deed filed. Same day Preliminary Trustee's [name not given] Bond approved & filed … September 15th 1885 Order of Final discharge filed." (Insolvent Docket A. L. J. No. 1, p. 98, in the Court Records Department of the Historical Society of Harford County). "Injunction.—On the application of Herman Stump and Hugh T. Stump, insolvent trustees of the Heaps Brothers, Tuesday last [March 24], the court granted an injunction restraining the Northern Harford Packing Association from shipping to Smith & Wicks, purchasers, the 2,000 [of] cases canned corn and 1,000 cases [of] canned tomatoes packed by the Heaps Bros., who were members of the Northern Harford Packing Association. The injunction was only preliminary, and the rights of the respective parties to the suit to the goods in question will be decided at a hearing to be had in a few days. The ultimate decisions in the case will be looked for with interest by other members of the Northern Harford Packing Association who have goods on hand not yet shipped by the Association." (*Harford Democrat*, March 27, 1885, p. 2). "Notice To Creditors of H. Henry Heaps, Wm. C. Heaps and John T. Heaps – You are hereby informed that the above named parties have applied for the benefit of the Insolvent Laws of the State of Maryland, and that there will be a meeting of their creditors at my office, in Bel Air, Harford county, Md., to elect a Permanent Trustee, on Monday, the 8th day of June, 1885, at 12 o'clock M., Herman Stump, Preliminary Trustee." (*The Aegis & Intelligencer*, May 29, 1885, p. 2) "Notice is hereby given to the creditors of H. Henry Heaps, William C. Heaps and John T. Heaps, who were such at the time of their application for the benefit of the Insolvent Laws of the State of Maryland, to file their claims with the Clerk of the Circuit Court for Harford county, duly authenticated and proven, on or before the first day of September, 1885. Herman Stump, Permanent Trustee." (*The Aegis & Intelligencer*, June 12, 1885, p. 2). **Genealogical Notes**: Hugh Henry Heaps, son of Alexander Heaps, was born on April 21, 1861, married Marion Virginia Scarborough (August 2, 1866 – April 3, 1933) circa December 24, 1884 (date of license) and died on January 9, 1942 in Baltimore. He was survived by two daughters, Miss Jessie Heaps and Frances (Mrs. Robert) Wallace, of Baltimore, and a brother W. Channel Heaps, of Street, MD. (Emory United Methodist Church tombstone inscription; *The Aegis*, April 7, 1933 and January 16, 1942)

Heaps, Thomas Franklin (Frank T.), 1892. "Insolvent Notice. In the Matter of the Insolvency of Frank T. Heaps ... Notice is hereby given to the creditors of Frank T. Heaps, that he has applied for the benefit of the Insolvent Laws of the State of Maryland, and that a meeting of the creditors of the said Heaps will be held at my office, in the town of Bel Air, on Friday, December 2nd, 1892, at 10 o'clock A. M., for the purpose of the selection of a permanent trustee for the estate of said insolvent. Septimus Davis, Preliminary Trustee." (*Harford Democrat*, December 23, 1892, p. 3). 1894. "Trustee's Sale. By virtue of an order of the Circuit Court for Harford county, passed in the matter of the insolvency of Thomas F. Heaps, the undersigned as permanent trustee will offer at Public Sale, at the residence of W. H. Tucker, near Hickory, on Wednesday, May 2nd, 1894, at 11 o'clock, A. M., the following Personal Property, belonging to the estate of said insolvent. To wit: One Bay Horse, 1 Dun Mare, 2 Cows, 1, 2 or 3-horse Wagon and Body, 1 Advance Plow, 1 Bradley Plow, 1 Bradley Horse Rake, Adriance [sic] Mowing Machine, Harrow, 2-Horse Carriage, 1 Buckboard, Double Cultivator, Iron Age Cultivator, Champion Binder, Hay Carriage, Bickford & Huffman Wheat Drill, Corn Drill, Harness, Forks, Hoes, Mattocks, and all other Personal Property belonging to the said Heaps. J. Thos. C. Hopkins, Permanent Trustee. J. S. Richardson, Auctioneer." (*The Aegis & Intelligencer*, April 20, 1894, p. 2). **Genealogical Notes:** Thomas Franklin Heaps, son of Robert Heaps and Mary A. Murphy, was born in 1859, married Ellen Jane Furlong (December 24, 1859 – June 14, 1943), of Harford Co., daughter of Patrick Furlong and Ann Rossiter, both from Ireland, worked as a farmer near Pylesville and died on May 28, 1910. The children of Thomas and Ellen Heaps were Thomas Augustus Heaps (1894-1946), Cletus Heaps, Mrs. John Hushon, Miss Pearl M. Heaps (1882-1959), all of Pylesville, Mrs. W. E. Orem, of Baltimore, and Robert Joseph Heaps (1885-1922). (Death certificates of Thomas F. Heaps and Ellen Jane Heaps; St. Mary's Catholic Church Cemetery tombstones; *The Aegis*, June 18, 1943)

Heaton, John H., 1885. "May 11th 1885. Petition, Schedules, Order, Deed, Order appointing Preliminary Trustee [name not given] & Trustee's Bond filed … September 14th 1885 Petitioner appeared in open court and was finally discharged by the Court." (Insolvent Docket A. L. J. No. 1, p. 97, in the Court Records Department of the Historical Society of Harford County). **Genealogical Notes:** John H. Heaton (January 22, 1839 – November 3, 1902), married Charlotte ---- (September 23, 1835 – January 26, 1913) by 1863 and daughter Ida H. Heaton (July 5, 1864 – August 13, 1864) and son Clarence T. Heaton (October 2, 1867 – July 22, 1868) are buried next to them in Angel Hill Cemetery. (tombstone inscriptions; *The Aegis and Intelligencer*, November 7, 1902, reported Heaton died from a stroke in an attorney's office in Springfield, OH, which may have been caused from over excitement relative to having received evidence that he had inherited a fortune of $160,000; they feared that his invalid wife in Havre de Grace might not survive the shock – but she did and lived over ten years longer)

Hendon, Josiah, 1834. "Petition, Affidavits, Schedule, personal discharge and order of publication, Bond for Appearance, Trustee's Bond, Trustee's Certificate and Deed to Trustee filed 11th Augt.1834. 14th March 1835. Petitioner appears, Certificate of Publication filed and finally discharged." (Insolvent Docket A, 1807-1843, p. 136, at Maryland State Archives)

Henry, Samuel, 1826. Insolvent debtor to be discharged from imprisonment. (*Independent Citizen*, December 3, 1829), "Petition, Schedule, bond, Sheriff's certificate and personal discharge and order for publication filed 24th March 1826. 19th March 1831 petitioner appears and cont'd. 16th August 1834 petitioner appears and cont'd … [case opened in 1829 and continued several times through 1836]. 16th Sept./56 [sic] Petition of Otho Scott & order filed appointing Daniel Scott Trustee of Insolvent." (Insolvent Docket A, 1807-1843, pp. 79, 98, at the Maryland State Archives; Insolvent Docket Prior to 1827, Court Records Accession #632 at the Historical Society of Harford County). 1864. William H. McConkey, et al., vs. Jeremiah Kirk, Jeremiah B. Haines and Daniel Scott. In the Circuit Court for Harford County, as a Court of Chancery. "The object of this suit is to procure a decree for partition or sale of certain lands and premises mentioned in the proceedings therein. The Bill states that Isaac

Henry, late of Harford county, died seized of one undivided third part of a certain tract or parcel of land, situate in said county, called *Partnership*, containing twenty-eight acres, more or less – the remaining undivided two-thirds of which were purchased by a certain Jeremiah B. Haines, on or about the 4th day of January, 1840. – That said Isaac Henry left four children, named Robert, Mary. Elizabeth and Samuel, his heirs at law, of whom Robert is since dead intestate, leaving Isaac, George, Robert, Samuel, William, Mary, Sarah E. and Caroline Henry his children and Ann Henry his widow, his only legal representatives. That said Mary (daughter of said Isaac Henry, deceased) is also since dead intestate, leaving Wm. H. McConkey and Mary A. Dorsey, her only children and heirs at law. That said Elizabeth is the widow of Sedgwick James, deceased, and that said Samuel [Henry] applied for the benefit of the insolvent laws, and all his interest in said land became vested in Daniel Scott, as his insolvent trustee." (*The Aegis & Intelligencer*, June 24, 1864, p. 3)

Herbert, Alvin C., 1861. "Petition, Schedule of property, List of debts due and owing to & from him, Affidavit, Order appointing Trustee, Trustee's Bond & approval & Deed to Trustee filed 12th Nov/61 … 28th April 1862 Petitioner appears, files Certificate of Publication of Notice to Creditors & finally discharged." (Insolvent Docket A.L.J. No. 1, p. 39, in the Court Records Department of the Historical Society of Harford County)

Heyer, Jacob, 1838. "Notice Is Hereby Given, to the creditors of Jacob Heyer, late an imprisoned debtor of Harford county, that on the application of said debtor by petition in writing to the Honorable Thomas A. Hays, one of the Justices of the Orphan's court for said county, for the benefit of the insolvent laws of Maryland, the said Judge on the 28th day of July, 1838, granted to the said debtor a discharge from imprisonment and appointed the first Saturday after the third Monday in November next, for his appearance before the Judges of Harford county court at the court house of said county, for a final hearing before said court, on said petition and to answer such interrogatories as his creditors may propose to him." (*The Madisonian and Harford and Baltimore Advertiser*, October 18, 1838, p. 3). 1838. "Petition, Schedule, Affidavits, personal discharge and order of publication, Bond for Appearance, Trustee's Bond, Trustee's Certificate and Deed to Trustee filed 30th July 1838. [nothing further recorded] (Insolvent Docket A, 1807-1843, p. 167, at the Maryland State Archives)

Hildt, William, 1878. "Petition, Schedule, List of Debts, Affidavit, Order, Trustee's Bond approved & Deed filed Oct. 29th 1878. Order of Court to sell property of the insolvent filed 6 Jany 1879 … May 10th 1879 Objections of Jas. A. Amos to the discharge of Wm. Hildt under the Insolvent Laws filed. Nov 17th 1879 Objections withdrawn & petitioner finally discharged … Recorded in Judgment Record H. D. G. No. 2, folio 267." (Insolvent Docket A. L. J. No. 1, p. 59, in the Court Records Department of the Historical Society of Harford County) "Notice is hereby given that William Hildt has made application to the Circuit Court of Harford county, for the benefit of the Insolvent Laws of Maryland, and that the second Monday in May, 1879, has been assigned for him to appear in said Court to answer such interrogatories as his creditors may propose or allege against him. A. L. Jarrett, Clerk." (*The Aegis & Intelligencer*, December 6, 1878, p. 2). "Trustee's Sale. In virtue of an order of the Circuit Court for Harford county, in the matter of the insolvency of William Hildt, the undersigned, as trustee, will offer at Public Sale, at Zachariah Amos's Mill, on the road leading from the Upper Cross Roads to Jarrettsville, on Friday, February 7th, 1879, at 12 o'clock, M., so much of those Tracts or Parcels of Land called *Addition* & *Saulsbury*, conveyed to James A. Amos and wife to William Hildt, by deed bearing date December 8th, 1888, and recorded in Liber A.L.J. No. 21, folio 234, one of the Land Records of Harford county, which is now in the possession of the said William Hildt, containing 22 acres, more or less. This property is situated on the road leading from the Upper Cross Roads to Jarrettsville, near Z. Amos's Mill. The improvements consist of a large new Frame Dwelling House, New Granary and other new Outbuildings. The fields are well watered, the land well fenced, and convenient to churches, schools, mills, stores, &c. Also at the same time will be sold, a small lot of Corn, 1 Harrow and 1 Horse Cart. Herman Stump, Jr., Trustee. J. S. Richardson, Auctioneer." (*The Aegis & Intelligencer*, January 10, 1879, p. 2). Cases disposed of in February term 1880: "James A. Amoss vs. Wm. Hildt; judgment subject to Hildt's discharge under insolvent laws. H. W. Archer and H. W. Archer, Jr., for plaintiff, Stump and Young for defendant." (*Havre de Grace Republican*, February 20, 1880, p. 3). **Genealogical Notes**: William Hildt, son of William Hildt, of Germany, married Mary Jane Fletcher (August 19, 1818 – September 9, 1898), daughter of Walter Fletcher (1793-1881, War of 1812 veteran) and Ellen Campbell, of Harford Co., and their son Everhart Hildt (September 19, 1850 – February 21, 1924) was a farmer and carpenter near Fallston. (Death certificates of Mary Jane Hildt and Everhart Hildt; *Harford Democrat*, September 23, 1898, stated Mary was the widow of William Hild (sic) and died at home in Norrisville [death certificate stated Fallston], left six children, names were not given, and was buried in West Liberty Cemetery)

Hill, Thomas, 1820. "Petition, Schedule, Bond, Sheriff's Certificate, order for publication and personal discharge filed 20th May 1820. Sepr. 2nd 1820 petr. appeared." [nothing further recorded]. (Insolvent Docket A, 1807-1843, p. 31, at the Maryland State Archives; Insolvent Docket Prior to 1827, Court Records Accession #632 at the Historical Society of Harford County).

Hilton, Miles, 1828. "Petition, Schedule, Affidavit, Certificate, Bond, Provisional Trustee's Bond, Trustee's Certificate, Discharge and Order of Publication filed 16th Septr. 1828 … 14th March 1829 Permanent Trustee [name not given] appointed. Bond filed and Petitioner finally discharged." (Insolvent Docket A, 1807-1843, p. 91, at the Maryland State Archives)

Hipkins, William W., 1885. "November 9th 1885. Petition, Schedules, Order, Insolvent's Deed & Preliminary Trustee's Bond approved & filed … Dec 5/85 … 2nd Report of Wm. M. Marine, Preliminary Trustee, filed, same day Bond of Permanent Trustee filed, same day Decree filed." [nothing further recorded] (Insolvent Docket A. L. J. No. 1, p. 102, in the Court Records Department of the Historical Society of Harford County). "William W. Hipkins made hi application for the benefit of the insolvent laws and William M. Marine was his preliminary trustee." (*Havre de Grace Republican*, November 27, 1885, p. 4). "Adjourned Creditors' Meeting In the Matter of the Insolvency of Wm. W. Hipkins. In the Circuit Court for Harford County. This is to give notice to the creditors of Wm. W. Hopkins that he has applied for the benefit of the Insolvent Laws of the State of Maryland and that I have been appointed Preliminary Trustee, and fixed Monday, November 23rd, 1885, at 11 o'clock A. M., as the time of meeting, but in the absence of said Insolvent and Creditors the meeting was adjourned until Saturday, December 14th, 1885, at 11 o'clock A. M., at the Clerk's office of the Circuit Court for Harford county as the time and place for the meeting of his creditors for the election of a Permanent Trustee and for other business. William M. Marine, Preliminary Trustee." (*Bel Air Times*, November 27, 1885, p. 3). "Notice to Creditors. Notice is hereby given to the creditors of William W. Hipkins, an insolvent debtor, who were such on the 9th day of November, 1885, the date of his application for the benefit of the Insolvent Laws, to file their claims against the estate of the said Insolvent, duly proven, with the Clerk of the Circuit Court for Harford county, on or before the 1st day of March 1886. William M. Marine. Permanent Trustee." (*Bel Air Times*. January 1, 1886, p. 3)

Hitchcock, Isaac, 1811. "Petition, Schedule, Bond and Notice to Creditors filed 24th June 1811. Augt. 17th 1811 petitioner appeared and the Court appointed Thomas W. Ayres [as] Trustee … Bond recorded 20th August 1811 and ordered by the Court that Isaac Hitchcock be discharged from his debts. Certificate of Trustee filed 14th April 1817." (Insolvent Docket A, 1807-1843, p. 10, at the Maryland State Archives; Insolvent Docket Prior to 1827, Court Records Accession #632 at the Historical Society of Harford County)

Hitchcock, John, 1811. "Whereas we the subscribers Justices of the Peace for Harford County together with John Moores, Esq., also one of the Justices of the Peace for said county, upon the petition of John Hitchcock, who set forth that he had been confined [in jail] twenty days and upwards for debts which he was unable to pay and finding the facts stated to be true together with the said John Moores, Esq. we did meet at the gaol of said county on the 19th Day of August last and did then and there appoint the 19th Day of September Instant to meet at the Court house of said county which said appointment we did then and there … at the request of the said Sheriff administer to the said John Hitchcock the following oath which was taken by the said John Hitchcock being first duly sworn on the holy Evangely of Almighty God in the words following, to wit – I John Hitchcock do solemnly swear that the schedule which I have delivered to the Sheriff of Harford County doth contain a full account to the best of my knowledge and remembrance of my whole estate both real and personal or that I have any title to or interest in and of all debts, credits and effects whatsoever which I or any in trust for me have or at the time of my petition had, or am or was in any respect entitled to in possession, remainder or reversion and that I have not directly or indirectly at any time since my imprisonment or before, sold, leased or otherwise conveyed or disposed of or intrusted all or any part of my estate, goods, stock, money or debts thereby to defraud my creditors or to secure the same to receive or expect any profit or advantage thereof so help me God, which said duplicate of the schedule aforesaid we have transmitted to the clerk of the county court to be by him preserved in his office for the information of the creditors of the said John Hitchcock. Given under our hands and seals this 18th Day of September 1811. Thomas A. Hays. Saml. Bradford." (Court Records Document 67.11.6(B) at the Historical Society of Harford County; a copy of the schedule to which "John Hitchcock" made his "X" mark was included, but no property was listed)

Hitchcock, John, Jr., 1810. "Whereas we the Subscribers, Justices of the Peace for Harford County upon the petition of John Hitchcock, Junr., who set forth that he had been confined in the Goal [jail] of said county twenty Days for Debts which he was unable to pay and finding the facts stated to be true we did meet at the county Gaol of said county on the 7th day of September last and did then and there appoint the 8th day of October Instant to meet at the Court House of said county which said appointment we did then and there … at the request of said Sheriff administer to the said John Hitchcock, Junr. the following oath which was taken by the said John Hitchcock, Junr. being first duly sworn on the holy Evangely of Almighty God in the words following, to wit, I John Hitchcock, Junr. do solemnly swear that the schedule which I have delivered to the Sheriff of Harford County doth contain a full account to the best of my knowledge and remembrance of my whole estate both real & personal or that I have any title to or interest in and of all debts, credits and effects whatsoever which I or any in trust for me have or at the time of my petition had, or am or was in any respect entitled to in possession, remainder or reversion and that I have not directly or indirectly at any time since my imprisonment or before, sold, leased or otherwise conveyed or disposed of or intrusted all or any part of my estate, goods, stock, money or debts thereby to defraud my creditors or to secure the same to receive or expect any profit or advantage thereof, which said duplicate of the schedule aforesaid we have transmitted to the clerk of the county court to be by him preserved in his office for the information of the creditors of the said John Hitchcock, Junr. Given under our hands & seals this 8th Day of October 1810. John Moores. Thomas A. Hays. Sam. Bradford." (Court Records Document 67.11.5(A) at Historical Society of Harford County; copy of schedule to which "John hitch Cock" signed his name was included, but no property was listed)

Hitchcock, Luther, 1828. "Petition, Schedule, Affidavit, Certificate, Bond, Deed, Provisional Trustee's Bond, Trustee's Certificate, Discharge and Order for Publication filed 19th August 1828." [nothing further recorded] (Insolvent Docket A, 1807-1843, p. 90, at the Maryland State Archives)

Hoffman, Allen, 1896. "In the matter of the Insolvency of Allen Hoffman ... This is to give notice to the creditors of Allen Hoffman, that he has applied for the benefit of the Insolvent Laws of the State of Maryland, and that we have been appointed Preliminary Trustees, and have fixed Saturday, October the 31st, 1896, at 11 o'clock, A. M., at the office of the undersigned, Walter W. Preston, Bel Air, Md., as the time and place for the meeting of his creditors of the said insolvent, for the election of a permanent trustee and for other business. William H. Harlan, Walter W. Preston, Preliminary Trustees." (*The Aegis & Intelligencer*, October 30, 1896, p. 2). "In pursuance of an order of Court passed in the above case on the 31st of October, in the year 1896, the undersigned hereby give notice to the creditors of said Allen Hoffman, who were such on the 17th day of October, 1896, to file their claims, duly authenticated, with the Clerk of the Circuit Court for Harford county, on or before the 1st day of February, in the year 1897. William H. Harlan, Walter W. Preston, Permanent Trustees." (*The Aegis & Intelligencer*, December 4, 1896, p. 2). "In pursuance of an order of Court passed in the above case on the 31st of October, in the year 1896, the undersigned hereby give notice to the creditors of said insolvent that he had been ordered to appear in the Circuit Court for Harford County on the first day of the February term 1897, the same being the 8th day of said month, to answer such interrogatories and allegations as his creditors, endorsers or sureties may propose or allege against him. William H. Harlan, Walter W. Preston, Permanent Trustees." (*The Aegis & Intelligencer*, December 4, 1896, p. 2). "Trustees' Sale. In pursuance of an order of Court ... the undersigned, the permanent trustees of said insolvent estate, will offer at public auction, at the court house door, in the town of Bel Air, on Monday, the 30th day of November, 1896, at 12 o'clock, M., the following Real Estate situate and lying in Harford county, Maryland, lately belonging to the said Allen Hoffman. 1. All that Farm or tract of land situate and lying near Doxen's Cross Roads, containing 71½ Acres of Land, More or Less, upon which James P. Beall now resides, being the same and all the land described in a deed from William H. Doxen, trustee to Allen Hoffman, dated November 18, 1887, and recorded amongst the Land Records of Harford county in Liber A.L.J., No. 60, folio 94. This parcel is improved by a comfortable frame Dwelling, Frame Barn Corn House and Wagon House, Canning House and other outbuildings and has on it a good Orchard. The land is of excellent quality and well improved and under good fence. 2. Said Hoffman's equity of redemption in all that lot or parcel of land lying in the town of Bel Air, fronting about 68 feet on the westerly side of Main street, and running back 166 feet more or less, upon which the said Hoffman now resides, being the same and all the land described in a mortgage from the said Hoffman and wife to Pamelia B. Raine, dated November 23, 1894, and recorded as aforesaid in Liber W.S.F, No. 82, folio 151, excepting two parcels included in said mortgage, heretofore sold by said Hoffman, without the concurrence of the mortgagee, one to John Smith by deed dated November 27, 1893, and recorded as aforesaid in Liber W.S.F., No. 86, folio 400, and the second to William C. Sheridan, by deed dated April 30th, 1896, and recorded as aforesaid in Liber W.S.F., No. 88, folio 103. This lot is sold subject to the aforesaid mortgage to Mrs. Pamelia B. Raine to secure the sum of $4,800 and interest, which mortgage also covers the adjoining property of John Smith and Wm. C. Sheridan conveyed by said deeds to said Smith and Sheridan, a part of the consideration of the deed to said Smith from the said Hoffman, being that the said Smith is to pay off the sum of $1,250 of said mortgage according to the terms thereof. This parcel is sold subject to the inchoate right of dower of Mrs. Hoffman. Interest on said mortgage will be adjusted to the day of sale. This property is improved by a fine Frame Mansion, Stable and all necessary and convenient outbuildings and is one of the most desirable residences in Bel Air. William H. Harlan, Walter W. Preston, Permanent Trustees. J. S. Richardson, Auctioneer." (*The Aegis & Intelligencer*, December 4, 1896, p. 2). "Order Nisi ... Ordered, this 1st day of December, 1896, that the sales made and reported in the above entitled cause by William H.

Harlan and Walter W. Preston, permanent trustees, be finally confirmed, unless cause to the contrary thereof be shown on or before the 26th day of December, 1896; provided, a copy of this order be inserted in some newspaper published in Harford county, once in each of three successive weeks, before the 26th day of December, 1896. The report states the amount of sale to be $1,975. Wm. S. Forwood, Jr., Clerk." (*The Aegis & Intelligencer*, December 18, 1896, p. 2). **Genealogical Notes:** Allen Hoffman, son of John Hoffman, of PA, later of Canada and Buffalo, NY, was born on August 4, 1846 in Waterloo, Ontario, Canada and was a merchant, hotel keeper, canned goods broker, insurance agent, bank director and Civil War veteran of Havre de Grace. He married 1st to Minerva J. Taylor on June 21, 1865 and divorced on September 29, 1877. Two months later, as a "widower" he married 2nd to Sallie R. Sheridan (May 5, 1851 - April 8, 1942), daughter of Richard C. Sheridan, on November 28, 1877 by Rev. W. R. Gwinn at Abingdon. Allen died on January 26, 1897. (Harford Co. marriage license in 1865 spelled his name Hoofman and the 1877 certificate spelled his name Hoffman and her name Shurdan; *Biographical Record of Harford and Cecil Counties, Maryland*, 1897, pp, 204-205, did not mention his first marriage; St. George's P. E. Church Records, 1834-1903, p. 146, spelled his name Allan Hoffman; Mt. Zion Methodist Church tombstones; Harford County Equity Court Case No. 2732 in 1877; *Harford Democrat*, October 19, 1877; *The Aegis & Intelligencer*, October 19, 1877; *The State Gazette and Merchants and Farmers' Directory, 1871*)

Holbrook, William, 1840. "Petition, Affidavits, Schedules, Order of appointment of Trustee, Certificate, Order of Discharge & Order of Publication, Appearance Bond, Trustee's Bond & Deed filed 21st Decr. 1840. Petitioner appears & files Certificate of Publication May 22, 1841 & finally discharged." (Insolvent Docket A, 1807-1843, p. 176, at the Maryland State Archives)

Holland, Nicholas B., 1857. "Petition, Schedules, Affidavits, Appointment of Trustee & order of notice, Trustee's Bond & deed filed 23rd May 1857. 14th Novr. 1857 Petitioner appears, files certificate of publication & discharged ... 22nd July 1878 Petition of S & R Hough & Co. Copy of order & Judgment of court appointing Henry W. Archer, Jr. Trustee in place of A. W. Bateman is filed. 15 September 1880 Trustee's report and order of Court filed. Jany 12, 1881 Petition of Otho S. Lee filed. Jany 15, 1881 Auditor's Report & Order Nisi filed. January 31st 1881 Final order on Auditor's Report filed." [nothing further recorded] (Insolvent Docket A. L. J. No. 1, p. 17, in the Court Records Department of the Historical Society of Harford County). **Genealogical Notes**: Nicholas Bond Holland, second child and oldest son of Robert William Holland (1793-1866) and Eliza Carnan Bond (b. 1795, d. after 1870), was born in 1828, married Mary Amanda Bouldin (April 19, 1829 – May 14, 1894) on November 27, 1854, died on May 8, 1885 and they were buried at Christ Episcopal Church, Rock Spring Parish. Their children were Mary Florence Holland Burnett and Carrie Isabelle Holland. (*Descendants of the Signers of the Bush Declaration of March 22, 1775, Harford County, Maryland*, by Christopher T. Smithson and Henry C. Peden, Jr., 2010, p. 185; Christ Church tombstones)

Hollingsworth, Jesse, 1830. "Petition, Schedule, Shffs. certificate, personal discharge and order of publication, Bond for Appearance, Trustee's Bond, Trustee's Certificate and Deed to Trustee filed 24th June 1830. March 19th 1831 Petitioner appears. Certificate of Publication [filed] and finally discharged." (Insolvent Docket A, 1807-1843, p. 106, at Maryland State Archives). Insolvent debtor to be discharged from imprisonment. (*Independent Citizen*, December 9, 1830) **Genealogical Note:** Jesse Hollingsworth was born on October 22, 1796, died on January 15, 1863 and was buried in Little Falls Friends Cemetery (tombstone).

Holloway, Richard, 1825. "Petition, Schedule, Bond, Shffs Certificate and personal discharge and order for publication filed 19th August 1825. Allegations filed March 18th 1826 and the petitioner appears in Court and order filed ... 19th August 1826 petitioner appears. August 21st 1826 answer of Richard Holloway filed ... 17th March 1827 petitioner appeared. Interrogatories withdrawn and petitioner personally discharged. 18th August 1827 assent of Creditors filed." (Insolvent Docket A, 1807-1843, p. 73, at the Maryland State Archives; Insolvent Docket Prior to 1827, Court Records Accession #632 at the Historical Society of Harford County). **Genealogical Note**: Richard Holloway was deposed on July 2, 1811, age 26. (Court Records Document 44.21.2(i) at the Historical Society of Harford County)

Hoopes, Dillwyn, 1896. "Dillwyn Hoopes, a merchant doing business at Bynum, has made application for the benefit of the insolvent laws. Mr. Joseph T. Hoopes, who was appointed preliminary trustee, gave bond for $5,000." (*Havre de Grace Republican*, April 18, 1896, p. 3; *Harford Democrat*, April 17, 1896, p. 2, reported a similar story that "Hoopes kept a store at Bynum and was a shipper of milk.")

Hoopman, H. B., 1890. "Another Harford canner, Mr. H. B. Hoopman, has applied to an insolvent court for relief; Wm H. Harlan, preliminary trustee." (*Havre de Grace Republican*, July 25, 1890, p. 3)

Hopkins, David, 1820. "Petition, Schedule, Bond, Sheriff's certificate, personal discharge and order for publication filed 24th November 1820 – March 17th 1821 petitioner appeared … Court appoints William S. Hays his Trustee, Trustee's bond filed 20th March 1821 – a personal discharge granted to the petitioner." [nothing further recorded] (Insolvent Docket A, 1807-1843, p. 39, at the Maryland State Archives; Insolvent Docket Prior to 1827, Court Records Accession #632 at the Historical Society of Harford County)

Hopkins, Edward C., 1886. "Insolvent Notice. This is to notify the creditors of Edward C. Hopkins, an insolvent debtor, that the second Monday of September, in the year 1886, has been fixed by the Court for the appearance of said insolvent to answer such interrogatories or allegations as his creditors, endorsers or sureties may propose or allege against him. Fred. R. Williams, Permanent Trustee." (*Bel Air Times*, May 7, 1886, p. 3). "Notice to Creditors. The creditors of Edward C. Hopkins, an insolvent debtor, are hereby notified to file their claims against said insolvent, duly, authenticated, with the Clerk of the Circuit Court for Harford county on or before the 1st day of October, in the year 1886. Fred. R. Williams, Permanent Trustee." (*Bel Air Times*, May 7, 1886, p. 3). **Genealogical Notes**: Edward C. Hopkins, third child and oldest son of Wakeman Bryarly Hopkins (1806-1860) and Hannah Richardson Worthington (1808-1885), was born on February 14, 1847, married Hannah P. Hopkins (1848-1890) circa November 1, 1872 (date of license) and worked as a farmer near Darlington. He drowned accidentally in Deer Creek on March 17, 1914 and was buried in Darlington Cemetery. The children of Edward and Hannah Hopkins were Raleigh W. Hopkins (1873-1898) and Richard Kenton Hopkins, of Philadelphia, PA. (*Descendants of the Signers of the Bush Declaration of March 22, 1775, Harford County, Maryland*, by Christopher T. Smithson and Henry C. Peden, Jr., 2010, pp. 234, 240; Death Certificate No. 2906 of Edward C. Hopkins; Darlington Cemetery tombstone inscriptions; *The Aegis & Intelligencer*, March 27, 1914)

Hopkins, George R., 1886. "Notice to Creditors. In the Matter of the Insolvency of George R. Hopkins … In pursuance of an order of Court, passed in the above matter on the 1st day of July, 1886, the undersigned hereby gives notice to the creditors of George R. Hopkins, an insolvent debtor, that Monday, the 13th day of September 1886, has been fixed by the Court for the appearance of said Insolvent, to answer such interrogatories or allegations as his creditors, endorsers or sureties may propose or allege against him. Wm. H. Harlan, Permanent Trustee." (*Bel Air Times*, July 16, 1886, p. 3). **Genealogical Notes**: George R. Hopkins, son of Wellmore Hopkins and Mary B. Bayless, was born on November 21, 1856, married Marceline Virginia Hoopman (1854-1930) on December 5, 1882 and died on November 1, 1913. Their children were Wellmore Hoopman Hopkins, Louise Hopkins Worthington, Ethel Hopkins Worthington, Harry Hopkins, Robert Milton Hopkins, and Levin Hopkins; four other children died in infancy. George was a railroad engineer at the time of his death. (*Barnes-Bailey Genealogy*, by Walter D. Barnes, 1939, pp. H-61, I-77; Harford County Death Certificate No. 15540 of George R. Hopkins; Harford County 1860 Census)

Hopkins, Harry F., 1886. "Insolvent Notice. In the matter of the Insolvency of Harry F. Hopkins ... In pursuance of an order passed in the above entitled cause, the undersigned hereby gives notice to the creditors of Harry F. Hopkins, an insolvent debtor, that the 14th day of February, 1887, has been fixed upon by the court for said insolvent to appear and answer such interrogatories or allegations, as his creditors, endorsers or sureties may propose or allege against him. Geo. L. Van Bibber, Permanent Trustee." (*Harford Democrat*, December 17, 1886, p. 2). "Notice to Creditors ... In pursuance of an order passed in the above entitled cause, the undersigned hereby gives notice to the creditors of Harry F. Hopkins, an insolvent debtor, who were such on the date of his application for the benefit of the insolvent laws of Maryland, to file their claims, duly proven, with the Clerk of the Circuit Court for Harford county on or before the 1st day of March, 1887. Geo. L. Van Bibber, Permanent Trustee." (*The Harford Democrat*, December 17, 1886, p. 2). **Genealogical Notes:** Harry F. Hopkins married Sallie Buck Lynch, daughter of William and Catherine C. R. Lynch, on October 23, 1881 at the bride's residence by Rev. Asbury Reilly and they had two children, Anna Kate Hopkins (born September 6, 1886) married Stephen Stewart Merritt, Jr. on November 23, 1911, and Irene Hopkins (1892-1893). ("Sallie Buck Lynch Bible," *Maryland Bible Records, Vol. 5*, by Henry C. Peden, Jr., 2004, pp. 110-111)

Hopkins, John E. and Samuel G., 1884. "John E. Hopkins & Samuel G. Hopkins, Co-partners doing business under the firm name of John E. Hopkins & Bro. October 10th 1884. Petition, Schedule, Deed, Order appointing Preliminary Trustee & Trustee's Bond filed ... 2/3/84 Order of Court appointing Stevenson Archer Permanent Trustee filed ... [numerous claims and notices filed from 1884 to 1886 such as The Rasin Fertilizing Co., and Samuel Wagner & Co.] ... 20 Nov/84 Order of Court for Sale of Real & Personal Property filed ... 20 Feby 1888 Order Nisi filed." (Insolvent Docket A. L. J. No. 1, pp. 92, 105, in the Court Records Department of the Historical Society of Harford County). "In the matter of the Application of John E. Hopkins and Samuel G. Hopkins for the benefit of the Insolvent Laws of the State of Maryland, In the Circuit Court for Harford County. This is to give notice to the creditors of John E. Hopkins and Samuel G. Hopkins, trading as John E. Hopkins and Brother, and their individual creditors, that they have applied for the benefit of the Insolvent Laws of the State of Maryland, and that I have been appointed preliminary trustee, and have fixed Wednesday, the 27th day of October 1884, at 11 o'clock, A. M., at my office in the town of Bel Air, Harford county, as the time and place for the meeting for the election of a Permanent Trustee, and other business. Herman Stump, Preliminary Trustee." (*The Aegis & Intelligencer*, October 17, 1884, p. 2). "Tuesday, 16th instant [December, 1884], Stevenson Archer as insolvent trustee of John E. and Samuel G. Hopkins, sold 44 acres of the insolvent's estate to Mrs. Etta Hopkins for $1,500; 4 acres, improved by a comfortable dwelling house and subject to widow's dower, to John W. Spencer, for $910; and 99 acres, subject to widow's dower, to Dr. John Sappington, for $2,700." (*Havre de Grace Republican*, December 26, 1884, p. 4; *Harford Democrat*, December 19, 1884, p. 2) **Genealogical Notes:** John E. Hopkins and Samuel G. Hopkins were farmers and sons of George W. Hopkins and Sophia Spencer. John was born in 1852, married Rachel Leetta "Etta" Hopkins (1844-1920) circa January 12, 1881 (date of license) and died at his residence near Level on October 6, 1886, age about 38 [which was reported in his obituary, but it was actually 34 years, 8 months and 20 days] and was survived by his wife and three young children (names were not given in his obituary). Samuel Gover Hopkins was born on March 1, 1853 and died on July 3, 1944, having predeceased his wife Annie S. Hetrick (1860-1932) whom he married circa February 15, 1882 (date of license). They are buried in Rock Run United Methodist Church Cemetery. (tombstone inscriptions; marriage records; *The Aegis & Intelligencer*, October 15, 1886; Death certificate of Samuel G. Hopkins)

Hopkins, John H., 1885. A deed "of trust for the benefit of creditors" [under the Insolvent Laws of the State of Maryland] has "lately been filed in the clerk's office [for] John H. Hopkins, canner, to Herman Stump." (*The Aegis & Intelligencer*, November 20, 1885, p. 2). **Genealogical Notes**: John Henry Hopkins, son of Henry Hopkins (1806-1834) and Ann E. "Nancy" Hughes (1809-1898), was born on November 15, 1834, married Mary Martha Martin (1839-1910), daughter of Henry Martin (1808-1855) and Susannah Hollis (1817-1842), on February 20, 1867 by Rev. John W. Bull at the home of Daniel Martin, worked as a farmer, canner and stone mason, and died on November 29, 1885 at his home near Perryman. The children of John and Nancy Hopkins were Harry Gover Hopkins, Annie Virginia Hopkins, William Martin Hopkins, John Oscar Hopkins, George H. Hopkins and Hollis Hughes Hopkins. (*Maryland Bible Records, Volume 1*, pp. 61-62, and *Volume 2*, pp. 67-68, by Henry C. Peden, Jr., 2003; *The Hughes Genealogy, 1636-1953*, by Joseph Lee Hughes, 1953, p. 106; *The Aegis & Intelligencer*, December 4, 1885)

Hopkins, John M., 1882. "Application for benefit of the Insolvent Laws, schedules, affidavit, order of Court appointing Herman Stump preliminary Trustee, Bond approved and deed filed June 6th 1882 … 26th June 1882 Report of the appointment of A. Preston Gilbert Permanent Trustee … Aug 7/84. Order of Court for appearance of Insolvent & copy sent. September 8th 1884 Certificate of Publication of insolvent notice filed. Same day Petitioner discharged per order of Court filed." (Insolvent Docket A. L. J. No. 1, p. 74, in the Court Records Department of the Historical Society of Harford County). "Upon the application of John M. Hopkins, of Harford county, for the benefit of the Insolvent Laws of the State of Maryland, I have been appointed preliminary Trustee, and I therefore give notice that there will be a meeting of his creditors at my office, in the town of Bel Air, Harford county, on Monday, the 26th day of June, 1882, for the purpose of electing a permanent trustee. Herman Stump, Preliminary Trustee." (*The Aegis & Intelligencer*, June 16, 1882, p. 2). "In the matter of the Insolvent Petition of John M. Hopkins, for the benefit of the Insolvent Laws … In Pursuance of an order of the Circuit Court for Harford county, notice is hereby given to the creditors, endorsers and sureties of John M. Hopkins, that he will appear in said court, on the 8th day of September, 1884, to answer such interrogatories as they may propose or allege against him, and warning them to show cause, if any they have, why said Insolvent should not be discharged. A. Preston Gilbert, Permanent Trustee." (*The Aegis & Intelligencer*, August 3, 1884, p. 2). **Genealogical Notes**: John Miller Hopkins, son of Philip Hopkins and Rachel Miller, was born on February 1, 1817, married Phoebe Ann "Phoebie" Huff (1814-1897) circa November 25, 1841 (date of license), worked as a farmer near Wilna, died on November 14, 1908 and they were buried in Cokesbury Memorial Methodist Church cemetery in Abingdon (tombstone inscribed as born on February 1, 1822, but his death certificates states he was 91, thus born 1817). At the time of his death he was survived by two daughters, Mrs. B. F. Cronin, of Wilna, and Miss Sarah Hopkins, of Baltimore. (*The Aegis & Intelligencer*, November 20, 1908)

Hopkins, Joseph R., 1892. "Notice to Creditors. In the matter of the Insolvency of Joseph R. Hopkins … Notice is hereby given to the creditors of Joseph R. Hopkins, of Harford county, that he has applied for the benefit of the Insolvent Laws of the State of Maryland, and that a meeting of the creditors of the said Joseph R. Hopkins will be held at my office, in Bel Air, on Monday, February 15th, 1892, at 12 o'clock, M., for the purpose of electing a permanent trustee of said insolvent. Edward M. Allen, Preliminary Trustee." (*Harford Democrat*, March 4, 1892, p. 3). **Genealogical Notes**: Joseph Reese Hopkins, Jr., son of Joseph Reese Hopkins and Leetta "Lettie" Miller (c1796-1871), was born on December 17, 1835, married Maria McCausland on January 5, 1865 in Baltimore by Rev. Samuel Spranklin, worked as a farmer and butcher in Darlington, died on February 13, 1907 and was buried in Rock Run United Methodist Church cemetery. The children of Joseph and Lettie Hopkins were Anna McCausland Hopkins and Dr. Murray Lindley Hopkins. (Death Certificate; *Maryland Bible*

Records, Volume 1, by Henry C. Peden, Jr., 2003, pp. 116-117; *The Aegis & Intelligencer,* February 15, 1907; Research by Reese E. Morgan, of Watertown, CT, in 2008)

Hopkins, Robert R., 1886. "Notice to Creditors. In the Matter of the Insolvency of Robert R. Hopkins ... In pursuance of an order of Court, passed in the above matter on the 1st day of July, 1886, the undersigned hereby gives notice to the creditors of Robert R. Hopkins, an insolvent debtor, that Monday, the 13th day of September 1886, has been fixed by the Court for the appearance of said Insolvent, to answer such interrogatories or allegations as his creditors, endorsers or sureties may propose or allege against him. Wm. H. Harlan, Permanent Trustee." (*Bel Air Times,* July 16, 1886, p. 3). **Genealogical Notes:** Robert R. Hopkins, son of Wellmore Hopkins (1813-1880) and Mary B. Bayless (1823-1893), was born in 1858, married Susan "Sue" Dever (b. 1860), worked as a farmer near Level, died July 29, 1905 and buried in Deer Creek Harmony Presbyterian Church Cemetery. (tombstones; Robert's death certificate gave his name as Robert B. Hopkins, stated he was age 45, and his wife Susan D. Hopkins was still living in 1905; *Our Silver Heritage,* by Benjamin Stump Silver and Frances Aylett (Bowen) Silver, 1976, p. 3190; *The Aegis & Intelligencer,* May 5, 1893)

Hopkins, William H., 1889. "George A. Barton and Wm. H. Hopkins, insolvents, appeared, and were finally discharged." (*Havre de Grace Republican,* February 15, 1889, p. 4). **Genealogical Note:** William H. Hopkins, of Aberdeen, was born in 1854, worked as a butcher and was an avid duck hunter by 1911 to at least 1922. (*Duck Hunters on the Susquehanna Flats, 1850-1930,* by Henry C. Peden, Jr. and Jack L. Shagena, Jr., 2014, p. 59)

Howard, Joseph, 1829. Insolvent debtor to be discharged from imprisonment. (*Independent Citizen,* April 30, 1829). "Petition, Schedule, Certificate and personal discharge and order for publication, Bond for Appearance, Trustee's Bond and deed to Trustee filed 7th March 1829. 15th August 1829 Petitioner appeared and finally discharged." (Insolvent Docket A, 1807-1843, p. 95, at Maryland State Archives). **Genealogical Notes:** Joseph Howard was born in 1797, died on September 9 1878 and was buried in Cokesbury Memorial Methodist Church cemetery (tombstone inscription).

Howard, Patrick, 1892. "Land Sold.—Friday last [December 30, 1892] the insolvent trustees of Patrick Howard, by John S. Richardson, auctioneer, sold the real and personal estate of the insolvent." (*Harford Democrat,* January 6, 1893, p. 2)

Howard, Samuel, 1841. "Petition, 2 Affidavits, 3 Schedules, Appointment of Trustee, Certificate, Order, Personal Discharge, Appearance Bond, Deed and Trustee's Bond filed 6th April 1841. 20th Novr. 1841 Certificate of Publication filed & Petitioner appears & finally discharged." (Insolvent Docket A, 1807-1843, p. 177, at the Maryland State Archives)

Howlett, William, 1844. "Notice Is Hereby Given to the creditors of *William Howlett,* late an imprisoned debtor of *Harford County,* that on the application of said debtor by petition in writing to the Hon. Robert W. Holland, chief justice of the Orphan's court of said county, for the benefit of the insolvent laws of Maryland, the said judge on the 14th day of March, 1845, granted to said debtor a discharge from imprisonment and appointed the first Saturday after the 3rd Monday in November next, for his appearance before the Judges of *Herford* county court at the court house of said county, for a final hearing before said court, on said petition and to answer such interrogatories as his creditors may propose to him." (*Harford Madisonian and Bel-Air & Havre de Grace Messenger,* October 18, 1844, p. 3)

Huff, John, 1838. "Notice Is Hereby Given, to the creditors of John Huff, late an imprisoned debtor of Harford county, that on the application of said debtor by petition in writing to the Honorable Samuel Bradford, one of the Justices of the Orphan's court for said county, for the benefit of the insolvent laws of Maryland, the said Judge on the 21st day of August, 1838, granted to the said debtor a discharge from imprisonment and appointed the first Saturday after the third Monday in November next, for his appearance before the Judges of Harford county court at the court house of said county, for a final hearing before said court, on said petition and to answer such interrogatories as his creditors may propose to him." (*The Madisonian and Harford and Baltimore Advertiser*, October 18, 1838, p. 3). 1838. "Petition, Schedule, Affidavits, personal discharge and order of publication, Bond for Appearance, Trustee's Bond, Trustee's Certificate and Deed to Trustee filed 21st August 1838. 24th Novr. 1838 Certificate of publication and allegations filed. Affidavit & order to remove proceedings to Baltimore County Court to May Term. Record transmitted to Baltimore County Court the 5th day of January 1839 by mail. 18th May 1839 Record transmitted to Harford County Court. 25th May 1839 cont'd. rule plea, affidavit filed, plea filed non cul [not guilty] & issue … [list of seven witnesses for creditors] … Novr 28th 1839 Jury sworn … [twelve men] … verdict for petitioner and finally discharged." (Insolvent Docket A, 1807-1843, p. 167, at the Maryland State Archives)

Huff, Thomas R., 1890. "Proceedings have been filed in the Circuit Court to declare Thomas R. Huff, of Scarborough P. O., insolvent. Messrs. J. Thos. C. Hopkins and F. R. Williams appear for the petitioners." (*The Aegis & Intelligencer*, January 17, 1890, p. 2). "Insolvent Notice. In the matter of the Insolvency of Thomas R. Huff. In the Circuit Court for Harford County In Insolvency. To the Creditors of Thomas R. Huff. Take notice that Thomas R. Huff, of Harford county, having been adjudicated an insolvent debtor, by the Circuit Court for Harford county, the proceedings under which the adjudication was made being now pending, a meeting of the creditors of said insolvent debtor will be held at my office, in Bel Air, on Tuesday, the 12th day of October, 1897, at 12 o'clock, M., for the purpose of selecting a permanent trustee. Thos. H. Robinson, Preliminary Trustee." (*The Aegis & Intelligencer*, October 8, 1897, p. 3)

Huff, Zachariah, 1817. "Whereas we the subscribers Justices of the Peace for Harford County upon the petition of Zachariah Huff setting forth therein that he had actually been confined in the jail of said county since the twentieth day of January last for debts which he is unable to pay and finding the facts therein stated to be true we did meet at the jail of said county on the ninth day of February last and did then and there appoint the thirteenth day of March instant to meet at the Court house of said county, which said appointment we did then and there … at the request of the said Sheriff administer to the said Zachariah Huff the following oath which was taken by the said Zachariah Huff being first duly sworn on the Holy Evangely of Almighty God in the words following to wit, I Zachariah Huff do solemnly promise and swear that the schedule which I have delivered to the Sheriff of Harford county doth contain a full account to the best of my knowledge and remembrance of my whole estate both real and personal or that I have any title to or interest in, and of all debts, credits and effects whatsoever which I or any in trust for me have or at the time of my petition had, or am or was in any respect entitled to in possession, remainder or reversion and that I have not directly or indirectly at any time since my imprisonment or before, sold, leased or otherwise conveyed or disposed of or intrusted all or any part of my estate, goods, stock, money or debts thereby to defraud my creditors or to secure the same to receive or expect any profit or advantage thereof so help me God, which said duplicate of the Schedule aforesaid we have transmitted to the clerk of the county court to be by him preserved in his office for the information of the creditors of the said Zachariah Huff. Given under our hands and seals this thirteenth day of March 1817. James Wallace. Joseph Robinson. Benjamin Richardson." (Court Records Document 67.11(3) at Historical Society of Harford County; a copy of the schedule to which "Zachariah Huff" signed his name was included and listed this property: "Three drawing knives, one Cooper's axe, one adz, two jointers, one crow, and one set of truss hoops")

Huggins, Henry S., 1857. "Petition, Schedules, Affidavits, Appointment of Trustee, Order of Notice, Trustee's Bond & Deed filed 9th December 1857. 2nd Aug/58 Petition & ordered filed. 13th Novr. 1858 Petitioner appears, files certificate of publication & finally discharged." (Insolvent Docket A. L. J.

No. 1, p. 22, in the Court Records Department of the Historical Society of Harford County). "Notice is hereby given that Henry S. Huggins, of Harford County, has made application to the Circuit Court of said County, for the benefit of the Insolvent Laws of Maryland, and that the first Saturday after the second Monday in May, 1858, has been assigned for him to appear in said Court to answer such interrogatories as his creditors may propose or allege against him. William Galloway, Clerk of Circuit Court for Harford County." (*The Southern Aegis*, December 12, 1857, Vol. I, No. 22, p. 177) "In the matter of the petition of Henry S. Huggins for the benefit of the Insolvent Laws. In the Circuit Court for Harford County, May term, 1858. Ordered by this Court, this 2nd day of August, 1858, that Henry S. Huggins be and appear before this Court on the first Saturday after the second Monday in November next, to answer such interrogatories or allegations as his creditors may propose or allege against him, and that he give notice of the day so fixed for his appearance, by publishing a copy of this order in some newspaper printed in Harford County, once a week for one month, the first assertion to be three months before the said first Saturday after the said second Monday in November next. John H. Price. True copy. Test: Wm. Galloway, Clk." (*The Southern Aegis*, August 21, 1858, p. 3). **Genealogical Notes**: Henry S. Huggins (born circa 1822) (gentleman) married Margaret A. Meyers (born circa 1834) on December 14, 1852 and their son Hugh Thompson Huggins was born on September 20, 1853 and son John Robert Henry Huggins was born on July 19, 1857. (Baltimore *Sun*, December 16, 1852; St. John's Episcopal Church, Havre de Grace Parish, Canonical Parish Register, Volume B, 1835-1858; 1860 Census mistakenly listed his name as Henry L. Huggins)

Hughes, Alexander, 1842. "Petition, Affidavits, Schedules, Appointment, certificate, order, personal discharge, appearance bond & trustee's bond filed 20th Decr. 1842. Petitioner appears & cont'd. 20 May 1843. 25 Nov 1843 Petitioner appears, files certificate & finally discharged." (Insolvent Docket A, 1807-1843, p. 186, at the Maryland State Archives)

Hughes, James, 1829. Insolvent debtor to be discharged from imprisonment. (*Independent Citizen*, November 16, 1829). "Petition, Schedule, Certificate of Sheriff, personal discharge, Order for Publication, Bond for Appearance, Trustee's Bond, Trustee's Certificate and Deed to Trustee filed 19th May 1829. 13th March 1830 Notice of Publication filed. 15th March 1830 Oath administered and Petitioner discharged." (Insolvent Docket A, 1807-1843, p. 97, at the Maryland State Archives)

Hughes, James P., 1871. "Petition, Schedules, Affidavit, Order, Trustee's Bond & Deed filed 22 May/71. 12th Sept. 1871 Certificate of Publication filed and final Order of Discharge ordered." (Insolvent Docket A. L. J. No. 1, p. 54, in the Court Records Department of the Historical Society of Harford County) **Genealogical Notes**: James P. Hughes, son of James Hughes and Hannah Elizabeth Gilbert, was born March 8, 1825, married Mary ---- (1818-1879), and died February 29, 1890. Their children were Eleanora "Ella" Jane (1855-1923, married S. John Galloway), Adolphus, James, and George Hughes. (*The Hughes Genealogy, 1636-1953*, by Joseph L. Hughes, 1953, p. 100; Angel Hill Cemetery)

Hughes, John T., 1810. "Whereas we the subscribers Justices of the Peace for Harford County upon the petition of John T. Hughes who set forth therein that he had been confined in the Gaol [jail] of said county twenty days for debts which he was unable to pay & finding the facts stated to be true we did meet at the county Gaol of said county on the 2nd Day of March last and we did then and there appoint the 2nd Day of April Instant to meet at the Court-House of said county which said appointment we did then and there … at the request of the said Sheriff administer to the said John T. Hughes the following Oath which was taken by the said John T. Hughes being first duly sworn on the Holy Evangely of Almighty God in the words following, I John T. Hughes do solemnly swear that the Schedule which I have delivered to the Sheriff of Harford County doth contain a full account to the best of my knowledge and remembrance of my whole estate both real and personal or that I have any title to or interest in and of all debts, credits and effects whatsoever which I or any in trust for me have or at the time of my petition had, or am or was in any respect entitled to in possession, remainder or reversion and that I have not directly or indirectly at any time since my imprisonment or before, sold, leased or otherwise conveyed or disposed of or intrusted all or any part of my estate, goods, Stock, money or Debts thereby to defraud my creditors or to secure the same to receive or expect any profit or advantage thereof so help me God, which said duplicate of the Schedule aforesaid we have transmitted to the clerk of the county court to be by him preserved in his Office for the information of the Creditors of the said John T. Hughes. Given under our hands & seals this 2nd Day of April 1810. Saml. Bradford. Thomas A. Hays. Jno. C. Bond." (Court Records Document 67.14.3(A) at the Historical Society of Harford County; a copy of the schedule to which he signed his name "Jno. T. Hughes" was included and listed this personal property: "1 Hog, 2 Cyder Barrels, 6 Chairs")

Hughes, Vincent, 1833. "Petition, Schedule, Affidavit, Personal discharge, Order for Publication, Bond for Appearance, Trustee's Bond, Trustee's Certificate and Deed to Trustee filed 3rd June 1833. 15th March 1834 Petitioner appears, Certificate of Publication filed and finally discharged." (Insol-vent Docket A, 1807-1843, p. 126, at the Maryland State Archives)

Hulshart, George W., 1879. "Petition, Schedules, Affidavits, Order appointing A. P. Gilbert & Geo. Y. Maynadier Trustees, Trustees Bond & Deed filed Sept 15th 1879 … September 13th 1880 Certificate of Publication of Notice & Petitioner finally discharged." [Auditor's Reports filed subsequently] (Insolvent Docket A. L. J. No. 1, p. 66, in Court Records Department of the Historical Society of Harford County spelled his name Hultzhart). "Trustees' Sale. By virtue of an order of the Circuit Court for Harford county, the undersigned, as trustees, in the matter of the insolvency of George W. Hulshart, will offer at public sale, on the premises, in Norrisville, Harford county, Md., on Saturday, October 18th, 1879, at 11½ o'clock, A. M., all the right, title, claim, interest and estate of said Hultshart, in and to the following Real & Personal Property, viz: 16½ Acres, More or Less, and described in a deed from Mary Channel to said Hultshart and wife, dated on 15th of June, 1866, and recorded in Liber W. H. D., No. 17, folio 412, one of the Land Records of the Circuit Court for Harford county, together with the buildings and improvements thereon. Also, Lot in Norrisville, improved by a Foundry, &c., and described in a deed from David A. Edie and wife to said Hultshart and Laban Lowe, containing 30¾ Square Perches, more or less, and recorded as aforesaid in Liber A. L. J., No. 38, folio 388. Also the following Personal Property! Two Brown Horses, 1 two-horse Spring Wagon, 1 Top Buggy, 2 sets Wagon Harness, 1 set Buggy Harness, 1 six-horse power Engine and Boiler, 1 Fan and Cups for melting iron, 8 sets Plow Patterns with Flasks and Fallow Boards, Cinder Mill, 3 Work Benches and Wooden Vises. George Y. Maynadier, A. Preston Gilbert, Trustees. John S. Richardson, Auctioneer." (*Harford Democrat*, October 3, 1879, p. 2). "Notice is hereby given that George W. Hultzhart, of Harford county, has made application to the Circuit Court for said county, for the benefit of the Insolvent Laws of Maryland, and that the second Monday of September, 1880 has been assigned for him to appear in said Court to answer such interrogatories as his creditors may propose or allege against him." (*The Aegis & Intelligencer*, February 27, 1880, p. 4). **Genealogical Notes**: George W. Hulshart (born c1837, PA) married Mary "Mollie" Whirley (born c1829, PA) circa 1858 and their son George W. Hulshart, Jr. was born in 1859 in MD (1860 Harford Co. Census misspelled his name Ulshart; *The Aegis and Intelligencer*, 4 Jan 1884, reported George W. Hulshart, Jr. won a watch on two separate occasions at Alexander Rigdon's store when he purchased plugs of tobacco and each contained the prize tag; Death certificate of William E. Hulshart, 1882-1950, stated his parents were George W. Hulshart and Mollie Whirley)

Hutchins, James B., 1881. "Petition, Schedules, Affidavit, Order of appointment of Herman Stump Trustee, Bond & Deed filed 5th Jany 1881." [nothing further recorded] (Insolvent Docket A. L. J. No.

1, p. 71, in Court Records Department of the Historical Society of Harford County). "Discharged by Judge Yellott. At the last November term of Court, James B. Hutchins was convicted on a charge of assaulting John Zimmerman, of Upper Cross Roads, and was sentenced to pay $1 fine and costs, and to imprisonment in the county jail for thirty days. He served out his term, paid his fine of $1 and Sheriff Morgan released him. A few days afterwards he was rearrested for non-payment of costs, which amounted to about $100. He then took benefit of the insolvent laws and his counsel. Hon. Herman Stump, sued out a writ of habeas corpus on his behalf. The case came up before Judge Yellott, of Towsontown, who discharged the petitioner, holding that the costs were in the nature of a debt, and he could not be detained therefore as the constitution of Maryland prohibited imprisonment for debt. The petitioner was represented by Hon. Herman Stump and the State by Hon. George Y. Maynadier, State's attorney for Harford county, and Wm. Young, Esq." (*The Aegis & Intelligencer*, January 14, 1881, p. 2). **Genealogical Notes:** James B. Hutchins (1852-1900), son of John Stansbury Hutchins (1818-1881) and Amanda Zana Nelson (1822-1901), married Caroline Katherine Thalwitzer (1861-1908) and resided in Towson, MD. He was known in his day as a fine tournament rider, the "Knight of My Lady's Manor." (*Nicholas Hutchins of My Lady's Manor*, by Elmore Hutchins, circa 1978, pp. 168-169)

Hutchins, Thomas, 1836. "Petition, Affidavits, Schedule, personal discharge and order of publication, Bond for Appearance, Trustee's Bond, Trustee's Certificate and Deed to Trustee filed 5th September 1836. 18th March 1837 Petitioner appears and order of Court filed & cont'd. 19th August 1837 Allegations filed. Certificate of Publication filed. Petitioner appears. O. S. [Otho Scott] appears as counsel for petitioner and petitioner discharged." (Insolvent Docket A, 1807-1843, p. 153, at the Maryland State Archives)

Hutchins, William, 1834. "Petition, Affidavits, Schedule, personal discharge and order of publication, Bond for Appearance, Trustee's Bond, Trustee's Certificate and Deed to Trustee filed 1st April 1834. 16th August 1834 Petitioner appears, Affidavit filed and continued, and petition and order filed. 14th March 1835 Petitioner appears, Certificate of Publication filed and finally discharged." (Insolvent Docket A, 1807-1843, p. 133, at Maryland State Archives)

Iley, John D., 1897. "Mr. John D. Iley, a farmer residing near Minefield, has made application for the benefit of the insolvent laws, and on Wednesday executed a deed of trust to Walter W. Preston, who gave bond in the sum of five hundred dollars." (*The Aegis & Intelligencer*, March 12, 1897, p. 3). "Insolvent Sale. By virtue of an order of the Circuit Court for Harford county, the undersigned, permanent trustee in insolvency for John D. Iley, will sell at Public Sale, on the farm now occupied by said Iley, near Minefield Station on the Baltimore and Lehigh Railroad, in Harford county, on Tuesday, April 6th, 1897, Commencing at 11 o'clock, A. M., the following Personal Property, to wit: Two good work Horses, 1 Spring Market Wagon, 1 three-horse Wagon, 2 Hay Carriage, 1 Buckeye Mower, 1 Roller, 1 lot Hay in mow, several barrels of Corn, about 1,000 feet Chestnut Boards and other lumber, a number of Posts, Pales, &c., Plows, Harrows, Cultivators and other Farming Implements. Walter W. Preston, Permanent Trustee. James T. Smithson, Auctioneer." (*The Aegis & Intelligencer*, March 26, 1897, p. 3). **Genealogical Notes:** John D. Iley (September 20, 1844 – April 20, 1910), son of Jacob Iley (born c1819) and Elizabeth Rigdon (born c1824), married Elizabeth P. Stansbury (June 23, 1852 – October 14, 1928) on July 6, 1868 by Rev. William Grafton at the minister's house. (Harford County license and marriage certificate; Highland Presbyterian Church tombstones; 1850 Census; Death certificate of John D. Iley – informant was their son Joe Iley; *The Aegis*, October 19, 1928, stated Ellizbaeth P. Iley had lived many years in the vicinity of Highland and she died in Baltimore City; her surviving children were Joseph Iley, of Baltimore, Walter Iley, of Highland, and Mrs. Walter L. Crowl, Mrs. William Heaps and Mrs. John Walters, all of Baltimore)

Inman, Jack, 1884. "March 21st 1884. Petition in Insolvency, affidavit and order of Court thereon filed … Same day Subpoena & copy of petition & order of Court delivered to Sheriff, Harford County … 28th March 1884 Order of Court extending time for respondent to answer … April 3rd 1884 Answer of Defendant filed." [nothing further recorded] (Insolvent Docket A. L. J. No. 1, p. 85, in Court Records Department of the Historical Society of Harford County)

Jackson, Edward, 1825. "Petition, Schedule, Bond, Schedule, Sheriffs Certificate and personal Discharge and order for Publication filed 14th June 1825 filed March 18th 1826 Printers Certificate." [nothing further recorded] (Insolvent Docket A, 1807-1843, p. 71, at the Maryland State Archives; Insolvent Docket Prior to 1827, Court Records Accession #632 at the Historical Society of Harford County)

Jackson, John, 1805. "Whereas we the subscribers Justices of the Peace for Harford County upon the petition of Jackson [sic] set forth therein that he had been confined in the goal [jail] of the said county twenty days for debts which he was unable to pay and finding the facts stated to be true we did meet at the county gaol of the said county on the 24th day of January 1805 and did then and there appoint the 24th day of February Inst. to meet at the court house of said county which said appointment we did then and there … at the request of the said sheriff administer to the said John Jackson the following oath which was taken by the said John Jackson being first duly sworn on the Holy Evangely of Almighty God in the words following, I John Jackson do solemnly swear that the schedule which I have delivered to the sheriff of Harford County doth contain a full account to the best of my knowledge and remembrance of my whole estate both real & personal or that I have any title to or interest in and of all debts, credits & effects whatsoever which I or any in trust for me have or at the time of my petition had, or am or was in any respect entitled to in possession, remainder or reversion and that I have not directly or indirectly at any time since my imprisonment or before, sold, leased or otherwise conveyed or disposed of or intrusted all or any part of my estate, goods, stock, money or debts thereby to defraud my creditors or to secure the same to receive or expect any profit or advantage thereof so help me God, which said duplicate of the schedule aforesaid we have transmitted to the clerk of the county court to be by him preserved in his office for the information of the creditors of the said John Jackson. Given under our hands and seals this 25th day of February 1805. John Moores. Wm. Smithson. Thos. A. Hays." (Court Records Document 67.21.3(b) at the Historical Society of Harford County; copy of the schedule was included to which "John Jackson" signed his name, but no property was listed)

James, Samuel S., 1874. "Petition, 3 Schedules, Affidavit, Order, Trustee's Bond & Insolvent Deed filed & Notice to Creditors issued 10th November 1874. 10th May 1875 Petitioner appears in Court, filed Certificate of Publication & notice & is finally discharged by the Court." (Insolvent Docket A. L. J. No. 1, p. 56, in the Court Records Department of the Historical Society of Harford County). "Notice is hereby given that Samuel S. James has made application to the Circuit Court of Harford county, for the benefit of the Insolvent Laws of Maryland, and that the second Monday in May, 1875 has been assigned for him to appear in said Court to answer such interrogatories as his creditors may propose or allege against him. A. L. Jarrett, Clerk." (*The Aegis & Intelligencer*, November 13, 1874, p. 2). 1896. "A petition in insolvency has been filed in the Harford County Circuit Court, by Mr. Samuel S. James and wife, of near Dublin, and one from his wife, both being made to Mr. J. Royston Stifler, attorney. He gave bond in the sum of $9,000 for both deeds." (*Havre de Grace Republican*, November 7, 1896, p. 3). **Genealogical Notes**: Samuel S. James (May 13, 1847 – June 23, 1928), son of Levi James (1813-1882) and Adaline Flowers (1817-1890), married Sarah E. Forsythe (May 11, 1852 – June 25, 1905), daughter of William Forsythe, Jr. (1819-1864) and Henrietta Forsythe (1833-1896), on March 23, 1875 by Rev. B. F. Clarkson [place of marriage not stated] and was a farmer and merchant at Cedarville near Dublin by 1880 to at least 1903 and was later a court crier in Bel Air. (Marriage records; West Harford Circuit M. E. Church South Records; *Country Stores: Harford County's Rural Heritage*, by Henry C. Peden, Jr. and Jack L. Shagena, Jr., 2015, p. 147; Mt. Zion Methodist Church tombstones; Dublin United Methodist Church tombstones; Death certificates of Samuel S. James and Sarah E. James; *Harford Democrat*, May 23, 1890; *Maryland Gazetteer, 1902-1903*)

James, Thomas, 1842. "Petition, Affidavits, Schedules, Appointment of trustee, certificate [and] order, personal discharge, deed, bond & trustee's bond & deed to trustee & appearance bond filed 15th June 1842. 26th Novr. 1842 Petitioner appears, files certificate of publication & cont'd. 20 May 1843 Petitioner appears & finally discharged." (Insolvent Docket A, 1807-1843, p. 182, at the Maryland State Archives)

Jarrett, A. L., 1834. "Petition, Affidavit, Schedule, personal discharge and order of publication, Bond for Appearance, Trustee's Bond, Trustee's Certificate and Deed to Trustee filed 17th May 1834. 16th Augt. 1834 Petitioner appears, Certificate of Publication filed and finally discharged. 11th July 1835 Trustee's Report filed and order of reference to Auditor filed ... 5th August 1836 Trustee's report and order filed." [nothing further recorded] (Insolvent Docket A, 1807-1843, p. 135, at Maryland State Archives). **Genealogical Notes**: Abraham Lingan Jarrett (better known as Capt. A. Lingan Jarrett), son of Abraham Jarrett and Elizabeth Smith Dallam, was born at Rock Run on September 5, 1808, married Mary Ann E. Jones (1810-1888), daughter of Stephen Jones and Mary Taylor, on November 3, 1836, served as the Clerk of the Circuit for Harford County from 1851 to 1858 and 1867 to 1891, died on February 18, 1894 and was buried on his home place south of Bel Air (now the site of the Lorien Nursing & Rehabilitation Center on Emmorton Road). They had no children. (*Descendants of the Signers of the Bush Declaration of March 22, 1775, Harford County, Maryland*, by Christopher T. Smithson and Henry C. Peden, Jr., 2010, pp. 343, 348; *Harford Democrat*, February 23, 1894)

Jarrett, Abraham, 1806. "June 4, 1806. To the Honorable the Judges of Harford County Court. Abraham Jarrett states to your Honors that he is named in the act passed at the late session of the General Assembly of Maryland entitled 'An act for the relief of sundry Insolvent Debtors,' the benefit of which law your petitioner wishes to obtain, he therefore offers to deliver to the use of his creditors, all his property, real, personal and mixed (the necessary wearing apparel and bedding of himself and family excepted), to which he is in any way entitled, a schedule whereof together with a list of his creditors as far as he can ascertain them is hereto annexed under oath of your petitioner as by the said act is directed. Your honors hereupon are solicited to grant your petitioner the benefit of the act aforesaid and to do herein which further shall appear right and proper, &c. &c., and your petitioner files herewith the assent in writing of his creditors to whom is due more than two-thirds of all the amount of Debts due from your petitioner. A Schedule of all my property ... One tract of Land called *Hill's Camp* containing about 350 acres, one tract of land containing about 171 acres called *Expence*, part of two tracts of Land, one called *Charley Roy*, the other called *Valencienes*, containing about 241 acres. [signed] Abrm. Jarrett." [Also, five pages of lists of debts due and debts owed, plus seven pages of objections, allegations and petitions through 1808. The final entry in the record book was as follows]: "31st August 1809. Petitions and issues withdrawn as per agreement filed." (Court Actions in Insolvencies, 1805-1807, Court Records Accession #605 at the Historical Society of Harford County). 1827. "Abraham Jarrett, Sr. Petition, Schedule, Bond, Sheriff's certificate and personal discharge and order for publication filed and Bond of provisional trustee filed and certificate for Trustee filed 24th March 1827 – 18th August 1827 certificate of notice to creditors filed." [nothing further recorded] (Insolvent Docket A, 1807-1843, p. 84, at the Maryland State Archives). **Genealogical Notes**: Abraham Jarrett, son of Abraham Jarrett and Martha Bussey, was born circa 1764, married Elizabeth Smith Dallam (1774-1825), widow of Herman Stump and daughter of Josiah William Dallam and Sarah Smith, on November 19, 1804 at *Mt. Friendship* and died in 1832. They had two children, Amanda C. Jarrett Cooley and Abraham Lingan Jarrett. (*Descendants of the Signers of the Bush Declaration of March 22, 1775, Harford County, Maryland,* by Christopher T. Smithson and Henry C. Peden, Jr., 2010, pp. 340-343; *Descendants of Abraham Jarrett,* by John D. Jarrett, an undated manuscript in The Henry C. Peden, Jr. Research Library at the Historical Society of Harford County). It is interesting to note that this could have been the Abraham Jarrett, age 50 (born circa 1764) who was born in Maryland, served as a seaman during the War of 1812 and his home port was Baltimore. On January 1, 1815 he was captured while serving on the privateer *Fox* by HM Brig *Barbadoes* off St. Bartholomew, West Indies, was then transported on HMS *Swiftsure* to Prison Depot Plymouth 2 in England, received on April 16, 1815 as Prisoner of War No. 483, was discharged on June 2, 1815 and released to the Cartel *Soverign* [no further information available]. (*Maryland Casualties in the War of 1812,* by Christos Christou, Jr. and Henry C. Peden, Jr., 2019, pp. 200-201)

Jarrett, Deveraux, 1855. "(For prior Entries see Old Docket page 26). 4th Sept. 1855 Petition of C. D. Bouldin Trustee … 25th Sept. 1855 Answer of Jesse B. Jarrett, admr. of Edward B. Jarrett filed … 4th Jan 1856 … Claims of C. D. Bouldin & Archer H. Jarrett filed … 11 Augt/56 Petition of Emmor Woodward & Answer of Trustee filed … 13th Novr. 1856 Petition of Emmor Woodward dismissed with costs & Auditor's Report finally certified." [nothing further recorded] (Insolvent Docket A. L. J. No. 1, p. 8, in the Court Records Department of the Historical Society of Harford County)

Jeffery, Alexander, 1816. "Whereas we the subscribers Justices of the Peace for Harford County upon the petition of Alexander Jeffery stating therein that he had actually been confined in the goal [jail] of said county since the seventeenth day of July last for debts which he is unable to pay and finding the facts therein stated to be true we did meet at the goal of said county on the sixth day of August last and did then and there appoint the second day of March Inst. to meet at the Court house of said county, which said appointment we did then and there … at the request of the said Sheriff administer to the said Alexander Jeffery the following oath which was taken by the said Alexander Jeffery being first duly sworn on the holy Evangely of Almighty God in the words following to wit, I Alexander Jeffery do solemnly promise and swear that the schedule which I have delivered to the Sheriff of Harford county doth contain a full account to the best of my knowledge and remembrance of my whole estate both real and personal or that I have any title to or interest in, and of all debts, credits and effects whatsoever which I or any in trust for me have or at the time of my petition had, or am or was in any respect entitled to in possession, remainder or reversion and that I have not directly or indirectly at any time since my imprisonment or before, sold, leased or otherwise conveyed or disposed of or intrusted all or any part of my estate, goods, stock, money or debts thereby to defraud my creditors or to secure the same to receive or expect any profit or advantage thereof so help me God, which said duplicate of the Schedule aforesaid we have transmitted to the clerk of the county court to be by him preserved in his office for the information of the creditors of the said Alexander Jeffery. Given under our hands and seals this ninth day of September 1816. James Wallace. Joseph Robinson." (Court Records Document 67.11(4) at Historical Society of Harford County; a copy of the schedule to which "Alexr. Jeffery" signed his name was included, but his personal property was listed in this way: ~~Property, 2 pair of plough chains, 2 clevises~~) [sic].
Genealogical Note: Alexander Jeffery married Adelia Barnes circa April 7, 1802 (date of license).

Jewett, Isaac W., 1847. "Petition, Affidavits, Bond & Deed filed 10th Augt/47 (see old Doc. page 63). 22nd Sept/55 Petition of Trustee & Order of Sale filed 25th Jan/56 … Order of final qualification of Trustee's Sale with certificate of publication of creditors filed. Recorded in Judgment Record Liber H. D. G. No. 2, folio 406." (Insolvent Docket A. L. J. No. 1, p. 7, in the Court Records Department of the Historical Society of Harford County)

Johns, Edward F., 1882. "Application for benefit of Insolvent Laws, 3 Schedules, Affidavit, Order appointing Trustee and day for hearing, Trustee's Bond & Deed filed 10th March 1882. Sept 12th 1882 Certificate of publication of Insolvent notice filed & same day Petitioner appeared in Court and was finally discharged." (Insolvent Docket A. L. J. No. 1, p. 72, in Court Records Department of the Historical Society of Harford County) "Notice is hereby given that Edward F. Johns, of Harford county, has made application to the Circuit Court for said county, for the benefit of the Insolvent Laws of Maryland, and that the second Monday of September, 1882 has been assigned for him to appear in said Court to answer such interrogatories as his creditors may propose or allege against him. A. L. Jarrett, Clerk." (*The Aegis & Intelligencer*, April 7, 1882, p. 2). **Genealogical Notes**: Edward Franklin Johns was born on August 31, 1822, married Jane R. Spicer (June 10, 1825 – December 17, 1902) circa July 9, 1845 (date of license) and died on March 8, 1908 at the home of his daughter Mrs. Agnes Eltonhead in Baltimore City. Their daughter Agnes Louise Johns (1847-1935) married William T. Eltonhead (1840-1880) on January 23, 1867. They are buried at Cokesbury Memorial Methodist Church in Abingdon. (*The Aegis & Intelligencer*, February 1, 1867 and March 13, 1908; Cokesbury Cemetery tombstone inscriptions)

Johnson, Abraham, 1842. "Petition, Affidavits, Schedules, Appointment, certificates, order, personal Discharge, Deed, Appearance & Trustee's Bonds filed 30th Augst. 1842." [nothing further recorded] (Insolvent Docket A, 1807-1843, p. 184, at Maryland State Archives). **Genealogical Note**: Abraham Johnson married Polly Donovan on September 9, 1802. (St. George's P. E. Parish Register)

Johnson, Alphonso C., 1828. "Petition, Schedule, Affidavit, Sheriffs Certificate, Bond, Deed, Provisional Trustee's Bond, Trustee's Certificate, Discharge and Order for Publication filed 7th January 1828. 12th March 1828 the appointment of Charles Carman [as] provisional trustee revoked and Abraham Jarrett, Jr. appointed … in his stead … 16th August 1828 Petitioner appeared … 22nd August 1828 adjudged by the Court that the petitioner hath been guilty of fraud and assent of his creditors after behaving himself unable to pay his debts and had been unable to pay them and that he is not entitled to the benefit of the insolvent laws of this State. 2nd March 1830 petition and order for discharge filed. 1st September 1836 petition and order filed and Trustee bond filed." [nothing further recorded] (Insolvent Docket A, 1807-1843, p. 87, at the Maryland State Archives)

Johnson, Charles, 1810. "Whereas we the subscribers Justices of the Peace for Harford County together with John Guyton, Esq., also one of the Justices of the Peace for said County, upon the petition of Charles Johnson who set forth therein that he had been confined in the Gaol [jail] of said county twenty Days for Debts which he was unable to pay and finding the facts stated to be true we together with John Guyton, Esquire, did meet at the county Gaol of said county on the 25th Day of January last and we did then and there appoint the 26th Day of February Instant to meet at the Court-House of said county which said appointment we did then and there … at the request of said Sheriff administer to the said Charles Johnson the following Oath which was taken by the said Charles Johnson being first duly sworn on the Holy Evangely of Almighty God in the words following, I Charles Johnson do solemnly swear that the Schedule which I have delivered to the Sheriff of Harford County doth contain a full account to the best of my knowledge and remembrance of my whole estate both real and personal or that I have any title to or interest in and of all debts, credits and effects whatsoever which I or any in trust for me have or at the time of my petition had, or am or was in any respect entitled to in possession, remainder or reversion and that I have not directly or indirectly at any time since my imprisonment or before, sold, leased or otherwise conveyed or disposed of or intrusted all or any part of my estate, goods, Stock, money or Debts thereby to defraud my creditors or to secure the same to receive or expect any profit or advantage thereof so help me God, which said duplicate of the Schedule aforesaid we have transmitted to the Clerk of the County Court to be by him preserved in his Office for the information of the Creditors of the said Charles Johnson. Given under our hands & seals this 26th Day of February 1810. Thomas A. Hays. Saml. Bradford." (Court Records Document 67.15(1) at the Historical Society of Harford County; a copy of the schedule was included to which Charles Johnson made his "x" mark that looked like a "+" mark, but listed no property)

Johnson, George M., 1839. "Petition, Schedule, Affidavits, personal discharge and order of publication, Bond for Appearance, Trustee's Bond, Trustee's Certificate and Deed to Trustee filed 16th July 1839. Novr. 23rd 1839 Petitioner appears and finally discharged." (Insolvent Docket A, 1807-1843, p. 170, at the Maryland State Archives)

Johnson, George W., 1859. "Petition, Schedule of property, List of debts, Affidavit, Order, Trustee's Bond, Appointment of Trustee and Deed to Trustee filed 31st May 1859. A. W. Bateman, Trustee. 19th Nov/59 Petitioner appears, files certificate of publication and was finally discharged by the Court." (Insolvent Docket A. L. J. No. 1, p. 28, in the Court Records Department of the Historical Society of Harford County) "Notice is hereby given that George W. Johnson, of Harford County, has made application to the Circuit Court of said County, for the benefit of the Insolvent Laws of Maryland, and that the 1st Saturday after the 2nd Monday in November, 1859, has been assigned for him to appear in said Court to answer such interrogatories as his creditors may propose or allege against him. Wm. Galloway, Clerk, Circuit Court for Harford County." (*The Southern Aegis*, June 11, 1859, p. 3). **Genealogical Notes**: George W. Johnson (1830 – November 2, 1893) married Julia Ann Taylor (August 17, 1839 – September 7, 1917), daughter of Benjamin Taylor, on August 6, 1857 and was a farmer at Joppa. Their son Thomas C. Johnson was 8 months old in July 1860. (Baltimore *Sun*, August 8, 1857; 1860 Harford Co. Census listed her as Julian and his name was written strangely as George Johnsonk; Cokesbury Memorial Methodist Church tombstones; Death certificate of Julia Ann Johnson; *The Aegis & Intelligencer*, November 10, 1893, listed him as George W. Johnson, Sr.)

Johnson, James, 1802. Petitioned for relief under the act for relief of sundry Insolvent Debtors (*Laws of Maryland*, Vol. III, 1802, Chapter 97, Liber JG No. 4, folio 308-314), 1811. "Whereas we the subscribers Justices of the Peace for Harford County upon the petition of James Johnson who set forth therein that he had been confined [in jail] twenty days and upwards for debts which he was unable to pay and finding the facts stated to be true we did meet at the jail of said county on the 24th of February last and did then and there appoint the 27th day of March Instant to meet at the court house of said county which said appointment we did then and there … at the request of the said sheriff administer to the said James Johnson the following oath which was taken by the said James Johnson being first duly sworn on the Holy Evangely of Almighty God in the words following, I do solemnly swear that the schedule which I have delivered to the sheriff of Harford County doth contain a full account to the best of my knowledge and remembrance of my whole estate both real & personal or that I have any title to or interest in and of all debts, credits & effects whatsoever which I or any in trust for me have or at the time of my petition had, or am or was in any respect entitled to in possession, remainder or reversion and that I have not directly or indirectly at any time since my imprisonment or before, sold, leased or otherwise conveyed or disposed of or intrusted all or any part of my estate, goods, stock, money or debts thereby to defraud my creditors or to secure the same to receive or expect any profit or advantage thereof so help me God, which said duplicate of the schedule aforesaid we have transmitted to the clerk of the county court to be by him preserved in his office for the information of the creditors of the said James Johnson. Given under our hands & seals this 27th Day of March 1811. Thomas A. Hays. Saml. Bradford. John Guyton." (Court Records Document 67.14.5(A) at the Historical Society of Harford County; schedule was included to which James Johnson signed his name and listed his property as "1 Old Mare, 4 Cyder Casks, 4 Winsor

Chairs"). **Genealogical Note**: James Johnson was deposed on February 19, 1801 and stated he was about 40 years old. (Court Records Document 56.16.16 at the Historical Society of Harford County)

Johnson, John, 1832. "Petition, Schedule, Affidavit, personal discharge, Order for Publication, Bond for Appearance, Trustee's Bond, Trustee's Certificate and Deed to Trustee filed the 25th April 1832. 28 May 1832 Petition, Exhibit and Order filed and petition and order for sale filed. 18th Augt. 1832 Allegations and Interrogatories filed, and petitioner appears, certificate of publication filed, and finally discharged … [numerous claims filed from 1832 through 1837] … 20th May 1839 Auditors Report No. 1 & 2 filed. 19th Sept. 1842 Affidavit filed. Order filed 4 Oct 1843. 4th Decr. 1844 Petition of John Johnson & Exhibit A – Answer of Constable & order filed." [nothing further recorded] (Insolvent Docket A, 1807-1843, pp. 117, 127, at the Maryland State Archives)

Johnson (Johnston), William, 1810. "Whereas we the subscribers Justices of the Peace for Harford County upon the petition of William Johnson who set forth therein that he had been confined in the Gaol [jail] of said county twenty days for debts which he was unable to pay & finding the facts stated to be true we did meet at the county Gaol of said county on the 13th day of August last and we did then and there appoint the 13th day of September Inst. to meet at the Court House of said county which said appointment we did then and there … at the request of said Sheriff administer to the said William Johnson the following Oath which was taken by the said William Johnson being first duly sworn on the Holy Evangely of Almighty God in the words following, I William Johnson do solemnly swear that the Schedule which I have delivered to the Sheriff of Harford County doth contain a full account to the best of my knowledge and remembrance of my whole estate both real and personal or that I have any title to or interest in and of all debts, credits and effects whatsoever which I or any in trust for me have or at the time of my petition had, or am or was in any respect entitled to in possession, remainder or reversion and that I have not directly or indirectly at any time since my imprisonment or before, sold, leased or otherwise conveyed or disposed of or intrusted all or any part of my estate, goods, Stock, money or Debts thereby to defraud my creditors or to secure the same to receive or expect any profit or advantage thereof so help me God, which said duplicate of the Schedule aforesaid we have transmitted to the clerk of the county court to be by him preserved in his Office for the information of the Creditors of the said William Johnson. Given under our hands and seals this 13th Day of Sepr. 1810. Thomas A. Hays. Saml. Bradford. Jno. C. Bond." (Court Records Document 67.14.6(A) at the Historical Society of Harford County included a copy of a schedule to which he signed his name "William Johnston," not Johnson, but he had no property)

Jolley, Edward, 1806. "August 21st 1806. To the Honorable the Judges of Harford County Court sitting. The petition of Edward Jolley of Harford County respectfully sheweth, That being rendered by misfortunes wholly unable to pay his debts he applied to the legislature at November Session 1805 for the benefit of an Act of Insolvency, that the same was granted and his name is included in the Act that entitled 'An Act for the relief of sundry insolvent debtors, that he hereby offers to deliver up to the use of his creditors, all his property, real, personal and mixed, to which he is in any way entitled, a schedule whereof an oath together with a list of his creditors also on oath as far forth as he can ascertain them, is annexed to and accompanies this petition, that he is ready to comply with the directions of the said Act and the orders of the court and in all respects confirm thereto, that he is in actual confinement and custody of the Sheriff of Harford County at the Suit of John Sample for a debt due before the passage of the Act aforesaid. Your Petitioner therefore prays he may be discharged from said confinement and that such further proceedings may be hereupon had by the Court as that he may have and obtain the benefits of the aforesaid Act as far as he shall be entitled now and hereafter to the same and he as in duty bond will ever pray and so forth. 16th Augt. 1806. [signed] Edwd. Jolley." [Several pages of debts owed and debts due and other statement, plus the following]: "A Schedule of Edward Jolley's property ... part of a Tract of Land called *Jolley's First Attempt* containing 538 acres or thereabouts; part of a Tract of Land called *Stapleton's Lott* containing 30 acres or thereabouts; one half of 5/6 of a tract of land purchased of the Heirs of Job Barnes, said to contain 50 acres; also a tract of land called *Dooley's Beginning* said to contain 100 acres; also one other tract of land called *Stapleton's Delight* said to contain 43 acres, the whole of the above lands mortgaged to William Jolley for the following sums, viz., in August 1803 for $1,262 with Interest thereon until paid. I have recd. from the said William Jolley since the said Mortgage was executed a sum the precise amt. of which I cannot ascertain at present does not exceed one hundred Dollars in cash. I have purchased of John Litton, deceased, a Tract of land called *Litton's Fancy* said to contain 80 acres not paid for (except it may be a small part) nor conveyed. I have also purchased one half of a Saw mill and 4½ acres of land of Robert McCoy and Brothers not paid for nor conveyed. 1 Walnut desk, 1 Saddle. Since the execution of the Mortgage to William Jolley as above expressed I have given a deed to him the said William Jolley for the aforesaid Tracts of Land called *Dooley's Beginning* and *Stapleton's Delight* for the consideration of $475 which Deed bears date in August 1803 with an understanding that upon the repayment of the money there was to be a reconveyance." [And also the following]: "I have carried on a saw mill in co. with Alexander Reese ... I was left executor of my father John Jolley's Estate which is unclosed. Also I took out letters *de bonis non* on a devise to my mother Elisabeth Jolly deceased, which is also unclosed." [The last entry in 1807 was as follows]: "Ordered by the Court that the Trustee sell the property mentioned in the schedule, on three months credit the purchaser to give bond with security to be approved by the Trustee." (Court Actions in Insolvencies, 1805-1807, Court Records Accession #605 at the Historical Society of Harford County)

Jones, Walter T., 1820. "Petition, Schedule, Bond, Sheriff's certificate, order for publication and personal discharge filed 27th June 1820." [nothing further recorded] (Insolvent Docket A, 1807-1843, p. 33, at the Maryland State Archives; Insolvent Docket Prior to 1827, Court Records Accession #632 at the Historical Society of Harford County). **Genealogical Note**: Walter T. Hall married Willamina Jones circa December 13, 1819 (date of license).

Jones, William, 1859. "Petition, Schedule, Affidavit, Appointment of Trustee, Order of Notice to Creditors, Trustee's Bond and Deed to Trustee filed 5th September/59 & A. W. Bateman, Esqr., appointed Trustee. 27th February 1860 Petitioner appears & files certificate of publication & finally discharged." (Insolvent Docket A. L. J. No. 1, p. 30, in Court Records Department of the Historical Society of Harford County). "Notice is hereby given that William Jones, of Harford County, has made application to the Circuit Court of said County, for the benefit of the Insolvent Laws of Maryland, and that the 4th Monday in February, 1860, has been assigned for him to appear in said Court to answer such interrogatories as his creditors may propose or allege against him. Wm. Galloway, Clerk, Circuit Court for Harford County." (*The Southern Aegis*, October 4, 1859, p. 3)

Jordan (Jordon), William, 1826. "Petition, Schedule, bond, Sheriff's certificate and personal discharge and order for publication filed 7th March 1826. 19th August 1827 Petitioner appears and printers certificate filed and finally discharged." (Insolvent Docket A, 1807-1843, at the Maryland State Archives; Insolvent Docket Prior to 1827, Court Records Accession #632 at the Historical Society of Harford County)

Keen, James W., 1844. "Notice Is Hereby Given, to the creditors of *James W. Keen*, late an imprisoned debtor of Harford county, that on the application of said debtor by petition in writing to the Hon. Robert W. Holland, chief justice of the Orphan's court of said county, for the benefit of the insolvent laws of Maryland, the said judge on the 17th day of May, 1844, granted to the said debtor a discharge from imprisonment and appointed the first Saturday after the 3rd Monday in November next, for his appearance before the Judges of Harford county court at the court house of said county, for a final hearing before said court, on said petition and to answer such interrogatories as his creditors may propose to him." (*Harford Madisonian and Bel-Air & Havre de Grace Messenger*, October 18, 1844, p. 3) "Notice is hereby given, to the creditors of *James W. Keen*, late an imprisoned debtor of Harford county, that on the application of said *Keen* by petition in writing to the Hon. John C. Legrand, one of the associate justices of the county court, of said county, for the benefit of the insolvent laws of Maryland, the said judge on the 19th day of November, 1844, granted to the said debtor a discharge from imprisonment and appointed the first Saturday after the 3rd Monday in May next, for his appearance before the Judges of Harford county court at the court house of said county, for a final hearing before said court, on said petition and to answer such interrogatories as his creditors may propose to him." (*Harford Madisonian and Bel-Air & Havre de Grace Messenger*, January 3, 1845, p. 3). **Genealogical Notes**: James W. Keen, of Harford Co., married Miss Anna Keen, of Baltimore Co., on December 4, 1823 by Rev. Healy (*Baltimore Patriot*, December 5, 1823). Ann M. Keen (1793 – February 15, 1854) and James W. Keen (December 13, 1800, Rock Run – September 12, 1880, Havre de Grace), who worked as a blacksmith and later as a butcher, were buried in Rock Run Methodist Church Cemetery (tombstones; *The Aegis & Intelligencer*, September 17, 1880).

Kemp, Nard, 1895. "Mr. Nard Kemp, druggist at Darlington, made application on Wednesday [January 9, 1895] for the benefit of the insolvent laws. Mr. J. Royston Stifler was appointed preliminary trustee." (*The Aegis & Intelligencer*, January 11, 1895, p. 2). "Notice to Creditors. In the matter of the Insolvency of Nard Kemp ... This is to give notice to the creditors of Nard Kemp, of Harford County, an insolvent debtor, of the pendency of proceedings in insolvency, in relation to his estate, and that Friday, January 18th, 1895 at 10 o'clock, A. M., at the office of J. Royston Stifler, in Bel Air, Md., is the time and place fixed for a meeting of the creditors of said insolvent to choose a permanent trustee or trustees for said estate and other business. J. Royston Stifler, Preliminary Trustee." (*The Aegis & Intelligencer*, January 11, 1895, p. 2). "Insolvency Notice ... By virtue of an order of said Court, passed on the 11th day of February, 1895, notice is hereby given that the 13th day of May, 1895, is fixed as the day for said Nard Kemp, insolvent, to appear in said Court, to answer such interrogatories or allegations as his creditors, endorsers or sureties may propose or allege against him. J. Royston Stifler, Permanent Trustee." (*The Aegis & Intelligencer*, February 22, 1895, p. 1). "Notice to Creditors ... Notice is hereby given to all creditors of Nard Kemp, who were such on the 8th day of January, 1895, to file their claims, duly proven with the Clerk of the Circuit Court for Harford County, on or before the 1st day of May, 1895. J. Royston Stifler, Permanent Trustee." (*The Aegis & Intelligencer*, February 22, 1895, p. 1)

Kennard, Isaac, 1822. "Petition, Schedule, Bond, Sheriff's certificate, personal discharge and order for publication filed 1st July 1822 – allegations filed 15th March 1823, petitioner appears 15th March and prays a continuance, which is granted. 30th Aug. 1823 Petitioner appears and continued. March 13th 1824 petitioner appears and continued. August 14th 1824 Petitioner appears and allegations withdrawn and petitioner discharged." (Insolvent Docket A, 1807-1843, p. 50, at the Maryland State Archives; Insolvent Docket Prior to 1827, Court Records Accession #632 at the Historical Society of Harford County)

Kerr, Edward, 1832. "Petition, Schedule, Affidavit, Personal discharge, and Order for Publication, Bond for Appearance, Trustee's Bond, Trustee's Certificate and Deed to Trustee filed 7th November 1832. 16th March 1833 Additional schedule filed. 4th Novr. 1833 Order for Sale filed. 14th March 1835 Trustee's Report filed ... 13th August 1836 ... Auditor's Report and Order of Confirmation filed. Recorded in Judgment Record A. L. J. No. 1, folio 348." (Insolvent Docket A, 1807-1843, p. 122, at the Maryland State Archives). **Genealogical Note**: Edward Kerr married Lucinda McGriger circa December 19, 1810 (date of license).

Kinsey, Elam and Seth L., 1890. "Elam Kinsey and Seth L. Kinsey, trading as Elam Kinsey & Son, of the fifth district, have applied for the benefit of the insolvent laws." (*Havre de Grace Republican*, August 29, 1890, p. 3)

Kinszel, Charles, 1810. "Whereas we the subscribers Justices of the Peace for Harford County, upon the petition of Charles Kinszel, who set forth that he had been confined [in jail] twenty days and upwards for debts which he was unable to pay and finding the facts stated to be true we did meet at the gaol of said county on the 14th Day of June last and did then and there appoint the 16th day of July Instant to meet at the Court house of said county which said appointment we did then and there … at the request of the said Sheriff administer to the said Charles Kinszel the following oath which was taken by the said Charles Kinszel being first duly sworn on the holy Evangely of Almighty God in the words following, to wit, I Charles Kinszel do solemnly swear that the schedule which I have delivered to the Sheriff of Harford County doth contain a full account to the best of my knowledge and remembrance of my whole estate both real and personal or that I have any title to or interest in and of all debts, credits and effects whatsoever which I or any in trust for me have or at the time of my petition had, or am or was in any respect entitled to in possession, remainder or reversion and that I have not directly or indirectly at any time since my imprisonment or before, sold, leased or otherwise conveyed or disposed of or intrusted all or any part of my estate, goods, stock, money or debts thereby to defraud my creditors or to secure the same to receive or expect any profit or advantage thereof so help me God, which said duplicate of the schedule aforesaid we have transmitted to the clerk of the county court to be by him preserved in his office for the information of the creditors of the said Charles Kinszel. Given under our hands and seals this 16th Day of July 1810. Thomas A. Hays. Jno. C. Bond." (Court Records Document 67.15.6(a) at the Historical Society of Harford County; a copy of the schedule was included to which "Charels Kenzel" signed his name, but no property was listed). **Genealogical Note**: Charles Kinszil married Ann Johnson on February 8, 1798 (St. James Parish Register; St. John's Parish Register spelled his name Kinzell).

Kirk, John R., 1857. "Petition, Schedules, Affidavits, Appointment of Trustee," etc. 16 Jany/57. 16 May/57 Petitioner appears, files certificate of publication and finally discharged." (Insolvent Docket A. L. J. No. 1, p. 15, in the Court Records Department of the Historical Society of Harford County). "Notice is hereby given that John R. Kirk, of Harford County, has made application to the Circuit Court of said County, for the benefit of the Insolvent Laws of Maryland, and that the first Saturday after the second Monday in May next has been assigned for him to appear in said Court to answer such interrogatories as his creditors may propose or allege against him. A. Lingan Jarrett, Clerk." (*Harford Democrat*, February 27, 1857, p. 3) **Genealogical Notes**: John R. Kirk was a school teacher in Harford County who later worked as a book keeper in Louisville, KY. He was never married and died on August 29, 1892, age 66, in Churchville at the home of Dr. Thomas H. Roberts (1840-1927) whose wife Susanna Davis (1835-1915) was Kirk's half sister. They are all buried in Churchville Presbyterian Church cemetery. (*The Aegis & Intelligencer*, September 2, 1892, p. 3; tombstones)

Kirwan, E. F., Company, 1895. "The E. F. Kirwan Company, of Baltimore, a tin can manufacturing firm well known to many Harford packers, made an assignment last Saturday [November 9, 1895]. Insolvency was alleged by creditors, and admitted. Messrs. Jas. H. Preston and D. L. Brinton are receivers, and gave bond in the sum of $70,000 each. Mr. Edgar F. Kirwan also made an individual assignment. A note for $1,500, purporting to be signed by Mr. John Finney Wells, of Aberdeen, and one for $1,050, with the name of Mr. Conrad Krouse, of Aberdeen, as endorser, and made payable to Mr. E. F. Kirwan, have been presented to our county banks for payment, and pronounced forgeries by both these gentlemen. There are said to be $15,000 of forged paper placed through this same channel." (*Havre de Grace Republican*, November 16, 1895, p. 3)

Knellinger, George, 1873. "Petition, 3 Schedules, Affidavit, Order, Trustee's Bond & Deed filed 26th May 1873. 8th September 1873 Petitioner appears in Court, files Certificate of Publication & is finally discharged by the Court." (Insolvent Docket A. L. J. No. 1, p. 58, in the Court Records Department of the Historical Society of Harford County). "Notice is hereby given that George Knellinger has made application to the Circuit Court of Harford county, for the benefit of the Insolvent Laws of Maryland, and that the 8th day of September, 1873 has been assigned for him to appear in said Court to answer such interrogatories as his creditors may propose or allege against him. A. L. Jarrett, Clerk." (*Harford Democrat*, May 30, 1873, p. 2). **Genealogical Notes**: George Knellinger (born 1827, Bavaria – June 3, 1883) married Elizabeth ---- (March 16, 1836 – December 12, 1921) circa 1852 and worked as a shoemaker in Forest Hill. Their children in 1860 were George H. Knellinger (age 7), William F. Knellinger (age 6), C. Edward Knellinger (September 15, 1856 – May 18, 1945) married Frances Carr on September 2, 1878, and Laura Knellinger (age 1), all born in Maryland. They also had a son David Knellinger (1861-1885). (1860 Harford County Census; 1878 marriage record; Mountain Christian Church Cemetery tombstone inscriptions)

Lake, Amos, 1823. "Petition, Schedule, Bond, Sheriff certificate and personal discharge and order for publication filed 15th day of November 1823. Certificate of publication of notice filed. March 13th 1824 Petitioner appears and discharged." [nothing further recorded] (Insolvent Docket A, 1807-1843, p. 59, at the Maryland State Archives; Insolvent Docket Prior to 1827, Court Records Accession #632 at the Historical Society of Harford County)

Lamborn, Daniel, 1817. "Petition, Schedule, Bond and Notice to Creditors filed 10th Decr. 1817 – Decr. 20th 1817 the Court appoints Jason Moore, trustee, and ordered to give Bond in $5000 penalty ... March 13th 1818 the petitioner appeared in Court ..." [list of creditors, nothing further recorded] (Insolvent Docket A, 1807-1843, p. 22, at Maryland State Archives; Insolvent Docket Prior to 1827, Court Records Accession #632 at Historical Society of Harford County). **Genealogical Notes**: Daniel Lamborn was born in 1777, came to Harford County from Kennett Twp., PA, married Elizabeth ----, possibly Elizabeth Smith, circa 1800 and a son John Smith Lamborn was born on the 2nd day of the 2nd month, 1801. He acquired a mill on Winters Run near Bel Air in 1808, signed a promissory note to Buckler Bond and proceeded to manufacture paper for several years. Faced with indebtedness in 1817 and in default of his promissory note, Bond brought suit to sell the land that was eventually acquired by Thomas A. Hays in 1818. Daniel continued to operate Lamborn's Mill, also known as Laurel Paper Mill, under the obligation of paying Hays $125.00 every three months. By 1831 Hays had taken possession of the property and "Lamborn removed to the vicinity of Elkridge, which is the last trace we have of him." (*Heavy Industries of Yesteryear: Harford County's Rural Heritage*, by Jack L. Shagena, Jr. and Henry C. Peden, Jr., 2015, pp. 171-173; *American Paper Mills, 1690-1832*, by John Bidwell (Hanover, NH: Dartmouth College Press, 2012), p. 232; Little Falls Quaker Records; *Harford Historical Bulletin No. 31*, 1987; Court Records Documents 55.23.1(H) and 82.19.2(F) in the Court Records Department at the Historical Society of Harford County)

Lancaster, William E., 1837. "Petition, Affidavits, Schedule, personal discharge and order of publication, Bond for Appearance, Trustee's Bond, Trustee's Certificate and Deed to Trustee filed 16th June 1837. 17th March 1838 Petitioner appears, certificate of publication filed and finally discharged." (Insolvent Docket A, 1807-1843, p. 156, at Maryland State Archives). 1839. "Petition, Schedule, Affidavits, personal discharge and order of publication, Bond for Appearance, Trustee's Bond, Trustee's Certificate and Deed to Trustee filed 21st June 1839. Novr. 23rd 1839 Petitioner appears and discharged." (Insolvent Docket A, 1807-1843, p. 170, at the Maryland State Archives). 1841. "Petition, 3 Schedules, 2 Affidavits, personal discharge, Certificate, Appearance Bond, Trustee Bond & Deed filed 8th July 1841. Novr. 20th 1841 Petitioner appears and Certificate of Publication filed & finally discharged." (Insolvent Docket A, 1807-1843, p. 178, at the Maryland State Archives). **Genealogical Note**: William E. Lancaster was deposed on December 19, 1829, aged 24 years and upwards, thus born in 1805. (Court Records Document 89.01.1(M) at the Historical Society of Harford County)

Lee, John, 1802. Petitioned for relief under the act for relief of sundry Insolvent Debtors (*Laws of Maryland*, Vol. III, 1802, Chapter 97, Liber JG No. 4, folio 308-314)

Lee, Washington, 1808. "Petition, Schedule & Bond filed 17th August 1808." [nothing further recorded] (Insolvent Docket A, 1807-1843, p. 3, at the Maryland State Archives; Insolvent Docket Prior to 1827, Court Records Accession #632 at the Historical Society of Harford County)

Leleve, Charles A., 1821. "Petition, Schedule, Bond, Sheriff's certificate, personal discharge and order for publication filed 2nd June 1821 – 15th March 1822 petitioner appeared ... Court appoints Henry Scarff Trustee." [nothing further recorded] (Insolvent Docket A, 1807-1843, p. 45, at the Maryland State Archives; Insolvent Docket Prior to 1827, Court Records Accession #632 at the Historical Society of Harford County)

Lewis, Edward I., 1831. "Petition, Schedule, Sheriff's Certificate, personal discharge and Order for Publication, Bond for Appearance, Trustee's Bond, Trustee's Certificate and Deed to Trustee filed the 16th January 1832. 18th Augt. 1832 Petitioner appears, certificate of publication filed, and finally discharged." (Insolvent Docket A, 1807-1843, p. 114, at the Maryland State Archives)

Lilly, James R., 1880. "Application for benefit of Insolvent Laws, Schedules, Affidavit, Order of Appearance, Trustee's bond & deed filed 10th April 1880. 13th Sept. 1880 Certificate of pub. on notice filed & Petitioner finally discharged." (Insolvent Docket A. L. J. No. 1, p. 69, in Court Records Department of the Historical Society of Harford County). "Notice is hereby given that James R. Lilly, of Harford county, has made application to the Circuit Court for said county for the benefit of the Insolvent Laws of Maryland, and that the second Monday of September, 1880 has been assigned for him to appear in said Court to answer such interrogatories as his creditors may propose or allege against him. A. Lingan Jarrett, Clerk, Circuit Court for Harford county." (*The Aegis & Intelligencer*, May 7, 1880, p. 3). **Genealogical Notes**: James Robert Lilly was born on October 30, 1832, married Sarah H. Divers (born circa 1835) circa December 28, 1854, worked as a farmer and died on September 30, 1918 in Havre de Grace. Their children in 1860 were Susan A. Lilly (age 4), Adaline Lilly (age 2), and Robert H. Lilly (1859-1934). (Harford Co. marriage license; 1860 Harford Co. Census; Smith's Chapel tombstones; Death certificate of James Robert Lilly stated he was a widower and the informant, George A. Davis, did not know parents' names, but father was born in Ireland)

Loflin, Albert, 1885. A deed "of trust for the benefit of creditors" [under Insolvent Laws of the State of Maryland] has "lately been filed in the clerk's office [for] Wm. Maxwell and Albert Loflin, canners, to A. P. Gilbert." (*The Aegis & Intelligencer*, November 20, 1885, p. 2). "Insolvent Notice. In the Matter of the Insolvency of Albert Loflin ... Notice is hereby given to the creditors of Albert Loflin, of Harford county, that he has applied for the benefit of the Insolvent Laws of the State of Maryland, and that a meeting of the creditors of the said Loflin will be held in my office, in the town of Bel Air, on Friday, March 14, 1886, at 10 o'clock, A. M., for the purpose of electing a permanent trustee for the estate of the said insolvent. Septimus Davis, Preliminary Trustee." (*Bel Air Times*, May 7, 1886, p. 3). "Notice to Creditors. The creditors of Albert Loflin, an insolvent debtor, are hereby notified to file their claims against said insolvent, duly authenticated, with the Clerk of the Circuit Court for Harford county on or before the 1st day of September, in the year 1886. Septimus Davis, Permanent Trustee." (*Bel Air Times*, June 4, 1886, p. 3). **Genealogical Notes**: Albert Loflin (1847 – January 10, 1915), son of John Smith Loflin (born 1817) and Ellen Bailey (born 1820), married Fannie M. Jewens (1852-1881), all of Harford Co., on May 20, 1874 by Rev. S. A. Hoblitzell at the Hopewell Methodist Protestant Church and worked as a farmer at Aberdeen. (Marriage records stated he was age 27 and she was age 21; *The Aegis and Intelligencer*, 29 May 1874; Informant for the death certificate of Albert Loflin was Edgar Loflin who stated Albert was born -- July 1848 and died at age 66 years and 6 months, but his tombstone at Rock Run United Methodist Church Cemetery is inscribed 1847-1915)

Loflin, William, 1844. "Notice Is Hereby Given, to the creditors of William Loflin, late an imprisoned debtor of Harford county, that on the application of said debtor by petition in writing to the Hon. Robert W. Holland, chief justice of the Orphan's court of said county, for the benefit of the insolvent laws of Maryland, the said judge on the 9th day of July, 1844, granted to the said debtor a discharge from imprisonment and appointed the first Saturday after the 3rd Monday in November next, for his appearance before the Judges of Harford county court at the court house of said county, for a final hearing before said court, on said petition and to answer such interrogatories as his creditors may propose to him." (*Harford Madisonian and Bel-Air & Havre de Grace Messenger*, October 18, 1844, p. 3). **Genealogical Notes**: William Loflin (October 20, 1804 – May 22, 1882) married Emily B. Bailey (May 13, 1812 – April 4, 1890), daughter of Aquila Bailey and Martha Evans, on April 21, 1831 by Rev. William Finney. Children buried next to them are Mary Martha Loflin (1834-1834), Alice E. Loflin (1850-1851), Martha Rebecca Loflin (1855-1857), and Charles Alfred Loflin (1857-1858). The obituary of Emily Loflin stated she died at the home of her daughter Mrs. William Chesney, near Churchville, and survived by two sons and four daughters, but no names were given. (*The Aegis & Intelligencer*, April 11, 1890; *Independent Citizen*, April 1831; Marriage license misspelled his name as Lofflin; Churchville Presbyterian Church Register of Communicants; Deer Creek Harmony Presbyterian Church tombstone inscriptions; *Barnes-Bailey Genealogy*, by Walter D. Barnes, 1939, p. G-18)

Long, Peter, 1805. "Whereas we the subscribers Justices of the Peace for Harford County together with Thomas A. Hays, Esq., also one of the Justices of the Peace for said County, upon the petition of Peter Long, who set forth that he had been confined [in jail] twenty days for debts which he was unable to pay and finding the facts stated to be true we together with Thomas A. Hays, Esq. we did meet at the gaol of said county on the 8th day of April 1805 and did then and there appoint the 9th day of May Instant to meet at the Court House of said county which said appointment we did then and there ... at the request of the said Sheriff administer to the said Peter Long the following oath which was taken by the said Peter Long being first duly sworn on the holy Evangely of Almighty God in the words following, I Peter Long do solemnly swear that the schedule which I have delivered to the Sheriff of Harford County doth contain a full account to the best of my knowledge and remembrance of my whole estate both real & personal or that I have any title to or interest in and of all debts, credits and effects whatsoever which I or any in trust for me have or at the time of my petition had, or am or was in any respect entitled to in possession, remainder or reversion and that I have not directly or indirectly at any time since my imprisonment or before, sold, leased or otherwise conveyed or disposed of or intrusted all or any part of my estate, goods, stock, money or debts thereby to defraud my creditors or to secure the same to receive or expect any profit or advantage thereof so help me God, which said duplicate of the schedule aforesaid we have transmitted to the clerk of the county court to be by him preserved in his office for the information of the creditors of the said Peter Long. Given under our hands and seals this 9th Day of May Anno Domini Eighteen hundred and five. Wm. Smithson. John Moores." (Court Records Document 67.18.5(1st) at the Historical Society of Harford County; copy of the schedule to which "Peter Long" signed his name was included, but no property was listed)

Love, Jacob, 1810. "Petition, Schedule, Bond, &c. filed 25th June 1810. Order for publication filed 18th Augt." [nothing further recorded]. (Insolvent Docket A, 1807-1843, p. 6, at the Maryland State Archives; Insolvent Docket Prior to 1827, Court Records Accession #632 at the Historical Society of Harford County). **Genealogical Note**: Jacob Love, a son of John Love and Margaret Preston, married

Mary ----, possibly Mary Smithson, daughter of Thomas Smithson, in 1800. (Court Record, c1819, Historical Society of Harford County; *Harford Historical Bulletin No. 11*, Spring-Summer 1977, p. 44)

Love, James, 1823. "Petition, Schedule, Certificate of Residence, Shff's Certificate, bond, personal discharge and order for publication filed 10th July 1823. March 14th 1824 Petioner [Petitioner] appears and continued." [nothing further recorded] (Insolvent Docket A, 1807-1843, p. 56, at the Maryland State Archives; Insolvent Docket Prior to 1827, Court Records Accession #632 at the Historical Society of Harford County). **Genealogical Note**: James Love, a son of John Love and Margaret Preston, served as a private in the War of 1812 and died after April 26, 1848 when last seen by Dr. Matthew J. Allen. (*Genealogical Gleanings from Harford County, Maryland Medical Records, 1772-1852*, by Henry C. Peden, Jr., 2016, p. 119; *Harford Historical Bulletin No. 11*, Spring-Summer 1977, p. 44)

Love, John, 1829. "Petition, Schedule, Certificate of Sheriff, personal discharge, Order for Publication, Bond for Appearance, Trustee's Bond, Trustee's Certificate and Deed to Trustee filed 4th July 1829. 13th March 1830 Petitioner appears and motion to withdraw petition." (Insolvent Docket A, 1807-1843, p. 97, at the Maryland State Archives). **Genealogical Note**: John Love, a son of John Love and Margaret Preston, married Susannah Green circa November 8, 1791 (date of license; *Harford Historical Bulletin No. 11*, Spring-Summer 1977, p. 44)

Mackin, Joseph, 1884. "Aug 9th 1884. Petition, Schedule, Order, Trustee's Bond & Insolvent Deed filed." [nothing further recorded] (Insolvent Docket A. L. J. No. 1, p. 86, in the Court Records Department of the Historical Society of Harford County). **Genealogical Note**: There was a Joseph L. Mackin, formerly of Havre de Grace, who was warden of the Baltimore County Jail by 1892 at which time he was very ill and suffering with typhoid fever. (*Havre de Grace Republican*, October 7, 1892)

Magness, Samuel, 1811. "Whereas we the subscribers Justices of the Peace for Harford County upon the petition of Samuel Magnes [sic] who set forth therein that he had been confined twenty days and upwards for debts which he was unable to pay and finding the facts stated to be true we did meet at the Goal [jail] of said county on the 25th of January last and did then and there appoint the 25th day of February Instant to meet at the court house of said county which said appointment we did then and there … at the request of the said Sheriff administer to the said Samuel Magnes [sic] the following oath which was taken by the said Samuel Magnes [sic] being first duly sworn on the holy Evangely of Almighty God in the words following to wit, I do solemnly swear that the schedule which I have delivered to the Sheriff of Harford County doth contain a full account to the best of my knowledge and remembrance of my whole estate both real & personal or that I have any title to or interest in and of all Debts, credits and effects whatsoever which I or any in trust for me have or at the time of my petition had, or am or was in any respect entitled to in possession, remainder or reversion and that I have not directly or indirectly at any time since my Imprisonment or before, Sold, leased or otherwise conveyed or disposed of or intrusted all or any part of my estate, goods, stock, money or Debts thereby to defraud my creditors or to secure the same to receive or expect any profit or advantage thereof so help me God, which said duplicate of the Schedule aforesaid we have transmitted to the Clerk of the County Court to be by him Preserved in his Office for the information of the Creditors of the said Samuel Magnes [sic]. Given under our hands and seals this 25th Day of February Eighteen hundred and Eleven. Saml. Bradford. John Moores. Thomas A. Hays." (Court Records Document 67.20.2(B) at the Historical Society of Harford County; a copy of the schedule was included to which "Samuel Magness" signed his name, but no property was listed). 1820. Samuel Magness. "Petition, Schedule, Bond, Order for publication, and personal discharge filed 8th January 1820. March 18th 1820 petitioner appeared." [nothing further recorded] (Insolvent Docket A, 1807-1843, p. 27, at the Maryland State Archives; Insolvent Docket Prior to 1827, Court Records

Accession #632 at the Historical Society of Harford County). **Genealogical Note**: Samuel Magness married Elizabeth Flanagan circa April 8, 1805 (date of license).

Magness, Thomas, 1820. "Petition, Schedule, Bond, Sheriff's certificate, personal discharge and order for publication filed 26th Sept. 1820. March 17th 1821 petitioner appeared, filed certificate of publication and Thomas A. Hays appointed Trustee and personal discharge granted the petitioner." (Insolvent Docket A, 1807-1843, p. 37, at Maryland State Archives; Insolvent Docket Prior to 1827, Court Records Accession #632 at the Historical Society of Harford County). **Genealogical Note**: Thomas Magness married Jemima Rockhold on December 22, 1803 (*Maryland Bible Records, Volume 1*, by Henry C. Peden, Jr., 2003, p. 149) and Thomas Magness married Mary Lee circa October 15, 1811 (date of license). It is possible that this was the same man, but additional research will be necessary.

Markland, Charles E., 1834. "Petition, Affidavits, Schedules, personal discharge and order of Publication, Appointment and Certificate of Trustee, Bond for Appearance, Trustee's Bond and Deed to Trustee filed 18th March 1834. 16th Augt. 1834 Petitioner appears, Certificate of Publication filed and finally discharged. 16th August 1837 Short copy of Judgment and Affidavit filed ... [two claims were filed] ... 30th Augt. 1838 Trustee's report, certificate of printer's order for reference to Auditor, Auditor's report and order of confirmation nisi filed." (Insolvent Docket A, 1807-1843, p. 132, at the Maryland State Archives)

Martin, Abraham, 1829. Insolvent debtor to be discharged from imprisonment. (*Independent Citizen*, May 14, 1829). "Petition, Schedule, Certificate of Sheriff, personal discharge, order for publication, Bond for Appearance, Trustee's Bond and deed to Trustee filed 7th March 1829. 15th August 1829 Petitioner appears and certificate filed. 17th March 1831 Petitioner appears and finally discharged." (Insolvent Docket A, 1807-1843, p. 94, at Maryland State Archives). **Genealogical Notes**: Abraham Martin was born on April 8, 1788, served in the War of 1812, married Mary Magness (November 3, 1793 – February 17, 1842) on September 26, 1816, received pension SC-11351, died on February 6, 1872 and was buried in Cokesbury Memorial Methodist Church Cemetery. The children of Abraham and Mary Martin were S. Jane Martin, Susan Anne Martin (married Thomas H. Magness in 1841), Clara or Clarissa Martin, and Mary Martin. (tombstones and military records; *Maryland Bible Records, Volume 1*, by Henry C. Peden, Jr., 2003, pp. 160-161)

Martin, John, 1821. "Petition, Schedule, Bond, Sheriff's certificate, personal discharge and order for publication filed 3rd March 1821 – 1st September 1821 John Martin appeared in Court & cont'd. 16th March 1822 petitioner appeared in Court & cont'd." [nothing further recorded] (Insolvent Docket A, 1807-1843, p. 43, at the Maryland State Archives; Insolvent Docket Prior to 1827, Court Records Accession #632 at the Historical Society of Harford County). 1837. "Petition, Affidavits, Schedule, personal discharge and order of publication, Bond for Appearance, Trustee's Bond, Trustee's Certificate and Deed to Trustee filed 4th Augt. 1837. 17th March 1838 Certificate of publication filed. Petitioner appears & finally discharged." (Insolvent Docket A, 1807-1843, p. 157, at the Maryland State Archives)

Martin, Robert, 1858. "Petition, Schedule of property, List of debts due & owing to & from, Affidavit, Order & Appointment of Daniel Scott Trustee, Trustee's Bond and Deed to Trustee filed 18th day of October 1858. 30th April 1859 Petitioner appears, files certificate of publication & finally discharged." (Insolvent Docket A. L. J. No. 1, p. 24, in the Court Records Department of the Historical Society of Harford County). "Notice is hereby given that Robert Martin, of Harford County, has made application to the Circuit Court of said County, for the benefit of the Insolvent Laws of Maryland, and that the 1st Saturday after the 4th Monday in February, 1859, has been assigned for him to appear in said Court to answer such interrogatories as his creditors may propose or allege against him. Wm. Galloway, Clerk, Circuit Court for Harford County." (*The Southern Aegis*, August 23, 1858, p. 3)

"Trustee's Sale. The undersigned, trustee of Robert Martin, an Insolvent Debtor, will sell at public sale, at the residence of the said Martin, on Saturday, the 6th day of November, at 10 o'clock, the following Personal Property and Effects, to wit: 1 two-horse Wagon, 2 double Shovels, 1 hinge Harrow, &c. Terms of sale cash. Dan Scott, Trustee." (*The Southern Aegis*, October 30, 1858, p. 3) **Genealogical Note**: Robert Martin married Susan McComas circa October 29, 1830 (date of license).

Martin, Samuel, 1825. "Petition, Schedule, Bond, Sheriffs Certificate and personal discharge and order for publication filed 15th day of November 1825. March 18th 1826 Certificate of publication filed. Petitioner appears by O. [Otho] Scott atty., continued by consent. Allegations filed. 19th Augt. 1826 Petitioner appears and cont'd. 17th March 1827 Petitioner appears, answers to interrogatories filed and petitioner discharged." (Insolvent Docket A, 1807-1843, at Maryland State Archives; Insolvent Docket Prior to 1827, Court Records Accession #632 at the Historical Society of Harford County, slightly differs in wording and contains less information than Insolvent Docket A)

Massey, John, 1810. "Whereas we the subscribers, Justices of the Peace for Harford County upon the petition of John Massey, who set forth that he had been confined in the goal [jail] of said county twenty days for debts which he was unable to pay and finding the facts stated to be true we did meet at the county gaol of sd. county on the 19th day of March last and did then and there appoint the 19th day of April Instant to meet at the Court House of said county which said appointment we did then and there ... at the request of the said Sheriff administer to the said John Massey the following oath which was taken by the said John Massey being first duly sworn on the holy Evangely of Almighty God in the words following, to wit, I do solemnly, sincerely & truly declare & affirm that the schedule which I have delivered to the Sheriff of Harford County doth contain a full account to the best of my knowledge and remembrance of my whole estate both real & personal or that I have any title to or interest in and of all debts, credits and effects whatsoever which I or any in trust for me have or at the time of my petition had, or am or was in any respect entitled to in possession, remainder or reversion and that I have not directly or indirectly at any time since my imprisonment or before, sold, leased or otherwise conveyed or disposed of or intrusted all or any part of my estate, goods, stock, money or debts thereby to defraud my creditors or to secure the same to receive or expect any profit or advantage thereof, which said duplicate of the schedule aforesaid we have transmitted to the clerk of the county court to be by him preserved in his office for the information of the creditors of the said John Massey. Given under our hands and seals this 19th Day of April Eighteen hundred and ten. Thomas A. Hays. Jno. C. Bond. Samuel Bradford." (Court Records Document 67.10.7(A) at the Historical Society of Harford County; a copy of the schedule to which "John Massey" signed his name was included, but no property was listed) **Genealogical Notes**: John Massey and Ann Birckhead obtained a marriage license on November 24, 1798, but did not marry at that time. They obtained another license on December 9, 1802 and were married by Rev. Wilmer. (Harford County marriage licenses; *Baltimore Federal Gazette* on January 4, 1803 reported "Mr. Massey and Miss Burkhead married lately in Harford Co.")

Mathews, Josiah (Josias), 1829. Insolvent debtor to be discharged from imprisonment. (*Independent Citizen*, December 3, 1829). "Petition, Schedule, Shff's. Certificate, personal discharge, Order for Publication, Bond for Appearance, Trustee's Certificate, Trustee's Bond and Deed to Trustee filed 30th Octr. 1829. 13th March 1830 Certificate of Publication filed & Petitioner appears. 15th March 1830 Oath administered and petitioner discharged. 9th June 1834 petition and order appointing Otho Scott Trustee ... 31st May 1836 Auditor's Report and Order of Confirmation Nisi filed. Recorded in Judgment Record A. L. J. No. 1, folio 219." (Insolvent Docket A, 1807-1843, p. 100, at the Maryland State Archives). **Genealogical Note**: Josiah Matthews married Jane Forwood on January 19, 1792 by Rev. John Ireland. (Scharf Papers, Harford County Returns of Ministers to Treasurer, Maryland State

Archives, published in *Harford County, Maryland Marriage Licenses, 1777-1865*, by Jon Harlan Livezey and Helene Maynard Davis, 1993, p. 274)

Mathews, Lloyd, 1829. Insolvent debtor to be discharged from imprisonment. (*Independent Citizen*, December 3, 1829)

Maulsby (Malsby), David, 1833. "Petition, Schedule, Affidavit, Personal discharge, and Order for Publication, Bond for Appearance, Trustee's Bond, Trustee's Certificate and Deed to Trustee filed 1st March 1833. 17th August 1833 Petitioner appears, Certificate of Publication filed, Interrogatories filed – Interrogatories answered and petitioner finally discharged." (Insolvent Docket A, 1807-1843, p. 124, at the Maryland State Archives). **Genealogical Notes**: David Maulsby, son of John and Mary Maulsby, married Mary Coale, daughter of Samuel and Lydia Coale, on the 2nd day of the 10th month 1806 at Deer Creek Monthly Meeting. (Deer Creek Quaker Records spelled his name Malsby)

Maulsby, Israel D., 1827. "Petition, Schedule, Bond, Sheriff's certificate and personal discharge and order for publication filed and Bond of provisional trustee filed and certificate for Trustee filed 11th August – 22nd Augt. 1827 the petitioner having taken the insolvent's oath is personally discharged … 15th March 1828 personally appeared … O. [Otho] Scott appointed Trustee and Bond filed and a personal discharged granted. 2nd June 1828 Petitioner appears & order for final discharge filed – 25th Augt. 1828 order for sale filed. 24th Augt. 1833 petition and order of sale filed." [nothing further] (Insolvent Docket A, 1807-1843, p. 85, at the Maryland State Archives). **Genealogical Notes**: Israel D. Maulsby was an attorney who married Jane Hall, daughter of John and Susannah Hall, on February 9, 1806 by Rev. John Coleman. He died on June 14, 1839, age 58, and she died on January 14, 1864, age 75. (St. James Parish Register; *Baltimore American*, February 21, 1806; Christ Church tombstones)

Maulsby (Malsby), Morris, 1836. "Petition, Affidavit, Schedule, personal discharge and order of publication, Bond for Appearance, Trustee's Bond, Trustee's Certificate and Deed to Trustee filed 8th August 1836. 18th March 1837 Petitioner appears, certificate of publication filed. Interrogatories filed. Judgment that Morris Maulsby is guilty of fraud in conveying to his son Lee Maulsby his real & personal estate, and that he forever be precluded from obtaining the benefit of the Insolvent laws of this State." (Insolvent Docket A, 1807-1843, p. 152, at Maryland State Archives). 1838. "Petition, Schedule, Affidavits, personal discharge and order of publication, Bond for Appearance, Trustee's Bond, Trustee's Certificate and Deed to Trustee filed 1st March 1838. 24th Novr. 1838 Petitioner appears, certificate of publication filed, & petitioner discharged." (Insolvent Docket A, 1807-1843, p. 164, at the Maryland State Archives). **Genealogical Note**: Morris Maulsby married Mary Lee on March 16, 1802. (St. George's Parish Register; marriage license spelled his name Malsby)

Maxwell, Walter S., 1885. "Nov 16th 1885. Petition, Schedules, Order, Insolvent's Deed & Preliminary Trustee's Bond approved & filed … Feby 8/86 Certificate of Publication of Notice to Insolvent to appear & answer interrogatories & Final Discharge of Insolvent filed … 6th July 1886 Final order filed." [nothing further recorded] (Insolvent Docket A. L. J. No. 1, p. 103, in the Court Records Department of the Historical Society of Harford County). "Insolvent Notice. Notice is hereby given to the creditors of Walter S. Maxwell, that he has made application for the benefit of the insolvent laws of the State of Maryland, and that a meeting of said creditors will be held at my office, in Bel Air, on Wednesday, the 25th day of November, 1885, at 12 o'clock, M., to choose a permanent trustee of the estate of said Walter S. Maxwell. A. Preston Gilbert, Preliminary Trustee." (*Harford Democrat*, November 20, 1885, p. 2). "Walter S. Maxwell, canner, has applied for the benefit of the insolvent laws, A. Preston Gilbert being preliminary trustee." (*The Aegis & Intelligencer*, November 20, 1885, p. 2; and, *Havre de Grace Republican*, November 27, 1885, p. 4). "In the matter of the Insolvency of Walter S. Maxwell … Notice is hereby given to Walter S. Maxwell, an insolvent debtor, to appear in said Court on the second Monday in February, 1886, to answer such interrogatories or allegations as his creditors, endorsers or sureties may propose or allege against him, and all creditors of said Maxwell are notified of the time aforesaid. A. Preston Gilbert, Permanent Trustee." (*Harford Democrat*, December 18, 1885, p. 3)

Maxwell, William, 1885. A deed "of trust for the benefit of creditors" [under the Insolvent Laws of the State of Maryland] has "lately been filed in the clerk's office [for] Wm. Maxwell and Albert Loflin, canners, to A. P. Gilbert." (*The Aegis & Intelligencer*, November 20, 1885, p. 2)

McCann, Charles A. L., 1871. "Petition, Schedules, Affidavit, Order, Trustee's Bond & Deed filed 21 March/71." [nothing further recorded] (Insolvent Docket A. L. J. No. 1, p. 54, in the Court Records Department of the Historical Society of Harford County)

McCaskey, Benjamin, 1816. "Whereas we the subscribers Justices of the Peace for Harford County upon the petition of Benjamin McCaskey stating therein that he had actually been confined in the gaol [jail] of said county since the nineteenth day of July last for debts which he was unable to pay and finding the facts therein stated to be true we did on the ninth day of July 1816 appoint the tenth day of August instant to meet at the Courthouse of said county which said appointment we did then and there … at the Request of the said Sheriff administer to the said Benjamin McCaskey the following oath which was taken by the said Benjamin McCaskey being first duly sworn on the Holy Evangely of Almighty God in the words following, to wit: I, Benjamin McCaskey do solemnly promise and swear that the Schedule which I have delivered to the Sheriff of Harford County doth contain a full account to the best of my knowledge and rembrance of my whole estate both real and personal or that I have any title to, or interest in, and of all debts, credits and effects whatsoever which I or any in trust for me, have or at the time of my petition had, or now or was in any respect entitled to in possession, remainder or reversion and that I have not directly or indirectly at any time since my imprisonment or before, sold, leased or otherwise conveyed or disposed of or intrusted all or any part of my estate, goods, stock, money or debts thereby to defraud his creditors or to secure the same to receive or expect any profit or advantage thereof, so help me God. Which said duplicate of the schedule aforesaid we have transmitted to the Clerk of the County Court to be by him preserved in his office for the information of the creditors of the said Benjamin McCaskey. Given under our hands ands seals this --- [blank] day of August 1816." [document was not signed] The schedule was dated August 10, 1816 and was signed by James Wallace, Benjn. Richardson and Joseph Robinson. (Court Records Document 67.02.6(A) at Historical Society of Harford County; copy of the schedule which he signed "Benjamin McCaskey" was included, but did not list any property)

McCaskey, Ellis, 1826. "Petition, Schedule, Bond, Sheriff's certificate and personal discharge and order for publication and Bond of provisional trustee and certificate for Trustee filed 16th August 1826. 17th March 1827 Cert. of publication filed and Insolvent personally discharged." (Insolvent Docket A, 1807-1843, p. 82, at the Maryland State Archives; Insolvent Docket Prior to 1827, Court Records Accession #632 at the Historical Society of Harford County)

McCleary, Robert, 1831. "Petition, Schedule, Sheriff's certificate, personal discharge and order for publication, bond for appearance, Trustee's bond, Trustee's certificate and Deed to Trustee filed 13th July 1831." [nothing further] (Insolvent Docket A, 1807-1843, p. 110, at the Maryland State Archives)

McClure, Albert, 1886. "Robert R. Boarman, Attorney. Order Publication. In the matter of the petition of Charles Francis vs. Albert McClure … The Object of this petition is to have Albert McClure declared and adjudicated an Insolvent. The petition stated that the said Albert McClure has departed from and quit from the State of Maryland for the purpose of defrauding his creditors, and to prevent the service of process upon him in any action for debt, and prays that he may be adjudicated an Insolvent. It is therefore, this 20th day of December, A. D. 1886, ordered by the Court, that the petitioner, by causing a copy of this order, together with the substance and object of the petition, to be inserted in some newspaper published in Harford county, once a week, for three successive weeks, before the 20th day of January, 1887, give notice to the said Albert McClure of the object and substance of the petition, and warning him to appear in this Court, in person or by solicitor, on or before the 20th day of January, 1887, to show cause, if any he has, why he should not be declared an insolvent as prayed. Jas. D. Watters. A. Lingan Jarrett, Clerk." (*The Aegis & Intelligencer*, December 31, 1886, p. 2). "In the matter of the Insolvency of Albert McClure ... Notice is hereby given that Albert McClure, formerly of Harford county, having been, by the Circuit Court for Harford county, adjudicated an insolvent debtor, the proceedings under which such adjudication was made being now pending, a meeting of the creditors of such Insolvent debtor will be held at the office of George L. Van Bibber in Bel Air, Md., on Saturday, February 5th, 1887, at 11 o'clock, A. M., for the purpose of proof of claims, propounding of interrogatories and selection of permanent trustee or trustees. George L. Van Bibber, Robert R. Boarman, Preliminary Trustees." (*The Aegis & Intelligencer*, January 28, 1887, p. 2). "Albert McClure, the runaway merchant of Bynum's Station, has been adjudged an insolvent debtor, by the Court." (*Havre de Grace Republican*, February 4, 1887, p. 4). "Notice is hereby given to the creditors of the said Albert McClure, who were such upon the date of the application to have him declared an insolvent, to file their claims duly proven, with the Clerk of the Circuit Court for Harford County, on or before the 1st day of May, 1887. Robert R. Boarman, George L. Van Bibber, Permanent Trustees." (*The Aegis & Intelligencer*, February 11, 1887, p. 2). "Trustee's Sale. By virtue of an order of the Circuit Court for Harford county, the subscribers, as permanent trustees, will offer at Public Sale, at the Court House door, in Bel Air, on Saturday, March 5th, 1887, at 11 o'clock, A. M., all that Tract or Parcel of Land, situate and lying in Harford county, at Bynum's Station, on the Maryland Central Railroad, containing 11 acres, 2 roods and 29 square perches, more or less, being the same and all the lad particularly described in two deeds to Albert McClure, one from James H. Quinby and wife, dated the 17th day of May, 1886, and recorded in Liber A. L. J., No. 56, folio 285, one of the Land Record Books of the Circuit Court for Harford county, and the other from John M. Blake and wife, dated the 14th day of June, 1886, and recorded in Liber A. L. J., No. 55, folio 408, one of the Land Records aforesaid. The improvements consist of a new two-story Frame Dwelling, Back Building, new Store House and Warehouse, Stable and other outbuildings. This property is mot eligibly located for doing a remunerative business. Bynum's Station is the natural outlet for a well-settled and thriving neighborhood. Robert R. Boarman, George L. Van Bibber, Trustees." (*The Aegis & Intelligencer*, February 11, 1887, p. 2)

McComas, Aquila, 1809. "Petition, Schedule, Bond, &c. filed 23rd Decr. 1809." Robert Amoss, Sr., was appointed trustee in August 1810 and a Bond of Trust was recorded on April 9, 1812 [nothing further recorded]. (Insolvent Docket A, 1807-1843, p. 5, at the Maryland State Archives; Insolvent Docket Prior to 1827, Court Records Accession #632 at the Historical Society of Harford County). **Genealogical Notes**: Aquila McComas, son of John McComas, was born on March 30, 1773, married Martha Amos (January 26, 1778 – March 4, 1858), daughter of Robert Amos (1741-1818) and Martha McComas (c1745-1832), worked as a farmer on his farm located between Jarrettsville and Upper Cross Roads (Old Corbin Amos Farm, later Fox Hill Farm, now Uphill Farm on Route 165), served as a lieutenant in the War of 1812, died on March 5, 1825 and was buried in the family burying ground on his farm. The children of Aquila and Martha McComas were Robert Amos McComas (1798-1844) and Gabriel A. McComas (c1800-1882). (*Children of Mt. Soma*, by Gertrude J. Stephens, 1992, pp. 381, 408; *Family Cemeteries and Grave Sites in Harford County, Maryland*, by Henry C. Peden, Jr., 2016, p. 1; 1804 deposition in Harford County Land Records HD No. 4, p. 67)

McComas, Nicholas Day, 1804. "Whereas we the Subscribers Justices of the Peace for Harford County upon the petition of Nicholas Day McComas, who set forth that he had been confined in the Gaol [the jail] of said county twenty Days for Debts which he was unable to pay & finding the facts stated to be true we together did meet at the County Gaol of said County on the 18th day of August Instant and did then and there appoint the 18th Day of August Instant to meet at the Court House of said county which said appointment we did then and there … at the request of said Sheriff administer to the said Nicholas Day McComas the following oath which was taken by the said Nicholas Day McComas being first duly sworn on the holy Evangels of almighty God in the words following, I Nicholas Day McComas do solemnly swear that the schedule which I have delivered to the Sheriff of Harford County doth contain a full account to the best of my knowledge and remembrance of my whole estate both real & personal or that I have any title to or interest in and of all debts, credits and effects whatsoever which I or any in trust for me have or at the time of my petition had, or am or was in any respect entitled to in possession, remainder or reversion and that I have not directly or indirectly at any time since my imprisonment or before, sold, leased or otherwise conveyed or disposed of or intrusted all or any part of my estate, goods, stock, money or debts thereby to defraud my creditors or to secure the same to receive or expect any profit or advantage thereof so help me God, which said duplicate of the schedule aforesaid we have transmitted to the clerk of the county court to be by him preserved in his office for the information of the creditors of the said Nicholas Day McComas. Given under our hands and seals this 18th Day of August 1804. John Moores. Wm. Smithson, Jacob Norris." (Court Records Document 67.10.2(A) at the Historical Society of Harford County; a copy of the schedule to which "Nich. D. McComas" signed his name was included, but no property was listed). **Genealogical Notes**: Nicholas Day McComas, son of Alexander McComas, married Elizabeth Onion on July 24, 1794 and died in 1816. (St. James Parish Register; St. John's Parish Register; Research by Christopher T. Smithson, of Darlington, MD, 1999)

McComas, William, 1840. "Petition, Schedule, Affidavits, personal discharge and order of publica-tion, Bond for Appearance, Trustee's Bond, Trustee's Certificate and Deed to Trustee filed July 28th 1840. 21st Novr. 1840 Petitioner appears & files Certificate of Publication and finally discharged." (Insolvent Docket A, 1807-1843, p. 172, at the Maryland State Archives). **Genealogical Note**: William McComas (1790-1857) married Ellen Fort (1798-1859), daughter of John and Elizabeth Fort, circa 1818. (Mountain Christian Church tombstone inscriptions)

McCoy, John G., 1886. "Insolvent Creditors' Notice. Bel Air, January 14, 1886. Notice is hereby given that John G. McCoy of Harford county, and State of Maryland, has applied for the benefit of the Insolvent Laws of said State. A meeting of his creditors to choose a Permanent Trustee will be held in Bel Air, on January 30, 1886, at 12 o'clock M., at the office of the undersigned. F. R. Williams, Preliminary Trustee." (*Bel Air Times*, January 22, 1886, p. 3). "Insolvent Notice. This is to notify the creditors of John G. McCoy, an insolvent debtor, that the second Monday of May, in the year 1886, has been fixed by the Court for the appearance of said insolvent to answer such interrogatories or allegations as his creditors, endorsers or sureties may propose or allege against him. Fred. R. Williams, Permanent Trustee." (*Bel Air Times*, February 19, 1886, p. 3). "Notice to Creditors. The creditors of John G. McCoy, an insolvent debtor, are hereby notified to file their claims against said insolvent, duly, authenticated, with the Clerk of the Circuit Court for Harford county on or before the 1st day of June, in the year 1886. Fred. R. Williams, Permanent Trustee." (*Bel Air Times*, February 19, 1886, p. 3)

McDonald, Alexander, 1851. "Notice Is Hereby Given, To the creditors of Alexander McDonald, late an imprisoned debtor of Harford County, that on the application of said debtor by petition in writing to the Hon. Samuel M. Magraw, one of the justices of the Orphan's Court of said County, for the benefit of the insolvent laws of Maryland, the said judge on the 10th day of July, 1851, granted to the said debtor a discharge from imprisonment and appointed the first Saturday after the 3rd

Monday in November next, for his appearance before the Judges of Harford county court at the court house of said county, for a final hearing before said court, on said petition and to answer such interrogatories as his creditors may propose to him." (*Harford Madisonian and Havre de Grace Weekly Advertiser*, October 9, 1851, p. 3)

McFadden (McFadin), Benjamin, 1813. "Harford County Gaol. To John Moores, John Guyton and Samuel Bradford, gentlemen justices of the peace for said county. The petition of Benjamin McFadden humbly sheweth that your petitioner hath actually remained in the jail of said county since the twelfth day of July last for debts which he is unable to ay, that he is willing to comply with the requisites of the Act of Assembly entitled 'an act for the relief of insolvent debtors' and prays you gentlemen to appoint a time and place for his discharge under said act. And your petitioner as in duty bound will ever pray &c. August 10th 1813. Benjamin McFadin." (Court Records Document 67.14.7(B) at the Historical Society of Harford County). "Whereas we the subscribers Justices of the Peace for Harford County upon the petition of Benjamin McFadden set forth therein that he had been confined [in jail] twenty days and upwards for debts which he was unable to pay and finding the facts stated to be true we did meet at the jail of said county on the 10th instant and did then and there appoint the 31st day of August instant to meet at the court house of said county which said appointment we did then and there … at the request of the said sheriff administer to the said Benjamin McFadden the following oath which was taken by the said Benjamin McFadden being first duly sworn on the Holy Evangely of Almighty God in the words following, I do solemnly swear that the schedule which I have delivered to the sheriff of Harford County doth contain a full account to the best of my knowledge and remembrance of my whole estate both real & personal or that I have any title to or interest in and of all debts, credits & effects whatsoever which I or any in trust for me have or at the time of my petition had, or am or was in any respect entitled to in possession, remainder or reversion and that I have not directly or indirectly at any time since my imprisonment or before, sold, leased or otherwise conveyed or disposed of or intrusted all or any part of my estate, goods, stock, money or debts thereby to defraud my creditors or to secure the same to receive or expect any profit or advantage thereof so help me God, which said duplicate of the schedule aforesaid we have transmitted to the clerk of the county court to be by him preserved in his office for the information of the creditors of the said Benjamin McFadden. Given under our hands and seals this thirty-first day of August 1813. John Moores. Saml. Bradford. John Guyton." (Court Records Document 67.14(7) at the Historical Society of Harford County; a copy of the schedule was included to which "Benjamin McFadin" signed his name, but no property was listed). **Genealogical Notes**: Benjamin McFadden married Sarah Horner, daughter of James and Mary Horner, by 1800. Their son John Harvey McFadden was born on January 22, 1801. (*Our Horner Ancestors*, by Virginia Hunter Hinds, 1974; St. George's Parish Register)

McFadden, William, Jr., 1835. "Petition, Affidavits, Schedule, personal discharge and order of publication, Bond for Appearance, Trustee's Bond, Trustee's Certificate and Deed to Trustee filed 7th September 1835. 19th Mar 1836 Petitioner appears, certificate of publication filed and finally discharged." (Insolvent Docket A, 1807-1843, p. 143, at Maryland State Archives)

McGaw, John, 1838. "Petition, Schedule, Affidavits, personal discharge and order of publication, Bond for Appearance, Trustee's Bond, Trustee's Certificate and Deed to Trustee filed 30th March 1838. 24th Novr. 1838 Petitioner appears, certificate of publication filed & discharged." (Insolvent Docket A, 1807-1843, p. 165, at the Maryland State Archives). **Genealogical Note**: John McGaw, son of Robert McGaw and Elizabeth Armstrong, was born on March 27, 1797 and died on April 5, 1863. (Grove Presbyterian Church tombstone)

McGonegal, Daniel, 1816. "Whereas we the subscribers Justices of the Peace for Harford County upon the petition of Daniel McGonegal setting forth therein that he had actually been confined in the goal [jail] of said county since the ninth of January last for debts which he is unable to pay and finding the facts therein stated to be true we did meet at the goal of said county on the twenty ninth day of said month and did then and there appoint the second day of March Inst. to meet at the Court house of said county, which said appointment we did then and there ... at the request of the said Sheriff administer to the said Daniel McGonegal the following oath which was taken by said Daniel McGonegal being first duly sworn on the Holy Evangely of Almighty God in the words following to wit, I Daniel McGonegal do solemnly promise and swear that the schedule which I have delivered to the Sheriff of Harford county doth contain a full account to the best of my knowledge and remembrance of my whole estate both real and personal or that I have any title to or interest in, and of all debts, credits and effects whatsoever which I or any in trust for me have or at the time of my petition had, or am or was in any respect entitled to in possession, remainder or reversion and that I have not directly or indirectly at any time since my imprisonment or before, sold, leased or otherwise conveyed or disposed of or intrusted all or any part of my estate, goods, stock, money or debts thereby to defraud my creditors or to secure the same to receive or expect any profit or advantage thereof so help me God, which said duplicate of the Schedule aforesaid we have transmitted to the clerk of the county court to be by him preserved in his office for the information of the creditors of the said Daniel McGonegal. Given under our hands & seals this Second of March 1816. James Wallace. Benj. Richardson. Joseph Robinson." (Court Records Document 67.14(8) at Historical Society of Harford County; a copy of the schedule to which "Danl McGonegal" signed his name was included, but he had no property). **Genealogical Notes**: Daniel McGonegal married Mary McLaughlin circa October 7, 1799 (date of license) and their three children, Hugh McGonegal (born September 22, 1800), Daniel McGonegal (born August 16, 1802) and Philip McGonegal (born September 29, 1808), were all baptized on October 22, 1808, by which time their mother had died. (St. George's Parish Register; Harford County General Entries Book; Harford County marriage license misspelled his name as "McCongall")

McIlvaine (McIlvain), Jeremiah, 1884/1896. "Court Proceedings. When we went to press week [May 23, 1896] the case of Bernard S. McIlvaine vs. S. A. Williams, executor of Wm. Woolsey, was on trial, before a jury. This was a suit on an administration bond of the late Jeremiah McIlvaine, Mr. Woolsey having been one of the sureties. George W. McIlvaine, the father of the plaintiff, died about 1884. Jeremiah McIlvaine, father of George W., became his administrator and took possession of the estate, but failed to pay over the net balance, about $1,100, to the heirs, who were the widow and three children. When Jeremiah McIlvaine died his estate was found to be insolvent, so recourse was had to his bondsmen who were Mr. George J. Finney and the late William Woolsey. It was claimed by the defence that while the administrator, Jeremiah McIlvaine, had not actually filed an account with the Orphans' Court, claiming credit for these balances, that he had paid out many times more than the amount left by George's estate in the maintenance and education of the children, and in fact, that this was the reason of his estate being insolvent. The case occupied the court until Tuesday morning when the jury brought in a sealed verdict for the plaintiff for $244.85 and $44.07 interest. The amount claimed by this particular plaintiff was $244.85, with interest since he became of age, at which time it was payable." (*Havre de Grace Republican*, May 30, 1896, p. 2) **Genealogical Notes**: Jeremiah McIlvain was born in 1808 and married Ann Crosby (1802 – March 30, 1866), a great-granddaughter of John Morton who gave the casting vote for American independence on July 4, 1776. Jeremiah died on May 26, 1893 and his only son George W. McIlvain was born on 9th day of 7th month and died on 20th day of 8th month 1884. George married Rachel A. Ramsey (1842-1924) and they had a son Bernard Stump McIlvain (1871-1908), the plaintiff aforesaid. (Darlington Cemetery tombstone inscriptions; Death certificate of Rachel McIlvain who was a daughter of Samuel Ramsey and Susanna Stump)

McJilton, William, 1830. Insolvent debtor to be discharged from imprisonment. (*Independent Citizen*, Nov 4, 1830). "Petition, Schedule, Shff's. Certificate, Personal Discharge, Order of Publication, Bond for Appearance, Trustee's Bond, Trustee's Certificate and Deed to Trustee filed 8th day of March 1830. 1st day of June 1830 petition filed and George H. Wilson appointed Trustee … 14th August 1830 Petitioner appears and cont'd … March 19th 1831 petitioner appears, certificate of publication filed & finally discharged." (Insolvent Docket A, 1807-1843, p. 103, at the Maryland State Archives). **Genealogical Note**: William McJilton married Ann Nevil circa May 30, 1804 (date of license).

McKee, David Jr. and Charles, 1884. "September 15th 1884. Petition, Schedule of Property, Affidavit, Order, Trustee's Bond & Insolvent Deed filed … [numerous claims and notices filed from 1884 to 1888] … 21 Novr 1888 Objections to discharge of Insolvents filed. 22 Dec 1888 Order of Court for Insolvents to appear 11 Feby 1889 & answer interrogatories filed [no record of their appearance] … 16 April 1889 Auditor's Report & Order Nisi filed. 24 May 1889 Notice of Motion & Final Order filed." [nothing further recorded] (Insolvent Docket A. L. J. No. 1, pp. 89, 106, in the Court Records Department of the Historical Society of Harford County). "David and Charles McKee, canners, of Thomas' Run, have made application for the benefit of the insolvent law. Messrs. Harlan and Webster have been appointed preliminary trustees." (*The Aegis & Intelligencer*, March 28, 1890, p. 2). "David & Charles McKee, members of a canning firm at Thomas' Run, have been obliged to yield under the pressure of the universal depression connected with the business, and have applied for the benefit of the insolvent laws." (*Havre de Grace Republican*, April 4, 1890, p. 3). "Trustee's Sale. In pursuance of an order of the Circuit Court for Harford county, the subscriber, permanent trustee of the insolvent estate of David McKee and Brother, will sell at public sale, at the M. C. R. R. depot, in Bel Air, Harford county, Md., on Thursday, November 20th, 1884, at 12 o'clock, M., about 2,000 Cases of Three Lb. Canned Tomatoes, of the pack of 1883, belonging to said insolvent estate, to the highest bidder for cash. Wm. H. Doxen, Permanent Trustee. J. S. Richardson, Auctioneer." (*Harford Democrat*, November 14, 1884, p. 3). "Trustee's Sale of Personal Property. In pursuance of an order of the Circuit Court for Harford county, the undersigned, Permanent Trustee, in the insolvency of David McKee & Bro., will sell on the farm lately occupied by them, near Thomas' Run post office, on Tuesday, April 15th, 1890, at 10 o'clock, A. M., the following Personal Property: One pair good Mules, 1 good work and driving Horse, 2 Mares with foal, 2 good Cows, 2 Steers, 1 four-horse Brown Wagon, 1 No-top Buggy, 1 Road Cart, 1 Hay Carriage, 1 Sleigh, 1 Superior Wheat Drill, 1 new Evans Corn Drill, 2 Plows, 2 Harrows, 2 Iron Age Cultivators, 1 Hill Marker, 1 Roller, 2 sets Lead Harness, Collars, Bridles, 4 Housings, 2 sets of Breechband Harness, 2 sets Plow Harness, 4 Choke Straps, I Check Line, 2 sets Buggy Harness, 1 Riding Bridle and Saddle, 2 sets Spreaders, 2 sets Double Trees, Single Trees, Forks, Rakes, Shovels, Mattocks, Hoes, 2 Grain Cradles, Briar Scythe, Corn Knives, Chains of all kinds, Meat Cask, together with a complete Canning House Outfit, One Platform Scales, 1 new Tomato Packer, 1 Carboy of Acid, lot of corn labels, lot of Pine and Poplar Lumber, lot of Tomato boxes, lot of Bricks, &c. Also some other articles. William H. Harlan, Permanent Trustee." (*The Aegis & Intelligencer*, April 11, 1890, p. 1), **Genealogical Notes**: David McKee, Jr. and Charles McKee were sons of David McKee (1810-1886) and Jane ---- (1812-1872). Charles McKee married Elva K. McMichael circa February 13, 1884 (date of license).

McKenny, John, of Peter, 1820. "Petition, Schedule, Bond, Sheriff's certificate, order for publication and personal discharge filed 30th May 1820. Sepr. 2nd 1820 petr. appeared." [nothing further was recorded] (Insolvent Docket A, 1807-1843, p. 32, at the Maryland State Archives; Insolvent Docket Prior to 1827, Court Records Accession #632 at the Historical Society of Harford County).

McLaughlin, Michael, 1810. "Whereas we the subscribers Justices of the Peace for Harford County upon the petition of Michael McLaughlin who set forth therein that he had been confined in the goal [jail] of said county twenty days for debts which he was unable to pay and finding the facts stated to be true we did meet at the county gaol of the said county on the 26th day of April last and did then and there appoint the 28th day of May Instant to meet at the court house of said county which said appointment we did then and there ... at the request of the said sheriff administer to the said Michael McLaughlin the following oath which was taken by the said Michael McLaughlin being first duly sworn on the Holy Evangely of Almighty God in the words following, I Michael McLaughlin solemnly swear that the schedule which I have delivered to the sheriff of Harford County doth contain a full account to the best of my knowledge and remembrance of my whole estate both real & personal or that I have any title to or interest in and of all debts, credits & effects whatsoever which I or any in trust for me have or at the time of my petition had, or am or was in any respect entitled to in possession, remainder or reversion and that I have not directly or indirectly at any time since my imprisonment or before, sold, leased or otherwise conveyed or disposed of or intrusted all or any part of my estate, goods, stock, money or debts thereby to defraud my creditors or to secure the same to receive or expect any profit or advantage thereof so help me God, which said duplicate of the schedule aforesaid we have transmitted to the clerk of the county court to be by him preserved in his office for the information of the creditors of the said Michael McLaughlin. Given under our hands and seals this 28th day of May 1810. Thomas A. Hays. Samuel Bradford. John C. Bond." (Court Records Document 67.21.2(a) at the Historical Society of Harford County; copy of the schedule to which Michael McLaughlin made his "X" mark was included, but no property was listed).
Genealogical Note: Michael McLaughlin, age not given, appeared in Court on August 29, 1816 and stated he was "a native of Ireland and at present residing in Harford County in the State of Maryland, appeared in open Court here and prays to become a citizen of the United States, and it appearing to the satisfaction of the court here that said Michael McLaughlin was a resident within the limits and under the jurisdiction of the United States between the twenty ninth day of January seventeen hundred and ninety five and the eighteenth day of June seventeen hundred and ninety eight, that he was a resident five years and upwards within and under the jurisdiction of the United States and one year and upwards immediately preceding this application within the State of Maryland and that during the said time of five years he has behaved as a man of good moral character attached to the principles of the Constitution of the United States, and well disposed to the good order and happiness of the same, and the said Michael McLaughlin having declared on oath taken within open Court here that he would support the Constitution of the United States, and that he doth absolutely and entirely renounce and adjure all allegiance and fidelity to the United Kingdoms of Great Britain and Ireland, and the said Michael McLaughlin also declared on oath taken as aforesaid, that he has never borne any hereditary title or been of any of the orders of nobility in any country whatever, the Court here thereupon admits the said Michael McLaughlin to become a citizen of the United States." (County Court Minutes, 1816-1822, pp. 8-9, at the Historical Society of Harford County)

McLaughlin, Patrick, 1816. "August Term 1816. Petitioner appeared in Court here and postponed until the first Thursday of next March Term and the Court appoints Benjn. G. Jones Trustee and ordered that he give Bond to the State of Maryland in the penalty of $1000." [nothing further recorded]. Another entry on a different page: "Petition, Schedule, Bond, Order to Sheriff, Sheriff's certificate, personal discharge and order of publication filed 28th Nov. 1818 – March 13th 1819 petr. appeared and filed a certificate of publication." [nothing further recorded] (Insolvent Docket A, 1807-1843, pp. 19, 24, at the Maryland State Archives; Insolvent Docket Prior to 1827, Court Records Accession #632 at the Historical Society of Harford County). **Genealogical Note:** Patrick McLaughlin, age not given, appeared in Court on August 22, 1806 and stated he was "a native of Ireland and at present residing in Harford County in the State of Maryland and prays to be admitted to become a citizen of the United States and it appearing to the satisfaction of the Court here that the same Patrick McLaughlin was a resident within the limits and under the jurisdiction of the United States before the twenty ninth day of January one thousand seven hundred and ninety five and the eighteenth day of June seventeen hundred and ninety eight, that he was resident five years and upwards within in and under the jurisdiction of the United States and one year and upwards immediately preceding this application within the State of Maryland. That during the said time of five years he has behaved as a man of a good moral character attached to the principles of the Constitution of the United States and well disposed to the principles of the same, and that the same Patrick McLaughlin having declared on oath taken in open Court that he would support the Constitution of the United States and that he doth absolutely and entirely renounce and abjure all allegiance and fidelity to every foreign Prince, Potentate, State or Sovereignty whatever and particularly all allegiance and fidelity to the King of Great Britain and the said Patrick McLaughlin also declaring on oath taken in open Court, that he has never borne hereditary title, or been of any of the orders of nobility in any country whatever, the court here thereupon admits the said Patrick McLaughlin to become a citizen of the United States." (County Court Minutes, 1798-1806, pp. 123-124, at the Historical Society of Harford County). He was deposed in 1826, aged 47 and upwards. (Equity Court Case No. 33, Jarrett vs. Wallace & Mitchell)

McNabb, Daniel, 1817. "Whereas we the subscribers Justices of the Peace for Harford County upon the petition of Daniel McNabb setting forth therein that he had actually been confined in the goal [jail] of said county since the eighteenth day of October last for debts which he is unable to pay and finding the facts therein stated to be true we did meet at the goal of said county on the seventh day November last and did then and there appoint the ninth day of December instant to meet at the Court house of said county, which said appointment we did then and there … at the request of the said Sheriff administer to the said Daniel McNabb the following oath which was taken by the said Daniel McNabb being first duly sworn on the Holy Evangely of Almighty God in the words following to wit, I Daniel McNabb do solemnly promise and swear that the schedule which I have delivered to the Sheriff of Harford county doth contain a full account to the best of my knowledge and remembrance of my whole estate both real and personal or that I have any title to or interest in, and of all debts, credits and effects whatsoever which I or any in trust for me have or at the time of my petition had, or am or was in any respect entitled to in possession, remainder or reversion and that I have not directly or indirectly at any time since my imprisonment or before, sold, leased or otherwise conveyed or disposed of or intrusted all or any part of my estate, goods, stock, money or debts thereby to defraud my creditors or to secure the same to receive or expect any profit or advantage thereof so help me God, which said duplicate of the Schedule aforesaid we have transmitted to the clerk of the county court to be by him preserved in his office for the information of the creditors of the said Daniel McNabb. Given under our hands and seals this ninth day of December 1817. James Wallace. Joseph Robinson. Benjn. Richardson." (Court Records Document 67.14(9) at Historical Society of Harford County; a copy of the schedule to which Daniel McNabb made his "X" mark was included, but no property was listed)

McNabb, John, 1806. "Whereas we the Subscribers Justices of the Peace for Harford County upon the petition of John McNabb, who set forth that he had been confined in the Gaol [jail] of the said county twenty Days for Debts which he was unable to pay and finding the facts stated to be true we together did meet at the County Gaol on the 24th day of June last and did then and there appoint the 25th of July Instant to meet at the Court House of said county which said appointment we did then and there … at the request of the said Sheriff administer to the said John McNabb the following oath which was taken by the said John McNabb being first duly sworn on the holy Evangels of Almighty God in the words following – I John McNabb do solemnly swear that the schedule which I have delivered to the Sheriff of Harford County doth contain a full account to the best of my knowledge and remembrance of my whole estate both real & personal or that I have any title to or interest in and of all debts, credits and effects whatsoever which I or any in trust for me have or at the time of my petition had, or am or was in any respect entitled to in possession, remainder or reversion and that I have not directly or indirectly at any time since my imprisonment or before, sold, leased or otherwise conveyed or disposed of or intrusted all or any part of my estate, goods, stock, money or debts thereby to defraud my creditors or to secure the same to receive or expect any profit or advantage thereof so help me God, which said duplicate of the schedule aforesaid we have transmitted to the clerk of the county court to be by him preserved in his office for the information of the creditors of the said John McNabb. Given under our hands and seals this --th [page torn] day of April 1806. John Moores. Thomas A. Hays. Bennet Bussey." (Court Records Documents 67.10.3(A) at the Historical Society of Harford County; a copy of the schedule to which "Jno. Mᶜnabb" signed his name was included, but no property was listed). 1833. "Petition, Schedule, Affidavit, Personal discharge, Order for Publication, Bond for Appearance, Trustee's Bond, Trustee's Certificate and Deed to Trustee filed 21st December 1833. 15th March 1834 Petitioner appears, Certificate of Publication filed and finally discharged." (Insolvent Docket A, 1807-1843, p. 129, Maryland State Archives)

McVey, John, 1811. "Whereas we the subscribers Justices of the Peace for Harford County upon the petition of John McVey who set forth therein that he had been confined in the goal [jail] of said county twenty days for debts which he was unable to pay and finding the facts stated to be true we did meet at the county gaol of said county on the first day of February last and did then and there appoint the 4th day of March Instant to meet at the court house of said county which said appointment we did then and there … at the request of the said sheriff administer to the said John McVey the following oath which was taken by the said John McVey being first duly sworn on the Holy Evangely of Almighty God in the words following, I John McVey do solemnly swear that the schedule which I have delivered to the sheriff of Harford County doth contain a full account to the best of my knowledge and remembrance of my whole estate both real & personal or that I have any title to or interest in and of all debts, credits & effects whatsoever which I or any in trust for me have or at the time of my petition had, or am or was in any respect entitled to in possession, remainder or reversion and that I have not directly or indirectly at any time since my imprisonment or before, sold, leased or otherwise conveyed or disposed of or intrusted all or any part of my estate, goods, stock, money or debts thereby to defraud my creditors or to secure the same to receive or expect any profit or advantage thereof so help me God, which said duplicate of the schedule aforesaid we have transmitted to the clerk of the county court to be by him preserved in his office for the information of the creditors of the said John McVey. Given under our hands and seals this 4th day of March 1811. Thomas A. Hays. Saml. Bradford." (Court Records Document 67.21.1(b) at Historical Society of Harford County; a copy of the schedule was included to which "John McVey" signed his name, but no property was listed)

Meads, James, 1825. James Meads, executor of James Meads vs. James Meads, Daniel Meads, Elisha Meads and Benedict Meads. Complaint stated James Meads died testate, leaving several children, and his personal estate was not sufficient to pay his debts, but he owned part of a tract called *Meads' Delight*. He requested that the Court order the land sold to pay the debts. James G. Davis was appointed to make the sale in 1825 and John McKinney, Jr. was appointed in 1826. Also mentioned money due Philip Echle and wife. Case was resolved in 1828. (Harford County Equity Court Book HD No. 1, pp. 281-286)

Michael, Caleb, 1840. "Petition, Schedule, Affidavits, personal discharge and order of publication, Bond for Appearance, Trustee's Bond, Trustee's Certificate and Deed to Trustee filed 7th February 1840. 23rd May 1840 Certificate of publication filed, petitioner appears and finally discharged." (Insolvent Docket A, 1807-1843, p. 171, at the Maryland State Archives). **Genealogical Note**: Caleb Michael was born in 1805 and died on August 22, 1849 (St. Ignatius Catholic Church cemetery).

Milhoof (Millhooff), John, 1822. "Petition, Schedule, Bond, Sheriff's certificate, and personal discharge & order for publication filed 17th September 1822 [with regards to "John Millhooff"]. Certificate of publication filed 15th March 1823. Aug 14th 1824 Richard Webster appointed Trustee, bond filed, and petitioner personally discharged." (Insolvent Docket A, 1807-1843, p. 51, at the Maryland State Archives; Insolvent Docket Prior to 1827, Court Records Accession #632 at the Historical Society of Harford County). **Genealogical Note**: "John Milhoof" married Polly --- before March 15, 1816 (Court Records Document 71.00.9 at the Historical Society of Harford County).

Miller, Samuel, 1822. "Petition, Schedule, Bond, Sheriff's certificate, personal discharge and order for publication filed 31st October 1822. March 15th 1823 printers certificate of publication filed. Petitioner appears and is discharged." (Insolvent Docket A, 1807-1843, p. 53, at the Maryland State Archives; Insolvent Docket Prior to 1827, Court Records Accession #632 at the Historical Society of Harford County). **Genealogical Note**: Samuel Miller was deposed on January 31, 1828 and stated he was aged 73 and upwards (Court Records Document 90.29.73 at Historical Society of Harford County).

Miller, William F., 1825. "Petition, bond, Schedule, Shffs Certificate, personal discharge and order for publication filed 21st May 1825. March 18th 1826 Nathaniel W. S. Hays appointed Trustee and Printers Certificate filed. 18th March 1826 Petitioner Discharged." 1829. Insolvent debtor. Samuel Bradford, trustee. (*Independent Citizen*, October 29, 1829) [various petitions and reports filed from 1826 through 1832] (Insolvent Docket A, 1807-1843, p. 70, at the Maryland State Archives; Insolvent Docket Prior to 1827, Court Records Accession #632 at the Historical Society of Harford County)

Milligan, James, 1856. Jesse Hillis vs. Ann Milligan and the Heirs at Law of James Milligan. Object of the Bill in this case was to obtain a decree for the sale of a house and lot in Havre de Grace, being part of Lot No. 7, and fronting 30 feet on Otsego St. The Bill states that James Milligan contracted about December 28, 1854 with Dorus Seneca to purchase the said house and lot for $300 and said Milligan borrowed the whole sum from Jesse Hillis, the complainant, with the promise and understanding that legal title shall be conveyed to him as security. Notwithstanding the agreement, the said Milligan, without the knowledge of the complainant, obtained from the said Seneca a deed of conveyance of said lot and afterwards died in August 1856 without having paid the money he borrowed except the sum of $70. James Milligan died intestate, without issue, leaving a widow, Ann Milligan, who is the only legal representative known to the complainant, and his estate is insufficient to pay his debts, or to justify an administration thereon. The complaint requests the said lot and house be sold to pay Milligan's debt to him and an order of publication be passed against said Milligan's heirs at law, if there be any. (*Harford Democrat*, May 1, 1857). **Genealogical Note**: James Milligan married Miss Annie Hagan, both of Harford Co., on December 22, 1853 by Rev. Reese. (*Baltimore Weekly American*, December 31, 1853, and Baltimore *Sun*, December 24, 1853, both noted "Harford papers please copy")

Minnick, Cyrus, 1869. "Petition, 3 Schedules, Affidavit, Order, Trustee's Bond & Deed filed 6th day of December 1869." [nothing further recorded] (Insolvent Docket A. L. J. No. 1, p. 53, in the Court Records Department of the Historical Society of Harford County). **Genealogical Notes**: Cyrus

Minnick (1839-1895) (broom maker), third son of Jacob Minnick (1800, MD - 1875) and Elizabeth P. ---- (1802, PA - 1898), married Margaret Keith (born c1838), daughter of John A. Keith (1805-1879) and Mary M. Burgoyne (1812-1903), of Cecil Co., later of Harford Co., circa 1863 and in 1870 their children were Elizabeth Minnick, age 6, and Maryetta Minnick, age 1. (1870 Harford Co. Census, 3rd District, stated "Syras Minck" was age 30, Margaret was age 20, thus born circa 1850, but that would mean she married at the age of 13; Emory United Methodist Church Cemetery monument for the Keith family includes Cyrus Minnick (1839-1895) and Marjorie Minnick (1855-1946), wife of Cyrus Minnick; *The Aegis & Intelligencer*, 9 Aug 1895, reported Mrs. Margaret Minnick died in Wilmington, DE and was brought to the home of her mother [name not given] near Prospect and buried in Emory M. E. Church Cemetery, but there is no tombstone for her; 1850 Harford County Census listed his name as Cilus Minnick and listed her name as Margaret Keath)

Mitaway (Mittaway), Pat (African American) 1826. "Negro Pat Mitaway. Petition, schedule, Bond, Shff's certificate, affidavit of residence, personal discharge and order for publication filed 3rd January 1826. Printers certificate filed and personal discharged filed 21st Augt. 1826." (Insolvent Docket A, 1807-1843, p. 76, at the Maryland State Archives; Insolvent Docket Prior to 1827, Court Records Accession #632 at the Historical Society of Harford County contained less information)

Mitchell, Edward, 1836. "Petition, Affidavits, Schedule, personal discharge and order of publication, Bond for Appearance, Trustee's Bond, Trustee's Certificate and Deed to Trustee filed 24th August 1836. 18th March 1837 Petitioner appears, Certificate of Publication filed & Petitioner discharged." (Insolvent Docket A, 1807-1843, p. 153, at Maryland State Archives). **Genealogical Note**: Edward Mitchell married Margaret Williams circa March 29, 1821 (date of license).

Mitchell, George L., 1882. "Petition of S. H. Levins Sons, affidavit, Order of Court filed January 1st 1883 & copy of order of Court & Subpoena delivered to sheriff … Jany 8/83 H. W. Archer appears for Geo. L. Mitchell per order filed … Mitchell notified not to remove any property in possession as per schedules. Jany 13th/83 Agreement & order of Court. Same day answer of Geo L. Mitchell filed …" [Two claims filed in 1883 and 1884, but final resolution of the case was not cited.] (Insolvent Docket A. L. J. No. 1, p. 77, in the Court Records Department of the Historical Society of Harford County). **Genealogical Notes**: George Lewis Mitchell, son of Joseph G. Mitchell (1822-1902) and his 1st wife Martha Elizabeth Michael (1818-1861), was born on March 21, 1851, married Mary Emma Bowman (1858-1940) on April 29, 1881 and died on September 28, 1922 in Oakington. Their children were Pearl Sylvia Mitchell, Rose Ella Mitchell, Mary Lillian Mitchell Bonnett, Helen Bowman Mitchell, Stella Elizabeth Mitchell Gilbert and George Corthell Mitchell. George L. was a retired railroad engineer at the time of his death. (*Barnes-Bailey Genealogy*, by Walter D. Barnes, 1939, pp. H-42, I-64a; Harford County Death Certificate No. 9856; Grove Presbyterian Church tombstone inscriptions)

Mitchell, James, 1844. "Notice Is Hereby Given, to the creditors of James Mitchell, late an imprisoned debtor of Harford county, that on the application of said debtor by petition in writing to the Hon. Robert W. Holland, chief justice of the Orphan's court of said county, for the benefit of the insolvent laws of Maryland, the said judge on the 21st day of May, 1844, granted to the said debtor a discharge from imprisonment and appointed the first Saturday after the 3rd Monday in November next, for his appearance before the Judges of Harford county court at the court house of said county, for a final hearing before said court, on said petition and to answer such interrogatories as his creditors may propose to him." (*Harford Madisonian and Bel-Air & Havre de Grace Messenger*, October 18, 1844, p. 3)

Mitten (Mitton), Job, 1814. "Petition, Schedule, Bond and Notice to Creditors filed 18th March 1814." [nothing further recorded] (Insolvent Docket A, 1807-1843, p. 14, at the Maryland State Archives; Insolvent Docket Prior to 1827, Court Records Accession #632 at the Historical Society of Harford County). 1827. "21st day of August 1827. Petition, Schedule, Bond, Sheriff's certificate and personal discharge and order for publication filed. Deed to provisional trustee filed." [nothing further recorded] (Insolvent Docket A, 1807-1843, p. 85, at the Maryland State Archives)

Monks, Francis E., 1817. "Petition, Schedule & Bond filed 30th August 1817, the necessary oath was administered to the petitioner and ordered that he give the usual notice to his creditors and also ordered that he be discharged from the custody of the Sheriff of Harford County … March 14th 1818 the Court appoints James G. L. Presbury trustee. Bond of trustee, Deed to Trustee and certificate filed." [nothing further recorded] (Insolvent Docket A, 1807-1843, p. 21, at Maryland State Archives; Insolvent Docket Prior to 1827, Court Records Accession #632 at the Historical Society of Harford County). 1833. "Petition, Schedule, Affidavit, Personal discharge, Order for Publication, Bond for Appearance, Trustee's Bond, Trustee's Certificate and Deed to Trustee filed 13th Nov. 1833. 15th March 1834 Petitioner appears, Certificate of Publication filed and finally discharged." (Insolvent Docket A, 1807-1843, p. 128, at the Maryland State Archives). **Genealogical Notes:** Francis E. Monks, son of John Monks aka Capt. John Clark Monk (1760-1827) and Mary ----, was born circa 1787 and was charged with having begotten an illegitimate male child on the body of Elizabeth Martin on November 17, 1821. Francis served in the War of 1812 and participated in the Battle of North Point in 1814. He married Ann Dawes circa February 5, 1825 (date of license) and twelve years later hung himself from the limb of a tree in George M. Wheeler's woods near Hickory. In October 1837 it was reported that he had been hanging for several days and had been in a state of mental derangement for several months; also noted he was about fifty years of age. (Harford County Will Book SR No, 1, p. 421; Harford County Land Records HD No. 21, p. 63; Baltimore *Sun*, October 26, 1837; Harford County Court Minutes, 1816-1822, p. 85, and Court Records Document 74.07.7 at the Historical Society of Harford County; John Clark Monk tomb in St. George's (Spesutia) P. E. Church cemetery)

Monks, James P., 1828. "Petition, Schedule, Affidavit, Certificate, Sheriffs Certificate, Bond, Trustee Bond, Discharge filed. 16th August 1828 Certificate of publication filed. Petitioner discharged. Edward Tredway appointed trustee … with security in the penalty of $500." [nothing further recorded] (Insolvent Docket A, 1807-1843, p. 89, at the Maryland State Archives). **Genealogical Notes:** James P. Monks, son of John Monks aka Capt. John Clark Monk (1760-1827) and Mary ----, was born on October 13, 1800, married Mary Amelia Tredway (April 26, 1811 – February 17, 1879) on February 12, 1828 and died on January 25, 1878. The children of James and Mary Monks were John C. Monks (b. 1829), Edward Tredway Monks (1831-1924), Ann Eliza Monks (b. 1833), James H. Monks (b. 1836), William T. Monks ((1837-1916, married Lucretia A. Tipton), Thomas A. Monks (1839-1860), Lewis W. Monks (b. 1841), Mary E. Monks (1842-1842), Catherine J. Monks (1843-1843), Sarah M. Monks (1844-1846), Coleman Y. Monks (1845-1848), Olivia C. Monks (b. 1847, married Ralph Ecoff), A. Coleman Monks (1849-1850), Robert A. Monks (1851-1883), Mary Addie Monks (1854-1906) and Sarah Lavinia Monks (1856-1877). (James P. Monks Bible, *Maryland Bible Records, Volume 1*, by Henry C. Peden, Jr., 2003, pp. 173-174; Watters Memorial Church tombstones; Harford County Will Book SR No. 1, p. 421; *The Aegis & Intelligencer*, February 15, 1878)

Mooberry, Robert, 1805. "Whereas we the Subscribers, Justices of the Peace for Harford County upon the petition of Robert Mooberry who set forth that he had been confined in the Gaol [the jail] of said county twenty Days for Debts which he was unable to pay & finding the facts stated to be true we together did meet at the County Gaol of said County on the 6th day of August 1805 and did then and there appoint the 6th Day of September Inst. to meet at the Court House of said county which said appointment we did then and there … at the request of said Sheriff administer to the said Robert Mooberry the following oath which was taken by the said Robert Mooberry being first duly sworn on the holy Evangels of almighty God in the words following – I Robert Mooberry do solemnly swear that the schedule which I have delivered to the Sheriff of Harford County doth contain a full account to the best of my knowledge and remembrance of my whole estate both real & personal or that I have any title to or interest in and of all debts, credits and effects whatsoever which I or any in trust for me have or at the time of my petition had, or am or was in any respect entitled to in possession, remainder or reversion and that I have not directly or indirectly at any time since my imprisonment or before, sold, leased or otherwise conveyed or disposed of or intrusted all or any part of my estate, goods, stock, money or debts thereby to defraud my creditors or to secure the same to receive or expect any profit or advantage thereof so help me God, which said duplicate of the schedule aforesaid we have transmitted to the clerk of the county court to be by him preserved in his office for the information of the creditors of the said Robert Mooberry. Given under our hands and seals this 18th Day of August 1804. John Moores. Wm. Smithson." (Court Records Document 67.10.1(A) at the Historical Society of Harford County; a copy of the schedule to which "Robert Mubary" made his "X" mark was included, but no property was listed). **Genealogical Notes**: Robert Mooberry, son of ---- and Mary Mooberry, was born on December 26, 1770 and was indentured (bound out) to Kidd Morsall to learn the joiner's trade in January 1782. (Harford County 1776 Census; Orphans Court Proceedings). Robert Mooberry apparently married later since he was head of household in the 1810 Harford County Census and he was still living in 1823. (Court Records Document 49.22.7 in the Court Records Department at the Historical Society of Harford County)

Moore, George, 1847. "Notice is hereby given, to the creditors of George Moore, late an imprisoned debtor of Harford county, that on the application of said debtor by petition in writing to the Hon. Henry Hall, one of the justices of the Orphan's Court of said county, for the benefit of the insolvent laws of Maryland, the said judge on the 17th day of August, 1847, granted to the said debtor a discharge from imprisonment and appointed the first Saturday after the 3rd Monday in November next, for his appearance before the Judges of Harford county court at the court house of said county, for a final hearing before said court, on said petition and to answer such interrogatories as his creditors may propose to him." (*Harford Madisonian and Havre de Grace Messenger*, Sept 4, 1847, p. 2)

Moore, Theodore R., 1879. "Petition, Affidavit, 2 Schedules, Appointment of Trustee, Order to appear & give notice, deed & Trustee's Bond filed 7th Jany 1879. Petition of G. Y. M. [George Y. Maynadier] Trustee filed 8th Jany 1879 … 12th May 1879 Petitioner appears, files Certificate of Publication & finally discharged by the Court." [also mentioned several claims filed by various individuals through 1883] (Insolvent Docket A. L. J. No. 1, pp. 60-61, in the Court Records Department of the Historical Society of Harford County, mistakenly listed him as "Theore R. Moore"). "Notice is hereby given that Theodore R. Moore has made application to the Circuit Court of Harford county, for the benefit of the Insolvent Laws of Maryland, and that the second Monday in May, 1879, has been assigned for him to appear in said Court to answer such interrogatories as his creditors may propose or allege against him. A. Lingan Jarrett, Clerk, Circuit Court for Harford County." (*The Aegis & Intelligencer*, January 10, 1879, p. 2). "Trustee's Sale. In virtue of an order of the Circuit Court for Harford county, in the matter of the insolvency of Theodore R. Moore, the undersigned, as trustee, will offer at Public Sale, on the premises, near Fallston, in said county, where said Moore now resides, on Tuesday, February 11, 1879, at 11 o'clock A. M., the following property, to wit: one undivided sixth part or interest in reversion in and to that certain Farm or Tract of Land, called *Moss Wood Farm*, situated near Fallston, in said county, whereon Benjamin P. Moore, Sr. resided at the time of his death, containing about 154 acres, more or less, subject to the life estate therein of Mary G. Moore, widow of said Benjamin P. Moore, Sr., deceased. Also the following Personal Property, to wit: Two young Mules, 1 Driving Horse, 8 Cows, four of them full Alderney, and two of them fresh; 2 Heifers, 18 months old, and 2 do. 6 months old; 4 steers, two suitable for oxen; 1 Alderney Bull, 1 registered Bull, 6 months old; 1 Berkshire Boar and Sow, 1 Heavy Wagon, 1 light Spring Wagon, double and single Express Harness, Wagon Harness, Collars and Bridles, two-horse Thresher, 2 Wheat Drills, one new; Champion Reaper and Mower, spring-tooth Horse Rake, Plows, Harrows, Cultivators, &c. Also Ice Cream and Dairy Fixtures, 1 Two-Horse Engine, good as new; 1 Ice Cream Machine, 10 Ice Cream Packers, 10 gallons each; 1½ dozen Milk Cans, Churn, Butter Worker, Belting, &c. Terms of Sale … George Y. Maynadier, Trustee." (*The Aegis*, January 17, 1879, p. 2)

Moore, William, 1840. "11th Augst. 1840. Petition, Schedule, Affidavits, personal discharge and order of publication, Bond for Appearance, Trustee's Bond, Trustee's Certificate and Deed to Trustee filed. 21st Novr. 1840 Petitioner appears & files Certificate of Publication and finally discharged." (Insolvent Docket A, 1807-1843, p. 173, at the Maryland State Archives)

Morgan, Robert, 1805. "March 27th 1805. To Henry Ridgely, Esqr., Chief Justice of Harford County Court and his associates. The Petition of Robert Morgan of Harford County & State of Maryland, respectfully sheweth that at a Session of Assembly begun and held at the City of Annapolis on Monday the fifth day of November in the year of our Lord one thousand eight hundred and four, he obtained an Act of Insolvency, Your Petitioner therefore prays that your honors will exonerate and discharge him from all Debts and Contracts prior to the passage of the law agreeably to the provisions prescribed by the aforesaid Act, an [sic[also appoint a Trustee, & your Petitioner as in duty bound will ever pray." [Lists of creditors and debts due were included, plus the following] "A return of the household furniture. One large looking glass, 1 small ditto, 16 oz. Plate, 2 dozn. China plates, 4 large ditto dishes, 3 dozn. plates Queen Ware, 3 large dishes ditto, 3 China Bowls, 1 ditto tea pot, 1 doz, Stone pots, ½ doz. Chairs, 1 Case Drawers, 1 Corner Cupboard walnut, 2 dining Table ditto, 1 Breakfast table ditto, 1 Tea table Cheritree, 1 Dressing ditto, 6 landscapes, 5 other prints, 1.2 doz, wine Glasses, 1½ doz, China Cups & Saucers, Kitchen furniture, two large Iron pots, 2 small ditto, 4 potracks. 1 large brass kettle, 1 large ditto skillet, Farming utensils, one wagon, 1 Wheat Fan, 3 ploughs, 1 Harrow, 4 sets Chains, 4 pair hames, 10 Shoots." [Among other Court record entries was the following]: "Know all men by these presents that I Robert Morgan of Harford County Maryland am held and firmly bound in the penal sum of three hundred Dollars of good and lawful money to be paid to the State of Maryland and for the true performance thereof I bind myself my heirs executors and administrators, firmly by these presents. Sealed with my Seal and dated this twenty-eighth day of March 1805 … Ro. Morgan." (Court Actions in Insolvencies, 1805-1807, Court Records Book Accession No. 605 at the Historical Society of Harford County). **Genealogical Notes**: Robert Morgan was born on May 24, 1755 in Baltimore County, married Martha Hamilton on May 30, 1780 in Prince George's Co., MD and died after 1821 in Harford County. Their children were Sarah H. Morgan Richardson, John Thomas Hamilton Morgan, Lurena Morgan Slade, Edward Morgan, William Morgan and Julia Ann Morgan Macatee. *Descendants of the Signers of the Bush Declaration of March 22, 1775, Harford County, Maryland*, by Christopher T. Smithson and Henry C. Peden, Jr., 2010, p. 212; St. James P. E. Parish Register)

Morrison, John, 1824. "Petition, Bond, Schedule, Sheriffs Certificate, personal Discharge and order for Publication filed 6th July 1824." [nothing further recorded] (Insolvent Docket A, 1807-1843, p. 64, at the Maryland State Archives; Insolvent Docket Prior to 1827, Court Records Accession #632 at the Historical Society of Harford County). **Genealogical Note**: John Morrison married Frances Webster circa September 1, 1791 (date of license).

Morton, Samuel, 1857. "Petition, Schedules, Affidavits, Appointment of Trustee & order of notice, Trustee's Bond & Deed to Trustee filed 7th July 1857." [nothing further recorded] (Insolvent Docket A. L. J. No. 1, p. 19, in the Court Records Department of the Historical Society of Harford County)

Moseman, Jacob, 1855. "Petition, Affidavits, Schedules, Appointment of Trustee [not named], Order, Deed & Trustee's Bond filed 27 Jul/55. 13th May/56 Petitioner appears, files certificate of publication

& finally discharged." [nothing further recorded] (Insolvent Docket A. L. J. No. 1, p. 7, in the Court Records Department of the Historical Society of Harford County). "Notice is hereby given that Jacob Moseman, of Harford County, has made application to the Circuit Court of said County, for the benefit of the Insolvent Laws of Maryland, and that the first Tuesday of May Term, 1856, has been assigned for him to appear in the said Court to answer such interrogatories as his creditors may propose or allege against him. A. Lingan Jarrett, Clerk." (*Harford Democrat*, January 18, 1856, p. 2) **Genealogical Notes**: Jacob Moseman married Mary Ann Allen (b. 3 Apr 1829) and their children were Sarah P. E. Moseman, Henry James Mosemanm John Jacob Moseman, Josepheain Moseman, Mary Louise Moseman, Thomas Samuel Moseman, Ellen Malindy Moseman, and Willie Ernest Mseman. (*Maryland Bible Records, Volume 2*, by Henry C. Peden, Jr., 2003, pp. 97-100)

Moulton, Thomas W., 1866. "Petition, Schedule of property, List of debts to & from Affidavit, Order, Bond & Deed filed 15th May 1866 … Richd. Loflin, Trustee. 17th Nov/66 … Petitioner appeared & was finally discharged." (Insolvent Docket A. L. J. No. 1, p. 46, in the Court Records Department of the Historical Society of Harford County). "Notice is hereby given that Thomas W. Moulton has made application to the Circuit Court of Harford county, for the benefit of the Insolvent Laws of Maryland, and that the first Saturday after the second Monday in November next has been assigned for him to appear in said Court to answer such interrogatories as his creditors may propose or allege against him. Wm. H. Dallam, Clerk, Circuit Court for Harford county." (*The Aegis & Intelligencer*, May 18, 1866, p. 2). **Genealogical Notes**: Thomas W. Moulton, of Harford Co., married Henrietta Katz, of Philadelphia, and their daughter Mary G. Moulton (1844-1937), of Philadelphia, later of Havre de Grace, married John L. Touchton. (Wesleyan Chapel tombstones; Death certificate of Mary G. Touchton; 1850 Harford County Census)

Munnikhuysen, Jacob H., 1839/1879. "Petition, Schedules, affidavits, personal discharge & order for publication for appearance, Trustee's Bond, Trustee's Certificate & deed to trustee filed 25th March 1839. May 25th 1839 Petitioner appears, Petition & Order filed & continued. 23rd Novr. 1839 Petitioner appears and finally discharged. [line drawn across middle of the page followed by] 19th Feby 1879 Report of Insolvent Trustee & Order of Notice to Creditors filed. 4th March 1879 Claim of Constable Executrix filed. 4th April 1869 Claim of Wm. Munnikhuysen, admr. of John A. Munnikhuysen, filed. April 22nd 1879 Claim of Lee Magness, use of E. L. Sawyer, filed … Dec 22nd 1883 Auditor's Report & Order Nisi filed … 9th April 1884 Final order on 2nd Report filed." (Insolvent Docket A, 1807-1843, p. 168, at the Maryland State Archives; Insolvent Docket A. L. J. No. 1, p. 65, in Court Records Department of the Historical Society of Harford County). "Notice to Creditors, Ordered, by the Circuit Court for Harford county, this 19th day of Feby, 1879, that the trustee of Jacob H. Munnikhuysen, as insolvent debtor, by publication of a copy of this order in some newspaper printed in Harford county, once in each of three successive weeks before the 18th day of March, 1879, give notice to all creditors of said insolvent debtor who were such at the date of his petition, viz., 26th day of February, 1839 [sic] to file their claims with the clerk of this Court, on or before the 18th day of March, 1879. James D. Watters. True copy--test: A. L. Jarrett, Clerk." (*Harford Democrat*, February 2, 1879, p. 2) **Genealogical Notes**: Jacob H. Munnikhuysen (1802-1892), son of John Munnikhuysen and Mary Howard Lee, married Charlotte E. Howard in 1844. (Information from findagrave.com)

Murphy, Ephraim H., 1858. "Petition, Schedules, Affidavits, Appointment of Trustee, Order of Notice, Trustee's Bond & Deed filed 13th January 1858. 2nd Aug 1858 Petition & ordered filed. 13th Nov/58 Petitioner appears, files certificate of publication & finally discharged." (Insolvent Docket A. L. J. No. 1, p. 23, in the Court Records Department of the Historical Society of Harford County). "Notice is hereby given that Ephraim H. Murphy, of Harford County, has made application to the Circuit Court of said County, for the benefit of the Insolvent Laws of Maryland, and that the first Saturday after the second Monday in May, 1858, has been assigned for him to appear in said Court to answer such interrogatories as his creditors may propose or allege against him. Wm. Galloway, Clerk of Circuit Court for Harford County." (*The Southern Aegis*, January 23, 1858, p. 3) "In the matter of the petition of Ephraim H. Murphy for the benefit of the Insolvent Laws. In the Circuit Court for Harford County, May term, 1858. Ordered by this Court, this 2nd day of August, 1858, that Ephraim H. Murphy be and appear before this Court on the first Saturday after the second Monday in November next, to answer such interrogatories or allegations as his creditors may propose or allege against him, and that he give notice of the day so fixed for his appearance, by publishing a copy of this order in some newspaper printed in Harford County, once a week for one month, the first assertion to be three months before the said first Saturday after the said second Monday in November next. John H. Price. Test: Wm. Galloway, Clk." (*The Southern Aegis*, August 21, 1858, p. 3)

Murphy, Gilbert, 1822. "Petition, Schedule, Bond, Sheriff's certificate, personal discharge and order for publication filed 26th Aug. 1823. March 13th 1824 printers certificate filed, petitioner appears and is discharged." (Insolvent Docket A, 1807-1843, p. 52, at the Maryland State Archives, spelled his name Murphey; Insolvent Docket Prior to 1827, Court Records Accession #632 at the Historical Society of Harford County)

Myers, Edward, 1846. "Notice is hereby given, to the creditors of Edward Myers, late an imprisoned debtor of Harford County, that on the application of said debtor by petition in writing to the Hon. Samuel Bradford, associate justice of the Orphan's Court of said county, for the benefit of the insolvent laws of Maryland, the said judge on the 23rd day of March, 1846, granted to the said debtor a discharge from imprisonment and appointed the first Saturday after the 3rd Monday in November next, for his appearance before the Judges of Harford county court at the court house of said county, for a final hearing before said court, on said petition and to answer such interrogatories as his creditors may propose to him." (*Harford Madisonian and Havre de Grace Messenger*, 20 Aug 1846, p. 3)

Myres, Alexander K., 1835. "Petition, Affidavits, Schedule, personal discharge and order of publication, Bond for Appearance, Trustee's Bond, Trustee's Certificate and Deed to Trustee filed 15th Augt. 1835. 19th Mar 1836 Petitioner appears, certificate of publication filed and finally discharged." (Insolvent Docket A, 1807-1843, p. 142, at Maryland State Archives) **Genealogical Note**: see below.

Myres, Henry K., 1824. "Petition, Bond, Schedule, Sheriffs Certificate, personal Discharge and order for Publication filed 27th July 1824. March 19th 1825 Petitioner appears." [nothing further] (Insolvent Docket A, 1807-1843, p. 65, at Maryland State Archives; Insolvent Docket Prior to 1827, Court Records Accession #632 at Historical Society of Harford County) **Genealogical Note**: Henry Kentle Myres and Alexander Kentle Myers, sons of John and Margaret (Estate Distributions, 1817 and 1829)

Nagle, John H., 1889. "Notice to Creditors. In the matter of the Insolvency of John H. Nagle ... Notice is hereby given to the creditors of John H. Nagle, that he has applied for the benefit of the Insolvent Laws of the State of Maryland, and that a meeting of the creditors of said insolvent will be held at the office of Geo. L. Van Bibber, in Bel Air, Harford county, on Tuesday, the 17th day of December, 1889, at 10 o'clock, A. M., for the purpose of electing a permanent trustee or trustees, proving claims, propounding interrogatories, &c. Geo. L. Van Bibber, Frank E. Gorrell, Preliminary Trustees." (*The Aegis & Intelligencer*, December 13, 1889, p. 2). "S. A. Williams and F. E. Gorrell, Solicitors. Notice to Creditors ... Ordered, this 6th day of March, 1890, by the Circuit Court for Harford County, that the permanent trustees of the estate of said insolvent give notice, by publication of this order in some newspaper printed and published in Harford County, for four successive weeks before the first day of April next, to the creditors of said John H. Nagle, insolvent, to file their claims duly proven, with the Clerk of said Court, on or before the 15th day of May next. James D. Watters. True copy, test, A. L. Jarrett, Clerk." (*The Aegis & Intelligencer*, March 28, 1890, p. 3). "S. A. Williams and F. E. Gorrell,

Solicitors. Order Nisi ... Ordered, this sixth day of March, 1890, by the Circuit Court for Harford County, that the within and aforegoing report of sale made and reported by Stevenson A. Williams and Frank E. Gorrell, permanent trustees of the estate of John H. Nagle, an insolvent, be finally ratified and confirmed, unless cause to the contrary thereof be shown on or before the sixth day of April next; provided, a copy of this order be inserted in some newspaper printed and published in Harford county, once in each of three successive weeks on or before the sixth day of April next. The report states the amount of sales to be $2,858.55. A. L. Jarrett, Clerk." (*The Aegis & Intelligencer*, March 28, 1890, p. 3) "S. A. Williams and Frank E. Gorrell, Trustees. Order Nisi ... Ordered, this 1st day of July, 1890, by the Circuit Court for Harford County, that the sale as reported by S. A. Williams and Frank E. Gorrell, permanent trustees, in their report No. 2, be ratified and confirmed, unless cause to the contrary thereof be shown on or before the 26th day of July, inst.; provided, a copy of this order be inserted in some newspaper printed and published in Harford county, once a week in each of three successive weeks, before the 26th day of July, inst. The report states the amount of sales to be $200.00. A. Lingan Jarrett, Clerk." (*The Aegis & Intelligencer*, July 4, 1890, p. 2) **Genealogical Notes**: John Henry Nagle, son of Emanuel Nagle and 2nd wife Elizabeth Howe, was born on March 23, 1864, married Florence Livezey (b. November 12, 1869) on August 4, 1886 and their children were Henry Cramp Nagle (1887-1888), James Stewart Nagle (b. 1889), Millard Howe Nagle (b. 1890), and Sylvania Gertrude Nagle (b. 1892). (*Maryland Bible Records, Volume 1*, by Henry C. Peden, Jr., 2003, pp. 183-187)

Negro Priss, 1823. "Petition, Schedule, Bond, Sheriff's certificate, personal discharge and order for publication filed 4th March 1823. 30th Aug. 1823 Petitioner appears & cont'd. 6th September 1823 objections filed by George Wilson ... 13th March 1824 Petitioner appears, certificate of publication of notice filed ... allegations withdrawn [and] released." (Insolvent Docket A, 1807-1843, p. 53, at the Maryland State Archives; Insolvent Docket Prior to 1827, Court Records Accession #632 at the Historical Society of Harford County)

Nelson, Jarrett, 1810. "Petition & Schedule filed 19th Augt. 1811. Ordered by the Court that the Sheriff of Harford County bring into Court the body of the said Jarrett Nelson tomorrow morning ... brought into Court ... ordered by the Court that [he] be discharged from his confinement ... Augt. 28th 1812 petitioner appeared and the Court appointed Abel Alderson his trustee and ordered to be discharged from his debts ... Certificate of the trustee that he has received all the property of the petitioner filed 28th Augt. 1812." (Insolvent Docket A, 1807-1843, p. 11, at the Maryland State Archives; Insolvent Docket Prior to 1827, Court Records Accession #632 at the Historical Society of Harford County)

Nelson, John, 1834. "Petition, Affidavits, Schedule, personal discharge and order of publication, Bond for Appearance, Trustee's Bond, Trustee's Certificate and Deed to Trustee filed 5th Augt.1834. 14th March 1835. Petitioner appears, Certificate of Publication filed and finally discharged." (Insolvent Docket A, 1807-1843, p. 135, at Maryland State Archives)

Nelson, William, 1866. "Petition, Schedule of property, List of debts to & from Affidavit, Order, Bond & Deed filed 12th June 1866 ... J. T. C. Hopkins, Trustee. 17th Nov/66 ... Petitioner appeared & was finally discharged." (Insolvent Docket A. L. J. No. 1, p. 47, in the Court Records Department of the Historical Society of Harford County). "Notice is hereby given that William Nelson has made application to the Circuit Court of Harford county, for the benefit of the Insolvent Laws of Maryland, and that the first Saturday after the second Monday in November next has been assigned for him to appear in said Court to answer such interrogatories as his creditors may propose or allege against him. Wm. H. Dallam, Clerk, Circuit Court for Harford county." (*The Aegis & Intelligencer*, June 15, 1866, p. 2)

Neuman, August, 1898. "Notice to Creditors. Notice is hereby given to the creditors of August Neuman, who were such on the 20th day of April in the year 1897, that said Neuman has been adjudicated an insolvent debtor, and that the undersigned have been appointed preliminary trustees for his estate and they have fixed Saturday, the 21st day of May, 1898, at eleven o'clock A. M. at the office of the undersigned, Frank E. Gorrell, in Bel Air, as the time and place for the meeting of the creditors of said insolvent to choose a permanent trustee for his estate. William G. Rouse, Frank E. Gorrell, Preliminary Trustees." (*The Aegis & Intelligencer*, May 20, 1898, p. 2)

Noonan, Michael, 1831. "Petition, Schedule, Shffs. certificate, personal discharge and order for publication, Bond for Appearance, Trustee's Bond, Trustee's Certificate and Deed to Trustee filed 21st April 1831. 13th August 1831 Petitioner appears, certificate of publication, oath administered and petitioner finally discharged." (Insolvent Docket A, 1807-1843, p. 109, at Maryland State Archives)

Norrington, Isaac, 1821. "To the Honorable Wm. H. Ward, one of the Justices of the Orphans Court of Harford County. The petition of Isaac Norrington of Harford County respectfully sheweth that your petitioner is now in actual confinement in Harford County Jail for debts which he is unable to pay, that he is willing and offers to deliver up to the use of his creditors all his property real, personal and mixed, the necessary wearing apparel and bedding of himself & family excepted, a schedule whereof together with a list of his creditors and debtors, as far as he can at present ascertain them is hereto on oath annexed, your petitioner also hereto annexes proof on oath that he has resided two years next preceding this his application within the State of Maryland. Your petitioner therefore prays your Honour to grant him the benefit of the insolvent laws of this State and to relieve him from his present confinement, and your Petitioner will ever pray. Isaac Norrington." (Court Records Document 68.05.6(a) at Historical Society of Harford County). "I hereby certify that Isaac Norrington the petitioner above named is now in actual confinement in Harford County Jail for debt at the suit of John Eaton and that is not upon a breach of peace or any of the penal Laws of the State of Maryland or of the United States. Given under my hand this 31st day of August 1821. Joshua Guyton, Sheriff." (Court Records Document 68.05.6(a) at the Historical Society of Harford County) "State of Maryland Harford County to wit. On this 31st day of August 1821 personally appeared Abel Watkins before me the subscriber one of the State of Maryland's Justices of the Peace in and for the county aforesaid and made oath on the Holy Evangely of Almighty God that Isaac Norrington the petitioner within named has resided within the State of Maryland the two years next preceding [sic] the date hereof and that he still resides therein. Sworn to before Saml. Bradford." (Court Records Document 68.05.6(a) included a copy of the schedule to which "Isaac Norrington" signed his name, but no property was listed). **Genealogical Note**: Isaac Norrington was a son of Mary Norrington who died testate in 1792. She may have been the widow of John Norrington. (Harford County Will Book AJ No. 2, pp. 488-490)

Norris, Charles W., 1879. "Petition, Schedules, Affidavits, Order, Appointment of Stevenson Archer Trustee, Trustee's Bond & deed filed 29 October 1879. Feby 9th 1880 Petitioner appears in Court, files printed notice of Insolvency with printer's certificate, no objections, he is by the Court finally discharged." (Insolvent Docket A. L. J. No. 1, p. 66, in Court Records Department of the Historical Society of Harford County). "Insolvent Notice. Notice is hereby given, that Charles W. Norris, of Harford county, has made application to the Circuit Court for said county for the benefit of the Insolvent Laws of Maryland, and that the second Monday of February, 1880, has been assigned for him to appear and answer such interrogatories as his creditors may propose or allege against him. A. Lingan Jarrett, Clerk, Circuit Court for Harford Co." (*Harford Democrat*, October 31, 1879, p. 2). **Genealogical Notes**: Charles Wesley Norris (1840 – March 28, 1914), son of Cardiff Dutton Norris (1806-1876) and Mary Frances Dutton (1813-1887), married Miss Elizabeth P. "Lizzie" Keene (1850-

1937), of Cambridge, MD, on October 22, 1873 at St. Paul's Church in Baltimore by Rev. William F. Brand, pastor of St. Mary's Episcopal Church at Emmorton, Harford County. Charles was a general store merchant in Bel Air and later employed at the B&O Station at Camden in Baltimore. Their only child Elizabeth K. Norris (1875-1964) is buried beside them in Union Chapel. (*The Aegis and Intelligencer*, October 24, 1873 and April 3, 1914; *The Norris Family of Maryland and Virginia*, by Harry Alexander Davis, 1941, pp. 321, 671; Union Chapel United Methodist Church tombstones). Charles W. Norris and his brother Frank C. Norris (1845-1905) kept a general store in Bel Air by 1869, trading as Charles W. Norris & Bro., and Walter Fraser was the store clerk in 1870. The newspaper reported in 1872, "These gentlemen understand and appreciate the value of advertising, and you can rely upon everything they tell you about their goods. Their stock is large, and embraces almost everything you desire. Go and see their Dolly Vardens." In December 1872 a seasonal comment about the store also appeared in the paper: "Here, too, may be found a rare assortment of Christmas good things, sufficient to please the palate and tempt the taste of old Epicurus himself." In 1875 he hired master builder Jacob E Bull and added a 12x20 feet extension to his storeroom and a 12x30 feet shed room for storage. His salesroom when completed was 20x50 feet. In 1878 Charles sold his stock of goods to John G. Rouse, formerly of Hopewell Cross Roads, who conducted the business in Bel Air. He was enumerated as a retired merchant living in the Abingdon District in the 1880 census and he later moved to Baltimore. His brother left the mercantile business for a short time, but returned to the trade when he bought the Moore Bros.' Store in Fallston in 1888. (Harford County Census; Harford County Directory, 1878; *Harford Democrat*, April 16, 1875; *The Aegis & Intelligencer*, April 19, 1869, September 2, 1870, May 3, 1872, December 20, 1872, February 1, 1878, and April 20, 1888)

Norris, George. 1825. "Petition, Bond, Schedule, Shffs Certificate, Certificate of Residence, personal discharge and order for publication filed 19th July 1825." [nothing further recorded] (Insolvent Docket A, 1807-1843, p. 72, at the Maryland State Archives; Insolvent Docket Prior to 1827, Court Records Accession #632 at the Historical Society of Harford County)

Norris, Luther A., 1830. Sale by trustees of Luther A. Norris, insolvent debtor of Baltimore Co., of his title to tracts in Harford Co. called *Elling*, part of *Swampy Point*, part of *Holly Hill*, part of *Islington*, part of *Planter's Neglect*, part of *Parker's Folly*, part of *Holling Refuge* and part of *Hanson's Regnedged Neck* – 200 acres – H. W. Bool, Jr., auctioneer. (*Independent Citizen*, November 11, 1830). **Genealogical Notes**: Luther Augustus Norris, son of Capt. Jacob Norris (1753-1806) and Avarilla Gallion, was born in 1800, married Mary Hollis, daughter of Clark Hollis, circa July 22, 1819 (date of license) and was listed in Baltimore in the 1830 census, but not listed in the 1840 census. The children of Luther and Mary Norris were Clarissa Norris Stauffer, Augustus Norris, James A. Norris, Mary Louisa Norris Ruck and John Julius Norris. (*The Norris Family of Maryland*, by Thomas M. Myers, 1916, p. 43; Harford County Estate Distribution, 1824; *The Norris Family of Maryland and Virginia, Genealogy of Thomas Norris 1361-1930*, by Harry Alexander Norris, 1941, Volume I, pp. 289-290)

Norris, Thomas, 1804. "Whereas we the Subscribers Justices of the Peace for Harford County upon the petition of Thomas Norris, who set forth that he had been confined in the gaol [jail] of the said county twenty Days for Debts which he was unable to pay & finding the facts stated to be true we together did meet at the County Gaol on the fourteenth day of October 1804 and did then and there appoint the fifth day of November Instant to meet at the Court House of said county which said appointment we did then and there … at the request of said Sheriff administer to the said Thomas Norris the following oath which was taken by the said Thomas Norris being first duly sworn on the holy evangels of almighty God in the words following, I Thomas Norris do solemnly swear that the schedule which I have delivered to the Sheriff of Harford County doth contain a full account to the best of my knowledge and remembrance of my whole estate both real & personal or that I have any title to or interest in and of all debts, credits and effects whatsoever which I or any in trust for me have or at the time of my petition had, or am or was in any respect entitled to in possession, remainder or reversion and that I have not directly or indirectly at any time since my imprisonment or before, sold, leased or otherwise conveyed or disposed of or intrusted all or any part of my estate, goods, stock, money or debts thereby to defraud my creditors or to secure the same to receive or expect any profit or advantage thereof so help me God, which said duplicate of the schedule aforesaid we have transmitted to the clerk of the county court to be by him preserved in his office for the information of the creditors of the said Thomas Norris. Given under our hands & seals this 5th day of November Eighteen hundred and four. John Moores. James Amos. Wm. Smithson." (Court Records Document 67.08.9(A) (B) at the Historical Society of Harford County; a copy of the schedule to which "Thomas Norriss" [sic] had signed his name was included, but no property was listed). **Genealogical Notes**: Thomas Norris, son of Alexander Norris and Sarah Norrington, was born in August 1771 and married Elizabeth Parker (b. 1772) by 1793 in Harford County, later moved to York Co., PA and both died there in the 1850s. The children of Thomas and Elizabeth Norris were Alexander Norris, John Norris, Elizabeth Jane Norris Parker, Salem Norris, Parker A. Norris, Martha Norris Boyd, Frances Ann Norris Crawford, Thomas Norris and Isaac Norris. (*The Norris Family of Maryland and Virginia, Genealogy of Thomas Norris 1361-1930,* by Harry Alexander Norris, 1941, Volume I, pp. 351, 717-719)

Norton, David (African American), 1822. "Harford County sct. On application to the subscriber as a Judge of the Orphans Court of Harford County by petition in writing of David Norton stating that he is an imprisoned debtor in actual confinement in the Gaol of said County and praying for a discharge from said confinement and for the benefit of the Act of the General Assembly of Maryland Entitled an 'Act for the relief of sundry insolvent debtors' passed at November session in the year eighteen hundred and five and the several supplements thereto on the terms therein mentioned, a Schedule of his property and a list of his Creditors on oath being annexed to his said Petition with competent and satisfactory testimony that he has resided two years within the State of Maryland next before the making of his application as aforesaid and the said David Norton having taken the oath prescribed by the said act prescribed for delivering up his property and given bond with security and in a penalty by me approved and prescribed for his appearance before the Judges of Harford County Court on the first Saturday after the second Monday in March next at the Courthouse of said County, being the time by me appointed for hearing before said Court in said petition to answer Interrogatories which his Creditors may propose to him according to the provisions of the said Original Act. I do hereby order and adjudge that the said David Norton be discharged from Imprisonment and direct that he give notice to his Creditors of his said application and discharge, and of the day so by me appointed for a hearing before said Court, by advertisement to be inserted in the Bond of Union once a week for three months before the day so appointed. Given under my hand this 29th day of August 1822. John Moores." (Court Records Document 68.05.3(b) at the Historical Society of Harford County). "Know all men by these presents that we David Norton & Thomas Norton all of Harford county and State of Maryland are held and firmly bound unto the said State in the full and just sum of one hundred dollars Current money To the payment whereof well and truly to be made to the said State or its certain Attorney, we bind ourselves and each of us, our and each of our heirs, executors and administrators firmly by these presents. Sealed with our seals and dated this 29th day of August eighteen hundred and twenty two. The Condition of the above obligation is such that if the above bound David Norton shall make his personal appearance before the Judges of Harford county Court at the Courthouse in said County on the first Saturday after the second Monday in March next to answer interrogatories which his creditor may propose to him and also to appoint a Trustee for the benefit of his Creditors. Then the above obligation to be void or else to be and remain in full force and virtue in Law. David "X" Norton. Thos. "X" Norton. Witness: John Moores." (Court Records Document 68.05.3(b), loc. cit.) "To the Honorable John Moores, Esq., Judge of the Orphans Court of Harford County. The petition of David Norton of Harford County respectfully sheweth that your petitioner is now imprisoned in the Gaol of Harford county for debts which he is unable to pay, that he is willing and offers to deliver up to the use of his creditors, all his property, real, personal and mixed to which he is in any way entitled (the necessary wearing apparel and bedding of himself and his family excepted), a Schedule whereof together with a list of his Creditors and debtors as far as he can ascertain them at present ascertain them are hereto on oath annexed. Your Petitioner also hereto annexes proof on oath that he has resided two years next preceding this his application within the State of Maryland. Your petitioner therefore prays your honors to grant him the benefit of the Insolvent Laws of this State and discharge him from his present imprisonment and he will pray &c. 29 August 1822. Daniel "X" Norton. Test: Saml. Bradford." (Court Records Document 68.05.3(a), loc. cit.; a copy of the schedule to which David Norton made his "X" mark was included, but he had no property to list). "I hereby certify that the within named David Norton now in actual confinement in the Gaol of Harford County is an Insolvent debtor, and that he is not confined on account of any breach of the Peace or for the nonpayment of any fine or penalty for a breach of the laws of this State or of the United States. 29th August 1822. Saml. Bradford, Shff." (Court Records Document 68.05.3(a), loc. cit.) "Petition, Schedule, Bond, Sheriff's certificate, and personal discharge & order for publication filed 29th Aug 1822. Petitioner has leave on 15th March 1823 to withdraw his petition." [nothing further recorded] (Insolvent Docket A, 1807-1843, p. 51, at the Maryland State Archives; Insolvent Docket Prior to 1827, Court Records Accession #632 at the Historical Society of Harford County)

Nourse, William B., 1890. "Insolvent's Notice. In the matter of the Insolvency of William B. Nourse ... Notice is hereby given to the creditors of William B. Nourse who were such upon his application for the benefit of the Insolvent Laws of the State of Maryland, to file their claims, duly proven, with the Clerk of said Court, on or before the first day of July, 1890. Frank E. Gorrell, Permanent Trustee." (*The Aegis & Intelligencer*, April 11, 1890, p. 2). "Insolvent's Notice ... Notice is hereby given to the creditors of William B. Nourse that the 12th day of May, 1890, has been fixed as the day that said Insolvent shall appear before the Circuit Court for Harford County, to answer such interrogatories or allegations as his creditors, endorsers or sureties propose or allege against him. Frank E. Gorrell, Permanent Trustee." (*The Aegis & Intelligencer*, Ibid.) **Genealogical Notes**: William B. Nourse (born 1843), of Prince George's Co., MD, worked as a farmer and married Rosa H. Raymond (born 1853), of Harford Co., on September 21, 1875 by Rev. Daniel Haskell, assisted by Rev. Robert Bolton, at the bride's parents at the Home Farm near Perrymansville. (Marriage records did not indicate place of marriage, but *The Aegis & Intelligencer*, October 1, 1875, did; also reported him as W. B. Nourse, Esq.)

O'Brien, William, 1829. "Petition, Schedule, Bond of Trustee, Certificate, Deed, Bond of Petitioner and Order of Publication filed 7th March 1829." [nothing further recorded] (Insolvent Docket A, 1807-1843, p. 93, at the Maryland State Archives)

O'Connor, Michael, 1806. "Whereas we the Subscribers Justices of the Peace for Harford County, together with William Wilson also one of the Justices of the Peace for said county, upon the petition of Michael O'Connah [sic] who set forth that he had been confined in the gaol [jail] of said county twenty days & upwards for Debts which he was unable to pay & finding the facts stated to be true we together with the said William Wilson did meet at the County Gaol of said county on the 20th day of March 1806 and did then & there appoint the 21st day of April Inst. [to meet at the Court House] which said appointment we did then and there ... at the request of said Sheriff administer to the said Michael O'Connah the following oath which was taken by the said Michael O'Connah being first duly sworn on the Holy Evangely of Almighty God in the words following, vizt., I Michael O'Connah do solemnly swear that the schedule which I have delivered to the Sheriff of Harford County doth contain a full account to the best of my knowledge and remembrance of my whole estate both real & personal or that I have any title to or interest in and of all debts, credits and effects whatsoever which I or any in trust for me have or at the time of my petition had, or am or was in any respect entitled to in possession, remainder or reversion and that I have not directly or indirectly at any time since my imprisonment or before, sold, leased or otherwise conveyed or disposed of or intrusted all or any part of my estate, goods, stock, money or debts thereby to defraud my creditors or to secure the same to receive or expect any profit or advantage thereof so help me God, which said duplicate of the schedule aforesaid we have transmitted to the clerk of the county court to be by him preserved in his office for the information of the creditors of the said Michael O'Connah. Given under our hands & seals this 21st Day of April 1806. John Moores. Thomas A. Hays." (Court Records Document 67.08.8(A) at the Historical Society of Harford County; copy of the schedule to which "Michael O'Connar" made his "X" mark was included, but no property was listed; Michael O'Conner's release was filed on the same day). **Historical Notes**: Michael O'Connor, aged 65, swore in open Court on March 12, 1821 "that he served in the Revolutionary War, as follows: That he enlisted under Lt. John W. Dorsey in Capt. Edward Norwood's Compy. of Infantry of Flying Camp, served out the period of his enlistment and returned to Baltimore after the Battle of White Plains, and in the spring of 1777 entered into Capt. Alexander Furnival's Compy. of Artillery stationed at Whetstone Point (now Fort McHenry) in the State of Maryland for the term of three years, from thence enlisted into Capt. Richard Dorsey's Compy. of Artillery for 3 years and was attached to Col. Charles Thompson's Artillery Regt. and after the Battle of Monmouth reenlisted for during the war, served out the period of his enlistment and was discharged at Annapolis after returning from James' Island. That he made his original declaration at Baltimore before the Honorable Judge Brice on or about the 8th of July 1818 and was placed on the Revolutionary Pension List of the Maryland Agency as will appear by his Certificate dated 27th January 1819 and numbered 5829 and I do solemnly swear that I was a resident citizen of the United States on the 18th March 1818, and that I have since that time by gift, sale or in any manner disposed of my property or any part thereof with intent thereby so to diminish it as to bring myself within provisions of an act of Congress entitled an act to provide for certain persons engaged in the land and naval service of the United States in the Revolutionary War, passed on the 18th day of March 1818, and that I have not nor has any person in trust for me, any property or securities, contracts or debts due to me nor have I any income other than what is contained in the schedule hereto annexed, and by me subscribed. That he hath no property of any kind or nature whatsoever, neither hath he any family. That he formerly obtained his support by common labouring work through the country, but now from advanced age and debility depends solely on his pension and the assistance of Friends. That in consequence of his reduced circumstances stands in need of the assistance of his country for support, not being able to support himself without public charity." Michael O'Connor made his "X" mark on the document. (Court Records Document 25.14.4 at Historical Society of Harford County)

O'Donnel, Edward, 1834. "Petition, Affidavits, Schedule, personal discharge and order of publication, Bond for Appearance, Trustee's Bond, Trustee's Certificate and Deed to Trustee filed 27th Decr. 1834. 15th Augt. 1835. Petitioner appears, Certificate of Publication filed and finally discharged." (Insolvent Docket A, 1807-1843, p. 137, at the Maryland State Archives)

O'Donnel, John, 1834. "Petition, Affidavits, Schedule, personal discharge and order of publication, Bond for Appearance, Trustee's Bond, Trustee's Certificate and Deed to Trustee filed 27th Decr. 1834.

15th Aug. 1835. Petitioner appears, Certificate of Publication filed and finally discharged. 12th Oct 1835 Petition and Order for Sale filed … May 16th 1836 Auditor's Report and order of ratification nisi filed." (Insolvent Docket A, 1807-1843, p. 137, at the Maryland State Archives)

Oliver, ----, 1884. "Injunction.—Saturday last [July 12, 1884] Sheriff Walker served an injunction on Major Hancock, agent for Thurber & Co., of New York, J. O. Becket and George Peacock, deputy U. S. Marshals, and Jacob Yumel, agent for the P., W. & B. R. R., to prevent the removal of canned goods that was conveyed to Harlan & Webster, trustees, for Oliver, an insolvent, for the benefit of his creditors. Before the arrival of the sheriff one thousand cases of the goods had gone beyond his jurisdiction. The remainder, about two thousand cases, are held at Aberdeen and Harford Furnace under the order of the court. Notwithstanding this injunction, on Monday Messrs. Peacock and Becket, in disregard of the orders of the court, continued the removal of the goods and succeeded in transferring five hundred cases from Harford Furnace to the warehouse at Aberdeen. In consequence of this action they were arrested on Tuesday morning and brought to Bel Air and placed in jail, charged with contempt of court. Judge Fowler came over to Bel Air, Tuesday evening, to her the contempt case, but before it was heard, a writ of habeas corpus from Judge Bond, of the U. S. Court, was served, and the case was adjourned to the U. S. Court in Baltimore, and yesterday it was to have been tried. Messrs. H. W. Archer and W. H. Harlan represented the Oliver creditors, Messrs. Hancock, Young and Blackisten [for] the Thurbers." (*Harford Democrat.* July 18, 1884, p. 2)

Onion, John B., 1805. "March 26th 1805. To Henry Ridgely, Esqr., Chief Justice of Harford County Court and his associates. The Petition of John B. Onion of Harford County humbly sheweth that he is included in an Act for the relief of sundry Insolvent Debtors passed November Session Eighteen hundred and four, that he has resided the last two preceding years in the State of Maryland, that he is willing to deliver to the use of his creditors, all his property, real, personal and mixed (the necessary wearing apparel & beding [sic] for himself & family excepted) to which he is in any way entitled, a Schedule whereof an oath together with a list of his Creditors also on oath as near as he can ascertain them, whereof two-thirds of said Creditors in value & amt. have assented in writing to your petitioners obtaining the benefits of said Act all which will more fully appear to your honors by the documents hereunto annexed, your petitioner therefore prays the full benefit of said Act, and your petitioner &c, &c. [signed] John B. Onion. A Schedule of the property, vizt., 300 acres of Land in the N. W. territory, 1½ acres of Land near the City of Annapolis which I hold a life estate in, one old horse." [Among other Court record entries were two lists of creditors and other statements including this final entry]: "July 8th 1805. The Creditors of the said John B. Onion not attending according to notice … the petition of the said John B. Onion be continued over and postponed to next Term. [Final entry, undated]: The original Papers delivered the Petitioner by the order of the Court And the Petition withdrawn." (Court Actions in Insolvencies, 1805-1807, Court Records Book Accession No. 605 at the Historical Society of Harford County). **Genealogical Notes:** John Barret Onion was born circa 1765, married Juliet M. Pendegras on March 26, 1789 and died on June 27, 1813 in Harford County. The children of John and Juliet Onion were Mabrey Onion (1790-1809), Caroline C. Onion (1792-1857), Matilda Onion (1794-1853), Thomas B. Onion (b. 1796), Elizabeth Onion (b. 1798), John B. Onion, Jr. (b. 1800, died young), Zacheus Onion (1802-1856), Juliet Onion (b. 1805), Rachael Onion (b. 1808) and Edward Mabrey Onion (1810-1876). (Edward M. Onion Bible, *Maryland Bible Records, Volume 5,* by Henry C. Peden, Jr., 2004, pp. 131-133; Harford County Equity Court Case No. 6, filed in 1816, Juliet Onion vs. John Rouse, now in possession of the Maryland State Archives)

Onion, Lloyd D., 1829. "Petition, Schedule, Sheriff's Certificate, personal discharge, Order for Publication, Bond for Appearance, Trustee's Certificate Trustee's Bond and Deed to Trustee filed 30th Oct 1829. 13th March 1830 Interrogatories filed. Printers certificate filed. Petitioner appears and cont'd.

14th August 1830 Petitioner appears and continued." [nothing further recorded] (Insolvent Docket A, 1807-1843, p. 99, at the Maryland State Archives). 1836. "Petition, Affidavits, Schedule, personal discharge and order of publication, Bond for Appearance, Trustee's Bond, Trustee's Certificate and Deed to Trustee filed 25th July 1836. 18th March 1837 Petitioner appears, certificate of publication filed and finally discharged." (Insolvent Docket A, 1807-1843, p. 149, loc. cit.). **Genealogical Notes**: Lloyd Day Onion, son of Thomas Bond Onion, of Baltimore County, married Elizabeth Rouse (b. February 17, 1803), daughter of John Rouse (1775-1832) and Sarah Cochran (1775-1850), of Harford Co., circa 22 Oct 1825 (date of license; *Heirs & Legatees of Harford County, Maryland, 1802-1846*, by Henry C. Peden, Jr., 1988, pp. 41, 43; Sarah Rouse's estate distribution on April 25, 1850; *The Rouse Family of Maryland*, by Nancy R. Rouse, 1989, p. 4; Harford County Equity Court Paper #77, Watters vs. Onion, at the Maryland State Archives)

Orr, James, 1816. "Petition, Schedule & Bond filed 15th March 1816 … ordered by the Court that he give notice in one of the Baltimore papers once a week for three months previous to the first Thursday of next Augt. term." [nothing further recorded] (Insolvent Docket A, 1807-1843, p. 17, at the Maryland State Archives; Insolvent Docket Prior to 1827, Court Records Accession #632 at the Historical Society of Harford County). 1821. "Harford County sct. On application to the subscriber as a Judge of the Orphans Court of Harford County by petition in writing of James Orr stating that he is an imprisoned debtor in actual confinement in the Jail of said County and praying for a discharge from said confinement, and for the benefit of the Act of the General Assembly of Maryland Entitled 'An Act for the relief of sundry insolvent debtors' passed at November Session, Eighteen hundred and five, and the several supplements thereto on the terms therein mentioned, a Schedule of his property and a list of his creditors on oath being annexed to his said petition with competent and satisfactory testimony that he has resided two years within the State of Maryland next before the making of his application as aforesaid and the said James Orr having taken the affirmation prescribed by the said act prescribed for delivering up his property and given bond with security and in a penalty by me approved and prescribed for his appearance before the Judges of Harford County Court on the first Saturday after the fourth Monday in August next at the Court house of said County, being the time by me appointed for hearing before said Court in said petition to answer interrogatories which his Creditors may propose to him according to the provisions of the said Original Act. I do hereby order and adjudge that the said James Orr be discharged from Imprisonment and direct that he give notice to his creditors of his said application and discharge and of the day so by me appointed for a hearing before said Court by advertisement to be inserted in the Bond of Union once a week for three months before the day so appointed. Given under my hand this 14th day of February 1821. John Moores." (Court Records Document 68.05.2(c) at Historical Society of Harford County). "Know all men by these presents that we James Orr and Samuel Bradford of Harford county and State of Maryland are held and firmly bound unto the State of Maryland in the sum of fifty dollars Current money of the United States to be paid to the said State or its certain attorney to which payment well and truly to be made and done, we bind ourselves, our heirs, executors and administrators firmly by these presents. Sealed with our seals and dated this 14th day of February 1821. The Condition of the above obligation is such that if the above bound James Orr shall make his personal appearance before the Judges of Harford county Court on the first Saturday after the fourth Monday in August next at the Court House in said County then and there to answer such Interrogatories and allegations as his creditors may propose to him, then the above obligation to be void and of no effect otherwise to remain in full force and virtue in Law. James Orr. Saml. Bradford. Signed and sealed in presence of John Moores." (Court Records Document 68.05.2(a), loc. cit.) "To the honorable John Moores, one of the Justices of the Orphans Court of Harford County. The petition of James Orr of

Harford County respectfully sheweth that your petitioner is now actual confinement in Harford County Jail for debts which he is unable to pay, that he is willing and offers to deliver up to the use of his creditors, all his property, real, personal and mixed to which he is in any way entitled, the necessary wearing apparel and bedding of himself and his family excepted, a schedule whereof together with a list of his creditors and debtors as far as he can at present ascertain them are hereto on oath annexed. Your Petitioner also annexes proof on oath that he has resided two years next preceding this his application within the State of Maryland. Your petitioner therefore prays your honour to grant him the benefit of the insolvent laws of this state and release him from his present imprisonment, and your petitioner will ever pray &c. 14 Feby. 1821, James Orr." (Court Records Document 68.05.2(b), loc. cit.; a copy of the schedule to which "James Orr" signed his name was included, but he had no property to list). "I hereby certify that the within named James Orr is now in actual confinement in Harford County Jail for debt at the suit of Benjamin Baxter and that it is not for any breach of the penal laws of the State of Maryland or of the United States. Given under my hand this 14 day of Febry 1821. Joshua Guyton, Shff." (Court Records Document 68.05.2(b), loc. cit.) "Petition, Schedule, Bond, Sheriff's certificate, personal discharge and order for publication filed 14th February 1821." [nothing further recorded] (Insolvent Docket A, 1807-1843, p. 42, at the Maryland State Archives; Insolvent Docket Prior to 1827, Court Records Accession #632 at the Historical Society of Harford County). **Genealogical Note:** James Orr, age not given, appeared in Court on August 21, 1805 and stated he was "a native of Ireland and at present residing in Harford County in the State of Maryland and prays to be admitted to become a citizen of the United States and it appearing to the satisfaction of the Court here that the same James Orr was a resident within the limits and under the jurisdiction of the United States before the twenty ninth day of January one thousand seven hundred and ninety five and the eighteenth day of June seventeen hundred and ninety eight, that he was resident five years and upwards within in and under the jurisdiction of the United States and one year and upwards immediately preceding this application within the State of Maryland. That during the said time of five years he has behaved as a man of a good moral character attached to the principles of the Constitution of the United States and well disposed to the principles of the same, and that the same James Orr having declared on oath taken in open Court that he would support the Constitution of the United States and that he doth absolutely and entirely renounce and abjure all allegiance and fidelity to every foreign Prince, Potentate, State or Sovereignty whatever and particularly all allegiance and fidelity to the King of Great Britain and the said James Orr also declaring on oath taken in open Court, that he has never borne hereditary title, or been of any of the orders of nobility in any country whatever, the court here thereupon admits the said James Orr to become a citizen of the United States." (County Court Minutes, 1798-1806, p. 110, at the Historical Society of Harford County)

Osborn, Henry A., 1897. "Henry A. Osborn Insolvent. Mr. Henry Amoss Osborn, of Oakington, one of the largest land owners and canners of Harford county, has been declared insolvent upon a petition filed against him in the Circuit Court by J. H. Duker, of Baltimore. Messrs. Stevenson A. Williams and Willard G. Rouse were appointed trustees on Tuesday [August 17] and furnished bond for $75,000, which indicates assets amounting to nearly $40,000. Mr. Osborn is the owner of several fine farms, but has made several heavy losses lately, by reason of depreciation in the value of real estate and of canned products, and this can be taken for a reason for his financial condition." (*The Aegis & Intelligencer*, August 20, 1897, p. 3). "Henry Amos Osborn Insolvent. We regret to note that Mr. Henry Amos Osborn, the well-known farmer and canned goods packer whose residence is near this city [Havre de Grace], has been forced into insolvency. A petition in insolvency was filed in our Circuit Court, Tuesday, by Mr. J. H. Duker of Baltimore. The petition of insolvency alleged failure to meet negotiable paper at maturity, and the creation of a preference to Conley & Flanigan, commission merchants of Philadelphia, by way of a mortgage for $15,000, executed to them on the 3rd of May. S. A. Williams and Willard G. Rouse were appointed preliminary trustees, and gave bond in the sum of $75,000, indicating assets amounting to between $35,000 and $40,000. It is understood that Mr. Osborn's liabilities amount to about $50,000, of which $20,000 is secured by mortgage on his real estate. Mr. Osborn has been one of our largest packers of canned goods, and this year has over three hundred acres in corn to be packed. He will commence operations next week, and expects to put up thirty thousand cases. His corn has an established reputation, and Mr. Osborn feels confident that he will be able to fully meet all his obligations and have a goodly margin – a hope that his friends and the community will be glad to see fully realized." (*Havre de Grace Republican*, August 21, 1897, p. 3; *Harford Democrat*, August 20, 1897, p. 2, reported a similar story that contained additional details). **Genealogical Notes**: Henry Amos Osborn, son of Cyrus Osborn and Susan Silver, was born on July 18, 1841, married Frances Almira Fletcher (1844-1932) and died on August 2, 1925. Their children were Inez Henry Osborn, Elizabeth Fletcher Osborn and Henry Amos Osborn, Jr.; all of them never married. Henry was a farmer and canner at *Blenheim* near Havre de Grace and he is buried in the Grove Presbyterian Church cemetery in Aberdeen. (*Barnes-Bailey Genealogy*, by Walter D. Barnes, 1939, pp. H-16, I-16; Harford County Death Certificate No. 9173)

Osmond, Herman C., 1896. "Mr. Herman C. Osmond, of this city, has applied for the benefit of the insolvent laws of the State. Mr. Jos. W. Chamberlaine has been appointed preliminary trustee." (*Havre de Grace Republican*, June 13, 1896, p. 3). "Notice to Creditors. In the matter of the Insolvency of Herman C. Osmond ... In pursuance of an order of Court passed in the above matter, notice is hereby given to all the creditors of Herman C. Osmond to file their claims against said insolvent, duly proven, with the Clerk of the Circuit Court, on or before the 14th day of September, 1896, and that said Herman C. Osmond has been directed to appear before the Court on Monday, September 14, 1896 to answer such interrogatories and allegations as his creditors, endorsers or sureties may propose or allege against him. Joseph W. Chamberlaine, Permanent Trustee." (*The Aegis & Intelligencer*, July 31, 1896, p. 2). **Genealogical Notes**: Herman Carroll Osmond, son of Jacob Osmond and Mary E. Johnson, was born on April 20, 1848, married Miss Clara Gallup (born c1848 – died before 1916), both of Havre de Grace, on January 5, 1871 by Rev. William Cooke, worked as a boat builder and fishing boat owner at Havre de Grace, and died on December 20, 1916. He was survived by two sons, H. Carroll Osmond, Jr., of Philadelphia, and Clarence Osmond, of Havre de Grace, and a daughter, Mrs. William Beck, in whose home he died on South Washington Street in Havre de Grace. (Harford County marriage license; *Havre de Grace Republican*, February 3, 1871 and December 23, 1916; Death certificate and obituary of Herman C. Osmond state he was a widower and buried in Angel Hill Cemetery, but there are no markers for him or his wife; *Heavy Industries of Yesteryear: Harford County's Rural Heritage*, by Jack L. Shagena, Jr. and Henry C. Peden, Jr., 2015, pp. 61, 62, stated Herman owned a fishing battery, or fishing float, in 1884)

Paca, William, 1820. "In Harford County Court, March Term, 1820. On application to the judges of Harford county Court, in court sitting by petition in writing of William Paca, of said county, stating that he is an imprisoned debtor in actual confinement. And for the benefit of the act of the General Assembly of Maryland entitled "An act for the relief of sundry solvent debtors" passed at November session in the year Eighteen hundred and Five, and the several supplements thereto, on the terms therein mentioned, a schedule of his property and a list of his creditors, on oath, being annexed to said petition, with competent and satisfactory testimony that he had resided two years within the State of Maryland before the making of his application as aforesaid, for delivering up in property and given bond, with security, on a penalty prescribed by the court and approved by the same, for his personal appearance before the judges of [the] Harford county court on the first Saturday after the Fourth Monday of August next, at the courthouse of said county, it being the time, by the said court appointed for a hearing before said court, on said petition, to answer such interrogatories as his creditors may propose to him, according to the provisions of the said original act. It is hereby ordered and adjudged that the said William Paca be discharged from imprisonment, and directed that he give notice to his creditors of his application and discharge, and of the day, so by the court appointed, for a hearing before the said court, by advertisement to be inserted in some one of the newspapers printed in the city of Baltimore, once a week for three months before the day so above appointed." (Court Records Document 67.23.5(c) at Historical Society of Harford County). "To the Honorable the judges of Harford county court. The petition of William Paca of Harford county respectfully shews that he is now in actual confinement in Harford county gaol for debts which he is unable to pay, that he is willing and offers to deliver up to the use of his creditors all his property real, personal and mixed (the necessary wearing apparel and bedding of himself and family excepted) A schedule whereof together with a list of his creditors and debtors, as far as he can, at present, ascertain them is hereto on oath annexed. Your petitioner also hereto annexes proof on oath that he has resided two years next preceding this his application within the State of Maryland. Your petitioner therefore prays your honors to grant him the benefit of the Insolvent law of this State and to relieve him from his present confinement (and) your petitioner will pray, &c. Wm. Paca." [15 Mar 1820]. (Court Records Document 67.23.5(a), loc. cit.) "I hereby certify that William Paca, the petitioner above named, is now in actual confinement in Harford county gaol for debt at the suit of James Billingslea and that is not in for a breach of peace or any of the penal laws of the State of Maryland or of the United States, or of anyone thereof. Given under my hand this Fifteenth day of March Eighteen Hundred and Twenty. Joshua Guyton, Sheriff." (Court Records Document 67.23.5(a), loc. cit.) "Harford County sct. On this 15th day of March Eighteen hundred and Twenty personally appeared Winston Smith before me the subscriber one of the State of Maryland's Justices of the Peace in and for Harford county aforesaid and made oath on the Holy Evangely of Almighty God that William Paca the Petitioner above named has resided within the State of Maryland the two years next preceding the date hereof, and that he still resides therein. Saml. Bradford." (Court Records Document 67.23.5(a), loc. cit.; a copy of the schedule for William Paca was included, but he did not sign it and no property was listed). "Know all men by these presents that we William Paca, John Chauncey and Winston Smith of Harford county and State of Maryland are held and firmly bound unto the said State in the full and just sum of Five thousand Dollars current money to the payment whereof well and truly to be made to the said State, we bind ourselves and each of us, our and each of our heirs, executors and administrators, jointly and severally, firmly by these presents, sealed with our seals and date this Fifteenth day of March Eighteen hundred and Twenty. The condition of the above obligation is such that if the above bound William Paca shall personally appear at such time or times as the judges of Harford county Court shall direct and not depart therefrom without leave of said Judges, to answer the allegations of his creditor or creditors according to the provisions of an act of the General Assembly of Maryland entitled an act for the relief of insolvent debtors passed at November Session Eighteen hundred and five and the supplements thereto, then this obligation to be null and void, else to be and remain in full force and virtue in law. Signed, sealed and delivered in the presence of Jas. G. Davis. Wm. Paca. John Chauncey, Winston Smith." (Court Records Document 67.20.23(b), loc. cit.) "Petition, Schedule, Bond, Sheriff's certificate, order for publication and personal discharge filed 15th March 1820." [nothing further recorded] (Insolvent Docket A, 1807-1843, p. 30, at the Maryland State Archives; Insolvent Docket Prior to 1827, Court Records Accession #632 at the Historical Society of Harford

County). **Genealogical Notes**: William Paca, son of Aquila Paca (1738-1788) and Helen Tootell, daughter of Dr. Richard Tootell and Elizabeth Frazier, married Harriet Matthews on June 23, 1808 in Harford County and died on May 19, 1834 in Baltimore County. They had no children. (*Descendants of the Signers of the Bush Declaration of March 22, 1775. Harford County, Maryland*, by Christopher T. Smithson and Henry C. Peden, Jr., 2010, pp. 296-297)

Parlet, James, 1839. "Petition, Schedule, Affidavits, personal discharge and order of publication, Bond for Appearance, Trustee's Bond, Trustee's Certificate and Deed to Trustee filed 18th January 1839. 25th Novr. 1839 Petitioner appears, certificate of publication filed and discharged." (Insolvent Docket A, 1807-1843, p. 168, at the Maryland State Archives)

Parsons, Abner, 1806. "Whereas we the Subscribers Justices of the Peace for Harford County upon the petition of Abner Parsons, who set forth that he had been confined in the Gaol [jail] of the said county twenty Days for Debts which he was unable to pay and finding the facts stated to be true we together did meet at the County Gaol on the 24th day of June last and did then and there appoint the 25th of July Instant to meet at the Court House of said county which said appointment we did then and there ... at the request of the said Sheriff administer to the said Abner Parsons the following oath which was taken by the said Abner Parsons being first duly sworn on the holy evangels of almighty God in the words following, I Abner Parsons do solemnly swear that the schedule which I have delivered to the Sheriff of Harford County doth contain a full account to the best of my knowledge and remembrance of my whole estate both real & personal or that I have any title to or interest in and of all debts, credits and effects whatsoever which I or any in trust for me have or at the time of my petition had, or am or was in any respect entitled to in possession, remainder or reversion and that I have not directly or indirectly at any time since my imprisonment or before, sold, leased or otherwise conveyed or disposed of or intrusted all or any part of my estate, goods, stock, money or debts thereby to defraud my creditors or to secure the same to receive or expect any profit or advantage thereof so help me God, which said duplicate of the schedule aforesaid we have transmitted to the clerk of the county court to be by him preserved in his office for the information of the creditors of the said Abner Parsons. Given under our hands and seals this 25th day of July 1806. Thomas A. Hays. John Moores. James Amos." (Court Records Documents 67.08.7(a) (b) at the Historical Society of Harford County; copy of the schedule to which "Abner Parsons" signed his name was included and this personal property was listed: "1 Set Truss Hooks, 2 Drawing Knives, 1 Jointer Stock, 1 Crose [sic], 1 Small Grindstone, 1 Pair Coopers Compasses, 1 Cooper Ax, 1 Shoe Hammer, 1 Pair Pinchers"). 1820. "I hereby certify, that the within named Abner Parsons is now in actual confinement in the common goal [jail] of Harford County, as an imprisoned debtor, and that he is not confined on account of any breach of the peace, or for the non-payment of any fine or penalty for a breach of the Laws of this State, or of the United States. Harford County, Joshua Guyton, Sheriff. March 16th 1820." (Court Records Document 68.00.7(a) at the Historical Society of Harford County contains a petition, a list of creditors and a schedule signed by "Abner Parsons," but no property was listed; other documents are enclosed in this file). "On application to the subscriber as a Judge of the Orphans Court of Harford County by petition in writing of Abner Parsons stating that he is an imprisoned debtor in actual confinement in the Gaol [Jail] of said County, and praying for a discharge from said Confinement and for the benefit of the Act of the General Assembly of Maryland entitled 'An Act for the relief of sundry Insolvent debtors' passed at November Session in the year eighteen hundred and five and the several supplements thereto, on the Terms therein mentioned. A schedule of his property and a list of his Creditors on oath being annexed to his said petition with Competent testimony that he has resided two years within the State of Maryland next before the making of his application as aforesaid and the said Abner Parsons having taken the oath prescribed by the said act for delivering up his property and given Bond with security and in a penalty by me approved and presented for his appearance before the Judges of Harford county Court on the first Saturday after the fourth Monday of August next at the Court house of said County being the time by me appointed for a hearing before said Court in said Petition to answer Interrogatories which his Creditors may propose to him according to the provisions of the said original act. I do hereby order and adjudge that the said Abner Parsons be discharged from Imprisonment and direct that he give Notice to his Creditors of his said application and discharge and of the day so by me appointed for a hearing before said Court by advertisement to be inserted in the Bond of Union newspaper once a week for three months before the day so appointed. Given under my hand this seventeenth day of March eighteen hundred and twenty. John Moores." (Court Records Document 68.00.7(c), loc. cit.) "Petition, Schedule, Bond, Sheriff's certificate, order for publication and personal discharge filed 17th March 1820." [nothing further recorded] (Insolvent Docket A, 1807-1843, p. 29, at the Maryland State Archives; Insolvent Docket Prior to 1827, Court Records Accession #632 at the Historical Society of Harford County). **Genealogical Notes**: Abner Parsons married Rachel Dyer, daughter of Joseph and Joanna Dyer, in 1790 and their children were: Elizabeth Parsons (b. 1791), Joseph Dyer Parsons (b. 1793), Abraham Parsons (b. 1795), Honnor Parsons (b. 1798) and Rachel Parsons (b. 1798). (Gunpowder and Little Falls Monthly Meetings)

Parsons, Abraham, 1810. "Whereas we the subscribers [and] Justices of the Peace for Harford County upon the petition of Abraham Parsons, who set forth that he had been confined in the Gaol [jail] of said county twenty days for debts which he was unable to pay & finding the facts stated to be true we did meet at the County Gaol of said county on the 5th day of April last and did then and there appoint the 7th day of May instant to meet at the Court House of said county which said appointment we did then and there ... at the request of the said Sheriff administer to the said Abraham Parsons the following Oath which was taken by the said Abraham Parsons being first duly sworn on the holy Evangely of Almighty God in the words following, to wit, I Abraham Parsons do solemnly swear that the Schedule which I have delivered to the Sheriff of Harford County doth contain a full account to the best of my knowledge & remembrance of my whole estate both real and personal or that I have any title to or interest in and of all debts, credits and effects whatsoever which I or any in trust for me have or at the time of my petition had, or am or was in any respect entitled to in possession, remainder or reversion and that I have not directly or indirectly at any time since my imprisonment or before, sold, leased or otherwise conveyed or disposed of or intrusted all or any part of my estate, Goods, Stock, money or Debts thereby to defraud my Creditors or to secure the same to receive or expect any profit or advantage thereof so help me God, which said duplicate of the Schedule aforesaid we have transmitted to the Clerk of the County Court to be by him preserved in his Office for the information of the Creditors of the said Abraham Parsons. Given under our hands and seals this 7th Day of May 1810. Thomas A. Hays. Saml. Bradford. John C. Bond." (Court Records Document 67.18.1(A) at the Historical Society of Harford County; copy of the schedule to which he signed his name "Abraham Parsons" was included, but no property was listed). 1815. "Petition, Schedule & Bond filed 2nd September 1815 ... Luke Amoss appointed Trustee to give bond in the penalty of $500, the petitioner to give notice in the usual manner to his creditors." [nothing further recorded] (Insolvent Docket A, 1807-1843, p. 15, at the Maryland State Archives; Insolvent Docket Prior to 1827, Court Records Accession #632 at the Historical Society of Harford County)

Parsons, John, 1806. "Whereas we the Subscribers Justices of the Peace for Harford County upon the petition of John Parsons, who set forth that he had been confined in the Gaol [jail] of the said county twenty Days for Debts which he was unable to pay and finding the facts stated to be true we together did meet at the County Gaol on the 24th day of June last and did then and there appoint the

25th of July Instant to meet at the Court House of said county which said appointment we did then and there ... at the request of the said Sheriff administer to the said John Parsons the following affirmation which was taken by the said John Parsons in the words following, I John Parsons do solemnly affirm and declare that the schedule which I have delivered to the Sheriff of Harford County doth contain a full account to the best of my knowledge and remembrance of my whole estate both real & personal or that I have any title to or interest in and of all debts, credits and effects whatsoever which I or any in trust for me have or at the time of my petition had, or am or was in any respect entitled to in possession, remainder or reversion and that I have not directly or indirectly at any time since my imprisonment or before, sold, leased or otherwise conveyed or disposed of or intrusted all or any part of my estate, goods, stock, money or debts thereby to defraud my creditors or to secure the same to receive or expect any profit or advantage thereof so help me God, which said duplicate of the schedule aforesaid we have transmitted to the clerk of the county court to be by him preserved in his office for the information of the creditors of the said John Parsons. Given under our hands and seals this 25th day of July 1806. Thomas A. Hays. John Moores. James Amos." (Court Records Document 67.08.6(A) at the Historical Society of Harford County; a copy of the schedule to which "John Parsons" signed his name was included and this personal property was listed as follows: 1 Scythe & Hangings, 2 Sets Truss Hoops, 1 Jointer, 1 Old Drawing Knives, 1 Cresset and frow, 1 Pair Compasses, 2 Planes, 3 Small Planes, 30 feet Walnut Plank, 5 Shoe Lasts part of Shoe Makers, 1 Small Keg). 1810. "Whereas we the subscribers Justices of the Peace for Harford County together with John Moores, Esq., also one of the Justices of the Peace for said county, upon the petition of John Parsons, who set forth that he had been confined [in jail] twenty days and upwards for debts which he was unable to pay and finding the facts stated to be true together with the said John Moores, Esq. we did meet at the gaol of said county on the 23rd Day of November last and did then and there appoint the 24th day of Decemr. Instant to meet at the Court house of said county which said appointment we did then and there ... at the request of the said Sheriff administer to the said John Parsons the following oath which was taken by the said John Parsons being first duly sworn on the holy Evangely of Almighty God [*Note:* Since he was a Quaker, the last part of this sentence should have been omitted from his statement.] in the words following, to wit, I John Parsons do solemnly, sincerely and truly declare and affirm that the schedule which I have Delivered to the Sheriff of Harford County doth contain A full account to the best of my Knowledge and remembrance of my whole Estate both real and personal or that I have any title to or interest in and of all debts, credits and Effects whatsoever which I or any in trust for me have or at the time of my petition had, or am or was in any respect entitled to in possession, remainder or reversion and that I have not directly or indirectly at any time Since my Imprisonment or before Sold, Leased or Otherwise conveyed or Disposed of or intrusted all or any part of my Estate, Goods, Stock, money or Debts thereby to defraud my Creditors or to Secure the same to receive or expect any Profit or Advantage thereof which said duplicate of the Schedule aforesaid we have transmitted to the clerk of the county court to be by him Preserved in his Office for the information of the Creditors of the said John Parsons. Given under our hands and seals this 24th Day of December 1810. Thomas A. Hays. Jno. C. Bond." (Court Records Document 67.10.8(A) at Historical Society of Harford County; a copy of the schedule to which "John Parsons" signed his name was included and listed this property: "1 Dozn. Lasts, Some Other Shoemaker Tools, Some Carpenter Tools, 1 Sett Truss Hoops"). **Genealogical Notes:** John Parsons married Susanna ---- circa 1790 and their children were Jessee Parsons (b. 1791) and Susanna Parsons (b. 1794). Susanna Parsons, the wife of John, died in childbirth on the 14th day of the 7th month, 1794. (Gunpowder Monthly Meeting Records)

Patterson, James H., 1895. "Last Saturday [May 18, 1895] a petition in insolvency was filed at Bel Air, for the benefit of James H. Patterson." (*Havre de Grace Republican*, May 25, 1895, p. 2). "Notice to Creditors. In the matter of the Insolvency of James H. Patterson ... To the creditors of James H. Patterson: Notice is hereby given to the creditors of James H. Patterson, who were such upon the date of his application for the benefit of the insolvent laws of the State of Maryland, that a meeting of the creditors of said insolvent will be held at the office of the undersigned, in Bel Air, Md., on Monday, May 27, 1895, at 10 o'clock, A. M., for the purpose of choosing a permanent trustee or trustees, propounding interrogatories, &c. J. Royston Stifler, Preliminary Trustee." (*The Aegis & Intelligencer*, May 17, 1895, p. 2). "Circuit Court Proceedings. Franklin Pennington vs. James H. Patterson; judgment on two notes for $1,241.66 and $148, being subject to his application in insolvency." (*Havre de Grace Republican*, May 25, 1895, p. 3). "Notice to Creditors ... In pursuance of an order of Court, dated the 6th day of August in the year 1895, notice is hereby given to the creditors of said James H. Patterson, an insolvent debtor, who were such on the 16th day of May, 1895, to file their claims, duly proven, with the Clerk of the Circuit Court for Harford county, on or before the 10th day of September 1895. J. Royston Stifler, Permanent Trustee." (*The Aegis & Intelligencer*, August 16, 1895, p. 2). "Notice to Creditors ... Ordered this 6th day of August, 1895, that James H. Patterson, appear before the Circuit Court for Harford county, in insolvency, on the second Monday of September, 1895, and answer such interrogatories and allegations as his creditors, endorsers or sureties may propose or allege against him, and that J. Royston Stifler, permanent trustee, give not less than one month's notice hereof to the creditors of said James H. Patterson. Jas. D. Watters. True copy, test: Wm. S. Forwood, Jr., Clerk." (*The Aegis & Intelligencer*, August 16, 1895, p. 2). **Genealogical Notes**: James H. Patterson, son of Samuel Patterson and ---- Garrett, was born on February 10, 1851, worked as a farmer near Rocks, married Rebecca J. McComas (June 27, 1850 – July 30, 1912), daughter of William McComas and Emily Wright, died on February 8, 1917 at home near Madonna and was buried in McKendree Church cemetery. Their children were Marie V. Patterson (1876-1956), of Chicago, ---- Patterson (infant son, 1877-1877), William M. Patterson, of Harford Co., Samuel J. Patterson, of Harford Co., J. Howard Patterson, of Baltimore, Edgar T. Patterson, of California, Benjamin Franklin Patterson, of Chicago, and Mrs. Elizabeth E. O'Ferrall, of Baltimore. (Death certificate of James H. Patterson; *The Aegis & Intelligencer*, August 2, 1912 and February 16, 1917; McKendree Cemetery tombstones)

Patterson, William C., 1857. "Petition, Schedules, Affidavits, Appointment of Trustee & order of notice, Trustee's Bond & Deed to Trustee filed 27th October 1857. 15th May 1858 Petitioner appears, files certificate of publication & discharged." (Insolvent Docket A. L. J. No. 1, p. 20, in the Court Records Department of the Historical Society of Harford County). "Notice is hereby given that William C. Patterson, of Harford County, has made application to the Circuit Court of said County, for the benefit of the Insolvent Laws of Maryland, and that the first Saturday after the second Monday in May, 1858, has been assigned for him to appear in said Court to answer such interrogatories as his creditors may propose or allege against him. A. Lingan Jarrett, Clerk." (*The Southern Aegis*, November 28, 1857, Volume I, No. 21, p. 161)

Pearce, John W., 1831. "Petition, Schedule, Shffs. certificate, personal discharge, order for publication, bond for appearance, Trustee's bond, Trustee's certificate and deed to Trustee filed 25th May 1831." [nothing further recorded] (Insolvent Docket A, 1807-1843, p. 110, at the Maryland State Archives). 1836. "Petition, Affidavits, Schedule, personal discharge and order of publication, Bond for Appearance, Trustee's Bond, Trustee's Certificate and Deed to Trustee filed 19th April 1836 ... March term 1837 Certificate of Publication filed and ordered by the Court that he give notice to his creditors. 19th August 1837 Petitioner appears, certificate of publication filed and finally discharged." (Insolvent Docket A, 1807-1843, p. 147, at the Maryland State Archives)

Pearce, William N., 1885. "June 3rd 1885. Petition, Affidavits, Schedules, Order of Court & Deed filed. Same day Preliminary Trustee's [name not given] Bond approved & filed ... Sept 22nd Order of Final discharge filed." (Insolvent Docket A. L. J. No. 1, p. 98, in the Court Records Department of the Historical Society of Harford County). "Insolvent Creditors' Notice. In the matter of the Insolvency of William N. Pearce. In the Circuit Court for Harford County In Equity. In pursuance of an order of the court, passed in the above cause, on the 22nd day of June, 1885, the subscriber hereby gives notice to William N. Pearce, an insolvent debtor, to be and appear in the Circuit Court for Harford county, on Tuesday, the 8th day of September, 1885, to answer such interrogatories or allegations, as his creditors, endorsers or sureties may propose or allege against him, and also to the creditors, that the said 8th day of September, 1885, has been fixed by the Court for the appearance of the said insolvent. Wm. H. Doxen, Permanent Trustee." (*Harford Democrat*, July 24, 1885, p. 3). **Genealogical Note**: William N. Pearce married Annie Griffin circa February 15, 1882 (date of license).

Pearson Brothers, 1895. "Mr. Oliver T. Rogers, of Havre de Grace, has been appointed permanent trustee of Pearson Bros., insolvents." (*The Aegis & Intelligencer*, April 26, 1895; *Havre de Grace Republican*,) April 27, 1895, p. 3, called them "Pearson & Bros., of this city"). "Insolvent Notice, In the Matter of the Insolvency of Frank C. Pearson and Harry C. Pearson, Co-Partners, Trading as Pearson & Bro. [sic] ... In Pursuance of an Order of the Circuit Court for Harford county, passed on the 18th day of May, 1895 in the above case, notice is hereby given to all creditors of the said Frank C. Pearson and Harry C. Pearson, co-partners, trading as Pearson & Bro., that *the 9th day of September, 1895*, has been fixed upon for them to appear before said Court, and answer such interrogatories and allegations as their creditors, endorsers or sureties may propose or allege against them." O. T. Rogers, Permanent Trustee." (*Havre de Grace Republican*, May 25, 1895, p. 2). **Genealogical Notes**: Frank C. Pearson (1864-1944), of Havre de Grace, later of Baltimore, and Harry Pearson were sons of Franklin D. Pearson (1828 – 10 Mar 1897) and Susanna E. Cook or Cooke (1834-1874), of Havre de Grace. (St. George's P. E. Church Records, 1834-1903, p. 142, and tombstone inscriptions; St. John's Episcopal Church, Havre de Grace Parish, Canonical Parish Register, Volume B, 1835-1858, spelled their mother's name Cooke; 1860 Harford County Census; *The Aegis & Intelligencer*, March 12, 1897; Death certificate for Mrs. Ada Kate Burns (1869-1937), sister of Harry C. and Frank C. Pearson)

Perryman, George H., 1842. "Petition, Affidavits, Schedules, Appointments, certificate, order, personal discharge, Deed, Appearance & Trustee's bonds filed 5th July 1842 – 25th Novr. 1842 Allegations filed. 26th Novr. 1842 Petitioner appears, files certificate of publication & cont'd. 20th May 1843 Allegations withdrawn. Petitioner appears & finally discharged & order appointing John H. Price Trustee filed. 1844 29th Novr. Petition & recommendation of trustee filed. 5 Decr, 1844 Order appointing H. D. Farnandis, Esqr., Trustee ... 3rd Feby 1847 Order of Sale filed ... 28th Decr./49 Certificate of Publication filed. Objections overruled & final order of ratification filed. 28 March/51 Auditor's Report & order of ratification filed." [nothing further recorded] (Insolvent Docket A, 1807-1843, p. 182, at Maryland State Archives). **Genealogical Note**: George H. Perryman married Isabella A. Gover (1806-1876) circa December 11, 1832 (date of license; St. George's P. E. Church tombstone)

Perveil, John, 1821. "To the Honorable Wm. H. Ward, one of the Justices of the Orphans Court of Harford County. The petition of John Peveil [sic] of Harford County respectfully sheweth that your petitioner is now in actual confinement in Harford County jail for debts which he is unable to pay, that he is willing and offers to deliver up to the use of his creditors all his property real, personal and mixed, the necessary wearing apparel and bedding of him-self & family excepted, a schedule whereof together with a list of his creditors and debtors, as far as he can at present ascertain them is hereto on oath annexed, your petitioner also hereto annexes proof on oath that he has resided two years next preceding this his application within the State of Maryland. Your petitioner therefore prays your Honour to grant him the benefit of the insolvent laws of this State and to relieve him from his present confinement, and your Petitioner will ever pray, &c. John Perveil." [9 Oct 1822] (Court Records Document 68.05.4(b) at the Historical Society of Harford County). "I hereby certify that John Peveil [sic] the petitioner above named is now in actual confinement in Harford County Jail for debt at the suit of Wallace & Quilder and that is not upon a breach of peace or any of the penal Laws of the State of Maryland or of the United States. Given under my hand this 9th day of October 1822. Saml. Bradford, Sheriff." (Court Records Document 68.05.4(b), loc. cit.) "State of Maryland Harford County to wit. On this 9th day of October 1822 personally appeared Christopher Wilson, Jr. before me the subscriber one of the State of Maryland's Justices of the Peace in and for Harford County and solemnly and sincearly [sic] & truly declared and affirmed that John Peveil the petitioner within named has resided within the State of Maryland the two years next preceding the date hereof and that he still resides therein. Affirmed before Joshua Guyton." (Court Records Document 68.05.6(a), loc. cit.; a copy of the schedule to which "John Perveil" signed his name was included, but no property was listed). "Harford County sct. On application to the subscriber as a Justice of the Orphans Court of Harford County by petition in writing of John Perveil stating that he is an imprisoned debtor in actual confinement in the jail of said County and praying for a discharge from said confinement and for the benefit of the Act of the General Assembly of Maryland entitled an 'Act for the relief of sundry insolvent debtors' passed at November session in the year eighteen hundred and five and the several supplements thereto on the terms therein mentioned, a schedule of his property and a list of his creditors on oath being annexed to his said petition with competent and satisfactory testimony that he has resided two years within the State of Maryland next before the making of his application as aforesaid and the said John Perveil having taken the oath prescribed by the said act prescribed for delivering up his property and given bond with security and in a penalty by me approved and presented [for] his appearance before the Judges of Harford County Court on the first Saturday after the second Monday in March next at the Court House of said County, being the time by me appointed for hearing before said court in said petition to answer interrogatories which his creditors may propose to him according to the provisions of the said original act. I do hereby order and adjudge that the said John Pevail [sic] be discharged from imprisonment and direct that he give notice to his creditors of his said application and discharge, and of the day so by me appointed for a hearing before said Court, by advertisement to be inserted in the Bond of Union once a week for three months before the day so appointed. Given under my hand this 9th day of October 1822. John Moores." (Court Records Document 68.05.4(a), loc. cit.) "I hereby certify that the annexed advertisement was published three months in the Bond of Union agreeably to the order therein specified. Wm. Coale, Jr." (Court Records Document 68.05.4(c), loc. cit.; a copy of the notice had been clipped from the newspaper and included in this file). "Petition, Schedule, Bond, Sheriff's certificate, personal discharge and order for publication filed 10th October Eighteen hundred and twenty-two. March 15th 1823 notice of publication filed. Petitioner appears and is discharged." (Insolvent Docket A, 1807-1843, p. 52, at the Maryland State Archives; Insolvent Docket Prior to 1827, Court Records Accession #632 at the Historical Society of Harford County)

Philips, Anthony, 1810. "Whereas we the subscribers Justices of the Peace for Harford County upon the petition of Anthony Philips, who set forth that he had been confined [in jail] twenty days and upwards for debts which he was unable to pay and finding the facts stated to be true we did meet at the gaol of said county on the 12th day of October last and did then and there appoint the 12th day of November instant to meet at the Court house of said county which said appointment we did then and there ... at the request of the said Sheriff administer to the said Anthony Philips the following oath which was taken by the said Anthony Philips being first duly sworn on the Holy Evangely of Almighty God in the words following, vizt., I Anthony Philips do solemnly swear that the schedule which I have delivered to the Sheriff of Harford County doth contain a full account to the best of my knowledge and remembrance of my whole estate both real & personal or that I have any title to or interest in and of all debts, credits and effects whatsoever which I or any in trust for me have or at the time of my petition had, or am or was in any respect entitled to in possession, remainder or reversion and that I have not directly or indirectly at any time since my imprisonment or before, sold, leased or otherwise conveyed or disposed of or intrusted all or any part of my estate, goods, stock, money or debts thereby to defraud my creditors or to secure the same to receive or expect any profit or advantage thereof so help me God, which said duplicate of the schedule aforesaid we have transmitted to the clerk of the county court to be by him preserved in his office for the information of the creditors of the said Anthony Philips. Given under our hands and seals this 12th Day of November 1810. Thomas A. Hays. Jno. C. Bond. Benjn. Richardson." (Court Records Document 67.02.7(A) at Historical Society of Harford County; a copy of schedule to which Anthony Philips made his "X" mark was included, but no property was listed)

Phillips, David, 1859. "Petition, Schedule, Affidavit, Appointment of A. W. Bateman, Esqr., Trustee, Order of Notice to Creditors, Trustee's Bond & approval & Deed to Trustee filed 20th September 1859." [nothing further recorded] (Insolvent Docket A. L. J. No. 1, p. 31, in the Court Records Department of the Historical Society of Harford County). "Notice is hereby given that David Phillips, of Harford County, has made application to the Circuit Court of said County, for the benefit of the Insolvent Laws of Maryland, and that the 4th Monday in February, 1860, has been assigned for him to appear in said Court to answer such interrogatories as his creditors may propose or allege against him. Wm. Galloway, Clerk, Circuit Court for Harford County." (*The Southern Aegis*, October 15, 1859, p. 3)

Plumer, Joseph, 1810. "Whereas we the subscribers Justices of the Peace for Harford County together with Thomas A. Hays, Esq., also a Justice of the Peace for said county, upon the petition of Joseph Plumer, who set forth that he had been confined [in jail] twenty days and upwards for debts which he was unable to pay and finding the facts stated to be true together with Thomas A. Hays we did meet at the gaol of said county on the 11th day of November last and did then and there appoint the 12th day of October Instant to meet at the Court house of said county which said appointment we did then and there ... at the request of the said Sheriff administer to the said Joseph Plumer the following oath which was taken by the said Joseph Plumer being first duly sworn on the holy Evangely of Almighty God in the words following, I do solemnly swear that the schedule which I have delivered to the Sheriff of Harford County doth contain a full account to the best of my knowledge and remembrance of my whole estate both real & personal or that I have any title to or interest in and of all debts, credits and effects whatsoever which I or any in trust for me have or at the time of my petition had, or am or was in any respect entitled to in possession, remainder or reversion and that I have not directly or indirectly at any time since my imprisonment or before, sold, leased or otherwise conveyed or disposed of or intrusted all or any part of my estate, goods, stock, money or debts thereby to defraud my creditors or to secure the same to receive or expect any profit or advantage thereof so help me God, which said duplicate of the schedule aforesaid we have transmitted to the clerk of the county court to be by him preserved in his office for the information of the creditors of the said Joseph Plumer. Given under our hands and seals this 12th Day of October 1810. Saml. Bradford. John Moores." (Court Records Document 67.14(10) at Historical Society of

Harford County; a copy of the schedule to which "Joseph Plumer" signed his name was included, but no property was listed)

Pogue, John, 1805. "Whereas we the subscribers Justices of the Peace for Harford County upon the petition of John Pouge [sic] set forth therein that he had been confined in the goal [jail] of the said county twenty days for debts which he was unable to pay and finding the facts stated to be true we did meet at the county gaol of the said county on the 5th day of February 1805 and did then and there appoint the 8th day of March Inst. to meet at the court house of said county which said appointment we did then and there ... at the request of the said sheriff administer to the said John Pouge the following oath which was taken by the said John Pouge being first duly sworn on the Holy Evangely of Almighty God in the words following, I John Pouge solemnly swear that the schedule which I have delivered to the sheriff of Harford County doth contain a full account to the best of my knowledge and remembrance of my whole estate both real & personal or that I have any title to or interest in and of all debts, credits & effects whatsoever which I or any in trust for me have or at the time of my petition had, or am or was in any respect entitled to in possession, remainder or reversion and that I have not directly or indirectly at any time since my imprisonment or before, sold, leased or otherwise conveyed or disposed of or intrusted all or any part of my estate, goods, stock, money or debts thereby to defraud my creditors or to secure the same to receive or expect any profit or advantage thereof so help me God, which said duplicate of the schedule aforesaid we have transmitted to the clerk of the county court to be by him preserved in his office for the information of the creditors of the said John Pogue. Given under our hands and seals this 8th day of March 1805. Thos. A. Hays. James Amos. Wm. Smithson." (Court Records Document 67.21.4(c) at the Historical Society of Harford County; a copy of the schedule was included to which "John Pogue" signed his name, but no property was listed). 1813. "Harford County Gaol. The petition of John Pogue humbly sheweth that your petitioner hath actually remained in the jail of said county since the twenty-first day of May last for debts which he is unable to ay, that he is willing to comply with the requisites of the Act of Assembly entitled 'an act for the relief of insolvent debtors' and prays you gentlemen to appoint a time and place for his discharge under said act. And your petitioner as in duty bound will ever pray &c. June 9th 1813. John Pogue." (Court Records Document 67.12.4(d) at Historical Society of Harford County). "Whereas we the subscribers Justices of the Peace for Harford County upon the petition of John Pogue set forth therein that he had been confined [in jail] twenty days and upwards for debts which he was unable to pay and finding the facts stated to be true we did meet at the jail of said county on the 9th day of June last and did then and there appoint the 10th day of July instant to meet at the court house of said county which said appointment we did then and there ... at the request of the said sheriff administer to the said John Pogue the following oath which was taken by the said John Pogue being first duly sworn on the Holy Evangely of Almighty God in the words following, I do solemnly swear that the schedule which I have delivered to the sheriff of Harford County doth contain a full account to the best of my knowledge and remembrance of my whole estate both real & personal or that I have any title to or interest in and of all debts, credits & effects whatsoever which I or any in trust for me have or at the time of my petition had, or am or was in any respect entitled to in possession, remainder or reversion and that I have not directly or indirectly at any time since my imprisonment or before, sold, leased or otherwise conveyed or disposed of or intrusted all or any part of my estate, goods, stock, money or debts thereby to defraud my creditors or to secure the same to receive or expect any profit or advantage thereof so help me God, which said duplicate of the schedule aforesaid we have transmitted to the clerk of the county court to be by him preserved in his office for the information of the creditors of the said John Pogue. Given under our hands and seals this 10th day of July 1812. John Moores. Thomas A. Hays.

Saml. Bradford." (Court Records Document 67.12.4(b) at the Historical Society of Harford County; a copy of the schedule to which "John Pogue" signed his name was included, but no property was listed). **Genealogical Notes**: John Pogue married Ann Greenland, daughter of Richard Greenland and Jane Hearn, on February 2, 1802, served in the War of 1812 and died on December 13, 1837, probably in Baltimore. (St. George's P. E. Parish Register; Baltimore *Sun*, December 18, 1837; military record states "deserted in 3 days" and marriage license mistakenly gave her surname as Greenfield).

Pooley Shirt Company, 1897. "Notice to Creditors. This is to give notice to the creditors of George F. Pooley and Andrew L. Stewart, trading as Pooley Shirt Company, Insolvent Debtors, of the pendency of proceedings in Insolvency in relation to their estate, and that Tuesday, the 16th Day of March, 1897, at 11 o'clock A. M., at the Office of S. A. and F. R. Williams, in Bel Air, MD, is the time and place fixed for a meeting of the creditors of said Pooley Shirt Company, to chooses a Permanent Trustee for said estate. Frank H. Jacobs, Preliminary Trustee." (*Havre de Grace Republican*, March 13, 1897, p. 2). "Notice to Creditors. Notice is hereby given to the creditors of George F. Pooley and Andrew L. Stewart, trading as Pooley Shirt Company, to file their claims, properly proven, with the Clerk of the Circuit Court for Harford county, on or before the 27th day of June 1898. Stephen J. Seneca, Permanent Trustee." (*Havre de Grace Republican*, June 11, 1898, p. 2). "In the Matter of the Insolvency of George F. Pooley and Andrew L. Stewart, trading as Pooley Shirt Company, In the Circuit Court for Harford County. In the above entitled matter, it is this 10th day of May, 1898, by the Circuit Court for Harford County, ordered that the said George F. Pooley and Andrew L. Stewart, trading as Pooley Shirt Company, be and appear in this Court on the 27th Day of June, 1898, to answer such interrogatories or allegations as their creditors, endorsers or sureties may propound or allege against them, why they should not be discharged under the insolvent laws of the State of Maryland, and that the permanent trustee of said insolvents give notice to their creditors, of the day so fixed upon, by the publication of this order in some newspaper published in Harford county, once a week for one month before the said 27th day of June, 1898. Jas. D. Watters. True copy—Test: Wm. S. Forwood, Jr., Clerk." (*Havre de Grace Republican*, June 11, 1898, p. 2)

Pope, Folger, 1826. "Petition, Schedule, Bond, Sheriff's certificate & personal discharge. Order for publication. Bond of provisional trustee and Certificate for Trustee filed 6th December 1826 … 17th March 1827 Certificate of publication filed and petitioner appeared & continued. 18th August 1827 petitioner appeared … Richard McGill appointed Trustee and that he give bond with security to be approved of by the Court in the sum of $500." [nothing further recorded] (Insolvent Docket A, 1807-1843, p. 82, at the Maryland State Archives)

Porter, John, 1820. "To the Honorable John Moores, one of the Justices of the Orphans Court of Harford County. The petition of John Porter of Harford County respectfully sheweth that your petitioner is now in actual confinement in Harford County Jail for debts which he is unable to pay, that he is willing and offers to deliver to the use of his creditors all his property real, personal and mixed, the necessary wearing apparel and bedding of himself and family excepted, a schedule whereof together with a list of his creditors and debtors, as far as he can at present ascertain them is hereto on oath annexed. Your petitioner also hereto annexes proof on oath that he has resided two years next preceding this his application within the State of Maryland. Your petitioner therefore prays your Honour to grant him the benefit of the Insolvent Laws of this State and to relieve him from his present Confinement. And your petitioner will pray, &c., 26 September 1820. John Porter." (Court Records Document 67.23.6(c) at the Historical Society of Harford County) "I hereby certify that John Porter the petitioner above named is now in actual confinement in Harford County Gaol for debt at the suit of James Criswell and that is not upon a breach of peace or any of the penal laws of this State or of the United States. Given under my hand this 24th day of July 1820. Joshua Guyton,

Sheriff." (Court Records Document 67.23.6(c), loc. cit.) "State of Maryland Harford County to wit. On this 26th day of Sept. 1820 personally appeared Moses St. Clair before me the subscriber one of the State of Maryland Justices of the Peace in and for the county aforesaid and made oath on the holy Evangely of Almighty God that John Porter the petitioner within named has resided within the State of Maryland the two years next preceding the date hereof, and that he still resides therein. Sworn to before Saml. Bradford." (Court Records Document 67.23.6(c), loc. cit.) "On application to the subscriber a Judge of the Orphans Court of Harford County by petition in writing of John Porter stating that he is an imprisoned debtor in actual confinement in the Jail of said County, and praying for a discharge from said confinement and for the benefit of the Act of the General Assembly of Maryland Entitled "An Act for the relief of sundry Insolvent debtors" passed at November session of eighteen hundred and five and the several supplements thereto, on the terms therein mentioned. A schedule of his property and a list of his creditors on oath being annexed to his said petition with competent and satisfactory testimony that he has resided for two years within the State of Maryland, next before the making of his application as aforesaid and the said John Porter having taken the oath by the said act prescribed for delivering up his property and given bond with security, and in a penalty by me approved and presented for his appearance before the Judges of Harford County Court on the first Saturday after the second Monday in March next at the Court House of said county being the time by me appointed for a hearing before said court in said petition to answer interrogatories which his creditors may propose to him according to the provisions of the said original act. I do hereby order and adjudge that the said John Porter be discharged from imprisonment, and direct that he give notice to his creditors of his said application and discharge and of the day so by me appointed for a hearing before said Court, by advertisement to be inserted in the Bond of Union newspaper once a week for three months before the day so appointed. Given under my hand this 26th day of Sepr. 1820. John Norris." (Court Records Document 67.23.6(d), loc. cit.) A copy of the schedule to which he signed his name "John Porter" was included, but no property was listed. (Court Records Document 67.13.6(c), loc. cit.) "I hereby certify that the annexed advertisement was published three months in the Bond of Union – Wm. Coale, Jr." (Court Records Document 67.23.6(E), loc. cit.; a copy of the notice was clipped from the newspaper and included in the file). "Petition, Schedule, Bond, Sheriff's certificate, personal discharge and order for publication filed 26th Sepr. 1820. March 17th 1821 petr. appeared. Allegations of fraud filed 20th March 1821." [nothing further recorded] (Insolvent Docket Prior to 1827, Court Records Accession #632 at the Historical Society of Harford County; Insolvent Docket A, 1807-1843, p. 38, at the Maryland State Archives). **Genealogical Notes**: John Porter married Catherine McNeuse on January 27, 1791 by Rev. John Ireland and their daughter Sarah Porter was born on June 11, 1791 [sic] and baptized on November 16, 1806. (Scharf Papers, Harford County Returns of Ministers to Treasurer, Maryland State Archives, published in *Harford County, Maryland Marriage Licenses, 1777-1865*, by Jon Harlan Livezey and Helene Maynard Davis, 1993, p. 274; St. George's P. E. Parish Register) Another interesting note: John Porter, aged 40, appeared in Court on August 27, 1817 and openly stated that he is "a native of Ireland at present residing in Harford County in the State of Maryland and declares on oath that it is bona fide his intention to become a citizen of the United States and to renounce forever all allegiance and fidelity to the United Kingdoms of Great Britain and Ireland whereof he is at this time a citizen." John Porter signed the statement. (County Court Minutes 1816-1822, p. 25, at the Historical Society of Harford County). [*Note*: It appears there were two men named John Porter at this time.]

Poultney, Evan, 1836. "Petition, Affidavits, Schedule, personal discharge and order of publication, Bond for Appearance, Trustee's Bond, Trustee's Certificate and Deed to Trustee filed 19th August 1836. 18th March 1837 Petitioner appears & cont'd. 23rd March 1837 Petitioner recommendation and

144

order appointing of John Glenn and Reverdy Johnson Trustees. 27th May 1837 Answer of Evan Poultney to the allegations of the Trustees of the Bank of Maryland filed … [long list of subpoenas for creditors and short list for witnesses] … 31st August 1837 Petitioner appears and application for the benefit of the Insolvent Laws withdrawn." (Insolvent Docket A, 1807-1843, pp. 152, 180, at the Maryland State Archives). 1837. "Petition, Affidavits, Schedule, personal discharge and order of publication, Bond for Appearance, Trustee's Bond, Trustee's Certificate and Deed to Trustee filed 14th December 1837. 12th March 1838 Allegations filed … [long list of witnesses for creditors] … 17th March 1838 Petitioner appears and case cont'd 24th November 1838 Petitioner's Death suggested." [nothing further recorded] (Insolvent Docket A, 1807-1843, p. 160, at the Maryland State Archives)

Presbury, James, 1806. "Whereas we the Subscribers Justices of the Peace for Harford County, together with William Wilson also one of the Justices of the Peace for said county, upon the petition of James Presbury who set forth that he had been confined in the Gaol [jail] of said county twenty days for Debts which he was unable to pay and finding the facts stated to be true we together with the said William Wilson did meet at the County Gaol of said county on the 19th day of March 1806 and did then and there appoint the 19th [April] Instant to meet at the Court House which said appointment we did then and there … at the request of the said Sheriff administer to the said James Presbury the following oath which was taken by the said James Presbury being first duly sworn on the Holy Evangely of Almighty God in the words following, I James Presbury do solemnly swear that the schedule which I have delivered to the Sheriff of Harford County doth contain a full account to the best of my knowledge and remembrance of my whole estate both real & personal or that I have any title to or interest in and of all debts, credits and effects whatsoever which I or any in trust for me have or at the time of my petition had, or am or was in any respect entitled to in possession, remainder or reversion and that I have not directly or indirectly at any time since my imprisonment or before, sold, leased or otherwise conveyed or disposed of or intrusted all or any part of my estate, goods, stock, money or debts thereby to defraud my creditors or to secure the same to receive or expect any profit or advantage thereof so help me God, which said duplicate of the schedule aforesaid we have transmitted to the clerk of the county court to be by him preserved in his office for the information of the creditors of the said James Presbury. Given under our hands & seals this 19th April 1806. John Moores. Thomas A. Hays." (Court Records Documents 67.08.8(A)(B) at the Historical Society of Harford County; a copy of the schedule to which "James Presbury" signed his name was included, but no property was listed)

Presbury, Roger, 1831. "Petition, Schedule, Sheriff's Certificate, personal discharge and Order for Publication, Bond for Appearance, Trustee's Bond, Trustee's Certificate and Deed to Trustee filed 12th Dec 1831." [nothing further recorded] (Insolvent Docket A, 1807-1843, p. 113, at the Maryland State Archives)

Presbury, William R., 1824. "Petition, bond, Schedule, Certificate of residence, Shff's Certificate, personal discharge and order for publication filed 14th Augt. 1824." [nothing further recorded] (Insolvent Docket A, 1807-1843, p. 68, at the Maryland State Archives; Insolvent Docket Prior to 1827, Court Records Accession #632 at the Historical Society of Harford County). **Genealogical Note**: William R. Presbury was a son of George Presbury, of William, and his father died in or about March 1821. (Equity Court Book HD No. 1, pp. 136-152, John Kirk vs. William R. Presbury and Stephen Watters, executors of George Presbury, of William, et al.)

Preston, Benjamin, 1812. "Petition, Schedule, and Notice to Creditors filed 9th May 1812, bond filed 1st Augt. 1812. 29th Augt. 1812 Petitioner appeared in Court." [nothing further recorded] (Insolvent Docket A, 1807-1843, p. 13, at the Maryland State Archives; Insolvent Docket Prior to 1827, Court Records Accession #632 at the Historical Society of Harford County)

Preston, Benjamin V., 1880. "Application for benefit of Insolvent Laws, Schedules, Affidavit, Order. Trustees Bond & Deed filed 30 March 1880. Nov 5th 1880 Certificate of publication of Insolvent notice filed. Petitioner appeared in open Court & finally discharged." (Insolvent Docket A. L. J. No. 1, p. 68, in Court Records Department of the Historical Society of Harford County). "Notice is hereby given that Benjamin V. Preston, of Harford county, has made application to the Circuit Court for said county for the benefit of the Insolvent Laws of Maryland, and that the second Monday of September, 1880 has been assigned for him to appear in said Court to answer such interrogatories as his creditors may propose or allege against him. A. Lingan Jarrett, Clerk, Circuit Court for Harford county." (*The Aegis & Intelligencer*, April 9, 1880, p. 3). **Genealogical Notes**: Benjamin V. Preston (May 10, 1840 – December 19, 1923), son of Thomas Preston and Jemima Barton, married 1st to Julia Ann Laye (1846 – November 9, 1886) on December 15, 1865 by Rev. William Finney at Churchville, married 2nd to Roberta J. Gilbert (1865-1936) in 1891, and worked as a farmer near Aberdeen. He was survived by his wife Bertha [probably meant Berta, short for Roberta], sons Sylvester Preston, Edward Preston, Gover Preston, Arthur Preston and Burdell Preston, and four daughters, names not given. (Harford Co. license and marriage certificate in 1865 mistakenly listed him as Benjamin B. Preston, but 1891 marriage certificate correctly listed him as Benjamin V. Preston; Calvary United Methodist Church tombstone for Julia Preston; Baker Cemetery tombstones for Benjamin V. Preston and Roberta J. Preston; Death certificate of Benjamin V. Preston; *The Aegis*, December 28, 1923)

Preston, Corbin, 1806. "June the 3rd 1806. To the Honorable the Judges of Harford County Court. The petition of Corbin Preston of Harford County humbly sheweth that your petitioner made application to the General Assembly of Maryland at their last session and was included in the act entitled 'An act for the relief of sundry Insolvent Debtors,' That your petitioner is ready and willing to deliver up to the use and benefit of his creditors, all his property, real, personal and mixed, your petitioner states that he has hereto annexed a list if his property an also a list of his creditors on oath as by the said act required. Your Petitioner further states to you Honors that he is in actual confinement from which he prays to be discharged, and likewise humbly begs your honors to extend to him all the benefits of said Law and your petitioner as in duty bond will pray, &c. [signed] Jno. Sanders for Petr." [Lists of debts owed and debts due were included, plus several pages of statements, and the following property]: " A List of goods and chattels held by me Corbin Preston: some few sadlers tools, part of 2 pieces straining web, 1 old trunk, 1 bridle bit, 1 small looking glass, 1 plated chane."[?] And the last entry on May 27, 1813 was as follows, in part: "It is therefore adjudged and ordered that the said Corbin Preston be discharged from all debts, covenants, contracts, promises and agreements due from or owing or contracted in his individual as also in a co-partnership capacity by him before the twenty-eighth day of January eighteen hundred and six on which day the last act of the General Assembly for the relief of sundry Insolvent Debtors was passed. Provided nevertheless that any property which he shall hereafter require by gift, descent, or in his own right by bequest, devise or in any course of distribution shall be liable to the payment of the said Debts." (Court Actions in Insolvencies, 1805-1807, Court Records Book Accession No. 605 at the Historical Society of Harford County)

Preston, Darby (African American), 1831. "Negro Darby Preston. Petition, Schedule, Sheriff's Certificate, Personal Discharge and Order for Publication, Bond for Appearance, Trustee's Bond, Trustee's Certificate and Deed to Trustee filed 12th Decr. 1831. March 17th 1832 Certificate of publication filed, petitioner appears and finally discharged." (Insolvent Docket A, 1807-1843, p. 114, at the Maryland State Archives). **Genealogical Notes**: Darby Preston, born circa 1762, was involved in other legal matters in 1809, 1817 and 1824. (Court Record Documents 42.12.5, 44.09.3, 60.05.5 and 97.09.14 at the

Historical Society of Harford County). He was head of household in 1820 (Census) and listed as age 70 in 1832. (A List of Free People of Colour taken in 1832 by Joshua Guyton, Sheriff)

Preston, Moses, 1829. "Petition, Schedule, Certificate of Sheriff, personal discharge, Order for Publication, Bond for Appearance, Trustee's Bond, Trustee's Certificate and Deed to Trustee filed 13th May 1829. 15th August 1829 Petitioner appears, certificate filed and finally discharged." (Insolvent Docket A, 1807-1843, p. 96, at Maryland State Archives). **Genealogical Notes**: Moses Preston was born circa 1793 and brother of Thomas Preston. He appeared in Harford County in the early 1800s, but his place of origin is unknown. He married Blanch Monohon circa April 6, 1819 (date of license) and died circa 1850. (Family research by Jim Hickson, of Cecil County, MD in 1999, now deceased)

Preston, William, 1810. "Whereas we the subscribers Justices of the Peace for Harford County upon the petition of William Preston who set forth that he had been confined in the Gaol [jail] of said county twenty days for debts which he was unable to pay and finding the facts stated to be true we did meet at the gaol of said county on the 4th day of March last and did then and there appoint the 14th day of April Inst. to meet at the Court House of said county which said appointment we did then and there ... at the request of the said Sheriff administer to the said William Preston the following Oath which was taken by the said William Preston being first duly sworn on the holy Evangely of Almighty God in the words following – I William Preston do solemnly swear that the Schedule which I have delivered to the Sheriff of Harford County doth contain a full account to the best of my knowledge & remembrance of my whole estate both real and personal or that I have any title to or interest in and of all Debts, credits and effects whatsoever which I or any in trust for me have or at the time of my petition had, or am or was in any respect entitled to in possession, remainder or reversion and that I have not directly or indirectly at any time since my imprisonment or before, sold, leased or otherwise conveyed or disposed of or intrusted all or any part of my estate, Goods, Stock, money or Debts thereby to defraud my creditors or to secure the same to receive or expect any profit or advantage thereof so help me God, which said duplicate of the Schedule aforesaid we have transmitted to the Clerk of the County Court to be by him Preserved in his Office for the information of the creditors of the said William Preston. Given under our hands and seals this 14th Day of April 1810. Saml. Bradford. Jas. McComas. Bennet Bussey." (Court Records Document 67.14(1) at the Historical Society of Harford County; copy of schedule to which he signed his name "William Preston" was included, but no property was listed)

Price, Charles, 1820. "To the Honorable John Moores, one of the Justices of the Orphans Court of Harford County. The petition of Charles Price of Harford County respectfully sheweth that your petitioner is now in actual confinement in Harford County Goal for Debts which he is unable to pay (not for any breach of the laws of this State or of the United States), that he is willing and offers to deliver up to the use of his creditors all his property real, personal and mixed, the necessary wearing apparel and bedding of himself and [his] family excepted. A schedule whereof together with a list of his Creditors and Debtors as far as he can at present ascertain them is hereto on oath annexed. Your petitioner also hereto annexes proof on oath that he has resided two years next preceding [sic] this his application within the State of Maryland. Your petitioner therefore prays your honour to grant him the benefit of the Insolvent Laws of this State and to relieve him from his present confinement, and your Petitioner will ever pray, &c. 5t Augt. 1820. Charles Price." (Court Records Document 68.05.1(F) at the Historical Society of Harford County included a copy of the schedule to which "Charles Price" signed his name, but no property was listed). "I hereby certify that Charles Price is in my custody in the common goal of the county for Debt and not for any breach of the laws of the State of Maryland or the United States. Harford County. 5th Augt. 1820. Joshua Guyton, Sheriff." (Court Records Document 68.05.1(b), loc. cit.) "Harford County to wit. On this 4th day of August

1820 personally appeared before me the subscriber (one of the State of Maryland's Justices of the Peace in and for the County aforesaid) Henry Webster and made oath on the Holy Evangels of Almighty God that Charles Price (who is about to make application for the benefit of the insolvent laws) has resided within the State of Maryland for upwards of two years next before the date of this affidavit. Sworn before Saml. Bradford." (Court Records Document 68.05.1(c), loc. cit.) "Harford County sct. On the application to the Subscriber as a Judge of the Orphans Court of Harford County by petition in writing of Charles Price stating that he is an imprisoned debtor in actual confinement in the Goal of said County and praying for a discharge from said confinement and for the benefit of the Act of the General Assembly of Maryland entitled 'An act for the relief of sundry Insolvent debtors' passed at November session Eighteen hundred and five and the several supplements thereto on the terms therein mentioned, a schedule of his property and a list of his creditors on oath being annexed to his said petition with competent and satisfactory testimony that he has resided two years within the State of Maryland next before the making of his application as aforesaid and the said Charles Price having taken the oath prescribed by the said act prescribed for delivering up his property and given bond with security and in a penalty by me approved and prescribed for his appearance before the Judges of Harford County Court on the first Saturday after the second Monday in March next at the Court House of said County, being the time by me appointed for a hearing before said court in said petition to answer interrogatories which his creditors may propose to him according to the provisions of the said Original Act. I do hereby order and adjudge that the said Charles Price be discharged from said Imprisonment and direct that he give notice to his creditors of his said application and discharge, and of the day so by me appointed for a hearing before said Court by advertisement to be inserted in the Bond of Union newspaper once a week for three months before the day so appointed. Given under my hand this fifth day of Augt. Eighteen hundred and twenty. John Moores." (Court Records Document 68.05.1(E), loc. cit.) "March 17th 1821. I hereby certify that the annexed advertisement was published three months in the Bond of Union. Wm. Coale, Jr." (Court Records Document 68.05.1(d), loc. cit.; a copy of the notice was clipped from the newspaper and included in this file). "Petition, Schedule, Bond, Sheriff's certificate, personal discharge & order for publication filed 5th August 1820. March 17th 1821 … The Court appointed Henry Webster Trustee and a personal discharge granted the petitioner." [nothing further recorded] (Insolvent Docket A, 1807-1843, p. 36, at Maryland State Archives; Insolvent Docket Prior to 1827, Court Records Accession #632 at the Historical Society of Harford County). **Genealogical Notes**: Charles Price was born circa 1783, married Hannah Swart circa January 2, 1805 (date of license), served as a private in the War of 1812 and died in late 1847. (*Harford Madsonian and Bel-Air & Havre de Grace Messenger*, January 13, 1848, administrator's notice, but no obituary)

Price, Charles H., 1857. "Petition, Schedules, Affidavits, Appointment of Trustee & order of notice, Trustee's Bond & Deed to Trustee filed 1st June 1857. 14th Novr. 18578 Petitioner appears, files certificate of publication & discharged." (Insolvent Docket A. L. J. No. 1, p. 18, in the Court Records Department of the Historical Society of Harford County). "Notice is hereby given that Charles H. Price. of Harford County, has made application to the Circuit Court of said County, for the benefit of the Insolvent Laws of Maryland, and that the first Saturday after the 2nd Monday in November next has been assigned for him to appear in said Court to answer such interrogatories as his creditors may propose or allege against him. A. Lingan Jarrett, Clerk." (*Harford Democrat*, June 5, 1857, p. 3)

Price, James H., 1859. "Petition, Schedule of property, List of debts due & owing to & from, Affidavit, Order, Appointment of Trustee, Trustee's Bond and Deed to Trustee & A. W. Bateman, Esqr., appointed Trustee, filed 30th July 1859." [nothing further recorded] (Insolvent Docket A. L. J. No. 1, p. 29, in the Court Records Department of the Historical Society of Harford County). "Notice is hereby given that James H. Price. of Harford County, has made application to the Circuit Court of said County, for the benefit of the Insolvent Laws of Maryland, and that the 1st Saturday after the 2nd Monday in November next, has been assigned for him to appear in said Court to answer such interrogatories as his creditors may propose or allege against him. Wm. Galloway, Clerk, Circuit Court for Harford County." (*The Southern Aegis*, August 6, 1859, p. 3)

Prigg, Carvill H., 1842. "Petition, Affidavits, Schedules, Appointment, certificates, order, personal discharge, deed, appearance & trustee bonds filed 13th Septr. 1842. 26th Novr. 1842 Petition filed & leave to withdraw application." (Insolvent Docket A, 1807-1843, p. 184, at Maryland State Archives). **Genealogical Note**: Carvill Hall Prigg married Christena Wheeler on November 9, 1819 by Rev. Roger Smith at St. Ignatius Catholic Church in Hickory. (Church Register spelled her name Christine and his surname Prig, but the marriage license spelled the names Christena and Prigg respectively)

Prigg, Joseph, 1842. "Petition, Affidavits, Schedules, Appointment, certificate, order, [and] personal discharge, appearance & trustee's bonds filed 18th Oct. 1842 – 20 May 1843 Petitioner appears, files certificate of publication & finally discharged. 21 Nov/48 Petition of Creditors filed & order appointing Wm. H. Dallam Trustee & Trustee's Bond filed." [nothing further recorded] (Insolvent Docket A, 1807-1843, p. 186, at Maryland State Archives)

Pyle, Amer, 1885. A deed "of trust for the benefit of creditors" [under the Insolvent Laws of the State of Maryland] has "lately been filed in the clerk's office [for] Amer Pyle, to William H. Doxen." (*The Aegis & Intelligencer*, November 20, 1885, p. 2). "Notice to Creditors. In the matter of the insolvency of Amer Pyle ... Notice is hereby given to the creditors of the Amer Pyle, who were such on the 29th day of March, 1886, the date of the application for the benefit of the insolvent laws of Maryland, to file their claims against the estate of said insolvent, duly proven, with the Clerk of the Circuit Court for Harford county, on or before the 17th day of May next. William H. Doxen, Permanent Trustee." (*Harford Democrat*, April 23, 1886, p. 3). "Insolvent Notice ... It is ordered, this 12th day of April, 1886, that the said Amer Pyle, the insolvent, be and appear in this court, on Monday, the 17th day of May, 1886, to answer such interrogatories or allegations, as his creditors, endorsers or sureties may propose or allege against him, and that the permanent trustee give notice by the publication of this order in some newspaper published at Bel Air, Md., once a week for three successive weeks, before the 17th day of May, 1886, to the creditors of said insolvent of the day so fixed upon. Jas. D. Watters. A. L. Jarrett, Clerk." (*Harford Democrat*, April 23, 1886, p. 3). **Genealogical Notes**: Amer Pyle was born in 1826 at Chestnut Hill, later worked as a farmer at Wilna, married Mary R. Wann (1834-1919) circa 20 Aug 1862 (date of license), died on May 15, 1906 and was buried at Union Chapel. Their children were Bertie Pyle, Harry S. Pyle, Frederick Pyle, Stanley Pyle, of Portland OR, Woodley Pyle, I. Vinton Pyle, Miller Pyle and Grason Pyle. (Death certificate did not name his parents; *The Aegis & Intelligencer*, May 18, 1908; Union Chapel tombstones)

Pyle, Amos, 1822. Jeremiah Brown vs. Samuel Pyle, Daniel Pyle, John Pyle, Phebe Pyle, Joseph Pyle, Ruth Pyle and Orpha Pyle, heirs of Amos Pyle, deceased. Bill concerns the sale of the real estate of Amos Pyle who died in debt to the complainant on or about January 1, 1822. Amos Pyle died seized of several land tracts, but there was insufficient personal estate to pay his debts. The complainant requested his land to be sold. Amos Pyle's heirs as named above all resided in Pennsylvania and Phebe, Joseph, Ruth and Orpha Pyle were all infants under the age of 21 years. Case was resolved by the Court and closed on March 18, 1826. (Harford County Equity Court Book HD No. 1, pp. 216-221; *Bond of Union*, July 28, 1825, abstracted by F. Edward Wright in *Newspaper Abstracts of Cecil and Harford Counties, 1822-1830*, p. 29). **Genealogical Notes**: Amos Pyle, son of Moses Pyle and Mary Cook, of Lancaster Co., PA, was born circa 1765, married Ruth Stubbs (1766-1816), daughter of Daniel Stubbs and Ruth Gilpin, on January 10, 1793, settled in Harford County and died in 1822.

(The Stubbs Family of Little Britain, Lancaster County, Pennsylvania, by Helen Swisher Davenport and Stokes Clement Swisher, 1992)

Pyle, Lewis, 1835. "Petition, Affidavits, Schedule, personal discharge and order of publication, Bond for Appearance, Trustee's Bond, Trustee's Certificate and Deed to Trustee filed 27th June 1835. 19th Mar 1836 Petitioner appears, certificate of publication filed and finally discharged." (Insolvent Docket A, 1807-1843, p. 141, at the Maryland State Archives). **Genealogical Note**: Lewis Pyle, of Harford County, married Ann Johnson, of Baltimore City, on November 11, 1830 by Rev. Samuel Park. (*Independent Citizen*, November 18, 1830)

Ramsey, John R., 1894. "Mr. John R. Ramsey, of the fourth district, has applied for the benefit of the insolvent laws and Mr. Stevenson A. Williams is his preliminary trustee." (*Havre de Grace Republican*, May 4, 1894, p. 3)

Raymond, Henry A., 1884. "September 24th 1884. Petition, Schedule of Property, List of Creditors & Debts, Affidavits & Order of Court thereon filed … [various notices and claims filed] … May 11/85 Petitioner appeared in open Court & was finally discharged … [several more claims and exhibits filed] … June 15/85 Final Order of Auditor's Report." [nothing further recorded] (Insolvent Docket A. L. J. No. 1, p. 90, in Court Records Department of the Historical Society of Harford County). "Trustee's Sale of Personal Property. In virtue of an order of the Circuit Court for Harford county passed in the matter of the insolvency of Henry A. Raymond, the undersigned as permanent trustee, will offer at public auction on the farm now occupied by said insolvent, in Bush river Neck, formerly the farm of William M. Elliott, on Saturday, November 8th, 1884, at 11 o'clock A. M., the following Personal Property. Two horses, 2 mules, 12 hogs, reaper, wheat drill, carriage, spring wagon, 1 horse road wagon, lot of farming implements and harness, about 20 bushels of potatoes, and tenant interest in 20? acres of corn in the field. William H. Harlan, Permanent Trustee. J. S. Richardson, Auctioneer." (*Bel Air Times*, October 31, 1884). **Genealogical Notes**: Henry Allen Raymond was born in 1843, married Mary Virginia Osborn (1850 – December 3, 1904), daughter of Bennett Osborn and Jane Cole, lived on the old Allen estate near Stepney and died on March 8, 1927 at the home of his son-in-law on Barclay Street in Baltimore. The children of Henry and Mary Raymond were Mary Alleine Raymond (1878-1913) married in 1901 to William H. Pentz, of Aberdeen, later of Baltimore, and Harry H. Raymond (1880-1928), of Baltimore. (St. George's P. E. Church tombstones; *The Aegis & Intelligencer*, December 9, 1904 and June 27, 1913; *The Aegis*, March 11, 1927)

Reckord, William H., 1891. "Notice to Creditors. In the matter of the insolvency of William H. Reckord … Notice is hereby given to the creditors of William H. Reckord, who were such upon the 1st day of December 1891, to file their claims, duly proven, with the Clerk of the Circuit Court for Harford county on or before the first day of November, 1892. Robert Archer, Septimus Davis, D. Meredith Reese, Permanent Trustees." (*Harford Democrat*, August 19, 1982, p. 3). "Trustee's Sale. By virtue of an order of the Circuit Court for Harford County, passed in the insolvent proceedings against William H. Reckord, the undersigned, trustee, will see at Public Sale at the Court House door, in Bel Air, at 12 o'clock, M., on the 5th Day of September, 1892, the following described Parcel of Real Estate, containing 98 Acres, More or Less, situated in said county, near Benson P. O., on the Harford Turnpike, and road from Benson to Fullerton, and adjoining the lands of George Steigler and Garrett Amos. This property is covered with a fine growth of Timber, and is conveniently located near Schools, Churches and Stores, and is about two miles from Fallston on the B. and L. Railroad, and five miles from Joppa on the B. and O. R. R. The undersigned, Trustee of said William H. Reckord, will also sell at the same time and place a one-fifth interest in a remainder, after the death of Mrs. Julia A. Reckord, in a Real Estate Mortgage for the sum of $4,527.94, from the Reckord Manufacturing Company to Julia A. Reckord, dated December 22nd, 1891, and recorded among the Land

Records of said Harford county in Liber A.L.J. No. 72, folio 356. Robert Archer, Septimus Davis, D. Meredith Reese, Permanent Trustees." (*The Aegis & Intelligencer*, Sept 2, 1892, p. 1). **Genealogical Notes**: William H. Reckord married ---- Mabbett, daughter of Abraham Joseph Mabbett (c1837-1893) and Annie S. Whitaker, of Harford Co., later of Baltimore. (Baltimore *Sun*, October 5, 1857, spelled his father-in-law's name Mabbitt; *The Aegis & Intelligencer*, March 17, 1893, spelled it Mabbett)

Reed, Harris, 1860. "Petition, List of debts, Schedule of property, Affidavit, Order of Notice to Creditors, Trustee's Bond and Deed filed 18th Feby 1861 and Stevenson Archer, Esqr., appointed Trustee. 26th March 1861 3 promissory notes of Joel Cook & 1 promissory note of Elisha Cook's executors filed. 5th August 1861 Certificate of Publication of Notice to Creditors & petitioner finally discharged." (Insolvent Docket A. L. J. No. 1, p. 38, in Court Records Department of the Historical Society of Harford County). "Notice is hereby given, that Harris Reed has made application to the circuit court of Harford county, for the benefit of the Insolvent Laws of Maryland; and that the 1st Monday in August, 1861, has been assigned for him to appear in said court to answer such interrogatories as his creditors may propose or allege against him. Wm. Galloway, Clerk, circuit court for Harford co." (*National American*, April 26, 1861, p. 3)

Reed, Thomas, 1833. "Petition, Schedule, Affidavit, Personal discharge, Order for Publication, Bond for Appearance, Trustee's Bond, Trustee's Certificate and Deed to Trustee filed 10th May 1833. 17th Augt. 1833 Petitioner appears, Certificate of Publication filed and petitioner finally discharged." (Insolvent Docket A, 1807-1843, p. 125, at the Maryland State Archives). 1840. "Petition, Schedule, Affidavits, personal discharge and order of publication, Bond for Appearance, Trustee's Bond, Trustee's Certificate and Deed to Trustee filed May 29th 1840. 21st November 1840 Petitioner appears & files Certificate of Publication and finally discharged." (Insolvent Docket A, 1807-1843, p. 172, at the Maryland State Archives)

Reese, Alexander, 1806. "August 21st 1806. To the Honorable the Judges of Harford County Court. The petition of Alexander Reese of Harford County respectfully sheweth, That by misfortunes being rendered wholly unable to pay his debts obtained from the Legislature the passage of a law for relief included in the act entitled an act for the relief of sundry Insolvent debtors passed at November Session 1805, that under the provisions of said Act he offers to deliver up to the use of his creditors, all his property, real, personal and mixed (the necessary wearing apparel and bedding of himself and is family excepted) to which he is in any way entitled, a schedule whereof an oath together with a list of his creditors also on oath as far forth as he can ascertain them, is annexed to and accompanies this petition, and that in all things he is ready to comply with the directions of the said Act and that there is hereto also annexed the assent in writing of so many of his creditors aforesaid as have due to them the amount of two-thirds of the debts due by him at the time of the passage of the act and at the time of this his application Your Petitioner therefore prays that such proceedings shall therefrom be had by the Court in the premises as that your petitioner may be discharged, as in the said act is provided, from all debts, accounts, contracts. Promises and agreements due from or owing and contracted in his individual and also in a co-partnership capacity by him before the passage of the acts or before this his application, and he as in duty bond will ever pray, &c. 16th Aug. 1806. [signed] Alexander Reese." [Lists of debts owed and debts due were included, but several pages of statements, and the last entry in 1807, were as follows]: "Ordered by the Court that the Trustee sell the property mentioned in the schedule, on three months credit the purchaser to give bond with security to be approved by the Trustee." (Court Actions in Insolvencies, 1805-1807, Court Records Book Accession No. 605 at the Historical Society of Harford County)

Reiley, James, 1826. "Petition, Schedule, Bond, Sheriff's certificate and personal discharge and order for publication and Bond of provisional trustee and certificate for Trustee filed 26th June 1826."

[nothing further recorded] (Insolvent Docket A, 1807-1843, p. 80, at the Maryland State Archives; Insolvent Docket Prior to 1827, Court Records Accession #632 at the Historical Society of Harford County)

Renshaw, Henry, 1820. "To the Honorable John Moores, one of the Justices of the Orphans Court of Harford County. The petition of Henry Renshaw of Harford County respectfully sheweth that your petitioner is now in actual confinement in Harford County Jail for debts which he is unable to pay and not for any breach of laws of this State or the United States, that he is willing and offers to deliver up to the use of his creditors all his property real, personal and mixed, the necessary wearing apparel and bedding of himself and family excepted, A schedule whereof together with a list of his creditors and debtors as far as he can at present ascertain them is hereto on oath annexed. Your petitioner also hereto annexes on oath proof [sic] that he has resided two years next preceeding this his application within the State of Maryland. Your petitioner therefore prays your honor to grant him the benefit of the insolvent laws of this State and to relieve him from his present confinement and your petitioner will pray, &c. Henry "x" Renshaw. March 21st 1821." (Court Records Document 68.11.1(C) at the Historical Society of Harford County included a schedule of creditors to which Henry Renshaw made his "x" mark, but no property was listed). "Know all men by these presents that we Henry Renshaw and James Thompson are held and firmly bound unto the State of Maryland in the sum of one hundred Dollars current money to be paid to the said State, its certain attorney or assigns to which payment well and truly to be made and done we bind ourselves, our heirs, executors and administrators jointly and severally firmly by these presents. Sealed with our seals and dated this 21st day of March 1821. The condition of the above obligation is such that if the above bound Henry Renshaw shall make his personal appearance before the Judges of Harford County Court at the Court house in the County on the first Saturday next after the fourth Monday in August next, then and there to answer such allegations as his creditors may make against him agreeably to the Insolvent laws of Maryland and not depart therefrom without permission of the said court but await their Order, then the above obligation to be null and void otherwise to be and remain in full force and virtue in law. Henry "x" Renshaw, James Thompson." (Court Records Document 68.12.1(b), loc. cit.) "I hereby certify that Henry Renshaw is in my custody in the common jail of this county for debt at the suit of James Preston to the use of William Galloway and not for any breach of the laws of the State of Maryland or the United States. Joshua Guyton, Shff. Harford County, March 21st 1821." (Court Records Document 68.11.1(e), loc. cit.; newspaper clipping in file attached to this note: "I certify that the annexed advertisement was published 13 weeks successively in the Bond of Union & Weekly Advertiser. Wm. Coale, Jr." (undated document 68.12.1(d), loc. cit., "filed 1st Sept. 1821") "Petition, Schedule, Bond, Sheriff's certificate, personal discharge and order for publication filed 21st March 1821 – 1st September 1821 petitioner appears and Solomon Ady appointed Trustee and ordered that he give bond in the penalty of $100." [nothing further recorded] (Insolvent Docket A, 1807-1843, p. 44, at the Maryland State Archives; Insolvent Docket Prior to 1827, Court Records Accession #632 at the Historical Society of Harford County)

Reynolds, David H., 1888. "On Tuesday [February 14, 1888] David H. Reynolds, insolvent, appeared in open court, and no objections being made was finally discharged." (*The Aegis & Intelligencer*, February 17, 1888, p. 3)

Richardson, Benjamin, of Samuel, 1820. "Petition, Schedule, Bond, Sheriff's Certificate, order for publication and personal discharge filed 14th April 1820. Sepr. 2nd 1820 petitioner appeared. The Court appoints William Richardson Trustee and on his Executing a Bond the petr. to have a personal discharge granted him. Trustee's bond recorded same day." (Insolvent Docket A, 1807-1843, p. 30, at the Maryland State Archives; Insolvent Docket Prior to 1827, Court Records Accession #632 at the

152

Historical Society of Harford County). "To the Honorable John Moores, one of the Justices of the Orphans Court of Harford County. The petition [of] Benjamin Richardson of Saml. of Harford County respectfully sheweth that your petitioner is now in actual confinement in Harford County Gaol for debts which he is unable to pay, that he is willing and offers to deliver up to the use of his creditors all his property real, personal and mixed, the necessary wearing apparel and bedding of himself and family excepted, a schedule whereof together with a list of his creditors and debtors as far as he can at present ascertain them is hereto on oath annexed. Your petitioner also hereto annexes proof on oath that he has resided two years next preceeding this his application within the State of Maryland. Your petitioner therefore prays your honour to grant him the benefit of the Insolvent Laws of this State and to relieve him from his present confinement and your petitioner will pray, &c. Benjamin Richardson (of Saml). Harford County, 14th April 1820." (Court Records Document 68.11.3(a) at the Historical Society of Harford County included a schedule of creditors, signed by Benjamin Richardson, but no property was listed). "Know all men by these presents that we Benjamin Richardson of Samuel and William Richardson of Henry are held and firmly bound unto the State of Maryland in the sum of one thousand and seventy dollars Current money of the United States to be paid to the said State, its certain attorney or assigns to which payment well and truly to be made and done we bind ourselves, our heirs, executors and administrators jointly and severally firmly by these presents. Sealed with our seals and dated this fourteenth day of April 1820. The condition of the above obligation is such that if the above bound Benjamin Richardson of Samuel shall make his personal appearance before the Judges of Harford County Court at the Court house in the said County on the Saturday next after the fourth Monday in August next, then and there to answer such allegations as his creditors may make against him agreeably to the insolvent laws of Maryland and not depart therefrom without permission of the said Court but await their order, then the above obligation to be null and void otherwise to be and remain in full force and virtue in law. Benjamin Richardson. Wm. Richardson. Witness: John Moores." (Court Records Document 68.11(3)b at the Historical Society of Harford County) "I hereby certify that Benjamin Richardson of Saml. is in my custody in the common jail of this county for debt and not for any breach of the laws of the state of Maryland or of the United States. Harford County, 14th April 2810. Joshua Guyton, Shff." (Court Records Document 68.11.3(a), loc. cit.; a schedule of creditors to which "Benjamin Richardson" signed his name was included among other documents, but no property was listed). "Notice Is Hereby Given, To the creditors of Benjamin Richardson, of Samuel, late an imprisoned debtor of Harford county, that on the application of the said debtor, by petition in writing to the Honorable John Moores, Chief Judge of the Orphans' Court of said county, for the benefit of the insolvent laws of Maryland, the said Judge on the 14th day of April, in the year 1820, granted to the said debtor a discharge from imprisonment, and appointed the Saturday next after the fourth Monday in August next, for his appearance before the Judges of Harford county court, at the Court-House of said county, for a hearing before said Court, on said petition, and to answer interrogatories which his creditors may propose to him." (Court Records Document 67.26(8), loc. cit., had a copy of a newspaper article in the file with this note attached: "I certify that the annexed advertisement was published thirteen weeks successively in the Bond of Union. Wm. Coale, Jr., Bel Air, Aug. 31st 1820)

Richardson, Henry, 1863. "Petition, Schedule of property, A List of debts due and owing to, A list of debts due and owing from, Affidavit, Order, Trustee's Bond & Deed to Trustee filed 22nd January 1863 & Daniel Scott, Esqr., appointed Trustee. 27th February 1863 ... Claim of Jas. S. Barrow for taxes filed ... 25th May 1863 Auditor's Reports No. 1 & 2 filed ... 3rd August 1863 Petitioner appears, files Certificate of Notice to Creditors & finally discharged ... 27th Nov/63 Petition & Exhibits of Jno. D.

Mitchell filed … 22nd January 1864 Petition of John Ward & copy of Judgment filed … 11th April 1864 Claim of David Streett, of David, filed and same day Claim of Joseph A. Wheeler filed … 1st Aug 1864 Petition of William M. Ady filed … 20th Feby/66 Final order of ratification of Auditor Reports Nos. 1 & 2 filed. Recorded in Judgment Record ALJ No. 1, folio 382." (Insolvent Docket A. L. J. No. 1, p. 42, in the Court Records Department of the Historical Society of Harford County). "In the matter of the insolvency of Henry Richardson … Ordered, this 6th day of April, 1863, that the sales made and reported by Daniel Scott, Trustee for the benefit of the creditors of the said Henry Richardson, be and the same is hereby confirmed, unless cause to the contrary be shown on or before the 2nd day of May next; provided a copy of this Order be published in some newspaper printed in Harford county, once in each of three successive weeks, before the said 2nd day of May next. The report states the amount of sale to be $2,704.80. John H. Price. True copy. Test: Wm. Galloway, Clerk." (*The Southern Aegis*, April 10, 1863, p. 2). "Notice is hereby given to the creditors of Henry Richardson, an Insolvent Creditor, that they file their claims with the vouchers thereof with the Clerk of the Circuit Court for Harford County, on or before the 11th day of May next." (*The Southern Aegis*, April 10, 1863, p. 2). "Notice Is Hereby Given, that Henry Richardson has made application to the Circuit Court of Harford county, for the benefit of the Insolvent Laws of Maryland; and that the first Monday of August next, has been assigned for him to appear in said court to answer such interrogatories as his creditors may propose or allege against him. Wm. Galloway, Clerk, Circuit Court for Harford County." (*National American*, May 8, 1863, p. 3). **Genealogical Notes**: Henry Richardson (1814-1894), son of Col. William Richardson, married Elizabeth Ann Macatee (1811-1902), daughter of Capt. Henry Macatee and Theresa Wheeler, circa 10 Jan 1837 (date of license; St. Ignatius Catholic Church tombstone inscriptions; Macatee (McAtee) Family typescript in The Henry C. Peden, Jr. Research Library at the Historical Society of Harford County, p. 13; *The Genealogical and Encyclopedic History of the Wheeler Family in America*, by Albert G. Wheeler, Jr., 1914, p. 531)

Richardson, Skelton S., 1825. "Petition, bond, Schedule, Shffs Certificate, personal discharge and order for publication filed 1st June 1825. Printers Certificate filed the 18th March 1826. Petitioner appeared. Edward Rutledge appointed Trustee and personally discharged by order of Court. March 20th 1826 ordered by the Court that the trustee give bond with security." [nothing further recorded] (Insolvent Docket A, 1807-1843, p. 70, at Maryland State Archives; Insolvent Docket Prior to 1827, Court Records Accession #632 at the Historical Society of Harford County)

Richardson, Spencer, 1829. "Petition, Schedule, Certificate of Sheriff, personal discharge, order for publication, bond for appearance, Trustee's Bond and Trustee's Certificate filed 13th May 1829." [nothing further recorded] (Insolvent Docket A, 1807-1843, p. 96, at Maryland State Archives)

Ricketts, Nathan, 1825. Insolvent debtor. (*Bond of Union and Harford County Weekly Advertiser*, July 28, 1825). "Petition, Bond, Schedule, Sheriffs Certificate, personal discharge and order for publication filed 16th February 1825. 13th August 1825 Petitioner appears and order for publication filed. 18th March 1826 objections filed. March 18th 1826 printers certificate filed." [nothing further recorded] (Insolvent Docket A, 1807-1843, p. 69, at Maryland State Archives; Insolvent Docket Prior to 1827, Court Records Accession #632 at the Historical Society of Harford County). **Genealogical Note**: This may be the Nathaniel Ricketts (1786-1867) who married Ruth Lancaster (1788-1875) on April 19, 1810 and later settled in Morgan Co., OH, apparently in or after 1826. (*Harford County, Maryland Marriage References and Family Relationships, 1774-1824*, by Henry C. Peden, Jr., 2011, p. 175)

Ricketts, Samuel J., 1884. "22nd Jany 1884. Petition, Schedules, Order, bond of trustee & deed filed … [claims filed by various persons through 1884 into 1885] … 21st September 1885 Submission and final ratification of Auditor's Report No. 1 filed." [nothing further recorded] (Insolvent Docket A. L. J. No. 1, p. 83, in Court Records Department of the Historical Society of Harford County). "Public Sale. By virtue of an order of the Circuit Court for Harford County, the subscriber as Insolvent Trustee, will sell at Public Auction, at Wilton Farm, near Havre de Grace, on Wednesday, March 12th, 1884 at 10 o'clock all the Goods and Chattels of Samuel J. Ricketts, consisting of Stock, Farming Implements, &c., to wit: "One pair Roan Work Horses, 1 Chestnut Mare, 2 Gray Mares, in foal; 1 Hay Mare, 1 Bay Horse, 1 Chestnut Mare, 1 Sorrel colt three years old, 5 excellent Milch Cows, 2 Heifers. 4 Yearling Calves, 3 Brood Sows, and 14 Pigs, 1 Champion Self-Hinder, new; 1 Mower, 2 Buckeye double Sulky Cultivators, good as new; 1 Roller, 1 Empire Drill, new; 1 four-horse Wagon, 2 two-horse Wagons. Horse Rake, Cutting Box, Grain Fan, about 200 barrels of Corn in the ear, 58 acres of wheat in the ground, Hay, Oats, 1600 lbs. Phosphate, Plows, Cultivators, and many other articles used on a first-class farm. Also Household and Kitchen Furniture. Herman Stump, Trustee. J. S. Richardson, Auctioneer." (*Havre de Grace Republican*, February 29, 1884, p. 3; *The Aegis & Intelligencer*, March 7, 1884, p. 3). "In the matter of the Insolvent Petition of Samuel J. Ricketts, for the benefit of the Insolvent Laws ... In Pursuance of an order of the Circuit Court for Harford county, notice is hereby given to the creditors, endorsers and sureties of Samuel J. Ricketts, that he will appear in said court, on the 8th day of September, 1884, to answer such interrogatories as they may propose or allege against him, and warning them to show cause, if any they have, why said Insolvent should not be discharged. Herman Stump, Permanent Trustee." (*The Aegis & Intelligencer*, August 3, 1884, p. 2). "Ordered, this twenty-eighth day of January, 1885, that the sales made and reported by Herman Stump, Permanent Trustee in the above case, be finally ratified and confirmed, unless cause to the contrary be shown on or before the 21st day of February 1885; provided, a copy of this order be published in a newspaper printed and published in Harford county for three successive weeks prior to the said 21st day of February, 1885. Report states the amount of sales to be $2,416. A. Lingan Jarrett, Clerk." (*The Aegis & Intelligencer*, February 5, 1885, p. 2). **Genealogical Notes**: Samuel J. Ricketts (March 6, 1825 – February 2, 1911), son of Thomas M. Ricketts and Caroline E. Strong, married Belinda Bowen (1838 – January 13, 1900), daughter of William Bowen and Amelia Griffith, on January 28, 1858 and their children were Thomas William Ricketts (born October 28, 1858, married Oneda L. Davis), John C. Ricketts (April 3, 1860 – July 1, 1872), Samuel J. Ricketts, Jr. (born April 18, 1863, married Ida Foard), Harry G. Ricketts (born July 2, 1864, marrried Nevie E. Miller), Lewis or Louis C. Ricketts (born February 15, 1867, married Effie E. Brannan), Lilly May Ricketts (January 22, 1870 – August 23, 1930, married James H. Baldwin), John Edward Ricketts (June 23, 1873 – February 2, 1951, married Dora Elizabeth Ford), Estella Ricketts (born January 22, 1877 unmarried in 1911) and Walter Scott Ricketts (born November 28, 1877). (Harford Co. license; *Maryland Bible Records, Volume 1*, by Henry C. Peden, Jr., 2003, pp. 208-209; Baltimore *Sun*, March 4, 1858, mistakenly stated they were married on February 28, 1858 and spelled her name Balinda; 1860 Harford Co. Census listed his occupation as a manager; Death certificate of Belinda Ricketts; Death certificate of Samuel Ricketts mistakenly listed his mother's name as Charlotte Strong; *The Aegis & Intelligencer*, February 10, 1911, stated Samuel J. Ricketts died at the home of his daughter Mrs. James H. Baldwin in Havre de Grace; Angel Hill Cemetery tombstone inscriptions)

Rigdon, John, 1815. "Whereas we the Subscribers Justices of the Peace for Harford County together with Thomas Jeffery, also a Justice of the peace for said County, upon the petition of John Rigdon stating therein that he had actually remained in the gaol [jail] of said county since the first day of July last for debts which he was unable to pay and finding the facts stated to be true we did meet at the gaol of said county on the fourteenth of April last and we did then and there appoint the first day of August instant last to meet at the Court house of said county which said appointment we did then and there ... at the request of said Sheriff administer to the said John Rigdon the following oath which was taken by the said John Rigdon being first duly sworn on the holy Evangels of Almighty

God in the words following, to wit, I John Rigdon do solemnly swear that the schedule which I have delivered to the Sheriff of Harford County doth contain a full account to the best of my knowledge and remembrance of my whole estate both real and personal or that I have any title to or interest in and of all debts, credits and effects whatsoever which I or any in trust for me have or at the time of my petition had, or am or was in any respect entitled to in possession, remainder or reversion and that I have not directly or indirectly at any time since my imprisonment or before, sold, leased or otherwise conveyed or disposed of or intrusted all or any part of my estate, goods, stock, money or debts thereby to defraud my creditors or to secure the same to receive or expect any profit or advantage thereof so help me God, which said duplicate of the Schedule aforesaid we have transmitted to the clerk of the county court to be by him preserved in his office for the information of the creditors of the said John Rigdon. Given under our hands and seals this first day of August 1815. James Wallace. Joseph Robinson." (Court Records Document 67.10.9(A) at the Historical Society of Harford County; a copy of the schedule to which "John Rigdon" signed his name was included, but he had no property to list)

Riley, James, 1841. "Petition, 2 Affidavits, Schedules, Appointment of Trustee, Certificate, order to appear & personal discharge, Deed, Trustee's Bond & Appearance Bond filed 29th Septr. 1841. 21st May 1842 Petitioner appears, files Certificate of Publication & finally discharged." (Insolvent Docket A, 1807-1843, p. 179, at Maryland State Archives). **Genealogical Note**: James Riley married Caroline M. Osborn circa June 16, 1819 (date of license).

Riley, Thomas, 1859. "Petition, Schedule of property, List of debts due & owing to & from, Affidavit, Order appointing Wm. H. Dallam, Trustee, Trustee's Bond and Deed to Trustee filed 23rd June 1859. 19th Nov/59 Petitioner appears, files certificate of notice and was finally discharged." (Insolvent Docket A. L. J. No. 1, p. 28, in the Court Records Department of the Historical Society of Harford County). **Genealogical Notes**: Thomas Riley was born on either November 25, 1824 or July 25, 1827, married Mary Catherine Amos (May 18, 1834 – April 1, 1909) circa 1851 and died on either June 2, 1861 or January 2, 1864. Their children in 1860 were William Joshua Riley (age 8) and Mary Riley (age 6). Mary Catherine Riley married 2nd to Isaac Van Horne and they had a son George Van Horne. (1860 Harford County Census; Ebenezer United Methodist Church cemetery tombstone inscriptions differ from the information cited in *Children of Mt. Soma*, by Geretrude J. Stephens, 1992, p. 410)

Rittenhouse, Smith B., 1842. "Petition, Affidavits, Schedules, Appointment, certificate, order, personal Discharge, deed, appearance & Trustee's Bonds filed 1st Augst. 1842." [nothing further recorded] (Insolvent Docket A, 1807-1843, p. 183, at the Maryland State Archives)

Robertson, Grafton N., 1836. "Petition, Affidavits, Schedule, personal discharge and order of publication, Bond for Appearance, Trustee's Bond, Trustee's Certificate and Deed to Trustee filed 23rd November 1836. 18th March 1837 Petitioner appears, Certificate of Publication filed & finally discharged." (Insolvent Docket A, 1807-1843, p. 154, at Maryland State Archives). 1842. "Petition, Affidavits, Schedules, Appointment of trustee, certificate, order, personal discharge, deed, bond & trustee's bond & deed to trustee & appearance bond filed 12th July 1842. 26th Novr. [1842] Petitioner appears & leave to withdraw application." (Insolvent Docket A, 1807-1843, p. 183, at the Maryland State Archives)

Robertson (Robinson), William, 1805. "Whereas we the Subscribers together with John Moores, Justices of the Peace for Harford County, upon the petition of William Robinson who set forth that he had been confined in the Gaol [jail] of said county twenty days for Debts which he was unable to pay and finding the facts stated to be true did meet at the County Gaol of said county on the 17th day of May 1805 and did then and there appoint the 18th day of June Instant to meet at the Court House of said county which said appointment we did then and there … at the request of the said Sheriff administer to the said William Robinson the following oath which was taken by the said William Robinson being first duly sworn on the Holy Evangels of Almighty God in the words following, I William Robinson do solemnly swear that the schedule which I have delivered to the Sheriff of Harford County doth contain a full account to the best of my knowledge and remembrance of my whole estate both real & personal or that I have any title to or interest in and of all debts, credits and effects whatsoever which I or any in trust for me have or at the time of my petition had, or am or was in any respect entitled to in possession, remainder or reversion and that I have not directly or indirectly at any time since my imprisonment or before, sold, leased or otherwise conveyed or disposed of or intrusted all or any part of my estate, goods, stock, money or debts thereby to defraud my creditors or to secure the same to receive or expect any profit or advantage thereof so help me God, which said duplicate of the schedule aforesaid we have transmitted to the clerk of the county court to be by him preserved in his office for the information of the creditors of the said William Robinson. Given under our hands & seals this 18th June 1805. Thomas A. Hays. Wm. Smithson." (Court Records Documents 67.08.4(A) and (B) in the Court Records Department at the Historical Society of Harford County; copy of the schedule to which "William Robertson" signed his name was included, but no property was listed)

Robinson, Daniel, Sr., 1802. Petitioned for relief under the act for relief of sundry Insolvent Debtors (*Laws of Maryland*, Vol. III, 1802, Chapter 97, Liber JG No. 4, folio 308-314)

Robinson, Daniel N., 1802. Petitioned for relief under the act for relief of sundry Insolvent Debtors (*Laws of Maryland*, Vol. III, 1802, Chapter 97, Liber JG No. 4, folio 308-314)

Robinson, Harry S., 1893. "Insolvent Notice. In the matter of the Insolvency of Harry S. Robinson ... In the above entitled case it is this 19th day of December, 1893, by the Circuit Court for Harford county, ordered that the said Harry S. Robinson, the insolvent, be and appear in this Court on the 12th day of February, 1894, to answer such interrogatories or allegations as his creditors, endorsers or sureties may propose or allege against him, why he should not be discharged under the insolvent laws of the State of Maryland, and that the permanent trustee of said insolvent give notice to the creditors of the day so fixed upon by the publication of this matter in some newspaper published in Harford county, once a week for one month before the said 12th day of February, 1894. Jas. D. Watters. True copy—test: Wm. S. Forwood, Jr., Clerk." (*Harford Democrat*, January 19, 1894, p. 2). "Notice to Creditors. In the matter of the Insolvency of Harry S. Robinson ... Notice is hereby given to the creditors of Harry S. Robinson, of Harford county, as insolvent debtor, to file their claims, properly proven, with the Clerk of the Circuit Court for Harford county, on or before the 1st day of May, 1894. Geo. L. Van Bibber, Permanent Trustee. December 21st, 1893." (*Harford Democrat*, Jan 19, 1894, p. 2) **Genealogical Note**: Harry S. Robinson, a son of Alphonso Robinson (1830-1907) and Charlotte M. Emory (1835-1881), was born circa 1863. (*The Aegis & Intelligencer*, April 12, 1907; Union Chapel tombstones)

Robinson, James, 1802. Petitioned for relief under the act for relief of sundry Insolvent Debtors (*Laws of Maryland*, Vol. III, 1802, Chapter 97, Liber JG No. 4, folio 308-314). **Genealogical Note**: James Robinson (Robison), Sr. was age 83 in 1819 and James Robinson (Robison), Jr. was age about 44 in 1819. (Court Records Document 73.04.1.CC at the Historical Society of Harford)

Robinson, Thomas, 1802. Petitioned for relief under the act for relief of sundry Insolvent Debtors (*Laws of Maryland*, Vol. III, 1802, Chapter 97, Liber JG No. 4, folio 308-314)

Rochester, Earl J. J., 1842. "Petition, Affidavits, Schedules, Appointments, discharge, certificate, order, deed & appearance & trustee's bonds filed [no date given]. 26th Novr. 1842 Petitioner appears, files certificate of publication & cont'd. 20 May 1843 Petitioner appears & finally discharged." (Insolvent Docket A, 1807-1843, p. 182, at the Maryland State Archives)

Rockhold, James R., 1823. "Petition, Schedule, Bond, Sheriff certificate and personal discharge and order for publication filed 4th day of October 1823. 13th March 1824 Petitioner appears." [nothing further recorded] (Insolvent Docket A, 1807-1843, p. 58, at the Maryland State Archives; Insolvent Docket Prior to 1827, Court Records Accession #632 at the Historical Society of Harford County). **Genealogical Note**: James Reason Rockhold married Martha Hollis circa November 25, 1813 (date of Harford County marriage license) and served as a private in the War of 1812 (military records).

Rockhold, John, 1822. "To the Honorable John Moores, one of the Justices of the Orphan's Court of Harford County. The petition of John Rockhold of Harford County respectfully sheweth that your petitioner is now imprisoned in the Jail of Harford County for debts which he is unable to pay, that he is willing and offers to deliver up to the use of his creditors all his property real, personal and mixed to which he is in any way entitled (the necessary wearing apparel and bedding of himself and family excepted) a schedule whereof together with a list of his creditors and debtors, as far as he can ascertain them at present ascertain are hereto on oath annexed. Your petitioner also hereto annexes proof on Oath that he has resided two years preceeding this his application within the State of Maryland. Your petitioner therefore prays your honor to grant him the benefit of the Insolvent Laws of this State and discharge him from his present imprisonment and he will for will for ever pray for the health and prosperity of Your Honor. John "X" Rockhold. March 20th 1822." (Court Records Document 68.11.1(d) at the Historical Society of Harford County). "I hereby certify that the within named John Rockhold is now in actual confinement in the Jail of Harford County as an imprisoned debtor and that he is not confined for any breach of peace or for the nonpayment of any fine on penalty for a breach of the laws of this State or of the United States. Saml. Bradford, Shff. March 20th 1822." (Court Records Document 68.011.1(d), loc. cit., also included a clipping from the *Bond of Union* newspaper and a schedule of creditors to which John Rockhold made his "X" mark, listing this property: "Two Ploughs, One Shovel Plough, One Sled, Eight Cider Casks, Six Windsor [chairs], One Copper Kettle"). Insolvent debtor to be discharged from imprisonment. (*Bond of Union and Harford County Weekly Advertiser*, July 25, 1822). "John Rockhold, Senr. Petition, Schedule, Bond, Sheriff's Certificate and personal discharge and order for publication filed 26th March 1822 – 31st August 1822 petitioner appears … Robert Richardson appointed Trustee and petitioner discharged. Novr. 4th 1822 the Court appoints Philip R. Dallam Trustee in room of Robert Richardson who refuses to act, and bond of trustee filed same day." [nothing further recorded] (Insolvent Docket A, 1807-1843, p. 49, at the Maryland State Archives; Insolvent Docket Prior to 1827, Court Records Accession #632 at the Historical Society of Harford County). **Genealogical Notes**: John Rockhold married Martha Waters on February 2, 1790 (St. James' Parish Register). There was John Rockhold who was aged about 66 in 1777 and John Rockhold who was aged about 68 in 1811 who could have been his father and grandfather, but this is speculation. (Harford County Land Records Book J. L. G. No. A, p. 58; Court Records Document 98.22.1(D) at the Historical Society of Harford County)

Rodley, Robert, 1810. "Whereas we the subscribers Justices of the Peace for Harford County together with John Moores, Esq., also one of the Justices of the Peace for said county, upon the petition of Robert Rodley, who set forth that he had been confined [in jail] twenty days and upwards for debts which he was unable to pay and finding the facts stated to be true together with the said John Moores, Esq. we did meet at the gaol of said county on the 26th Day of November last and did then and there appoint the 27th day of December Instant to meet at the Court house of said county which said appointment we did then and there … at the request of the said Sheriff administer to the said Robert Rodley the following oath which was taken by the said Robert Rodley being first duly sworn on the holy Evangely of Almighty God in the words following, vizt., I Robert Rodley do solemnly swear that the schedule which I have delivered to the Sheriff of Harford County doth contain a full account to the best of my knowledge and remembrance of my whole estate both real and personal or that I have any title to or interest in and of all debts, credits and effects whatsoever which I or any in trust for me have or at the time of my petition had, or am or was in any respect entitled to in possession, remainder or reversion and that I have not directly or indirectly at any time since my imprisonment or before, sold, leased or otherwise conveyed or disposed of or intrusted all or any part of my estate, goods, stock, money or debts thereby to defraud my creditors or to secure the same to receive or expect any profit or advantage thereof so help me God, which said duplicate of the schedule aforesaid we have transmitted to the clerk of the county court to be by him preserved in his office for the information of the creditors of the said Robert Rodley. Given under our hands and seals this 27th Day of December 1810. Thomas A. Hays. Jno. C. Bond." (Court Records Document 67.18.3(A) at the Historical Society of Harford County; a copy of the schedule to which "Robert Rodley signed his name was included, but no property was listed)

Rogers, John O., 1886. "Notice to Creditors. In the matter of the Insolvency of John O. Rogers ... Notice is hereby given to the creditors of the said John O. Rogers, who were such on the 29th day of March, 1886, the date of his application for the benefit of the insolvent laws, to file their claims against the estate of said insolvent, duly proven, with the Clerk of the Circuit Court for Harford county, on or before the 10th day of May next. Walter W. Preston, Permanent Trustee." (*Harford Democrat*, April 23, 1886, p. 3). "Insolvent Notice ... It is ordered, this 8th day of April, 1886, that the said John O. Rogers, the insolvent, be and appear in this Court, on the 10th day of May, 1886, to answer such interrogatories or allegations, as his creditors, endorsers or sureties may propose or allege against him; and that the permanent trustee give notice, by the publication of this order in some newspaper published at Bel Air, in Harford county, once a week for three successive weeks, before the 10th day of May, 1886, to the creditors of said insolvent of the day so fixed upon. Jas. D. Watters. A. L. Jarrett, Clerk." (*Harford Democrat*, April 23, 1886, p. 3). **Genealogical Notes**: John O. Rogers, son of John O. Rogers (1821-1865) and Margaret A. Grafton (1816-1891), was born on June 24, 1855, married Eliza Stewart (1860-1947), worked as a farmer and died on April 9, 1932 in Aberdeen. The children of John and Eliza Rogers were M. Estelle Rogers (1882-1972), of Aberdeen, Rev. Milton Rogers, of Baltimore, and Raymond Rogers, of Emmorton. (*The Aegis*, April 15, 1932; Mt. Zion Methodist Church and Old Brick Baptist Church cemetery tombstones)

Rogers, Rowland, 1809. "Petition, Schedule, Bond, &c. filed 22nd Augt. 1809 ... March 20th 1810. Petition Withdrawn." (Insolvent Docket A, 1807-1843, p. 4, at the Maryland State Archives; Insolvent Docket Prior to 1827, Court Records Accession #632 at the Historical Society of Harford County). 1815. "Whereas we the subscribers Justices of the Peace for Harford County upon the petition of Rowland Rogers setting forth therein that he had actually remained in the goal [jail] of said County since the twentieth day of February last for debts which he was unable to pay and finding the facts therein stated to be true we did meet at the goal of said County on the eighteenth day of March last and did then and there appoint the eleventh day of April instant to meet at the Courthouse of said County, which said appointment we did then and there ... at the request of the said Sheriff administer to the said Rowland Rogers the following oath which was taken by the said Rowland Rogers being first duly sworn on the Holy Evangels of Almighty God in the words following to wit, I do solemnly promise and swear that the schedule which I have delivered to the Sheriff of Harford County doth contain a full account to the best of my knowledge and remembrance of my whole estate both real and personal or that I have any title to or interest in, and of all debts, credits and effects whatsoever which I or any in trust for me have or at the time of my petition had, or am or was in any respect entitled to in possession, remainder or reversion and that I have not directly or indirectly at any time since my imprisonment or before, sold, leased or otherwise conveyed or disposed of or intrusted all or any part of my estate, goods, stock, money or debts thereby to defraud my creditors or to secure the same to receive or expect any profit or advantage thereof so help me God, which said duplicate of the Schedule aforesaid we have transmitted to the Clerk of the County Court to be by him preserved in his office for the information of the creditors of the said Rowland Rogers. Given under our hands and seals this eleventh day of April 1815. James Wallace. Joseph Robinson." (Court Records Document 67.02.8(A) at the Historical Society of Harford County; copy of the schedule to which he signed his name "Rowland Rogers" was included and listed this personal property: "3 Hoes, 1 cutting knife"). **Genealogical Notes**: Rowland Rogers (1775-1848) married Catherine "Kitty" Rogers (1779-1855) circa December 3, 1800 (date of license) and was a Justice of the Peace. (Mt. Zion Methodist Church tombstone; 1818 Equity Court Paper #45 at the Maryland State Archives)

Ross, Abraham T., 1841. "Feby 12th 1841. Petition, Affidavits, Schedules, Order of appointment of Trustee, Trustee Certificate, Order of Discharge & Order of Publication, Appearance Bond, Trustee Bond & Deed filed. Petitioner appears & files Certificate of Publication and finally discharged 22 May 1841." (Insolvent Docket A, 1807-1843, p. 176, at the Maryland State Archives). **Genealogical Notes**: Abraham T. Ross was born October 5, 1806, married Sarah J. ---- (January 1, 1806 – December 17, 1880) probably circa 1830 and died on August 7, 1875. He wrote his will on July 8, 1875 and only mentioned his wife and executrix Sarah Ross. (Holy Trinity Episcopal Church tombstone inscriptions; Harford Co. Will Book WSR No. 9, p. 59)

Ross, Joseph, 1860. "Petition, Schedule of property, A list of debts due to & from, Affidavit, Order & appointment of Archer H. Jarrett, Trustee, Trustee's Bond & Deed to Trustee filed 12th April 1860. 20th July/60. Petition of J. Ross filed. 11th Sep 1860 Claim No. 1 filed. 12th November 1860 Petitioner appeared, filed certificate and was finally discharged." (Insolvent Docket A. L. J. No. 1, p. 33, in the Court Records Department of the Historical Society of Harford County). **Genealogical Notes**: Joseph Ross was born in October 1815, married Rachel ---- (1817 – February 17, 1872) probably circa 1840 and died on April 26, 1891. For many years he was the keeper of the Conowingo Bridge, was partly blind for many years and at the time of his death he was entirely blind. He left a daughter. Virginia M. Caldwell (b. 1843), wife of Charles C. Caldwell (b. 1854), of Cecil County, who were married on April 20, 1877. (Southern Cemetery tombstone inscriptions; *The Aegis & Intelligencer*, March 1, 1872 and May 1, 1891; Cecil County marriage license)

Rowe, Elizabeth, 1816. "Petition, Schedule and Bond filed 3rd Sepr. 1816 and ordered the petitioner be brought into Court immediately. The petitioner having appeared and taken the necessary oaths and given satisfactory security it is ordered by the Court that she be discharged from the custody of the Sheriff of Harford County and that she give the necessary notice required by Law. Notice sent petitioner by Richard Ward." (Insolvent Docket A, 1807-1843, p. 19, at the Maryland State Archives; Insolvent Docket Prior to 1827, Court Records Accession #632 at the Historical Society of Harford County). **Genealogical Note**: Elizabeth Rowe may have been the wife of Thomas Rowe and, if so, they were married before March 4, 1806. (Court Records Document 35.13.1 and Document 37.06.8 at the Historical Society of Harford County)

Ruff, John, 1821. "To the Honorable John Moores, one of the Justices of the Orphans Court of Harford County. The petition of John Ruff of Harford County respectfully sheweth that your petitioner is now in actual confinement in Harford County Gaol [Jail] for debts which he is unable to pay, that he is willing and offers to deliver to the use of his creditors all his property real, personal and mixed (the necessary wearing apparel and bedding of himself and family excepted) a schedule whereof together with a list of his creditors and debtors, as far as he can at present ascertain them, is hereto on oath annexed. Your petitioner also hereto annexes proof on oath that he has resided two years next preceeding this his application within the State of Maryland. Your petitioner therefore prays your honour to grant him the benefit of the insolvent laws of this State and to release him from his present confinement and your petitioner will pray, &c. &c. John Ruff." (Court Records Document 68.08.4(a) at the Historical Society of Harford County). "I hereby certify that John Ruff the petitioner above named is now in actual confinement in Harford County Gaol for debt at the suit of James Gilbert and that it is not upon a breach of peace or any of the penal Laws of the State of Maryland or of the United States. Given under my hand this 18th day of April 1821. Joshua Guyton, Sheriff." (Court Records Document 68.08.4(a), loc. cit., also included a schedule of creditors signed by John Ruff, but no property was listed, and a newspaper clipping from the *Bond of Union* was included in the file). "Petition, Schedule, Bond, Sheriff's certificate, personal discharge and order for publication filed 18th April 1821 – 1st September 1821 petitioner appears and Hosier Barnes appointed Trustee and ordered that he give bond in the penalty of $582." [nothing further recorded] (Insolvent Docket A, 1807-1843, p. 45, at the Maryland State Archives; Insolvent Docket Prior to 1827, Court Records Accession #632 at the Historical Society of Harford County). **Genealogical Note**: John Ruff was born in 1784, married Elizabeth Nelson circa March 1, 1814 (date of license), died February 22, 1831 and was buried in Cokesbury Memorial Methodist Church cemetery (tombstone for him, none for wife).

Ruff, Richard, 1820. "Petition, Schedule, Bond, Sheriff's certificate, order for publication and personal discharge filed 20th March 1820." (Insolvent Docket A, 1807-1843, p. 28, at Maryland State Archives; Insolvent Docket Prior to 1827, Court Records Accession #632 at the Historical Society of Harford County). "To the Honorable John Moores, one of the Justices of the Orphans Court of Harford County. The petition of Richard Ruff of Harford County respectfully sheweth that your petitioner is now in actual confinement in Harford County Gaol [Jail] for debts which he is unable to pay, that he is willing and offers to deliver to the use of his creditors all his property real, personal and mixed (the necessary wearing apparel and bedding of himself and family excepted) a schedule whereof together with a list of his creditors and debtors, as far as he can at present ascertain them, is hereto on oath annexed. Your petitioner also hereto annexes proof on oath that he has resided two years next preceeding this his application within the State of Maryland. Your petitioner therefore prays your honour to grant him the benefit of the insolvent laws of this State and to releive [sic] him from his present confinement and your petitioner will pray, &c. March 20th 1820. Richard Ruff." (Court Records Document 68.01.1(b) at the Historical Society of Harford County). "I hereby certify that Richard Ruff the petitioner above named is now in actual confinement in Harford County Gaol for debt at the suit of John H. Foard and that is not upon a breach of peace or any of the penal Laws of the State of Maryland or of the United States. Given under my hand this 20th day of March 1820. Joshua Guyton, Sheriff." (Court Records Document 68.01.1(b), loc. cit., also included a schedule of creditors signed by Richard Ruff, but no property was listed; yet, a newspaper clipping from the *Bond of Union* was included in the file with the following notice in 1823 indicating he had died and left personal property: "Trustee's Sale. The subscriber will sell for Cash, at Bush Town, on the 25th of April next, if fair, if not the next fair day thereafter, at 10 o'clock, sundry articles of Personal Property, which formerly belonged to Richard Ruff, deceased – consisting of Negroes, Horses, Cows, work Oxen, & Sheep; one road Waggon and one log Waggon, with many other articles of Farming Utensils, &c. &c. George Bradford, Trustee. April 2." (Court Records Document 68.01.1(E), loc. cit.) "March 25th 1823. Ordered by the Court that the Trustee sell all the property of the petitioner for cash, first giving 20 days public notice … Trustee's report of sales … filed 15th Aug. 1825." (Insolvent Docket A, 1807-1843, at the Maryland State Archives; Insolvent Docket Prior to 1827, Court Records Accession #632 at the Historical Society of Harford County). **Genealogical Note**: Richard Ruff was born circa 1755, served as a private in the militia in 1775, married Mary Ross circa 1778 and their son Richard Ruff was born on September 10, 1779. Richard, the father, died in 1823 as noted above. (St. George's P. E. Parish Register; Harford County Revolutionary War records)

Rush, Arnold, 1836. "Petition, Affidavits, Schedule, personal discharge and order of publication, Bond for Appearance, Trustee's Bond, Trustee's Certificate and Deed to Trustee filed 25th July 1836. 18th Mar 1837 Petitioner appears & cont'd. 31st March 1840 Petition and crave to withdraw petition." (Insolvent Docket A, 1807-1843, p. 149, at the Maryland State Archives). **Genealogical Note**: Arnold Rush married Esther Conn circa June 21, 1813 (date of license).

Rush, Jacob, 1836. "Petition, Affidavits, Schedule, personal discharge and order of publication, Bond for Appearance, Trustee's Bond, Trustee's Certificate and Deed to Trustee filed 25th July 1836. 18th March 1837 Petitioner appears, certificate of publication filed and finally discharged." (Insolvent Docket A, 1807-1843, p. 150, at the Maryland State Archives). **Genealogical Note**: Jacob Rush married Rachel Bull circa February 4, 1806 (date of license).

Rutledge, C. A. & Bro., 1889. "Messrs. Kirwan & Tyler, can manufacturers, of Baltimore, through their counsel, Messrs. Williams and Van Bibber, have filed a petition to the court to adjudge the firm of C. A. Rutledge & Bro. insolvent. Their claim upon the firm is $11,800. Answer must be made by Monday next." (*The Aegis & Intelligencer*, February 8, 1889, p. 2). "On Wednesday [February 20, 1889] Judge Watters heard argument in the matter of the petition of Kirwan & Tyley [Tyler], of Baltimore, to adjudge C. A. Rutledge & Bro. insolvents. Injunctions were granted to restrain the trustee and other parties in interest from selling the property under the deed of trust, and the insolvency proceedings will be tried before a jury. Messrs. Van Bibber and Williams appeared for the petitioners and Stump and Young for the respondents." (*The Aegis & Intelligencer*, February 22, 1889, p. 2; *Havre de Grace Republican*, February 22, 1889, p. 3, added "case was continued until next week.") **Genealogical Notes**: Charles Abram Rutledge (March 9, 1840 – May 24, 1924), Confederate veteran, hardware merchant and physician at Rocks, son of John Wheeler Rutledge (1800-1873) and Julia Ann Ward (1808 VA – 1889), married Elizabeth Warner Hanway (1850-1936), daughter of David Hanway (1807-1893) and Mary Ann Warner (1818-1898), on April 30, 1874 at Christ Church (Rock Spring Parish) by Rev. W. E. Snowden. He died at his home at Rutledge and was survived by his wife, a son J. Charles Rutledge, of Rutledge, and daughters Martha Rutledge and Julia Rutledge, of Baltimore. (Harford Co. marriage records; "Tinsmithing in 19th Century Harford County," by Henry C. Peden, Jr. and Jack L. Shagena, Jr., *Harford Historical Bulletin No. 103*, Summer 2006, pp. 50-51; *The Aegis*, May 30, 1924; Death certificate gave Charles' name as "Dr. Charles Abrahm Rutledge, C.S.A.")

Sankey, George W., 1810. "Petition, Schedule and Bond filed 15th March 1811 … Ordered by the Court ordered that George W. Sankey be discharged from confinement and ordered that he give notice in some of the newspapers printed in the City of Baltimore to his creditors to appear at next August term … [case continued] … 10th March 1812 George W. Sankey appeared in Court and his securities discharged … Court appoints Benjamin Rigdon as trustee … Bond of Trustee filed 29th August 1812." [nothing further was recorded]. (Insolvent Docket A, 1807-1843, p. 9, at the Maryland State Archives; Insolvent Docket Prior to 1827, Court Records Accession #632 at the Historical Society of Harford County)

Sappington, John, 1838. "Petition, Schedule, Affidavits, personal discharge and order of publication, Bond for Appearance, Trustee's Bond, Trustee's Certificate and Deed to Trustee filed 6th March 1838. 24th Novr. 1838 Interrogatories & answers filed. Petitioner appears, certificate of publication filed, and petitioner discharged." (Insolvent Docket A, 1807-1843, p. 163, at the Maryland State Archives). **Genealogical Notes**: John Sappington (1801-1869), son of Richard K. Sappington and Cassandra Frances Durbin, was a physician and married 1st to Sarah Lavinia Bagley (1807-c1837), daughter of William Bagley (c1765-1815) and Susannah Orrick Husband, on November 13, 1826 and they had a son Richard Sappington who became a prominent physician at Waverly in Baltimore. John married 2nd to Mary Ann O'Neill, daughter of Henry O'Neill, on December 30, 1838 by Rev. Goff and they had three children, Florence Sappington, John Sappington (b. 1847) and Walter Sappington. John lived in Darlington and was also a member of the constitutional convention that met in Annapolis in 1851. (*Biographical Record of Harford and Cecil Counties, Maryland* (1897), pp. 331-332; *Independent Citizen*, November 18, 1826; *Harford Republican*, January 10, 1839; *Descendants of William Bagley 1790-2000*, by Harlin Bagley (2001); Holy Trinity Episcopal Church tombstone for John Sappington, but no marker for either wife)

Scarborough, Benjamin W., 1885. "October 23rd 1885. Petition, Affidavits, Schedules, List of Creditors & Debts, Order & Insolvent's Deed filed. Same day Bond of Preliminary Trustee [name not given] approved & filed … Feby 2/86 Certificate of Publication of Notice to Insolvent to answer Interrogatories & Notice to Creditors filed. Feby 8/86 Final Order of Discharge filed." (Insolvent Docket A. L. J. No. 1, p. 101, in the Court Records Department of the Historical Society of Harford County). "Trustee's Sale. By virtue of a decree of the Circuit Court for Harford county, as a Court of Equity, the subscriber, as Trustee, will offer at Public Sale, at the Court House door, in Bel Air, on Monday, November 23rd, 1885, at 12 o'clock, M., all that Tract or Parcel of Land, situate in Dublin District, in said county, containing 120 acres, more or less, in which Benjamin W. Scarborough now resides, which is conveyed by and described in a deed from Stevenson Archer, Trustee, to Samuel J. and Benjamin W. Scarborough, dated on the 26th day of January in the year 1886, and recorded among the Land Records of Harford county, in Liber A.L.J. No. 16, folio 403. The improvements consist of a large Brick House, good Barn and other outbuildings. The land is in good condition and is well fenced. This property is about two miles from Delta Station and is convenient to churches, schools, mills, &c. J. Thomas C. Hopkins, Trustee." (*The Aegis & Intelligencer*, October 23, 1885, p. 2). "In the matter of the Insolvency of Benj. W. Scarborough … This is to give notice to the creditors of Benjamin W. Scarborough that he has applied for the benefit of the Insolvent Laws of the State of Maryland, and that we have been appointed Preliminary Trustees, and have fixed Saturday, the 14th day of November, 1885, at 11 o'clock, A. M., at the office of the undersigned, J. Thos. C. Hopkins, in the town of Bel Air, Harford county, as the time and place for the meeting of his creditors for the election of a permanent trustee and for other business. J. Thos C. Hopkins, Stevenson A. Williams, Preliminary Trustees." (*The Aegis & Intelligencer*, November 6, 1885, p. 2). "Notice Is Hereby Given, to the creditors of Benjamin W. Scarborough, an insolvent debtor, who were such on the 23rd day of October, 1885, the date of his application for the benefit of the insolvent laws, to file their claims against the estate of the said insolvent, duly proven, with the clerk of the Circuit Court for Harford county, on or before the first day of February, 1886. J. Thos C. Hopkins, Stevenson A. Williams. Permanent Trustees." (*The Aegis & Intelligencer*, November 20, 1885, p. 2). "In the matter of the Insolvency of B. W. Scarborough … In the above matter it is ordered, this second day of January, 1886, that the said Benjamin W. Scarborough, the insolvent, be and appear in this court, on Monday, the 8th day of February, 1886, to answer such interrogatories or allegations, as his creditors, endorsers or sureties may propose or allege against him, and that the permanent trustee give notice by the publication of this order in some newspaper published at Bel Air, in Harford county, once a week for three successive weeks, before the first day of February, 1886, to the Creditors of said insolvent of the day so fixed upon. Jas. D. Watters. A. L. Jarrett, Clerk." (*The Aegis & Intelligencer*, January 8, 1886, p. 2)

Scarborough (Scarbrough), John, 1822. Harvey Stokes and wife Martha, John Lewin and wife Lydia, Michael Huff and wife Rachel, Hezekiah Scarbrough, and John Sloan and wife Mary vs. John Scarbrough, Joseph Scarbrough, Daniel Jones and Rebecca his wife, and Thomas Williamson and

Sarah his wife. On July 17, 1823 the petitioners stated that John Scarbrough died in 1822 indebted to a number of individuals including the said orators and left an inconsiderable personal estate that is insufficient to pay his debts; however, he owned the following tracts in Harford Co., namely *Clark's Dunmurry, Antrim, Centre, John's Expences, Richmond's Enlargement, Renshaw's Delight*, and *Peace Proclaimed*. The petitioners requested that the said lands be sold to pay the debts of the said John Scarbrough, dec. The Court subsequently ordered that said lands shall be sold at public auction and William Richardson was appointed trustee for that purpose. The file included several pages of sales and distributions to the aforesaid heirs. (Harford County Equity Court Book HD No. 1, pp. 388-398). **Genealogical Notes**: John Scarborough (Quaker) was aged 61 and upward in 1801 and died in 1822. He left heirs at law, namely Martha Scarborough (1777-1866) who married Harvey Stokes (1773-1859) in 1804, Lydia Scarborough (1771-1841) who married John Lewin (1771-1868) circa 1792-1793, Rachel Scarborough (1780-1862) who married Michael Huff (1779-1850), Mary Scarborough who married John Sloan, Rebecca Charlotte Scarborough (1787-1825) who married Daniel Jones (1784-1848), Sarah Scarborough who married Thomas Williamson, and also Hezekiah, John and Joseph Scarborough. (Court Records Document 75.00.1.B and 75.00.1.O at the Historical Society of Harford County; Harford County Equity Court Book HD No. 1, pp. 388-398; Broad Creek Friends and Jones Family Cemetery tombstone inscriptions)

Scarborough, Mordecai S., 1891. "Notice to Creditors. "In the matter of the Insolvency of Mordecai S. Scarborough ... Notice is hereby given to the creditors of Mordecai S. Scarborough of Harford county, that he has made application for the benefit of the insolvent laws of the State of Maryland, and that a meeting of his creditors will be held at the office of Frank E. Gorrell, in the town of Bel Air, on Saturday, the 15th day of August, 1891, at 10 o'clock, A. M., for the purpose of choosing a permanent trustee for the estate of said insolvent. Frank E. Gorrell, Preliminary Trustee." (*The Aegis & Intelligencer*, August 7, 1891, p. 2). "Notice to Creditors ... Notice is hereby given to the creditors of Mordecai S. Scarborough, who were such on the 3rd day of August, 1891, to file their claims, duly proven, with the Clerk of the Circuit Court for Harford County, on or before the first day of January, 1892. Frank E. Gorrell, Permanent Trustee." (*The Aegis & Intelligencer*, October 16, 1891, p. 1). "Notice to Creditors ... Notice is hereby given to the creditors of Mordecai S. Scarborough, that the Second Monday in November, 1891, has been fixed as the day when said insolvent shall appear and answer such interrogatories or allegations as his creditors, endorsers or sureties may propose or allege against him. Frank E. Gorrell, Permanent Trustee." (*The Aegis & Intelligencer*, October 16, 1891, p. 1). "Mordecai S. Scarborough and A. S. Watters, insolvent debtors, were finally discharged." (*Havre de Grace Republican*, November 13, 1891, p. 2) **Genealogical Note**: Mordecai Silas Scarborough was the son of Mordecai Scarborough (May 27, 1815 – June 24, 1889) and Lydia Forwood Carr (April 1, 1830 – June 13, 1911). (*The Family of Scarborough*, by C. J. Scarborough Thomas, 1940, p. 233; Church of the Ascension tombstone for Mordecai Scarborough, but no tombstone for his wife Lydia Scarborough, just a footstone with her initials and year of death; *The Aegis & Intelligencer*, June 23, 1911)

Scarborough, Samuel J., 1885. "October 23rd 1885. Petition, Affidavits, Schedules, List of Creditors & Debts, Order and Insolvent's Deed filed. Same day Bond of Preliminary Trustee [name not given] approved & filed ... Feby 2/86 Certificated of Publication of Notice to Insolvent to appear & answer Interrogatories & Notice to Creditors filed. Feby 8/86 Final Order of Discharge filed." (Insolvent Docket A. L. J. No. 1, p. 102, in the Court Records Department of the Historical Society of Harford County). "Insolvent Creditors' Notice. In the matter of the Insolvency of Samuel J. Scarborough ... In the above matter it is ordered, this 2nd day of January, 1886, that Samuel J. Scarborough, the insolvent, be and appear in this court, on Monday, the 29th day of February, 1886, to answer such interrogatories or allegations, as his creditors, endorsers or sureties may propose or allege against him, and that the permanent trustee give notice by the publication of this order in some newspaper published at Bel Air, in Harford county, once a week for three successive weeks, before the 1st day of February, 1886, to the creditors of said insolvent of the day so fixed upon. Jas. D. Watters. A. L. Jarrett, Clerk." (*Bel Air Times*, January 22, 1886, p. 3) **Genealogical Notes**: Samuel John Scarborough (June 10, 1842 – October 29, 1923), son of Joseph Harvey Scarborough (1816-1863) and Elizabeth C. Weeks (1806-1857), of Harford Co., married Amelia J. Miller (10 Mar 1845 – 2 Jul 1910), daughter of Joseph Miller (1811-1876) and Martha ---- (1809-1878) of Delta, York Co., PA, in January 1865 and was a stage coach driver in Cecil Co., Civil War GAR veteran, miller, farmer and canner at Prospect in Harford County and a furniture store owner in Delta, PA. The children of Samuel and Amelia Scarborough were Joseph Harvey Scarborough, William Elmer Scarborough (1868-1890), Adda May Scarborough, Herman Miller Scarborough (1873-1875) and Charles Howard Scarborough. (*The Family of Scarborough*, by C. J. Scarborough Thomas, 1940, p. 254; 1870 Harford County Census, 5th District; Slateville Presbyterian Cemetery, Peach Bottom, York Co., PA, tombstones)

Schaffer, Augustus, 1840. "Petition, Schedule, Affidavits, personal discharge and order of publication, Bond for Appearance, Trustee's Bond, Trustee's Certificate and Deed to Trustee filed December 12th 1840. 22nd May 1841 Petition & Order of Court filed & time extended – Certificate of Publication filed – 20th Novr. 1841 Petitioner appears & finally discharged." (Insolvent Docket A, 1807-1843, p. 174, at the Maryland State Archives)

Scott, Aquila, 1826. Henry Dorsey, of Edward, Otho Scott, Martha Scott, Sarah Scott, and Mary Scott vs. Clemency Scott, executrix, heir at law and devisee of Aquila Scott, deceased, James P. Scott, Elizabeth McComas, John Norris and Sophia his wife, Aquila Scott McComas, Ann McComas, and Moses McComas, Mary McComas and Thomas McComas, infants. Bill of Complaint stated that Aquila Scott died testate about November 15, 1826 and was seized of three land tracts that had been mortgaged to said complainants. The said Martha Scott, Sarah Scott and Clemency McComas and Elizabeth Scott are his daughters and his son James P. Scott, are all of Harford County, and Aquila Scott McComas resides in Baltimore. Ann McComas, a minor, resides in Harford Co. Sophia Scott married John Norris and resides in Baltimore. Moses, Mary and Thomas McComas are minors and do not resident in Maryland. The personal estate of said Aquila Scott being insufficient to pay his debts they requested that the Court order his land to be sold to satisfy his debts. John Robinson was appointed by the Court as guardian of Ann McComas in 1828 and was then replaced by Israel D. Maulsby since the said John Robinson had become the land commissioner in this case. Clemency Scott, of lawful age, stated Aquila Scott, deceased, had borrowed $600 from his daughters Sarah, Mary and Martha Scott in 1802 and had never repaid them. John Robinson was appointed trustee to sell the land in question in order to settle the debts of Aquila Scott. Otho Scott bought the said three tracts of land called *Trust, Addition to Trust,* and *Beall's Camp* for $2,000 on September 8, 1828 and the case was resolved on November 17, 1828. A copy of the will of Aquila Scott written on August 28, 1826 was included, naming his daughters Clementine [sic], Martha, Mary and Sarah Scott, grandson Aquila Scott McComas, and appointing his aforesaid daughters as his executors. (Harford County Equity Court Book HD No. 1, pp. 286-301, included numerous other exhibits and statements). 1834. "Petition, Schedule, Affidavit, personal discharge and order for publication, Bond for Appearance, Trustee's bond, Trustee's certificate and Deed to Trustee filed 13th March 1834." [nothing further recorded] (Insolvent Docket A, 1807-1843, p. 131, at the Maryland State Archives)

Scott, Mordecai, 1810. "Whereas we the subscribers Justices of the Peace for Harford County upon the petition of Mordecai Scott, who set forth that he had been confined in the Gaol [jail] of said county twenty days for debts which he was unable to pay & finding the facts stated to be true we did meet at the county Gaol of said county on the 14th day of March last and we did then and there appoint the 14th day of April Inst. to meet at the Court House of said county which said appointment we did then and there … at the request of the said Sheriff administer to the said Mordecai Scott the following Oath which was taken by the said Mordecai Scott being first duly sworn on the Holy Evangely of Almighty God in the words following, I Mordecai Scott do solemnly swear that the Schedule which I have delivered to the Sheriff of Harford County doth contain a full account to the best of my knowledge and remembrance of my whole estate both real and personal or that I have any title to or interest in and of all debts, credits and effects whatsoever which I or any in trust for me have or at the time of my petition had, or am or was in any respect entitled to in possession, remainder or reversion and that I have not directly or indirectly at any time since my imprisonment or before, sold, leased or otherwise conveyed or disposed of or intrusted all or any part of my estate, goods, Stock, money or Debts thereby to defraud my creditors or to secure the same to receive or expect any profit or advantage thereof so help me God, which said duplicate of the Schedule aforesaid we have transmitted to the clerk of the county court to be by him preserved in his Office for the information of the Creditors of the said Mordecai Scott. Given under our hands and seals this 14th Day of April 1810. Samuel Bradford. John McComas. Bennet Bussey." (Court Records Document 67.12(1) at the Historical Society of Harford County; copy of schedule to which he signed his name "Mordecai Scott" was included, but no property was listed)

Scotten, Joseph E., 1841. "Petition, Affidavits, Schedules, Appointment of Trustee, Certificate, order, personal discharge, Trustee's Bond, deed to Trustee & Appearance Bond filed 5th Novr. 1841. 26th April 1842 Petitioner appears, files certificate & finally discharged." (Insolvent Docket A, 1807-1843, p. 181, at Maryland State Archives). 1871. "Petition, Schedules, Affidavit, Order, Trustee's Bond & Deed filed 31 March/71." [nothing further recorded] (Insolvent Docket A. L. J. No. 1, p. 55, in the Court Records Department of the Historical Society of Harford County). **Genealogical Note**: Joseph E. Scotten (1817 – August 11, 1872) married Agnes J. ---- (1812-1885) circa 1841 and they are buried in Deer Creek Quaker Cemetery in Darlington (tombstones).

Shade, Eliza, 1858. William Carty vs. Mathew Carty. The object of this Bill of Complaint was to procure a decree for the sale of a certain house and lot in Havre de Grace formerly owned by Eliza Shade, deceased. "The original and supplemental Bills state that heretofore, to wit: on or about the 1st of March, 1858, Eliza Shade, late of said [Harford] County, departed this life, unmarried, and without issue, leaving the complainant and one Mathew Carty (who are brothers of the deceased) her heirs at law; that the said Eliza Shade left no personal estate and was indebted to the complainant in a large sum of money for board, &c., to wit: in the sum of *Four Hundred Dollars*, and that the only property left by the said Eliza Shade was the House and Lot aforesaid; that the said Mathew Carty is a non-resident of the state of Maryland and without the jurisdiction of this court. The Bill then prays a sale of the land, &c., and that the proceeds of said sale be applied to the payment of the debts of said deceased." The Court ordered on August 19, 1859 that a notice be published in the newspaper giving notice to the said non-resident defendant to appear in Court on or before December 10, 1859 to answer the complaint and if in default thereof the Court will pass a decree of *pro confesso* against him. (*National American*, August 26, 1859)

Shannon, John, 1858. Sarah Shannon vs. Thomas Shannon, et al. Bill of Complaint alleged that the complainant, then being Sarah Maxwell, married on November 12, 1850 with John Shannon, now deceased, and during her coverture she loaned to him of her own separate funds the sum of $410, a part of which he laid out in the purchase of a parcel called *Kimble's Double Purchase* containing 30 acres. The money was loaned with the understanding that the said John Shannon would secure the same to her by a lien upon the said land, but the said Shannon died in February 1858 and before his death, with a view to secure the complainant the sum so loaned by her, he made a paper purporting to be his last will and testament and devising all his real estate to the said complainant, but the will was not executed according to the laws of this state so as to pass real estate. The Bill further states the personal estate of the deceased was insufficient to pay his debts and she, the complainant Sarah Shannon, requests the sale of said real estate for that purpose. John Shannon left at his death the following heirs at law: Thomas Shannon, a brother; Adaline Shannon, daughter of Samuel Shannon, a deceased brother; John Shannon and Luther Shannon, sons of Joseph Shannon, a deceased brother; George J. Shannon, John H. Shannon, Richard Shannon and Catharine Shannon, children of George S. Shannon, another deceased brother; Hutson Wood, son of deceased sister Jane who intermarried with James Wood, also deceased; Eliza Baker, daughter of said Jane Wood, who is now the wife of Aaron Baker; Effa Knight, another daughter of said Jane Wood, who is now wife of Thomas Knight. The said Thomas Shannon, Hutson Wood and Adaline Shannon reside in Harford Co. The said George J., John H., Richard and Catharine Shannon reside in Cecil Co. The said Eliza Baker resides in Baltimore. The said Effa Knight resides in Baltimore Co. The said Luther and John Shannon reside in Indiana. All of the parties are believed to be of full age. The Court ordered the bill to be published in the paper for all to appear on or before November 11, 1858 and answer the complaint, otherwise the same will be taken as confessed against them. (*The Southern Aegis*, July 3, 1858)

Shay, Thomas, 1804. "Whereas we the Subscribers Justices of the Peace for Harford County upon the petition of Thomas Shay, who set forth that he had been confined in the Gaol [jail] of the said county twenty Days for Debts which he was unable to pay & finding the facts stated to be true we together did meet at the County Gaol on the 10th Day of April 1804 and did then and there appoint the 12th day of May Instant to meet at the Court House of said county which said appointment we did then and there ... at the request of the said Sheriff administer to the said Thomas Shay the following oath which was taken by the said Thomas Shay being first duly sworn on the holy evangels of almighty God in the words following, I Thomas Shay do solemnly swear that the schedule which I have delivered to the Sheriff of Harford County doth contain a full account to the best of my knowledge and remembrance of my whole estate both real & personal or that I have any title to or interest in and of all debts, credits and effects whatsoever which I or any in trust for me have or at the time of my petition had, or am or was in any respect entitled to in possession, remainder or reversion and that I have not directly or indirectly at any time since my imprisonment or before, sold, leased or otherwise conveyed or disposed of or intrusted all or any part of my estate, goods, stock, money or debts thereby to defraud my creditors or to secure the same to receive or expect any profit or advantage thereof so help me God, which said duplicate of the schedule aforesaid we have transmitted to the clerk of the county court to be by him preserved in his office for the information of the creditors of the said Thomas Shay. Given under our hands & seals this 12th day of May 1804. Wm. Smithson. John Moores. William Wilson." (Court Records Document 67.08.3(A)(B) at the Historical Society of Harford County; a copy of the schedule to which "Thomas Shay" signed his name was included and listed this personal property: "one squirl [squirrel] gun, 1 tabel [table] & some cups & sassers [saucers], six tea spoons silver, one chest, one case and bottles"). 1817. "Petition, bond & schedule filed 12th March 1817 and ordered that the petitioner be brought before the Court immediately. The petitioner having taken the necessary oaths and given satisfactory security it is here ordered that he be discharged from the custody of the Sheriff of Harford County and that he give the notice required by law." (Insolvent Docket A, 1807-1843, p. 20, at the Maryland State Archives; Insolvent Docket Prior to 1827, Court Records Accession #632 at the Historical Society of Harford County). **Genealogical Notes**: Thomas Shay married Clarissa "Clare" Everist, widow of Joseph Everist, on March 1, 1810. (St. George's P. E. Parish Register; Harford County marriage license; Joseph Everist Estate Distribution, 1811). He may have been the son of Thomas

Shay who was age 56 in 1820. (Archives Folder No. 484, "Josias W. Dallam – Bush River Properties," at the Historical Society of Harford County)

Sherburne, Charles F., 1818. "Petition, Schedule, Bond, Order to Sheriff, Shff.'s certificate, personal discharge and order of publication filed 11th Sepr. 1818." [nothing further recorded] (Insolvent Docket A, 1807-1843, p. 23, at the Maryland State Archives; Insolvent Docket Prior to 1827, Court Records Accession #632 at the Historical Society of Harford County)

Sheredine (Sheridan), James, 1821. "Harford County sct. On application to the Subscriber as a Judge of the Orphans Court of Harford County by petition in writing of James Sheredine stating that he is an imprisoned debtor in actual confinement in the gaol [jail] of said County and praying for a discharge from said confinement, and for the Benefit of the Act of the General Assembly of Maryland entitled An Act for the Relief of Sundry Insolvent Debtors passed at November Session Eighteen hundred and five and the Several Supplements thereto on the terms therein mentioned, a Schedule of his property and a list of his creditors on oath being annexed to his said petition with competent and satisfactory testimony that he has resided two years within the State of Maryland next before the making of his application as aforesaid and the said James Sheredine having takeing [sic] the Oath prescribed by the said act prescribed for Delivering up his property and given Bond with Security and in a penalty by me approved and prescribed for his appearance before the Judges of Harford County Court on the first Saturday after the fourth Monday of August next at the Court house of said County, being the time by me appointed for a hearing before said Court to answer interrogatories which his Creditors may propose to him according to the provisions of the said Original Act. I do hereby order and adjudge that the said James Sheredine be discharged from said Imprisonment and Direct that he give Notice to his creditors of his said application and of the day so by me appointed for a hearing before said Court by advertisement to be inserted in the Bond of Union newspaper once a week for three months before the day so appointed. Given under my hand & seal this first day of February 1821. John Moores." (Court Records Document 68.08.2(E) at the Historical Society of Harford County which included a newspaper clipping from the *Bond of Union and Weekly Advertiser*). "Know all men by these presents that we James Sheredine, Lloyd Morris and John Sheredine are held and firmly bound unto the State of Maryland in the sum of six hundred dollars Current money to be paid to the said State, its certain attorney or assigns to which payment well and truly to be made and done, we bind ourselves, our heirs, executors and administrators jointly and severally by these presents. Sealed with our seals and dated this first day of February 1821. The Condition of the above obligation is such that if the above bound James Sheredine shall make his personal appearance before the Judges of Harford county Court at the County house in said County on the Saturday next after the fourth Monday in Augt. next then and there to answer such allegations as his creditors make against him agreeable to the Insolvent laws of Maryland and not depart therefrom without permission of said Court but await their order then the above obligation to be null and void otherwise to remain in full force [and] Virtue and [in]7 law. James Sheredine. Lloyd Morris. John "X" Sheredine. Witness: John Moores." (Court Records Document 68.08(C), loc. cit.) "I do hereby certify that James Sheredine is now in my custody in the common gaol of Harford County for debt and not for any breach of the laws of the State of Maryland or the United States. Given under my hand this first day of February 1821. Joshua Guyton, Shff." (Court Records Document 68.08.2(d) at the Historical Society of Harford County). "Petition, Schedule, Bond, Sheriff's certificate, personal discharge and order for publication filed 1st February – 1st September 1821 petitioner appeared, Bennet Love appointed Trustee and ordered that he give bond in the penalty of $500." [nothing further recorded] (Insolvent Docket A, 1807-1843, p. 32, at Maryland State Archives; Insolvent Docket Prior to 1827, Court Records Accession #632 at the

Historical Society of Harford County). **Genealogical Notes**: James Sheridan (1773-1838) married 1ˢᵗ to Elizabeth ---- by 1791 (daughter Elizabeth Sheridan born January 27, 1792), and she died in 1794. James married 2ⁿᵈ to Elizabeth Gorthrop circa December 4, 1794 (date of license. St. James P. E. Parish Register spelled his name Sheredine; Research by descendant Helene M. Davis, deceased, formerly of Street, MD, 1988)

Shertzer, Abraham, 1891. "Mr. Edward M. Allen has been appointed trustee of the insolvent estate of Abraham Shertzer, of Churchville." (*Havre de Grace Republican*, April 3, 1891, p. 3). "Notice to Creditors. In the matter of the Insolvency of Abraham Shertzer ... Notice is hereby given to the creditors of Abraham Shertzer that the 11th day of May, 1891, has been fixed as the day when said insolvent shall appear to answer such interrogatories or allegations as his creditors, endorsers or sureties may propose or allege against him. Edward M. Allen, Permanent Trustee." (*Harford Democrat*, April 3, 1891, p. 3). "Notice to Creditors ... Notice is hereby given to the creditors of Abraham Shertzer, who were such upon the date of his application for the benefit of the insolvent laws of the State of Maryland, to file their claims, duly proven, with the Clerk of the Circuit Court for Harford county on or before the 15ᵗʰ day of May, 1891. Edward M. Allen, Permanent Trustee." (*Harford Democrat*, April 3, 1891, p. 3). "May Term of Court ... Abraham Shertzer, insolvent, appeared, and was discharged." (*Havre de Grace Republican*, May 15, 1891, p. 3) **Genealogical Notes**: Abraham Shertzer (1828, PA – 1894), a farmer at Churchville, married Elizabeth Kessell (August 20, 1833, PA – April 1, 1908), daughter of Jacob Kessell and Mary Grosh, circa 1857-1858 and their oldest daughter Sarah Shertzer was born circa 1859 in Maryland. (1880 Harford County Census; Mt. Zion Methodist Church tombstones; 198 death certificate of Elizabeth Shertzer; *The Aegis & Intelligencer*, April 3, 1904)

Shertzer, Jacob H., 1890. "Jacob H. Shertzer, formerly of this county, but now of Baltimore county, has applied for the benefit of the insolvent laws." (*Havre de Grace Republican*, October 24, 1890, p. 3)

Shewel, Benjamin, 1812. "Whereas we the subscribers, Justices of the Peace for Harford County upon the petition of Benjamin Shewel, who set forth that he had been confined [in jail] twenty days and upwards for debts which he was unable to pay and finding the facts stated to be true we did meet at the gaol of said county on the 5ᵗʰ day of March last and did then and there appoint the 6ᵗʰ day of April instant to meet at the Court house of said county which said appointment we did then and there ... at the request of the said Sheriff administer to the said Benjamin Shewel the following oath which was taken by the said Benjamin Shewel being first duly sworn on the Holy Evangely of Almighty God in the words following, I do solemnly swear that the schedule which I have delivered to the Sheriff of Harford County doth contain a full account to the best of my knowledge and remembrance of my whole estate both real & personal or that I have any title to or interest in and of all debts, credits and effects whatsoever which I or any in trust for me have or at the time of my petition had, or am or was in any respect entitled to in possession, remainder or reversion and that I have not directly or indirectly at any time since my imprisonment or before, sold, leased or otherwise conveyed or disposed of or intrusted all or any part of my estate, goods, stock, money or debts thereby to defraud my creditors or to secure the same to receive or expect any profit or advantage thereof so help me God, which said duplicate of the schedule aforesaid we have transmitted to the clerk of the county court to be by him preserved in his office for the information of the creditors of the said Benjamin Shewel. Given under our hands and seals this 6ᵗʰ Day of April 1812. Samuel Bradford. Thomas A. Hays. John Moores." (Court Records Document 67.12(2) at Historical Society of Harford County; a copy of schedule to which "Benjamin Shewel" made his "| |" mark was included)

Shields, John, 1805. "Whereas we the subscribers Justices of the Peace for Harford County upon the petition of John Shields who set forth therein that he had been confined in the goal of the said county [twenty days] for debts which he was unable to pay and finding the facts stated to be true we did meet at the county gaol of the said county on the 13th day of February 1805 & did then and there appoint the 16th day of March Instant to meet at the Court House of said county which said appointment we did then and there … at the request of the said sheriff administer to the said John Shields the following oath which was taken by the said John Shields being first duly sworn on the Holy Evangels of Almighty God in the words following – I John Shields do solemnly swear that the schedule which I have delivered to the sheriff of Harford County doth contain a full account to the best of my knowledge and remembrance of my whole estate both real & personal or that I have any title to or interest in and of all debts, credits & effects whatsoever which I or any in trust for me have or at the time of my petition had, or am or was in any respect entitled to in possession, remainder or reversion and that I have not directly or indirectly at any time since my imprisonment or before, sold, leased or otherwise conveyed or disposed of or intrusted all or any part of my estate, goods, stock, money or debts thereby to defraud my creditors or to secure the same to receive or expect any profit or advantage thereof so help me God, which said duplicate of the schedule aforesaid we have transmitted to the clerk of the county court to be by him preserved in his office for the information of the creditors of the said John Shields. Given under our hands and seals this 16th day of March 1805. John Moores. Thos. A. Hays. Wm. Smithson." (Court Records Documents 67.02.5(A)(B)(C) at the Historical Society of Harford County; a copy of the schedule to which "John Shields" made his mark that resembled a "2" was included, but no property was listed). 1815. "Petition, Schedule & Bond filed 17th March 1815 … Samuel Bradford appointed his Trustee … petr. appeared agreeably to the tenor of his bond." [nothing further recorded] (Insolvent Docket A, 1807-1843, at Maryland State Archives; Insolvent Docket Prior to 1827, Court Records Accession #632 at Historical Society of Harford County)

Shields, William, 1805. "Whereas we the Subscribers Justices of the Peace for Harford County, together with William Wilson, Esq., also one of the Justices of the Peace for said county, upon the petition of William Shields who set forth that he had been confined in the gaol [jail] of said county twenty days for debts which he was unable to pay and finding the facts stated to be true we together with the said William Wilson, Esq., did meet at the County Gaol of said county on the 30th day of January 1805 and did then and there appoint the 2nd day of March Inst. to meet at the Court House which said appointment we did then and there … at the request of the said Sheriff administer to the said William Shields the following oath which was taken by the said William Shields being first duly sworn on the Holy Evangely of Almighty God in the words following, vizt., I William Shields do solemnly swear that the schedule which I have delivered to the Sheriff of Harford County doth contain a full account to the best of my knowledge and remembrance of my whole estate both real & personal or that I have any title to or interest in and of all debts, credits and effects whatsoever which I or any in trust for me have or at the time of my petition had, or am or was in any respect entitled to in possession, remainder or reversion and that I have not directly or indirectly at any time since my imprisonment or before, sold, leased or otherwise conveyed or disposed of or intrusted all or any part of my estate, goods, stock, money or debts thereby to defraud my creditors or to secure the same to receive or expect any profit or advantage thereof so help me God, which said duplicate of the schedule aforesaid we have transmitted to the clerk of the county court to be by him preserved in his office for the information of the creditors of the said William Shields. Given under our hands & seals this 2nd day of March Eighteen hundred and five. James Amos. Thomas A. Hays."

(Court Records Documents 67.08.2(A)(B) at the Historical Society of Harford County; a copy of the schedule to which "William Shields" made his "X" mark was included, but no property was listed)

Simmons, Joseph M., 1856. "Petition, Schedules, Affidavits, Appointment of H. W. Archer as Trustee," etc., 6 Feb 1856. "14th Nov. 1857 Certificate of publication & final order of ratification of sales filed. Recorded in Judgment Record Liber HDG No. 2, folio 336." (Insolvent Docket A. L. J. No. 1, p. 10, in the Court Records Department of the Historical Society of Harford County). 1893. "Notice to Creditors. This is to give notice to the creditors of Joseph M. Simmons, of Harford County, an Insolvent debtor, of the pendency of proceedings in Insolvency, in relation to his estate, and that Saturday, October 28th, 1893, at 11 o'clock, A. M., at the office of George Y. Maynadier, in Bel Air, Md., is the time and place fixed for a meeting of the creditors of said insolvent to choose a permanent trustee or trustees for said estate and other business. George Y. Maynadier, Preliminary Trustee." (*The Aegis & Intelligencer*, October 20, 1893 p. 3) "Notice to Creditors. In the matter of the Insolvency of Joseph M. Simmons ... Notice is hereby given to the creditors of Joseph M. Simmons, that by an order of the Circuit Court for Harford County, Tuesday, the 9th day of January, 1894, is fixed as the day for said insolvent to appear in said court, to answer such interrogatories or allegations as his creditors, endorsers or sureties may propose or allege against him. George Y. Maynadier, Permanent Trustee." (*The Aegis & Intelligencer*, December 8, 1893, p. 2). "Notice to Creditors ... Notice is hereby given to the creditors of Joseph M. Simmons, who were such at the date of their application for the benefit of the insolvent laws, to file their claims, properly authenticated, with the Clerk of the Circuit Court for Harford County, on or before the 9th day of January, 1894, as directed by an order of said court passed in the above case; provided, a copy of this order be published in some newspaper printed [in Harford county] once a week for four successive weeks before the 9thday of January, 1894. George Y. Maynadier, Preliminary Trustee." (*The Aegis & Intelligencer*, December 15, 1893, p. 2)

Singleton, James, 1831. "Petition, Schedule, Shffs. certificate, personal discharge and order for publication, bond for appearance, Trustee's bond, Trustee's certificate and deed to Trustee filed 25th May 1831. 13th Augt. 1831 Petitioner appears, order that petitioner gives notice and cont'd." [nothing further recorded] (Insolvent Docket A, 1807-1843, p. 110, at Maryland State Archives) **Genealogical Note**: James Singleton married Miss Martha Ann Clark on March 23, 1830 by Rev. Samuel Park. (*Independent Citizen*, April 1, 1830)

Singleton, John, 1844. "Notice Is Hereby Given, to the creditors of John Singleton, late an imprisoned debtor of Harford co., that on the application of said debtor by petition in writing to the Hon. Robert W. Holland, chief justice of the Orphan's court of said county, for the benefit of the insolvent laws of Maryland, the said judge on the 18th day of June, 1844, granted to the said debtor a discharge from imprisonment and appointed the first Saturday after the 3rd Monday in November next, for his appearance before the Judges of Harford county court at the court house of said county, for a final hearing before said court, on said petition and to answer such interrogatories as his creditors may propose to him." (*Harford Madisonian and Bel-Air & Havre de Grace Messenger*, October 18, 1844, p. 3) **Genealogical Note**: John Singleton married Mary Holly on August 17, 1840. (St. John's Episcopal Church, Havre de Grace Parish, Marriage Register, 1835-1868)

Slee, George and Clarence C. Kenly, 1891. "Circuit Court Proceedings. On Tuesday [May 26, 1891] the insolvency case of Quigly & Mullen vs. Slee & Kenly was taken up, and was on trial yesterday." (*Havre de Grace Republican*, May 29, 1891, p. 3). "Court Proceedings.—The jury in the insolvency case of Quigly & Mullen vs. Slee & Kenly, brought in a sealed verdict, on Friday morning, on issues in the case, in favor of the plaintiffs, but it remains for the court to determine whether the defendants shall be declared insolvent or not. James J. Archer and Hope H. Barroll appeared for the plaintiffs and S. A. Williams and [George L.] Van Bibber for the defendants." (*The Aegis & Intelligencer*, June 5, 1891, p. 2). "Notice to Creditors. In the matter of the insolvency of Slee & Kenly ... *To the Creditors of the firm of Slee & Kenly:* Take Notice, that George Slee and Clarence C. Kenly, partners, trading as Slee & Kenly, of Harford county, Md., having been, by the Circuit Court for Harford County, adjudicated insolvent debtors, the proceedings under which such adjudication was made being now pending, a meeting of the creditors of said insolvent debtors will be held on the 31st July, 1891, at 11 o'clock, A. M., at the office of James J. Archer, in the town of Bel Archer, for the purpose of proof of claims, propounding of interrogatories and the selection of permanent trustee or trustees. James J. Archer, Preliminary Trustee." (*The Aegis & Intelligencer*, July 31, 1891, p. 3). **Genealogical Notes**: George Slee, born in 1862, was proprietor of a general store over 60 years in Aberdeen; an avid duck hunter and co-owner in 1928 of the gunning boat *King Tut*, he died on May 4, 1951, survived by several nieces and nephews, with burial in Spesutia Cemetery. (*Duck Hunters on the Susquehanna Flats, 1850-1930*, by Henry C. Peden, Jr. & Jack L. Shagena, Jr., 2014, p. 107; *The Aegis*, May 11, 1951)

Sly, William (African American), 1825. "Negro William Sly. Petition, schedule, bond, Sheriff's Certificate, affidavit of residence, personal discharge and order for publication filed 18th October 1825. 19th Augt. 1826 petitioner appears and costs." [nothing further recorded] (Insolvent Docket A, 1807-1843, p. 75, at the Maryland State Archives; Insolvent Docket Prior to 1827, Court Records Accession #632 at the Historical Society of Harford County, slightly differed in its wording and date of petition)

Slymer, Andrew F., 1884. "August 9th 1884. Petition, Schedule, Order, Trustee's Bond & Insolvent Deed filed." [nothing further recorded] (Insolvent Docket A. L. J. No. 1, p. 86, in the Court Records Department of the Historical Society of Harford County)

Smith, Charles F., 1855. "Petition, Affidavits, Schedules, Appointment of Trustee [not named], Order, Deed filed 22nd Jany/55. 13 May/56 Petitioner appeared & filed certificate of publication & finally discharged." (Insolvent Docket A. L. J. No. 1, p. 6, in the Court Records Department of the Historical Society of Harford County). **Genealogical Notes**: Charles F. Smith married Caroline H. ---- (April 10, 1827 – March 10, 1869) circa 1845-1850 and Caroline H. Smith died at Maxwell's Point. (*Harford Democrat*, March 19, 1869)

Smith, Christopher, 1819. "Petition, Schedule, Bond, Order for publication, and personal discharge filed 2nd October 1819." [nothing further recorded] (Insolvent Docket A, 1807-1843, p. 27, at the Maryland State Archives; Insolvent Docket Prior to 1827, Court Records Accession #632 at the Historical Society of Harford County). "To the Honorable James Wallace, a Judge of the Orphans Court of Harford County. The petition of Christopher Smith of Harford County respectfully sheweth, That your petitioner is now imprisoned in the gaol of Harford County, for debts which he is unable to pay; that he is willing, and offers to deliver to the use of his creditors, all his property, real, personal and mixed, to which he is in any way entitled, (the necessary wearing apparel and bedding of himself and his family excepted), a schedule whereof, together with a list of his creditors, and debtors, as far as he can at present ascertain them, are hereunto on oath annexed. Your petitioner also hereto annexes proof on oath, that he has resided two years next preceding this his application, within the State of Maryland: Your petitioner therefore, prays your Honour to grant him the benefit of the Insolvent Laws of this state, and discharge him from his present imprisonment, and he will pray. Christopher "X" Smith. Filed 2nd October 1819. (Court Records Document 68.08.3(C) at the Historical Society of Harford County; a copy of the schedule to which "Christopher Smith" made his "X" mark was included, but listed no property). "On application to the subscriber, as a Judge of the Orphans Court of Harford County, by petition in writing of Christopher Smith stating that he is an imprisoned debtor in actual confinement in said county, and praying for a discharge from said confinement and for the benefit of the Act of the General

Assembly of Maryland, entitled, 'An act for the relief of sundry insolvent debtors,' passed at November Session, in the year eighteen hundred and five, and the several supplements thereto, on the terms therein mentioned, a schedule of his property and a list of his creditors on oath being annexed to his said petition, with competent and satisfactory testimony that he has resided for two years within the State of Maryland next before the making of his application as aforesaid and the said Christopher Smith having taken the oath prescribed by the said act for delivering up his property, and given bond with security and in a penalty by me approved and presented for his appearance before the Judges of Harford County Court, on the first Saturday after the second Monday of March next, at the Court House of said County, being the time by me appointed, for a hearing before said Court in said petition, to answer interrogatories which his creditors may propose to him according to the provisions of the said original Act: I do hereby order and adjudge that the said Christopher Smith be discharged from imprisonment; and direct that he give notice to his creditors of his said application and discharge, and of the day so by me appointed for a hearing before said Court, by advertisement to be inserted in the Federal Gazette Newspaper, once a week for three months before the day so appointed. Given under my hand this fourteenth day of September in the year eighteen hundred and nineteen. James Wallace." (Court Records Document 68.08.3(a) in the Court Records Department of the Historical Society of Harford County)

Smith, Gideon G., 1859. "Petition, Schedule of property, List of debts due and owing to and from, Affidavit, Order & Appointment of Caleb Emlin Trustee, Trustee's Bond approved and Deed to Trustee filed 5th February 1859 … 25th July/59 List of Sales & Trustee's Report of Sales & Order Nisi filed … 12th June/60 Auditor's Report & Objections thereto filed … 10th July/60 Auditor's Report No. 2 filed. 6th aug/60 Final Order of Ratification of Auditor's Report No. 2 filed. Recorded in Liber ALJ No. 1, Judgment Record, folio 59." (Insolvent Docket A. L. J. No. 1, p. 25, in the Court Records Department of the Historical Society of Harford County) "Notice Is Hereby Given that Gideon G. Smith has made application to the Circuit Court of Harford county, for the benefit of the Insolvent Laws of Maryland, and that the *First Saturday after the First Monday in August, 1859* has been assigned for him to appear in said Court to answer such interrogatories as his creditors may propose or allege against him. Wm. Galloway, Clerk, Circuit court for Harford County." (*National American*, February 25, 1859, p. 3). 1859 – Henry Fowler vs. Caleb Emlen, Gideon G. Smith, John G. Pusey, John A. Hopper, John H. Stokes and Isaac Thompson. The object of this Bill was to enforce the execution of a deed of trust made by Gideon G. Smith to Caleb Emlen. The Bill stated Gideon G. Smith is indebted to Henry Fowler in the sum of $5 with interest from August 20, 1858, and said Smith is also indebted to various persons in large sums of money. The said Smith on December 6, 1858 conveyed by deed to said Emlen all of his personal estate (Land Records WG No. 10, p. 274) and also assigned to him all debts and sums of money due him in trust for the benefit of his creditors, and after payment of all debts due and owing by said Smith, the surplus, if any, the said Emlen was to pay the same over to the said Smith. That prior to the execution of said deed of trust to the said Caleb Emlen, the said Gideon G. Smith had executed mortgages to several persons: the first to John G. Pusey for $2,050; the second to John A. Hopper for $1,828.50; the third to John H. Stokes for $1,000; and, the fourth to Isaac Thompson for $1,000, all with interest. John G. Pusey lives in Pennsylvania and John H. Stokes lives in New Jersey and the others live in Maryland. Caleb Emlen has neglected to proceed to execute the trust and the Court is requested to order him to give bond for the faithful performance of the trust and in default thereof some other person be appointed trustee and the trust property be sold. The Court ordered the defendants to appear on or before May 9, 1859 to show cause to the contrary or a decree *pro confesso* would then be ordered by the Court. (*The Southern Aegis*, January 8, 1859). **Genealogical Notes**: Gideon G. Smith, of Chester, PA, later of Darlington,

MD, was born on 7th day of 3rd month 1808, married Elizabeth Cowgill (born on 28th day of 7th month 1814, died on 11th day of 6th month 1871), and died on 12th day of 8th month 1885. The children of Gideon G. and Elizabeth Smith were Sarah C. Smith (1835-1888), Ann Smith (1839-1898) married Thomas Waring (1834-1908), Nathaniel Newlin Smith (1841-1915) married Clara H. Hopkins (1841-1928), Elizabeth C. Smith (1845-1900), Martha C. Smith (1847-1918), Mary N. Smith (1849-1902), Bernard Gilpin Smith (1853-1925) married Rebekah Wright (1855-1938) and Joshua Cowgill Smith (1856-1911) married Edith Mason (1857-1944). (Darlington Cemetery tombstone inscriptions; *The Aegis & Intelligencer*, August 17, 1885)

Smith, Henry, 1832. "Petition, Schedule, Affidavit, personal discharge and order for publication, Bond for appearance, Trustee's Bond, Trustee's Certificate and Deed to Trustee filed 8th May 1832. 28th May 1832 Petition and Order for Sale filed … [various claims and reports filed through 1836] … Recorded in Judgment Record A.L.J. No. 1, folio 301." (Insolvent Docket A, 1807-1843, p. 118, at the Maryland State Archives)

Smith, John, 1805. "March 27th 1805. To Henry Ridgely, Esqr., Chief Justice of Harford County Court and his associates. The Petition of Doctor John Smith of Harford County humbly sheweth that he is included in an Act for the relief of sundry Insolvent Debtors passed November Session Eighteen hundred and four, that he has resided the last two preceeding years in the State of Maryland, that he is willing to deliver to the use of his creditors, all his property, real, personal and mixed (the necessary wearing apparel & beding [sic] for himself & family excepted) to which he is in any way entitled, a Schedule whereupon an oath together with a list of his Creditors also on oath as near as he can ascertain them, he being now in actual confinement all of which will more fully appear to your Honors by the documents hereunto annexed – Your Petitioner therefore prays the full benefit of said Act & your petitioner &c, &c. [signed] John Smith. A Schedule of Property viz., 50 acres of Land called *Drouth* in Anne Arundel County in dispute … John Smith, an Insolvent Debtor … now confined in Harford County Goal [jail] … It is thereupon adjudged and ordered that the person of the said John Smith be discharged forthwith from arrest until the final determination of the Court upon the said Petition … July 8th 1805. The Creditors of the said John Smith not attending according to notice it is ruled and ordered here by the Court that the further consideration of the petition of the said John Smith be continued over and postponed to next Term." (Court Actions in Insolvencies, 1805-1807, Court Records Book Accession No. 605 at the Historical Society of Harford County)

Smith, John, 1841. "Petition, 2 Affidavits, Schedules, Appointment of Trustee, Certificate, order to appear & personal discharge, Deed, Trustee's Bond & Appearance bond filed 31 Aug 1841. 20th Novr. 1841 Petitioner appeared. 21st May 1842 Petitioner filed & time extended & Notice of Publication filed. 21st May 1832 Petitioner appears, files Certificate of Publication & finally discharged." (Insolvent Docket A, 1807-1843, p. 179, at Maryland State Archives)

Smith, Jonathan, 1805. "Whereas we the subscribers Justices of the Peace for Harford County upon the petition of Jonathan Smith set forth therein that he had been confined in the Gaol [jail] of the said county twenty days for debts which he was unable to pay & finding the facts stated to be true we did meet at the County Gaol of the said county on the 4th day of February 1805 and did then and there appoint the 6th day of March Instant to meet at the Court House of said county which said appointment we did then and there … at the request of the said Sheriff administer to the said Jonathan Smith the following oath which was taken by the said Jonathan Smith being first duly sworn on the holy Evangels of Almighty God in the words following – I Jonathan Smith solemnly swear that the schedule which I have delivered to the Sheriff of Harford County doth contain a full account to the best of my knowledge and remembrance of my whole estate both real and personal or that I have any title to or interest in and of all debts, credits and effects whatsoever which I or any in trust for me have or at the time of my petition had, or am or was in any respect entitled to in possession, remainder or reversion and that I have not directly or indirectly at any time since my imprisonment or before, sold, leased or otherwise conveyed or disposed of or intrusted all or any part of my estate, goods, stock, money or debts thereby to defraud my creditors or to secure the same to receive or expect any profit or advantage thereof so help me God, which said duplicate of the schedule aforesaid we have transmitted to the clerk of the county court to be by him preserved in his office for the information of the creditors of the said Jonathan Smith. Given under our hands and seals this 6th day of March Eighteen hundred & five. Thos. A. Hays. James Amos. Wm. Smithson." (Court Records Documents 67.08.1(A)(B) at Historical Society of Harford County; a copy of the schedule was included to which "Jonathan Smith" signed his name, but listed no property). **Genealogical Note:** Jonathan Smith married Jane Ramsay, daughter of William and Mary Ramsay, before 1799. (Harford County Will Book AJ, No. C, p. 26)

Smith, Joseph, 1824. "Petition, Bond, Schedule, Sheriffs Certificate and personal Discharge and order for Publication filed 17th June 1824." [nothing further recorded] (Insolvent Docket A, 1807-1843, p 64, at the Maryland State Archives; Insolvent Docket Prior to 1827, Court Records Accession #632 at the Historical Society of Harford County)

Smith, William P., 1834. "Petition, Affidavits, Schedule, Sheriff's certificate, personal discharge, Appointment and Certificate of Trustee, Bond for Appearance, Trustee's Bond and Deed to Trustee filed 18th March 1834. 16th March 1834 [actually 1835] Petitioner appears, Certificate of Publication filed and finally discharged." (Insolvent Docket A, 1807-1843, p. 132, at Maryland State Archives)

Smith, Winston D., 1834. "Petition, Schedule, Affidavits, Sheriff's certificate, personal discharge, Bond for Appearance, Trustee's Bond, Trustee's Certificate and Deed to Trustee filed 18th March 1834. 16th Augt. 1834 Petitioner appeared, certificate of publication filed and finally discharged." (Insolvent Docket A, 1807-1843, p. 131, at the Maryland State Archives)

Smithson, Thomas P., 1857. "Petition, Schedules, Affidavits, Appointment of Trustee & order of notice, Trustee's Bond & deed filed 30th day of May 1857. 14th Novr. 1857 Petitioner appears, files certificate of publication & discharged." (Insolvent Docket A. L. J. No. 1, p. 17, in Court Records Department of the Historical Society of Harford County). **Genealogical Notes:** Thomas Poteet Smithson, son of Thomas Smithson (1789-1859) and Cassandra Poteet, was born on September 20, 1814, married 1st to Lucretia Bosley circa February 12, 1849 (date of license), divorced some time after March 27, 1854, married 2nd to Mary Bull Smithson (1820-1864), daughter of William Bull Smithson (1796-1860) and Elizabeth Lee (17896-1838) on June 5, 1859 and Mary died on July 31, 1864. Thomas married 3rd to Mary Elizabeth Smithson (1848-1927), daughter of Thomas Edward Smithson (1825-1895) and Mary Jane Phelps (1828-1887), on June 9, 1865. His 2nd wife Lucretia Smithson, of Baltimore County, had changed her name legally back to Lucretia Bosley by court order dated January 18, 1860. Thomas P. Smithson died on October 21, 1876. The children by his 1st wife were Laura Smithson (b. c1852) and Thomas Smithson (b. c1854), and the children by his 2nd were William Valiant Smithson (b. 1861) and Mary Bull McClanahan Smithson (1863-1894), and the children by his 3rd wife were Thomas Poteet Smithson (1865-1940), Olevia Smithson (1867-1904), Grace Fife Smithson (1869-1889), Lee Smithson (1870-1872), Rumsey Edward Smithson (1872-1951), Wilbert Wallice Smithson (1874-1951) and Sarah Ann Smithson. (*Thomas Smitbson (1675-1732) of Baltimore County, Maryland and His Descendants*, by Diane Dieterle, 1993, pp. 123-124, 566-567; *Harford County, Maryland Divorce Cases, 1827-1912: An Annotated Index*, by Henry C. Peden, Jr., 1999, p. 29; *Divorces and Names Changed in Maryland by Act of the Legislature, 1634-1867*, by Mary K. Meyer, 1991, p. 110)

Sooy, Lee, 1890. "The creditors of Mr. Lee Sooy, an insolvent debtor, at their meeting in Bel Air, last week, elected Messrs. S. A. Williams and P. L. [Lesley] Hopper as permanent trustees, to settle the insolvent estate." (*Havre de Grace Republican*, January 3, 1890, p. 3). "Trustees' Sale. In pursuance of an order of the Circuit Court for Harford County, the undersigned, Permanent Trustees in Insolvency for Lee Sooy, will sell at Public Auction at Airalie Farm, bout two miles from Havre de Grace, on the Hopewell road on Wednesday, January 22, 1890, beginning at 11 o'clock A. M., the following Personal Property: of said insolvent, that is to say: Four good Work Horses, 4 Cows, 5 Wagons, a lot of Harness, 6 Hogs, Oats by the bushel, Corn by the barrel, Turnips, Potatoes, Cabbage, Hay, Fodder and Straw, Agricultural Implements, Dairy Utensils, Household and Kitchen Furniture. P. Lesley Hopper, S. A. Williams, Permanent Trustees. John S. Richardson, Auctioneer." (*Havre de Grace Republican*, January 17, 1890, p. 3). "On Tuesday [May 7, 1895], the case of Amos Spencer vs. Stephen J. Seneca was taken up and tried before a jury. This case grew out of the canning transactions of Lee Sooy, who became insolvent a few years ago. An agreement was drawn up between Messrs. Spencer, Seneca and Sooy under which Mr. Seneca was to furnish Mr. Sooy with cans, etc., and to sell all of his goods, paying over one third to Mr. Seneca on account of certain advances to Sooy and retaining two-thirds for himself and Sooy. Mr. Spencer sued for his third, but Mr. Seneca claims as a defense that Mr. Spencer's share had been paid by the taking up of certain notes. The jury on Thursday morning [May 9, 1895] brought in a sealed verdict for the plaintiff for $1,546.16. [George L.] Van Bibber and Albert Constable for the plaintiff, S. [Stevenson] A. Williams for defendant." (*The Aegis & Intelligencer*, May 17, 1895, p. 3; *Havre de Grace Republican*, May 18, 1895, p. 3, added "nearly $800 less than the amount asked for"). **Genealogical Note:** Lee Sooy married Sarah E. Allen circa June 5, 1880 (date of license).

Spencer, Jarrett, 1850. Docket entries were abbreviated: "(See old book page 88) Petition, Affidavits, Schedules, Appointment Order, bond & discharged filed 6th June/50. 25th Nov 1850 Petitioner appears, files certificate of publication & finally discharged. 22nd Sept/55 Petition & Order of Notice to Creditors filed … 28 May/56 Petition of Jarrett Gilbert & objections to Auditor's Report." [nothing further recorded] (Insolvent Docket A. L. J. No. 1, p. 6, in the Court Records Department of the Historical Society of Harford County). **Genealogical Notes:** Jarrett Spencer, son of John Walter Spencer (1793-1855) and Rebecca Keen (1796-1873), was born on September 12, 1822, married Elizabeth Cole Herbert (August 13, 1830? – April 13, 1910), daughter of Joseph Herbert, of Maryland, and Axa Ward, of Virginia, circa September 2, 1844 (date of license), worked as a farmer in Lapidum and died on November 11, 1900. The children of Jarrett and Elizabeth Spencer were Joseph E. Spencer, Philip M. Spencer and J. Herman Spencer. (Harford County Death Certificates; *The Aegis & Intelligencer*, November 16, 1900 and April 22, 1910; *Spencer Family History*, by Margaret Spencer Bishop (1933-2011), formerly of Cooptown, MD, 1986, p. 8, stated Elizabeth was born in 1833 and married in 1844, but she would have been only 11 years old at the time. Unfortunately, her death certificate did not indicate her age, but her obituary in *The Aegis & Intelligencer* on April 22, 1910 stated she was 80 years old, thus born in 1830. If that was the case then she was married at age 14.)

Spicer, Samuel L., 1827. "11th Decr. 1827. Petition, Schedule, Affidavit, Sheriffs Certificate, Bond, Deed, Trustee Bond, Discharge and Order for Publication filed. 15th March 1828 Petitioner appeared. … Stephen Jones appointed permanent trustee … personal discharge granted." (Insolvent Docket A, 1807-1843, p. 87, at the Maryland State Archives)

Spicer, W. Hicks, 1884. "October 24/84. Petition, Schedule of Property, List of Debts & Creditors, Affidavits & Order of Court appointing Preliminary Trustee [name not given] … Nov 21/84 Reports of Clerk & Preliminary Trustee & Order of Court thereon filed." [nothing further recorded] (Insolvent Docket A. L. J. No. 1, p. 93, in the Court Records Department of the Historical Society of Harford County)

St. Clair, David V., 1891. "Notice to Creditors. In the matter of the Insolvency of David V. St. Clair ... This is to give notice to the creditors of David V. St. Clair, an insolvent debtor, of the pendency of proceedings in insolvency in regard to the estate of said St. Clair, and that Saturday, the 23rd day of January, 1892, at 10 o'clock, A. M., at my office in Bel Air, in said county, is the time and place fixed for a meeting of the creditors of said insolvent to choose a permanent trustee for said estate. John A. W. Richardson, Preliminary Trustee." (*The Aegis & Intelligencer*, January 15, 1892, p. 2). "Notice to Creditors ... Notice is hereby given to the creditors of David V. St. Clair, that the 9th day of May, 1892, has been fixed as the day when said Insolvent shall appear to answer such interrogatories or allegations as his creditors, endorsers or sureties may propose or allege against him. John A. W. Richardson, Permanent Trustee." (*The Aegis & Intelligencer*, February 12, 1892, p. 3). "Notice to Creditors ... Notice is hereby given to the creditors of David V. St. Clair, who were such upon the date of his application for the benefit of the insolvent laws of the State of Maryland, to file their claims, duly proven, with the Clerk of the Circuit Court for Harford County, on or before the 9th day of May, 1892. John A. W. Richardson, Permanent Trustee." (*The Aegis & Intelligencer*, February 12, 1892, p. 3). **Genealogical Note**: David St. Clair married Lavinia Grafton circa December 24, 1884 (date of license).

St. Clair, Moses, 1833. "Petition, Schedule, Affidavit, Personal discharge, Order for Publication, Bond for Appearance, Trustee's Bond, Trustee's Certificate and Deed to Trustee filed 31st Decr. 1833. 16th Augt. 1834 Petitioner appears ... Judgment that the petitioner had before his application for the benefit of the Insolvent Laws conveyed away a part of his property with a view to receive advantage, thereby contrary to the 8th Section of the Act of 1805, Chap. 110." [nothing further recorded] (Insolvent Docket A, 1807-1843, p. 130, at the Maryland State Archives). **Genealogical Note**: Moses St. Clair married Ann Blaney on September 28, 1809 (St. James P. E. Parish Register).

Stansbury, Elizabeth, 1837. "Petition, Schedule, Affidavits, personal discharge and order of publication, Bond for Appearance, Trustee's Bond, Trustee's Certificate and Deed to Trustee filed 14th December 1837. 17th March 1838 Certificate of Publication filed. Petitioner appears and finally discharged." (Insolvent Docket A, 1807-1843, p. 161, at the Maryland State Archives)

Starr, John M., 1884. "October 13th 1884. Petition, Schedule of Property, List of Creditors & Debts, Affidavits & Order of Court thereon filed ... 29th Oct/84 Order of Court appointing Wm. H. Harlan Permanent Trustee ... [several claims and notices were filed in 1884 and 1885] ... 3 Feby 1888 Final Ratification of Auditor's Report No. 2 filed." [nothing recorded thereafter] (Insolvent Docket A. L. J. No. 1, pp. 93, 104, in the Court Records Department of the Historical Society of Harford County). "Trustee's Sale of Personal Property. In virtue of an order of the Circuit Court for Harford county passed in the matter of the insolvency of John M. Starr, the undersigned as permanent trustee, will offer at public auction on the farm of Thomas B. Swartz, near Hall's Shops, on Tuesday, November 11th, 1884, at 11 o'clock A. M., the following Personal Property. One black mare, 1 Alderney cow, 7 hogs, 5 pigs, lot chickens, 1 four horse wagon, 1 two wagon, hay carriage, ox cart, buggy, mower, grain fan, plows, harness, horse rake, cultivators and other farming implement [etc.] and Household Furniture, lot of canning fixtures, --?--, and many other articles. William H. Harlan, Permanent Trustee. J. S. Richardson, Auctioneer." (*Bel Air Times*, November 7, 1884). "Insolvent Notice. In the Matter of the Insolvency of John M. Starr ... In the above matter the insolvent having failed to appear upon the 11th day of May, 185, as required by an order of this Court passed on the 10th day of February last, and proper notice not having been given to said insolvent as required by a second order of the court directing his appearance, It is therefore, this 21st day of September, in the year 1885, ordered that John M. Starr, the insolvent, be and appear in this Court on Monday, the 24th day of November next, to answer interrogatories or allegations as his creditors, endorsers or sureties may propose or allege against him, and that the permanent trustee give notice, by the publication of this order in some newspaper published at Bel Air, in Harford county, once a week for three successive weeks before the 1st day of November next to the creditors of said insolvent of the say so fixed upon. Jas. D. Watters. A. L. Jarrett, Clerk." (*Bel Air Times*, October 9, 1885). **Genealogical Note**: John M. Starr married Mary K. Tollenger circa March 20, 1877 (date of license).

Steiner, Henry, 1856. "Petition, Schedules, Affidavits, Appointment of Trustee, Trustee's Bond, deed & order of appearance & notice to Creditors filed. 27 Jun/56." [nothing further recorded] (Insolvent Docket A. L. J. No. 1, p. 13, in Court Records Department of Historical Society of Harford County)

Stephenson, James, 1840. "Petition, Schedule, Affidavits, personal discharge, order of publication, Trustee's Bond, appearance bond, Trustee's Certificate, Deed filed 8th Decr. 1840. Petitioner appears & Certificate of Publication filed and finally discharged 22 May 1841." (Insolvent Docket A, 1807-1843, p. 175, at the Maryland State Archives). **Genealogical Note**: This may be the James Stephenson who married Priscilla Hopkins circa July 30, 1799 (date of license).

Stockham, Grant, 1898. "Point of Law Discussed. An interesting point of law was decided by Judge Watters last Wednesday [September 7, 1898] in the case of Otho N. Johnson vs. Grant Stockham and wife, in the Circuit Court for Harford county. A petition was filed by the plaintiff on July 10 [1898], praying that Mrs. Stockham be adjudicated an insolvent debtor. The defendants demurred to the jurisdiction of the court, on the ground that the passage of a general bankrupt law by Congress on July 1 [1898] has superseded the operation of all State bankrupt laws while it remains in effect, and also filed an answer denying the allegations of the petition. The court sustained the demurrer and dismissed the petition. S. A. Williams appeared for the plaintiff, and Register and Field, of Baltimore, and Harold Scarboro for the defendants." (*The Aegis & Intelligencer*, September 9, 1898, p. 2). "Judge Watters, on Wednesday last [September 7, 1898], passed an order dismissing the petition and rescinding the injunction in solvency against Clara E. Stockham and Grant Stockham, her husband." (*Havre de Grace Republican*, September 10, 1898, p. 3)

Stockham, Margaret E., 1894. "Insolvent Notice. George L. Van Bibber, Solicitor. Notice is hereby given to the creditors of Margaret E. Stockham, sometimes known as Margaret E. Michael, who were such on the 2nd day of October, 1894, that she has applied for the benefit of the Insolvent Laws of the State of Maryland, and that a meeting of her creditors will be held at the office of George L. Van Bibber, in the town of Bel Air, on Thursday, November 1, 1894, at 10 o'clock A. M., for the purpose of proving claims and choosing a permanent trustee for her estate. William H. Hinchman, Preliminary Trustee." (*Harford Democrat*, October 26, 1894, p. 2). "Margaret E. Stockham, of Perryman, has applied for the benefit of the insolvent laws. William H. Hinchman has been appointed preliminary trustee." (*The Aegis & Intelligencer*, November 2, 1894, p. 3; *Havre de Grace Republican*, November 2, 1894, p. 3, added "Margaret E. Stockham, sometimes known as Margaret E. Michael, of Bush River Neck"). "Insolvent Sale. The subscriber, as permanent trustee of Margaret E. Stockham, an insolvent, at Woodley Cottage Farm, near Perryman, on Wednesday, December 12th, 1894, Commencing at 10 o'clock, A. M., the following Personal Property: Ten Hogs, 7 Shoats, 7 Pigs, 16 Sheep, 1 pair Mules, 7 Mares, 2 Colts, 15 Milk Cows, 8 Yearling Calves, 1 Corn Planter. 3 Corn Workers, 3 Plows, 2 Wagons, 2 Harrows, 1 Buggy, 1 Milk Wagon, lot Harness, lot of Household and Kitchen Furniture, consisting in part of Beds, Bedding, Stoves, Chairs, China Ware, &c. Also, lot of Corn which will be sold by the barrel. William H. Hinchman, Permanent Trustee. J. S. Richardson, Auctioneer." (*The Aegis & Intelligencer*, November 30, 1894, p. 2). **Genealogical Notes**: Margaret E. Stockham, daughter of John Stockham (1783-1855) and Elizabeth Palmer (1801-1878), was born on November 27, 1842 near Perryman, never married, moved to Baltimore circa 1902, died at home at 6 E. Randall Street on

February 4, 1904 and was buried in St. George's P. E. Church cemetery. (tombstone; *The Aegis & Intelligencer*, January 22, 1904 and February 12, 1904; Death certificate of Susan S. Gallion, 1920)

Stover, Francis G., 1829. "Petition, Schedule, Certificate of Sheriff, Certificate of Personal Discharge, Order for Publication, Bond for Appearance, Trustee's Bond, Trustee's Certificate, Deed to Trustee filed 7th March 1829. 15th August 1829 Order for Sale filed. Order copied for W. B. Bond, Esqr., 16th Sepr. 1829" [nothing further] (Insolvent Docket A, 1807-1843, p. 94, at the Maryland State Archives)

Stover, Jacob, 1824. "Petition, Bond, Schedule, certificate personal discharge and order for publication filed 21st Sept. 1824. March 19th 1825 Printers Certificate filed. Petitioner appears and is discharged." (Insolvent Docket A, 1807-1843, p. 68, at Maryland State Archives; Insolvent Docket Prior to 1827, Court Records Accession #632 at the Historical Society of Harford County)

Streett, John M. and Richard, 1890. "Messrs, John M. and Richard Streett, canners, this week made application to our County Court for the benefit of the insolvent law." (*Havre de Grace Republican*, June 27, 1890, p. 3)

Streett, Lawrence, 1889. "An Insolvency Case.—The examination of witnesses before Judge Watters and a jury in the insolvency case of Lawrence Streett, began in the Court House, on Friday last. The petition to declare Streett insolvent was made by Messrs. Kirwan & Tyler, of Baltimore, to whom Streett is indebted for 10,000 cases of empty cans. The firm was represented by Messrs. S. A. Williams and Geo. L. Van Bibber. Messrs. Wm. Young, [George Y.] Maynadier and J. M. Stump prepared for the defendant. In May last, some months after buying the cans, Streett sold a piece of land to his brother Kennedy Streett, and subsequently sold his farm of 75 acres, being the home place, to his brother, Dr. ---- [illegible due to the paper being water damaged] Streett, of Baltimore, for ---- [illegible] and the remainder ---- [illegible] the property [illegible] in cash ---- [illegible] Thomas H. ---- [illegible]. On the 1st of November Lawrence Streett ---- [illegible] a deed of trust of the remainder of his ---- [illegible] being ---- [illegible] Mr. J. M. Streett ---- [illegible] amounting to about $1,600 ---- [illegible] witnesses were examined, including the defendant himself who was called on to account for the ---- [illegible] sums of money which had come into his possession from the sale of canned goods and other property. The case will be resumed on Monday next." (*The Aegis & Intelligencer*, December 27, 1889, p. 2). "The insolvency case of Lawrence Streett which was to have been resumed on Tuesday was postponed on account of the sickness of counsel and jurymen until January 28th" [1890]. (*The Aegis & Intelligencer*, January 17, 1890, p. 2). "The circuit court on Tuesday [January 28, 1890] took up the Streett insolvent case, and prayers argued." (*Havre de Grace Republican*, January 31, 1890, p. 3). "Mr. Lawrence Streett has been declared insolvent, by a Court jury, and all the deeds, except one, he made to his brother, Dr. David Streett, have been set aside." (*Havre de Grace Republican*, February 14, 1890, p. 3). "The petit jury for the May term of the Circuit Court was called together at Bel Air, last Monday [September 1, 1890], in the case of Kirwan & Tyler, of Baltimore, against Lawrence Streett, a canner. The proceedings were for the purpose of adjudicated the affairs of Streett, an insolvent, this being the cases in which Judge Watters granted a new trial, last spring, because one of the parties to the suit treated some of the jurors on the panel to whiskey. On a suggestion of defendant's counsel for removal, Judge Watters decided that there is no provision of law under which an insolvent case can be removed, and it went over to [the] next day." (*Havre de Grace Republican*, September 5, 1890, p. 3). "The insolvent case of Kirwan & Tyler vs. Lawrence Streett will go to the Court of Appeals, on the question [of] whether Judge Watters had a right to refuse defendant's application for the removal of the case to another court." (*Havre de Grace Republican*, September 12, 1890, p. 3). "The Lawrence Streett insolvency case, which has occupied so much of the time of our County Court, has been settled, and the insolvency proceedings dismissed." (*Havre de Grace Republican*, September 26, 1890, p. 3)

Streett, St. Clair, 1857. "Petition, Schedules, Affidavits, Appointment of Trustee & order of notice, Trustee's Bond & Deed to Trustee filed 30th June 1857. 14th Novr. 1857 Petitioner appears, files certificate of publication & discharged." (Insolvent Docket A. L. J. No. 1, p. 19, in the Court Records Department of the Historical Society of Harford County). "Notice is hereby given that St. Clair Streett, of Harford County, has made application to the Circuit Court of said County, for the benefit of the Insolvent Laws of Maryland, and that the first Saturday after the second Monday in May next has been assigned for him to appear in said Court to answer such interrogatories as his creditors may propose or allege against him. A. Lingan Jarrett, Clerk." (*The Southern Aegis*, July 18, 1857, Vol. I, No. 3, p. 15). **Genealogical Notes**: Dr. St. Clair Streett, son of Col. John Streett (1762-1836) and Martha St. Clair, was born on February 1, 1788, served in the War of 1812, married 1st to Ariel Hope Jarrett (1793-1849) on December 17, 1816, married 2nd to Susan Stubblefield (widow) (1797-1872), of Baltimore City, on October 24, 1850 by Rev. M. L. Forbes and died at *Farmington* in Harford Co. on November 16, 1864. The children of St. Clair and Ariel Streett were Sarah Jane Streett (married Hamilton Lefever), John Rush Streett (married Elizabeth Hope), Martha Streett (married Matthew Forbes) and Cecelia Streett (married Thomas Green). St. Clair and Susan Streett had one child, Susan Cornelia Streett. (*Baltimore American*, December 25, 1816; Baltimore *Sun*, October 26, 1850; *The Family of John Streett and Martha St. Clair of Harford County, Maryland*, by Anitra R. Streett (1998), pp. 72, 73, 353; *Harford Democrat*, May 17, 1872; St. James P. E. Church tombstone inscriptions; military records)

Streett, William, 1833. "Petition, Schedule, Affidavit, Personal discharge, Order for Publication, Bond for Appearance, Trustee's Bond, Trustee's Certificate and Deed to Trustee filed 3rd August 1833 ... [various allegations and answers filed in 1834] ... 16th Augt. 1834 Petitioner appears and finally discharged." (Insolvent Docket A, 1807-1843, p. 126, at the Maryland State Archives). **Genealogical Notes**: William Streett, son of Col. John Streett and Martha St. Clair, was born on December 3, 1795, served in the War of 1812, married 1st to Eliza Crook, eldest daughter of Walter Crook, of Baltimore Co., on 13 Apr 1819 by Rev. Jennings, married 2nd to Mary Ann Montgomery (1799-1874), widow of William B. Montgomery (1796-1838) and daughter of Thomas Butler and Jane Macatee, on June 23, 1841 by Rev. James Reid (witnesses were Abraham Streett and Elizabeth Wheeler), died on March 6, 1860 and was buried in St. Mary's Roman Catholic Church cemetery. The children of William and Eliza Streett were Mary Martha Streett, Virginia Streett, John Walter Streett, Olivia Streett and William Bernard Streett. (*The Family of John Streett and Martha St. Clair of Harford County, Maryland*, by Anitra R. Streett, 1998, p. 195; St. Mary's Catholic Church tombstones; marriage licenses; military records; Macatee (McAtee) Family typescript at the Historical Society of Harford Co., p. 8; St. Ignatius Catholic Church, Marriage Register, 1817-1854, p. 26, listed their names in Latin as "Gulielmum Street et Mariam Montgomery, alias Butler")

Strong, Maximillion, 1831. "Petition, Schedule, personal discharge and order for publication, bond for appearance, Trustee's bond, Trustee's certificate and deed to Trustee filed 10th Oct 1831. 17th March 1832 Certificate of publication filed & Petitioner appears and finally discharged." (Insolvent Docket A, 1807-1843, p. 112, at the Maryland State Archives). **Genealogical Note**: Maximillion Maxwell Strong married Frances Ann Allender circa September 14, 1825 (date of license).

Stump, Herman, 1841. "Petition, Affidavits, Schedules, Appointment of Trustee, Certificate, Order, Personal Discharge, Trustee's Bond, deed to Trustee & Appearance Bond filed 22nd Octr. 1841. 20th Novr. 1841 on application of the Petitioner the Court have [sic] examined the Insolvent papers of Herman Stump & find several errors in the proceedings & do order the proceedings [sic] & do order them to be dismissed 21st May 1842, Petitioner appears." [nothing further recorded] (Insolvent Docket A, 1807-1843, p. 180, at Maryland State Archives). **Genealogical Notes**: Herman Stump, son and youngest child of John Stump, of Stafford (1752-1816), and Cassandra Willson, was born on

180

August 13, 1798 and was the proprietor of Stafford Mills. He died on March 13, 1881, unmarried, at the home of Col. Thomas Smithson, the husband of his niece, near Port Deposit in Cecil County and was buried in the family burial ground at Stafford in Harford County. (*Substantial Copy of Genealogical Record of the Stump Family of Maryland*, compiled by Albert P. Silver and Henry W. Archer, 1891, pp. 1-3; *The Aegis & Intelligencer*, March 18, 1881)

Sunderland, Benjamin, 1818. "Petition, Schedule, Bond, Order to Sheriff – Shff.'s certificate, personal discharge and order of publication filed 11th Sepr. 1818 – March 15th 1819 petr. appeared and ordered by the Court that he give notice in any newspaper." [nothing further recorded] (Insolvent Docket A, 1807-1843, p. 23, at the Maryland State Archives; Insolvent Docket Prior to 1827, Court Records Accession #632 at Historical Society of Harford County). **Genealogical Note**: Benjamin Sunderland married Elizabeth ---- by 1805 and their daughter Mary Ann Sunderland was born on January 20, 1806 (St. George's P. E. Parish Register).

Susquehanna and Tidewater Canals, 1887. "The Tide-Water Canal. The State Board of Public Works is taking considerable interest in the affairs of the Susquehanna and Tide-Water Canal. Two meetings have been held this week, and Ex-Governor Philip Francis Thomas has been retained to represent the State in the application, now pending in Philadelphia Courts, made by the Reading Railroad Company to be released from the canal leases. At the meeting of the Public Works Board yesterday (Thursday) some of the canal officials from this vicinity were to be present, in connexion [sic] with its affairs. On Wednesday, Messrs. Robert A. Dobbin, of Baltimore, and Henry W. Archer, Jr., of Bel Air, attorneys for George W. Dobbin, filed in the Circuit Court of this county, a bill in equity, praying that a receiver be appointed for the canal, and that a decree be passed for the sale of the property.—The bill alleges that the complainant is owner of a number of priority bonds of the canal company, payment of interest on which has been refused. In 1839 the canal company borrowed from the State of Maryland $1,000,000, and being in arrears for the interest in 1842, the State permitted the company to issue certain bonds to take precedence of the State's claim. It is upon these bonds that the present suit is brought, the bill alleging that the canal company is insolvent." (*Havre de Grace Republican*, March 4, 1887, p. 4). "Attorney General John P. Poe, Solicitor. Order of Publication. The State of Maryland vs. the Susquehanna Canal Company, the Tide Water Canal Company, the Philadelphia and Reading Railroad Company, the Unknown Holders of the Susquehanna Canal Preferred Bonds which matured on January 1, 1894, and the Unknown Holders of the Tide Water Canal Priority Bonds which matured on January 1, 1894. In the Circuit Court for Harford County, In Equity. The Object of the bill in this case is to procure a decree for sale of the Susquehanna and Tide Water Canal, its property and franchises and for a distribution of the proceeds of such sale amongst its creditors, according to their several rights and priorities; and also for the appointment in the meantime of a Receiver to take charge of the affairs of the said Susquehanna Canal Company and the said Tide Water Canal Company, respectively, of and all their property of every description; and to hold, preserve, manage and operate the same, if the operation of said Canal shall be deemed desirable under the order of this Court. The bill states that the Defendant Corporations, chartered respectively by the States of Pennsylvania and Maryland, are the owners of a contiguous canal extending from Havre de Grace, Maryland, to Wrightsville, Pennsylvania; that under the Maryland Act of 1838, chapter 416, entitled "An Act to ensure the completion of the Susquehanna Canal and of the Tide Water Canal," the Susquehanna Canal Company and the Tide Water Canal Company mortgaged their Canal and property to the State of Maryland and to secure the sum of one million dollars and interest, as in said Act provided, and that under the Act of 1843, Chapter 363, they executed a further mortgage to Dennis Claude, Treasurer of the Western Shore of Maryland, to secure the indebtedness therein mentioned; that under the provisions of said Act of 1843, Chapter

363, the Tide Water Canal Company was authorized to issue and did issue Priority Bonds for the purpose specified in said Act, the amount issued being believed to be about $97,800; and that the Susquehanna Canal Company also issued similar Preferred Bonds amounting to $200,000 or thereabouts; that said Preferred and Priority Bonds respectively, matured on the 1st of January, 1894, and are claimed to be still outstanding and unpaid as a prior lien upon the property of said Canal Companies respectively; that said Preferred and Priority Bonds are believed to be owned or controlled by the Philadelphia and Reading Railroad Company, a Pennsylvania Corporation, and if not so owned and controlled are claimed by parties unknown to the plaintiff. The said Canal Companies on the second day of January, 1872, made a lease of their Canal and all their works and property to the said Philadelphia and Reading Railroad Company for nine-hundred and ninety-nine years for the rent and upon the terms set out and charged in the lease; and that said lease was surrendered by the receivers of said Railroad Company on the 27th of April, 1894. That for many years said Canal Companies made default upon their mortgages to the State of Maryland, and that on the 31st of January, 1889, under authority conferred by the Maryland Act of 1888, Chapter 154, a settlement and compromise was effected by L. Victor Baughman, Comptroller of the Treasury, with the approval of Elihu E. Jackson, Governor, and Stevenson Archer, Treasurer of Maryland, whereby in consideration of the payment of $127,500.00, being twenty-five per cent of the over due and unpaid interest upon said mortgages to the State of Maryland, a released was executed to said Canal Companies of the balance of said unpaid interest; the time for the payment of the principle of one million dollars was extended for fifty years maturing in 1938, and the rate of interest on said mortgage debt was reduced from six per cent to two per cent per annum; that said Canal Companies paid said interest up to and including the first day of January, 1893, but have paid no interest since that time. That the Canal was operated by said Philadelphia and Reading Railroad Company under the lease of January 2, 1872, until the 27th of April, 1894, when it was abandoned, and that the Canal is now lying idle and daily deteriorating in value, and that it has no business or revenues sufficient to pay the operating expenses and interest on the debts of said Canal Companies; that the said companies owe a mortgage due in 1918, bearing six per cent interest, amounting to $1,336,000; also a mortgage due in 1902, bearing interest at the rate of seven per cent, amounting to $257,000; also unfunded debt for equipment, etc., amounting to $21,282.33; also unfunded debt being unpaid interest on their bonded debt, amounting to $538,235.18, in addition to the unpaid interest due the State of Maryland, and that said companies are hopelessly insolvent. It is thereupon, this 7th day of December, 1894, by the Circuit Court for Harford county, sitting in Equity, ordered that the plaintiff, by causing a copy of this order to be inserted in two newspapers, once a week, for four consecutive weeks before the 12th of January, 1895, give notice to the Philadelphia and Reading Railroad Company, a non-resident corporation, and to the unknown holders of the Susquehanna Canal Preferred Bonds which matured on January 1, 1894, and the unknown holders of the Tide Water Canal Priority Bonds which matured on January 1, 1894, non-residents as well as residents of this State, of the object and substance of the said bill, and warning them to be and appear in this court, in person or by solicitor, on or before the 30th day of January, 1895, to answer said bill, and to show cause if any they have, why a decree should not pass as prayed. Wm. S. Forwood, Jr., Clerk." (*The Aegis & Intelligencer*, December 14, 1894, p. 2). Under the heading of "To Sell The Canal" the paper further stated, in part, "It is to be hoped that it may fall into the hands of some company that will build a first-class railroad along the line. In the event of the failure to be operated as a canal the title would probably revert to the original owners, but they would no doubt gladly give the right of way to any good company." (*The Aegis & Intelligencer*, December 14, 1894, p. 3)

Sutton, Samuel, 1831. "Petition, Schedule, Shffs. certificate, personal discharge and order for publication, Bond for Appearance, Trustee's Bond, Trustee's Certificate and deed to Trustee filed 21st March 1831. 31st August 1831 Petitioner appears. Certificate of Publication filed & oath administered and finally discharged." (Insolvent Docket A, 1807-1843, p. 108, at the Maryland State Archives). **Genealogical Notes**: Samuel Sutton was born in 1795, served in the War of 1812, participated in the Battle of North Point on September 12-14, 1814, married 1st to Martha ---- (1794-1824), served in the Maryland Legislature, married 2nd to Susan Chauncey (1792-1879) circa March 26, 1832 (date of license) and died at his home at *Mount Hope Retreat* on March 8, 1878 in his 83rd year. (St. George's Parish tombstone inscriptions; military records; *The Aegis & Intelligencer*, March 15, 1878)

Tayson, Elijah, 1863. "Petition, Schedule of property, a List of debts due & owing to him & a List of debts due & owing from him, Affidavit, Order, Trustee's Bond & Deed to Trustee filed 4th March 1863 & R. W. Whaland appointed Trustee. 3rd August 1863 Petitioner appears and files Certificate and finally discharged." (Insolvent Docket A. L. J. No. 1, p. 43, in the Court Records Department of the Historical Society of Harford County). "Notice Is Hereby Given, that Elijah Tayson has made application to the Circuit Court of Harford county, for the benefit of the Insolvent Laws of Maryland; and that the first Monday of August next, has been assigned for him to appear in said court to answer such interrogatories as his creditors may propose or allege against him. Wm. Galloway, Clerk, Circuit Court for Harford county." (*National American*, May 8, 1863, p. 3). **Genealogical Notes**: Elijah Tayson was born circa 1831), married Arabella Ross (born circa 1835) circa 10 Nov 1857 (date of license), worked as a farmer and their son Hall R. Tayson was 1 year old in 1860. (Harford County marriage license; 1860 Harford County Census)

Thompson, Amos, 1883. "July 17th 1883. Petition, Schedule, Order of Court, Bond of preliminary trustee & Insolvent deed filed … Aug 30th 1883 Order of court filed appointing Wm. M. Marine permanent Trustee filed … Nov 12, 1883 Petitioner appeared in open Court & was finally discharged." (Insolvent Docket A. L. J. No. 1, p. 82, in Court Records Department of the Historical Society of Harford County). **Genealogical Notes**: Amos Thompson, son of Elijah Thompson and Martha Forsythe, was born in 1847 at Robin Hood near Aberdeen, MD, married Ada Treadway (1853-1932) on April 24, 1878, worked as a farmer and a canner, and died at Robin Hood on May 8, 1910. (marriage license; Wesleyan Chapel tombstone inscriptions; death certificate of Amos Thompson)

Thompson, Archibald, 1812. "Petition, Schedule, Bond and Notice to Creditors filed 13th March 1812 … August 25th 1812 petitioner appeared agreeably to the tenor of his bond." [nothing further recorded] (Insolvent Docket A, 1807-1843, p. 12, at the Maryland State Archives; Insolvent Docket Prior to 1827, Court Records Accession #632 at the Historical Society of Harford County). **Genealogical Note**: Archibald Thompson marred Elizabeth (Wheeler) Whitaker, widow of Abraham Whitaker who died in 1804. (Harford County Land Records Liber HD No. 8, pp. 145-147; *Descendants of the Signers of the Bush Declaration of March 22, 1775, Harford County, Maryland*, by Christopher T. Smithson and Henry C. Peden, Jr., 2010, p. 367)

Thompson, Bernard, 1821. "Petition, Schedule, Bond, Sheriff's certificate, personal discharge and order for publication filed 29th January 1821 – 1st September 1821 petitioner appeared – Nathaniel Hays appointed Trustee and ordered that he give bond in the penalty of $500." [nothing further recorded] (Insolvent Docket A, 1807-1843, p. 41, at the Maryland State Archives; Insolvent Docket Prior to 1827, Court Records Accession #632 at the Historical Society of Harford County). **Genealogical Note**: Bernard Thompson married Martha Renshaw circa January 3, 1811 (date of license).

Thompson, Isaac H., 1859. "Petition, Schedule of property, List of debts due & owing to & from, Affidavit, Order & Appointment of A. Lingan Jarrett, Esqr., Trustee, Trustee's Bond approved and filed 28th February 1859 and Deed to Trustee made & filed. 25th August/59 Petition of Insolvent &

order filed. 14th Nov/59 Petitioner appears and files certificate of publication upon petition & finally discharged." (Insolvent Docket A. L. J. No. 1, p. 27, in the Court Records Department of the Historical Society of Harford County). "Notice is hereby given that Isaac H. Thompson, of Harford County, has made application to the Circuit Court of said County, for the benefit of the Insolvent Laws of Maryland, and that the 1st Saturday after the 1st Monday in August, 1859, has been assigned for him to appear in said Court to answer such interrogatories as his creditors may propose or allege against him. Wm. Galloway, Clerk, Circuit Court for Harford County." (*The Southern Aegis*, March 19, 1859, p. 3) "In the matter of the insolvency of Isaac H. Thompson ... Upon the Petition of Isaac H. Thompson, an Insolvent debtor, it is ordered this 25th day of August, 1859, that said Insolvent appear in the Circuit Court for Harford county on the 2nd Monday of November next, to answer such interrogatories or allegations as his creditors, endorsers or securities may propose or allege against him, and that he give notice thereof to his creditors by publication of this order in some newspaper printed in Harford county, for four successive weeks one month before the said 2nd Monday in November. John H. Price. True copy. Test: Wm. Galloway, Clk." (*The Southern Aegis*, September 3, 1859, p. 3) **Genealogical Notes**: Isaac H. Thompson was born c1831 in Pennsylvania, married Sarah H. ---- (born c1839, PA) circa 1859 and worked as a farmer. (1860 Harford County Census listed them in the Darlington area of the 5th District, but with no children at that time)

Thompson, James, 1830. "Petition, Schedule, Shffs. certificate, personal discharge and order of publication, Bond for Appearance, Trustee's Bond, Trustee's Certificate and Deed to Trustee filed 15th day of June 1830." [nothing further recorded] (Insolvent Docket A, 1807-1843, p. 106, at Maryland State Archives)

Thompson, Joshua, 1826. "Petition, Schedule, Bond, Sheriff's certificate and personal discharge and order for publication and Bond of provisional Trustee and certificate for trustee filed 8th Jul 1826. 17th March 1827 Certificate of publication filed and petitioner finally discharged." (Insolvent Docket A, 1807-1843, p. 80, at the Maryland State Archives; Insolvent Docket Prior to 1827, Court Records Accession #632 at the Historical Society of Harford County). **Genealogical Note**: Joshua Thompson married Ann --- probably circa 1791 and her tombstone states "Ann Thompson died February 6, 1815, age 41, wife of Joshua" (Mitchell-Osborn family cemetery).

Thompson, Mahlon, 1860. "Petition, Schedule of property, List of debts due & owing, Affidavit, Order appointing Trustee & notice to creditors, Trustee's Bond and Deed to Trustee filed 21st Decr. 1860, A. W. Bateman, Esqr., appointed Trustee ... 22nd April 1861 Petitioner appears & files Certificate of Notice to Creditors & finally discharged." (Insolvent Docket A. L. J. No. 1, p. 37, in the Court Records Department of the Historical Society of Harford County). "Notice is hereby given that Mahlon Thompson, has made application to the Circuit Court of Harford county, for the benefit of the Insolvent Laws of Maryland, and that the 4th Monday in April, 1861, has been assigned for him to appear in said Court to answer such interrogatories as his creditors may propose or allege against him. Wm. Galloway, Clk." (*The Southern Aegis*, January 19, 1861, p. 3) **Genealogical Notes**: Mahlon Thompson (c1819 – July 21, 1891), farmer, miller and storekeeper, son of Mahlon and Martha Thompson, married Angeline Whitaker (July 24, 1830 – December 13, 1892), daughter of Isaac Whitaker (1792-1875) and Mary McConnell (1799-1867), on December 16, 1851 in Havre de Grace and their son Isaac W. Thompson was 5 years old in 1860. (Harford Co. license; Baltimore *Sun*, February 4, 1852; 1860 Harford Co. Census; *Ancestral Charts Volume 4*, Harford County Genealogical Society, 1988, pp. 188-189, stated Angeline Whitaker was born on the 24th day of the 7th month 1830, her father Isaac Whitaker was born on October 27, 1782 and her mother Mary McConnell was born on the 24th day of the 1st month 1799; Christ Episcopal Church tombstone inscriptions)

Thompson, William, 1842. "Petition, Affidavits, Schedules, Appointment, Certificate, Order, personal discharge, Appearance bond & Trustee's bond filed 12th Oct. 1842 – 20 May 1843 Petitioner appears, files certificate of publication & finally discharged." (Insolvent Docket A, 1807-1843, p. 185, at Maryland State Archives)

Thompson, William S., 1859. "Petition, Schedule, Affidavit, Appointment of A. W. Bateman, Esqr., Trustee, Order of Notice to Creditors, Trustee's Bond & approval & Deed to Trustee filed 8th November 1859. 27th February 1860 Petitioner appears & files certificate of publication & finally discharged." (Insolvent Docket A. L. J. No. 1, p. 31, in Court Records Department of the Historical Society of Harford County). "Notice is hereby given that William S. Thompson, of Harford County, has made application to the Circuit Court of said County, for the benefit of the Insolvent Laws of Maryland, and that the 4th Monday in February, 1860, has been assigned for him to appear in said Court to answer such interrogatories as his creditors may propose or allege against him. Wm. Galloway, Clerk, Circuit Court for Harford County." (*The Southern Aegis*, November 19, 1859, p. 3)

Thorn, John, 1803. "Whereas we the subscribers Justices of the Peace for Harford County upon the petition of John Thorn who set forth therein that he had been confined in the goal of the said county twenty days for debts which he was unable to pay and finding the facts stated to be true we did meet at the county gaol of the said county on the 26th day of December 1803 & did then and there appoint the 25th day of January Inst. to meet at the Court House of said county which said appointment we did then and there … at the request of the said sheriff administer to the said John Thorn the following oath which was taken by the said John Thorn being first duly sworn on the Holy Evangels of Almighty God in the words following, I John Thorn do solemnly swear that the schedule which I have delivered to the sheriff of Harford County doth contain a full account to the best of my knowledge and remembrance of my whole estate both real & personal or that I have any title to or interest in and of all debts, credits & effects whatsoever which I or any in trust for me have or at the time of my petition had, or am or was in any respect entitled to in possession, remainder or reversion and that I have not directly or indirectly at any time since my imprisonment or before, sold, leased or otherwise conveyed or disposed of or intrusted all or any part of my estate, goods, stock, money or debts thereby to defraud my creditors or to secure the same to receive or expect any profit or advantage thereof so help me God, which said duplicate of the schedule aforesaid we have transmitted to the clerk of the county court to be by him preserved in his office for the information of the creditors of the said John Thorn. Given under our hands & seals this 25th day of January 1804. John Moores. Wm. Smithson. James Amoss." (Court Records Documents 67.02.4(A)(B) at the Historical Society of Harford County; a copy of the schedule was included to which "John Thorn" signed his name, but no property was listed)

Toogood, William (African American), 1820. "Petition, Schedule, Bond, Sheriff's certificate, order for publication and personal discharge filed 1st July 1820." [nothing further recorded] (Insolvent Docket A, 1807-1843, p. 34, at the Maryland State Archives; Insolvent Docket Prior to 1827, Court Records Accession #632 at the Historical Society of Harford County). **Genealogical Notes**: William Toogood aka Bill Toogood aka Bill Howe, was born circa 1786, was involved in legal matters in 1811 and 1812 and was listed on the criminal docket from 1811 to 1814 (Court Records Document 99.04.6 and Criminal Docket Book 1810-1821 at the Historical Society of Harford County). William Toogood (alias William Howe) was involved in a legal matter in 1829 and William Toogood was also involved in legal matters in 1823 and 1833 (Court Record Documents 74.09.5, 94.16.2 and 105.10.2, loc. cit.) Bill Toogood (Twogood) was head of household in the 1820 census. Bill Toogood was involved in legal matters from 1819 to 1822 (Court Records Document 111.08.1). Bill Twogood was listed as age 46 in 1832 (A List of Free People of Colour taken in 1832 by Joshua Guyton, Sheriff). Bill

Toogood (alias Bill Howe) was involved in a legal matter in 1836 (Court Records Document 94.22.3, loc. cit.) and Bill Toogood (alias Bill Howe) was listed on the criminal docket in 1836 and 1837 (Criminal Docket Book, 1831-1838, loc. cit.)

Touchstone, Henry, 1820. Nathan Touchstone vs. John Touchstone, Henry Touchstone, Thomas Shannon and his wife Ann, and William Butler and his wife Sarah, Bill of Complaint stated Henry Touchstone, father of the complainant, died testate in 1820, leaving these children: John Touchstone of Baltimore Co., and Ann Touchstone (who married Thomas Shannon), Sarah Touchstone (who married William Butler) of Harford Co., and Henry Touchstone, an infant under the age of 20 years, and all of Harford County [and also the complainant Nathan Touchstone]. The said Henry Touchstone died in debt to sundry persons and it was requested that his land, being part of *Land of Promise* and *Eyetrap* [*Eightrupp*] located near Rock Run on the road to Quaker Bottom, should be sold to pay his debts. Abraham Jarrett was appointed guardian of the said minor Henry Touchstone. All parties agreed to sell the land, the matter was resolved and the case was closed in 1829. (Harford County Equity Court Book HD No. 1, pp. 170-177)

Trago, John, 1856. "Petition, Schedules, Affidavits, Appointment of Trustee A. W. Bateman," etc., 26 Feb 1856. "11 November 1856 Petitioner appears, files certificate of publication of notice to creditors & finally discharged." (Insolvent Docket A. L. J. No. 1, p. 11, in the Court Records Department of the Historical Society of Harford County). "Notice is hereby given that John Trago, of Harford County, has made application to the Circuit Court of said County, for the benefit of the Insolvent Laws of Maryland, and that the first Tuesday of November term, 1856, has been assigned for him to appear in said Court to answer such interrogatories as his creditors may propose or allege against him. A. Lingan Jarrett, Clerk." (*Harford Democrat*, March 14, 1856, p. 3)

Travis, John, 1821. "To the Honorable John Moores, one of the Justices of the Orphans Court of Harford County. The petition of John Travis of Harford County respectfully sheweth that your petitioner is now in actual confinement in Harford County Jail for debts which he is unable to pay, that he is willing and offers to deliver to the use of his creditors all his property real, personal and mixed, the necessary wearing apparel and bedding of himself and family excepted, a schedule whereof together with a list of his creditors and debtors, as far as he can at present ascertain them, is hereto on oath annexed. Your petitioner also hereto annexes proof on oath that he has resided two years next preceeding this his application within the State of Maryland. Your petitioner therefore prays your Honour to grant him the benefit of the insolvent laws of this state and to relieve him from his present confinement and your petitioner will pray, &c. John "X" Travis" (Court Records Document 68.08(.1(b) at the Historical Society of Harford County). "Know all men by these presents that we John Travis and Henry H. Johns of Harford County and State of Maryland are held and firmly bound unto the State of Maryland in the sum of one hundred dollars Current money of the United States to the payment whereof well and truly to be made of us our [sic] and each of our heirs, executors and administrators jointly and severally by these presents with our seals and dated this 15th day of January 1821. The condition of the above obligation is such that if the above bound John Travise shall make his personal appearance in Harford County Court on the first Saturday after the fourth Monday in August next then, before the judges thereof, then and there to answer such allegations or interrogatories, as his creditors make propose to him, then the above obligation to be void else to remain in full force and virtue in law. John "X" Travis. Henry H. Johns." (Court Records Document 68.08.1(A), loc. cit.) "I hereby certify that John Travis the petitioner above named is now in actual confinement in Harford County Jail for debt at the suit of Thomas W. Bond and that it is not upon a breach of peace or any of the penal Laws of the state of Maryland or of the united States, given under my hand this 15 day of January 1821. Joshua Guyton, Sheriff." (Court Records

Document 68.08.1(b), loc. cit., included a schedule of creditors to which John Travis made his "X" mark, but no property was listed). "Petition, Schedule, Bond, Sheriff's certificate, personal discharge and order for publication filed 15th January 1821." [nothing further recorded] (Insolvent Docket A, 1807-1843, p. 40, at the Maryland State Archives). 1823. "Petition, Shff's. certificate, schedule, bond, certificate of residence, personal discharge and order for publication filed 30th June 1823. Petitioner appears on the 13th March 1824 & files a certificate of publication of notice, and Ordered that he be discharged." (Insolvent Docket A, 1807-1843, p. 56, at the Maryland State Archives; Insolvent Docket Prior to 1827, Court Records Accession #632 at Historical Society of Harford County). **Genealogical Note**: John Travis married Catherine Bodden circa February 27, 1817 (date of license).

Treadway, Amos, 1861. "Petition, Schedule of property, A List of debts due & owing to him, A list of debts due & owing from him, Order appointing Trustee, Trustee's Bond & approval and Deed to Trustee filed 12th Sept. 1861 … 21st April 1862 Cont'd. 4th Aug/62 finally charged." (Insolvent Docket A. L. J. No. 1, p. 39, in the Court Records Department of the Historical Society of Harford County). "Notice is hereby given, that Amos Treadway has made application to the Circuit Court of Harford county, for the benefit of the Insolvent Laws of Maryland; and that the 4th Monday of February next, has been assigned for him to appear in said court to answer such interrogatories as his creditors may propose or allege against him. Wm. Galloway, Clerk, Circuit Court for Harford County." (*National American*, October 11, 1861, p. 3). **Genealogical Notes**: Amos Treadway was born in 1818, moved to Illinois, returned to Harford County, married Margaret Jane Carroll (April 26, 1826 – May 19, 1909), daughter of Aquilla Carroll and Rachel Whitaker, circa June 17, 1847 (date of license), moved to Richmond Co., VA, returned to Harford Co., engaged in farming and canning business with son-in-law Amos Thompson and died at home at Robin Hood near Aberdeen on February 3, 1889. The children of Amos and Margaret Treadway were Dr. Paca H. Treadway (removed near Little Rock, Arkansas), Mrs. Emma Touchton (wife of Samuel W. Touchton), Mrs. Adah Thompson (wife of Amos Thompson), Elsie Treadway and Otis A. Treadway. Their son Marian Treadway was born on October 26, 1857 and died on June 19, 1858 in Richmond Co., VA. (Harford County marriage license spelled his surname Tredaway; Aquilla Carroll Family Records in *Maryland Bible Records, Volume 2*, by Henry C. Peden, Jr., 2003, pp. 16-17, contains Carroll family information only; Wesleyan Chapel tombstone inscriptions; *Havre de Grace Republican*, February 8, 1889 and May 22, 1909)

Treadway, Otis A., 1890. "Otis A. Treadway has applied for the benefit of the Insolvent laws. Mr. Septimus Davis has been appointed preliminary trustee." (*The Aegis & Intelligencer*, November 21, 1890, p. 2). "Insolvent Notice. In the matter of the Insolvency of Otis A. Treadway … In pursuance of an order of Court passed in the above matter, notice is hereby given that the second Monday in February, in the year 1891, is fixed as the day for the said Otis A. Treadway, insolvent, to appear in said Court to answer such interrogatories or allegations, as his creditors, endorsers or sureties may propose or allege against him. Septimus Davis, Permanent Trustee." (*Harford Democrat*, December 12, 1890, p. 2). 1896. "Notice to Creditors, In the Matter of the Insolvency of Otis A. Treadway … To the Creditors of Otis A. Treadway. Take notice that Otis A. Treadway, of Harford county, Maryland, has been adjudicated an insolvent debtor by the Circuit Court for Harford County. The proceedings under which said adjudication was made being now pending, a meeting of the creditors of said insolvent debtor will be held on the *27th day of January, 1896*, at 11 o'clock A. M., at the office of Septimus Davis in the town of Bel Air, Maryland for the purpose of electing a permanent trustee for the estate of said insolvent. Septimus Davis, Preliminary Trustee." (*Havre de Grace Republican*, January 18, 1896, p. 2). "Trustee's Sale. In pursuance of an order of the Circuit Court for Harford County, Md., the undersigned, as permanent trustee in insolvency of Otis A. Treadway, will sell at Public Sale, at the Court House door, in Bel Air, on Monday, March 9th. 1896, at 12 o'clock, M., All

That Land situated in Harford county, near Aberdeen, and lately occupied by said Otis A. Treadway, and being all the lands mentioned and described in a deed from Septimus Davis, trustee, to Francis A. Davis, bearing date December 19th, 1892, and is recorded amongst the land records of said Harford county in Liber W. S. F. No. 76, Folio 298, containing in all 129 Acres of Land, More or Less, being composed of two tracts of land, one called *Robin Hood Forest* containing about 39 acres, and the other called *Paradise* and containing about 90 acres. The improvements consist of a Comfortable Dwelling House, Canning House, and necessary out buildings, there is also a Large Brick Mill on the property. About two-thirds of the land is in cultivation and of good quality. Septimus Davis, Trustee." (*Havre de Grace Republican*, February 29, 1896, p. 2) **Genealogical Notes**: Otis Amos Treadway, son of Otis Treadway and Margaret Carroll, was born on September 14, 1860 at Paradise near Aberdeen, MD, married Oleita Virginia Briney, daughter of John E. and Mary Briney (born October 3, 1873, tombstone states Victoria B. Treadway, 1873-1956) on February 8, 1894, worked as a farmer, stone mason and rural mail carrier near Havre de Grace, died on March 30, 1944 and was buried in Wesleyan Chapel Cemetery. The children of Otis and Victoria Treadway were Newell O. E. Treadway, Wendell Treadway, Mrs. Otis Snyder and Mrs. Frances Jones. (Wesleyan Chapel tombstones; death certificate and obituary of Otis Amos Treadway; *The Aegis*, April 7, 1944)

Tredway, William, 1820. "I hereby certify that William Tredway is in my custody in the common jail of Harford County for debt and not for any breach of the laws of the State of Maryland or of the United States. Harford County, 22nd March 1820. Joshua Guyton, Sheriff." (Court Records Document 67.28.2(D) at the Historical Society of Harford County). "To the Worshipfull John Moores, Esq., Chief Justice of the Orphans Court of Harford County. The petition of William Tredway respectfully represents to your Worship that by unforeseen accidents and misfortunes, he has been reduced to poverty and distress and rendered totally unable to pay his debts. He is therefore under the painful necessity of applying to you for the benefit of the Insolvent Laws passed at November Session 1805 and the several supplements thereto. Your petitioner represents to you that he is now in confinement in the common jail of the County as appears by the certificate of the Sheriff accompanying this petition for debt and not for any breach of the laws of this State or of the United States, and that he offers to delivered [sic] up all his property of whatever nature, kind or description, whether real, personal or mixed, to the use of his creditors, a list whereof is herewith exhibited upon oath together with a list of his debts and creditors so far as he can ascertain them and that he is prepared to prove his residence within this State for two years last before this his application. He therefore humbly prays that you will issue your order to the Sheriff of Harford County directing and commanding him to have your petitioner before you on a day in the order to be named and that you will then direct and order your petitioner be released from confinement and the custody of the Sheriff aforesaid and extend to your petitioner such other and further relief as is contained in the provisions of the Insolvent Laws aforesaid. And your petitioner as in duty bound will pray and so forth [March 22, 1820]. William Tredway." (Court Records Document 67.28.2(A), loc. cit.; a schedule signed by "William Tredway" was included, but no property was listed; a copy of the newspaper clipping from the *Bond of Union* was also enclosed). "Petition, Schedule, Bond, Sheriff's certificate, order for publication & personal discharge filed 22nd March 1820 – Sepr. 2nd 1820 petitioner appeared and Court appointed Edward Tredway Trustee and on his executing a Bond the petr. to have a personal discharged granted him, Bond recorded same day." (Insolvent Docket A, 1807-1843, p. 29, at Maryland State Archives; Insolvent Docket Prior to 1827, Court Records Accession #632 at the Historical Society of Harford County). **Genealogical Note**: William Tredway married Amelia Magness circa December 21, 1809 (date of license).

Troyer, Charles C., 1895. "Insolvency of Charles C. Troyer. This is to give notice of the pendency of proceedings in Insolvency, in relation to the estate of Charles C. Troyer, an insolvent debtor, and that a meeting of the creditors of said insolvent will be held at the office of the undersigned, at Bel Air, Harford county, Md., on Wednesday, January 16th, 1886, at 11 o'clock A. M., to choose a permanent trustee for the estate of said insolvent. Gilbert S. Hawkins, Preliminary Trustee." (*Harford Democrat*, January 11, 1895, p. 2). "Insolvency Notice. In the matter of the Insolvency of Charles C. Troyer … By virtue of an order of said Court, passed on the 28th day of January, 1895, notice is hereby given that the 13th day of May, 1895, is fixed as the day for said Charles C. Troyer, insolvent, to appear in said Court, to answer such interrogatories or allegations as his creditors, endorsers or sureties may propose or allege against him. Gilbert S. Hawkins, Permanent Trustee." (*The Aegis & Intelligencer*, February 1, 1895, p. 2). "Notice is hereby given to all creditors of Charles C. Troyer, who were such on the 4th day of January, 1895, to file their claims, duly proven with the Clerk of the Circuit Court for Harford County, on or before the 1st day of May, 1895. Gilbert S. Hawkins, Permanent Trustee." (*The Aegis & Intelligencer*, February 1, 1895, p. 2). "Order Nisi. Sarah Robinson vs. Charles C. Troyer and wife et al. In the Circuit Court for Harford County, In Equity. Ordered, this 39th day of January, 1895, that the sales made and reported in the above entitled cause by Thomas H. Robinson, Trustee, be finally confirmed, unless cause to the contrary thereof be shown on or before the 23rd day of February, 1895; provided, a copy of this order be inserted in some newspaper published in Harford county, once in each of three successive weeks, before the 23rd day of February, 1895. The report states the amount of sale to be $1,625. Wm. S. Forwood, Jr., Clerk." (*The Aegis & Intelligencer*, February 1, 1895, p. 2). "Trustee's Sale of Personal Property. By virtue of an order of the Circuit Court for Harford county, sitting in Insolvency, passed in the matter of the insolvency of Charles C. Troyer, the subscriber, as permanent trustee, will offer at Public Sale on the farm formerly owned by Charles C. Troyer, near Black Horse post office, in Harford county, on Tuesday, February 26, 1895, at 10 o'clock. A. M., the following Personal Property, to wit: Lot of Farming Implements, consisting of Forks, Shovels, Hoes, Mattock, &c., lot of Chickens, Household Furniture and other articles. Gilbert S. Hawkins, Permanent Trustee. W. Crawford Norris, Auctioneer." (*The Aegis & Intelligencer*, February 1, 1895, p. 2). Charles C. Troyer, an insolvent debtor, was discharged by the Court on May 13, 1895. (*The Harford Democrat*, May 17, 1895, p. 2) **Genealogical Notes**: Charles C. Troyer was born on July 6, 1858, married Mary Elizabeth Miles (1859-1923) and died on November 19, 1927 in New Freedom, York Co., PA. Their children were Susan Alvirda Troyer (1885-1955) who married James Ross Hanna (1896-1961), Cecelia E. Troyer (1887-1964) who married William E. Kincaid (1885-1948), Maud Ethel Troyer (1888-1914), William Howard Troyer (1890-1954) who married Marian Lovesiah Stifler (1891-1963), and Mary Elizabeth Troyer (1891-1940) who married a Markley. (Bethel Presbyterian Church Cemetery tombstones; McKendree Methodist Episcoopal Cemetery tombstones; Norrisville Methodist Church Cemetery tombstones; Historical Society of Harford County cemetery files and other family records)

Truss, William, 1811. "Petition, Schedule, Bond and Notice to Creditors filed 13th December 1811 … Augt. Term 1812 petr. appeared. Sept 2nd 1812 application withdrawn." (Insolvent Docket A, 1807-1843, p. 12, at the Maryland State Archives; Insolvent Docket Prior to 1827, Court Records Accession #632 at the Historical Society of Harford County). **Genealogical Notes**: William Truss was born circa 1755, served in the militia in 1781, married Catherine Ricketts (b. 1758), daughter of Samuel Ricketts and Hannah Mead, by 1789 and their son William Truss was born on April 9, 1790. (St. George's P. E. Parish Register; Ricketts folder in the George W. Archer Collection in the Archives Department at the Historical Society of Harford County; Revolutionary War military records)

Tucker, James, 1831. "Petition, Schedule, Sheriff's certificate, personal discharge and order of publication, Bond for Appearance, Trustee's Bond, Trustee's Certificate and deed to Trustee filed 11th April 1831. 13th August 1831 Petitioner appears, order filed & cont'd. 17th March 1832 Certificate of Publication filed, petitioner appears and finally discharged." (Insolvent Docket A, 1807-1843, p. 108, at Maryland State Archives). **Genealogical Notes**: James Tucker was the eldest son of David Tucker (born in 12th month 1760) and Elizabeth ---- (born in 10th month 1763, but apparently not a Quaker since David was condemned by Friends for marrying outside the good order in 1789). James was born in 7th month 1791 and married by 1814 to Rachel Tucker (born in 6th month 1794, but apparently not a Quaker as she requested to become a member of the Society of Friends in the 4th month of 1815). Their son Ely Tucker was born on 26th day of 3rd month 1815 and son Aaron Harkins Tucker was born on 14th day of 1st month 1817. (Little Falls Friends Monthly Meeting Records)

Turner, George W., 1809. "Petition, Schedule, Bond, &c. filed 23rd Decr. 1809." Daniel Turner was appointed trustee in August 1810 [nothing further recorded]. (Insolvent Docket A, 1807-1843, p. 5, at the Maryland State Archives; Insolvent Docket Prior to 1827, Court Records Accession #632 at the Historical Society of Harford County)

Van Bibber, George L., 1890. "Trustees' Sale. By virtue of an order of the Circuit Court for Harford county, passed on the 18th day of August, 1890, in the matter of the insolvency of George L. Van Bibber, the subscribers will offer for sale by public auction, on Monday, September 15th, 1890, at 11 o'clock, A. M., at the residence of said George L. Van Bibber, near the Toll-Gate, on the Baltimore and Harford Turnpike, the following Real and Personal Property, to wit: 1. All that Parcel of land whereon the said Van Bibber now resides, containing 17 Acres, More or Less, described in a deed to him from Stevenson Archer et al. dated the 4th day of September, 1876, and recorded amongst the Land Records of Harford County, in Liber A.L.J. No. 34, folio 14. This piece of land is improved by a Large Frame Dwelling House, in good repair, Stable, Woodhouse and Ice House, and commands a very extended view of the valley of Winter's Run. 2. All that Parcel of Land fronting about 20 feet on Main Street, in the Town of Bel Air, adjoining the lots of David Maxwell and Mrs. Elizabeth G. Lee, being a part of the land described in a deed to said Van Bibber from Stevenson Archer, trustee, dated the 27th day of September, 1876, and recorded as aforesaid in Liber A.L.J., No. 37, folio 315. This lot is improved by a two-story Frame Building and Spring-House. 3. Also the following Personal Property: Household and Kitchen Furniture, 2 Horses, 5 Cows, 1 Carriage, 1 Express Wagon, 1 Buggy, 1 Cart, 1 Harrow, 1 Plow, 1 Cultivator, Shovels, Forks, 1 set Double Harness, 3 sets Single Harness, 1 set Cart Harness, Saddle and Bridle. S. A. Williams, Fred. R. Williams, Permanent Trustees. J. S. Richardson, Auctioneer." (*The Aegis & Intelligencer*, April 21, 1890, p. 2). "Notice to Creditors. Notice is hereby given to all creditors of George L. Van Bibber, an insolvent debtor, to file their claims, properly proven, with the Clerk of the Circuit Court for Harford county on or before the 1st day of March, 1891. S. A. Williams, Fred R. Williams, Permanent Trustee." (*The Aegis & Intelligencer*, August 29, 1890, p. 2). "All of the real and personal property of Mr. Geo. L. Van Bibber, of Bel Air, was sold at public sale, last Monday, under insolvency proceedings. His horse [sic] and seventeen acres of ground were bought by Mr. James Lee, for $2,500, subject to the wife's right of dower." (*Havre de Grace Republican*, Sept. 19, 1890, p. 3). **Genealogical Notes**: George Lindenberger Van Bibber, Jr., son of George Lindenberger Van Bibber (1814-1855) and Hannah Catherine Archer (1815-1906), was born on December 14, 1845 in Churchville, Harford Co., MD, married Adele Franklin (November 29, 1845 – December 5, 1921) in Beersheba Springs, TN on August 3, 1871, worked as an attorney in Bel Air, MD and died on October 5, 1911. The children of George and Adele Van Bibber were Dr. Armfield Franklin Van Bibber (1872-1953) married Susanna Rebecca Michael, Harriet Lewis Van Bibber (b. 1873) married Joseph Alexis Shriver, Lena Chew Van Bibber

(1875-1962), George Lindenberger Van Bibber III (b. 1878), and Claude Noel Van Bibber (b. 1881). (*Descendants of the Signers of the Bush Declaration of March 22, 1775, Harford County, Maryland*, by Christopher T. Smithson and Henry C. Peden, Jr., 2010, pp. 50-51)

Vandegrift, John, 1821. "I hereby certify that John Vandagrift [sic] is in my custody in the common jail of Harford County for debt and not for any breach of the penal laws of the State of Maryland or of the United States. Harford County, March 1st, 1821. Joshua Guyton, Sheriff." (Court Records Document 67.28.1(C) at the Historical Society of Harford County). "To John Norris, Esquire, Justice of the Orphans Court of Harford County. The petition of John Vandagrift [sic] of Harford County respectfully represents, that from circumstances not now within his controul [sic], he has been rendered totally unable to pay his debts, and reduced to the humiliating necessity of applying for the benefit of the insolvent law passed [in] November Session Eighteen hundred and five and the several supplements thereto. Your petitioner represents that he is now in confinement in the common jail of the County (as appears by the Certificate of the Sheriff accompanying his petition) for debt and not for any breach of the laws of this State or of the United States, and that he offers to deliver up all his property of whatever nature, kind or description, whether real, personal or mixed, to the use of his creditors, a list whereof is here exhibited upon oath, together with a list of his debts and creditors so far as he can ascertain them, and that he is prepared to prove his residence within this State for two years last before this his application he therefore prays that you will issue your order to the Sheriff of Harford County directing and commanding him to have your petitioner before you forth with or at such other time as to you shall seem meet [probably meant to write fit instead of meet] and that you will direct that your petitioner be released and discharged from confinement and the custody of the Sheriff aforesaid, and that you will be pleased to extend to your petitioner such other and further relief as is contained in the provisions of the insolvent laws aforesaid, and your petitioner will &c. March 2nd, 1821. John Vandegrift." (Court Records Document 67.28.1(E), loc. cit.; a schedule signed by "John Vandegrift" was included, but no property was listed; a copy of the newspaper clipping from the *Bond of Union and Weekly Advertiser* was also enclosed)."Petition, Schedule, Bond, Sheriff's certificate, personal discharge and order for publication filed 2nd March 1821 – 1st September 1821 petitioner appeared and the Court appointed James Herbert appointed Trustee and ordered that he give bond in the penalty of $1200." [nothing further recorded] (Insolvent Docket A, 1807-1843, p. 43, at the Maryland State Archives; Insolvent Docket Prior to 1827, Court Records Accession #632 at the Historical Society of Harford County). **Genealogical Note**: John Vandegrift married Mary Mitchell, daughter of John and Mary Mitchell, before 1811. (Harford County Estate Distribution in 1811; Court Records Document 64.09.5 dated in 1815 at the Historical Society of Harford County)

Varney (Vernay), Peter, 1825. John Clendinen vs. Mary Varney (widow of Peter Varney), Eleanor Varney, Jane Varney, Ann Varney, David Varney, John Varney, Mary Varney, Sarah Varney, Noellis Varney, Baily St. Clair and Elizabeth his wife, Sophia Varney, and Martha Varney, the heirs and representatives of the said Peter Varney, deceased. Bill of Complaint filed March 13, 1825 by John Clendinen who stated he was security for Peter Varney when he was Deputy Sheriff under Joshua Guyton, High Sheriff, in 1819, 1820 and 1821. At the end of that time said Varney was indebted to said Guyton who subsequently died, followed by the death of Peter Varney in 1824 intestate. As his security aforesaid Clendinen became liable to pay said monies to said Guyton. Clendinen filed for administration of the estate of Varney and it was granted by the Orphans Court, but the personal estate of Varney was insufficient to pay his debts, including the monies Varney owed to Guyton that Clendinen became responsible for paying. He requested that lands, being part of tracts called *Spittle Craft*, *Collins' First Shift*, *Addition to Bond's Gratuity* and *Orr's Survey*, situated near the Rocks of Deer

Creek and owned by Peter Varney, be sold to pay his debts. Clendinen also requested a guardian be appointed for minor children Sophia and Martha Varney. The Court passed an order on November 6, 1824 for all parties to appear. A subpoena was issued on March 12, 1825 and it was renewed on May 18, 1825. Summons for Walter Martin and wife Ann was subsequently issued on July 19, 1825 for them to appear, and also one for John Varney of Baltimore County. On August 12, 1825 Thomas A. Hays was assigned by the Court to appoint a guardian to the two minor Varney children aforesaid. The case was later continued until August Term 1826 and an order passed to summons Eleanor Varney, David Varney, Mary Varney Jr., Sarah Varney, Baily St. Clair and Elizabeth his wife, Noellis Lafayette Varney, Walter Martin and Ann his wife, formerly Varney, John Varney, and Israel Curry and Jane his wife, formerly Varney. Harry D. Gough had been appointed guardian for minor children Sophia and Martha Varney, both being under the age of 21 years. On August 24, 1826 all defendants present agreed with the facts as stated in the bill filed by John Clendinen in 1825. Ultimately the Court ordered Peter Varney's land to be sold for the benefit of his creditors and the sale was acknowledged on May 28, 1827, with the trustees reporting the amount of the sale was $1010. Yet, a subsequent objection was filed about the wording of the initial bill of complaint in which the land had not been properly described and the entitlement of the widow to her dowry had not been addressed. As a result, the parties in the case refused to give up possession of the said lands. A writ of *habere facias possession* was then issued on March 24, 1828, an injunction served on the defendants, and Clendinen prayed for a remedy. The Court ordered that the dower right of the widow Mary Varney be admeasured and that one-third of the lands be delivered to her and the case was finally resolved. (Harford County Equity Court Book HD No. 1, pp. 318-332). **Additional Genealogical Notes**: Peter Vernay was born circa 1765 and reportedly fought in France with Gen. Lafayette as aide de camp. He came to America, settled near Federal Hill in Harford County and married Mary Tate (1768 – July 29, 1838), daughter of John or David Tate, circa 1789. Of their children named above Elizabeth Vernay was born in 1790, Jane Vernay married Israel Curry (1784 – December 29, 1861) and died on May 31, 1879 in her 85th year, Eleanor Vernay married Joshua Amos, Elizabeth Vernay married Bailey St. Clair, Ann Vernay and Sarah Vernay remained single, John Vernay married Margaret A. Bayley, Mary Vernay married Samuel Murray, Noellis Lafayette Vernay married Michael Buckingham, Sarah Vernay was born on April 10, 1806 and died on April 22, 1881, Sophia Vernay married William Hollifield, Martha Vernay remained single and died on August 19, 1891 in her 81st year, and Daniel Vernay moved west. Mary Tate Vernay has a tombstone at Bethel Church, but not Peter Vernay because he went back to France for a visit in 1824, which happened to be the same year that Gen. Lafayette visited America, and he died while there. (Bethel Presbyterian Church Cemetery Records; Harford County Equity Court Book HD No. 1, p. 316; *Jarrettsville Past and Present*, compiled by the Bicentennial Committee, 1975-1976, p. 39)

Visage, James, 1816. "Petition, Schedule and Bond filed 28th Augt. 1816 and ordered that the petitioner be brought before the Court immediately – James Visage the petitioner having taken the necessary oath and given the satisfactory security it is here ordered that he be discharged from the custody of the Sheriff of Harford County and that he give the notice required by law ... Augt. 28th 1817 petitioner appeared ... Christopher Wilson appointed Trustee ... ordered by the Court that the petitioner be discharged from his debts ... certificate of trustee filed 10the Augt. 1818 and certificate of discharge granted petitioner same day." (Insolvent Docket A, 1807-1843, p. 18, at the Maryland State Archives; Insolvent Docket Prior to 1827, Court Records Accession #632 at the Historical Society of Harford County). **Genealogical Note**: James Visage married Susannah ---- some time before 1819. (Court Records Document 82.20.4 at the Historical Society of Harford County)

192

Wakeford, William H., 1895. "Mr. J. F. Boyd has filed a petition in insolvency against Wm. H. Wakeford, formerly manager of the flouring mills in this city." (*Havre de Grace Republican*, March 16, 1895, p. 3)

Walker, George F., 1891. "Trustee's Sale. By virtue of an order of the Circuit Court for Harford County, passed in the matter of the insolvency of George F. Walker, the undersigned, permanent trustee of said insolvent, will sell at Public Auction, at the Court House door, in Bel Air, on Saturday, January 17th, 1891, at 12 o'clock, M., All that Valuable Farm situate in the Third Election District of Harford County, whereon the said Geo. F. Walker now resides, containing 168 Acres, More or Less, adjoining the lands of John Winkler, John S. Young and others, and more particularly described in a deed from Susan E. Morrison and others to the said Geo. F. Walker, dated the 27th day of February in the year 1883, and recorded amongst the Land Records of Harford County in Liber A.L.J. No. 53, folio 299. This farm is about two miles from Bel Air, on the road leading to Emmorton, most desirably situated and highly improved. The improvements consist of a Large Frame Dwelling, in excellent order, Wagon House, Granary, stable with capacity for fourteen head horses and twelve head cattle, Barrack, also Two Tenant Houses, one double, the other single, Ice House, and other buildings. Stevenson A. Williams, Permanent Trustee." (*The Aegis & Intelligencer*, January 2, 1891, p. 2). "Trustee's Sale! In pursuance of an order of the Circuit Court for Harford County, the subscriber, permanent trustee of George F. Walker, an insolvent debtor, will sell at Public Auction, at the residence of said Walker, on the road leading from Bel Air to Abingdon, about two miles from the former place, on Friday, February 20th, 1891, Beginning at 10 o'clock, A. M., all the Personal Property belonging to the estate of said insolvent, consisting in part of 4 mules, 2 Work Mares, one Shoreham Driving Mare, 1 Plutus Driving Mare, one Cyclops Driving Horse, four years old; one Marshal Ney Colt, two years old; one Steve Bailey Colt, 2 years old; 2 Registered Holstein Cows, 1 Registered Holstein Bull, 2 years old; 1 Standard Holstein Calf, 8 weeks old; 1 Standard Holstein Heifer, one year old; 1 four-horse Wagon, 2 two-horse Wagons, two old Wagons, two Hay Carriages, 1 Stone Bed, 1 Roller, 1 Osborne Binder, 1 Osborne Mower, 1 Farmers' Friend Double Corn Planter, 1 Empire Bone Spreader, 1 Buckeye Wheat Drill, Wheat Fan, Corn Sheller, Cutting Box, 2 Sulky Cultivators, 2 Hinge Harrows, 1 A Harrow, Plows, Cultivators, Shovel Plows, Dayton Wagon and Pole, 1 Buggy, Double Trees, Log Chains, 2 sets Breeching Harness, 5 sets Plow Harness, 4 sets Lead Harness, 1 set Double Harness, Tomato Crates, Hay by the ton, Corn by the barrel, Corn Fodder, 1 Tare Beam, 500 feet Fencing Boards, 15 Posts for board fence, 60 White Oak Posts with 5 post-holes, 45 Oak Posts, not hewn, Also a lot of Canning House Fixtures, now in and about the canning-house recently occupied by said Walker, on the farm of Mr. Isaac Amos, at Emmorton, consisting in part of 1 Fisher Kettle, capacity 900 two-pound cans; 2 Warfield Corn Cutters, Corn Fan and Briner, 1 Stevens' Tomato Packer, one seven-horse Engine, 1 Steam Pump, lot of Pulleys, Belting and Piping, 6 large Crates, 2 Exhaust Crates, 2 Exhaust Tubs, 1 Scalding Tub, one Packing Table, lot Trays, 3 Hull Fire Pots, lot of Baskets and Buckets, Capping Irons, 1 Wheelbarrow, 1 five-ton Fairbanks' Scales, one 1,000 pounds Fairbanks' Scales, and various other articles. Also one Men's Shanty, 16 by 30 feet, and one large Husking Shed. S. A. Williams, Permanent Trustee. J. S. Richardson, Auctioneer." (*The Aegis & Intelligencer*, February 13, 1891, p. 2). **Genealogical Notes:** George F. Walker (June 11, 1837 – May 24, 1903, son of James T. Walker and Elizabeth Keen, lived near Perryman and married Laura H. Elliott (May 1, 1840 – June 8, 1921), daughter of William M. Elliott (1810-1882), of Bush River Neck, and Catharine A. M. Barron (1805-1889), of New Jersey, on November 27, 1862 by Rev. Dr. Frederick Swentzell at the bride's father's home. He served as county sheriff, 1883-1885, and was later employed at the Baltimore Custom House. (Harford Co. marriage license; 1850 Harford Co. Census mistakenly listed her as Laura H. Eliott, daughter of William M. Eliott, age 37, and Catharine

A. Eliott, age 41; *The Southern Aegis*, December 13, 1862; Baltimore *Sun*, December 1, 1862; St. Mary's Episcopal Church tombstones; *The Aegis & Intelligencer*, May 29, 1903, stated he died at the home of E. Stanley Patterson, his son-in-law, near Emmorton; Death certificates of George F. Walker and Laura H. Walker; *History of the Harford County Sheriff's Office*, by Terry A. Noye, 2006, pp. 14, 79, 81)

Walker, Jacob P., 1892. "Notice to Creditors. In the matter of the Insolvency of Jacob P. Walker ... In Pursuance of an order of Court passed in the above case on Dec. 29th, 1892, notice is hereby given to the creditors of the insolvent Jacob P. Walker, that the 13th day of February, 1893, has been fixed as the day when said Insolvent shall appear in the Circuit Court for Harford County and answer such interrogatories or allegations as his creditors, endorsers or sureties may propose or allege against him. Edwin H. Webster, of J., Permanent Trustee." (*The Aegis & Intelligencer*, January 20, 1893, p. 1). "Notice to Creditors ... The undersigned, as trustee, pursuant to an order of Court in the above case, passed December 29th, 1892, hereby gives notice to all persons having claims against Jacob P. Walker, as of the 14th of December last, to file their claims, properly proven, with the Clerk of the Circuit Court for Harford county, on or before the first day of April, 1893. Edwin H. Webster, of J., Permanent Trustee." (*The Aegis & Intelligencer*, January 20, 1893, p. 1). **Genealogical Notes**: Jacob Porter Walker, son of Robert Walker (1795-1865) and Catherine Hoopman (1801-1865), was born on July 15, 1840, married Rebecca Louisa Hoopman (1856-1946) on November 27, 1895 and died on February 24, 1934 at home in Havre de Grace. They are buried at Wesleyan Chapel (which was built by his grandfather Christian Hoopman). Their son M. Barrett Walker was an attorney in Baltimore. Jacob "was born at the old Walker homestead near Level in the Second District, and for many years was a prominent farmer and canner in that locality, known for his ability to raise unusually large crops." (*Barnes-Bailey Genealogy*, by Walter D. Barnes, 1939, pp. H-61; Wesleyan Chapel tombstone inscriptions; Harford County Death Certificate No. 01670; *The Aegis*, March 2, 1934)

Wallis, Randall, 1802. Petitioned for relief under the act for relief of sundry Insolvent Debtors (*Laws of Maryland*, Vol. III, 1802, Chapter 97, Liber JG No. 4, folio 308-314). **Genealogical Notes**: Randall Wallis was born in 1763, married Ann Worthington (1774-1846), a Quaker, on the 25th day of the 6th month 1795, after obtaining a marriage license on June 1, 1795, and died in 1822. Ann Wallis, late Worthington, "has gone out in her marriage to a man not in membership with assistance from a Baptist Teacher." (Deer Creek Friends Monthly Meeting Records and tombstone inscriptions)

Walton, Elijah, 1836. "Petition, Affidavits, Schedule, personal discharge and order of publication, Bond for Appearance, Trustee's Bond, Trustee's Certificate and Deed to Trustee filed 18th March 1836 ... [several petitions filed from 1836 through 1846; petitioner appears several times and the case was continued] ... 20 Nov 1847 Petitioner appears by W. B. Bond [attorney] & cont'd. with consent." [nothing further recorded] (Insolvent Docket A, 1807-1843, p. 146, at Maryland State Archives)

Ward, Charles, 1816. "Whereas we the subscribers Justices of the Peace for Harford County upon the petition of Charles Ward stating therein that he had been actually confined in the gaol [jail] of said county since the twelfth day of March last for debts which he was unable to pay and finding the facts therein stated to be true we did on the ninth day of May 1816 appoint the Eighth day of June then next to meet at the Courthouse of said county which said appointment we did there ... at the Request of the said Sheriff administer the above and annexed Oath to the said Charles Ward. Given under our hands and Seals this Eighth day of June Eighteen hundred and Sixteen. James Wallace, Jos. Robinson. On this 8th day of June 1816 personally appeared Charles Ward the Petitioner within named and made oath on the Holy Evangels of Almighty God that the Schedule which he hath delivered to the Sheriff of Harford County doth contain a full account to the best of my knowledge and Remembrance of his whole Estate both real and personal or that he has any title to or interest in and of all Debts, Credits and Effects whatsoever which he hath or any in Trust for him, have or at the time of his Petition had, or now or was in any respect entitled to in possession, Remainder or Reversion and that he hath not directly or indirectly at any time since his Imprisonment or before, sold, leased or otherwise conveyed or disposed of or Intrusted all or any part of his Estate, goods, stock, money or Debts thereby to defraud his Creditors or to secure the same to receive or expect any profit or advantage thereof. James Wallace. Jos. Robinson. (Court Records Document 67.12(3) at Historical Society of Harford County; a copy of the schedule to which he signed his name "Charles Ward" was included). **Genealogical Notes**: Charles Ward, son of Richard Ward (1755-1834) and Jane Smith, was born on January 19, 1791, married Elizabeth White circa June 14, 1832 (date of license) and died on August 15, 1865. The children of Charles and Elizabeth Ward were Sarah Ward, Charles Ward, Jr., Samuel Ward, and John S. Ward (1845-1868). (*Descendants of the Signers of the Bush Declaration of March 22, 1775, Harford County, Maryland*, by Christopher T. Smithson and Henry C. Peden, Jr., 2010, pp. 360, 362; Dublin United Methodist Church Cemetery tombstone inscriptions)

Ward, John S., 1899. Circuit Court cases set for trial in November term 1899 included "Insolvency case of John S. Ward, J. J. Archer for plaintiff. S. A. Williams for defence." (*The Aegis & Intelligencer*, November 17, 1899, p. 2). "On Wednesday [November 14, 1899] the insolvency case of John S. Ward was concluded, the prayers of the defendant, [Stephen J.] Seneca, being granted by the court. The claim of the plaintiff that 2,400 cases of canned goods had been delivered to said Seneca, within four months anterior to the insolvency, and therefore to the prejudice of the other creditors, was not substantiated." (*The Aegis & Intelligencer*, November 17, 1899, p. 2) **Genealogical Notes**: John S. Ward, son of Jarrett E. Ward (1802-1898) and Elizabeth Barnes (1823-1902), was born on March 24, 1859, married Margaret P. Gorrell (1866-1941) on April 26, 1893 and died on August 8, 1903 in Havre de Grace. (Death certificate of John S. Ward; Baltmore *Sun*, October 29, 1941, p. 20; Wesleyan Chapel Methodist Church tombstone inscriptions; Historial Society of Harford County cemetery files)

Wareham, John T., 1859. "Petition, Schedule of property, List of debts due & owing to & from, Affidavit, Order & Appointment of A. L. Jarrett, Esquire, Trustee, Trustee's Bond approved and Deed to Trustee filed 28th December 1858 … 28th August/59 Petition & order filed." [nothing further recorded] (Insolvent Docket A. L. J. No. 1, p. 25, in the Court Records Department of the Historical Society of Harford County). "Notice is hereby given that John T. Wareham, of Harford County, has made application to the Circuit Court of said County, for the benefit of the Insolvent Laws of Maryland, and that the 1st Saturday after the 4th Monday in April, 1859, has been assigned for him to appear in said Court to answer such interrogatories as his creditors may propose or allege against him. Wm. Galloway, Clerk, Circuit Court for Harford County." (*The Southern Aegis*, January 8, 1859, p. 3) "Trustee's Sale. The Undersigned, as Insolvent Trustee of John T. Wareham, will sell at public sale, on Wednesday, the 2nd Day of February next, at the residence of said Wareham, all the Personal Property conveyed to him by said Insolvent, consisting of Corn, Wheat, Mill Feed and a Wheat Fan. Sale to take place at 12 o'clock M., A. L. Jarrett, Trustee." (*The Southern Aegis*, January 22, 1859, p. 2) "In the matter of the petition of John T. Wareham for the benefit of the Insolvent Laws. In the Circuit Court for Harford County, August Term, 1849 [1859]. Ordered that the Creditors of the above named Insolvent, file their claims with the Auditor of this Court on or before the 1st day of October next, provided a copy of this order be published in some newspaper printed and published in said County, for three successive weeks before the 10th day of September next. John H. Price. True copy. Test: Wm. Galloway, Clk." (*The Southern Aegis*, August 13, 1859, p. 3) "In the matter of the insolvency of John T. Wareham ... Upon the Petition of John T. Wareham, an Insolvent debtor, it is Ordered that said Insolvent appear in the Circuit Court for Harford county on the 2nd Monday of November next, to answer such interrogatories or allegations as his creditors, endorsers or securities may propose or allege against him, and that he give at least four successive weeks notice thereof to his creditors by publication of this order in some newspaper printed in Harford county, the first publication to be at least two months before the day so appointed for his appearance. John H. Price. True copy. Test: Wm. Galloway, Clk." (*The Southern Aegis*, September 3, 1859, p. 3). **Genealogical Notes**: John T. Wareham married Miss Susan E. Keen on July 6, 1853 at Abingdon by Rev. T. S. C. Smith [who was pastor of Bethel Presbyterian Church at Madonna near Jarrettsville]. (Harford Co. license; Baltimore *Sun*, July 7, 1853; *The Harford Madisonian*, July 7, 1853, mistakenly listed his name as George T. Wareham)

Washington, Amos N. (African American), 1890. "Amos N. Washington, colored, has made application for the benefit of the Insolvent Law. Mr. W. Beatty Harlan has been appointed preliminary trustee." (*The Aegis & Intelligencer*, March 14, 1890, p. 2; *Havre de Grace Republican*, March 21, 1890, p. 2, added that he was a well-known colored man of the second district)

Watkins, Tobias, 1806. "Harford County Court. Ordered on the petition of Tobias Watkins, an Insolvent debtor in actual confinement under an execution founded on a Judgment obtained against him in the name of Adam Whan for a debt due before the passage of the act entitled 'An act for the relief of Sundry Insolvent debtors' passed at the last General Assembly, that the Sheriff of Harford County in whose Custody he is, discharge the said Tobias Watkins he having given bond with approved Security for his appearance to answer the interrogatories of his Creditors." (Court Records Document 67.27.1(k) [unsigned and undated; filed June 3, 1806] and there is additional information in Court Actions on Insolvencies, 1805-1807, Court Records Accession #605 at the Historical Society of Harford County). "Schedule of the property of the petitioner, real, personal & mixed – One house & Lot whereon the petitioner resides in Havre de Grace under mortgage & subject to --?-- [illegible] of purchase money, One unimproved Lot in Do., One Negro boy aged about 12 yrs. [and] One Negro girl aged about 3 years } both in Baltimore concealed(?) by the father – George Cook, 1 Carpet, 1 Doz. Windsor chairs, 2 Tables, 2 pr. candlesticks, 1 large looking glass, 2 small Do., 1 Franklin stove, 1 Oplate(?) stove, 30 volumes of books, 1 Pine book case & table, 1 case Medicine drawers, 2½ Doz. Double flint glass bottles, a quantity of medicine, 1 Chariot, 1 horse and 2 cows" (Court Records Document 67.27.1(m) was not dated and not signed by petitioner). Letter dated March 17, 1806 from John W. Pratt, of Washington, addressed to Dr. Tobias Watkins, of Havre de Grace, MD, letter dated April 9, 1806 from Adam Whann, of Elkton, MD, addressed to Dr. Tobias Watkins, of Havre de Grace, MD, and a copy of a newspaper notice published in the *Philadelphia Register* is among other documents contained in this file at the Historical Society of Harford County). **Genealogical Note**: Tobias Watkins married Mary ---- by 1803 and their son William Henry Watkins was born on April 8, 1804. (St. George's P. E. Parish Register)

Watt, Joseph, 1816. "Petition, Schedule & Bond filed 14th March 1816 … ordered by the Court that he give notice in one of the Baltimore papers once a week for three months previous to the first Thursday of next Augt. term. Certificate of notice filed." [nothing further recorded] (Insolvent Docket A, 1807-1843, p. 16, at the Maryland State Archives; Insolvent Docket Prior to 1827, Court Records Accession #632 at the Historical Society of Harford County). **Genealogical Note**: This may be the Joseph Watt, son of Robert Watt and Sarah Streett, who married Mary Hitchcock circa September 7, 1817 (license date). (*The Whiteford Genealogy*, by Hazel Whiteford Baldwin, 1992, p. 344)

Watters, A. S., 1891. "Mordecai S. Scarborough and A. S. Watters, insolvent debtors, were finally discharged." (*Havre de Grace Republican*, November 13, 1891, p. 2)

Watters, Abner, 1817. "Whereas we the subscribers Justices of the Peace for Harford County upon the petition of Abner Watters setting forth therein that he had actually been confined in the jail of said County since the 21st day of April last for debts which he is unable to pay and finding the facts therein stated to be true we did meet at the jail of said County on the twelfth day May last and did then and there appoint the thirteenth day of June instant to meet at the Court house of said county, which said appointment we did then and there … at the request of said Sheriff administer to the said Abner Watters the following oath which was taken by the said Abner Watters being first duly sworn on the Holy Evangely of Almighty God in the words following to wit, I Abner Watters do solemnly promise and swear that the Schedule which I have delivered to the Sheriff of Harford county doth contain a full account to the best of my knowledge and remembrance of my whole estate both real and personal or that I have any title to or interest in, and of all debts, credits and effects whatsoever which I or any in trust for me have or at the time of my petition had, or am or was in any respect entitled to in possession, remainder or reversion and that I have not directly or indirectly at any time since my imprisonment or before, sold, leased or otherwise conveyed or disposed of or intrusted all or any part of my estate, goods, stock, money or debts thereby to defraud my creditors or to secure the same to receive or expect any profit or advantage thereof so help me God, which said duplicate of the Schedule aforesaid we have transmitted to the clerk of the county court to be by him preserved in his office for the information of the creditors of the said Abner Watters. Given under our hands and seals this thirteenth day of June 1817. James Wallace. Joseph Robinson. Benjamin Richardson." (Court Records Document 67.12(4) at Historical Society of Harford County; a copy of the schedule to which he signed his name "Abnor Waters" was included)

Watters, Robert A., 1840. "1st September. Petition, Schedule, Affidavits, personal discharge and order of publication, Bond for Appearance, Trustee's Bond, Trustee's Certificate and Deed to Trustee filed. 21st Novr. 1840 Allegations filed. 22nd May 1841 Certificate of Publication filed, Petitioner appears. 25th May 1841 Petitioner appears & cont'd. Novr. 20th 1841 Petitioner appears and Judge Archer withdrew from the bench – the petitioner examined upon oath – Petitioner finally discharged." (Insolvent Docket A, 1807-1843, p. 174, at Maryland State Archives). **Genealogical Note**: Robert A. Watters married Elizabeth Harlan (died June 28, 1880 in her 59th year) circa February 21, 1846 (date of license) and died March 3, 1885 in his 70th year. (Fallston United Methodist Church tombstones)

Watters, William, 1811. "Petition, Schedule, Bond, and Notice to Creditors filed 2nd April 1811. Objections filed. Augt. 20th 1811 the petitioner appeared and with leave of the Court withdrew his petition." (Insolvent Docket A, 1807-1843, p. 10, at the Maryland State Archives; Insolvent Docket Prior to 1827, Court Records Accession #632 at the Historical Society of Harford County). 1823. "Petition, Schedule, certificate of residence, Shff's certificate, bond, personal discharge and order for publication filed 16th July 1823. 13th March 1824 Petitioner appears and files a certificate of publication of notice, and ordered that he be discharged. Nathaniel W. S. Hays appointed Trustee March 20th 1826 ordered by the Court that the trustee give bond with security." [nothing further recorded] (Insolvent Docket A, 1807-1843, p. 57, at the Maryland State Archives; Insolvent Docket Prior to 1827, Court Records Accession #632 at the Historical Society of Harford County). **Genealogical Note**: There were two men named William Watters at this time: one married Elizabeth Brown circa July 1, 1799 (date of license) and the other married Sarah Wilson circa April 14, 1808 (date of license).

Way, Samuel, 1825. "Petition, Schedule, Bond, Shffs Certificate and personal discharge and order for publication filed 13th July 1825. Printer's Certificate of publication filed on the 16th March 1826. Petitioner appears." [nothing further recorded] (Insolvent Docket A, 1807-1843, p. 71, at the Maryland State Archives; Insolvent Docket Prior to 1827, Court Records Accession #632 at the Historical Society of Harford County). **Genealogical Note**: Samuel Way married Mary Smith circa May 8, 1821 (date of license).

Webb, Samuel, 1841. "Petition, 2 Affidavits, 3 Schedules, Appointment of Trustee, Certificate, Order, Personal Discharge, Appearance Bond, Deed and Trustee's Bond filed 29th June 1841. 20th Novr. 1841 Petitioner appears & files Certificate & finally discharged." (Insolvent Docket A, 1807-1843, p. 177, at the Maryland State Archives). **Genealogical Note**: There were two men named Samuel Webb at this time: one married Belinda ---- by 1790 and their son Isaac Webb was born on June 2, 1791 (St. James P. E. Parish Register) and the other married Elizabeth Dawney circa July 7, 1814 (date of license).

Webster, Isaac, 1804. "Whereas we the subscribers Justices of the Peace for Harford County upon the petition of Isaac Webster who set forth therein that he had been confined in the gaol [jail] of said county for debts which he was unable to pay and finding the facts stated to be true we did meet at the county gaol of the said county on the 11th day of September 1804 and did then and there appoint the 12th day of October Instant to meet at the Court House of said county which said appointment we did then and there … at the request of the said sheriff administer to the said Isaac Webster the following oath or affirmation which was taken by the said Isaac Webster being first duly affirmed according to law in the words following, I Isaac Webster do solemnly, sincerely and truly declare and affirm that the schedule which I have delivered to the Sheriff of Harford County doth contain a full account to the best of my knowledge and remembrance of my whole estate both real and personal or that I have any title to or interest in and of all debts, credits & effects whatsoever which I or any in trust for me have or at the time of my petition had, or am or was in any respect entitled to in possession, remainder or reversion and that I have not directly or indirectly at any time since my imprisonment or before, sold, leased or otherwise conveyed or disposed of or intrusted all or any part of my estate, goods, stock, money or debts thereby to defraud my creditors or to secure the same to receive or expect any profit or advantage thereof so help me God, which said duplicate of the schedule aforesaid we have transmitted to the clerk of the county court to be by him Preserved in his Office for the information of the Creditors of the said Isaac Webster – Given under our hands & seals this 12th day of October 1804. John Moores. Wm. Smithson. Thos. A. Hays." (Court Records Documents 67.02.1(A)(B) at the Historical Society of Harford County; a copy of the schedule was included to which "Isaac Webster" signed his name, but no property was listed). **Genealogical Note**: There were four men with this name at this time, but since the aforementioned Isaac Webster affirmed, rather then swore to the holy evangels of almighty God, this would indicate he was a Quaker; therefore, he would be the Isaac Webster, of Harford Co., who married Elizabeth Hopkins, daughter of Samuel and Sarah Hopkins, of Baltimore Co., on the 12th day of the 4th month 1799 at the Baltimore Monthly Meeting, having obtained a certificate from Deer Creek Monthly Meeting in Darlington to accomplish his marriage in Baltimore City. (*Quaker Records of Northern Maryland, 1716-1800*, by Henry C. Peden, Jr., M.A., 1993, pp. 160, 214)

Webster, John W., 1851. "Petition &c. 17th Feby/51 … 22nd March/51 Order of Sale filed. [* see below] May/52 … Judgment for Petitioner. Agreement & Order of final Discharge filed." (Insolvent Docket A.L.J. No. 1, p. 3, in Court Records Department of the Historical Society of Harford County). [* insert above] "William T. Watters & Charles Harvey vs. John W. Webster … 19th May/51 Judgt. confessed for $400, subject to defendant's application for the benefit of insolvent laws …" (Judgment Docket 1846-1850, p. 80, Court Records Accession #187 at the Historical Society of Harford County) **Genealogical Notes**: John Wesley Webster, son of Henry Webster (1793-1872) and Martha Hanson (1796-1850), was born on September 22, 1819 at Webster's Forest, Harford County, married Priscilla Frances Smithson (1821-1919), daughter of William Smithson (1779-1836) and Margaret Hall Lee (1782-1858), on December 2, 1844 and died on June 23, 1872 at Bald Hill, Harford County. Their children were Mary Priscilla Webster (1845-1850), John Ann Webster (1847-1850), Anna Mary Webster (1851-1918), Henry Webster (1855-1939), John Wesley Webster (1857-1916), Edwin Hanson Webster (1859-1929), Benjamin Franklin Webster (1862-1947), and William Webster (1865-1923). (*Maryland Bible Records, Volume 2*, by Henry C. Peden, Jr., 2014, p. 172; Death certificate of Priscilla F.

Webster; Calvary Methodist Church cemetery tombstones; Historical Society of Harford County cemetery files; Research by Christopher T. Smithson, of Darlington, MD, 2019)

Webster, Samuel, of Isaac, 1804. "Whereas we the Subscribers Justices of the Peace for Harford County upon the petition of John Wilson, who set forth that he had been confined in the Gaol [jail] of the said county twenty Days for Debts which he was unable to pay & finding the facts stated to be true we together did meet at the County Gaol on the 17th day of April 1804 and did then and there appoint the 18th day of May Inst. to meet at the Court House of said county which said appointment we did then and there ... at the request of the said Sheriff administer to the said Samuel Webster, of Isaac, the following oath which was taken by the said Samuel Webster, of Isaac, being first duly sworn on the holy evangels of almighty God in the words following, I Samuel Webster, of Isaac, do solemnly swear that the schedule which I have delivered to the Sheriff of Harford County doth contain a full account to the best of my knowledge and remembrance of my whole estate both real and personal or that I have any title to or interest in and of all debts, credits & effects whatsoever which I or any in trust for me have or at the time of my petition had, or am or was in any respect entitled to in possession, remainder or reversion & that I have not directly or indirectly at any time since my imprisonment or before, sold, leased or otherwise conveyed or disposed of or intrusted all or any part of my estate, goods, stock, money or debts thereby to defraud my creditors or to secure the same to receive or expect any profit or advantage thereof so help me God, which said duplicate of the schedule aforesaid we have transmitted to the clerk of the county court to be by him preserved in his office for the information of the creditors of the said Samuel Webster, of Isaac. Given under our hands & seals this 18th day of May 1804. James Amos. John Moores. Wm. Smithson." (Court Records Document 67.26.3(c) at the Historical Society of Harford County; a copy of the schedule to which "Samuel Webster, (of Isaac" [sic] signed his name was included, but no property was listed), **Genealogical Notes**: Samuel Webster, of Isaac, was a Quaker until he was charged on the 27th day of the 11th month 1794 "with fornication and marrying by the assistance of a hireling teacher." This would explain why he swore rather than affirmed when he took the oath in 1804. (*Quaker Records of Northern Maryland, 1716-1800*, by Henry C. Peden, Jr., M.A., 1993, p. 154)

Weeks, Benjamin, 1857. "Petition, Schedules, Affidavits, Appointment of Trustee & order of notice, Trustee's Bond & deed filed 9 May 1857. 15th May 1858 Petitioner appears, files certificate of publication & discharged." (Insolvent Docket A. L. J. No. 1, p. 16, in the Court Records Department of the Historical Society of Harford County). "Notice is hereby given that Benjamin Weeks, of Harford County, has made application to the Circuit Court of said County, for the benefit of the Insolvent Laws of Maryland, and that the first Saturday after the second Monday in May, 1858, has been assigned for him to appear in said Court to answer such interrogatories as his creditors may propose or allege against him. Wm. Galloway, Clerk of Circuit Court for Harford County." (*The Southern Aegis*, December 19, 1857, Vol. I, No. 24, p. 185)

Welch, William, 1812. "Petition & Schedule filed 26th Augt. 1812, bond filed Augt. 27th 1812 ... Court appoints William D. Lee trustee, the petitioner to give notice in the usual manner" [nothing further recorded]. (Insolvent Docket A, 1807-1843, p. 13, at the Maryland State Archives; Insolvent Docket Prior to 1827, Court Records Accession #632 at the Historical Society of Harford County). **Genealogical Note**: William Welch married Elizabeth Horton, sister of Edward W. Horton, circa 29 Jul 1794 (date of license). (*Maryland Genealogical Society Bulletin*, Volume 36, No. 1, 1995, p. 29)

Wells, James, 1828. "Petition, Schedule, Affidavit, Certificate, Bond, Deed, Trustee's Bond, Trustee's Certificate, Discharge and Order of Publication filed 26th Novr. 1828. 14th March 1829 Notice to Creditors filed. Petitioner appeared in Court and discharged." (Insolvent Docket A, 1807-1843, p. 91, at the Maryland State Archives). **Genealogical Note:** James Wells married Eleanora ---- by 1805 (Ward-Wells family records show daughter Sarah born circa 1805; Baltimore *Sun*, August 21, 1863)

Wells, Joseph, 1884. "November 24th 1884. Petition in Insolvency Affidavit & Order of Court thereon filed … [several claims and notices filed in 1884] … 1/85 Order of Court dismissing petition filed." [nothing further recorded] (Insolvent Docket A. L. J. No. 1, p. 94, in the Court Records Department of the Historical Society of Harford County).

Wernweg, Lewis, 1821. "Petition, Schedule, Bond, [Sheriff's] Certificate, personal discharge and order for publication filed [on] 13 November 1821. 16th March 1822 petitioner appeared, certificate of publication filed, John Forwood appointed Trustee and ordered that the petitioner be discharged." (Insolvent Docket A, 1807-1843, p. 47, at Maryland State Archives; Insolvent Docket Prior to 1827, Court Records Accession #632 at the Historical Society of Harford County). **Genealogical Notes:** Lewis Wernweg (1769-1843) was a civil engineer from Wurtemberg, Germany who immigrated to America in 1786 and moved to the town of Conowingo in Cecil County in 1819 to work on the Conowingo Bridge. He was also involved in rebuilding the Rock Run Bridge over the Susquehanna River in 1830-1831. ("Abstracts of the Minutes of the Susquehanna Bridge and Bank Co., 1815-1831, in the Col. Benjamin Silver Collection at the Historical Society of Harford County; *Timber Bridges: Covered and Uncovered*, by Jack L. Shagena, Jr. and Henry C. Peden, Jr., 2010, pp. 55-56)

West, David, 1808. "Petition, Schedule, Bond, &c. filed the 26th July 1808." [nothing further recorded]. (Insolvent Docket A, 1807-1843, p. 3, at the Maryland State Archives; Insolvent Docket Prior to 1827, Court Records Accession #632 at the Historical Society of Harford County)

West, Samuel, 1824. "Petition, Bond, Schedule, Sheriffs Certificate and Personal Discharge and order for Publication filed 10th August 1824. 19th March 1825 Printers Certificate filed and petitioner appears and is discharged." (Insolvent Docket A, 1807-1843, p. 66, at the Maryland State Archives; Insolvent Docket Prior to 1827, Court Records Accession #632 at the Historical Society of Harford County). **Genealogical Note:** He may have been the Samuel West who married Catherine Mason circa January 6, 1824 (date of license).

Westfall, Edward, 1885. "Proceedings of the Commissioners. The collector for the 3rd district was instructed to return the taxes of Edward Westfall as insolvent." (*Havre de Grace Republican*, May 1, 1885, p. 1). **Genealogical Notes:** Edward Westfall was born circa 1846 in Prussia, worked as a carpenter, married Mary ---- (born circa 1835, Prussia) circa 1868 and their son Edward Westfall, Jr. was one year old in 1870 and he was born in Maryland. (1870 Harford Co. Census, 3rd District)

Wetherill, Solomon S., 1879. "Petition, Schedules, Appointment of Trustee, Order of appearance, Deed & Trustee's Bond filed 12th February 1879 … 15th September 1879 Petitioner finally discharged … [but later stated] … 15th May 1880 Petitioner appears, files Certificate of Publication & final discharge granted … [also mentioned several claims filed by various individuals through 1880] … Recorded in Judgment Record Liber H. D. G. No. 2, folio 229." (Insolvent Docket A. L. J. No. 1, p. 62, in Court Records Department of the Historical Society of Harford County). "Insolvent Notice. Notice is hereby given, that Solomon S. Wetherill, of Harford county, has made application to the Circuit Court for said county for the benefit of the Insolvent Laws of Maryland, and that the second Monday of September, 1879, has been assigned for him to appear and answer such interrogatories as his creditors may propose or allege against him. A. Lingan Jarrett, Clerk, Circuit Court for Harford Co." (*Harford Democrat*, February 14, 1879, p. 2). "Trustee's Sale. In virtue of an order of the Circuit Court for Harford county, in the matter of the insolvency of Solomon S. Wetherill, the undersigned, as Trustee, will offer at Public Sale, on the premises, near Jarrettsville, in said county, where said Wetherill now resides, on Wednesday, March 26, 1879, at 10 o'clock, A. M., the following Property! To wit: All that Tract or Parcel of Land composed of part of tract of land called *Glady Ground* containing 128 Acres, More or Less, particularly described in a deed of mortgage from Solomon S. Wetherill to Priscilla Worthington, which mortgage is recorded in Liber A. L. J. No. 26, folio 17, one of the Land Records of Harford county, which tract will be offered in two parcels: The first, containing 25 acres, which lies south of Cooptown and Baltimore road; and second, containing 103 acres, on north side of said road. The first tract is well fenced and in good state of cultivation. The second tract is improved by [a] comfortable Brick Dwelling House, and good new frame Barn and other outbuildings; is well watered and fenced. Also the following Personal Property: Three horses, 5 cows, 2 Sows, one with pigs; Farm Wagon and Bed, light Spring Wagon, 1 two horse Carriage, one two horse Sleigh and Bells, Wheelbarrow, Plow, 1 two and 1 three horse Hinge Harrow, Double and Single Shovel Plows, Cultivators, Horse Power and Threshing Machine, World Mowing Machine, Hay Carriage, Bark Carriage, Double and Single Trees, Wagon & Carriage Harness, Plow Harness, Wagon Saddle, Bridles and Collars, Riding Bridle, Grain Cradles, Horse Rake, Post Digger, Forks, Rakes, Hoes, Shovels, Mattock, Barrels and Boxes, Clover Hay, Wheat and Oat Straw, Corn Fodder, Oats by the bushel, Corn by the barrel, 2 hives of Bees, ⅝ Walnut Boards, 1¼ Whiteoak Plank, Horse Blankets, 15 acres of Wheat in the ground, 3 acres of Rye in the ground, 1 Coat Stove, Tables, Settee, Chairs, Clock, Pots and Jars, Pots and Buckets, lot Dairy Fixtures, Butter Tub, Cream Can, Tin Milk Pans and various other articles." (*Harford Democrat*, February 28, 1879, p. 2) **Genealogical Notes**: Solomon S. Wetherill was born on October 31, 1824 in Bucks Co., PA, married Jane V. Johnson (1825-1876) probably circa 1850 and died on December 9, 1895 in Baltimore City. They had a son Alfred J. Wetherill (1866-1872) who died young and no children were mentioned in Solomon's obituary. (*The Aegis & Intelligencer*, December 13, 1895, p. 3; Historical Society of Harford County cemetery files)

Whann, Samuel, 1856. "Petition, Schedules, Affidavits, Appointment of Trustee (A. W. Bateman)," etc., 7 April 1856. "18th Novr. 1856 Petitioner appears, files certificate of publication to creditors & finally discharged." (Insolvent Docket A. L. J. No. 1, p. 12, in the Court Records Department of the Historical Society of Harford County) "Notice is hereby given that Samuel Whann, of Harford County, has made application to the Circuit Court of said County, for the benefit of the Insolvent Laws of Maryland, and that the first Tuesday of November term, 1856, has been assigned for him to appear in said Court to answer such interrogatories as his creditors may propose or allege against him. A. Lingan Jarrett, Clerk." (*Harford Democrat*, April 11, 1856, p. 3). **Genealogical Notes**: Samuel Whann, a shoemaker and widower), age 51 (or 57?), married Sarah E. Flaharty (widow), age 28, on November 25, 1869 by Rev. George M. Berry at the home of Samuel Whann (Harford Co. license and marriage certificate; *The Aegis & Intelligencer*, December 17, 1869)

Wheeler, Benjamin, 1813. "Whereas we the Subscribers, Justices of the Peace for Harford County upon the petition of Benjamin Wheeler setting forth therein that he had actually remained in the Goal [jail] of said County since the seventh day of September last for debts which he was unable to pay and finding the facts therein stated to be true we did meet at the Goal of said County on the first day of October instant and did then and there appoint the 27th day of October inst. to meet at the Court house of said County, which said appointment we did then and there … at the request of the said Sheriff administer to the said Benjamin Wheeler the following oath which was taken by the said Benjamin Wheeler being first duly sworn on the Holy Evangels of Almighty God in the words following to wit, I do solemnly promise and swear that the schedule which I have delivered to the Sheriff of Harford County doth contain a full account to the best of my knowledge and remembrance of my whole estate both real and personal or that I have any title to or interest in, and of all debts, credits and effects whatsoever which I or any in trust for me have or at the time of my petition had, or am or was in any respect entitled to in possession, remainder or reversion and that I have not directly or indirectly at any time since my imprisonment or before, sold, leased or otherwise conveyed or disposed of or intrusted all or any part of my estate, goods, stock, money or debts thereby to defraud my creditors or to secure the same to receive or expect any profit or advantage thereof so help me God, which said duplicate of the Schedule aforesaid we have transmitted to the Clerk of the County Court to be by him preserved in his office for the information of the creditors of the said Benjamin Wheeler. Given under our hands and seals this twenty-seventh day of October 1813. Saml. Bradford. John Guyton." (Court Records Document 67.24.1(A) at the Historical Society of Harford County; a copy of the schedule to which he signed his name "Benj. Wheeler" was included, but no property was listed). **Genealogical Notes**: Benjamin Wheeler, son of Thomas and Elizabeth Wheeler, married Elizabeth Green (1761-1802), daughter of Benjamin and Elizabeth Green, circa February 4, 1793 (date of license). (*History of the Wheeler Family in America*, by Albert Gallatin Wheeler, 1914 p. 528, states he was born in 1731 and his first wife was Mary Neal)

Wheeler, Bennett, 1805. To the Honorable the Judges of Harford County to wit. The petitioner Bennett [sic] Wheeler sheweth that your petitioner at November Session Eighteen hundred and five applied to the Legislature of Maryland for an Act of Insolvency, that he was included in the law for the relief of sundry Insolvent Debtors, that your petitioner has hereto annexed a schedule of his property which he is willing and ready to deliver up to the use and for the benefit of his creditors, that he has likewise hereto annexed a list of his creditors and debtors on oath as far as he can ascertain them as the law required. He therefore prays your Honors to extend to him the benefit of the act passed at November Session 1805 for the relief of Insolvent Debtors and he as in duty bound will pray &c. [signed] Bennet Wheeler." (Court Records Document 67.24.1(c) at the Historical Society of Harford County). "A Schedule of Bennet Wheeler's property as given in by him to the Judges of Harford County Court: part of *Wheeler's & Clark's Contrivance* in dispute contg. 100 acres, 40 acres of land lying in Harford County; part of *Benjamin's Camp*, pt. of *Pearson's Range*, part of *Brotherly Love*, part of *Children's Rolung House*, Subject to Mortgage & Sale under Chancellors Decree but now in dispute; 1 negro woman named Nan, 1 negro girl named Rachel, 1 negro boy named Joe, one colt, Subject to a Bill of Sale to Delaporte; and, 1 negro woman named Sarah, 1 negro man named Robin, 1 dining table, 1 breakfast ditto, 1 tea do., 2 large spinning wheels, 2 small do., I iron pot rack, 2 flatt irons, 1 wash stand, 4 chests, 8 cyder Hogsheads, 4 sixtys, 2 ploughs, 10 bushels of lime, 1 crosscut saw, 7 or 8 shoots, 5 harrow teeth" … [also] debts due Bennet Wheeler [from] Isaac Emmons (New Jersey suit now pending) and the Estate of Ignatius Wheeler (about $200), plus a long list of Bennet Wheeler's creditors. (Court Records Document 67.24.2(B), loc. cit.) "June 3, 1806. We the Subscribers, Creditors of Bennett Wheeler, an applicant for the benefit of the 'Act for the relief of Sundry Insolvent Debtors' do assent to his obtaining the benefit of said law. [signed by] John Reardon, James Wallace, Michl. McElhiney, Joseph Johnson, Edwd. W. Norton, Saml. Jay, Jos. Wheeler, Edwd. Prigg, Jno. Johnston, Ro. [Robert] Morgan, Frs. [Francis] Delaporte." Last entry in book: "Postponed until Saturday the 23rd August, 1806." (Court Records Document 67.24.2(D) and Court Actions in Insolvencies, 1805-1807, Court Records Accession #605, both at the Historical Society of Harford County). 1807. "Petition and Schedule filed 19th August 1807. Assent of Creditors filed and ordered that notice be given three months prior to the Saturday after the second Monday of March next in the [Baltimore] American … March 19th 1908 Petition Withdrawn." (Insolvent Docket A, 1807-1843, p. 7, at the Maryland State Archives; Insolvent Docket Prior to 1827, Court Records Accession #632 at the Historical Society of Harford County). 1810. "Notice. I shall apply to the Judges of Harford county court, at their next session, for the benefit of the Act of Assembly of the state of Maryland, for the relief of sundry insolvent debtors, passed at November session, eighteen hundred and five, and the acts supplementary hereto. Bennet Wheeler. June 15." [same notice was inserted in the *Baltimore American* beginning June 16, 1810]. "I do hereby certify that the annexed advertisement Signed [by]

Bennet Wheeler giving notice to his creditors of his intention to apply to Harford County Court for the benefit of the insolvent Laws of the State of Maryland, was duly inserted in the Baltimore Evening Post once a week for Eight successive weeks. Given Under my Hand at the City of Baltimore this fifteenth day of August 1810. H. Niles." (Court Records Document 67.24.2(C) at the Historical Society of Harford County; copies of the newspaper notices were clipped and included in the file). Under a $2000 bond Henry McAtee was appointed trustee on August 22, 1810 and the Court subsequently ordered that Wheeler be discharged from his debts [no date given]. (Insolvent Docket A, 1807-1843, p. 7, at the Maryland State Archives; Insolvent Docket Prior to 1827, Court Records Accession #632 at the Historical Society of Harford County). **Genealogical Notes**: Bennett Wheeler, son of Ignatius Wheeler and Elizabeth Rosier, was born circa 1745-1750 and never married. "Bennett Wheeler was apparently a poor manager. He mortgaged his lands, sold off his slaves and was involved in many court actions … In 1803 Bennett Wheeler filed a complaint in Chancery Court vs. Francis Ignatius Mitchell, his nephew. The complaint 'sheweth' that Bennett Wheeler mortgaged some land and slaves to Mitchell in order to secure a debt. The said Mitchell proceeded to exercise his rights and took away a number of negros [sic] and cattle and sold them to others. (Chancery Papers 5751). In 1796 Bennett Wheeler mortgaged to Samuel Lee two tracts called *Benjamin's Camp* and *Wheeler's and Clark's Contrivance*, 1,000 acres. Evidently he did not pay the mortgage as fore-closure was made and part of Bennett's land was sold by the sheriff. In 1807 Bennett protested the sale, claiming Francis Wheeler was the high bidder but the trustees would not accept his bid as he could not furnish the required bond, In Dec. 1808 Edward F. Bussey petitioned the court to force Bennett Wheeler to vacate the lands sold to said Bussey. (Chancery Papers 3097)." Bennett Wheeler apparently died between 1810 and 1820 since he did not appear in the 1820 Harford County census.

Wheeler, Francis I., 1829. "Petition, Schedule, Shff. Certificate, personal discharge, [and] Order for Publication, Bond for Appearance, Trustee's Certificate, Trustee's Bond and Deed to Trustee filed 30th Octr. 1829. Petitioner appeared on the 13th March 1830 and cont'd." [nothing further recorded] (Insolvent Docket A, 1807-1843, p. 100, at Maryland State Archives). **Genealogical Notes**: Francis Ignatius "Frank" Wheeler, son of Ignatius Wheeler and Henrietta Maria (Neale) Smith, was born in 1782, married Mary Ann Macatee (1782-1855), daughter of George and Elizabeth Macatee, circa July 4, 1814 (date of license which mistakenly gave his name as Francis A. Wheeler) and died in 1863. (*History of the Wheeler Family in America*, by Albert Gallatin Wheeler, Jr., 1914, p. 530; "Macatee (McAtee) Family" manuscript in The Henry C. Peden, Jr. Research Library at the Historical Society of Harford County)

Wheeler, Henrietta, 1816. "Petition, Schedule & Bond filed 14th March 1816 … ordered by the Court that she give notice to her creditors in one of the Balt. papers once a week for three months previous to next August Term. Aug. 31st 1816 the petitioner appeared and term of publication extended until the first Thursday of next March term." [nothing further recorded] (Insolvent Docket A, 1807-1843, p. 16, at the Maryland State Archives; Insolvent Docket Prior to 1827, Court Records Accession #632 at the Historical Society of Harford County)

Wheeler, James B., 1819. "Petition, Schedule, Bond, Order for publication, Sheriff's certificate and personal discharge filed 16th August 1819 – Augt. 28th 1819 petitioner appeared and prays leave to withdraw his petition. Petition withdrawn. April 25th 1820 papers d'd. Jas. B. Wheeler." (Insolvent Docket A, 1807-1843, p. 31, at the Maryland State Archives; Insolvent Docket Prior to 1827, Court Records Accession #632 at the Historical Society of Harford County). 1820. "I hereby certify that James B. Wheeler is in my custody in the common jail of Harford county for debt and not for any breach of the law of the State of Maryland or of the United States. Harford County, May 20th, 1820. Joshua Guyton, Sheriff" (Court Records Document 67.20.4(F) in the Historical Society of Harford

County). "To John Moores, Esquire, Chief Justice of the Orphans Court of Harford County. The petition of James B. Wheeler of Harford County respectfully represents, that from circumstances not now within his controul [sic], he had been rendered totally unable to pay his Debts, and reduced to the humiliating necessity of applying for the benefit of the ensolvent [sic] Law passed [in] November Session Eighteen hundred and five and the several supplements thereto. Your petitioner represents that he is now in confinement in the common gaol of the County (as appears by the Certificate of the Sheriff accompanying this petition) for debt and not for any breach of the laws of this State or of the United States, and that he offers to deliver up all his property of whatever nature, kind or description, whither real, personal or mixed, to the use of his creditors, a list whereof is here exhibited upon oath, together with a list of his debts and creditors so far as he can ascertain them, and that he is prepared to prove his residence within this State for two years last before this his application he therefore prays that you will issue your order to the Sheriff of Harford County directing and commanding him to have your petitioner before you forthwith or at such other time as to you shall seem meet [probably meant to write fit instead of meet] and that you will direct that your petitioner be released and discharged from confinement and the custody of the Sheriff aforesaid, and that you will be pleased to extend to you petitioner such other and further relief as is contained in the provisions of the ensolvent [sic] laws aforesaid, and your petitioner will &c. May " 1820. Jas. B. Wheeler." (Court Records Document 67.20.4(B), loc. cit.; a schedule signed by James B. Wheeler was included, but no property was listed). "Harford County sct. On application to the subscriber as a Justice of the Orphans Court of Harford County by petition in writing of James B. Wheeler of said county stating that he is an imprisoned debtor in actual confinement in the Gaol of said County and praying for a discharge from said confinement and for the benefit of the Act of the General Assembly of Maryland entitled an Act for the relief of sundry insolvent debtors, passed at [the] Novr. session in the year eighteen hundred and five and the several supplements thereto, on the terms therein mentioned, a schedule of his property and a list of his creditors on oath being annexed to his said petition with competent and satisfactory testimony that he has resided two years within the State of Maryland next before the making of his application as aforesaid and the said James B. Wheeler having taken the oath prescribed by the said act prescribed for delivering up his property and given bond with security and in a penalty by me approved and presented [for] his appearance before the Judges of Harford County Court on the first ---- [Saturday] after the fourth Monday in August next at the Court House of said County, being the time by me appointed for hearing before said court in said petition to answer interrogatories which his creditors may propose to him according to the provisions of the said original act. I do hereby order and adjudge that the said James B. Wheeler be discharged from Imprisonment, and direct that he give notice to his creditors of his said application and discharge, and of the day so by me appointed for a hearing before said Court, by advertisement to be inserted in the Bond of Union once a week for three months before the day so appointed. Given under my hand this 20th day of May 1820. John Moores." (Court Records Document 67.29.4(c), loc. cit. "Know all men by these presents that we James B. Wheeler, Samuel Bradford and William Richardson are held and firmly bound unto the State of Maryland in the sum of four thousand Dollars current money to be paid to the said State or its certain attorney or assigns to which payment well and truly to be made and done, we bind ourselves, our heirs, executors and administrators jointly and severally firmly by these presents sealed with our seals and date this 20th day of May 1820. The condition of the above obligation is such that if the above bound James B. Wheeler shall make his personal appearance before the Judges of Harford County court at the Court house in the said County in the 1st Saturday after the fourth Monday of August next, then and there to answer such allegations which creditors may make against him, agreeably to the ensolvent [sic] laws of Maryland, and no depart therefrom without permission of the said Court but await their order, then the obligation to be null and void, otherwise to be and remain in full force and virtue in law. Signed, sealed and delivered in the presence of Jas. B. Wheeler. Saml. Bradford. Wm. Richardson." (Court Records Document 67.20.4(D), loc. cit.; Document 67.20.4(A) in this file is a copy of an objection and allegation of fraud filed by Stevenson Archer, attorney for the Susquehanna Bridge Company, in this case). "Petition, Schedule, Bond, Sheriff's Certificate, order for publication and personal discharge filed 20th May 1820. Sepr. 2nd 1820 petr. appeared. March 14th 1821 leave to amend objections. March 17th 1821 petitioner appeared." [nothing further recorded] (Insolvent Docket A, 1807-1843, p. 25, at the Maryland State Archives; Insolvent Docket Prior to 1827, Court Records Accession #632 at the Historical Society of Harford County).

Whitaker, Dorsey H., 1823. "Petition, Shffs. certificate, Schedule, bond, certificate of residence, personal discharge and order for publication filed 12th April 1823." [nothing further recorded] (Insolvent Docket A, 1807-1843, p. 55, at Maryland State Archives; Insolvent Docket Prior to 1827, Court Records Accession #632 at Historical Society of Harford County). 1831. "Petition, Schedule, personal discharge and order for publication, Bond for appearance, Trustee's Bond, Trustee's Certificate and Deed to Trustee filed 12th Dec 1831. 17th March 1832 Certificate of publication filed discharged." (Insolvent Docket A, 1807-1843, p. 112, at the Maryland State Archives) **Genealogical Notes**: Dorsey Howard Whitaker, son of Joshua Whitaker (1761-1818) and Ruth Howard, was born in 1796, married Sarah G. Galloway (1802-1890), daughter of Absolom Galloway and Mary Merritt, on October 26, 1828 and died on November 4, 1876 in Baltimore City. (Harford County marriage record; Baltimore *Sun*, November 6, 1876, p. 2, reported his name as Dorsey H. Whitaker, Sr.)

Whitaker, Isaac, 1825. "Petition, Schedule, Bond, Sheriffs certificate and personal discharge and order for Publication filed 20th December 1825." (Insolvent Docket A, 1807-1843, p. 76, at the Maryland State Archives; Insolvent Docket Prior to 1827, Court Records Accession #632 at the Historical Society of Harford County). 1827. "Petition, Schedule, Bond, Sheriff's certificate and personal discharge and order for publication filed and Bond of provisional trustee filed and certificate for trustee filed 16th February 1827. 18th Augt. 1827 Petitioner appeared. Certificate of publication filed and Petitioner personally discharged." (Insolvent Docket A, 1807-1843, p. 83). 1829. "Petition, Schedule, Certificate of Sheriff, personal discharge, order for publication, bond for appearance, Trustee's Bond and deed to Trustee filed 12th May 1829. 15th August 1829 Petitioner appears. Certificate of Notice filed and order for final discharge and Order for Sale filed." (Insolvent Docket A, 1807-1843, p. 95).

Whitaker, Joshua, 1824. "Petition, Bond, Schedule, Sheriffs Certificate and personal Discharge and order for Publication filed 10th Augt. 1824." [nothing further recorded] (Insolvent Docket A, 1807-1843, p. 66, at the Maryland State Archives; Insolvent Docket Prior to 1827, Court Records Accession #632 at the Historical Society of Harford County). 1829. Insolvent debtor to be discharged from imprisonment. (*Independent Citizen*, December 10, 1829). "Petition, Schedule, Shff's. Certificate, personal discharge, Order for Publication, Bond for Appearance, Trustee's Certificate, Trustee's Bond and Deed to Trustee filed 28th Decr. 1829. 13th March 1830 Petitioner appears and Certificate of Publication filed. 15th March 1830 Oath administered and petitioner discharged." (Insolvent Docket A, 1807-1843, p. 101, at the Maryland State Archives). **Genealogical Notes**: Joshua Whitaker, son of Isaac Whitaker and Elizabeth Hill, died in 1818, age 61. He married Ruth Howard, daughter of Lemuel Howard and Martha Scott, before 1792 (son Isaac born on October 27, 1792). (Research by descendant Mary-Lynne (Thompson) Livezey, wife of Jon Harlan Livezey, Esq., of Aberdeen, 1988)

White, Robert, 1802. Petitioned for relief under the act for relief of sundry Insolvent Debtors (*Laws of Maryland*, Vol. III, 1802, Chapter 97, Liber JG No. 4, folio 308-314). **Genealogical Note**: Robert White married Mary Ann ---- by 1799 and their daughter Cassandra White was born on March 17, 1800 (St. George's P. E. Parish Register)

Whitelock, Andrew J., 1860. "Petition, Schedule of property, A list of debts due to & from, Affidavit, Order & appointment of James Moores, Trustee, Trustee's Bond and Deed to Trustee filed 23rd March 1860. 6th August 1860 Petitioner appeared, filed certificate of publication of notice to creditors and was finally discharged." (Insolvent Docket A. L. J. No. 1, p. 32, in the Court Records Department of the Historical Society of Harford County). "Notice is hereby given, that Andrew J. Whitelock has made application to the circuit court of Harford county, for the benefit of the Insolvent Laws of Maryland, and that the *1st Monday of August next*, has been assigned for him to appear in said court to answer such interrogatories as his creditors may propose or allege against him. Wm. Galloway, Clerk, circuit court for Harford co." (*National American*, March 30, 1860, p. 2). **Genealogical Notes**: Andrew Jackson Whitelock (born 1838 – died after 1897), son of John Whitelock (1785-1858), of Cecil Co., later of Harford Co., and Ann Gorrell, married Sarah Dixon (born 1836) circa November 2, 1863 (date of Harford Co. license; 1870 Harford County Census; *Portrait and Biographical Record of Harford and Cecil Counties, Maryland*, 1897, p. 267)

Whittemore, Henry, 1830. "Petition, Schedule, Shff's. Certificate, personal discharge and Order for Publication, Bond for Appearance, Trustee's Bond, Trustee's Certificate and Deed to Trustee filed 11th May 1830. 15th August 1830 Petitioner appears and cont'd. 19th March 1831 Certificate and Sundry accts. Filed, petitioner appears and finally discharged." (Insolvent Docket A, 1807-1843, p. 102, at Maryland State Archives). 1835. "Petition, Affidavits, Schedule, personal discharge and order of publication, Bond for Appearance, Trustee's Bond, Trustee's Certificate and Deed to Trustee filed 24th day of February 1835. 15th Augt. 1835. Petitioner appears, Certificate of Publication filed and finally discharged." (Insolvent Docket A, 1807-1843, p. 139, at the Maryland State Archives). **Genealogical Note**: Henry Whittemore married Mary Ann Bell circa November 20, 1821 (date of license) in Harford County. (*Baltimore Patriot*, December 1, 1821, gave her name as "Miss Mary Bell")

Wiggins, John, 1820. "To the Honorable John Norris, a Judge of the Orphans Court of Harford County. The petition of John Wiggins of Harford County respectfully sheweth that your petitioner is now imprisoned in the gaol of Harford County, for debts which he is unable to pay; that he is willing, and offers to deliver to the use of his creditors, all his property, real, personal and mixed, to which he is in any way entitled, (the necessary wearing apparel and bedding of himself and his family excepted), a schedule whereof, together with a list of his creditors, and debtors, as far as he can at present ascertain them, are hereunto on oath annexed. Your petitioner also hereto annexes proof on oath, that he has resided two years next preceding this his application, within the State of Maryland: Your petitioner therefore, prays your Honour to grant him the benefit of the Insolvent Laws of this state, and discharge him from his present imprisonment, and he will pray. John Wiggins. (Court Records Document 67.13.1(b) at the Historical Society of Harford County). "On application to the subscriber, as a Judge of the Orphans Court of Harford County, by petition in writing of John Wiggins stating that he is an imprisoned debtor in actual confinement, and praying for a discharge from said confinement and for the benefit of the Act of the General Assembly of Maryland entitled 'An act for the relief of sundry insolvent debtors,' passed at November Session of eighteen hundred and five, and the several supplements thereto, on the terms therein mentioned, a schedule of his property and a list of his creditors on oath being annexed to his said petition with competent and satisfactory testimony that he has resided for two years within the State of Maryland next before the making of his application as aforesaid and the said John Wiggins having taken the oath by the said act prescribed for delivering up his property and given bond with security, and in a penalty by me approved and presented for his appearance before the Judges of Harford County Court, on the 1st Saturday after the 2nd Monday of March next, at the Court House of said County being the time by me appointed for a hearing before said Court in said petition, to answer interrogatories which his creditors may propose to him according to the provisions of the said original Act. I do hereby order and adjudge that the said John Wiggins be discharged from imprisonment, and direct that he give notice to his creditors of his said application and discharge, and of the day so by me appointed for a hearing before said Court, by advertisement to be inserted in the Bond of Union Newspaper, once a week for three months before the day so appointed. Given under my hand this 25th day of September 1820. John Norris." (Court Records Document 67.13.1(c), loc. cit.; a copy of the schedule to which he signed his name "John Wiggins" was included and listed this property: one case of drawers and three hogs)."Petition, Schedule, Bond, Sheriff's certificate, personal discharge and order for publication filed 25th Sepr. 1820. March 17th 1821 petitioner appeared." [nothing further recorded] (Insolvent Docket A, 1807-1843, p. 37, at the Maryland State Archives; Insolvent Docket Prior to 1827, Court Records Accession #632 at the Historical Society of Harford County). 1834. "Petition, Affidavits, Schedule, personal discharge and order of publication, Bond for Appearance, Trustee's Bond, Trustee's Certificate and deed to Trustee filed 27th Decr. 1834. August 15th 1835 Allegations filed … Petitioner appears, Certificate of Pub-lication filed … finally discharged." (Insolvent Docket A, 1807-1843, p. 138, at Maryland State Archives). **Genealogical Notes**: John Wiggins, son of Joseph and Sarah Wiggins (the mother being deceased), married Sarah Norton, daughter of Stephen and Sophia Norton, all of Harford County, on Thursday the 3rd day of the 11th month 1803 at Deer Creek Friends Monthly Meeting. Family members present were Joseph Wiggins, Anna Wiggins, Stephen Norton, Elizabeth Barton, Philip A. Barton, Bazel Wiggins, Margaret Wiggins, Sally Wiggins, Margery Wiggins, Elizabeth Wiggins, Thomas Norton and Nathaniel Norton. (Deer Creek Monthly Meeting Minutes; *Baltimore Telegraphe*, November 5, 1831, spelled his name "Wiggons")

Wiles, Aquila, 1842. "Petition, Affidavits, Schedules, Appointment, certificates, order, personal Dis-charge, Deed, Appearance & Trustee's Bonds filed September 2nd 1842. Order for Sale filed 24th Novr. 1842. – 20th May 1843 Petitioner appears, files certificate of publication & finally discharged. Trustee Report filed 4th Oct 1843. – 27th Novr. 1843 Auditor's Report filed. 30th Novr. 1843 Order of ratification filed. Recorded in Judgment Record A.L.J. No. 1, folio 143." (Insolvent Docket A, 1807-1843, p. 184, at Maryland State Archives). **Genealogical Note**: Aquila Wiles married Miss Mary Bayless on December 10, 1829 by Rev. William Finney. (*Independent Citizen*, December 24, 1829)

Wiley, David E., 1885. "September 19th 1885. Petition, Schedules, Affidavit, Order appointing Prelimi-nary Trustee [name not given], Bond & Deed filed … 11th Feby 1887 Objections withdrawn. Same day Final order of discharge filed." (Insolvent Docket A. L. J. No. 1, p. 100, in the Court Records Department of the Historical Society of Harford County). "In the matter of the Insolvency of David E. Wiley ... In pursuance of an order passed by the Circuit Court for Harford County, notice is hereby given to the Creditors of David E. Wiley, an insolvent debtor, to file their claims, duly authenticated and proven, with the Clerk of said court, on or before the second Monday of February, 1886. Herman Stump, Permanent Trustee." (*The Aegis & Intelligencer*, November 27, 1885, p. 3). "To the Creditors of David E. Wiley. Take notice that David E. Wiley, of Harford county, an Insolvent Debtor, having filed his petition to be discharged from all his debts and liabilities under the provisions of the Insolvent Laws of the State of Maryland, and such petition being now pending, a meeting of the creditors of said insolvent debtor will be held at my office, in the town of Bel Air, Harford county, Md., on the 22nd day of October, 1885, at 12 o'clock, M., for the purpose of proof of claims, propounding interrogatories, selection of a permanent Trustee and for such other business as may properly come before said meeting. Herman Stump, Preliminary Trustee." (*The Aegis & Intelligencer*, October 16, 1885, p. 2)

Wilkinson, Joseph H., 1859. "Petition, Schedule of property, List of debts due & owing to & from, Affidavit, Order & Appointment of Stevenson Archer, Esqr., Trustee, Trustee's Bond approved and Deed to Stevenson Archer filed 14th February 1859. 6th August 1859 Petitioner appears, files certificate of publication & finally discharged." (Insolvent Docket A. L. J. No. 1, p. 26, in the Court Records Department of the Historical Society of Harford County). "Notice Is Hereby Given that Joseph H. Wilkinson has made application to the Circuit Court of Harford county, for the benefit of the Insolvent Laws of Maryland, and that the *1st Saturday after the First Monday in February, 1859* has been assigned for him to appear in said Court to answer such interrogatories as his creditors may propose or allege against him. Wm. Galloway, Clerk, Circuit court for Harford County." (*National American*, February 25, 1859, p. 3). "The undersigned, as Trustee for the benefit of the creditors of Joseph H. Wilkinson, will sell on the 17th day of March, 1859, At the residence of Ezekiel Moulton, near Hoopman's Chapel, One Horse Power and Thresher, Turning Lathe and Tools Belonging Thereto; One Doz. Chairs, One Bedstead, One Parlor Stove, One Sweep Power, One Sett of Chair Stuff. Terms—Cash. Sale to commence at 11 o'clock, A. M. Stevenson Archer, Trustee of Joseph H Wilkinson." (*National American*, February 25, 1859, p. 3). 1874. "Petition, 3 Schedules, Affidavit, Order, Trustee's Bond and deed filed 30th November 1874 & Notice to Creditors issued" [nothing further recorded] (Insolvent Docket A. L. J. No. 1, p. 57, in the Court Records Department of the Historical Society of Harford County). "Notice is hereby given that Joseph H. Wilkinson has made application to the Circuit Court of Harford county, for the benefit of the Insolvent Laws of Maryland, and that the second Monday in May, 1875 has been assigned for him to appear in said Court to answer such interrogatories as his creditors may propose or allege against him. A. L. Jarrett, Clerk." (*The Aegis & Intelligencer*, December 4, 1874, p. 2). **Genealogical Notes**: Joseph Harkins Wilkinson (February 22, 1834 – September 10, 1911), son of Thomas Wilkinson and Sarah Harkins, married Amelia Elizabeth Moulton (August 16, 1835 – January 8, 1907), daughter of Ezekiel Moulton, of Maryland, and Rebecca A. Bailey, of Pennsylvania, circa December 6, 1854 (date of license) and worked as a farmer, canner and wheelwright near Aberdeen. Their daughter Rachael H. Elizabeth Wilkinson was born circa 1858 and married ---- Myers, of Baltimore; they also had a son W. W. Wilkinson in whose house Joseph died. (Harford County 1860 Census; Wesleyan Chapel tombstone for Amelia E. Wilkinson, but no marker for Joseph H. Wilkinson; Death certificates of Amelia E. Wilkinson and Joseph Harkins Wilkinson; *Havre Grace Republican*, September 16, 1911)

Willey, Isaac, 1837. "Petition, Affidavits, Schedule, personal discharge and order of publication, Bond for Appearance, Trustee's Bond, Trustee's Certificate and Deed to Trustee filed 25th March 1837. 19th August 1837 Petitioner appears, Certificate of Publication filed and finally discharged." (Insolvent Docket A, 1807-1843, p. 155, at Maryland State Archives)

Willey, William, 1841. "Petition, Affidavits, Schedules, Appointment of Trustee, Certificate, order, personal discharge, Trustee's Bond & Deed to Trustee & Appearance Bond filed 26th Novr. 1841. 22nd May 1842 Petitioner appears, files certificate of publication & finally discharged." (Insolvent Docket A, 1807-1843, p. 181, at Maryland State Archives)

Williams, Benjamin J., 1893. "Mr. Benjamin J. Williams, of Darlington, has applied for the benefit of the insolvent laws. Mr. F. R. Williams has been appointed preliminary trustee." (*The Aegis & Intelligencer*, February 24, 1893, p. 3) **Genealogical Notes**: Benjamin J. Williams, son of Benjamin H. Williams and Zenith Denton, was born on April 1, 1849 in Calvert Co., MD, worked as a merchant in Darlington, married 1st to Mary Susie Humes (1850-1908), daughter of Thomas Humes, Jr. and Annie S. Spilman (d. 1905), in 1872, married 2nd to Mrs. R. G. Allen, formerly Elizabeth Cooke Forwood

208

(1864-1933), daughter of Dr. William Stump Forwood (1830-1892) and Jane Adeline Bond (1835-1888), in 1909 and died on November 26, 1925 at home in Darlington. (Darlington Cemetery tombsones; Baltimore *Sun*, January 2, 1905; *The Aegis*, December 4, 1925)

Williams, Ephraim, 1804. "Whereas we the Subscribers Justices of the Peace for Harford County together with William Smithson, one of the associate Justices of Harford County Court, upon the petition of Ephraim Williams, who set forth that he had been confined in the gaol [jail] of the said county twenty Days for Debts which he was unable to pay & finding the facts stated to be true we together with the said William Smithson did meet at the County Gaol on the 17th day of February 1804 and did then and there appoint the 19th day of March Inst. to meet at the said place which said appointment we did then and there … at the request of the said Sheriff administer to the said Ephraim Williams the following oath which was taken by the said Ephraim Williams being first duly sworn on the holy Evangels of Almighty God in the words following, I Ephraim Williams do solemnly swear that the schedule which I have delivered to the Sheriff of Harford County doth contain a full account to the best of my knowledge and remembrance of my whole estate both real & personal or that I have any title to or interest in and of all debts, credits and effects whatsoever which I or any in trust for me have or at the time of my petition had, or am or was in any respect entitled to in possession, remainder or reversion and that I have not directly or indirectly at any time since my imprisonment or before, sold, leased or otherwise conveyed or disposed of or intrusted all or any part of my estate, goods, stock, money or debts thereby to defraud my creditors or to secure the same to receive or expect any profit or advantage thereof so help me God, which said duplicate of the schedule aforesaid we have transmitted to the clerk of the county court to be by him preserved in his office for the information of the creditors of the said Ephraim Williams. Given under our hands & seals this 19th Day of March 1804. John Moores. James Amos." (Court Records Document 67.02.3(C) at the Historical Society of Harford County; a copy of the schedule to which Ephraim Williams signed his name was included, but no property was listed). **Genealogical Note**: Ephraim Williams married Agness ---- before 1800. (Court Records Document 26.26.5, loc. cit.)

Williams, Ezekiel, 1802. Petitioned for relief under the act for relief of sundry Insolvent Debtors (*Laws of Maryland*, Vol. III, 1802, Chapter 97, Liber JG No. 4, folio 308-314)

Williams, Hiram N., 1884. "August 20th 1884. Petition, affidavit, Schedules, Order of Court appointing preliminary trustee [name not given] & Bond & Deed filed … [various claims and notices filed from 1884 to 1886] … 22nd Jany 1887 Final order of ratification of Auditor's Report filed." [nothing further recorded] (Insolvent Docket A. L. J. No. 1, p. 87, in the Court Records Department of the Historical Society of Harford County). "In pursuance of an order of the Circuit Court for Harford county, the undersigned, permanent trustee of the estate of Hiram N. Williams, an insolvent debtor, will sell at Public Auction, at the residence of said Williams, about one mile southerly from Perryman Station, in Bush River neck, on Saturday, November 1st, 1884, beginning at 11 o'clock, A. M., all the Personal Property, belonging to said estate, consisting in part of 3 Horses, 2 Cows, 1 two-horse Wagon, 2 covered Wagons, 1 Sleigh, 1 Wheel Cultivator, 1 Shovel Plow, a lot of Hot-Bed Sash, 1 Process Kettle, 1 Scalding Kettle, 2 large Crates, 2 small Crates, 1 Crane, Fire Pot and Tank, Scalding Baskets, Capping Iron, Buckets, Fruit Boxes, and various other articles. Stevenson A. Williams, Permanent Trustee. George A. Cairnes, Auctioneer." (*The Aegis & Intelligencer*, October 24, 1884, p. 2). "Notice to Creditors. In the Matter of the Insolvency of Hiram N. Williams … Ordered this 18th day of June, in the year 1886, that Monday, the 13th day of September, 1886, be, and the same is hereby fixed as the day for said insolvent to appear and answer such interrogatories or allegations as his creditors or sureties may propose or allege against him, and the permanent trustee of said insolvent is hereby directed to give notice of the day so fixed upon to the creditors of said insolvent by inserting this order in some newspaper published in Harford county once a week for five successive weeks prior to the 1st day of August next. Jas D. Watters. True copy—Test: A. L. Jarrett, Clerk." (*Bel Air Times*, July 16, 1886, p. 3)

Williams, Lelburn (Lilburn), 1816. "Petition, Schedule, Bond and Notice to Creditors filed 15th July 1816. March 15th 1817 Application withdrawn." (Insolvent Docket A, 1807-1843, p. 17, at the Maryland State Archives; Insolvent Docket Prior to 1827, Court Records Accession #632 at the Historical Society of Harford County). **Genealogical Note**: Lilburn Williams married Hannah ---, possibly Hannah McGuire, by 1803 and their son Allen McGuire Williams was born on July 14, 1804. (West Harford Circuit of the Methodist Church Birth Register)

Williams, Robert, 1894. "Notice to Creditors. In the Matter of the Insolvency of Robert Williams. In the Circuit Court for Harford County. In the above matter it is this 26th day of November, 1894, ordered that the said Robert Williams, the insolvent, be and appear in this court on the second Monday of February, 1895, to answer such interrogatories or allegations as his creditors, endorsers, or sureties may propose or allege against him, and that the Permanent Trustees give notice, by the publication of this order in some newspaper for four successive weeks before the 15th day of January next, to the creditors of the said insolvent of the day so fixed upon. Jas. D. Watters. Notice is hereby given to the creditors of Robert Williams, an insolvent debtor, who were such at the time of the filing of his application for the benefit of the insolvent laws of the State of Maryland, to file their claims, duly proven, with the Clerk of the Circuit Court for Harford County, *on or before the 1st day of May, 1895*. S. E. Penning, P. L. Hopper, Permanent Trustee." (*Havre de Grace Republican*, January 5, 1895, p. 3)

Williams, William M., 1849. "John Mitchell, use of Samuel Russell, vs. William M. Williams … 19th Nov/49 Judgment confessed (subject to Deft. application for the Insolvent Laws) for $500 …" (Judgment Docket 1846-1850, p. 61, Court Records Accession No. 187 at the Historical Society of Harford County). John, George E. & William Brock & Henry Emory, trading under the firm of Brock's Son & Co. vs. William M. Williams … 21st May/49 Judgt. confessed (subject to defts. applict. for the benefit of Insolvent laws) for $500 …" (Judgment Docket 1846-1850, p. 54, loc. cit.)

Wilson, Bill (African American), 1821. "To the Honorable John Moores, one of the Justices of the Orphans Court of Harford County. The petition of Negro Bill Wilson of Harford County respectfully sheweth that your petitioner is now in actual confinement in Harford County Jail for debts which he is unable to pay, that he is willing and offers to deliver up to the use of his creditors all his property real, personal and mixed, the necessary wearing apparel and bedding of himself and family excepted, a schedule whereof together with a list of his creditors and debtors, as far as he can at present ascertain them is hereto on oath annexed, your petitioner also hereto annexes proof on oath that he has resided two years next preceding this his application within the State of Maryland. Your petitioner therefore prays your Honour to grant him the benefit of the insolvent laws of this State and to release him from his present confinement, and your Petitioner will pray &c &c. 1st Novr. 1821. Bill "X" Wilson." (Court Records Document 67.22.7(a) at the Historical Society of Harford County). "I hereby certify that Negro Bill Wilson the petitioner above named is now in actual confinement in Harford County Jail for debt at the suit of John C. Norris and John Robinson and that is not upon a breach of peace or any of the penal Laws of the State of Maryland or of the United States. Given under my hand this 1st day of Novr. 1821. Saml. Bradford, Sheriff." (Court Records Document 67.22.7(a), loc. cit.) "State of Maryland Harford County to wit. On this 21st day of Novr. 1821 personally appeared Washington Bond before me the subscriber one of the State of Maryland Justices of the Peace in and for the county aforesaid and made oath on the holy Evangely of Almighty God that Negro Bill Wilson the petitioner within named has resided within the State of Maryland the two years next preceeding the date hereof and that he still resides therein. Sworn to before Jason Moore." (Court Records Document 67.22.7(a), loc. cit.) "On application to the subscriber as a Justice of the Orphans Court of Harford County by petition in writing of Negro Bill Wilson stating that he is an imprisoned debtor in actual confinement in the Jail of said County and praying for a discharge from said confinement and for the benefit of the Act of the General Assembly of Maryland, Entitled An Act for the relief of sundry insolvent debtors, passed at November session eighteen hundred and five and the several supplements thereto, on the terms therein mentioned, a schedule of his property and a list of his creditors on oath being annexed to his said petition with competent and satisfactory testimony that he has resided for two years within the State of Maryland, next before the making of his application as aforesaid and the said Negro Bill Wilson having taken the oath by the said act prescribed for delivering up his property and given bond with security, and in a penalty by me approved and presented for his appearance before the Judges of Harford County Court on the first Saturday after the second Monday in March next at the Court House of said County being the time by me appointed for a hearing before said court in said petition to answer interrogatories which his creditors may propose to him according to the provisions of the said original act. I do hereby order and adjudge that the said Negro Bill Wilson be discharged from imprisonment and direct that he give notice to his creditors of his said application and discharge and of the day so by me appointed for a hearing before said Court by advertisement to be inserted in the Bond of Union newspaper once a week for three months before the time so appointed. Given under my hand this 1st day of Novr. 1821. John Moores." (Court Records Document 67.13.2(c), loc. cit.; a copy of the schedule to which Bill Wilson made his "X" mark was included and listed two guns as his property). "Know all men by these presents that we Bill Wilson and Washington Bond of Harford County and State of Maryland are held and firmly bound unto the State of Maryland in the full and just sum of fifth Dollars current money of the United States to the payment whereof well and truly to the said State, we bind ourselves, our heirs, executors and administrators, jointly & severally firmly by these presents sealed with our seals and date this 1st day of Novr. 1821. The condition of the above obligation is such that if the above bound Negro Bill Wilson shall make his personal appearance in Harford County Court on the first Saturday after the second Monday in March next before the Judges thereof then and there to answer such allegations or interrogatories as his creditors may propose to him then the above obligation to be void, else to remain in full force and virtue in law. Signed, sealed and delivered in the presence of John Moores. Bill "X" Wilson. Washington "2" Bond." (Court Records Document 67.22.7(b), loc. cit.) "Petition, Schedule, Bond, Sheriff's certificate, personal discharge and order for publication filed 1st Novr. 1821." [nothing further recorded] (Insolvent Docket A, 1807-1843, p. 47, at the Maryland State Archives; Insolvent Docket Prior to 1827, Court Records Accession #632 at the Historical Society of Harford County)

Wilson, Isaac T., 1828. Trustee's Sale of five negroes, late the property of Isaac T. Wilson, an insolvent debtor. J. D. Learned, Baltimore, trustee. (*Bond of Union and Harford County Weekly Advertiser*, August 28, 1828). "Farm for sale in pursuance of general order of Baltimore County Court in relation to insolvent debtors, trustee of Isaac T. Wilson will sell tract called *Bell Tavern*, lately in possession of said Wilson, binding upon Bush River in Harford County; see George Bradford adjoining the land or J. D. Learned, trustee, Baltimore." (*Independent Citizen*, December 3, 1829) **Genealogical Notes**: Isaac T. Wilson married Mary Brookes on November 7, 1807 and they had one known child, Sarah Louise T. Wilson (1813-1869) who married George Thomas Gilbert (1811-1884) on July 18, 1835. (Old Brick Baptist Church tombsones; Will of Mary Wilson in Harford County Liber TSB No. 6, p. 309)

Wilson, James, 1845. "Notice is hereby given, to the creditors of James Wilson, late an imprisoned debtor of Harford county, that on the application of said debtor by petition in writing to the Hon. Alexander Norris, one of the associate justices of the county court, of said county, for the benefit of the insolvent laws of Maryland, the said judge on the 23rd day of November, 1844, granted to the said debtor a discharge from imprisonment and appointed the first Saturday after the 3rd Monday in May next, for his appearance before the Judges of Harford county court at the court house of said county, for a final hearing before said court, on said petition and to answer such interrogatories as his creditors may propose to him." (*Harford Madisonian and Bel-Air & Havre de Grace Messenger*, April 11, 1845, p. 3)

Wilson, John, 1804. "Whereas we the Subscribers Justices of the Peace for Harford County upon the petition of John Wilson, who set forth that he had been confined in the Gaol [jail] of the said county twenty Days for Debts which he was unable to pay & finding the facts stated to be true we together did meet at the County Gaol on the 19th Day of November 1804 and did then and there appoint the 20th day of December Instant to meet at the Court House of said county which said appointment we did then and there ... at the request of the said Sheriff administer to the said John Wilson the following oath which was taken by the said John Wilson being first duly sworn on the holy evangels of almighty God in the words following, I John Wilson do solemnly swear that the schedule which I have delivered to the Sheriff of Harford County doth contain a full account to the best of my knowledge and remembrance of my whole estate both real and personal or that I have any title to or interest in and of all debts, credits & effects whatsoever which I or any in trust for me have or at the time of my petition had, or am or was in any respect entitled to in possession, remainder or reversion & that I have not directly or indirectly at any time since my imprisonment or before, sold, leased or otherwise conveyed or disposed of or intrusted all or any part of my estate, goods, stock, money or debts thereby to defraud my creditors or to secure the same to receive or expect any profit or advantage thereof so help me God, which said duplicate of the schedule aforesaid we have transmitted to the clerk of the county court to be by him preserved in his office for the information of the creditors of the said John Wilson. Given under our hands & seals this 20th day of December 1804. Wm. Smithson. Thos. A. Hays. John Moores." (Court Records Document 67.26.2(b) at the Historical Society of Harford County; a copy of the schedule to which "John Wilson" made his "X" mark was included, but no property was listed). **Genealogical Notes**: There were two men named John Wilson at this time: one married Norry Brady on April 20, 1797 (St. George's Parish Register) and one married Margaret Smith circa November 22, 1799 (date of license).

Wilson, John C., 1844. "Notice is hereby given, to the creditors of John C. Wilson, late an imprisoned debtor of Harford county, that on the application of said debtor by petition in writing to the Hon. John C. Legrand, one of the justices of the county court of said county, for the benefit of the insolvent laws of Maryland, the said judge on the 27th day of November, 1844, granted to the said debtor a discharge from imprisonment and appointed the first Saturday after the 3rd Monday in May next, for his appearance before the Judges of Harford county court at the court house of said county, for a final hearing before said court, on said petition and to answer such interrogatories as his creditors may propose to him." (*Harford Madisonian and Bel-Air & Havre de Grace Messenger*, January 3, 1845, p. 3)

Wilson, John S., 1854. "Petition, 2 Affidavits, 3 Schedules, Appointment of A. W. Bateman, Esq., Trustee. Order to give Bond & Deed filed 29th Oct/54. 13 May/56 Certificate of publication filed." [nothing further recorded] (Insolvent Docket A. L. J. No. 1, p. 5, in the Court Records Department of the Historical Society of Harford County)

Wilson, William H., 1844. "Notice Is Hereby Given, to the creditors of William H. Wilson, late an imprisoned debtor of Harford co., that on the application of said debtor by petition in writing to the Hon. Robert W. Holland, chief justice of the Orphan's court of said county, for the benefit of the insolvent laws of Maryland, the said judge on the 16th day of July, 1844, granted to the said debtor a discharge from imprisonment and appointed the first Saturday after the 3rd Monday in November next, for his appearance before the Judges of Harford county court at the court house of said county, for a final hearing before said court, on said petition and to answer such interrogatories as his creditors may propose to him." (*Harford Madisonian and Bel-Air & Havre de Grace Messenger*, October 18, 1844, p. 3)

Wood, Elisha, 1842. "Petition, Affidavits, Schedules, appointment, certificate order, personal discharge, Appearance & Trustee's bonds filed 18th Oct. 1842. 20 May 1843 Petitioner appears, files certificate of publication & finally discharged." (Insolvent Docket A, 1807-1843, p. 185, at the Maryland State Archives)

Wood, John P., 1850. "James A. Mallory vs. John P. Wood … 20th May/50 Judgt. confessed for $1000 (subject to defendant's application for the benefit of insolvent laws …" (Judgment Docket 1846-1850, p. 67, Court Records Accession #187 at the Historical Society of Harford County)

Woodland, William, 1820. "To the Honorable John Moores, one of the Justices of the Orphans Court of Harford County. The petition of William Woodland of Harford County respectfully sheweth that your petitioner is now in actual confinement in Harford County Gaol for debts which he is unable to pay, that he is willing and offers to deliver to the use of his creditors all his property real, personal and mixed (the necessary wearing apparel and bedding of himself and family excepted), a schedule whereof together with a list of his creditors and debtors, as far as he can at present ascertain them is hereto on oath annexed. Your petitioner also hereto annexes proof on oath that he has resided two years next preceding this his application within the State of Maryland. Your petitioner therefore prays your honour to grant him the benefit of the insolvent laws of this State and to relieve him from his present confinement, and your petitioner will pray. Wm. W. Woodland." [signed 24 July 1820]. (Court Records Document 67.13.2(c) at the Historical Society of Harford County). "I hereby certify that William Woodland the petitioner above named is now in actual confinement in Harford County Gaol for debt at the suit of James Criswell and that is not upon a breach of peace or any of the penal laws of this State or of the United States. Given under my hand this 24th day of July 1820. Joshua Guyton, Sheriff. State of Maryland Harford County, to wit. On this 4th day of July 1820 personally appeared Christopher Wilson before me the subscriber one of the State of Maryland justices of the peace in and for the county aforesaid and solemnly affirmed (being a Quaker) that William Woodland the petitioner within named has resided within the State of Maryland the two years next preceeding the date hereof and that he still resides therein. Affirmed to before Saml. Bradford. On application to the subscriber a Judge of the Orphans Court of Harford County by petition in writing of William Woodland stating that he is an imprisoned debtor in actual confinement in the Gaol of said County, and praying for a discharge from said confinement and for the benefit of the Act of the General Assembly of Maryland entitled an Act for the relief of sundry Insolvent debtors, passed at [the] November session of eighteen hundred and five and the several supplements thereto, on the terms therein mentioned, a schedule of his property and a list of his creditors on oath being annexed to his said petition with competent and satisfactory testimony that he has resided for two years within the State of Maryland, next before the making of his application as aforesaid and the said William Woodland having taken the oath by the said act prescribed for delivering up his property and given bond with security, and in a penalty by me approved and presented for his appearance before the Judges of Harford County Court on the first Saturday after the second Monday in March next at the Court House of said county being the time by me appointed for a hearing before said court in said petition to answer interrogatories which his creditors may propose to him according to the provisions of the said original act. I do hereby order and adjudge that the said William Woodland be discharged from imprisonment, and direct that he give notice to his creditors of his said application and discharge and of the day so by me appointed for a hearing before said Court, by advertisement to be inserted in the Bond of Union newspaper once a week for three months before the day so appointed given under my hand this 24th day of July 1820. John Moores." (Court Records Documents 67.13.2(b)(d), loc. cit.; a copy of the schedule to which he signed his name "Wm. W. Woodland" was included, but no property was listed for him). "Notice Is Hereby Given, To the creditors of William Woodland, late an imprisoned debtor of Harford county, that on the application of the said debtor, by petition in writing to the honorable John Moores, chief Judge of the Orphans' Court of said county for the benefit of the insolvent laws of Maryland, the said Judge on the 1st day of September, in the year 1820, granted to the said debtor a discharge from imprisonment, and appointed the first Saturday in after the second Monday in March next, for his appearance before the Judges of Harford county, at the court-house in said county, for a hearing before said court, on said petition, and to answer interrogatories which his creditors may propose to him. March 17th 1821, I hereby certify that the annexed advertisement was published three months in the Bond of Union – Wm. Coale, Jr." (Court Records Document 67.13.2(a), loc. cit.; a copy of the notice was clipped from the newspaper and included in this file). "Petition, Schedule, Bond, Sheriff's certificate, order for personal discharge and publication filed 24th July 1820 … Christopher Wilson appointed Trustee and the petitioner personally discharged." [nothing further recorded] (Insolvent Docket A, 1807-1843, p. 35, at the Maryland State Archives; Insolvent Docket Prior to 1827, Court Records Accession #632 at the Historical Society of Harford County)

Worsley, William, 1810. "Whereas we the subscribers Justices of the Peace for Harford County together with John C. Bond, Esq., also one of the Justices of the Peace for said County, upon the petition of George Wosley [sic] who set forth therein that he had been confined in the Gaol [jail] of said county twenty Days for Debts which he was unable to pay and finding the facts stated to be true we together with John C. Bond, Esq., did meet at the County Gaol of said county on the 26th Day of April last and we did then and there appoint the 28th Day of May Inst. to meet at the Court House of said county which said appointment we did then and there … at the request of the said Sheriff administer to the said George Wosley the following Oath which was taken by the said George Wosley being first duly sworn on the holy Evangely of Almighty God in the words following, to wit, I George Wosley [sic] do Solemnly swear that the Schedule which I have delivered to the Sheriff of Harford County doth contain a full account to the best of my Knowledge & Remembrance of my whole estate both real and personal or that I have any title to or interest in and of all debts, credits and effects whatsoever which I or any in trust for me have or at the time of my petition had, or am or was in any respect entitled to in possession, remainder or reversion and that I have not directly or indirectly at any time since my imprisonment or before, sold, leased or otherwise conveyed or disposed of or intrusted all or any part of my estate, goods, Stock, money or Debts thereby to defraud my creditors or to secure the same to receive or expect any profit or advantage thereof so help me God, which said duplicate of the Schedule aforesaid we have transmitted to the Clerk of the County Court to be by him preserved in his Office for the information of the Creditors of the said George Wosley. Given under our hands and seals this 28th Day of May 1810. Saml. Bradford. Thomas A. Hays." (Court Records Document 67.09.2(C) at the Historical Society of Harford County included a copy of the schedule and "George Worsley" signed his name, but no property was listed)

Worthington, Joseph, 1836. "Petition, Affidavits, Schedule, personal discharge and order of publication, Bond for Appearance, Trustee's Bond, Trustee's Certificate and Deed to Trustee filed 18th January 1836 … [some petitions and interrogatories filed] … 12th August 1836 Petitioner appears, certificate of publication filed and finally discharged." (Insolvent Docket A, 1807-1843, p. 146, at Maryland State Archives)

Wright, Thomas, 1837. "Petition, Affidavits, Schedule, personal discharge and order of publication, Bond for Appearance, Trustee's Bond, Trustee's Certificate and Deed to Trustee filed 16th October 1837. 17th March 1838 Certificate of Publication filed. Petitioner appears and finally discharged." (Insolvent Docket A, 1807-1843, p. 160, at the Maryland State Archives)

Young, Hugh, 1805. "Whereas we the Subscribers Justices of the Peace for Harford County upon the petition of Hugh Young, who set forth that he had been confined in the Gaol [jail] of the said county twenty Days for Debts which he was unable to pay & finding the facts stated to be true we together did meet at the County Gaol on the 10th Day of January 1805 and did then and there appoint the 11th Day of February Instant to meet at the Court House of said county which said appointment we did then and there … at the request of the said Sheriff administer to the said Hugh Young the following oath which was taken by the said Hugh Young being first duly sworn on the holy evangels of almighty God in the words following, I Hugh Young do solemnly swear that the schedule which I have delivered to the Sheriff of Harford County doth contain a full account to the best of my knowledge and remembrance of my whole estate both real and personal or that I have any title to or interest in and of all debts, credits & effects whatsoever which I or any in trust for me have or at the time of my petition had, or am or was in any respect entitled to in possession, remainder or reversion & that I have not directly or indirectly at any time since my imprisonment or before, sold, leased or otherwise conveyed or disposed of or intrusted all or any part of my estate, goods, stock, money or debts thereby to defraud my creditors or to secure the same to receive or expect any profit or advantage thereof so help me God, which said duplicate of the schedule aforesaid we have transmitted to the clerk of the county court to be by him preserved in his office for the information of the creditors of the said Hugh Young. Given under our hands & seals this 11th day of February 1805. Thomas A. Hays. Wm. Smithson. James Amos." (Court Records Document 67.26.4(a) at the Historical Society of Harford County; a copy of the schedule to which "Hugh Young" signed his name was included and listed this property: "1 Plow, 1 Hoe, 1 Ax, 1 Mattock, 1 Dutch Oven, 2 Pots")
Genealogical Notes: There were two men with this name at this time: one was Hugh Young, son of Robert Young (d. 1777) who married Eleanor Durbin (b. 1761) and the other Hugh Young married Amelia Barton, daughter of James Barton and Margaret Smithson, circa December 22, 1806 (date of license). (Will of Robert Young, Liber AJ No. R, p. 266; Land Records Liber HD No. Q, pp. 360-362)

Young, John, 1824. "Petition, Bond, Schedule, Sheriffs Certificate and personal Discharge and order for Publication filed 10th Augt 1824." [nothing further recorded] (Insolvent Docket A, 1807-1843, p. 67, at the Maryland State Archives; Insolvent Docket Prior to 1827, Court Records Accession #632 at the Historical Society of Harford County). **Genealogical Note**: John Young married Susan Rogers circa November 8, 1810 (date of license).

Zimmerman, ----, 1891. "Circuit Court Proceedings. Messrs. John Axer and ---- Zimmerman, insolvents, appeared at bar and asked to be discharged." (*Havre de Grace Republican*, November 18, 1892, p. 3)

Zollinger, Henry A. and Maria, 1848. "Joseph S. Burnett, Joseph N. Withers & Marshall S. Shafleigh, trading under the firm of Burnett, Withers & Co. vs. Henry A. Zollinger … 15th May/48. Judgt. confessed for $500 (subject to defendant's application for the benefit of insolvent laws …" (Judgment Docket 1846-1850, p. 43, Court Records Accession #187 at the Historical Society of Harford County), 1848. "John Walker vs. Henry A. Zollinger and Maria Zollinger … 20th Nov/48 Judgt. confessed (subject to Henry A. ---- [sic] application for the Insolvents Laws) for $200 …"(Judgment Docket 1846-1850, loc. cit., p. 44)

Hill, Margaret, 25
Hill, Martha, 45
Hill, Thomas, 45, 79
Hill's Camp, 92
Hillis, Jesse, 116
Hilton, Miles, 79
Hinchman, Willliam H., 177
Hinkle, Charles M., 70
Hipkins, William W., 79
Hitchcock, Elizabeth Ann, 6
Hitchcock, Isaac, 79
Hitchcock, John, 80
Hitchcock, John Jr., 80
Hitchcock, Luther, 80
Hitchcock, Mary, 195
Hoblitzell, S. A., 101
Hoffman, Allen, 81, 82
Hoffman, John, 82
Hoke, Jacob, 54
Holbrook, William 82
Holland, Amanda Jane, 4
Holland, Carrie Isabelle, 82
Holland, James, 4
Holland, Mary Florence, 82
Holland, Nicholas B., 82
Holland, Nicholas Bond, 82
Holland, Robert Holland, 82
Holland, Robert W., 2, 12, 17, 24,
    86, 97, 102, 117, 170
Hollifield, William, 191
Holling Refuge, 125
Hollingsworth, Jesse, 82
Hollis, Clark, 125
Hollis, Frances, 20
Hollis, Mary, 125, 157
Hollis, Semelia Ann, 10
Hollis, Susannah, 85
Holloway, Richard, 82, 83
Holloway, Sarah, Mrs., 66
Holly Hill, 125
Holly, Mary, 170
Holmes, Jane, 31
Home Farm, 127
Hoopes, Dillwyn, 83
Hoopes, Joseph T., 83
Hoopman, Catherine, 193
Hoopman, H. B., 83
Hoopman, Marceline Virginia, 83
Hoopman, Rebecca Louisa, 193
Hope, Daniel, 12
Hope, Elizabeth, 179

Hopkins, Angie V., 66
Hopkins, Anna Kate, 84
Hopkins, Anna McCausland, 85
Hopkins, Annie Virginia, 85
Hopkins, Clara H., 173
Hopkins, David, 83
Hopkins, Edward C., 83
Hopkins, Elizabeth, 197
Hopkins, Etta, Mrs., 84
Hopkins, George H., 85
Hopkins, George R., 83
Hopkins, George W., 84
Hopkins, Hannah P., 83
Hopkins, Harry, 83
Hopkins, Harry F., 84
Hopkins, Harry Gover, 85
Hopkins, Hollis Hughes, 85
Hopkins, Irene, 84
Hopkins, J. T. C., 5, 77, 123
Hopkins, J. Thomas C., 87, 162
Hopkins, John E., 84
Hopkins, John H., 85
Hopkins, John Henry, 85
Hopkins, John M., 85
Hopkins, John Miller, 85
Hopkins, John Oscar, 85
Hopkins, Joseph R., 85
Hopkins, Joseph Reese, 85
Hopkins, Joseph Reese Jr., 85
Hopkins, Levin, 83
Hopkins, Louise, 83
Hopkins, Maria Louisa, 6
Hopkins, Murray Lindley, 85
Hopkins, Philip, 85
Hopkins, Priscilla, 177
Hopkins, Rachel Leetta, 84
Hopkins, Raleigh W., 83
Hopkins, Richard Kenton, 83
Hopkins, Robert Milton, 83
Hopkins, Robert R., 86
Hopkins, Samuel, 197
Hopkins, Samuel G., 84
Hopkins, Samuel Gover, 84
Hopkins, Sarah, 85, 197
Hopkins, Susan D., 86
Hopkins, Wakeman Bryarly, 83
Hopkins, Wellmore, 83, 86
Hopkins, Wellmore Hoopman, 83
Hopkins, William H., 17, 86
Hopkins, William Martin, 85
Hopper, Harry, 70

Hopper, John A., 172
Hopper, P. Lesley, 174, 175, 209
Hopper, Peter Lesley, 40
Horner, James, 110
Horner, Mary, 110
Horner, Sarah, 110
Horton, Edward W., 198, 201
Horton, Elizabeth. 198
Houseman and Walworth, 14
Howard, Charlotte E., 121
Howard, Joseph, 86
Howard, Lemuel, 204
Howard, Patrick, 86
Howard, Ruth, 204
Howard, Samuel, 86
Howe, Elizabeth, 123
Howe, William (Bill), 184, 185
Howlett, William, 86
Hudson, Mary Roberta, 4
Huff, John, 86
Huff, Michael, 162, 163
Huff, Phoebe Ann, 85
Huff, Rachel, 162
Huff, Thomas R., 87
Huff, Zachariah, 87
Huggins, Henry S., 87, 88
Huggins, Hugh Thompson, 88
Huggins, John Robert Henry, 88
Hughes, Adolphus, 88
Hughes, Alexander, 88
Hughes, Eleanora Jane, 88
Hughes, George, 88
Hughes, James, 88
Hughes, James P., 88
Hughes, John T., 88, 89
Hughes, Mary, 88
Hughes, Peter, 75
Hughes, Vincent, 89
Hulshart, George W., 89
Hulshart, George W. Jr., 89
Humes, Mary Susie, 207
Humes, Thomas Jr., 207
Husband, Susannah Orrick, 161
Hushon, John, Mrs., 77
Hutchins, James B., 89, 90
Hutchins, John Stansbury, 90
Hutchins, Thomas, 90
Hutchins, William, 90
Iley, Elizabeth P., 90
Iley, Jacob, 90
Iley, John D., 90

226

McCoy, Robert, 97
McDonald, Alexander, 109
McDonald, James, 49
McElhiney, Michael, 201
McFadden, Benjamin, 110
McFadden, Hannah Jane, 43
McFadden, John, 43
McFadden, John Harvey, 110
McFadden, William Jr., 110
McGaw, John, 110
McGaw, Robert, 110
McGill, Richard, 142
McGonegal, Daniel, 111
McGonegal, Hugh, 111
McGonegal, Philip, 111
McGriger, Lucinda, 98
McGuire, Hannah, 209
McIlvain, Bernard Stump, 112
McIlvain, George W., 111
McIlvain, Jeremiah, 111
McIlvain, Rachel, 112
McIlvaine, Bernard S., 111
McIlvaine, George W., 111
McIlvaine, Jeremiah, 111
McJilton,William, 30, 112
McKee, Charles, 112
McKee, David, 112
McKee, David Jr., 112
McKee, Jane, 112
McKee, John A., 20
McKenny, John, 112
McKenny, Peter, 112
McKinney, John Jr., 116
McLaughlin, Mary, 111
McLaughlin, Michael, 113
McLaughlin, Patrick, 113, 114
McMath, William, 28
McMichael, Elva K., 112
McNabb, Daniel, 114
McNabb, J. Martin, 8
McNabb, James W., 42
McNabb, John, 114, 115
McNeuse, Catherine, 143
McVey, John, 115
Mead, Hannah, 188
Meads, Benedict, 115
Meads, Daniel, 115
Meads, Elisha, 115
Meads, James, 115
Meads' Delight, 115
Merriken, Joseph, 24

Merritt Farm, 5
Merritt, Mary, 204
Merritt, Stephen Stewart Jr., 84
Meyers, Margaret A., 88
Michael & Malcolm, 22
Michael, Caleb, 116
Michael, Charles W., 22
Michael, Jacob, 43
Michael, Margaret E., 177
Michael, Martha Elizabeth, 117
Michael, Susanna Rebecca, 189
Middleton, Ann Elizabeth, 73
Miles, Mary Elizabeth, 188
Milhoof, John, 116
Milhoof, Polly, 116
Miller, Amelia J., 164
Miller, Caroline Amos, 4
Miller, John H., 13
Miller, Joseph, 164
Miller, Leetta, 85
Miller, Martha, 164
Miller, Nevie R., 154
Miller, Rachel, 85
Miller, Samuel, 116
Miller, Sophia A. H., 6
Miller, William F., 116
Millhooff, John, 116
Milligan, Ann, 116
Milligan, James, 116
Minnick, Cyrus, 116, 117
Minnick, Elizabeth, 117
Minnick, Elizabeth P., 117
Minnick, Jacob, 117
Minnick, Margaret, 117
Minnick, Marjorie, 117
Minnick, Maryetta, 117
Mitaway (Mittaway), Pat, 117
Mitchell, Clemency G., 26
Mitchell, Edward, 117
Mitchell, Elizabeth, 16
Mitchell, George Corthell, 117
Mitchell, George L., 117
Mitchell, George Lewis, 117
Mitchell, Helen Bowman, 117
Mitchell, James, 117
Mitchell, John, 190
Mitchell, John [Jno.] D., 152, 153
Mitchell, John H., 63, 64, 65
Mitchell, Joseph G., 117
Mitchell, Mary, 190
Mitchell, Mary Lillian, 117

Mitchell, Pearl Sylvia, 117
Mitchell, Rose Ella, 117
Mitchell, Stella Elizabeth, 117
Mitten (Mitton), Job, 117
Monk, John Clark, 118
Monk, Mary, 118
Monks, Ann Eliza, 118
Monks, Edward Tredway, 118
Monks, Elecia Melvina, 3
Monks, Florence B., 75
Monks, Francis E., 118
Monks, James H., 118
Monks, James P., 118
Monks, John, 118
Monks, John C., 118
Monks, Lewis W., 118
Monks, Mary E., 118
Monks, Olivia C., 118
Monks, Sarah Lavinia, 118
Monks, Thomas A., 118
Monks, William T., 118
Monohon, Blanch, 146
Montgomery, Mary Ann, 179
Montgomery, William B., 179
Mooberry, Mary, 119
Mooberry, Robert, 118, 119
Moore, Benjamin P. Sr., 119
Moore, Caleb J., 14, 15
Moore, Caroline F., 4
Moore, George, 119
Moore, Jason, 3, 100, 210
Moore, Theodore R., 119
Moore, William, 120
Moores, John, 80, 91, 102, 103, 109, 110, 115, 119, 127, 130, 134, 135, 136, 139, 140, 141, 142, 144, 147, 151, 152, 156, 157, 160, 166, 167, 168, 169, 184, 197, 198, 208, 209, 210, 211
Morgan, Cassandra E., 10
Morgan, Edward, 120
Morgan, John Thos. Hamilton, 120
Morgan, Julia Ann, 120
Morgan, L. F., 23
Morgan, Lurena, 120
Morgan, Ro. [Robert], 201
Morgan, Robert, 120
Morgan, Sarah H., 120
Morgan, William, 120
Morris, Lloyd, 167
Morrison, John, 120